SECOND EDITION

Windows XP Annoyances

for Geeks

David A. Karp

O'REILLY®

Beijing · Cambridge · Farnham · Köln · Paris · Sebastopol · Taipei · Tokyo

Windows XP Annoyances for Geeks, Second Edition
by David A. Karp

Printed in the United States of America.

Published by O'Reilly Media, Inc., 1005 Gravenstein Highway North, Sebastopol, CA 95472.

O'Reilly books may be purchased for educational, business, or sales promotional use. Online editions are also available for most titles (*safari.oreilly.com*). For more information, contact our corporate/institutional sales department: (800) 998-9938 or *corporate@oreilly.com*.

Editors:	Tim O'Reilly
	Robert Luhn
Production Editor:	Sanders Kleinfeld
Cover Designer:	Ellie Volckhausen
Interior Designer:	David Futato

Printing History

November 2004:	Second Edition, *Windows XP Annoyances for Geeks.*
October 2002:	First Edition, *Windows XP Annoyances.*

Portions of this book have been previously published as follows:

March 2001:	*Windows Me Annoyances.*
October 1998:	*Windows 98 Annoyances.*
April 1997:	*Windows Annoyances.*

This book uses RepKover™, a durable and flexible lay-flat binding.

ISBN: 0-596-00876-7
[M] [4/05]

Windows XP Annoyances

for Geeks

Other Microsoft Windows resources from O'Reilly

Related titles

Windows XP Pro: The Missing Manual
Windows XP Home: The Missing Manual
Windows XP Power Hound
Windows XP Unwired
Windows XP Personal Trainer
Windows XP in a Nutshell
Windows XP Hacks
Windows XP Pocket Reference
Learning Windows Server 2003
Windows Server Hacks

Windows Books Resource Center

windows.oreilly.com is a complete catalog of O'Reilly's Windows and Office books, including sample chapters and code examples.

oreillynet.com is the essential portal for developers interested in open and emerging technologies, including new platforms, programming languages, and operating systems.

Conferences

O'Reilly brings diverse innovators together to nurture the ideas that spark revolutionary industries. We specialize in documenting the latest tools and systems, translating the innovator's knowledge into useful skills for those in the trenches. Visit *conferences.oreilly.com* for our upcoming events.

Safari Bookshelf (*safari.oreilly.com*) is the premier online reference library for programmers and IT professionals. Conduct searches across more than 1,000 books. Subscribers can zero in on answers to time-critical questions in a matter of seconds. Read the books on your Bookshelf from cover to cover or simply flip to the page you need. Try it today with a free trial.

Table of Contents

Preface

What IS an Annoyance?

If you're using Microsoft Windows, I shouldn't have to tell you what an annoyance is. To put it simply, an annoyance is a problem to be solved, and Windows certainly has no shortage of those.

An annoyance is the way Windows keeps forgetting your settings, rearranging your desktop icons, and constantly changing the order of items in your Start Menu. An annoyance is the inconsistent way Windows handles the dragging and dropping of files. An annoyance is the fact that Microsoft gave Windows a fancy face lift in Windows XP, but didn't bother to fix a nearly decade-old problem with File → Open and File → Save dialogs (more on that later). An annoyance is Service Pack 2, which contains as many new bugs as it fixes, and only provides superficial protection in an age of viruses, Trojan horses, and spyware.

More often than not, an annoyance is the result of bad design, as opposed to a garden-variety bug.

Now, if we had a large selection of compatible operating systems from which to choose, the point would be almost moot; each of us would simply choose the most appropriate (and, of course, least annoying) software available. However, the real world isn't like that, and most of us who use Microsoft Windows are doing so out of necessity rather than personal choice. That puts Microsoft in a position to control what we see and how we work. Realizing you're not alone is the first step to improving your experience with Windows XP and regaining control of your machine before it assumes control of you.

But the purpose of this book is not to complain or criticize, but rather to acknowledge and understand the problems and shortcomings of the operating system in an effort to overcome them.

Windows XP Annoyances for Geeks presents solutions that enable you to both customize and troubleshoot Windows. This is an important distinction, because effective problem solving often requires that you know whether an annoyance is an inadvertent bug or an intentional feature of the software, and the dividing line isn't always clear. It's important to realize that if software doesn't act in a way that *you* think it should, it should be regarded as poor design and not necessarily the result of a bug. A bug is an action carried out by a piece of software that wasn't intended by the *designers* of the product. Ultimately, this distinction doesn't make any particular annoyance any less annoying, but it goes a long way toward helping you come up with a solution.

Thinking Inside the Box

Here's a simple, yet not readily apparent, example of an intentional design decision that has led to a tangible annoyance in Windows:

Common file dialog boxes—the little windows that appear when you go to **File → Open** or **File → Save** in most applications—look basically the same, regardless of the application you're using, essentially because they're a function provided by Windows XP. This concept of *common* dialogs (in the Windows world, anyway) was introduced in the 1980s in Windows 3.1 and has since undergone an evolutionary process as they've been reworked in each successive version of the operating system.

An annoyance that plagued these boxes from the start was that they were not resizable and were therefore awkward to use with large displays (or, conversely, too large on small displays). Fortunately, this problem has since been fixed, and in Windows XP, we enjoy resizable file dialog boxes most of the time. And although each application's file dialog will remember its size temporarily, this information is forgotten when the application is closed. Of course, this means that if you want a larger dialog box, you'll have to enlarge it again and again, and do it separately for each application.

However, a more serious problem (in my opinion), still not remedied in XP, is that of the **Look in** (or **Save in**) list at the top of these dialogs. When you're opening or saving a file, the only clue to the location of the current folder is the *name*—not the entire path—of the folder. So, for example, if the current folder shown in a file dialog box is called *images*, there's no way to immediately determine if the folder you're looking at is *c:\projects\images* or *d:\webpages\personal\images*.

What's worse is that Microsoft *knows* about the problem and has done nothing about it; in fact, they've taken steps to hide it. In some earlier versions of Windows, if you clicked the [?] button and then clicked the **Look in** list, you would see this note: "To see how the current folder fits in the hierarchy on your computer, click the down arrow." In later releases of Windows, Microsoft simply removed the explanatory text, and did so instead of simply improving the interface.

The simple truth is that this would be very easy for Microsoft to remedy, and has been for years. In fact, Explorer has an option that allows you to fix a similar problem with folder windows by going to **Control Panel → Folder Options → View** tab and turning on the **Display the full path in title bar** option. Yet this option has no effect on file dialog boxes, despite the fact that they've been designed to mimic folder windows in most other ways.

So, why has Microsoft neglected to fix this very basic design flaw? One might assume that it's part of Microsoft's ongoing strategy to hide as much information as possible from the user, in an effort to make the computer *appear* easier to use. This is the same type of backward thinking that resulted in hidden filename extensions (see the discussion of file types in Chapter 4). The goal? Hide as much information as possible from the user, even at the expense of usability.

Perhaps it's merely a matter of priority. Perhaps the decision makers at Microsoft feel that "cute" dialog boxes will sell more copies of Windows than functional ones. Or maybe it's just another aspect of self-preservation in the computer industry: if Microsoft ever released the perfect product, nobody would upgrade ever again!

Now, we can speculate as to the intentions of the various developers of Windows until we're blue in the face, but what it really comes down to is *attitude*. By labeling something a bug, we are placing the burden of resolving the problem on Microsoft, and waiting for Microsoft developers to fix a bug that they consider to be a feature can definitely be considered a lost cause.

However, if we lump together the crash-a-day tendency of Windows, the irritating little animations, the clutter on the desktop, the lack of decent documentation, and the fact that performance rarely meets expectations, and call them all *annoyances*, we assume the burden of solving our own problems. This is a valuable attitude to adopt; it motivates us to learn more about the operating system so that we can work more efficiently. And, more importantly, it gives us the power to resolve the problems we encounter, so that we can get through the day with some degree of sanity.

Simply put, you should *not* be required to adjust the way you think in order to complete a task on a computer; rather, you should learn how to adjust the computer to work in a way that makes sense to you.

Take the solutions in this book seriously, but don't follow them blindly. Anything that indeed improves the interface can streamline your work and make the overall Windows experience less painful and more enjoyable. However, one person's annoyance is another's feature; what's important is to construct the interface that works best for you.

How This Book Came to Be

Back in early 1995, I was using a beta (pre-release version) of Windows 95 on my machine. Only a few hours after installing it, I became aware of the extent to which the previous version of Windows (Windows for Workgroups 3.11) had *stunted* my machine. A well-designed operating system can unleash the power of the hardware on which it runs, just as a poorly designed operating system can make you want to throw all of your expensive hardware in the thresher. Windows is a little bit from column A and a little bit from column B.

Now, not being the complacent type, I immediately started hacking away at Windows, compiling a list of questions and complaints about the operating system, some of which had solutions and some of which did not. This was the start of the *Windows 95 Annoyances* web site, which turned out to be one of the very first web sites devoted to Windows 95. Later, in the summer of 1995, other pre-release users began writing me with their own questions and complaints, and even with occasional solutions to the problems I hadn't yet solved.

As readers' requests for information and additional solutions became more diverse, so did the web site. The site quickly evolved from a simple list of annoyances to an extensive collection of tips and tricks, and eventually to a more comprehensive support center for Windows 95.

Then, in 1996, I wrote the book *Windows Annoyances* for O'Reilly, followed by *Windows 98 Annoyances* in 1998, and *Windows Me Annoyances* in 2000. As these books were written and released, the web site was expanded to include other versions of Windows, and now, as *Annoyances.org*, serves as the home for this book and its predecessors, the ever-increasing collection of online tips and tricks, and several very popular threaded discussion forums.

The first edition of *Windows XP Annoyances* was written in 2002 to cover the original release of Windows XP. This new edition, *Windows XP Annoyances for Geeks,* covers the benefits and pitfalls of Microsoft's latest edition of Windows XP: Service Pack 2.

I've written this book with the philosophy that the more you know about a tool you use—specifically, Microsoft Windows XP—the better your day-to-day experience with it will be. If this contradicts what you've seen in other books or the Windows manual, you're getting the idea.

But I prattle on. Feel free to dive in to any part of the book and start eliminating annoyances.

Organization of This Book

Chapter 1, *Getting Started with Windows XP*, discusses not only some of the more common annoyances in the operating system and why they're there, but also many of the improvements in this version over its successors. It's good stuff for gaining perspective on the operating system and its history of annoying behavior. Learn the best ways to install (and reinstall) Windows XP, including some advanced tips, such as setting up a dual-boot system and activation.

Chapter 2, *Basic Explorer Coping Skills*, starts by examining the Windows user interface and some of the settings that can significantly impact its usefulness. This is followed by a discussion of the way you work with Windows and how to take advantage of some of its lesser-known tricks and customization features, including advanced tips on Explorer: file-manipulation tricks, undocumented interface tweaks, and, best of all, some workarounds for Explorer's annoying Search tool. Finally, information on customizing skins and creating your own startup screen should whet your appetite for some of the real meat in the rest of the book.

Chapter 3, *The Registry*, reveals the structure of the Registry, Windows's giant database of settings and system configuration data, as well as the use of the Registry Editor application. This information is especially important, as most of the rest of the book depends on a working knowledge of the Registry. In addition to Registry basics, this chapter includes some advanced topics, such as effective searching techniques, finding the right Registry keys, and even a way to change certain Registry settings from within Explorer!

Chapter 4, *Tinkering Techniques*, continues with customization and problem-solving topics that take advantage of the Registry techniques discussed earlier. You'll find in-depth solutions for reducing clutter, protecting your file types, and customizing Windows XP beyond Microsoft's intentions; editing the Start Menu acquires a whole new meaning in this chapter.

Chapter 5, *Maximizing Performance*, presents an often-neglected topic. The goal is to get the best possible performance from your system without spending a lot of money or time. Learn about fine-tuning your applications, hardware, and processes to make your system run its best. Manage your hard disk space effectively with multiple partitions, advanced NTFS features, and virtual memory.

Chapter 6, *Troubleshooting*, starts with Windows startup and shutdown issues, error messages, application crashing, and the Windows Update feature. And that's only the first section. The next two sections cover drivers and hardware problems, documentation about which is often neglected. Eliminate the Blue Screen of Death, and use the Recovery Console when Windows won't start. Finally, you'll find tips on safeguarding your data in preparation for the worst disasters, as well as data recovery tips for those for whom the disasters have already happened.

Chapter 7, *Networking and Going Wireless*, allows you to expand your desktop and your repertoire by setting up a local-area network and connecting to the Internet. More than just the basics, this chapter explores protocols, troubleshooting, and advanced technologies, such as Internet Connection Sharing, Remote Desktop Sharing, virtual private networking, security, and WiFi. Plus, discover the ins and outs of the new Windows Security Center in Service Pack 2.

Chapter 8, *User Accounts and Administration*, covers user accounts, permissions, encryption, as well as resource sharing. This is essential material for anyone concerned about security, even if you're the only user on your machine. Bypass the logon box, share files and printers, and implement automatic file encryption and compression.

Chapter 9, *Scripting and Automation*, starts with a discussion of simple programming using the flexible Windows Script Host (WSH) included in Windows XP. In addition, you'll find advanced solutions, such as functions for accessing the Registry, working with files, and even making CGI programs for a web server. The chapter wraps up with several cool examples and a look at the Scheduled Tasks feature and how it can be used in conjunction with scripts for a truly automated environment.

Chapter 10, *The Command Prompt*, rounds out the book with coverage of what used to be called DOS. The Command Prompt is still a valuable tool in Windows XP, and can serve as an essential safety net in the event of a problem. Here, you'll find coverage of DOS commands, batch files (an alternative to the Windows Script Host), and, of course, the system path.

Appendix A, *Setting Locator*, is a comprehensive list of nearly every setting scattered throughout Windows XP, from folder options to removing tray icons.

Appendix B, *BIOS Settings*, is a glossary of the often-neglected motherboard settings that can significantly affect the stability and performance of your system.

Appendix C, *TCP/IP Ports*, is a discussion and listing of network ports, used to identify data travelling on a network (or over the Internet) and essential for networking configuration and security.

Appendix D, *Class IDs (CLSIDs) of System Objects*, lists the Registry codes used to identify certain system objects (such as My Computer and the Recycle Bin), useful when hacking the Registry.

Getting the Most Out of This Book

This book is arranged to be used as a learning tool, as well as a reference. More than just a bag of tricks, it covers a wide range of topics, some informational and some instructional. Although you certainly don't need to read the chapters in order, it is structured so that you can progress easily from one topic to the next, expanding your knowledge and experience as you go. You should be able to jump to any topic as needed; if you find that you don't have the proficiency required by a particular solution, such as knowledge of the Registry, you should be able to learn about it elsewhere in the book (Chapter 3, in the case of the Registry). For additional software and corrections, check out the *Annoyances.org* web site at *http://www.annoyances.org/*.

Most topics are presented as problems or annoyances with corresponding solutions. Topics usually begin with a few introductory paragraphs explaining something you don't often find in other references: why you'd want to complete the particular solution (and sometimes, why you wouldn't). In some cases, you may want to skip ahead to the actual solution procedure, easily identifiable by bullets or numbered steps.

Software Depository

Throughout this book, various add-on software is mentioned in the solutions to various problems. Now, wherever possible, I try not to make a particular solution absolutely dependent on add-on software—after all, I'd rather you carry around this book than a CD packed with useless, obsolete shareware.

In some cases, of course, a solution involving add-on software is either the preferable or only recourse. Fortunately, nearly all the software necessary to fill the holes in Windows as discussed in this book is freely available on the Internet. However, instead of including a list of web addresses here, all the software mentioned in this book, as well as software yet to be discovered, can be found at *http://www.annoyances.org*—just click the **Software** link on your left.

In addition to links for the downloadable software, you'll also find updates and additional information for the book. Also available is Creative Element Power Tools, a collection of tools specifically designed to help solve some of the Annoyances discussed in this book. You can download it from *http://www.creativelement.com/powertools/*.

Using Code Examples

This book is here to help you get your job done. In general, you may use the code in this book in your programs and documentation. You do not need to contact us for permission unless you're reproducing a significant portion of the code. For example, writing a program that uses several chunks of code from this book does not require permission. Selling or distributing a CD-ROM of examples from O'Reilly books does require permission. Answering a question by citing this book and quoting example code does not require permission. Incorporating a significant amount of example code from this book into your product's documentation does require permission.

We appreciate, but do not require, attribution. An attribution usually includes the title, author, publisher, and ISBN. For example: "*Windows XP Annoyances for Geeks*, by David A. Karp. Copyright 2005 O'Reilly Media, Inc., 0-596-00876-7."

If you feel your use of code examples falls outside fair use or the permission given above, feel free to contact us at *permissions@oreilly.com*.

Conventions Used in This Book

The following typographical conventions are used in this book:

`Constant width`
: Indicates command-line computer output, code examples, commands, text to type, and paths to Registry keys.

`Constant width italic`
: Indicates user-defined elements within constant-width text (such as filenames or command-line parameters). For example, Chapter 8 discusses a file encryption utility, *cipher.exe*, which has a variety of command-line options. A particular solution might instruct you to type:

```
cipher /r:filename
```

The italic portion of the above code, `filename`, signifies the element you'll need to replace with whatever is applicable to your system or needs. The rest—the non-italicized portion—should be typed exactly as shown.

Bold
: Identifies captions, menus, buttons, checkboxes, tabs, keyboard keys, and other interface elements. By bolding interface elements, it makes it easy to distinguish them from the rest of the text. For example, you may wish to turn off the **Force Windows to crash** option.

Window/dialog titles and icon captions are typically not bolded, but some objects (such as Control Panel contents) can appear as icons or menu items, and therefore typically appear bolded.

Italic
: Introduces new terms and indicates web site URLs, file and folder names, and variables.

"Quotation marks"
: Are used sparingly in this book, and are typically used to indicate references to topic headings and emphasize new concepts. Note that if you see quotation marks around something you're supposed to type, you should type the quotation marks as well (unless otherwise specified).

Path Notation
: Occasionally, the following shorthand path notation is used to show you how to reach a given user-interface element or option. The path notation is always presented relative to a well-known location. For example, the following path:

Control Panel → Date and Time → Internet Time tab

means "Open the Control Panel, then open **Date and Time**, and then choose the **Internet Time** tab."

Keyboard shortcuts
: When keyboard shortcuts are shown, a hyphen (such as **Ctrl-Alt-Del**) means that the keys must be held down simultaneously.

This is an example of a tip, often used to highlight a particularly useful hint or time-saving shortcut. Tips often point to related information elsewhere in the book.

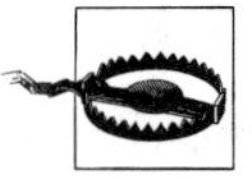

This is an example of a warning, which alerts to a potential pitfall of the solution or application being discussed. Warnings can also refer to a procedure that might be dangerous if not carried out in a specific way.

Request for Comments

Please address comments and questions concerning this book to the publisher:

O'Reilly Media, Inc.
1005 Gravenstein Highway North
Sebastopol, CA 95472
(800) 998-9938 (in the United States or Canada)
(707) 829-0515 (international/local)
(707) 829-0104 (fax)

You can also send us messages electronically. To be put on the mailing list or request a catalog, send email to:

elists@oreilly.com

To comment or ask technical questions about this book, send email to:

bookquestions@oreilly.com

The O'Reilly web site has a section devoted especially to this book, on which can be found errata, sample chapters, reader reviews, and related information:

http://www.oreilly.com/catalog/winxpannoy2/

For software mentioned in this book, as well as additional tips, online discussion forums, and Windows news, visit:

http://www.annoyances.org/

For more information about books, conferences, software, Resource Centers, and the O'Reilly Network, see the O'Reilly web site at:

http://www.oreilly.com/

Acknowledgments

I'd like to start by thanking the folks at O'Reilly Media, Inc. It's a supreme pleasure to work with people who are dedicated to quality and are passionate about their work. Special thanks to Tim O'Reilly for his enthusiasm, support, and commitment to quality. Thanks to Robert Luhn for helping me get this edition together and out in time.

Thanks also to everyone on the team who worked on this book.

I'd like to thank my family, friends, and well-wishers (in that they didn't wish me any specific harm), all of whom put up with my deadlines and late-night writing binges. Additional thanks to Ruth Kampmann. Finally, my immeasurable gratitude to Torey Bookstein, the love of my life.

And, as always, I thank you for your continued support. Without the people who read this book, it's nothing more than a test subject for Newton's first law of motion.

CHAPTER 1

Getting Started with Windows XP

Windows XP is easily the most stable, most powerful, and most seamless operating system ever to come from Microsoft. Whether or not that's saying something depends on how much time you've personally spent with Windows 95 or DOS.

Do you get a sinking feeling every time you're about to install new software on your computer? Do you get tired of having to turn off all the bells and whistles integrated into a new product just to make it usable? Does your day-to-day experience with Windows make you want to chuck the whole system out the window? Have you calmly accepted the fact that your new operating system will most likely contain more bugs than improvements?

Why fight it? Why not simply join the masses and slip into the mind-numbing abyss of acquiescence, feeling powerless whenever computers don't work as seamlessly as promised by those who market them?

Because you know there's a better way. You know there's more to Windows XP than what's mentioned in the documentation, such as it is, and in Microsoft's press clippings. And you know you're not alone.

A Brief History of Time, Re: MS Windows

As time progresses, the lineage of Windows becomes less linear. Windows XP, despite its name, is *not* the direct successor to Windows Me, nor is Windows 2000 the direct successor to Windows 98 and Windows 95. Instead, Windows XP is the latest installment to the historically less-consumer-oriented Windows NT line of operating systems, developed in parallel to the Windows 9x/Me line.

So why the distinction between these two product lines? The first release of Windows NT, arbitrarily assigned the 3.1 version number, was released in the middle of 1993. At the time, Microsoft's marketing department asserted that NT was an acronym for New Technology, which was actually quite an accurate description. The NT kernel, or underlying code upon which the interface (Explorer) runs, was completely new and did not rely on DOS,* despite the fact that it shared the same shell (interface) as Windows 3.1. This resulted (theoretically) in a more stable environment, much better security, and the ability to be easily ported to work on other processors (such as Compaq's Alpha chip).

Over the years, this "portability" has become much less emphasized. More recently, the NT line (Windows NT 4.0 in 1996 and Windows 2000 in 2000) has been improved and remarketed as a web, intranet, and network server; a challenger to Unix; and now, with Windows XP, a viable home-office operating system.

One of the problems with earlier releases of NT (from NT 3.1, which nobody liked, to NT 4.0, most commonly used as a web server, to Windows 2000, which made inroads among businesses and power users) was that they offered the enhanced features of the NT kernel without most of the perks and polish prized by the average consumer. What had plagued NT most, however, was the abysmal industry support for the platform. Given the overwhelming majority of Windows 9x users, a sizeable percentage of the hardware and software available for the PC—even released as recently as the time of this writing—was simply not supported in Windows NT/2000. The result was a platform that was really inappropriate for most users.

Windows XP changed all that way back in 2001. Among other things, Windows XP—known internally as Windows NT 5.1 (Windows 2000 is version 5.0)—replaces Windows Me completely and marks the end of the DOS-based Windows 9x/Me line. Not that we're sorry to see it go.

XP finally puts the stability and security of NT into the hands of *all* Windows users, while giving power users such perks as Plug and Play,† good

* DOS, or "Disk Operating System," was the first operating system available for the IBM PC (released in 1981). The first versions of Microsoft Windows (Versions 1.x-3.x) were simply applications that ran on top of DOS. Windows 9x and Me are no different, although Microsoft went to great lengths to hide the dependence on DOS. *Historical trivia: Microsoft purchased the code for DOS 1.0 for $50,000 and used it as the basis for their operating systems for more than twenty years.*

† Plug and Play was also included in Windows 2000, but has been improved in Windows XP with improved streamlining and automation, knowledge of far more devices, and much better industry support.

support for games, and most importantly, the industry support that is now possible due to the fact that Windows XP is the sole operating system platform sold by Microsoft (at least at the time of this writing).

Windows Editions and Service Packs

Windows XP is actually available in several different flavors, each of which is intended for a different market:

Windows XP Professional
: The power-user edition of Windows XP, and the subject of most of this book.

Windows XP Home
: This less-expensive edition of Windows XP is nearly identical to the Professional edition, with only a few minor exceptions. For instance, a few administrative tools present in XP Pro are missing from the Home edition.

Windows 2003 Server
: This edition is designed for those running a web server, domain server, or another mission-critical application (and if you don't like Unix). It's effectively the same platform as Windows XP, also with only a few minor exceptions when it comes to the end-user experience and the topic of conversation in this book.

On top of this assortment, Microsoft releases bug fixes and security patches for all editions of Windows several times a month, and if you have XP's auto-update feature enabled (Chapter 6), you likely have most or all of those updates already installed.

Now, from time to time, Microsoft consolidates all these patches into Service Packs, theoretically making it easier to assert precisely which version of Windows you're using. As of this writing, two service packs have been released for Windows XP:

Service Pack 1 (SP1), released in September 2002
: Released roughly a year after Windows XP first hit store shelves, SP1 contained nearly all the maintenance fixes to date, as well as a beefed-up Activation system (explained later in this chapter). Since hoards of phony Microsoft serial numbers floating around the web were instantly rendered useless, this update understandably caused a stir.

  However, the real problem with SP1 was the fact that it was issued as just another entry in the Windows Update catalog. For those with the aforementioned auto-update feature enabled, this meant that SP1 was installed automatically on millions of computers. A 160+ MB download requiring at least three times as much free disk space, it brought many otherwise-functioning systems to their knees for no other reason than insufficient disk space.

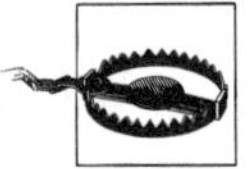

Let this be a lesson to you to avoid installing any subsequent service påck in this way; instead, download the standalone "network" version and run the update manually (after backing up your entire system) to avoid the worst of the SP-related problems.

Service Pack 2 (SP2), released in August 2004

SP2 was a more significant update than merely the sum of the bug-fix updates it contained. Among other things, SP2 replaced the weak wireless-networking support found in earlier versions with a new WiFi sniffer and configuration utility (Chapter 7). Plus, Microsoft has actually started pretending to take security seriously with this release and has changed a few of the operating system's defaults to plug the holes that so much malware (Chapter 6) had exploited previously (while, at the same time, opening up a few new ones). Finally, it comes with an improved firewall and a new Security Center utility to help protect the system. See Chapter 7 for complete coverage.

If you purchased Windows XP recently, either by itself or preinstalled on a new computer, then you likely already have either SP1 or SP2 preinstalled and are using a more recent edition than the one originally released in 2001. If you don't yet have Service Pack 2, it's considered essential, especially if you use wireless networking. That said, see Chapter 6 for a way to prevent SP2 from being installed on your system.

What You Get with Windows XP

If Windows XP is your foray into Windows, you're lucky to have escaped the early days of changing jumpers, editing the *config.sys* file, running out of "system resources," and suffering with the Windows 3.x Program Manager. However, dealing with the problems of the early days of Windows is a good way to build coping skills and is the only way to appreciate some of the things we now take for granted, such as Plug and Play and fast Internet connections.

Getting under the hood of Windows is not only a great way to take charge of the operating system and make it conform to the way you work and think, but it's also a very effective method for learning more about your computer and the technology that makes it work.

The basic "shell" interface (Explorer, the Desktop, and the Start Menu) in Windows XP is not that different from that of its immediate predecessors, Windows Me and Windows 2000. The new "Windows XP Style" (discussed at more length in Chapter 2) adds an optional new look to all dialogs, controls, windows, and even the Start Menu, but everything still works pretty much the same as it did in every version of Windows since 95.

What follows are a few highlights and lowlights of Windows XP, most notably for those who have upgraded or who are thinking of upgrading from a previous version. Some may seem insignificant; others may mean the difference between upgrading to Windows XP and waiting for something better to come along. All of these, naturally, add up to the total Windows XP experience.

Note that whether any particular thing is actually new to you depends on which version of Windows you were using previously.

Drag-and-drop of EXE files finally makes sense

After years of customer complaints, Microsoft has finally fixed the absurd way Windows handled the drag-and-drop of *.exe* files. As one visitor to *Annoyances.org* wrote several years ago, "whoever came up with the 'dragging an application creates a shortcut' behavior must be shot immediately." Now, dragging an *.exe* file works the same as dragging any other type of file. See Chapter 2 for details on drag-drop, plus a few nasty exceptions and plenty of helpful tips.

Enhanced file dialog boxes

As described in "Thinking Inside the Box" in the preface, nearly all of the file dialog boxes in Windows XP are resizable, fixing a long-standing annoyance with this common interface component. Unfortunately, however, file dialogs still don't remember their size, position, sort order, or display format (Details, Large Icons, etc.).

Also relatively new to file dialog boxes is the "Places Bar," a gray stripe down the left side of most dialog boxes containing icons for prominent file locations. Introduced first in Microsoft Office 2000, it contained links to the Desktop, the *My Documents* folder, and, among other things, *Web Folders*. The default Places Bar in Windows XP is far more useful, doing away with the useless *Web Folders* shortcut, instead including direct links to networked resources, My Computer, the Desktop, and History. See "Customize the Places Bar" in Chapter 4 for details on making these dialog boxes more useful.

A new look for Find, uh...I mean Search

The new Search tool doesn't really add any functionality over the Find tool found in Windows 98 and NT 4.0, but the interface has changed. Instead of a separate window, Search appears as a pane in Explorer, which tends to be confusing, frustrating, and just plain annoying.

For those users of Windows Me and 2000 who may have become accustomed to the Search pane in Explorer, XP's Search tool adds several layers of complexity with separate pages of options and a "helpful" puppy-dog assistant.

The good news is that the arbitrary 10,000-file limit on search results has been lifted, but there are plenty of flaws (such as the fact that the "search for text" feature often doesn't work at all). See "Fix the Search Tool" in Chapter 2 for fixes and workarounds.

Folder Shortcuts

It's finally possible to create a shortcut to a folder that behaves like a folder, instead of like a file. For example, an ordinary shortcut to your *c:\windows\temp* folder cannot be used as part of a path, but a Folder Shortcut can. Say you have a Folder Shortcut called *Cletus*, located in *c:*, that points to *c:\windows\temp*. You could then reference a file called *c:\Cletus\filename.txt*. The problem is that Folder Shortcuts are difficult to make and have their drawbacks as well. See "Mirror a Folder with Folder Shortcuts" in Chapter 4 for details, as well as some other cool things you can do with folders and drives.

Say goodbye to DOS

If you're coming from Windows 95, 98, or Me, DOS was always a sort of safety net: an easy way to replace system files, reinstall the operating system, or effect other repairs in case Windows wouldn't start. Although DOS is not part of Windows XP, there are a number of tools at your disposal, most of which are better than their counterparts in earlier versions of Windows. See Chapter 2 for details on replacing in-use files, Chapter 6 for troubleshooting a system that won't boot, including details on the System Recovery Console.

Although some of you may not appreciate it yet, the true death of DOS* is a blessing in disguise and is responsible for the stability and security that Windows XP offers. For example, see Chapter 5 for more information on the robust NTFS filesystem, previously unavailable on any DOS-based Windows computer.

* Don't confuse the DOS operating system with the Command Prompt, which is still alive and well, and discussed in Chapter 10.

Better hardware support

Each new version of Windows comes with more drivers than any of its predecessors, supporting a larger range of hardware, and Windows XP is no exception. In reality, though, we use new computers with old sound cards and new sound cards with old computers, meaning that upgrading is not always as seamless as Microsoft claims on the outside of the box. See Chapter 6 for troubleshooting and maintenance tips.

Dynamic system resources

Every time you open an application, it loads all of its visual components, such as windows, menus, text boxes, buttons, checkboxes, and lists, into memory. Windows keeps track of the visual components of all open applications so that, for example, when you drag a window across the screen, it knows what's behind the window and is able to redraw it when it becomes visible. These visual components are stored in an area of memory called System Resources.

The problem is that the System Resources consumed by an application aren't necessarily released when the application is closed.

In Windows 9x/Me, the amount of memory set aside for System Resources was a fixed amount, regardless of the amount of physical RAM installed in the machine. This meant that you could open and close an application several times and actually run out of System Resources. That's why Windows would complain that it was out of memory, even when you had only two or three applications open. Other symptoms included slow performance, application windows not displaying and updating properly, applications hanging, and the entire system crashing. The only fix was to clear out the System Resources by restarting Windows. This design was one of the biggest drawbacks of the platform.

In Windows XP (and Windows 2000), memory is allocated to System Resources dynamically; that is, System Resources grows as needed. This means that instead of having to restart the computer every few hours, as needed with Windows 9x/Me, you can theoretically leave a Windows XP machine running for days, weeks, or even months.

Performance, for better or worse

Anyone familiar with software upgrades has come to expect that any new version of an application or operating system will require more disk space and will run slower than its predecessor on the same hardware. This, of course, means lots of dollars spent on lots of gigabytes and lots of gigahertz. Microsoft is no stranger to what has become known as "bloat-ware," and Windows XP is, of course, no exception.

The reason that successive versions of software products do not get leaner and faster is that they don't have to. This is because for every additional megabyte of hard disk space an operating system requires, the available storage on the average new computer increases by ten megabytes.

At the same time, Windows XP actually does have some functionality that may result in improved performance over previous versions of Windows. For instance, it should outperform a Windows 2000–based system on the same hardware and will definitely boot faster in most cases. But, there is much more going on "under the hood" in Windows XP, so while it probably won't outperform its meager DOS-based ancestors on slower hardware, it will take better advantage of faster, newer hardware (and will literally scream on a dual-processor system).

An operating system being simultaneously slower and faster than its predecessor may seem like bit of a paradox, but that's the reality behind the evolution of personal computers. The key is to make the most of what you've got, and that's what this book is all about.

Suffice it to say, there are actually quite a few goodies that have been added to Windows XP, including lots of little touches here and there that actually work to improve the product.

So, assuming you haven't done so already, let's get right to installing the product on your computer!

Installing Windows XP

Installing an operating system is not an especially pleasant activity for most Windows users. Depending on your hardware, just booting up the setup CD can be a headache. Then you have to type that ridiculous 25-digit CD key and then make a bunch of choices about your network (all of which really could be made after setup, by the way). You then must sit and wait...and wait...for Windows to copy some two thousand files to your hard disk and then go through the excruciating process of "configuring" your computer. When it finally boots—assuming it even makes it this far—you then have the unenviable task of having to download and install more than a hundred megabytes worth of updates and fixes. And when all is said and done, you still will need to go through and turn off all of the annoying "features" littered throughout the interface and then fix the myriad of problems that are sure to pop up.

But the worst part is the feeling you can't shake: that you chose to install Windows XP on your machine, and now you've got to live with it.

Since a significant percentage of Windows XP users will obtain the OS preinstalled on their computers, many reading this will be fortunate enough to not have had to endure the installation of an operating system. That doesn't mean, however, that the task won't come back to haunt you later on, such as when you need to reinstall Windows or upgrade to the next version.

Both the steps to begin the installation procedure and the procedure itself can vary, depending on what's already installed on your system (if anything) and how you choose to approach the task.

Windows XP setup can be run from within an installed copy of Windows XP, Windows 2000, Windows NT 4, Windows Me, or Windows 98/95. You can also run setup from DOS (also known as the Windows 9x Command Prompt). Or, if you have no operating system at all, you can boot off the CD and install it fresh. The following sections cover the advantages and drawbacks of each type of install.

Anyone installing Windows XP on a hard disk that has data on it would be wise to back up the entire system before starting the install process. Make sure the backup software you use will also operate in Windows XP so you can read the media after the install is complete; otherwise, your backup will be worthless. See Chapter 6 for more information.

Installing on a New (Clean) System

The Windows XP installation CD is bootable, which means you can put it in the drive, turn on your computer, and installation will start automatically.

If you have an older (pre-SP2) installation CD, it's possible to create a new CD with Service Pack 2 preinstalled. See the "Slipstreaming XP and SP2" sidebar for details.

While most modern systems support bootable CDs, very few are configured to actually boot off such a CD when one is inserted. If your computer doesn't boot off the Windows setup CD, you'll need to change your BIOS settings accordingly. Start by entering your system's BIOS setup utility (discussed in Appendix B), going to the boot section, and changing the "boot device priority" or "boot sequence" so that your CD drive appears *before* your hard disk.* Exit the BIOS setup when you're finished.

* If you have a SCSI-based CD drive, look in your SCSI controller's BIOS setup screen and enable support for bootable CDs. If your SCSI controller is built into your motherboard, you'll probably need to first specify your SCSI controller as a boot priority over your hard disk, and then enable bootable CDs in your SCSI BIOS.

Slipstreaming XP and SP2

If you've upgraded the original release of Windows XP with Service Pack 2, you'll soon learn that you can no longer use your original CD to reinstall Windows in the event your PC won't boot. The solution is to integrate Service Pack 2 with your Windows XP installation CD, a process commonly called "slipstreaming." (Note that this won't work on a CD with SP1 or any OEM "recovery" CDs.) Here's how you do it:

1. Copy the entire contents of your XP install CD to a folder on your hard disk (e.g. *c:\xp*); just highlight everything in the root folder and do a drag-drop.
2. Download the Full Network Install release of Service Pack 2, *WindowsXP-KB835935-SP2-ENU.exe*, available at *http://microsoft.com*, and save it to a folder on your hard disk (e.g. *c:\sp2*).
3. Open a Command Prompt window (see Chapter 10) and type:

   ```
   cd c:\sp2
   WindowsXP-KB835935-SP2-ENU /integrate:c:\xp
   ```

   (Naturally, you'll need to change `c:\sp2` and `c:\xp` if you placed the files elsewhere.) If you get an error stating that "This Service Pack cannot be integrated into a destination that also has integrated Software Updates," the CD you're using can't be slipstreamed.
4. Next, extract the boot loader from your original XP installation CD using IsoBuster (*http://www.smart-projects.net/isobuster/*). When you start IsoBuster, select your CD drive from the list and then highlight the *Bootable CD* folder on the left. Drag the file *BootImage.img* from IsoBuster onto your hard disk.
5. Open a CD burning program that can create bootable CDs (e.g. Nero Burning ROM 6.0 or Roxio Easy Media Creator), and start a "Bootable CD" project. When prompted, specify *BootImage.img* file for the boot image data, select "4" for the sector count, choose "n emulation" for the bootable disc type, and type **0x7C0** for the load segment.
6. Add the entire contents of the `c:\xp` folder to your project, and burn the CD.
7. Boot off your new CD to install Windows XP along with Service Pack 2.

Note that there are a number of utilities that will help you further customize the Windows XP installation CD. nLite (*http://nuhi.msfn.org/nlite.html*), for instance, allows you to remove unwanted components before you install XP.

If you're unable to boot off the Windows XP CD, you'll need to use a bootable floppy, either one made from a previous version of Windows (see "Installation from the Command Prompt," later in this chapter) or one that comes with the full version of Windows XP. See "Creating a Bootup Floppy," later in this chapter, for more information.

Otherwise, Setup will display a welcome screen and spend several minutes loading drivers for your hardware. This ensures that Setup will properly support your hard drive, CD drive, and mass storage controllers; when Windows XP is installed, only the drivers you specifically need are loaded. But since Setup hasn't been prepared in this way (for obvious reasons), it must load (or attempt to load) every possible driver.

When the initialization is done, you'll be presented with several choices. The first screen instructs you to press **Enter** to set up Windows XP now, or press **R** to repair a Windows XP installation using the Recovery Console (an advanced diagnostic and repair tool covered in Chapter 6). Unless you specifically need to use the Recovery Console, press **Enter** to continue (even if you're here to repair a Windows installation).

Next, Setup will look for an existing Windows XP installation. If one is found, you'll have the opportunity to repair it now (see "Reinstalling Windows XP," later in this chapter for details). Just press **ESC** to continue.

The next screen will allow you to choose a drive and partition on which to install Windows. Here, you'll have the option of installing onto an existing drive or making changes to your partition table to add or remove partitions. See "Working with Partitions," in Chapter 5, for more information. Note that Setup will not allow you to choose the installation folder, but instead will simply place the files in the *\Windows* folder.

During the installation of some earlier versions of Windows, you could choose the name of the folder in which Windows is stored (by default, *\Windows*). This can be a problem if you're upgrading a Windows 2000 or Windows NT system, which, by default, store their files in *\WINNT*. If this applies to you, it's better to use the procedure outlined in "Upgrading from a Previous Version of Windows," later in this chapter. In this case, Setup will use whatever folder name is used by the current Windows installation.

If you're installing on a clean system (with a new, empty hard disk), you'll want to create a new partition using all of the available space (or several partitions, as desired). If your hard disk already has data on it, you'll be given the opportunity here to repartition your drive or simply install Windows XP on an existing partition (usually the first one, *C:*).

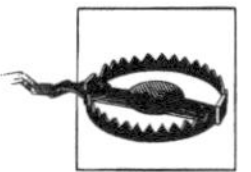

Repartitioning your drive involves deleting one or more existing partitions so that one or more new partitions can be created. It's important to realize that if you delete any partition that has data on it, all of the data will be erased. And without a complete backup, there will be no way to get it back.

When asked about the filesystem, you'll want to choose the NTFS filesystem in most cases; see "Choosing the Right Filesystem" in Chapter 5 for more information.

At this point, Windows setup will begin to copy files and configure your system. The rest of the installation process should be fairly straightforward; if you run into a problem, see "Dealing with Potential Problems During Setup," later in this chapter.

Upgrading from a Previous Version of Windows

The preferred way (at least according to Microsoft) to upgrade to Windows XP from a previous version is to install from within the existing copy of Windows. With Windows running, insert the Windows XP installation CD into your drive, and it should start automatically.*

When Setup starts, you'll be given four choices:

Install Windows XP
: This opens the main Windows Setup program (also accessible by launching *\i386\Winnt32.exe*). When it starts, your first choice will be between **Upgrade (Recommended)** and **New Installation (Advanced)**. Choose the upgrade option only if you want to install Windows XP over your existing installation, replacing your current OS with Windows XP and migrating all your settings and applications in one step.

  On the other hand, you may wish to choose **New Installation** if you want to install on another partition or on a clean hard disk (see "Installing on a New (Clean) System," earlier in this chapter). This option is instrumental in setting up a dual-boot system (discussed later in this chapter).

Install Optional Windows Components
: This is the same as opening **Add or Remove Programs** in Control Panel, and clicking **Add/Remove Windows Components**. Place a checkmark next to components you want installed, or clear the checkmark next to components you want removed.

Perform Additional Tasks
: This page contains links to several, mostly self-explanatory, tasks. Click **Set up Remote Desktop Connection** to install the Remote Desktop Connection software (described in "Controlling Another Computer

* If you have the AutoPlay feature disabled (see Chapter 4), or Setup doesn't start automatically for some reason, open Windows Explorer, navigate to your CD drive, and double-click *Setup.exe*.

Remotely (Just Like in the Movies)" in Chapter 6) on another computer. Click **Set up a home or small office network** to run the Network Setup Wizard, also discussed in Chapter 7. Finally, click **Transfer files and settings** to run the Files and Settings Transfer Wizard, discussed in "Transfer Windows to Another Hard Disk or System," in Chapter 5.

Check system compatibility
: This runs the Microsoft Windows Upgrade Advisor, which looks for potential problems, such as incompatible software and hardware, and lists them in a report. See "Casualties of the Upgrade," later in this chapter, for additional issues.

At this point, Windows Setup will begin to copy files and configure your system. The rest of the installation process should be fairly straightforward; if you run into a problem, see "Dealing with Potential Problems During Setup," later in this chapter.

Installing from the Command Prompt

If you need to install Windows XP on a new system and you are unable to boot off the CD, you can optionally install from a DOS boot disk (created on a Windows 9x/Me system by going to **Control Panel → Add/Remove Programs**, or from within Windows XP as described in Chapter 6). Just insert the floppy in your *A:* drive and power on your computer. If it's a Windows 98 or Windows Me floppy, it should contain all the necessary drivers for your CD drive,* required to access the setup program on the Windows XP CD.

When you get to the command prompt (`A:\>`), change to your CD drive by typing `D:` or `E:` (including the colon), depending on the letter on which the drive is installed. Then, type `\i386\winnt.exe` to start the DOS-based setup utility. The setup utility will copy the necessary boot files to your hard disk, reboot your computer, and run the same installer discussed in "Installing on a New (Clean) System," earlier in this chapter.

Reinstalling Windows XP

You may find yourself in a position where you'll need to reinstall Windows XP, either to solve a configuration problem or to repair a damaged installation. The procedure you choose depends on the current state of your computer.

* If you're using a Windows 95 startup disk, you'll need to obtain DOS drivers from the manufacturer of your CD drive and install them according to the included instructions.

If you're able to start Windows XP and access your CD drive, your best bet is to reinstall from within Windows. See "Upgrading from a Previous Version of Windows," earlier in this chapter, for details.

Otherwise, if Windows XP won't start, you should use the following procedure to repair the installation:

1. Boot off the XP CD, as described in "Installing on a New (Clean) System," earlier in this chapter.
2. When Setup begins, it will display two timed choices (timed, in that they disappear in 2–3 seconds if not activated). The first allows you to load a third-party SCSI or RAID controller driver by pressing **F6**. Use this only if Setup is unable to access your hard drive without them.

   The second option allows you to repair your system with the Automated System Recovery (ASR) feature by pressing **F2**. If you have a dual-boot system or other special arrangement, I recommend avoiding ASR, as it will attempt to repair your installation based on a few predetermined scenarios. The assumptions made by such an "automated" feature can wreak havoc if they're wrong.

   If you're unable to repair your system using the subsequent steps listed here, and you're unable to start the Windows Recovery Console due to a lost administrator password, you may wish to return here and try ASR as a last resort.

3. After Setup loads the hardware drivers, you'll then be presented with several choices. Press **R** at this point to start the Recovery Console (discussed later in this chapter). If you wish to repair XP without using the Recovery Console, press **Enter** here instead (I know, it's a bit counterintuitive). Or press **F3** to abort Setup and reboot the computer.
4. Next, Setup will look for an existing Windows XP installation and will hopefully find the one you're trying to repair here. Each Windows XP installation on your system will be listed here (you'll see only one if you don't have a dual-boot system). If it finds the installation you wish to repair, make sure it's highlighted and press **R** to begin the repair procedure, which, essentially, is an express reinstallation of the OS.

   If Setup can't find your installation, it means that one or more key system files are corrupted or missing. If you have a backup of your system, now would be the time to pull it out and think about restoring said files (see Chapter 6).

   Otherwise, your best bet is to use the Windows Recovery Console, discussed in Chapter 6.

If you try to repair Windows by pressing **ESC** here to start a new install, it may not work as expected. For example, even if you install to the same partition as the installation you're trying to repair, Setup may place the new copy of Windows in a different folder (i.e., *Winnt* vs. *Windows*).

5. The rest of the repair procedure should be relatively automated and fairly self-explanatory. For more troubleshooting information, see "Dealing with Potential Problems During Setup." See also Chapter 6 for more general troubleshooting tips.

Dealing with Potential Problems During Setup

No single book could possibly document every possible problem and incompatibility you might encounter while trying to install Windows XP. Luckily, about 95% of the problems you're likely to encounter fall under these six categories.

Motherboard BIOS
: The most common cause of a failed installation of Windows XP is an out-of-date BIOS. Fortunately, nearly all motherboards made in the last decade have software-upgradable flash BIOSes. Contact the manufacturer of your system or motherboard for any BIOS updates they have available, but don't bother unless a BIOS upgrade is absolutely necessary. (A failed BIOS upgrade will make your motherboard unusable.) See Appendix B for more information.

Video card
: Another common stumbling block to a successful Windows XP setup is your video card (display adapter). If Setup stops with an unintelligible error message, reboots unexpectedly during setup, or just hangs at a blank screen, your video card may be at fault. Some older video cards are simply not supported by Windows XP, but Setup will rarely, if ever warn you about such an incompatibility before you begin. If replacing the video card permits Windows XP to install, then the culprit is obvious. Note that while many video cards have upgradable flash BIOSes, I've never seen an instance where a BIOS upgrade can solve this type of incompatibility (although, it may be worth a shot). See the discussion of video cards in Chapter 6 for more troubleshooting advice.

Hardware inconsistencies and other problems
: Windows XP is a little more touchy about improper hardware configurations than previous versions of Windows. If, for example, your memory (RAM) is not all the same rated speed, is not the correct type for your motherboard, or is malfunctioning in some way, it will prevent

Windows XP from installing or running. Other potential problems include insufficient processor cooling, incorrect SCSI termination, improper jumpers on your IDE devices, bad cables, and even an older power supply. Chapter 6 includes troubleshooting tips for many kinds of hardware. See also Appendix B for system BIOS settings that may prevent Windows XP from installing.

Driver roadblocks
: Windows XP attempts to install drivers for all detected hardware towards the end of the setup process. If Setup crashes at the same point each time, try temporarily removing any extraneous devices (unneeded drives, cards, and external peripherals).

CD drive
: Since Windows XP installs from a CD, your CD drive may be to blame if the installation fails. A drive that delivers corrupt data to the computer will certainly cause problems, as will a drive that isn't accessible during the entire installation process. The same goes for older controllers (RAID and SCSI units, for example).

Dust in the wind
: Lastly, I've seen Setup fail from nothing more than excessive dust on the CD. Wipe the disk against your shirt and try again.

Setting Up a Dual-Boot System

With a dual-boot (or multiboot) setup, you can install multiple operating systems side by side on the same computer and simply choose which one to use each time you boot. So, why would you want to do this?

- If you rely on some software or hardware that will not operate in Windows XP, you can install Windows XP and the other OS on the same system simultaneously. This includes any previous version of Windows, as well as Linux, FreeBSD, Unix, BeOS, and even NeXTStep.
- If you're in the process of upgrading from an earlier version of Windows to Windows XP, you may wish to set up a dual-boot system. That way, you can test XP with your existing software and hardware without having to commit to the new OS until you're certain it will meet your needs.
- Some people install two copies of Windows XP on their system, one for normal use, and one as a testbed for new software and hardware. That way, you can try out a potentially buggy product without jeopardizing the main OS on which you must rely.

- Software developers often have several versions of Windows on the same machine so that they can test out their products on a variety of configurations without having to purchase a bunch of separate computers.

Windows XP comes with built-in support for a dual-boot system. The dual-boot feature (called the Boot Manager) is installed automatically when you install Windows XP. If, at the end of the installation, Windows XP is the only operating system on your computer, it will boot automatically without giving you a choice. Otherwise, you'll see a menu of installed operating systems, from which you can choose the OS you wish to use.

So, if you're installing Windows XP on a system with another OS, such as Windows 98, and you don't replace it with Windows XP (instead, you choose to install it into a different directory or partition), you'll get a dual-boot system without even trying.

In most cases, the boot manager of the last operating system installed is the one that will be used for all operating systems. For this reason, the order in which you install the operating systems is important; for example, it's typically desirable to install older operating systems *before* newer ones.

Some other operating systems, such as FreeBSD and Windows 2000, have boot managers of their own and can therefore be installed either before or after XP is installed with little additional fuss. However, operating systems *without* their own boot managers, such as Windows 9x/Me, will break the Windows XP boot manager if installed afterwards.

But what if you already have a Windows XP system and you need to add the dual-boot capability to it? Fortunately, there is a way to install other operating systems on top of an existing Windows XP installation, although it takes a little extra preparation.

The following procedure assumes that you already have a working installation of Windows XP:

1. Each operating system must have its own partition, assuming you have only one hard disk. See "Working with Partitions" in Chapter 5 for details on resizing drives and adding partitions.

   Note that since resizing partitions can be difficult without the proper third-party tools, you can simply add another hard disk instead of repartitioning your existing drive.

It's actually possible for Windows XP to share a partition with a Windows 9x/Me installation but only if they're installed into different folders. Since they'd share the *Program Files* folder, though, you'd be opening the door for conflicts and other problems.

2. Create a bootable floppy, as described in Chapter 6. The key is to back up the *ntdetect.com*, *ntldr*, and *boot.ini* files, which are the key to the Windows XP boot manager. See the next section for more information on the *boot.ini* file.

   You'd also be wise to back up your entire system at this point (see Chapter 6).

3. Install the other operating system; naturally, the installation procedure will vary, depending on the product you're installing. Be extremely careful not to install it into the same folder or partition as the existing copy of Windows XP.

4. When installation of the other product is complete, try starting the system. In some cases, the other product will have a suitable boot manager, and everything will work fine. If it doesn't, the procedure to repair the Windows XP boot manager depends on the other operating system you've just installed:

   Windows 2000 or Windows NT 4.0

   These earlier versions of Windows NT have boot managers similar to Windows XP's, but they may not work with Windows XP specifically. To repair the boot manager here, just copy the files *ntdetect.com*, *ntldr*, and *boot.ini* that you backed up in step 2 into the root directory of your boot drive (usually C:\), replacing the older ones that should be there.

   Windows 9x/Me

   Since these DOS-based versions of Windows (see Chapter 1) don't have boot managers of their own, the XP boot manager will be subdued by their installation. Although the files *ntdetect.com*, *ntldr*, and *boot.ini* should remain intact after installation, your hard disk's Master Boot Record (MBR) will have to be updated to once again recognize the Windows XP boot manager.

   This is done by starting the Windows Recovery Console (described in Chapter 6). Start by issuing the `fixmbr` command to restore the Windows XP boot manager, and then `bootcfg /rebuild` to force the boot manager to recognize the newly installed operating system.

Linux, FreeBSD, and others
: Each of these Unix flavors comes with its own boot manager that, for the most part, appears to be compatible with Windows XP. If in doubt, check the documentation for the specific operating system and version you're installing.

5. When you're done, create another bootable floppy (repeat step 2), so that you have an up-to-date backup of the *boot.ini* file.

> ### A Word About Filesystems and Dual-Boot
>
> Windows XP supports both the NTFS and FAT32 filesystems. If you need to set up a dual-boot machine with Windows 9x/Me and Windows XP, you'll need to use FAT32 on any drives that you want to access from the older Windows, as only Windows 2000, NT, and XP support NTFS.

Editing the Boot Manager configuration file (boot.ini)

The Windows XP boot manager is responsible for loading Windows XP, and, optionally, allowing you to boot into any other operating systems you may have installed. If you've set up a dual-boot (or multiboot) system, as described in the previous section, the list of operating systems that is presented when you first turn on your computer is stored in the Boot Manager configuration file (*boot.ini*).

The *boot.ini* file is, by default, a hidden file, located in the root directory of your primary partition (usually *C:*). If you can't see it, you'll have to configure Explorer to display hidden and system files by going to **Control Panel → Folder Options → View** tab, and selecting the **Show hidden files and folders** option and turning off the **Hide protected operating system files** option.

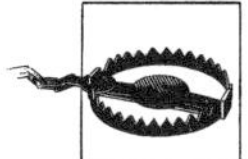

> If you screw up your *boot.ini* file, Windows XP won't load. Before editing the file directly, make sure to back it up as described in "Create a Boot Disk" in Chapter 6, so it can be easily restored if necessary. If worst comes to worst, start the Windows Recovery Console (discussed in Chapter 6) and issue the `bootcfg /rebuild` command to delete and then rebuild the *boot.ini* file.

The structure of *boot.ini*, similar to other *.ini* files, is explained in "Using INI Files" in Chapter 3. You can view and modify *boot.ini* in any plain-text editor, such as Notepad. A typical *boot.ini* file is shown in Example 1-1.

Example 1-1. The Boot Manager configuration file (boot.ini) is used to define the operating systems available in the boot menu

```
[boot loader]
timeout=20
default=multi(0)disk(0)rdisk(0)partition(2)\WINDOWS
[operating systems]
multi(0)disk(0)rdisk(0)partition(2)\WINDOWS="Windows XP Pro" /fastdetect
multi(0)disk(0)rdisk(0)partition(3)\WINNT="Windows 2000 Pro" /fastdetect
C:\="Microsoft Windows Me"
```

The two sections of the *boot.ini* file are as follows:

`[boot loader]`
: This section determines the default operating system—loaded automatically if no selection is made—and the timeout, the amount of time (in seconds) the Boot Manager waits before said selection is made.

`[operating systems]`
: This section lists each of the individual operating systems installed on the computer. The syntax is fairly simple: a "pointer" to the drive and folder containing the operating system is shown to the left of the equals sign, and the caption shown in the boot menu is shown to the right.

  The aforementioned pointer can appear in one of several different ways. The first two entries shown in Example 1-1 point to Windows NT installations (XP and 2000, respectively); the numbers in parentheses specify the disk and volume numbers of the respective partition, followed by the folder in which Windows is installed. The third entry points to a DOS partition (Windows Me in this case), where the syntax is merely the drive letter of the volume containing the OS.

  You'll notice that one of these entries matches the value of the `default` entry in the `[boot loader]` section.

To change the default OS and the timeout without editing *boot.ini* directly, go to **Control Panel → System** and click **Settings** in the **Startup and Recovery** section. Unfortunately, if you want to rename one or more of the captions in the menu, you'll have to open *boot.ini* and change the text in the quotation marks.

See "Using the Windows Recovery Console," in Chapter 6, for additional tools you can used to repair a damaged Windows XP installation and rebuild the *boot.ini* file.

Activating Windows XP

Product Activation is the euphemistic name given to the new system in Windows XP intended to curb software piracy. It effectively requires every

Windows XP user to call Microsoft (or connect via the Web) to obtain a long product activation key for each installation of the product. As though the hefty price tag and 25-character CD key on the back of the CD package in previous versions of Windows weren't enough, most users of Microsoft's latest OS are now required to take an additional step to complete the installation procedure.

If you don't enter the product key within a certain period after installing, Windows XP will expire and subsequently cease to function.* In theory, you'll only have to do this once for each computer running Windows XP, but the activation code is just as susceptible to bugs as any other component of Windows.

Here's how activation works:

1. When Windows XP is installed, the 25-character CD Key printed on the CD sleeve is typed by the user and stored in the Registry. The CD Key distinguishes one end-user license of Windows XP from another.

   Windows then generates a 20-digit product ID based on the CD Key and the Windows version.

2. After Windows has been installed, the Activate Windows XP utility is started. The "Installation ID," comprising the 20-digit product ID plus an 8-digit hardware ID, is then transmitted to Microsoft. This is either done transparently over a network connection or manually over the telephone.

   The hardware ID, a unique number based on values obtained from hardware in your computer, distinguishes one computer from another. The hardware ID is based on a *hardware hash*, a long sequence of numbers based on information found in your computer's hardware. The specific devices used are as follows:

   - Display adapter (video card)
   - SCSI adapter (if available)
   - IDE adapter
   - Network adapter MAC address (if available)
   - RAM amount range
   - Processor type
   - Processor serial number†

* Depending on your outlook, this may be a blessing in disguise.

† The processor serial number, in most cases, is not accessible to Windows. See Appendix B for the BIOS setting that affects this.

- Hard drive
- Hard drive volume serial number
- CD-ROM, CD-RW, or DVD-ROM

3. Microsoft then generates a 42-digit "Confirmation ID," which is sent back to the Activate Windows XP application (or read back verbally if you're activating XP over the phone). The machine is officially activated when the confirmation ID is received, cross-checked with the hardware ID and product ID, and finally stored on your computer.

It should be clear that since the confirmation ID is based upon the unique CD key and the unique hardware ID, it represents a single, unique combination of hardware and software. Change any of these components, and the confirmation ID will no longer be valid.

If you attempt to activate Windows with the same CD Key and a different hardware key (effectively installing the same copy of Windows on a different computer), the copy protection will kick in and the product activation will fail. The gray area is what happens when you upgrade part or all of your system.

Now, there is some margin for error built in, so upgrading only one or two of the aforementioned components should not cause a problem. However, simultaneously upgrading your motherboard, processor, memory, and video card will probably raise a red flag, and you'll probably have to get a new key. Likewise, if you purchase an entirely new computer and install your existing copy of XP on the new machine, you'll certainly have to obtain a new key from Microsoft.

It probably goes without saying that the automated activation will probably fail at this point, meaning that you'll have to speak with a Microsoft representative and explain that you're merely reinstalling and not pirating the software. It remains to be seen how much hassle reactivation will be; suffice it to say that those who upgrade often will bear the brunt of that hassle.

Note that if your system crashes, or if you simply need to wipe everything and reinstall for some reason, the confirmation ID from the previous activation should still be valid. Note that the confirmation ID is only shown if you activated over the phone, and is otherwise invisible; if you used the automated activation over the Internet, all you'll need to do is run the activation again. Since the hardware supposedly is no different, Microsoft shouldn't give you any trouble.

Many users may not be confronted with the hassle of product activation at all, for one of several possible reasons. Those systems purchased with Windows XP preinstalled may be preactivated as well, in one of two possible ways. Either the manufacturer may choose to activate Windows before shipping using the method described above, or by a separate mechanism called *System Locked Pre-installation* (SLP). SLP ties the hardware ID to the system BIOS, rather than the discrete components listed earlier. The resulting system may be upgraded more freely, but if the motherboard is replaced or the BIOS is upgraded (see Appendix B), the owner will have to reactivate the software. The other exception is the version of Windows XP sold with a volume license, usually to large businesses, which doesn't include the product activation feature at all.

Migrating to Windows XP

Migration is typically a term used by system administrators to describe the lengthy process of upgrading some or all the computers in an organization to a new software product, but nearly all of the issues faced apply to anyone upgrading to Windows XP from an earlier version.

While the previous section covered issues dealing with the actual installation of Windows XP, the following topics discuss the steps you may need to take after the upgrade has taken place.

Casualties of the Upgrade

As you've probably discovered on your own, there are a number of hardware and software products that simply won't work with Windows XP. Some of these products are simply awaiting driver updates from their respective manufacturers, while others have been abandoned by their manufacturers with no hope of future support.

If you haven't yet upgraded to Windows XP, it's best to first check with the manufacturers of each and every card, drive, printer, input device, and other peripheral you use to make sure your devices are supported under Windows XP, either out of the box or via a driver update. Naturally, it wouldn't be the least bit practical to try and list each individual incompatible device here, but the following list should give you an idea of the types of products that may cause problems with Windows XP (or any new operating system, for that matter).

Also available is the Microsoft Windows Upgrade Advisor (MSUA), mentioned in "Upgrading from a Previous Version of Windows," earlier in this chapter. The MSUA scans your system and compares it to a list of devices and software known to cause problems with Windows XP. While its internal list is far from complete, it will certainly warn you of any incompatibilities of which Microsoft is aware. Start it by inserting the Windows XP CD and clicking **Check system compatibility** and then **Check my system automatically**.

You can also download it from *http://www.microsoft.com/windowsxp/pro/howtobuy/upgrading/*.

As with the move to any new operating system, there are some software and hardware components that either won't be compatible with the new version, or are version-dependant, and must be updated to work with the new version.

Any versions of the following products not specifically designed to work with Windows XP will most likely need to be updated or removed:

- Any software that works with settings specific to any single version of Windows, such as Microsoft TweakUI (versions 1.33 and earlier). See Appendix A for details.
- Older backup software, such as Veritas Backup (all versions) and Seagate Backup Exec. However, any backup software made for Windows 2000 should work in Windows XP equally well. This is of special importance, because whatever software you use to back up Windows before upgrading will need to be supported in Windows XP. Otherwise, the backup you create will most likely be inaccessible.
- Antivirus and low-level disk utility software, such as Norton Utilities and Norton Antivirus, tend to cause problems when used in any operating system other than the one for which they were specifically designed.
- CD-R/DVD±R burning and CD-RW packet-writing software not designed specifically for Windows XP may interfere with the built-in CD burner features in Windows XP, or may stop functioning because of said features. Examples include Roxio Easy CD Creator (versions 5.0 and earlier) and any version of DirectCD released before 2002.
- Games, especially the more graphic-intensive and 3D-accelerated ones, frequently have problems with newer versions of Windows, especially those based on Windows NT (such as Windows 2000, and yes, Windows XP). While you won't have to remove these games before you upgrade to Windows XP, you may need to contact the manufacturers of any games that won't function in XP for any patches, updates, or special settings required for their games to run on Windows XP. Since games are rarely updated to work with newer versions of Windows, you may need to set up a dual-boot system (as described later in this chapter) just to run older games.
- Any software that requires that you boot directly into DOS will not function on a Windows XP system, as DOS is no longer part of the operating system. Try launching the program in compatibility mode, as described in Chapter 6.

- Certain types of hardware are more dependent on features found in specific operating systems and are less likely to be supported under newer versions of Windows. Such devices typically include TV and radio cards, webcams, video capture devices, digital cameras and memory-card readers, flatbed scanners, film scanners, synchronization cradles for handheld computers, older digitizers (tablets), oddball printers and pointing devices, CD changers, and DVD decoders. If you can't obtain newer drivers and software for any of these less-common peripherals, they may not work in Windows XP at all.

Few, if any, of the aforementioned issues should apply to the upgrade from Windows XP to XP Service Pack 2. However, the security changes discussed in Chapter 7 may cause some network-enabled software to break. Fortunately, these types of problems can typically be fixed by changing settings in the Windows Firewall or the software at issue.

If you find that one or more software or hardware products won't work in Windows XP, setting up a dual-boot system with an older version of Windows, as described later in this chapter, may be the answer.

Adjusting Windows XP to Smooth Out the Migration

Aside from the hardware and software incompatibilities discussed in the preceding section, the task of undoing some of the changes made by Setup is what will be on most users' minds right after upgrading to Windows XP. Fortunately, there are several things you can do to ease the transition:

Visual style of screen elements
: Make Windows XP look more like previous versions of Windows by going to **Control Panel** → **Display** → **Appearance** tab, and choose **Windows Classic style** from the **Windows and buttons** list.

Overly complex Start Menu
: To revert to the simpler single-column Start Menu found in earlier versions of Windows, go to **Control Panel** → **Taskbar and Start Menu** → **Start Menu** tab, and select the **Start menu** option.

Animation and other eye candy
: The animation and other eye candy used with windows, menus, lists, and even your mouse cursor is more prevalent in Windows XP than any previous version of Windows. See "Tame Mindless Animation and Display Effects" in Chapter 5 for details.

Categories in Control Panel

The categories in Control Panel, which are somewhat superfluous, can be removed by opening the Control Panel window (not the Control Panel menu in the Start Menu, nor the Control Panel folder in Windows Explorer, however), and clicking **Switch to Classic View** in the Common Tasks pane. If Control Panel appears as a menu in the Start Menu, you can open it in its own window by double-clicking or by right-clicking the **Control Panel** item and selecting **Open**. If you don't want a Common Tasks pane, see the next topic.

Common Tasks pane in folder windows

The Common Tasks pane is supposed to show links to additional programs and features, depending on the folder currently being viewed, but most of the time, it's just unnecessary clutter. If you prefer the simpler, cleaner folders found in earlier versions of Windows, go to **Control Panel → Folder Options → General** tab, and select the **Use Windows classic folders** option.

Hijacking of file types

Every time you run Windows Setup, it will reclaim a bunch of different file-type associations without asking. For example, your default applications for *.html* files (web pages), *.jpg* images, and *.zip* files (archives), are all forgotten in favor of Microsoft's replacements. The fact that Windows doesn't preserve your associations, or at least ask before overwriting them, should be attributed to nothing more than laziness on the part of Microsoft's developers.

See "File Types: The Link Between Documents and Applications" in Chapter 4 for details. See "Turn off the Windows Picture and Fax Viewer" in Chapter 4, for more information on the treatment of image files in Windows XP.

To turn off Windows built-in support for *.zip* files, wherein they're treated like folders instead of files, see "Fix the Search Tool" in Chapter 2.

New Search tool

See "Fix the Search Tool" in Chapter 2 to work around the consequences of the changes in Window XP's Search tool from previous sections.

Icons for system and desktop objects

The icons used for the system objects, such as My Computer and the Recycle Bin, have a new look in Windows XP. If you prefer the icons used in earlier versions of Windows, see "Cleaning Up Desktop Clutter" in Chapter 4. Note that nearly all of the older icons can be found in the file, *\Windows\System32\SHELL32.dll*.

Where to find it in Windows XP

A common problem encountered by those who are new to Windows XP, yet familiar with a previous version, is that some features are no longer found in the same places or simply have different names. The following lists some of the more major components that have been moved or renamed:

Network Neighborhood
: This is now called My Network Places and works pretty much the same (albeit a bit more reliably) as in earlier versions of Windows. Note that the networks and computers previously directly accessible through Network Neighborhood in some earlier versions of Windows are now buried under *Entire Network\Microsoft Windows Network*. To counteract this, Windows XP will automatically place shortcuts to some remote folders right in the My Network Places folder."

My Computer icon on the desktop
: By default, the My Computer icon is not shown on the Windows XP desktop, but all the entries it contained can be found in both the Start Menu and Windows Explorer. To put the icon back on the desktop, go to **Control Panel** → **Display** → **Desktop** tab → **Customize Desktop**, and turn on the **My Computer** option.

Control Panel in My Computer
: By default, Control Panel no longer appears in the My Computer window, but it's still available in the Start Menu. You can also go to **Control Panel** → **Folder Options** → **View** tab, and turn on the **Show Control Panel in My Computer** option. Confusingly, it will still appear under the My Computer branch in Windows Explorer, regardless of this setting.

Dial-up networking
: Dial-up connections are now considered ordinary network connections, and can be found in the Network Connections window.

DOS
: Although some earlier versions of Windows (e.g., Windows 9x/Me) relied on the old DOS operating system (described in Chapter 10), Windows XP is based instead on the more robust Windows NT kernel. This means, among other things, that you'll no longer be able to boot directly to DOS, unless you've set up a dual-boot system, as described later in this chapter. The good news is that booting to DOS is really not necessary any more.

Boot disk

Mostly because of the absence of DOS, Windows XP has no provision for making a boot disk that can start Windows XP. See "Create a Boot Disk" in Chapter 6 for applicable alternatives.

Web View

The Web View, at least as it existed in Windows 98, Me, and 2000, is thankfully gone in Windows XP. Although it can't be customized in the way that the Web View could, the Common Tasks pane (described in "Adjusting Windows XP to Smooth Out the Migration," earlier in this chapter) accomplishes most of what Microsoft originally intended the Web View to do. And fortunately, Common Tasks can be switched off much more easily than the Web View ever could.

CHAPTER 2

Basic Explorer Coping Skills

The part of Windows XP with which we interact most frequently is Windows Explorer, commonly referred to simply as "Explorer." The Explorer application (*Explorer.exe*) is known as the shell, since it's the pretty face that is used to conceal what lies under the hood of the operating system. Although Explorer is really only an application like any other, it is responsible for the desktop, the Start Menu, Recycle Bin, Control Panel, folder windows, and a million other things.

Given the amount of time you probably spend starting programs, copying files and folders, and looking for documents—not to mention actually writing all those documents—it makes sense to invest a little time to find better ways to accomplish these tasks. By following some of the solutions in this book, you can make your experience with Windows a lot more pleasurable, reducing stress and your recurring urges to toss your computer out a window seven stories off the ground.

The ideal user interface should adapt to you rather than the other way around. Indeed, one of the primary goals of this book is to show you how to change the way Windows looks, feels, and operates so that it is more closely in tune with the way you think and work. The problem is that there are some fundamental features of the interface that simply can't be changed, so some of the time you'll simply have to settle for the best compromise between the ideal solution and what is actually possible.

A classic example is the Search tool in Windows XP. When you begin a search from an open Explorer window, the Search pane replaces the folder tree, forcing you either to open a new Explorer window or to turn the folder tree back on by going to **View → Explorer Bar → Folders** (which incidentally is the only entry in this menu without a keyboard shortcut). And let's not forget the little puppy dog with its incessant scratching noises. Although these problems can't be completely fixed without a third-party add-on, there are several workarounds discussed in "Fix the Search Tool," later in this chapter. A little knowledge of the alternative methods will save you tons of aggravation.

Many of the topics discussed throughout this book require knowledge of the Windows Registry, with the exception of this chapter—I figured you'd want to jump right in. In addition to the Explorer-related tips and tricks, many of the topics of this chapter document the subtle interface differences in Windows XP from previous releases, especially useful for those who have recently upgraded—it's all good stuff. Chapter 3 provides thorough coverage of the Registry, a working knowledge of which will be employed by material found later in this book.

Lastly, it should be pointed out that this chapter assumes that you have a basic working knowledge of Windows: files and folders, double-clicking, right-clicking, using menus, and so on, although those who are just getting started with Windows should be able to catch on without too much effort.

Working with Explorer

One of the primary roles of Explorer is to provide the basic working interface that allows you to manage the files, folders, and applications on your system. This is why it's so baffling why Microsoft has buried the Windows Explorer icon so deep in the Start Menu, rather than giving it a more prominent position.

As stated earlier, the Windows desktop, the My Computer window, the single-folder windows, the folder-tree pane window, and the Start Menu are all services provided by the single Explorer application. However, in most Windows lore and in the solutions in this book, the term Explorer refers specifically to the window that has the hierarchical tree view in the left pane (referred to by Microsoft as the Folders Explorer bar). This window can be opened by going to **Start → Programs → Accessories → System Tools → Windows Explorer**, or by launching `Explorer.exe` from the Start Menu's **Run** command. All other windows used to browse folders—such as those windows accessible from the My Computer window—are commonly referred to as single-folder windows.

It's important to realize that Explorer, your single-folder windows, and even your desktop are all essentially the same interface (with a few subtle exceptions). File and folder icons look and behave the same, regardless of the way they're viewed.

Interface consistency is one of the most important aspects of interface design, but, unfortunately, it often contradicts other factors, such as intuition and historical consistency. For example, drag-drop in Explorer behaves differently when you're dragging from one drive to another (*d:* to *c:*) than when dragging from one folder to another on the same drive (*c:\docs* to *c:\files*). Why the inconsistency? Because that's the way it has been done in Windows for years, and fixing it would likely confuse too many users. (At least from the perspective of the company that otherwise would have to answer all the technical support calls.)

Actually, I've found that Windows XP has better consistency in its interface than most of its predecessors. In Windows 98, for example, keystrokes that worked in one situation in Explorer didn't work in other situations, and this has been fixed in this latest version for the most part. And Microsoft has done away with the "drag an EXE file to create a shortcut" behavior—found in some earlier versions of Windows—which was terribly inconsistent with the way other files were drag-dropped, not to mention really annoying. But, XP is still far from perfect; the way Control Panel categories appear in some cases but not in others end up making the tool that much harder to use.

One of Explorer's primary annoyances—and, paradoxically, one of its essential features—is the mandatory use of special combinations of keystrokes and mouse clicks to perform simple operations, such as using the **Ctrl** key to copy a file or having to make sure the source and destination folders are both visible before trying to copy or move an object. This behavior, for the most part, can't be changed—but there's enough flexibility and alternative methods built into the interface to allow you to accomplish just about any task.

Exploring Basic Explorer Settings

Many aspects of the way Windows works can be controlled by changing certain settings, which are scattered throughout Explorer. These settings can be changed quite easily, quickly making Windows behave the way you expect—which, of course, depends on your level of experience and how you work. The Folder Options dialog box is a good place to start (see Figure 2-1). Select **Folder Options** from Explorer's **Tools** menu (or double-click **Folder Options** in Control Panel).

The first page—or the **General** tab—of the Folder Options dialog box allows you to control three different options; their connection is that they all affect the way Explorer looks. The options are explained as follows:

Tasks

The **Show common tasks in folders** option, enabled by default, is responsible for the information pane shown on the left side of single-

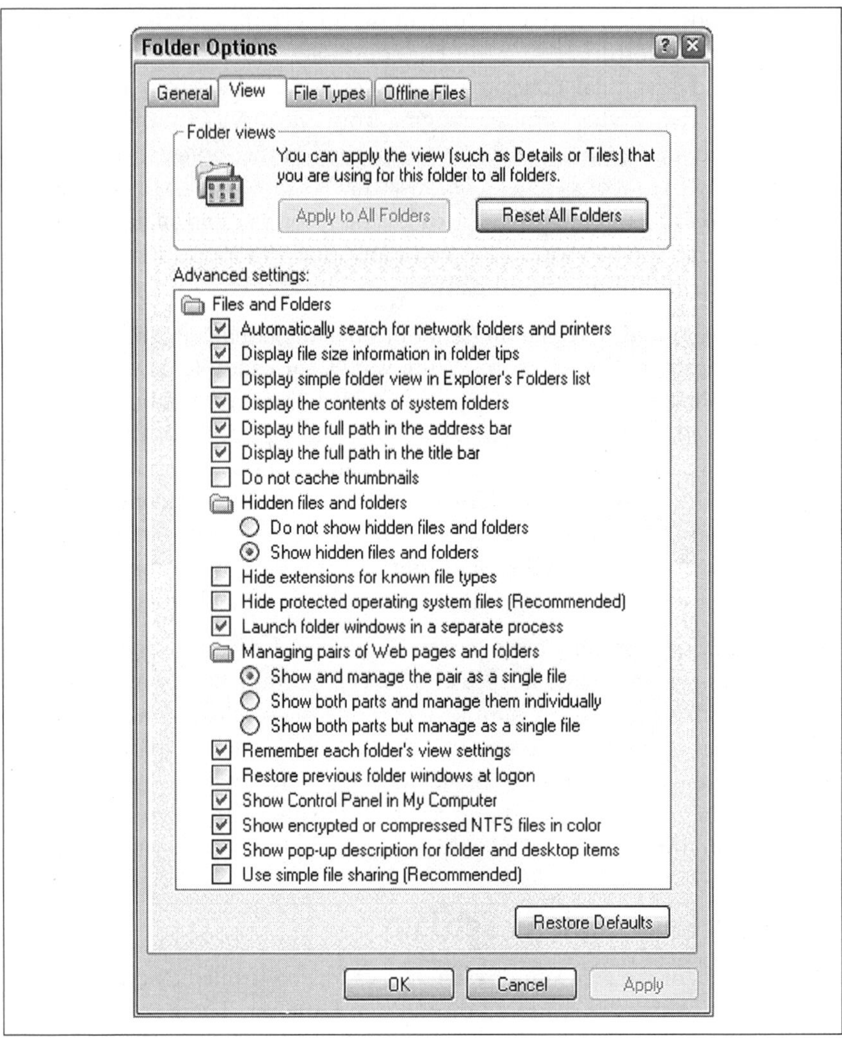

Figure 2-1. The Folder Options dialog box is a good place to start messing around with some basic Explorer settings

folder windows, or between the tree and the folder view in Explorer windows. With the exception of the option to enable or disable categories in Control Panel, the common tasks pane can be turned off (by selecting **Classic Folders**) with no loss in functionality.

The common tasks pane takes the place of the Web View found in earlier versions of Windows.

Browse folders

The **Browse folders** option determines whether or not a new window appears when you open a folder icon from within another open single-folder window. This setting is ignored when the folder tree pane is visible.

Note that the **Ctrl** key can be used to override whatever option you chose for **Browse folders**. For example, if you've opted to **Open each folder in its own window**, holding the **Ctrl** key while double-clicking a folder icon will force the folder to open in a new window.

Click items as follows

The **Single-click to open an item** option is included primarily as a hold-over from the Web View feature found in earlier versions of Windows, but it does have the advantage of allowing you to navigate most of Windows without having to double-click (something you can also do with the right mouse button).

Note that if you choose the single-click interface, you can no longer click twice slowly on an item to rename it; instead, you must either right-click on it and select **Rename** or carefully move the mouse pointer so that it is hovering over the icon (which is how icons are normally selected with this option) and press the **F2** key.

The **Double-click to open an item** option can certainly be a pain in the neck for beginners and experienced users alike, but there are significant advantages of requiring double-clicks to open icons. For example, it virtually eliminates the possibility of accidentally opening a program or folder when you try to select, delete, move, copy, or rename an item.* More importantly, double-clicking is consistent with all other operating systems, such as Macintosh and Unix, as well as with previous versions of Windows. This may not seem like a great argument, but a primary factor of good user-interface design is the use of familiar elements.

The next tab, **View**, shows settings that affect how much information Explorer shows you; unfortunately, the defaults are set in favor of a "simpler" view, which ironically can make Windows more difficult to use. Some of the more interesting settings include the following:

The use of some of the following options can be very confusing, in that enabling them ends up turning something *off* in the interface, or vice versa. But that's the nature of the beast...

* Most pointing devices (mice, styli, trackballs) with more than two buttons allow the additional buttons to be programmed. I've found that the third mouse button (or the second barrel switch, if you're using a stylus) is ideal for double-clicking.

Display the simple folder view in Explorer's Folders list

This misnamed option is merely responsible for showing or hiding the dotted lines shown in Explorer's folder tree. Although the default is *on*, you can turn it *off* to make the tree look more like earlier versions of Windows. Personally, I feel the lines make the tree a little clearer and easier to use, so I'd suggest turning this option off.

Display the contents of system folders

Enable this option (the default is *off*) to eliminate the warning that appears when you attempt to view the contents of certain folders, such as *\Windows* and *\Windows\System*.

Display the full path in the Address Bar/titlebar

By default, when viewing the folder, *c:\Documents and Settings\Agnes\Documents\Stuff* in Windows Explorer, only *Stuff* will actually appear in the titlebar and Address Bar. This can be extremely confusing, especially when you also have a *d:\Other Documents\Maddie\Stuff* folder. Why Microsoft insists on hiding pertinent information continually baffles me. I strongly recommend enabling both of these options to display the full path in all Explorer and single-folder windows. Note that these options have no affect on File Open/Save dialogs.

Hidden files and folders

Explorer does not show hidden files by default in Explorer. If set to **Show hidden files and folders**, any files with the "hidden" file attribute will be shown in Explorer, but their icons will still appear faded. To hide or unhide a file or folder, right-click it, select **Properties**, and change the **Hidden** option.

Hide extensions for known file types

I believe this feature to be one of Microsoft's biggest blunders; it's turned *on* by default, and has been in every Windows release since Windows 95. Filename extensions determine how Windows interacts with your documents, and hiding these extensions limits users' understanding of this technology and how it affects them. See "File Types: The Link Between Documents and Applications" in Chapter 4 for a further explanation of why this option should be turned *off*.

Hide protected operating system files

When this option is turned *on*, files with the "system" file attribute are hidden in Explorer. This is similar to the **Hidden files and folders** option, discussed earlier. So-called "system" files include the *boot.ini* file discussed in Chapter 10 and all *\Recycler* folders (responsible for the Recycle Bin).

Launch folder windows in a separate process

By default, the desktop, Start Menu, and all open Explorer and single-folder windows are handled by the same instance of Explorer. That is, only one copy of the *Explorer.exe* application is ever in memory. If you enable this option, each Explorer window will use a new instance of the program. Although this takes slightly more memory and may slightly increase the time it takes to open Explorer windows, it means that if one Explorer window crashes, it won't bring them all down. See the "What Happens When Explorer Crashes" sidebar for more information.

What Happens When Explorer Crashes

There's a little program that runs invisibly in the background that automatically restarts Explorer if it ever crashes. This is what is happening when your desktop spontaneously disappears and then reappears a few seconds later.

If you enable the **Launch folder windows in a separate process** option, it will separate the process that controls your desktop from those that control all open Explorer windows. This means that if one Explorer window crashes, they won't all crash. One side effect of this is that if the instance of Explorer that controls your desktop and Start Menu crashes, and there's another Explorer window open, that little background program will instantly open another Explorer window. This is the same thing that happens if you try to launch Explorer manually; Explorer will only load your desktop if no other instances of Explorer are detected. In this circumstance, you can be caught without a desktop or Start Menu at all.

To work around this, start by closing all Explorer windows. Then, press **Ctrl-Alt-Del** to display the Windows Security dialog, and click **Task Manager**. In the Task Manager window that appears, go to **File → New Task (Run)**. Type `explorer` and then click **OK**. Your desktop and Start Menu will then appear normally.

Managing pairs of Web pages and folders

The "pair" mentioned here refers to what you get when you save a web page in Internet Explorer and choose the **Web Page, complete** option in the Save Web Page dialog. By default, all of the images on a page are saved along with the original HTML file in their own folder: if you save a page called *Homepage of Mr. X*, the image folder will be automatically named *Homepage of Mr. X_files*.

Internet Explorer (IE) creates an invisible link between web pages saved in this way and their associated image folders, in that if you copy, move, or delete the HTML file, the image folder follows automatically. (Strangely, the same is not true for renaming.) The three options here relate to how Explorer handles this invisible link. Unfortunately, these options don't really work as you'd expect; they basically all end up doing the same thing.

If you don't want the image folder created when you save a web page in IE, just select **Web Page, HTML only** from the **Save as type** list in IE's Save Web Page dialog.

Remember each folder's view settings
: This option, when enabled, forces Explorer to remember the "View" settings for the 20–30 most recently opened folders, such as the sort-order and icon-size settings. This "memory" overrides the default view settings, but only for the folders you've recently customized. To change the defaults used by *all* folders, see "Force Explorer to Remember Its Own Settings," later in this chapter.

Show encrypted or compressed NTFS files in color
: Among the additional services provided by the NTFS filesystem (discussed in Chapter 5) are support for on-the-fly encryption and compression of certain files. Turn *on* this option to visually distinguish encrypted and compressed files and folders by displaying their names in blue. See Chapter 8 for more information on NTFS encryption.

Use Simple File Sharing
: Despite the fact that Microsoft apparently recommends enabling this setting, you should disable it immediately for security purposes. See Chapter 7 for more information.

What it comes down to, of course, is that you should use what works best for you. Don't blindly accept the defaults just because it came out of the box that way.

The third Folder Options tab, **File Types**, is discussed in detail in Chapter 4. In addition to the settings in the Folder Options dialog, there are other, less-conspicuous settings in the main Explorer window.

Details
: The Details view (go to **View → Details**) is easily the most useful format for folder listings, but not surprisingly, Microsoft has made the prettier but less useful Icons view the default for all versions of Windows since 95. The Details view displays file and folder names, along with their sizes, types, and dates in a tabular format.

  The list is easily sorted by clicking the appropriate column header. Right-click any column header to show or hide columns as needed, or go to **View → Choose Details** for the complete selection.

You can resize the column widths by dragging between the column headers; double-click the space between column headers to automatically resize the column to fit its contents. Finally, columns can be rearranged by dragging the column headers.

> You can also get the Details view in Windows's **File → Open** and **File → Save** dialog boxes. Just click the right-most icon on the top row of the dialog, and choose **Details** from the list that appears. Unfortunately, but not surprisingly, your setting here will not be saved, nor will it follow the defaults set in Explorer, as described later in this section.

Customize This Folder
: This opens the **Customize** tab of the current folder's Properties sheet. These settings affect the appearance of the folder's icon, but to change the appearance of all folders, see "Customize Drive and Folder Icons" in Chapter 4. Note that the **Customize This Folder** option is not available for special folders, such as *My Documents* and *My Pictures*.

Arrange Icons By
: This is the long-winded way of saying "sort." The quickest way to set the sort order of the current folder is to click the appropriate column header in the Details view, discussed above.

  Of note here is the **Show in Groups** option, which is new in Windows XP. This setting is responsible for the book-index-like capital letters in file listings and other headings in the My Computer and My Network Places folders. It doesn't actually change the order in which items are displayed, nor does it add any information to the listing. However, it can make a long listing less intimidating for inexperienced users.

See the next section for ways to force Explorer to remember your settings made here.

Force Explorer to Remember Its Own Settings

One of the most common annoyances users have with a lot of different software products is their inability to remember their state from session to session. For example, how many times have you selected the Details view in Explorer, only to find that it has been turned back to Icons or Tiles the next time the folder is opened?

For the most part, Explorer's apparent inability to remember settings is fairly easy to fix. All that is required is an understanding of the battle between Microsoft's default settings, your most recent choices, and the preferences you wish to make permanent.

There are two ways to save *most* of your preferences in Explorer:

Setting defaults for all new folders

Choose the icon size, sort order, and—if using the Details view—the column widths and positions you want to keep as the defaults. Then, go to **Tools → Folder Options → View** tab, and click **Apply to All Folders**. The settings you've set for the current folder will be used for all newly opened Explorer and single-folder windows.

The only exception is if you've configured individual folders to remember their settings, as follows:

Remembering settings for individual folders

Go to **Tools → Folder Options → View** tab, and turn on the **Remember each folder's view settings** option. With this option enabled, Explorer will temporarily save the settings for approximately 30 of the most recently viewed folders. These saved settings will override the defaults (set as described above), at least until Explorer forgets them.

Your choices are stored in the Registry (discussed in Chapter 3) rather than in the folders themselves, which not only explains the limit on the number of folders Explorer can remember but also exposes a rather annoying system flaw. Say you choose the view settings for a folder called *Lenny*. When you close and reopen *Lenny* right away, your settings will remain. However, if you rename the *Lenny* folder to, say, *Karl*, it will instantly revert to Explorer's defaults and forget the settings you made only seconds earlier.

Table 2-1 shows how—and when—each of the different settings in Explorer are saved.

Table 2-1. Different Explorer preferences are saved in different ways

Setting	Default set immediately	Default set in Folder Options[a]	Default set when window is closed	Default never set
Arrange Icons by		✓		
Customize Folder				✓
Explorer Bar				✓
Desktop icon layout				✓
Details view column settings		✓		
Icon size/view		✓		
Selected folder				✓
Sort order		✓		
Toolbars/Status	✓			
Window size and position			✓	

[a] These settings are also saved independently for the last 20–30 folders when the **Remember each folder's view settings** option is enabled.

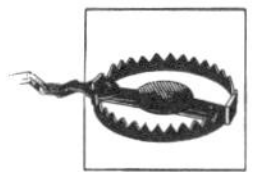

If you don't use the **Apply to All Folders** feature after changing Explorer's view settings, and the **Remember each folder's view settings** option is turned off, your settings will be forgotten as soon as you close the current window or switch to a different folder.

Helpful Explorer Keystrokes

Certain keyboard shortcuts can be real time savers in Explorer, especially when used in conjunction with the mouse.

The following tips assume you're using standard double-clicking, as explained in the previous section. If you've chosen to have icons respond to a single click, just replace "double-click" here with "single-click."

- Hold the **Alt** key while double-clicking on a file or folder to view the Properties sheet for that object.

  Although this is often quicker than right-clicking and selecting **Properties**, the right-click menu—also known as the context menu—has a bunch of other options, most of which are not accessible with keystrokes. For more information on context menus, see "File Types: The Link Between Documents and Applications" in Chapter 4.
- Hold the **Shift** key while double-clicking a folder icon to open an Explorer window at that location (as opposed to a single-folder window). Be careful when using this, because **Shift** is also used to select multiple files. The best way is to select the folder first.
- Press **Backspace** in an open folder window or in Explorer to go to the parent folder.
- Hold **Alt** while pressing the left cursor key to navigate to the previously viewed folder. Note that this is not necessarily the *parent* folder, but rather the last folder in Explorer's *history*. You can also hold **Alt** while pressing the right cursor key to move in the opposite direction (i.e., forward). Explorer's toolbar also has **Back** and **Next** buttons by default, which work just like their counterparts in Internet Explorer.
- With the focus on Explorer's folder tree, use the left and right arrow keys to collapse and expand folders, respectively. Press the asterisk (*) key to expand all the folders in the currently selected branch.
- Hold the **Shift** key while clicking on the close button [X] to close *all* open folder windows in the chain that was used to get to that folder. (This, of course, makes sense only in the single-folder view and with the **Open each folder in its own window** option turned on.)
- Select one icon, then hold the **Shift** key while clicking on another icon in the same folder to select it and all the items in between.

- Hold the **Ctrl** key to select or de-select multiple files or folders, one by one. Note that you can't select more than one folder in the folder tree pane of Explorer, but you can in the right pane.

  You can also use the **Ctrl** key to modify your selection. For example, if you've used the **Shift** key or a rubber band to select the first five objects in a folder, you can hold **Ctrl** while dragging a second rubber band to highlight additional files *without* losing your original selection.

You can select multiple files without using the keyboard by dragging a *rubber band* around them. Start by holding down the left mouse button in a blank portion of a folder window, then drag the mouse to the opposite corner to select everything that appears in the rectangle you just drew.

- Press **Ctrl-A** to quickly select all of the contents of a folder: both files and folders.
- In Explorer or any single-folder window (even in the folder-tree pane), press a letter key to quickly jump to the first file or folder starting with that letter. Continue typing to jump further. For example, pressing the **T** key in your *\Windows* folder will jump to the *Tasks* folder. Press **T** again to jump to the next object that starts with *T*. Or, press **T** and then quickly press **A** to jump to the first file that starts with *TA*, *taskman.exe*. If there's enough of a delay between the **T** and the **A** keys, Explorer will forget about the *T*, and you'll jump to the first entry that starts with *A*.
- Press **F6** to jump between the file pane and the address bar (if it's visible). If the Folders tree or Search Companion pane is open, **F6** will also jump to the close [**X**] button for that pane, but, strangely, not any of the controls within the pane itself. (**F6** also works the same way in most web browsers, incidentally.)

Convince Explorer to Start with the Folder You Want

There are several ways to open an Explorer window, but the most direct method is to use the **Windows Explorer** shortcut in the Start Menu. This has the same effect as selecting **Run** in the Start Menu and typing `explorer.exe`. That is, the Explorer application is run without any command-line arguments.

When Explorer is run without any arguments, it opens to its default location, the *My Documents* folder in the Desktop folder (even if you've deleted the *My Documents* icon from your Desktop). You may want to have Explorer open to a custom folder each time, saving the time required to repeatedly navigate through all the folders on your hard disk.

Launch Explorer from a shortcut

The following steps show how to modify your existing Windows Explorer shortcut in your Start Menu. If, instead, you wish to create a new shortcut, right-click on an empty portion of your desktop or the currently open folder, and select **New** and then **Shortcut**. When prompted for an application, point to *explorer.exe* (located in your *\Windows* folder):

1. Right-click on the Windows Explorer shortcut, select **Properties**, and click on the **Shortcut** tab.
2. Change the text in the **Target** field so it reads:

   ```
   explorer.exe /n,/e,d:\myfolder
   ```

   where *d:\myfolder* is the full path of the folder where you want Explorer to start. You might see the text, `%SystemRoot%` in front of `explorer.exe`, which can be left alone or removed, as desired.
3. Click **OK** when you're done. The next time you use the shortcut, Explorer will open to the specified location.

You may have to use a little trial and error to get the desired results. Now, the full syntax is as follows:

```
explorer.exe [/n][,/e][,/root,object][[,/select],subobject]
```

The square brackets (`[...]`) show the optional nature of the parameters. Note the use of commas between parameters, which aren't typical in command-line parameters.

`/n`
: This switch ensures that the folder will always be opened in a new window, even if the specified folder is already open elsewhere.

`/e`
: Use this option to open a standard Explorer window with the folder-tree pane, as opposed to the default single-folder view. In most cases, you'll want to also specify `/n` when using `/e`, but don't forget the comma.

`subobject`
: Specify *`subobject`* to force Explorer to automatically navigate to a particular folder. The folder is highlighted in the left pane, and its branch is expanded to show any subfolders.

`/select`
: If you also include the `/select` switch—only used in conjunction with the *`subobject`* parameter—only the *parent* of the folder specified by *`subobject`* is opened, and *`subobject`* is selected on the right side instead of the left.

`/root,`*`object`*
: Finally, the `/root,`*`object`* parameter allows you to choose what appears as the root of all folders in the new window, useful if you want an

Explorer Coping Skills

abbreviated tree. The default, of course, is the Desktop. You can specify an ordinary folder to be the root of the tree (i.e., `/root,c:\stuff`), or a system object by specifying the Class ID.

So, for example, if you want Explorer to open to the *My Computer* folder so that no drive branches are initially expanded (handy if you have several drives), type the following:

```
explorer.exe /n,/e,/select,c:\
```

Or, to display an Explorer window rooted at *c:*, use this:

```
explorer.exe /n,/e,/root,c:\
```

Exploring in context

In addition to launching Explorer with any number of parameters, you can open an Explorer window in the context of any object on the screen and Windows will choose the parameters accordingly.

For example, you can right-click on any visible folder icon (on your desktop, in an open folder, and even in the tree pane of another Explorer window) and select **Explore** to open a new Explorer window with the folder in question highlighted.

You can also explore from various system objects by right-clicking and selecting **Explore**. This works on the **Start** button, the My Computer icon, the My Network Places icon, any folder in your Start Menu, and many other places. Figure 2-2 shows the context menu for the **Start** button; note the default **Open** command shown in bold.

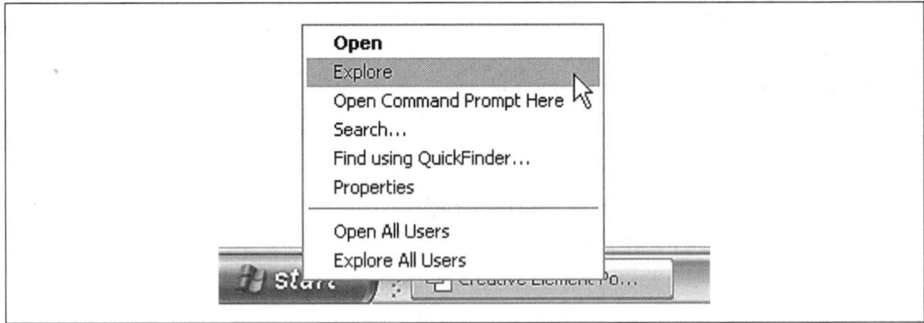

Figure 2-2. Right-click the Start button for quick access to the current user's Start Menu folder

Handling Files and Folders

Much of the work we do on a computer either involves creating or modifying documents. The rest of the time, it seems like all we do is move those documents around. The next few topics will help make file manipulation easier and hopefully a lot more pleasurable.

Take Charge of Drag-Drop

Intuitively, when one drags an object from one place on the screen to another, it would seem reasonable that the object would then appear in the new place and disappear from the old place. In other words, what happens to a file when you drag it from the left side of your desktop to the right side of your desktop should be exactly the same as what happens when you drag a file from one folder to another or from a floppy disk to your hard drive.

The problem is that drag-drop is handled differently in different situations. The decision of what action to take in each situation was made by a committee at Microsoft; I'd be willing to bet that you didn't have a personal representative at that meeting.

So, our aim here is to force Windows to work the way we think, keeping in mind the practical limitations of the operating system. Here's the way Explorer works (note that "object" is a file, folder, shortcut, system object, or anything else with an icon that can be knocked around with your mouse):

- If you drag an object from one place to another on the same physical drive (*c:\docs* to *c:\files*), the object is moved.
- If you drag an object from one physical drive to another physical drive (*c:\docs* to *d:\files*), the object is copied, resulting in two identical files on your system.

  This means that if you drag an object from one physical drive to another physical drive and then back to the first physical drive, but in a different folder (*c:\docs* to *d:\files* to *c:\stuff*), you'll end up with three copies of the object.
- If you drag an application executable (an *.exe* file), the same rules apply to it that apply to other objects, with the following unfortunate exceptions:*
  - If you drag *any* file named *setup.exe* or *install.exe* from one place to another, Windows will create a shortcut to the file, regardless of the source or destination folder.
  - If you drag any file with the *.exe* filename extension into any portion of your Start Menu or into any subfolder of your *Start Menu* folder, Windows will create a shortcut to the file. Dragging other

* In Windows 95, 98, and NT 4.0, dragging any *.exe* file anywhere would cause a shortcut to be created. This behavior, which nobody liked, has been mostly, but not entirely, abandoned in Windows XP.

file types (documents, script files, other shortcuts) to the Start Menu will simply move or copy them there, according to the previous rules.

- If these weren't enough, there are further exceptions. If you drag a file named *setup.exe* into a recordable CD drive, it will be copied. And if you drag a bunch of files of different types (including, say, *setup.exe*), then the create-a-shortcut rules above will be ignored, and they'll just be copied or moved as appropriate.

- If you drag a system object (such as a Control Panel icon), a warning is displayed, and a shortcut to the item will be created. This, of course, is a consequence of the fact that these objects aren't actually files and can't be duplicated or removed from their original locations.
- If you drag certain icons that appear on the desktop, such as My Documents, Internet Explorer, or the Recycle Bin, any number of different things can happen, each depending on the specific properties of the object.

The best way to cope with this confusion is to use a combination of certain keystrokes and the right mouse button to ensure the desired results every time you drag an object. That way, you don't have to predict what will happen based on some rules you won't likely remember.

- To *copy* an object in *any* situation, hold the **Ctrl** key while dragging. If you press **Ctrl** *before* you click, Windows assumes you're still selecting files (as described earlier in this chapter), so make sure to press it only *after* you've started dragging but before you let go of that mouse button. Of course, this won't work for system objects like Control Panel items—a shortcut will be created regardless.

  Using the **Ctrl** key in this way will also work when dragging a file from one part of a folder to another part of the same folder. See "Make a Duplicate of a File or Folder" later in this chapter for more information.
- To *move* an object in any situation, hold the **Shift** key while dragging. Likewise, if you press **Shift** before you click, Windows assumes you're still selecting files, so make sure to press it only after you've started dragging but before you let go of that mouse button. Like above, this doesn't apply to system objects like Control Panel icons.
- To create a shortcut to an object under any situation, hold the **Alt** key while dragging. Note that this is different than in previous versions of Windows.
- To choose what happens to dragged files each time *without* having to press any keys, drag your files with the *right mouse button*, and a special

menu like the one shown in Figure 2-3 will appear when the files are dropped. This context menu is especially helpful, because it will display only options appropriate to the type of object you're dragging and the place where you've dropped it.

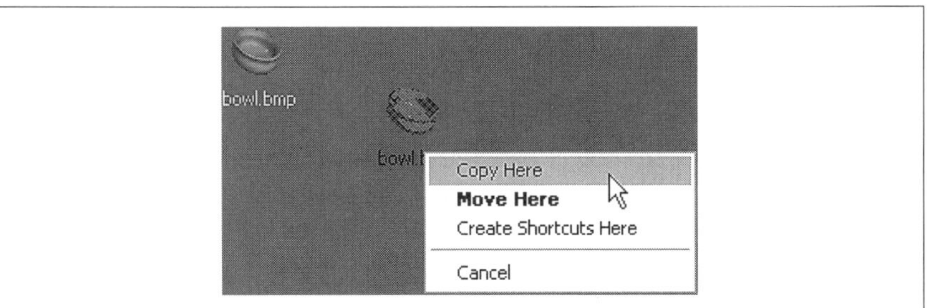

Figure 2-3. Drag files with the right mouse button for more control

To aid in learning the keystrokes, notice that the mouse cursor changes depending on the action taken. A small plus sign [+] appears when copying, and a curved arrow appears when creating a shortcut. If you see no symbol, the object will be moved. This visual feedback is very important; it can eliminate a lot of stupid mistakes if you pay attention to it.

There is no way to set the default action when dragging files and therefore no way to avoid using keystrokes or the right mouse button to achieve the desired results. Even if there were a way to change the default behavior, you probably wouldn't want to do it. Imagine if someone else sat down at your computer and started dragging icons: oh, the horror.

Explorer's **Undo** command (in the **Edit** menu, as well as available by right-clicking in an empty area of Explorer or the desktop) allows you to undo the last few file operations.* If you've copied, moved, or renamed one or more objects, the command will read **Undo Copy**, **Undo Move**, or **Undo Rename**, respectively. Additionally, if your Recycle Bin is configured to store files, **Undo Delete** may also appear. However, if you're doing a lot of copying, moving, and deleting of files, it's hard to know to which particular operation the **Undo** command refers at any given time. The easiest way to tell is to click and hold the mouse button over the **Undo** menu item and look in the status bar (select **Status Bar** from the **View** menu if it's not visible), which will tell you exactly with which files the operation dealt. This, of course, is not available on the desktop, but luckily, the **Undo** command works the same regardless of the folder from which you use it.

* **Ctrl-Z** is a keyboard shortcut for Undo.

Copy or Move to a Specified Path

Dragging and dropping is generally the quickest and easiest way to copy or move files and folders from one place to another. Typically, you must have both the source folder and the destination folder open and visible, which can add several steps to what should be a simple process. Furthermore, there's no provision for specifying a destination folder with the keyboard. The following procedures can be used to overcome these basic limitations.

Solution 1: Drag patiently

1. Open Explorer (with the folder-tree pane), and navigate to the source folder.
2. Drag one or more items over the tree pane on the left, then hold the mouse cursor over the visible branch of the destination folder. After two or three seconds, Explorer will automatically expand the branch and make the subfolders visible.
3. If the destination folder you're looking for is buried several layers deep, you'll have to wait for Explorer to expand each level. This requires a steady hand and a lot of patience.

Solution 2: Use cut, copy, and paste

This solution isn't exactly intuitive, but it can be convenient if you don't have a mouse or if your screen size limits the number of open windows:

1. Select the file(s) you want to copy, right-click on it, and select **Copy** to copy the file or **Cut** to move the file. The keyboard shortcuts for the cut, copy, and paste operations are **Ctrl-X**, **Ctrl-C**, and **Ctrl-V**, respectively.

   If the file is cut, its icon will appear faded (as though it were a hidden file). If the file is copied, there will be no visual distinction.
2. Open the destination folder (or click on the desktop), right-click on an empty area (or open the **Edit** menu), and select **Paste**. Whether the file is copied or moved—or a shortcut is made—depends on the same criteria as if you had dragged and dropped the item. Unfortunately, modification keystrokes discussed earlier in this chapter (**Ctrl**, **Shift**, and **Alt**) have no effect here, so you'll probably need a little trial and error.

Although Explorer uses the familiar cut, copy, and paste commands to accomplish this solution, they don't work exactly the same way for files as they do in other applications when you're manipulating text, for example.

If you cut a file and never get around to pasting it, or cut a second file without pasting the first, the first file that was cut is *not* deleted as you might expect. Cut, copy, and paste in the context of files work with file *references* rather than the files themselves, so unless you cut a file and then paste it into the Recycle Bin, there isn't much danger of losing anything. You can abort any cut operation by pressing **Esc**; the only visual feedback you'll get is that any "faded" file icons will return to their normal state.

Also, while you can drag-drop files from Explorer or the desktop into a running application to open the file in that application, the same isn't necessarily true for copy and paste. If you try to copy a file and then paste it into an application such as Word or Word Perfect, the file is inserted as an icon object directly into the document, which is not likely to be of much use to most people.

Solution 3: Use the Explorer toolbar

The standard Windows Explorer toolbar has two buttons, **Move To** and **Copy To**, that allow you to point to a location when moving and copying, respectively. Unfortunately, these functions can't be found in Explorer's menus or in the context menus of any files or folders; they're only available on the toolbar.

If Explorer's toolbar isn't currently visible, go to **View → Toolbars → Standard Buttons** to turn it on. By default, the **Move To** and **Copy To** buttons are in the sixth and seventh positions on the toolbar, respectively. If they're not, right-click on the toolbar, and select **Customize**.

Solution 4: Use a third-party add-on

The final solution is to install a separate utility to extend Explorer's capabilities. For example:

1. Install Creative Element Power Tools (*http://www.creativelement.com/powertools/*).
2. Enable the **Copy or Move files anywhere** tool.
3. Right-click on any file or folder, select **Move To** or **Copy To**, and then type or point to the destination folder. You can also create new folders on the fly and duplicate paths in the destination folder; the software even remembers the last dozen destinations you specified.

Make a Duplicate of a File or Folder

Windows lets you copy and move files from one folder to another by dragging them with different combinations of keystrokes, as described earlier in this chapter. You can also rename a file by clicking on its name or highlighting it and pressing the **F2** key. However, if you want to make a *duplicate* of a file in the *same* directory and assign it a different name, the process might not be as obvious. There are several different ways to do it:

- Hold the **Ctrl** key while dragging a file from one part of the window to another part of the *same* window. This works in single-folder windows, on the desktop, and in Explorer.
- Use the right mouse button to drag the file from one part of the window to another part of the same window, and then select **Copy Here**, as shown in Figure 2-3.
- For keyboard enthusiasts, press **Ctrl-C** and then **Ctrl-V** to create a duplicate of a file using the clipboard.

Regardless of which solution you use, the duplicate of a file called, say, *Myfile.txt* will be automatically named *Copy of Myfile.txt*. An additional copy of *Myfile.txt* will be called *Copy (2) of Myfile.txt*, while a copy of *Copy of Myfile.txt* will be called *Copy of Copy of Myfile.txt*. Because the filename keeps changing (albeit somewhat inconveniently), you can duplicate multiple files simultaneously to fill a directory quickly with dozens of identical files.

If you need a bunch of duplicates of a file or folder, start by duplicating it once. Then, select both the original and the copy, and duplicate them both. Then, select the now four objects and duplicate them to make eight. Once you have all the duplicates you need, see "More Ways to Rename Files," later in this chapter, for help in giving your duplicates more appropriate names.

If you duplicate a folder, all the contents of the folder will be duplicated, but only the name of the single folder will be changed—the names of the files and folders therein will remain intact.

The Power Rename utility, part of Creative Element Power Tools (*http://www.creativelement.com/powertools/*), allows you to duplicate large numbers of files quickly, while controlling how the duplicates are named. See the next section for details.

More Ways to Rename Files

Renaming files is just as common a task as copying or moving, but it ends up being much more tedious to accomplish, at least when using Explorer.

In its simplest form, Explorer's rename feature works like this: highlight a file, wait a second (to avoid double-clicking) then click the filename, type a new name, and press **Enter**. You can rename an object by right-clicking and selecting **Rename**, or by selecting and pressing **F2**.

However, this method is laborious, especially if you need to rename a whole bunch of files or folders. And if you need to change a filename extension (see "File Types: The Link Between Documents and Applications" in Chapter 4), then Explorer interrupts each renaming operation with a stern warning. The following solutions show other ways to rename files and overcome these limitations.

Solution 1: Select multiple files in Explorer

The following is the result of a new feature for Windows XP, though it leaves a lot to be desired:

1. Select multiple files in Explorer, on your desktop, in a single-folder window, or in a Search Results window. See "Helpful Explorer Keystrokes," earlier in this chapter, for different ways to select multiple files.
2. Although multiple files will be highlighted, only one file will be the "active" file. At first, there will be no visual distinction, but if you press and release the **Ctrl** key, a dotted rectangle will appear around the name of the active file.
3. The active file is important, since its name will be used as a template to rename the other selected files. If the file marked as active is not the one you want to use, hold the **Ctrl** key while clicking another file. If the new file was highlighted, it will become de-selected—in this case, just **Ctrl**-click the file once more to re-select it.
4. Press the **F2** key to rename the active file. Nothing will happen to the other selected files, at least not yet.
5. Rename the active file as desired. When you're done, press **Enter** (or, press **Esc** to abort the operation without renaming any files). The active file will retain the newly typed name. Furthermore, all of the other selected files will assume the name of the active file, plus a number in parentheses.

The rules that Explorer uses for renaming multiple files are as follows:

- Each new filename begins with the full filename of the active file. Then, for all files except the active file, a blank space followed by a number in parentheses is appended to the filename.
- The order in which the files currently appear in the folder is used to determine the numbers. The file that appears closest to the top of the listing is numbered "1," followed by "2," and so on.

- File extensions are never changed, even if you purposely change the file extension of the active file. See "File Types: The Link Between Documents and Applications" in Chapter 4 for more information on filename extensions.

Table 2-2 shows an example of what happens to five files renamed in this way.

Table 2-2. What happens when you try to rename multiple files in Explorer; the first file listed here is the "active" file, as described in Solution 1

Old filename	New filename
My file.doc	*The Penske File.rtf*
Grandma.jpg	*The Penske File (1).jpg*
Readme.1st	*The Penske File (2).1st*
Purchases.mdb	*The Penske File (3).mdb*
Chapter 2 (a folder)	*The Penske File (4)*

Although there's no way to preview what your filenames will look like, you can undo a multiple rename operation as easily as a single rename operation. Simply press **Ctrl-Z** to revert the filenames, or in an Explorer or single folder window, go to **Edit → Undo**. Even though multiple files can be renamed in a single step using this procedure, each file is given its own individual place in the "undo history." This means that if you rename seven files in a single step, you'll have to use the undo command seven times to revert them all.

Solution 2: Use the Command Prompt

This next solution uses the `ren` command, discussed in Appendix C, to rename any number of files using the traditional wildcard syntax:

1. Open a Command Prompt window by going to **Start → Programs → Accessories → Command Prompt**, or by launching *cmd.exe*.
2. Use the `cd` command, also explained in Appendix C, to change the working directory to the folder containing the files you wish to rename. For example, type:

   ```
   cd c:\stuff
   ```

   to change to the *c:\stuff* folder. For long folder names, there's a shortcut: just type `cd`, followed by a space, and then drag a folder icon onto the Command Prompt window. The full path of the folder will be typed for you.

Since the ren command only works in one folder at a time, you can't rename files in multiple folders in a single step, like you can with the other solutions in this section. However, you can use batch files or WSH scripts, discussed in Appendix C and Chapter 9, respectively, for more flexibility and automation.

3. The syntax of the ren command is as follows:

   ```
   ren source destination
   ```

   where both *source* and *destination* can be any combination of permissible characters and wildcards. Two wildcards are allowed: an asterisk (*), which is used to match any number of characters, and a question mark (?), which is used to match only a single character.

The following examples illustrate the use of the ren command:

Rename a single file

```
ren oldfile.txt newfile.txt
```

Change the extension of all .txt files to .doc

```
ren *.txt *.doc
```

Rename the first part of a filename without changing the extension

```
ren document.* documentation.*
```

Remove the extensions of all files in the folder

```
ren *.* *.
```

Change the first letter of all files in a folder to "b"

```
ren *.* b*.*
```

Add a zero in front of numbered chapter files

```
ren "chapter ??.wpd" "chapter0??.wpd"
```

Note the use of quotation marks here to accommodate the spaces in the filenames. Also, note how the zero fills the space in the original filenames; "inserting" a zero is a bit more complicated.

Rename all files with a "s" in the fourth position so that a "t" appears there instead

```
ren ???s*.* ???t*.*
```

Truncate the filenames of all files in the folder so that only the first four characters are used

```
ren *.* ????.*
```

Here are few additional notes for using ren to rename files:

- Using wildcards takes a bit of practice and patience. The more you do it, the better intuitive sense you'll have of how to phrase a rename operation. To make things simpler, try issuing several successive ren commands instead of trying to squeeze all your changes into a single step.
- If a naming conflict occurs, the ren command will never overwrite a file. For example, if you try to rename *Lisa.txt* to *Bart.txt*, and there's already another file called *Bart.txt*, ren will display an error and no renaming will occur.
- The *source* is always case-insensitive, in that capitalization doesn't matter when matching files. However, the capitalization you use for *destination* is preserved.
- ren isn't able to insert characters, only replace them. This makes it difficult to make filenames shorter or longer using wildcards.
- You can use batch files to execute a series of ren statements, as described in Appendix C.

Solution 3: Use a third-party add-on

The third solution is to install a separate utility to allow more sophisticated renaming operations:

1. Install Creative Element Power Tools (*http://www.creativelement.com/powertools/*).
2. Enable the **Rename files with ease** tool.
3. Select one or many files to rename, right-click, and select **Power Rename**. Or open the Power Rename utility and drag-drop the files onto the window.
4. Select the desired renaming criteria to your right. The first option, **As Specified**, allows you to type a file specification with wildcards, as described in Solution 2, earlier.

   Otherwise, choose **With Operation**, and then choose the options later, such as **Append filename**, **Re-number**, **Change Case**, or **Replace**.
5. Turn on the **Show what files will look like** option to see a preview of the filename(s).
6. Click **Apply** when you're done.

   If you wish to make duplicates (see "Make a Duplicate of a File or Folder," earlier in this chapter), turn on the **Leave original files (copy)** option and click **Apply** repeatedly, once for each duplicate you wish to create.

Make It Easier to Delete Files

Deleting files and folders is something we do every day, but under Windows XP's default settings, deleting a single file or a group of files can incur a whole slew of confirmation messages, and the results can be somewhat unpredictable.

The number and type of confirmation messages you get depends on settings in your Recycle Bin. For example, if your Recycle Bin is configured to store deleted files (the default), but not confirm their deletion, you may not see any warning message at all. The key is to cut out the unnecessary messages without completely eliminating the safeguards that help prevent accidental deletion.

Let's start by examining some of the Recycle Bin settings and their consequences. Right-click the Recycle Bin icon on your desktop, and select **Properties**. The various options here are pretty self-explanatory, but the following tips may help:

- If your Recycle Bin is configured to store deleted objects, you can get back accidental deletions by opening the Recycle Bin and dragging items out of it. If, instead, you've configured the Recycle Bin to delete files immediately, you'll need an undelete program (such as the one that comes with Norton Utilities) to get them back.

  You can also right-click any empty area of a folder or the desktop and select **Undo Delete** (assuming the last thing you did was delete an object), but only if you've configured the Recycle Bin to store your deleted objects.

- If you highlight an object and press the **Del** key, or right-click an object and select **Delete**, it has the same effect as dropping the object into the Recycle Bin. All the Recycle Bin settings apply regardless of the method used to actually delete the object. The exception is the Command Prompt's `del` command (discussed in Appendix C), which deletes files without confirmation screens and without storing them in the Recycle Bin.

  In fact, you may want to use `del` to quickly and easily delete one or more files sharing a common trait, such as the filename extension. Just type `del *.tmp` to delete all files with the *.tmp* extension in the active folder, for example (see Solution 2 in "More Ways to Rename Files," earlier in this chapter for more information on this syntax). The `del` command often completes its tasks more quickly than the Recycle Bin, especially for large numbers of files. Command-prompt commands also have the added benefit of deleting files without forcing you to stare at the flying-paper animation.

- It's possible to permanently delete an object in Windows XP without any confirmation dialog box whatsoever, a feature you should, of course, use with caution. To do this, open the **Recycle Bin Properties**, and turn on the **Do not move files to the Recycle Bin** option. Next, turn off the **Display delete confirmation dialog box**, and click **OK** when you're done. This doesn't get rid of all nag windows, though—only the ones for ordinary files. See below for exceptions.
- If you have more than one drive, the settings for each drive's Recycle Bin (shown as separate tabs in the Recycle Bin Properties window) can be set independently. Settings for a particular drive apply to all files deleted on that drive. For example, if drive *C:* is set to store deleted files, but drive *D:* is not, then only files deleted from drive *C:* will be recoverable. For this reason, it's usually best to specify **Use one setting for all drives** in the **Recycle Bin Properties**.
- The amount of disk space devoted to the Recycle Bin is specified as a percentage of the amount of free disk space per drive, rather than a fixed number of megabytes. This means that the size of your Recycle Bin will constantly change as the amount of free space changes, and the size of the Recycle Bin on each of your drives will always be different. Now, if you delete a 15 MB file and only 10 MB are available to the Recycle Bin, Windows will delete the file outright instead of storing it (it may warn you first).
- If you have your Recycle Bin configured to store deleted files, it will hold them until it becomes full and then will permanently erase the oldest contents to prevent "overflow." This means you will never be able to predict how long a deleted file will remain in the Recycle Bin: a sensitive file may stay in there for weeks, presenting a possible security hazard. Likewise, an accidentally deleted file may disappear after only a few hours (or less), long before it occurs to you to double-check the contents.

  The lesson: be careful when deleting files, be diligent about checking your Recycle Bin, and give some thought to the Recycle Bin settings.

Why would you want files to be stored in the Recycle Bin? It gives you a way out: if you find that you are careless and delete important files accidentally, you should definitely exploit this feature.

Why would you *not* want files to be stored in the Recycle Bin? First of all, those files don't exist in a vacuum; they take up valuable hard-disk space and can slow system performance. Deleted files are a security risk; it's one of the first places I'd look for sensitive information if I were breaking into someone's system. And having unwanted files remain on your hard disk can make your system more vulnerable to hard disk crashes (from corrupted files) and viruses (from email attachments you thought you deleted right away).

There are a few workarounds for whatever Recycle Bin settings you choose, allowing more flexibility and control. For example, if you've configured your Recycle Bin to store deleted files, you can still hold the **Shift** key while deleting any given object to permanently erase the object. The files currently stored in the Recycle Bin (if any) will not be affected.

The following are all of the confirmation and warning messages you may receive when deleting files, and, where applicable, how to bypass them:

- By default, you'll get a nag window when you first drop any file or folder onto the Recycle Bin or delete them with the **Del** key. This can be bypassed by turning off the **Display delete confirmation dialog** option.
- You'll be warned if you try to delete a file that has the read-only or system attributes set. The only way to curb this is to first turn off said attributes by right-clicking the file(s) and selecting **Properties**.
- Explorer will warn you if the file that's being deleted is an *.exe* file. However, it won't warn you when deleting *.dll* or *.ocx* files, even though they're just as necessary as *.exe* files for the applications that own them. There's no way to change this behavior.
- If you delete certain shortcuts in your Start Menu, Explorer will stop you to explain that you're not actually deleting the software to which it links. This is actually a property of said shortcuts and cannot be changed globally.
- You'll get a warning message if the files you're trying to delete are larger than the space you've allocated for the Recycle Bin. You can fix this by increasing the allocated space (move the slide bar to the right). This doesn't apply if you've enabled the **Do not move files to the Recycle Bin** option.
- Windows will give you a stern warning if you try to delete (or rename) a folder that contains (or once contained) an application, explaining that the application will no longer work. This only happens if the folder is referenced in the Registry. Since it's easier to just click **OK** rather than first removing all Registry references, there's no practical workaround to this one, either.
- Finally, you'll be asked to confirm that you actually wish to empty the Recycle Bin, regardless of the size or number of files currently inside.

How to Delete or Replace In-Use Files

Regardless of the number of confirmation windows Explorer throws at you, eventually you'll be allowed to delete the file or folder you're trying to get rid of. The only case when Windows XP simply won't allow you to delete (or replace) something is when that file or folder is "in use" by a running application or by Windows itself.

This is a safety mechanism, not only in place to prevent a running application executable or support file from being deleted while said application is running, but to prevent a document from being modified or deleted by an application other than that which has opened the document.

Remember, Windows makes it difficult to delete files that are in use for a reason. If you delete certain files located in your *\Windows* or *\Windows\System* folders, you can render Windows inoperable. However, there are plenty of files that can be deleted or replaced safely. Use these solutions at your own risk, and check out Chapter 6 for tips on securing your system with a backup.

Solution 1: Close the application

The easiest way to delete an in-use file is to simply close the application that owns it. If the file belongs to an invisible background program, use the Windows Task Manager (*taskmgr.exe*) to end the process. If it belongs to a service, use the Services window (*services.msc*) to stop it.

But what happens if the file is in use by the operating system? If you need to replace a *.dll* file in the *\Windows\System* folder, for example, Windows won't let you do it. But never fear! The remaining solutions should take care of it.

Solution 2: Use the Command Prompt

The Command Prompt, discussed in Appendix C, is sometimes able to access files that Explorer won't let you touch.

1. Open a Command Prompt window by going to **Start → Programs → Accessories → Command Prompt**, or by launching *cmd.exe*.
2. Use the `cd` command to change the working directory to the folder containing the file(s) you wish to delete. See Solution 2 in "More Ways to Rename Files," earlier in this chapter, for additional tips on the `cd` command.
3. Use the `del` command to delete the file, like this:

   ```
   del filename.ext
   ```

   where *`filename.ext`* is the name of the file.

If this doesn't work, try the next solution.

Solution 3: Brute force

Occasionally, simply renaming the file is enough to break Windows's hold on a shared file. If this doesn't work, restart Windows, and then try deleting again.

Solution 4: Use the Safe Mode with Command Prompt

Windows XP has a special way to get to the Command Prompt (discussed in Appendix C) without loading most of the rest of the operating system. Here's how to get to it:

1. Restart your computer.
2. Just after the system beep, but before the Windows startup logo appears, press the **F8** key to display the Windows Advanced Options Menu.
3. Use the up and down arrow keys to highlight **Safe Mode with Command Prompt** (the third one from the top), and press the **Enter** key.
4. When the Command Prompt window appears, use the `del` or `ren` commands discussed in Appendix C to delete or rename the file in question.
5. When you're done, restart your computer by typing:

   ```
   shutdown -s -t 0
   ```

   Or, press **Ctrl-Alt-Del** and then click **Shut Down**.

Solution 5: Use the Recovery Console

The Recovery Console is essentially a way to get to the Command Prompt when Windows isn't running at all. The Recovery Console operates at a lower level than the Safe Mode with Command Prompt, discussed in the previous solution, and will allow you to delete in-use files that otherwise can't be touched. It also provides access to your system when Windows won't start. See Chapter 6 for more information on the Windows Recovery Console.

Solution 6: Use Wininit.ini

The final solution is that which is implemented by the installation programs used to install software on your computer.

1. Open Explorer, and navigate to your *\Windows* folder.
2. Double-click the *Wininit.ini* file to open it in Notepad (or any other standard plain-text editor).

   If the file isn't there, just create a new empty text file, and name it *Wininit.ini*, and type the following line at the top:

   ```
   [rename]
   ```

In most cases, the *Wininit.ini* file will exist but will be empty, with the exception of the [rename] line. Any other lines here would have been added by a recent application install. See "Using INI Files" in Chapter 3 for more information on the structure of this type of file.

3. Under the [rename] section header, type the following line:

```
NUL=c:\folder\filename.ext
```

where *c:\folder\filename.ext* is the full path and filename of the file you wish to delete. You can specify as many files here as you want, one on each line.

If you wish to replace a file rather than simply deleting it, the syntax is a little different:

```
c:\folder\existing.ext=c:\folder\replacement.ext
```

where *c:\folder\existing.ext* is the full path and filename of the file you're trying to replace, and *c:\folder\replacement.ext* is the full path and filename of the new file to take its place. If the file specified on the right side of the equals sign doesn't exist, then the *existing.ext* file will be moved/renamed to *c:\folder\replacement.ext*.

4. Restart Windows. The files will be deleted or replaced as specified during the startup procedure.

Fix the Search Tool

Most of us rely on the Windows Search tool on a daily basis to find and organize files in Explorer. However, Microsoft has redesigned the Search tool in Windows XP in an effort to make it more inviting for novice users, but at the expense of the simplicity and efficiency found in earlier versions.

There are two primary issues with the Search tool that we'll address here: the cumbersome new interface and the fact that starting Search from within Explorer doesn't open it in a new window. Finally, we'll end the discussion with a bunch of Search tips. Together, these solutions should help make the Windows XP Search tool a lot more useful and a lot less annoying.

Part 1: The new Search interface

Okay, I'll admit it. The dog is cute. Being an animal lover, you'd think I'd appreciate having him down there wagging his tail and "helping" me find my files. But it took me less than two minutes to get tired of the cumbersome wizard-like interface, the overabundance of unnecessary choices, and the little scratching sounds the puppy makes while you're trying to work.

Ideally, when one opens a Search window, all of the important fields and options should be accessible immediately, without any additional nonsense and without disrupting the existing workspace. Unfortunately, that's not what Microsoft had in mind, as shown in Figure 2-4.

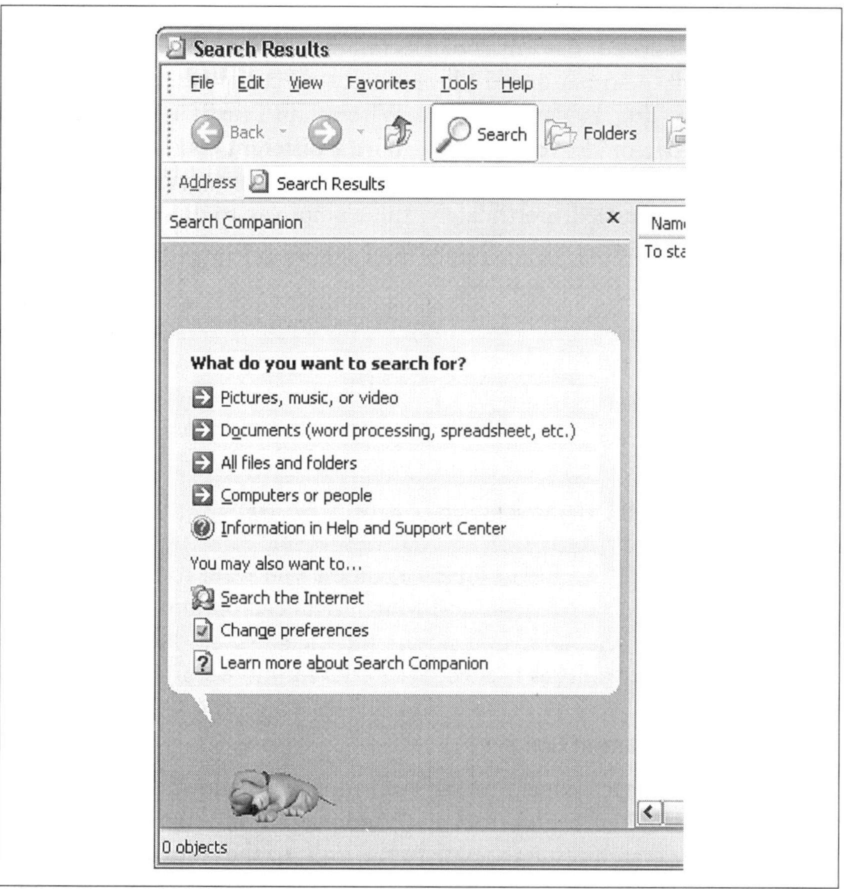

Figure 2-4. The puppy sleeps while you wade through the cumbersome Search menus

When you open the Search tool (see Part 2 for ways to start a Search), you're presented with a menu asking, "What do you want to search for?" and eight possible destinations. The first three destinations all basically do the same thing, but require that you first make a distinction about what type of file you're looking for, or rather, try to predict how Windows will categorize the file for which you're looking. For example, is that Photoshop document you were working on a "picture" or is it a "document?"

All files and folders is the obvious choice, as it will likely be in most situations. To skip this menu in the future and go straight to the **All files and folders** search tool, click **Change Preferences**, then **Change files and folders**

search behavior, and then choose **Advanced**. Fortunately, Explorer will remember your preference, and you won't have to deal with the menu again unless you want to.

You may have noticed that this choice is rather buried in the **Change Preferences** menu; all the other options here simply affect the Search Companion (the little puppy dog, by default). Click **Without an animated screen character** to say bye-bye to "Rover," or click **With a different character** to choose between Rover, Merlin (a wizard), Earl (a surfboarding banana), or Courtney (anybody's guess). Unfortunately, there's no way to disable the sounds the different characters make; if it weren't for this limitation, I'd probably still have the puppy on my system.

If you like the puppy, you'll be happy to know that he won't leave if you choose the **Advanced** option, described earlier, to bypass the menus and go straight to the Search form. Double-click the animated character at any time to turn him/her off, choose a different character, or to make him/her do a trick for you.

Once you're looking at the so-called "Advanced" view of the Search tool, any searches you perform will be relatively open. That is, you won't be restricted by a "type" of file to look for, unless you want to be. The **When was it modified**, **What size is it**, and **More advanced options** choices allow you to refine your search beyond simply the filename and location, further filtering the search results as needed. See Part 3 for more search tips.

Part 2: The Search pane in Explorer

If you've become accustomed to the Find tool in Windows 95/98/NT 4.0, you'll notice that the Search tool in Windows XP is roughly equivalent, except that the search results appear to the right of the controls rather than beneath them. Other than this horizontal layout, more closely resembling the standard Explorer window, and the extraneous menus discussed previously in Part 1, there's not a whole lot different with this new tool. (Windows Me and Windows 2000 have something much closer to the Windows XP Search tool, though.)

The problem becomes obvious when the Search tool is invoked from within an open Explorer window: the left pane containing the folder tree simply disappears! Furthermore, the contents of the currently selected folder remain visible in the right pane, but vanish as soon as a search is performed. The two ways to reproduce this are as follows:

- Press **Ctrl-F**, **Ctrl-E**, or **F3** in Explorer or any single-folder window.
- Select **Explorer Bar** and then **Search** from Explorer's **View** menu, or click the **Search** button on the Explorer toolbar.

The fact that the current window is reused for the Search tool has no apparent benefit, yet it inconveniently and frustratingly interrupts your workspace, which is the last thing you want when you're looking for something.

The only way to return to the previous view at this point is to select **Explorer Bar** and then **Folders** from Explorer's **View** menu—unfortunately, there's no keyboard shortcut, so this procedure is especially cumbersome. When the folder tree pane is reinstated, a new folder, *Search Results*, appears at the bottom of the tree. However, if you select another folder and then return to this *Search Results* folder, neither the search criteria nor the search results from your last search are retained. In other words, there's absolutely no point to this design.

The solution is to find a way to activate the Search tool so this doesn't happen, which essentially involves opening Search in a new window, leaving any open Explorer windows intact. There are four ways to do this:

- Select **Search** and then **For Files or Folders** from the Start Menu. **Local Hard Drives** will be automatically selected in the **Look in** list. If you want to start your search from the folder you were viewing, you'll have to select it manually from the **Look in** list.
- Click on the desktop, and then press **F3**. The Desktop will automatically be selected in the **Look in** list. Likewise, you'll have to select another folder manually from the **Look in** list if the Desktop is not where you wish to search. (Strangely, the **Ctrl-F** keyboard shortcut doesn't work on the Desktop, even though it works everywhere else.)
- Right-click on any folder icon on the desktop or in either pane of an Explorer window (drive icons also work), and select **Search**. A new window will appear, and the selected folder or drive will automatically appear in the **Look in** list.
- Obtain Creative Element Power Tools (*http://www.creativelement.com/powertools/*), which comes with a fix for the Search tool. With this utility, pressing **Ctrl-F** or **F3** in an open Explorer window will force a new Search window to open and the current folder to be placed in the **Look in** list.

Part 3: Search tips

Here are some additional tips for working with the Search tool:

Working with Search Results

The Search Results listing is an *active* list of the files and folders that match your search criteria. This means that you can double-click any found document, application, or folder to open it. You can also drag icons from the Search Results window or right-click them in place to view their context menus, just as though you were looking at them in their native folders.

For broader context, just highlight any single item and select **Open Containing Folder** from the **File** menu, and its parent folder will be opened with said object selected automatically.

Stretch out

The Search Results window is usually not large enough to display all pertinent information. Make it bigger so you can see the **In Folder** column, for example (Details view only), which tells you the full path of each item in the listing.

While we're at it, make sure the Status Bar is visible (go to **View → Status Bar**). The Search tool displays both its progress and a summary of its results in the Status Bar at the bottom of the Search window.

Sometimes it's easier to search for everything

If you initiate a search and leave the **All or part of the file name** field empty, the search results will just fill up with all files and folders in the specified location. This is very useful, as it will quickly allow you to find the newest or even largest files in the specified location. Just make sure you're using the Details view (select **View → Details**), and then click the appropriate column headers to sort the listing accordingly.

Note that the arbitrary 10,000-file limit imposed in some earlier versions of Windows has been lifted in Windows XP. For anyone who has been around long enough to remember XTree, this is equivalent to its fabulous "Show All" feature.

Save your search settings

There's also another way to open a Search window without disrupting an Explorer window. This solution has the added benefit of allowing you to save the default search location (sort of) and any other search options:

a. Open a Search window and select a search location and any other search options. Leave the **All or part of the file name** field empty for now.

b. Click **Search Now** to perform a search. The specific results that appear right now aren't important, though.

c. When the search is complete, select **Save Search** from the **File** menu. When prompted, navigate to the Desktop and type whatever you like for the filename; something generic, such as *Search.fnd*, might be suitable.

d. Double-click on the new *Search.fnd* file at any time to open a new Search window with your settings. You can make as many of these as you like, and place them in on your Desktop, in your Start Menu, or even on a QuickLaunch toolbar for quick access.

e. If you want to assign a keyboard shortcut to this new Search icon, start by moving the saved search file to a safe, out-of-the-way location. Create a shortcut to the file and place it in the same folder, in your Start Menu, or anywhere else that is convenient.

   Right-click on the new shortcut, click **Properties**, click on the **Shortcut key** field, and press the desired keystroke combination. Unfortunately, Windows won't let you choose a shortcut key combination with only the **Ctrl** key, so you can't redefine **Ctrl-F** for this window (believe me—this is the first thing I tried). However, **Ctrl-Shift-F** is almost as convenient and may serve as a suitable compromise. Click **OK** when you're done, then try it out!

Looking for text in files

If you're looking for text in a file, as opposed to the filename, the Windows XP Search tool doesn't actually work that well. Several times I've tested it by looking for text in a folder full of ordinary text files (no exotic file formats or anything), and Search couldn't find the text I *knew* to be in there. If you run into this problem, try UltraEdit-32 (*http://www.ultraedit.com*), and use the **Search → Find in Files** command instead.

Stop Search from looking in ZIP files

As described in the topic "Working with ZIP Files," later in this chapter, support for the ZIP file format is built into Windows XP. Whether you like this ZIP integration or not, it does mean that the Search tool will include the files *inside* of any ZIP archives it encounters, just as though they were in ordinary folders.

This negatively impacts the Search tool in two ways. First, it can increase search time considerably; every ZIP file found in your search will have to be opened and its contents extracted. Second, if any files matching your search criteria are found inside a ZIP file, they will appear normally in the search results, but the **In Folder** column will be blank for these items, making it that much more difficult to find where said files are actually located.

Unfortunately, there's no way to stop Search from looking in your ZIP files without disabling Windows XP's built-in support for ZIP files. But if you do disable ZIP integration, you can always install a separate ZIP utility that won't interfere with searches and may provide more functionality as well.

The places Search won't look

The following folders are places in which Search won't look for files:

- Your Fonts folder: *\Windows\Fonts*
- Deleted files stored in the Recycle Bin: *\Recycler*
- Restore points for System Restore: *\System Volume Information*

Furthermore, unless you turn on the **Search system folders** and **Search hidden files and folders** options (located under **More advanced options**), hidden and system files will be ignored in searches. Strangely, these settings are not connected to the settings in the Folder Options window that affect the visibility of hidden and system files in Explorer (discussed earlier in this chapter).

A Crash Course on File Organization

One of the best ways to improve file searches is to organize your files more efficiently in the first place. When you're saving files, Windows takes a few measures to ensure your files are at least placed in the *My Documents* folder, but beyond that, it's up to you.

The "old school" methodology is to place your personal files in folders designated for the applications that created them: all your spreadsheet files in one folder, all your word processor documents in another, and all photos in yet another. The problem with this is that the context of your files is so easily lost.

The most efficient way to organize your personal files is to group them by project or topic, rather than by the applications that created them. Figure 2-5 shows the tree view of a typical *My Documents* branch organized in this way.

Here are some tips for organizing your files:

Ignore file types

All your files, regardless of the programs that created them, should be organized without regard for the file types: your word processor documents, email attachments, database files, photos, drawings, and downloaded Acrobat (*.pdf*) documents can all sit side by side in the same folders, separated only by topic.

Just open a folder corresponding to the project on which you wish to work, and double-click a document to open the appropriate application to edit or view it. See "File Types: The Link Between Documents and Applications" in Chapter 4 for more information on the link between your documents and applications.

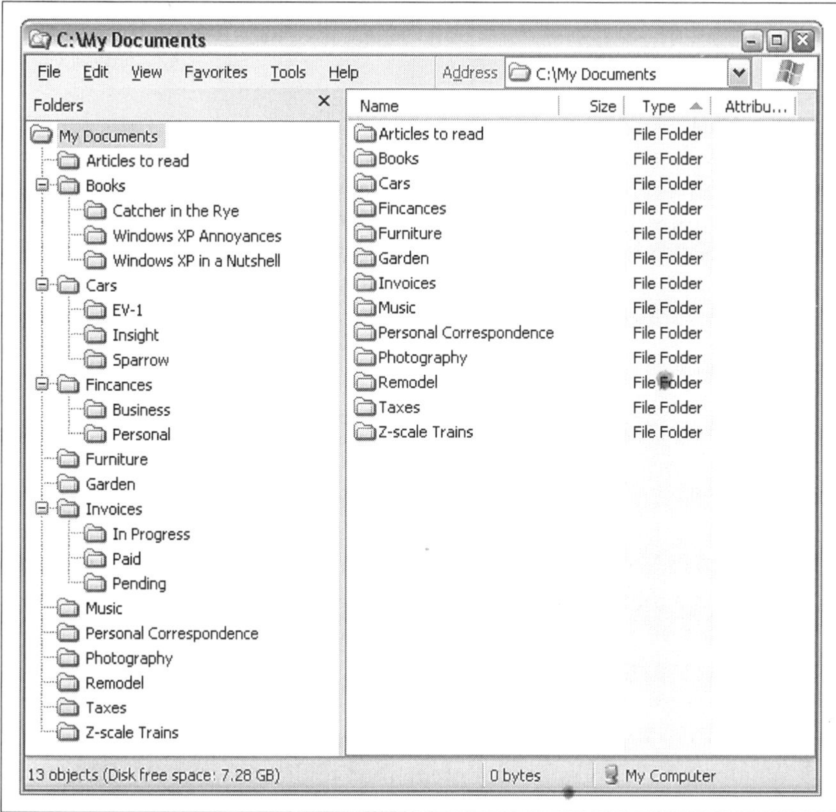

Figure 2-5. An example of how to organize your personal documents into descriptively named top-level folders

The same applies to your Internet Explorer Shortcuts and Netscape Bookmarks. Rather than grouping all your links in the same place, create Internet Shortcuts in these project folders. Place links to online gardening web sites in the *Garden* folder, right next to the spreadsheet containing an index of all your plants and the email attachments sent by your gardening friends. Then, just double-click your Internet Shortcuts to open the corresponding pages in your default web browser.

Keep it simple

It's best not to introduce too many levels of organization (i.e., folders within folders within folders), as these end up just making the data harder to find. For example, I could have grouped the *Furniture*, *Garden*, and *Remodel* folders and put them in another folder called *Home Improvement*, but what would have been the point? This way, all of my categories, so to speak, are visible right at the top level, and I can find the ones I want without having to hunt for them or open a bunch of intermediate folders.

Keep your Desktop clean

The Desktop is commonly a receptacle for files of all types, but this often leads to a ton of clutter. Instead of placing your working documents on your Desktop, put them in your projects folders right away. Then, to provide quicker access, make Windows Shortcuts to your most frequently accessed projects folders; see "Convince Explorer to Start with the Folder You Want," earlier in this chapter, for instructions on opening an Explorer window rooted in an arbitrary location, like the one shown in Figure 2-5.

A common root pays off down the road

It's a good idea to root all your projects folders in the same place. The *My Documents* folder is an especially convenient location for this, mostly because many **File → Open** and **File → Save** dialogs open to *My Documents* by default. Note that you can rename the *My Documents* folder to something a little less cutesy, or you can even change the location of the folder using TweakUI (see Appendix A). Another advantage to rooting all your projects folders in the same place is that it makes it easier to collect all your personal data, both for backups and when it comes time to upgrade your computer.

When to use My Pictures, My Videos, My eBooks, etc.

Windows XP installs several predefined folders in your *My Documents* folder, such as *My Pictures* and *My Music*, in an attempt to influence you to organize your files by content type, rather than topic or project. This, of course, contradicts the strategy explained here, as well as the system imposed by some of Microsoft's earlier efforts, such as the *My Documents* folder.

But why is Microsoft trying to organize your documents for you? Well, there are three reasons for the existence of these folders:

- First, if you have the common tasks pane enabled (discussed at the beginning of this chapter), certain additional links will appear for different folders. For example, when you open *My Pictures*, a special **Picture Tasks** will appear at the top of the tasks pane, with links to such features as **View as a slide show** and **Order prints online**.
- Next, some folders have different default view settings; for example, the default view in *My Pictures* is **Thumbnails**. This is intended to be convenient but doesn't always end up that way. See "Disable the Automatic Display of Thumbnails in Certain Folders" in Chapter 4 for more information.

- Finally, certain applications are designed to look in these folders for the types of files they typically support. The Windows Movie Maker, for example, opens by default to the *My Videos* folder (if it exists).

Naturally, though, it sometimes does make sense to use these folders. For example, any MP3s you've downloaded or ripped from CDs are likely to be all located in the same place anyway and putting them in the *My Music* folder will afford you these advantages.

Note that you can change the location of any of these system folders using TweakUI (see Appendix A), either to redirect them to existing folders or to consolidate them into a single folder. You can also safely and easily delete any of these folders, allowing you to organize your documents more appropriately. The exception is the *My Pictures* folder, which, if deleted, will be automatically re-created the next time Windows starts.

Working with ZIP Files

Phillip Katz conceived of the ZIP file format at his mother's kitchen table in 1986 and soon thereafter wrote a little program called PKZip. Although his program, capable of encapsulating and compressing any number of ordinary files and folders into a single archive file, was not the first of its type, it quickly became a standard and ended up revolutionizing the transfer and storage of computer data.

Although ZIP files have been the de facto standard in file compression for more than fifteen years, Windows XP is the first version of Windows to come with support for ZIP files built into the operating system.

ZIP files work somewhat like folders in that they "contain" files, so its not surprising that they're represented as folders in Explorer. But a ZIP file is typically smaller than the sum of its contents, thanks to the ZIP compression scheme. For example, a folder with ten spreadsheet documents might consume 8 MB of disk space, but when zipped might only consume 3 MB (or even less). The level of compression varies with the type of data being compressed; zipped text documents can be as small as 4% or 5% of the size of the original source files, but since movies and images are already compressed, they'll only compress to 95% to 98% of their original size, if that.

This compression makes ZIP files great for shrinking data down before emailing or otherwise transmitting over an Internet or network connection, since smaller files can be sent more quickly. Furthermore, since a single ZIP file can encapsulate a bunch of separate files, sending ZIPs is that much more convenient.

There are other compression schemes out there, although none have achieved the popularity of ZIP. In fact, a few years back, a new archive format was introduced that claimed much better compression than ZIP: archives made with this new scheme ended up being roughly one hundredth the size of corresponding ZIP files. The only problem was that this was a one-way process; files that were compressed and later extracted unfortunately bore no resemblance to the original source files. Might as well stick with ZIP…

To open a ZIP file, just double-click it. You can extract files from ZIP archives by dragging them out of the ZIP folder window. You can also right-click a ZIP file and select **Extract All**, but you'll have to deal with a more cumbersome wizard interface.

You can create a new ZIP file by right-clicking on an empty portion of the desktop or in any open folder, and selecting **New → Compressed (zipped) folder**. (The name here is actually misleading, since ZIP archives are actually files and not folders.) You can compress new files into ZIP archives by simply dragging them onto the *New Compressed (zipped) folder.zip* file icon, or into an open ZIP folder window.

Another way to compress a file, folder, or group of files and folders into a ZIP archive is to select them, right-click, select **Send To**, and then **Compressed (zipped) folder**. This is especially convenient, as there's no wizard or other interface to get in the way. For example, if you send the folder *CompuGlobalHyperMegaNet* to a ZIP file, Windows will compress the folder's contents into *CompuGlobalHyperMegaNet.zip* and place the new archive alongside the source folder.

The ZIP archive format has built-in error checking. If you find that certain file types become corrupted when emailing or downloading from the web, try putting them in a ZIP file to "protect" them.

There are some drawbacks to the integration with ZIP files in Windows XP. For example, it can interfere with searches, as described in "Fix the Search Tool," earlier in this chapter. It can also interfere with third-party ZIP utilities, many of which provide more functionality than the rudimentary ZIP support in Windows XP. For example, the WinZip utility (*http://www.winzip.com*) adds a bunch of handy commands to your context menus and even to the right-drag menus (discussed in "Take Charge of Drag-Drop," earlier in this chapter). Also, it treats ZIP archives more like files and less like folders, which many users may prefer.

If you wish to use another program to work with ZIP files, you should first disable Windows's built-in ZIP integration:

1. Go to **Start → Run**.
2. Type the following at the prompt and click **OK** when you're done:

```
regsvr32 /u %windir%\system32\zipfldr.dll
```

3. The change will take effect immediately, but you may have to restart Windows for all traces of the built-in ZIP support to disappear.

If, at any time, you wish to re-enable Windows XP's built-in ZIP support, just follow these steps:

1. Go to **Start → Run**.
2. Type the following at the prompt and click **OK** when you're done:

```
regsvr32 %windir%\system32\zipfldr.dll
```

3. The change will take effect immediately, but you may have to restart Windows for all traces of the built-in ZIP support to once again become available.

Clean up Windows Shortcuts

Windows Shortcuts are nothing special; they're just files (with the *.lnk* extension)* that contain "pointers" to the files, folders, programs, or system objects to which they link.

Windows gives you four ways of distinguishing shortcuts from other files:

- When created, a shortcut's caption begins with the text, "Shortcut to."
- The shortcut's icon also has a small curved arrow in the lower-left corner, as shown in the "before" icon in Figure 2-6.

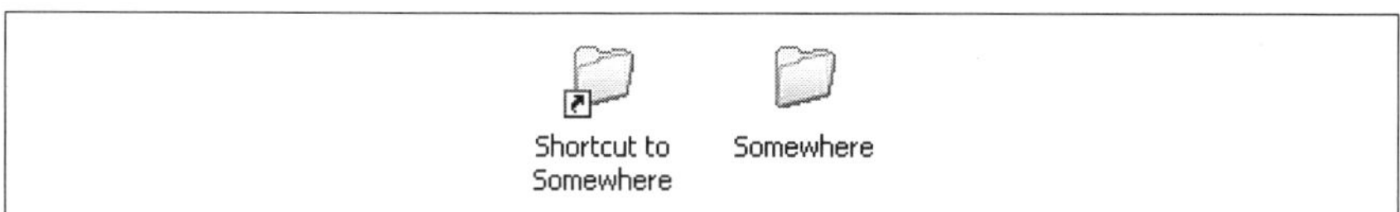

Figure 2-6. Cleaning up Windows shortcuts: before and after

- If you're viewing the folder containing the shortcut in **Details** mode, the **Type** column will read either **Shortcut**, **Shortcut to MS-DOS Program**, or **Internet Shortcut** for *.lnk*, *.pif*, and *.url* shortcut files, respectively. This information is also available in the shortcut's Properties sheet.

* The *.lnk* extensions for Windows Shortcuts will always be hidden, even if you've configured Windows to display your filename extensions, as described earlier in this chapter.

- Finally, shortcuts are small: typically only a few hundred bytes, regardless of the size of the objects to which they link.

Naturally, you can rename a single shortcut to get rid of the aforementioned "Shortcut to," but ensuring that the text isn't added to newly created shortcuts is a different matter. And there's no setting anywhere in the Windows interface for removing the little arrow icon. To turn off these artifacts for good on all shortcuts, use the following instructions.

Part 1: Remove the "Shortcut to" prefix

1. Create a shortcut—any shortcut.
2. Rename the shortcut (right-click and select **Rename** or select and press **F2**) and manually remove the "Shortcut to" portion of the name.
3. Delete the shortcut when you're done.
4. Repeat these steps eight times in succession. You'll know when the change has been made when the ninth shortcut is created without the "Shortcut to" prefix.

Keep in mind that this is a one-way change; there's no way to undo it without using the TweakUI utility, described next.

Part 2: More complete control

This next solution uses Microsoft's TweakUI utility for more control over the appearance of Windows Shortcuts.

1. Open TweakUI (see Appendix A) and expand the **Explorer** category.
2. The **Prefix "Shortcut to" on new shortcuts** option appears in the **Settings** list. If you've used the previous solution to disable the "Shortcut to" prefix, the option will already be turned off. Turn it off or on as desired.
3. Next, open the **Shortcut** category (it's under **Explorer**).
4. To disable or change the curved arrow icon, choose the desired option in the **Shortcut overlay** section: **Arrow** (the default), **Light arrow**, or **None** to disable it completely. If you choose **Custom**, you can choose any icon, although it should be 16×16 or smaller, or partially transparent, so as not to obscure the original icon.
5. Click **OK** when you're done. The changes should take effect immediately.

Note that if you disable the "Shortcut to" prefix with either of these two solutions, the change will be in effect for newly created shortcuts only; naturally, it won't automatically change the filenames of existing shortcuts.

Customizing the Interface

Microsoft has positioned the Desktop as the root of all other objects in the imaginary hierarchy depicted by Explorer's tree. This includes all drives, the Control Panel, *My Network Places*, *My Documents*, and—in terms of the layout of the interface—the Start Menu and all running applications.

The following topics cover some fundamental tasks when dealing with the desktop and other aspects of the shell, such as making sure your desktop layout remains intact and tweaking the Start Menu.

Dealing with Themes, Schemes, Styles, and Skins

Windows XP has a bunch of ways for you to save—and later retrieve—your preferences, but the inconsistent way Microsoft uses and names these features can be confusing and irritating. The best way to deal with schemes, styles, and themes is to understand their scope and learn when to use them.

Part 1: Schemes

A scheme is a saved collection of settings in a *single* dialog box. For example, you can save your current mouse pointer selections under a scheme name by going to **Control Panel → Mouse → Pointers**. This not only makes it easier to quickly switch between multiple sets of mouse pointers (such as one for when you're wearing your glasses and one for when you're not), but it allows you to quickly undo changes made by Windows and other applications.

Other dialogs that use schemes include **Control Panel → Power Options → Power Schemes** tab and **Control Panel → Sounds and Audio Devices → Sounds** tab. In previous versions of Windows, you could also save your Display Settings into a scheme, but in Windows XP, this functionality has been replaced with "themes."

Part 2: Themes

Themes work similarly to schemes, described above, in that several individual settings can be saved under a single theme name. The difference is that there's only one place in Windows to save and retrieve themes, and your theme selection affects settings in several dialogs.

Themes can be managed by going to **Control Panel → Display → Themes**. To load a theme and replace your current settings with those found therein, select a theme from the **Theme** list, and click **Apply**.

To save your current settings into a new theme (or replace an existing theme), click **Save As**. Another difference between themes and schemes is that while schemes are saved in the Registry, themes are saved in individual *.theme* files. By default, new themes are saved in the *My Documents* folder, although only themes found in the *\Windows\Resources\Themes* folder are used to populate the **Theme** list, so that's where you really should be placing your custom *.theme* files.

Settings saved with the current theme include your wallpaper, your custom desktop icons (**Desktop** tab → **Customize Desktop**), your screen saver, your current style (see below), and color selections. Themes essentially cover all of the tabs in the Display Properties dialog, except for the **Settings** tab.

According to the Windows documentation, themes are supposed to also encapsulate your mouse pointers, sounds, and Windows Media Player skin settings. Unfortunately, this simply doesn't work as it's supposed to. When you save a custom theme, these extra settings are ignored. But when you subsequently load a theme, the mouse pointers, sounds, and WMP skins are all simply reverted to their defaults. You'll need to use schemes (as described earlier) to save your mouse and sound settings and protect them from the themes feature.

The format of *.theme* files, should you ever need to edit them, is the same as for standard *.ini* files, discussed in "Using INI Files" in Chapter 3.

Part 3: Styles and skins

Styles (sometimes called "skins") are what are responsible for the new, cartoonish interface in Windows XP. They also have the capability to "skin" Windows XP, wherein a new custom look can be given to all Windows and controls. Rather than a way to save multiple settings, though, the current style is a single setting, found in **Control Panel → Display → Appearance**, in the **Windows and buttons** drop-down list.

By default in Windows XP, you have a choice between two styles: **Windows Classic style** and **Windows XP style**, both of which are pretty self-explanatory.

What isn't obvious is how to customize the new styles feature. Sure, if you select **Windows Classic Style** and then click **Advanced**, you can choose colors for just about any screen element. However, many of the options in the Advanced Appearance dialog have no effect when used with the **Windows XP style**, and, of course, there's no hint to this fact in the interface. About half of the settings in the **Item** list have meaning with the **Windows XP style**; for example, if you choose **Active Title Bar**, you'll be able to change the titlebar thickness (size) but not the color.

The only other choice you have when it comes to style customization is the **Color scheme** (see the discussion of schemes, earlier). Regardless of the currently selected style, the **Color scheme** list contains several preconfigured color combinations. When used with the **Windows Classic Style**, you can select from 22 available color schemes and then customize your choice by clicking **Advanced**.* But when used with the **Windows XP style**, your choice is restricted to three measly color schemes, none of which can be customized as much as the **Windows Classic Style**.

Fortunately, all hope is not lost. It is indeed possible to add new styles to Windows XP or even create your own, but only with a third-party add-on. Probably the best such utility is WindowBlinds (available at *http://www.stardock.com/*), which extends the default selection of styles with about a dozen new entries and allows you to install any number of freely available skins made by other users (check out *http://www.wincustomize.com/*). WindowBlinds is not free, but you can try it before you buy. Figure 2-7 shows an example of a dialog with a custom skin.

I've found WindowBlinds and other such utilities to be somewhat buggy. Once Windows is "skinned" with one of these tools, you may find that applications don't display correctly, and even Windows itself may behave strangely. Typically, the problems aren't that bad, but you may want to play with the software's list of exclusions, so that you can disable skins for applications that don't support them.

But many of you will want to create your own styles (skins), and fortunately, there are at least two ways to do it.

Solution 1: Create your own styles with WindowBlinds

This solution uses one of the skins that comes with the WindowBlinds program as a template for creating a new skin. It takes a considerable amount of time to customize a skin, but with a little patience and some skill with an image editor, you can give Windows XP a completely unique interface.

1. Install the WindowBlinds software (discussed previously), but leave it disabled for the time being. If it's already running, go to **Control Panel → Display → Appearance** and choose **Windows Classic style** to ensure that it's not currently loaded.

* Unlike other dialogs that use schemes, this one doesn't let you save new schemes or delete existing ones, which means the only way to customize this list is to edit the Registry (discussed in Chapter 3).

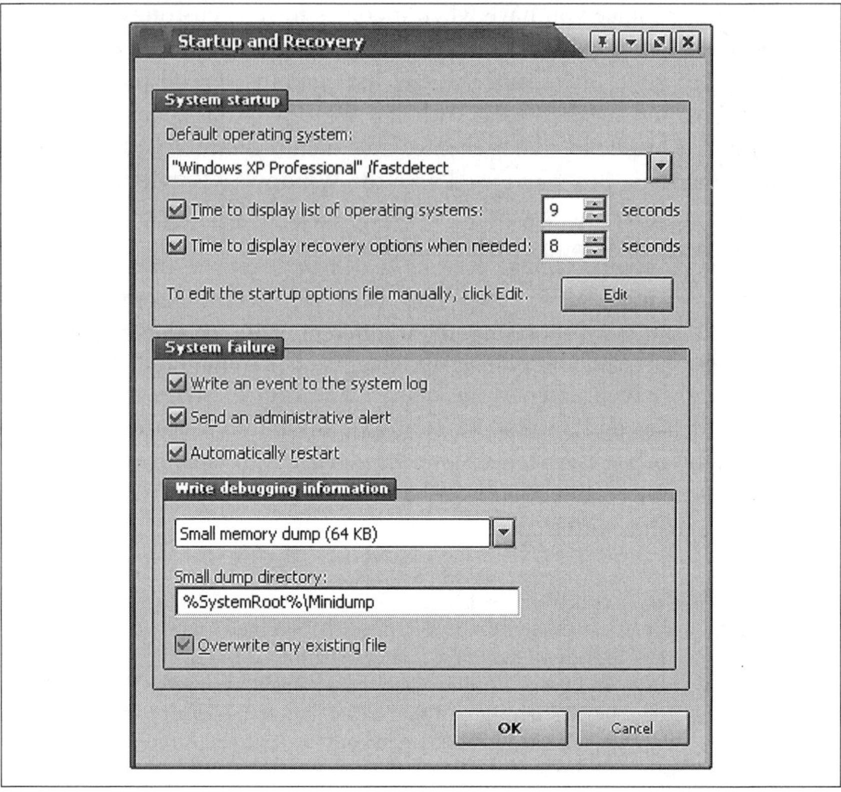

Figure 2-7. A third-party program is required to add custom styles (skins) to Windows XP

2. Open Explorer and navigate to the WindowBlinds program folder (e.g., *c:\Program Files\WindowBlinds*). In this folder, you'll see several subfolders, one for each of the example skins that come with the program. Choose a skin you'd like to customize, create a duplicate of the corresponding folder (see "Make a Duplicate of a File or Folder," earlier in this chapter, for details), choose a descriptive name for the new folder, and then open it in Explorer.
3. Each WindowBlinds skin folder has a *.uis* file that defines the skin. Start by renaming the existing *.uis* file so that it matches the folder name. For example, if you're in *\Program Files\WindowBlinds\Annoyances*, then the skin definition file would be named *Annoyances.uis*.
4. Open the *Annoyances.uis* file (or whatever you've named it) in your favorite text editor (or Notepad). The syntax of this file is the same as for standard *.ini* files, documented in "Using INI Files" in Chapter 3.

Most of the fields in the first section, `TitlebarSkin`, should be self-explanatory. For example, set the `SkinName` entry to the name you wish to give to the skin you're customizing. Change the other entries here as needed.

5. Each screen element (titlebar, title buttons, **Start** button, etc.) is represented by a single *.bmp* file. For example, the file *checkbox.bmp* contains the images used for standard checkbox controls in dialog boxes.

   Using your favorite image editor (or MS Paint), open the bitmap you wish to change. Most *.bmp* files here will actually contain several images, each corresponding to a different state of the control. For instance, the aforementioned *checkbox.bmp* file contains four images, side by side: unchecked with focus, checked with focus, unchecked without focus, and checked without focus. Use the existing *.bmp* file as a template; naturally, some experimentation will be required.

   To make things easier, your custom images should all be the same size as the images they're replacing. If, however, you wish to have, say, larger checkboxes than the skin you've used as a template, you'll have to make the appropriate change in the *.uis* file discussed in Step 3 as well. Just search the file for *checkbox.bmp* (or whatever filename you're changing), and enter new values for the `TopHeight`, `BottomHeight`, `LeftWidth`, and `RightWidth` entries.

6. When you're at a good stopping place, test your new skin. Enable WindowBlinds by going to **Control Panel → Display → Appearance** tab and selecting your newly created skin. Note that new skins may have to be added using the main WindowBlinds window.

   Continue to edit the files that comprise the skin until you achieve the desired results. Create backups as you work.

Solution 2: Poor-man's custom styles

This next solution also requires third-party add-on programs but utilizes only freely available utilities. It would have been nice if Microsoft provided some way to customize the styles (skins) in Windows XP that didn't require users to purchase additional products, but until they get around to adding the functionality to Windows, the following will allow you to customize a skin without spending any money.

1. Another program that allows you to add additional styles to Windows XP is StyleXP (available at *http://www.tgtsoft.com/*). Like WindowBlinds, StyleXP is not free, but TGTSoft does make a free "preview" version of the software available. Download and install one of the previews available on their web site.

2. Open Explorer, and create a new working folder in which to save the files associated with your new custom skin. Place the folder somewhere convenient, such as on your Desktop or in your *My Documents* folder.
3. Then, navigate to the *\Windows\Resources\Themes* folder in Explorer. There should be at least two subfolders here: *Luna*, corresponding to the default "Windows XP style," and *styleXP_1*, corresponding to the newly installed StyleXP preview. Open the *styleXP_1* folder. (Note that the folder name may be different for the preview you've downloaded.)

   In the *styleXP_1* folder, you'll find a single file, *stylexp_1.msstyles*. Place a copy of this file in the working folder you created in the previous step.
4. Download and install the free Resource Hacker utility (available at *http://www.users.on.net/johnson/resourcehacker/*). Resource Hacker allows you to modify the bitmaps embedded in certain types of files, including *.exe* and *.dll* files, as well as the *stylexp_1.msstyles* file that concerns us here.

   Start Resource Hacker, and drag-drop the newly created copy of *stylexp_1.msstyles* onto the Resource Hacker window to open it (or use **File → Open**).
5. Highlight the **Bitmap** branch in the left pane and, if you like, expand the branch to see the entries contained therein.
6. Select **Save [Bitmap] resources** from the **Action** menu and then specify a new filename in the folder you created above. In addition to the filename you specify, all of the bitmaps in the *stylexp_1.msstyles* file will be saved into individual *.bmp* files. The new *.bmp* files will have generic filenames (such as *Bitmap_1.bmp*), but the *.rc* file you save contains a "map" that links each file with its proper location in the Resource Hacker, and will be used later.
7. Edit the newly created *.bmp* files using your favorite image editor (or MS Paint). See the previous solution in this section for more information on the format of these files.
8. When you've modified all the bitmaps, return to Resource Hacker, and select **Replace Bitmap** from the **Action** menu. Select the first entry in the **Select bitmap to replace** list, click **Open file with the new bitmap**, and select the *Bitmap_1.bmp* file. Finally, click **Replace** to update the library with the new *.bmp* file.

   Repeat this step for each of the bitmaps you've modified. They're in order, so it should go fairly quickly: *Bitmap_2.bmp* corresponds to the second entry in the list, *Bitmap_3.bmp* corresponds to the third, and so-on. If you get confused, open the *.rc* file you created in Step 6 using your favorite text editor (or Notepad) and look up the filename associated with the names of the bitmap entries in the Resource Hacker.

9. When you're done, close the Replace bitmap dialog and then go to **File → Save** to save your changes.
10. The next step is to replace the existing *stylexp_1.msstyles* file (located in the *\Windows\Resources\Themes\styleXP_1* folder discussed at the beginning of this procedure) with the modified version. Note that if the style you're modifying is active, you'll have to select a different style before you can replace the file.
11. Finally, go to **Control Panel → Display → Appearance** tab and select your newly modified style from the list to see the new changes.

Special case: When an application ignores your selected style

The style you choose in **Control Panel → Display → Appearance** tab affects not only the titlebars of your applications, but also the push buttons, menus, toolbars, drop-down lists, and other screen elements. Some older applications, however, may not utilize the style you've chosen to its fullest extent.

To force a single application to update all of its push buttons, menus, etc., follow this procedure:

1. Start by typing the following into a plain text editor, such as Notepad:

```
<?xml version="1.0" encoding="UTF-8" standalone="yes"?>
<assembly xmlns="urn:schemas-microsoft-com:asm.v1" manifestVersion=
"1.0"><assemblyIdentity version="1.0.0.0" processorArchitecture="X86"
name="COMPANYNAME.PRODUCTNAME.PROGRAMNAME" type="win32"/><description>MY
DESCRIPTION</description>
<dependency><dependentAssembly><assemblyIdentity type="win32"
name="Microsoft.Windows.Common-Controls" version="6.0.0.0"
processorArchitecture="X86" publicKeyToken="6595b64144ccf1df"
language="*" /></dependentAssembly></dependency></assembly>
```

   Note that the bits of text appearing in ALL CAPS can be customized, although the rest must appear exactly as shown. If you don't feel like typing all this yourself, you can simply download it from *http://www.annoyances.org/downloads/manifest.txt*

2. The name into which this text is to be saved is based on the main application executable (*.exe* file) of the program you wish to update, followed by `.manifest`.

   For example, if you're trying to update Adobe Photoshop, and it has been installed in *c:\Program Files\Adobe\Photoshop*, then the application-executable filename would be *c:\Program Files\Adobe\Photoshop\Photoshp.exe*

   In this case, the filename you'd type would be `photoshp.exe.manifest`, and you'd place it in the *c:\Program Files\Adobe\Photoshop* folder.

3. The next time you start the application, all of its screen elements should now utilize the selected style.

Note that not all programs can be forced to use styles in this way, and of those that support it, not all will do it properly.

Make the Control Panel More Accessible

The settings accessible from the Control Panel affect all parts of the Windows interface, everything from your fonts and screen colors to your computer's network IP address and the refresh rate of your monitor. You may find yourself repeatedly returning to some Control Panel dialogs, while never opening others.

The Control Panel is a system folder, which means that it looks and behaves like a normal folder, but it doesn't actually exist as a folder on your hard drive, nor does it contain any files. That's why you can't easily add to, rename, or delete any of the Control Panel's contents.

Each icon in your Control Panel is really just a separate program or folder on your system, which means the Control Panel itself is nothing more than a glorified menu. Look through the solutions in this section for ways to exploit the Control Panel's flexibility.

See Appendix A for an alphabetical index of settings, many of which can be found in the Control Panel.

Part 1: Categories

A new addition in Windows XP is the way Control Panel icons, by default, are organized into categories. On the surface, it appears as though categories make Control Panel easier, but all they end up doing is adding an extra, unnecessary step to any task involving the Control Panel. Instead of simply opening the icon for the setting you wish to change, you now have to hunt for the icon by trying to guess how it has been categorized. And some icons don't even have categories, which means you'll need to know the "backdoor" method for getting to those items (discussed below).

Probably the most confusing aspect of this new design is that categories are only used under certain circumstances. In other words, depending on how you access the Control Panel, you may or may not have to make a category selection. For example, if you open the Control Panel in a single-folder window (the default when launched from the Start Menu), you'll only see the category view. But if you view the Control Panel folder in Explorer (with the folder-tree pane) or if you've configured Control Panel to display as a menu in the Start Menu (see Part 3), there will be no sign of categories.

To turn off categories in Control Panel and make its interface more consistent, you'll need to have the task pane visible: go to **Control Panel → Folder Options → General** tab, and select **Show common tasks in folders**. Then, open the Control Panel in a single-folder window and click **Switch to Classic View** at the top of the task pane. You can then turn off the task pane or leave it enabled as desired.

Explorer Coping Skills

For the sake of simplicity, the category selection is simply omitted in the solutions in this book. For example, if a solution instructs you to open **Control Panel → System**, and you have categories enabled, you'll need to open the **Performance and Maintenance** category before opening **System**. For the locations of each of the Control Panel icons in the category interface, see Table 2-3, later in this topic.

Part 2: Make shortcuts to Control Panel icons

Creating a shortcut to an individual Control Panel icon is an easy way to provide quick access to commonly used settings. This solution is really easy to do, but it's fairly limited. Part 3 offers more flexibility, at the expense of some simplicty.

1. Open any view of the Control Panel.
2. Drag any item onto your desktop or into an open folder window.
3. Windows will complain that it can't copy or move the item; confirm that you'll settle for a shortcut.
4. Double-click on the shortcut to quickly access the specific Control Panel icon.

Part 3: Search tips

Many Control Panel applets have multiple tabs, each with its own collection of settings and sub-dialog boxes. Anything you can do to decrease the steps in a repetitive task can be helpful. Here's how to make a shortcut to a particular tab of a particular dialog box:

1. Right-click in an empty area of your desktop or an open folder window, select **New**, then select **Shortcut**.
2. In the field labeled **Type the location of the item** (they're really looking for the full path and filename of the item, not just the location), type:

   ```
   control.exe sysdm.cpl ,3
   ```

   This command has three parts. The first, `control.exe`, is the executable that opens the Control Panel (the `.exe` extension is optional). The second, `sysdm.cpl`, is the Control Panel module you'd like to open, as listed in Table 2-3; omit the module name to open the standard Control Panel folder. Finally the number is the tab you'd like to switch to, where `0` is the first, `1` is the second, and so on—note the space *before* the required comma. The command in this example opens the fourth tab of the System dialog box, **Advanced**.

3. Click **Next**, type whatever you like for the name of this shortcut, and click **Finish** when you're done. To make any changes or to choose an icon for the shortcut, right-click on the shortcut and select **Properties**.

Table 2-3 shows all the standard Control Panel icons, the categories in which they're located, and the associated command-line equivalents.

Table 2-3. How to find each of the standard Control Panel icons using Categories or the Command Prompt

Applet name	Category	Command line
Accessibility Options	Accessibility Options	`control access.cpl`
Add Hardware	*n/a - see Notes*	`control hdwwiz.cpl`
Add or Remove Programs	Add or Remove Programs	`control appwiz.cpl`
Administrative Tools	Performance and Maintenance	`control admintools`

Date and Time	Date, Time, Language, and Regional Options	`control timedate.cpl`
		or
		`control date/time`

Display	Appearance and Themes	`control desk.cpl`
		or
		`control desktop`
		or
		`control color`
		(opens the Appearance tab automatically)

Folder Options	Appearance and Themes	`control folders`
Fonts	*n/a - just open \Windows\Fonts in Explorer*	`control fonts`
Game Controllers	Printers and Other Hardware	`control joy.cpl`
Internet Options	Network and Internet Connections	`control inetcpl.cpl`

Keyboard	Printers and Other Hardware	`control main.cpl Keyboard`
		or
		`control keyboard`

Mouse	Printers and Other Hardware	`control main.cpl`
		or
		`control mouse`

Table 2-3. How to find each of the standard Control Panel icons using Categories or the Command Prompt (continued)

Applet name	Category	Command line

Network Connections	Network and Internet Connections	`control ncpa.cpl`
		or
		`control netconnections`

Phone and Modem Options	Printers and Other Hardware	`control telephon.cpl`
		or
		`control telephony`

Power Options	Performance and Maintenance	`control powercfg.cpl`
Printers and Faxes	Printers and Other Hardware	`control printers`

Regional and Language Options	Date, Time, Language, and Regional Options	`control intl.cpl`
		or
		`control international`

Scanners and Cameras	Printers and Other Hardware	n/a

Scheduled Tasks	Performance and Maintenance	`control sticpl.cpl`
		or
		`control schedtasks`

Sounds and Audio Devices	Sounds, Speech, and Audio Devices	`control mmsys.cpl`
Speech	Sounds, Speech, and Audio Devices	`control speech`
System	Performance and Maintenance	`control sysdm.cpl`
Taskbar and Start Menu	Appearance and Themes	n/a

User Accounts	User Accounts	`control nusrmgr.cpl`
		or
		`control userpasswords`

Solution 4: Remove unwanted Control Panel icons

To remove almost any icon from the Control Panel, follow these steps:

1. Open TweakUI (see Appendix A) in Control Panel, and choose the **Control Panel** category.
2. Uncheck any entries you'd prefer weren't displayed in the Control Panel. Since TweakUI's descriptions aren't very good, you may want to look up any questionable items in Table 2-3. Unfortunately, only those entries that have *.cpl* files can be hidden here, which means you're stuck with such items as **Fonts** and **Scheduled Tasks**, whether you want them or not.

3. Click **OK** when you're done. Your changes will take effect immediately in the Control Panel folder, but you may need to log out and log back in to see the change in the Control Panel menu in the Start Menu.

Part 5: Add a cascading Control Panel menu to the Start Menu

The following simple solution allows you to turn your Control Panel into a menu in your Start Menu, providing quicker access to Control Panel icons.

1. Go to **Control Panel → Taskbar and Start Menu**, and choose the **Start Menu** tab.
2. Click the currently enabled **Customize** button.
3. If you're using the new Windows XP–style Start Menu (**Start menu** in the last dialog), choose the **Advanced** tab, and then select **Display as a menu** under the **Control Panel** entry.

   If you're using the **Classic Start menu**, turn on the **Expand Control Panel** option in the **Advanced Start menu options** list.
4. Either way, click **OK** when you're done.

Now, instead of a single menu item in the Start Menu, all the Control Panel icons will be listed individually. To open the separate Control Panel folder window from this interface, simply right-click **Control Panel** and select **Open**. The same goes for its submenus, such as **Fonts**, **Network Connections**, and **Scheduled Tasks**.

Another way to get a Control Panel menu in your Start Menu is to make a new Start Menu folder called *Control Panel*, and then create shortcuts to some or all Control Panel icons in the new folder, as described in the previous solutions in this section. This also affords you the opportunity to add additional icons for items that should have been included in the Start Menu, such as Device Manager (*devmgmt.msc*), Disk Manager (*diskmgmt.msc*), and the Volume Control (*sndvol32.exe*).

Massaging the Start Menu

It's unfortunate that, by default, so many of Windows XP's functions and components are accessible only through the Start Menu, because strictly speaking, it's not a very good interface. Now, I never liked the Start Menu found in earlier versions of Windows, now referred to as the "Classic" Start Menu, but I'm starting to miss it. The new Windows XP version is just a mess.

Figure 2-8 and Figure 2-10 show the two different Start Menus supported by Windows XP.

Figure 2-8. As though we didn't have enough clutter on our desktops, the new Windows XP Start Menu is a mess of icons and menus

You can choose between the two by going to **Control Panel → Taskbar and Start Menu → Start Menu** tab. Note that this option has no effect on the appearance of the **Start** button or taskbar; to change these, you'll need to go to **Control Panel → Display → Appearance** tab, as explained in "Dealing with Themes, Schemes, Styles, and Skins," earlier in this chapter.

Customizing the new XP-style Start Menu

While the Classic Start Menu is a simple, single-column list, the new Start Menu is an overblown hodgepodge of icons and buttons that, like the rest of Windows XP, tries too hard to be friendly.

Despite the new problems it introduces, it fortunately fixes several problems with the Classic Start Menu. For example, by placing more items in the main menu, Microsoft has reduced the need to delve into the awkward cascading **All Programs** menus. Also, the Control Panel has its own menu, rather than being buried in the **Settings** menu. Finally, dissimilar items such as **Shut Down** and **Control Panel** are physically separated and more easily distinguishable, which helps prevent accidentally clicking the wrong item.

The contents of the new XP-style Start Menu are divided into seven sections:

- Across the top is a huge banner simply containing the name of the currently logged-in user. This cannot be turned off or customized, except for the name and (optional) picture specified in the User Accounts window, described in Chapter 8.
- The **Log Off** and **Shut Down** commands are found along the bottom. Instead of **Shut Down**, you may see **Turn off Computer** here instead, depending on your user account settings, of all things (see Chapter 8). Or you may see **Disconnect** if you're using the Remote Desktop feature discussed in Chapter 7.
- On your left, above the horizontal line, are permanently installed shortcuts to programs. You can add new entries here by right-clicking any program executable (*.exe* file) or any Shortcut to a program and selecting **Pin to Start menu**. Such programs can be subsequently removed by right-clicking and selecting **Unpin from Start menu**.

  Although you can place shortcuts to programs here, you can't pin folders to your Start Menu, which means that the only way to organize your programs in folders is to bury them in the **All Programs** menu.

  By default, you'll see two special icons in this section that aren't pinned or unpinned like other shortcuts: Internet Explorer and Outlook Express. These items can be changed by going to **Control Panel** → **Taskbar and Start Menu** → **Start Menu** tab → **Customize** → **General** tab → **Show on Start menu** section, and changing the **Internet** and **E-mail** options.
- Below the permanent program shortcuts on the left side is a dynamic list of recently used programs. The problem with this list is that it is always changing—never a good sign of a well-thought-out interface. You can control how many programs are shown here in the **Programs** section of the Customize Start Menu dialog. Set this option to zero (0) to hide the list completely.
- At the very bottom of the left column is a single entry, **All Programs**, which has the distinction of being the only menu item here that can't easily be removed from the Start Menu (for good reason). The contents of this menu mirror the *\Documents and Settings\{username}\Start Menu\Programs* folder, and can be easily customized by dragging and

dropping, either in the menu itself or in Explorer. To quickly open the *Start Menu* folder in Explorer, right-click any of the folders in the **All Programs** menu and select **Explore**.

The **All Programs** menu is the counterpart to the **Programs** menu found in the Classic Start Menu. In the Classic Start Menu, described in the next section, any shortcuts placed directly in the *Start Menu* folder (as opposed to the *Programs* folder) are shown at the top of the Start Menu itself. In the new XP-style Start Menu, any such shortcuts are placed at the top of the **All Programs** menu instead, separated from the rest of the menu's contents by a horizontal bar.

To remove the **All Programs** item from the Start Menu, open the Group Policy editor (*gpedit.msc*) and expand the branches to `User Configuration\Administrative Templates\Start Menu and Taskbar`. Double click **Remove All Programs list from the Start menu**, select **Enabled**, and click **OK**. You'll have to log out and then log back in for this change to take effect.

- At the top of the right column are all of the Start Menu elements that begin with "My," which, I suppose, is Microsoft's way of being cute. These items don't necesssarily belong together, and all can be selectively removed in the **Advanced** tab of the Customize Start Menu dialog. See Chapter 4 for more information on the **My Recent Documents** menu and the My Computer icon on the Desktop. See Chapter 7 for more information on **My Network Places**.
- Finally, the standard Windows features are shown in the lower-right, such as **Run**, **Search**, and **Control Panel**. Although every one of these items can be turned off (a welcome change from the Classic Start Menu), resulting in a completely empty righthand column (as shown in Figure 2-9), there's no way to remove the second column from the Start Menu.

Regardless of the Start Menu style you prefer, spending a little time clearing out the junk you don't use will result in a simpler, cleaner interface. Figure 2-9 shows an extreme example of this; you'll probably want to either keep a few of the more useful items here, such as **Run**, **Search**, and **Control Panel**, or revert to the Classic Start Menu.

Customizing the Classic Start Menu

The Classic Start Menu style is not quite as flexible as the new XP-style Start Menu in terms of the items that can be removed, but it's much more flexible in the custom items that can be added. The Classic Start Menu also has the advantage of greater simplicity and a smaller footprint, both good for the minimalists among us. Figure 2-10 shows a somewhat slimmed-down Classic Start Menu.

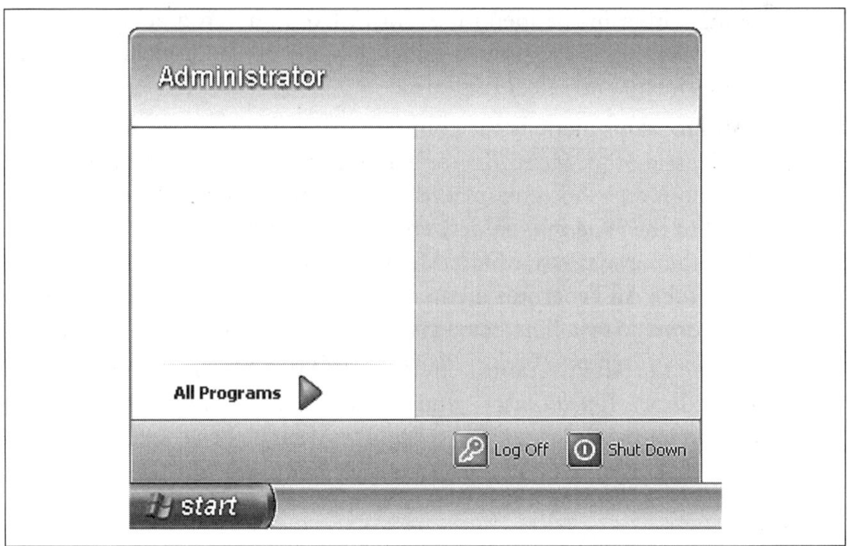

Figure 2-9. After cleaning out all optional items from the Start Menu, a great deal of empty space remains

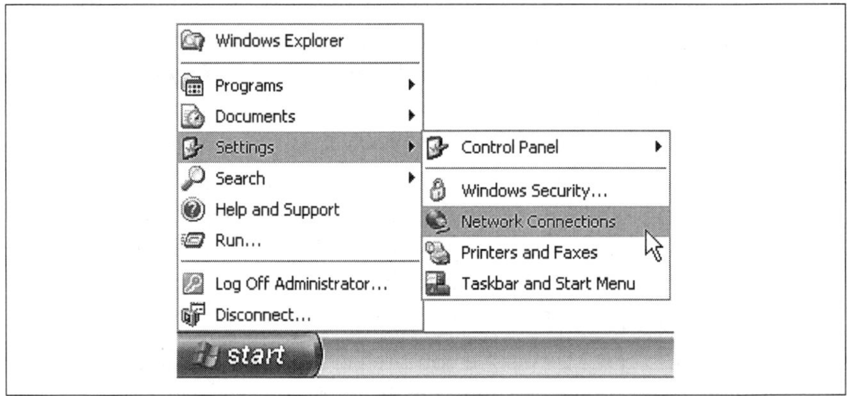

Figure 2-10. The Classic Start Menu is simpler and cleaner than the new XP-style Start Menu but relies more heavily on overly jumpy cascading menus

The Classic Start Menu is divided into only three sections:

- The lower part contains the seemingly "hard-coded" portions of the menu, corresponding to such features as **Search**, **Settings**, and **Run**. If you go to **Control Panel** → **Taskbar and Start Menu** → **Start Menu** tab → **Customize**, you'll be able to turn off the **Favorites**, **Log Off**, and **Run** entries.

  To remove the **Documents** menu, see "Taming Recent Documents" in Chapter 4. Some additional entries, such as **Search** and some of the items in the **Settings** menu, can be turned off by opening the Group Policy editor (*gpedit.msc*) and expanding the branches to `User Configuration\Administrative Templates\Start Menu and Taskbar`. The naming of the options here (in the right pane) is typically self-explanatory. To enable any of these options, double-click, select **Enable**, and then click **OK**. Depending on the option, you may have to log out and then log back in for the change to take effect.

- Above the so-called "hard-coded" entries is a single entry, **Programs**, which is the "classic" counterpart to the **All Programs** menu in the new XP-style Start Menu. The contents of this menu mirror the *\Documents and Settings\{username}\Start Menu\Programs* folder and can be easily customized by dragging and dropping, either in the menu itself or in Explorer. To quickly open the *Start Menu* folder in Explorer, right-click **Programs** and select **Explore**.
- Finally, the space above the horizontal bar is a fully customizable free-for-all, which can be thought of as the saving grace of the Classic Start Menu. In the example shown in Figure 2-10, there's a single shortcut to Explorer here, but you can place any type of shortcut here, and even include folders for further organization. This portion of the Start Menu mirrors the *\Documents and Settings\{username}\Start Menu* folder, with the exception of the *Programs* folder, discussed earlier.

  This compares to the top-left portion of the new XP-style Start Menu, discussed in the previous section, which can only accept programs (no folders or other file types are allowed there).

Unlike the new XP-style Start Menu, you can drag icons from the Desktop or an open folder window and drop them on any part of the Classic Start Menu above the horizontal line, or anywhere in the **Programs** menu.

Sorting Start Menu items

One thing you can do to streamline your Start Menu, regardless of the style you've chosen, is to rearrange items in the Start Menu, eliminating all the unnecessary levels and superfluous shortcuts. For example, instead of the Photoshop shortcut appearing in **Start → Programs → Adobe → Photoshop** (four levels deep), you can simply move the shortcut so it appears in the **Programs** menu. This isn't a great solution, but it's a good place to start.

A consequence of being able to drag-drop Start Menu items in place is that new items are added to the ends of menus, rather than sorted alphabetically with the existing entries. To manually resort any single menu in the Start Menu, right-click on any menu item, and select **Sort by Name**. To sort all your Start Menu folders in one step, you'll need to write a script. (See "Wacky Script Ideas" in Chapter 9 for details.)

The Curse of Personalized Menus

One of the biggest flaws in the Classic Start Menu is a feature called Personalized Menus, which is turned on by default. This remarkably awful feature made its debut in Microsoft Office 2000 and, unfortunately, found its way into Windows 2000 and Me, and yes, Windows XP. It's a design by which certain Start Menu entries indiscriminately and suddenly disappear, based on how recently those options have been used.

It's best to turn off this feature, and then manually and intentionally hide only those items which you know you never use. Go to **Control Panel → Taskbar and Start Menu → Start Menu** tab **→ Customize**, and turn off the **Use Personalized Menus** option.

Note that this option isn't available if you're using the new XP-style Start Menu. Instead of the Personalized Menus fiasco, there is a slightly more acceptable feature that changes only specific and well-defined regions of the Start Menu to reflect the most recently used entries. See "Customizing the new XP-style Start Menu," earlier in this topic, for details.

Dealing with overflow: scrolling vs. multiple columns

When there are too many items in a Programs folder to fit on the screen, one of two things can happen. The default is to "scroll" the menu, forcing you to click the arrow at the bottom of the menu to see more items. The alternative is to display the overflow in multiple columns, which can be a very clumsy interface. Neither choice is a perfect solution, but everyone has a preference.

If you prefer multiple columns to scrolling, go to **Control Panel → Taskbar and Start Menu → Start Menu** tab **→ Customize**. If you're using the Classic Start Menu, turn off the **Scroll Programs** option in the **Advanced Start menu options** list; if you're using the new XP-style Start Menu, choose the Advanced tab and turn off the **Scroll Programs** option in the **Start menu items** list.

Alternatives to the Start Menu

The best thing about the Start Menu is that you don't have to use it. You can start programs by opening associated documents, double-clicking shortcuts on the desktop, or any number of other means:

- Although the desktop is certainly not a great place to store a shortcut to every program on your computer, it's a great location for the most frequently used programs, and certainly better than burying them under several layers of menus. If you only use your computer for a handful of applications, you can move their shortcuts onto the Desktop by dragging (hold the **Ctrl** key to copy) and forget about the Start Menu entirely.

- As a partial fix for the inaccessibility of items in the Start Menu, Windows has configurable, dockable toolbars. Like the **All Programs** and **Programs** menus in the Start Menu, these toolbars just reflect the contents of one or more folders on your hard disk. By placing icons for your most frequently used applications, folders, and documents in these tiny toolbars, you can make it easier and quicker to open the tasks you need. You can drag toolbars anywhere on the screen, docking them to the taskbar or any other edge of your desktop.

  To display one of the preconfigured toolbars, right-click on an empty area of the taskbar, select **Toolbars**, and choose the one you want. In addition to the **Address** and **Links** toolbars, similar to those found in Internet Explorer, there's the **Desktop** toolbar that mirrors the contents of your desktop (good for when the desktop is covered by other windows) and the customizable Quick Launch* toolbar. Select **New Toolbar** to make a new, blank toolbar.

  The problem with these toolbars is that they're rather inflexible and, by default, are extremely small. And although they may be convenient for three or four items, they become clumsier with more icons.

If you find that you can't drag toolbars on or off the taskbar, your taskbar may be locked. Right-click an empty area of the taskbar, and turn off the **Lock the taskbar** option to allow dragging and resizing of the taskbar toolbars.

- Keyboard shortcuts are a convenient way to supplement whatever scheme you decide to use. Just right-click on any shortcut file, Start Menu entry, or taskbar toolbar icon, and select **Properties**. Click in the **Shortcut key** field, and press the desired keystroke combination. For example, you can set up **Ctrl-Shift-E** to open an Explorer window.
- There's nothing stopping you from using another program to augment or replace the Start Menu. In fact, I urge you to explore alternatives to all of the components Microsoft puts in the box, including Notepad,

* The folder containing the Quick Launch shortcuts is *\Documents and Settings\{username}\Application Data\Microsoft\Internet Explorer\Quick Launch*. However, when you create a new toolbar, the folder can be located anywhere—odds are you want to put it somewhere more convenient.

Outlook Express, and Internet Explorer. See *http://www.annoyances.org* for a few suggestions.

For example, Route 1 Pro (available at *http://www.creativelement.com/route1pro/*) implements one or more simple rows of buttons providing quick access to all your programs and files. It's quite a bit slicker and more flexible than either the Start Menu or the taskbar toolbars mentioned earlier.

Refresh the Desktop Without Restarting Windows

When Windows starts, it loads the Explorer application, which provides several services, including the desktop and the Start Menu. While it's loading, Explorer reads its settings from the Registry (see Chapter 3). If you make a change to the Registry, such as when following one of the procedures in this book, it might not take effect until you reload Explorer, which usually means restarting Windows.

However, restarting Windows can take several minutes and will mean shutting down all running applications, which can be a real pain. In many cases, you can put your changes into effect without restarting Windows, as explained in the following solutions. Whether any of these solutions work depends on the type of setting you've changed.

Solution 1

This, the simplest of the solutions in this topic, can be useful to force Explorer to update the contents of the Desktop with any changes, such as newly added or deleted icons:

1. Click on any empty area of your Desktop or select any Desktop icon.
2. Press the **F5** key.

F5 can be used to refresh the display of most other windows, such as folders in Explorer, Registry keys in the Registry Editor, and even web pages in Internet Explorer.

Solution 2

In cases where Solution 1 is not sufficient to implement your changes, you can force Explorer to reload without restarting:

1. Open the Windows Task Manager by right-clicking an empty area of your taskbar and selecting **Task Manager**.
2. Choose the **Processes** tab.

3. Select **explorer.exe** from the list, and click **End Process**.

   If you see more than one instance of **explorer.exe**, it means that one or more Explorer or single-folder windows are open and you've enabled the **Launch folder windows in a separate process** option described in "Exploring Basic Explorer Settings," earlier in this chapter. The one with the largest value in the **Mem Usage** column is the one responsible for the Start Menu and Desktop. If you're still not sure, close the extra Explorer windows and then return to the Task Manager window.

4. Your Desktop and Taskbar will disappear and then reappear after a few seconds. This means that Explorer has been shut down and that Windows has automatically loaded it back into memory.

   If the desktop doesn't reappear, you'll have to relaunch Explorer as explained in the "What Happens When Explorer Crashes" sidebar in the beginning of this chapter.

Solution 3

In cases where Solution 2 is not sufficient to implement your changes, the following solution will not only reload Explorer, but reinitialize all your user settings for all applications. Unfortunately, it will cause all your running applications to close, but it still doesn't take nearly as long as restarting your computer:

1. Open your Start Menu, and click **Log Off**. If you see a warning message, confirm that you indeed wish to log off by answering **Yes**.

   If the **Log Off** option doesn't appear in your Start Menu, go to **Control Panel** → **Taskbar and Start Menu** → **Start Menu** tab → **Customize** and turn on the **Display Logoff** option.

2. Depending on your user account settings, explained in Chapter 8, one of several different "log on" boxes will appear. Just log on as you normally would at this point.

Typically, the only time when none of these solutions will work is when you've installed a new hardware driver or application that must restart in order to replace one or more in-use files. See "How to Delete or Replace In-Use Files," earlier in this chapter, for details.

Customize the Windows Startup Logo

The pompous Microsoft Windows XP logo that appears for the 30 seconds or so it takes to boot your computer can be replaced with any image you choose; it just takes a little hacking.

In some previous versions of Windows, the logo was stored in an ordinary *.bmp* file, but in Windows XP, that bitmap is embedded in a system file. The following procedure shows how to extract the bitmap, modify it, and then reinsert it so it will appear the next time you start up. On the surface, it's a rather long process, but it's actually simpler than it looks.

1. Open Explorer, and navigate to your *\Windows\System32* folder.
2. Place a copy of the file, *ntoskrnl.exe* somewhere convenient, such as on your Desktop or in your *My Documents* folder. Then, make another copy of the file, to be used as a backup in case something goes wrong.
3. Download and install the free Resource Hacker utility (available at *http://www.annoyances.org/*). Resource Hacker allows you to modify the bitmaps embedded in certain types of files, including *.exe* and *.dll* files.

   Start Resource Hacker, and drag-drop the newly created copy of *ntoskrnl.exe* onto the Resource Hacker window to open it (or use **File → Open**).
4. Expand the branches to `Bitmap\1\1033` (click the plus sign next to **Bitmap**, then **1**, then **1033**), and then highlight the **1033** entry. In the right pane, you'll see a large black rectangle; although it doesn't look like it yet, this is the startup logo.
5. Select **Save [Bitmap : 1 : 1033]** from the **Action** menu, and then specify a filename for the logo file, such as *Startup Logo.bmp*.
6. Next, you'll need an image editor that has good control over palettes, such as Adobe Photoshop (*http://www.adobe.com*) or Paint Shop Pro (available at *http://www.jasc.com*). This was tested with Photoshop 7.0 and Paint Shop Pro 7.0, but any modern version of either program should work the same. MS Paint, the rudimentary image editor included with Windows XP, is insufficient for this task.

   The subsequent steps assume you're using Paint Shop Pro, since you can download an evaluation copy for free from the Jasc web site. I'm also including instructions for Photoshop for the graphics nuts among us. If you're using a different image editor, you'll have to adjust the next few steps for the specific features available in your software.
7. Open the newly saved *Startup Logo.bmp* file in your image editor. The image will appear all black at first; this is normal.
8. In Paint Shop Pro, select **Save Palette** from the **Colors** menu, and save the current color palette as *Black.pal*.

   Or, in Photoshop, go to **Image → Mode → Color Table**, and click **Save**. Save the palette into *Black.act*.

Either way, you'll need this later to revert the image when you're done editing.

9. In Paint Shop Pro, select **Edit Palette** from the **Colors** menu.

   Or, in Photoshop, go to **Image → Mode → Color Table**.

   You'll need to change the colors in the palette so that you can distinguish one color from another. The first two entries will remain black. Double-click the third entry (Palette Index 2), and change the **Red**, **Green**, and **Blue** values to 32, 26, and 21, respectively. Repeat this step for the other thirteen colors in this image, using the values in Table 2-4.

Table 2-4. Required color palette entries in order to view and edit the Windows XP startup logo

Palette Index	Red	Green	Blue
0	0	0	0
1	0	0	0
2	32	26	21
3	45	62	210
4	83	101	1
5	178	53	5
6	70	70	70
7	137	146	0
8	74	127	252
9	247	107	32
10	141	166	255
11	142	220	4
12	243	188	27
13	188	188	188
14	255	255	255
15	255	255	255

If you prefer, you can download the required palette file instead of entering it by hand:

Paint Shop Pro
: Download the palette file from *http://www.annoyances.org/download/startuplogo.pal*, then select **Load Palette** from Paint Shop Pro's **Colors** menu. Choose the *startuplogo.pal* file you just downloaded, make sure that the **Maintain indexes** option is selected below, and click **Open**.

Photoshop

Download the palette file from *http://www.annoyances.org/download/startuplogo.act*. In Photoshop, go to **Image → Mode → Color Table**, and click **Load**. Choose the *startuplogo.act* file you just downloaded and click **Load**.

If you're using an image editor other than Paint Shop Pro or Photoshop, you'll have to hand-enter the palette as described earlier.

10. Either way you do it, when you're done updating the palette, the Startup logo will be fully visible. If you hand-entered the palette in the previous step, take this opportunity to save the palette for later use:

    In Paint Shop Pro, go to **Colors → Save Palette**.

    Or, in Photoshop, go to **Image → Mode → Color Table**, and click **Save**.

11. Modify the image to your heart's content. Note that since this is only a 16-color image, you won't be able to get nice photographic tones or even gradients, but your logos should appear nice and crisp!

    Make sure not to alter the palette of the image. Also, make sure to accommodate the revolving blue stripe (which incidentally is another bitmap in the *ntoskrnl.exe* file). Figure 2-11 shows an example of a customized startup logo.

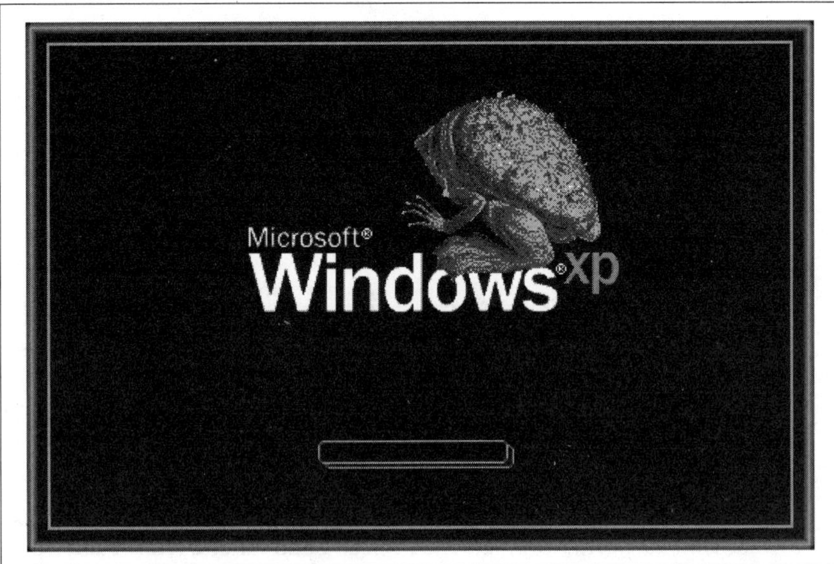

Figure 2-11. Have a little fun with the Windows startup logo

12. When you're done editing, you need to revert the color palette back to the all-black palette we saved at the beginning of this procedure (*Black.pal*):

    In Paint Shop Pro, select **Load Palette** from the **Colors** menu. Choose the *Black.pal* file, make sure that the **Maintain indexes** option is selected below, and click **Open**.

    In Photoshop, go to **Image** → **Mode** → **Color Table**, and click **Load**. Choose the *Black.act* file and click **Load**.

13. If you haven't done so already, save your work. Then, return to Resource Hacker, and select **Replace Bitmap** from the **Action** menu. Select the first entry in the **Select bitmap to replace** list (1), click **Open file with the new bitmap**, and select the *Startup Logo.bmp* file you modified. Finally, click **Replace** to update the library with the new image.
14. Close the Replace bitmap dialog, and then go to **File** → **Save** to save your changes.

If you are wise, you will take this opportunity to make sure you have a safe backup of the original *ntoskrnl.exe* before you replace it. That way, if the modified version is corrupted in any way, you'll be able to repair your system without having to reinstall.

15. The last step is to replace the in-use version of *ntoskrnl.exe* with the one you've just modified. You should be able to just drag the modified version right into your *\Windows\System32* folder, replacing the one that's there.

    If Windows complains that the file is in use and can't be replaced, you'll have to follow the steps outlined in "How to Delete or Replace In-Use Files," earlier in this chapter.

16. The new logo should appear the next time you start Windows. If, for some reason, the logo doesn't appear or Windows won't start, the problem is most likely caused by a corrupt *ntoskrnl.exe* file. This can be repaired by using the instructions in the previous step to replace the modified version with the original version you backed up—you did back it up, didn't you?

See "Customize the Welcome Screen" in Chapter 8 for a related solution.

CHAPTER 3

The Registry

Every time you change a setting in Control Panel, add hardware to your system, install an application, or even rearrange icons on your desktop, Windows stores the corresponding data in your Registry. The Registry is a database containing all the settings for Windows XP, as well as the applications installed on your system. Knowing how to use the Registry effectively is important for improving performance in Windows, troubleshooting all kinds of problems, and, most importantly, customizing Windows XP beyond what is possible with the dialog boxes scattered throughout the interface.

All of your file types (also known as associations; see "File Types: The Link Between Documents and Applications" in Chapter 4) are stored in the Registry, as well as all of the network, hardware, and software settings for Windows XP, and all of the particular configuration options for most of the software you've installed. The particular settings and data stored by each of your applications and by the various Windows components vary substantially, but you can use some special techniques to figure out undocumented settings and uncover hidden functionality, regardless of how the data is stored. What's especially helpful is that most of the settings stored in the Registry are named in plain English rather than with obscure codes and acronyms. You shouldn't take this fact for granted, as it does help quite a bit in finding settings and troubleshooting problems.

Word to the wise: you can irreversibly disable certain components of Windows XP—or even prevent Windows from running—by changing certain settings in the Registry. Now, the vast majority of settings in the Registry are mostly harmless, but nonetheless, I strongly recommend taking the steps outlined in this chapter to prevent making irreversible changes, such as taking advantage of Registry patches to back up portions of the Registry before you edit a single value. Furthermore, backing up your *entire system* will ensure that none of your valuable data or programs are compromised and will undoubtedly save you hours of hassle in the event of a stupid mistake. Believe me, I've been there.

The Registry Editor

Although the Registry is stored in multiple files on your hard disk, it is represented by a single logical hierarchical structure, similar to the folders on your hard disk. The Registry Editor (*Regedit.exe*) is included with Windows XP to enable you to view and manually edit the contents of the Registry.

Don't confuse the Registry with the Registry Editor. *Regedit.exe* is just another application; most of the access to the Registry is performed behind the scenes by the applications that you run, as well as by Windows; settings and other information are read from and written to the Registry constantly.

When you open the Registry Editor, you'll see a window divided into two panes (as shown in Figure 3-1). The left side shows a tree with folders, and the right side shows the contents of the currently selected folder. Now, these aren't really folders—it's just a convenient and familiar method of organizing and displaying the information stored in your Registry.

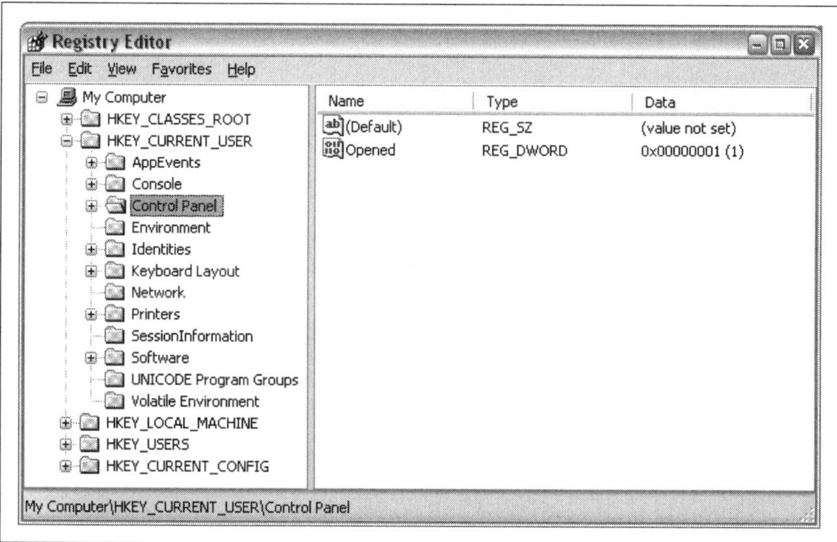

Figure 3-1. The Registry Editor lets you view and change the contents of the Registry

Each branch (denoted by a folder icon in the Registry Editor) is called a *key*. Each key can contain other keys, as well as *values*. Values contain the actual information stored in the Registry, and keys are used only to organize the values. Keys are shown only in the left pane; values are shown only in the right pane (unlike Windows Explorer, where folders are shown in both panes).

To display the contents of a key (folder), simply click the desired key name on the left, and the values contained within the key will be listed on the right side. To expand a certain branch to show its subkeys, click on the plus sign [+] to the left of any folder or double-click on the name of the folder.

Editing the Registry generally involves navigating down through branches to a particular key and then modifying an existing value or creating a new key or value. You can modify the contents of any value by double-clicking it.

To add a new key or value, select **New** from the **Edit** menu, select what you want to add (Figure 3-2), and then type a name. You can rename any existing value and *almost* any key with the same method used to rename files in Windows Explorer: right-click on an object and click **Rename**, click on it twice (slowly), or just highlight it and press the **F2** key. Lastly, you can delete a key or value by clicking on it and pressing the **Del** key or by right-clicking on it and selecting **Delete**.

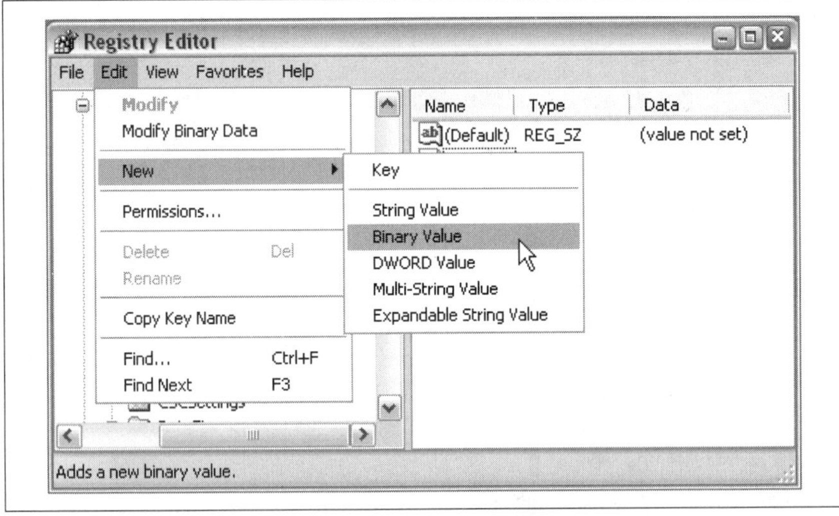

Figure 3-2. Select New from the Edit menu to add a new key or value to any part of the Registry

You can't drag-drop keys or values here as you can with files in Windows Explorer. There is very little reason to drag a key or value from one place to another in the Registry, as the settings are highly location-dependent. A value in one key may have a different meaning than the same value in a different key. The exception is when you want to duplicate a key and all its contents (such as a file-type key), which is something you can do with Registry patches, explained later in this chapter.

You can search for text in key and value names by selecting **Find** from the **Edit** menu. See "Search the Registry Effectively," later in this chapter, for tips on using this deceptively simple function. Lastly, select **Refresh** from the **View** menu to refresh the displayed portion of the Registry, in case another running application has changed, added, or removed a key or value since the Registry Editor last read the data.

The Registry's notion of a *path* is similar to Windows Explorer's. A Registry path is a location in the Registry described by the series of nested keys in which a setting is located. For example, if a particular value is in the `Microsoft` key under `SOFTWARE`, which is under `HKEY_LOCAL_MACHINE`, the Registry path would be `HKEY_LOCAL_MACHINE\SOFTWARE\Microsoft`. Elsewhere in this book, when a setting is changed in the Registry, this type of Registry path is always provided. If you find that you're viewing the same Registry path often, you can use the **Favorites** menu to bookmark the item, allowing you to return to it easily (similar to the operation of the **Favorites** menu in Internet Explorer).

The Structure of the Registry

There are five primary, or *root*, branches of the Registry, each containing a specific portion of the information stored therein. These root keys can't be deleted, renamed, or moved, because they are the basis for the organization of the Registry. They are:

`HKEY_CLASSES_ROOT`
: This branch contains the information that comprises your Windows file types. See the discussion of file types in Chapter 4 for details on the structure of most of the entries in this branch. A few special keys here, such as `CLSID` (short for *Class ID*), contain "registered" components of Windows and your installed applications. The contents of

HKEY_CLASSES_ROOT are generally easy to edit, but it's best not to mess with anything in the CLSID branch, because almost none of it is in plain English.

This entire branch is a symbolic link,* or "mirror," of HKEY_LOCAL_MACHINE\SOFTWARE\Classes but is displayed separately in this branch for clarity and easy access.

HKEY_USERS

This branch contains a sub-branch for the currently logged-in user, the name of which is a long string of numbers, which will look something like this:

```
S-1-5-21-1727987266-1036259444-725315541-500
```

This number is the SID (security identifier), a unique ID for each user on your system. See Chapter 8 for more information on SIDs.

While it may sound like a good idea to edit the contents of this branch, you should instead use the HKEY_CURRENT_USER branch described later, which is a symbolic link, or "mirror," of this branch. No matter which user is logged in, HKEY_CURRENT_USER will point to the appropriate portion of HKEY_USERS.

Because Windows only loads the profile (this portion of the Registry) of the currently logged-in user, only one user branch will ever be shown here. However, there will be a few other branches here, such as .default (used as a template when creating new user accounts), and a few others that will be of little interest to most users.

HKEY_CURRENT_USER

This branch simply points to a portion of HKEY_USERS, signifying the currently logged-in user. This way, any application can read and write settings for the current user without having to know which user is currently logged on.

In each user's branch are the settings for that user, such as Control Panel settings and Explorer preferences. Most applications store user-specific information here as well, such as toolbars, high scores for games, and other personal settings.

The settings for the current user are divided into several categories; among them are AppEvents, Control Panel, Identities, RemoteAccess, Software,

* A symbolic link is different from a Windows shortcut you'd find on your hard disk. Information in a linked branch appears twice and can be accessed at two different locations, even though it's stored only once. This means that Find may stop in both places if they contain something you're looking for and, as you might expect, changes in one place will be immediately reflected in the mirrored location.

and System. The most useful of these branches, Software, contains a branch for almost every application installed on your computer, arranged by manufacturer. Here and in HKEY_LOCAL_MACHINE\SOFTWARE (discussed later) can be found all of your application settings. As though Windows were just another application on your system, you'll find most user-specific Windows settings in HKEY_CURRENT_USER\Software\Microsoft\Windows.

HKEY_LOCAL_MACHINE
: This branch contains information about all of the hardware and software installed on your computer that *isn't* specific to the currently logged-in user. The settings in this branch are the same for all users on your system.

The sub-branch of most interest here is the SOFTWARE branch, which contains all of the information specific to the applications installed on your computer. Both this branch and the aforementioned HKEY_CURRENT_USER\Software branch are used to store application-specific information. Those settings that are specific to each user (even if your computer has only one user), such as toolbar configurations, are stored in the HKEY_CURRENT_USER branch; those settings that are not user-dependent, such as installation folders, are stored in the HKEY_LOCAL_MACHINE branch. You'll want to look in both places if you're trying to find a particular application setting, because most manufacturers (even Microsoft) aren't especially careful about which branch is used for any given setting.

HKEY_CURRENT_CONFIG
: This branch typically contains a small amount of information, most of which is simply symbolic links, or "mirrors," of other keys in the Registry. There's little reason to mess with this branch.

The Meat of the Registry: Values

Values are where Registry data are actually stored (keys are simply used to organize values). The Registry contains several types of values, each appropriate to the type of data they are intended to hold. There are seven types of values that are displayed in the Registry Editor, each of which is known by two different names (see Table 3-1).* Each type is known by at least two different names, the common name and the symbolic name (shown in parentheses).

* Another type of value, known as REG_LINK, is invisible in the Registry Editor. It facilitates symbolic links; the HKEY_CURRENT_USER branch, discussed earlier in this chapter, is an example.

Table 3-1. Value types visible in the Registry Editor

Value type	Icon used in RegEdit	Can be created in RegEdit?
String (REG_SZ)		Yes
Multi-String[a] (REG_MULTI_SZ)		Yes
Expandable String (REG_EXPAND_SZ)		Yes
Binary (REG_BINARY)		Yes
DWORD (REG_DWORD)		Yes
DWORD (REG_DWORD_BIGENDIAN)		No
Resource List (REG_RESOURCE_LIST, REG_RESOURCE_REQUIREMENTS_LIST, or FULL_RESOURCE_DESCRIPTOR)		No

[a] Multi-String values are also sometimes called String Array values.

Although the Registry Editor allows you to view and edit all seven types of values, it only allows you to create the five most common (and not surprisingly, most useful) types.* Although each of these value types is explained below, they'll make more sense when discussed in the context of the solutions throughout the rest of this book.

String values

String values contain *strings* of characters, more commonly known as plain text. Most values of interest to us will end up being string values; they're the easiest to edit and are usually in plain English.† String values are easy to edit; just double-click and type a string of text into the text field (Figure 3-3).

In addition to standard strings, there are two far less common string variants, used for special purposes:

String array value

Contains several strings, concatenated (glued) together and separated by null characters. Although the Registry Editor now lets you create these values, it's impossible to type null characters (character #0 in the ASCII character set) from the keyboard. The only way to place a null character into a Registry value is either programmatically or via cut-and-paste from another application.

* In previous versions of Windows, the Registry Editor only allowed you to create String, Binary, and DWORD values. The ability to create Multi-String and Expandable String values is new in Windows XP. Note that you'll find little reason to ever create the other two available types shown in Table 3-1.

† Although Windows is available in a wide variety of localized languages, most of the internal Registry data will still be in English, primarily because Microsoft is located in the United States, but also because the programming languages used to write Windows components and applications are all based on American English.

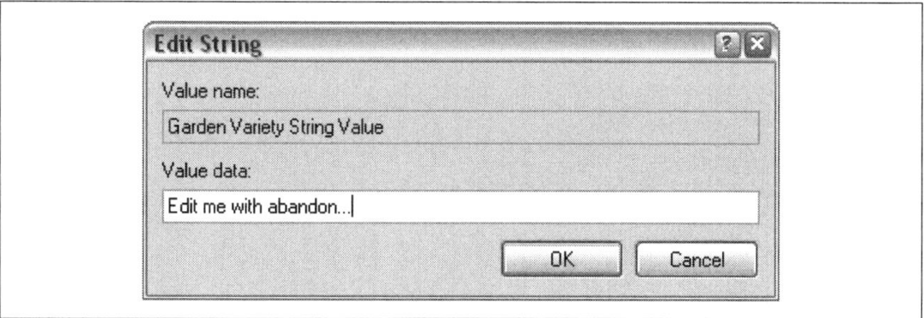

Figure 3-3. Edit a string value by typing text into this box

Expanded string value

Contains special variables, into which Windows substitutes information before delivering it to the owning application. For example, an expanded string value intended to point to a sound file may contain `%SystemRoot%\Media\doh.wav`. When Windows reads this value from the Registry, it substitutes the full Windows path for the variable, `%SystemRoot%`; the resulting data then becomes (depending on where Windows is installed) `c:\Windows\Media\doh.wav`. This way, the value data is correct regardless of the location of the Windows folder.

Binary values

Similarly to string values, binary values hold strings of characters. The difference is the way the data is entered. Instead of a standard text box, binary data is entered with hexadecimal codes in an interface commonly known as a *hex editor*.* Each individual character is specified by a two-digit number in base-16 (e.g., the number 6E in base-16 is the number 110 in good-ol' base-10), which allows characters not found on the keyboard to be entered. See Figure 3-4 for an example. Note that you can type hex codes on the left or normal ASCII characters on the right, depending on where you click with the mouse.

The contents of binary values often don't appear in plain English, making understanding their use, not to mention modifying them, that much more difficult. Figure 3-4 shows a binary value that just happens to have readable text.

Note also the various Resource List value types (see Table 3-1), which are just special cases of binary values; you'll find very little reason to ever mess with these.

* See "Thinning Out Explorer's New Menu" in Chapter 4 for an example of how a hex editor is used.

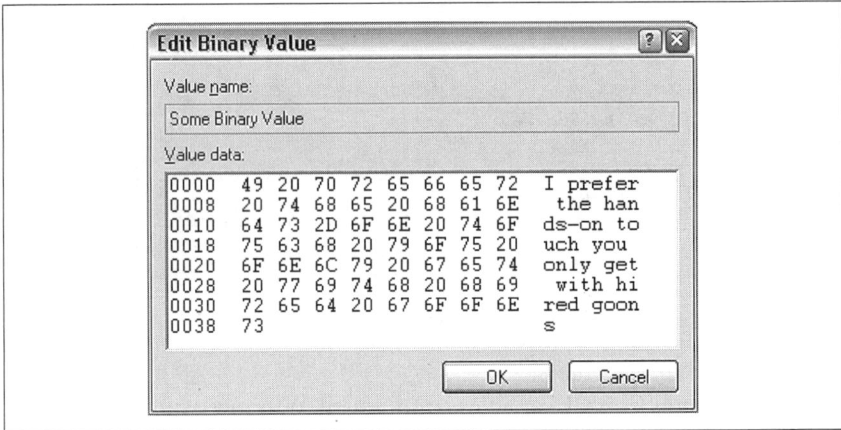

Figure 3-4. Binary values are entered differently from the common string values, but the contents are sometimes nearly as readable

DWORD values

Essentially, a DWORD is a number. Often, the contents of a DWORD value are easily understood, such as `0` for no and `1` for yes, or `60` for the number of seconds in some timeout setting. A DWORD value is used where only numerical digits are allowed, whereas string and binary values allow anything.

In the DWORD value editor (Figure 3-5), you can change the base of the number displayed. For values of 9 or smaller, this option won't make any difference. For 10 and larger, however, the wrong selection will result in the wrong value being entered. In most cases, you'll want to select **Decimal** (even though it's not the default), since decimal notation is what we use for ordinary counting numbers. Note that if there's already a number in the **Value data** field, it will be instantly converted when you switch the **Base**, which is a good way to illustrate the difference between the two.

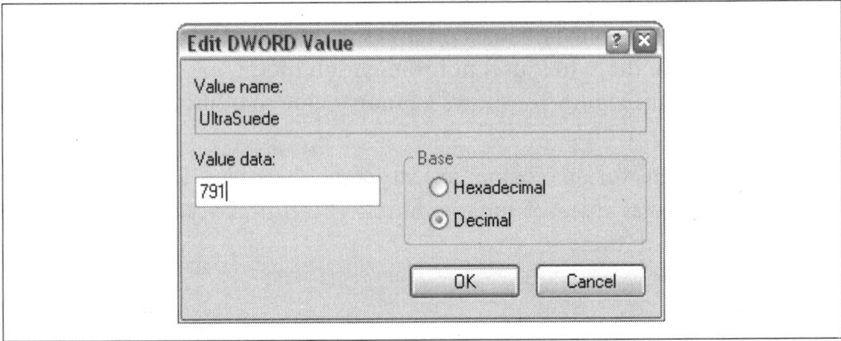

Figure 3-5. DWORD values are just numbers, but they can be represented in Decimal or Hexadecimal notation

In some circumstances, the particular number entered into a DWORD value is actually made up of several components, called bytes. This way, several values can be represented by a single number. While this notation is often convenient for programmers, it's decidedly inconvenient for lowly users fishing around in the Registry. The REG_DWORD_BIGENDIAN type is a variant of the DWORD type, wherein said bytes are simply represented in the opposite order.

You can create a value (or key) anywhere in the Registry and by any name and type that suits your whim. However, unless Windows or an application is specifically designed to look for the value, it will be ignored and your addition will have absolutely no effect.

Most Registry editing involves modifying existing values, as opposed to creating new ones. This often makes things easier, as the existing value and its contents can be used as an example.

The application that creates each value in the Registry solely determines the particular type and purpose of the value. In other words, no strict rules limit which types are used in which circumstances or how values are named. A programmer may choose to store, say, the high scores for some game in a binary value called `High Scores` or in a string value called `Lard Lad Donuts`.

An important thing to notice at this point is the string value named `(default)` that appears at the top of every key.* The default value cannot be removed or renamed, although its contents can be changed; an empty default value is signified by `value not set`. The `(default)` value doesn't necessarily have any special meaning that differentiates it from any other value, apart from what might have been assigned by the programmer of the particular application that created the key.

Registry Procedures

The solutions in the rest of this chapter will show you how to use the Windows Registry: how to find keys, how to automate changes, how to back up, and more. Use these techniques throughout the rest of the book, whether you're just playing around or trying to solve a problem.

* In the more simplistic Registry found in Windows 3.1 and Windows NT 3.x, each key had only one value. Starting in Windows 95, a key could contain any number of values; the default value simply took the place of the lone value from previous versions, allowing compatibility with older applications that were written before the change took effect. In fact, many things you'll find in the Registry are designed with such "legacy" support in mind.

Note that there are a few programs designed to make working with the Registry and its settings easier. For instance:

TweakUI
: The options in this little Microsoft add-on make certain Windows settings more accessible, settings that would otherwise require editing the Registry. Note that the version of TweakUI used with older versions of Windows should not be used in Windows XP. TweakUI is available directly from Microsoft, as well as from *http://www.annoyances.org*. See Appendix A for a list of TweakUI settings, arranged by task.

Creative Element Power Tools
: This collection of tools for Windows XP, Windows 2000, and Windows Me includes a bunch of settings, utilities, and context-menu addons that aren't otherwise possible with simple changes to the Registry. Among other things, a tool allowing you to search and replace in the Registry is included.

Backing Up the Registry

Taking a few minutes to make sure you have a good backup of your Registry now will save you hours of headaches later. But backing up the files that contain your Registry data (called *hives*) can be tricky.

`HKEY_USERS` and `HKEY_LOCAL_MACHINE` are, essentially, the only *true* root keys, because the Registry's three other root keys are simply symbolic links, or "mirrors," of different portions of the first two (see "The Structure of the Registry," earlier in this chapter). This means that only these two branches actually need to be physically stored on your hard disk.

Since the files in which the Registry is stored are never edited directly, you're likely to never need to know what they're called or where they're located. In fact, they can't even be copied while Windows is running, so you won't be able to back them up directly. However, sooner or later, you'll run into them, so the following is a list of all of the hive files in which the Registry is physically stored on your hard disk.

`HKEY_LOCAL_MACHINE`
: Each subkey of `HKEY_LOCAL_MACHINE` is stored in its own file in the folder, *\Windows\System32\Config*. For example, the contents of `HKEY_LOCAL_MACHINE\Software` is stored in the file *software* (no extension). The only exception to this is `HKEY_LOCAL_MACHINE\Hardware`, which is a dynamically generated branch, and therefore not stored on the hard disk at all.

`HKEY_USERS\{SID of current user}`
: This key, which is the same as `HKEY_CURRENT_USER`, is stored a file named *NTUSER.DAT*, located in the user's home directory, which is usually *\Documents and Settings\{username}*. See Chapter 8 for more information on user accounts and the SID.

> You may notice a copy of *NTUSER.DAT* in *\Documents and Settings\Default User*. However, this is not the template used for creating new users, as you might expect. Instead, this is merely a remnant of the installation process and does not appear to be used by Windows XP. When a new user account is created, the user hive is built using the data in *HKEY_USERS\.Default*, which is stored in the *default* file in *\WINDOWS\system32\config*.

Now, since these hive files are in use whenever Windows is running, they can't be read or modified by any other processes. This means that there is no direct way to back up or restore your entire Registry simply by copying these files (as is possible in some earlier versions of Windows). There are, however, several ways to achieve an effective Registry backup:

Use Registry-enabled backup software
: The most painless way to back up your entire Registry is to do so while backing up the rest of your system. Any decent backup software designed for Windows XP, including the Backup utility that comes with it, will be able to include the Registry in the backup. See Chapter 6 for more information.

Make Registry patches
: Registry patches are the quick and easy way to store small portions of your Registry, useful for transferring Registry data to other computers or simply backing up a key before you mess with it. This is similar, at least conceptually, to a local anesthetic. See "Using Registry Patches" later in this chapter for details.

Go behind Windows's back
: The only time when you are permitted to copy or overwrite the hive files is when Windows isn't running. If you have a dual-boot system (Chapter 1) or wish to use the Windows Recovery Console (Chapter 6), you'll be able to read and modify the hive files.

  The exception to this rule is the user hive, *NTUSER.DAT*, for users *other* than the one currently logged on. Say you have three users: Katie, Cat, and Sara. If Cat is currently logged in, the *NTUSER.DAT* files in both *\Documents and Settings\Katie* and *\Documents and Settings\Sara* will be ripe for the plucking.

The implications of this can be interesting. For example, you can back up or replace your own *NTUSER.DAT* hive simply by logging out and then logging in as another user (as long as that user has administrative privileges). You can also copy one user's settings to another user's account simply by duplicating the user's hive file, which is a quick and easy way to set the default profiles for a large number of user accounts. See Chapter 8 for more information on the administration of user accounts. Note that if you delete a user's hive, it will be reconstructed from data in *HKEY_USERS\.Default* the next time the user logs in.

Use the Windows Recovery Console

The Windows Recovery Console, discussed in Chapter 6, is a back door of sorts, allowing you to access Windows files while Windows isn't running and effect repairs if Windows won't start. This means that you can use the Recovery Console to copy the hive files.

Now, this isn't exactly the most convenient means of backing up the Registry, but if you create copies of the hives in another folder on your hard disk, you can use those copies should your Registry ever become corrupted. For instance, if your `HKEY_LOCAL_MACHINE` branch gets screwed up, all you'd need to do is replace the active hive files with backups made on an earlier date. See "How to Delete or Replace In-Use Files" in Chapter 2 for more tips.

If your HKEY_CURRENT_USER branch should ever become corrupted, you can restore it from a backup, as described here. Or, you can log on as the Administrator (or another existing account), and effect repairs from within Windows. Unfortunately, you can't create new user accounts on the fly from the Logon or Welcome screens, as you could in some earlier versions of Windows.

The important thing to realize with all of these backup solutions is that they require advanced planning. Don't wait until your system won't start before you start thinking about backing up. See Chapter 6 for simple backup tips.

Finding the Right Registry Key

The two main obstacles you'll encounter when trying to make a change to the Registry are (1) finding where a setting is located in the Registry, and (2) determining what modifications are necessary to affect the desired changes.

Sometimes it's obvious, such as a theoretical value called `ShowSplashScreen`, with its contents set to `1` (one); changing the `1` to a `0` (zero) would most likely result in turning the option off.* Other times you'll see a long, seemingly meaningless series of numbers and letters. Although there are no strict rules as to how values and keys are named or how the data therein is arranged, a little common sense and intuition will get you through most situations.

Here's a solution that will help you find the corresponding Registry key for a particular setting in Windows. For this example, we'll find the Registry setting associated with showing or hiding hidden files in Windows Explorer, and then we'll create the appropriate Registry patch.

A Registry patch is a convenient way of automating changes to the Registry, and therefore to Windows and your applications, and is useful if you frequently change a setting or a group of settings. It's also a convenient way to propagate a group of settings on one or more other computers. This solution provides a way to come up with a Registry patch that corresponds to one or more options in the interface.

The Registry

The idea is to take *snapshots* (make Registry patches) of your entire Registry *before* and *after* a change is made in Explorer (or any other program). By comparing the two snapshots, we can easily see which Registry keys and values were affected:

1. Make sure no unnecessary applications are running (check your Windows system tray/notification area), because they could write to the Registry at any time, adding unexpected changes.
2. Open the Registry Editor, and highlight the `HKEY_CURRENT_USER` branch.
3. Select **Export** from the **File** menu. Specify a filename (e.g. *User1.reg*), place it somewhere convenient (such as your Desktop), and click **Save** to export the entire branch to the file.

   Then, select the `HKEY_LOCAL_MACHINE` branch and repeat the steps, exporting it instead to *Machine1.reg*.†
4. Next, we will make our desired change. In this case, go to **Control Panel → Folder Options → View** tab. In the **Advanced Settings** list, change the **Hidden Files and Folders** option, and click **OK** when you're done.

* Zero and one, with regard to Registry settings, typically mean false and true (or off and on), respectively. However, sometimes the value name negates this—if the value in the example were instead called `DontShowSplashScreen`, then a `1` would most likely turn off said splash screen.

† Although the Registry has five main branches, the others are simply symbolic links of portions of these two. See "Backing Up the Registry," earlier in this chapter, for details.

5. Immediately switch back to the Registry Editor, and re-export the HKEY_CURRENT_USER and HKEY_LOCAL_MACHINE branches into new files, such as *User2.reg* and *Machine2.reg*, respectively, as described earlier in step 2.
6. What we now have is a *snapshot* of the entire Registry taken before and after the change (or changes) was made. It's important that the snapshots be taken immediately before and after the change, so that other trivial settings, such as changes in Explorer window positions, aren't included with the changes we care about.
7. All that needs to be done now is to distill the *changed* information into a useful format. Windows comes with the command-line utility File Compare (*fc.exe*), which can be used to find the differences between our *before* and *after* files.*

   At the command prompt, first use the cd command to change to the directory containing the Registry patches, such as *\Windows\Desktop*, if they're on your desktop (see Chapter 10 for more information on the cd command), and then type the following two lines:

   ```
   fc /u user1.reg user2.reg > user.txt
   fc /u machine1.reg machine2.reg > machine.txt
   ```
8. These commands will instruct File Compare to scan both pairs of files and write *only* the differences between the files into new text files: *user.txt* for the changes in HKEY_CURRENT_USER and *machine.txt* for the changes in HKEY_LOCAL_MACHINE.

   The *user.txt* file should look something like this:

   ```
   Comparing files user1.reg and USER2.REG

   ***** user1.reg
   [HKEY_CURRENT_USER\Software\Microsoft\Windows\CurrentVersion\
        Explorer\Advanced]
   "Hidden"=dword:00000001
   "ShowCompColor"=dword:00000000
   ***** USER2.REG
   [HKEY_CURRENT_USER\Software\Microsoft\Windows\CurrentVersion\
        Explorer\Advanced]
   "Hidden"=dword:00000002
   "ShowCompColor"=dword:00000000
   *****
   ```

   From this example listing, it's evident that the only applicable change was the Hidden value, located deep in the HKEY_CURRENT_USER branch.

* There are several superior, Windows-based third-party alternatives, such as UltraEdit-32 (available at *http://www.ultraedit.com*). See "Windows XP in a Nutshell" (O'Reilly) for complete documentation on the File Compare utility (*fc.exe*).

(There may be some other entries, but if you inspect them, you'll find that they relate only to MRU lists from RegEdit and can be ignored.)*

Note that for this particular setting, no changes were recorded in the HKEY_LOCAL_MACHINE branch, so *machine.txt* ends up with only the message, "FC: No differences encountered." This means our changes were only reflected in the HKEY_CURRENT_USER branch.

9. You'll also notice that the lines immediately preceding and following the line we care about are also shown; they're included by FC as an aid in locating the lines in the source files. We're lucky in that one of the surrounding lines in this example happens to be the section header (in brackets), which specifies the Registry key in which this value is located.†

   In most cases, you'll have to search the Registry snapshots (often easier than searching the Registry) for the changed line; in this example, you'd search *USER2.REG* for "Hidden"=dword:00000002 and then make note of the line enclosed in square brackets ([...]) immediately *above* the changed line. This represents the key containing the Hidden value.

   In *user2.txt,* the Hidden line is located in the section:

   ```
   [HKEY_CURRENT_USER\Software\Microsoft\Windows\CurrentVersion\
       Explorer\Advanced]
   ```

10. The next step is to convert the output from File Compare into a valid Registry patch. Because the FC output is originally derived from Registry patches, it's already close to the correct format. Start by removing all of the lines from *user.txt*, except the *second* version of the *changed* line—this would be the value in its *after* setting, which presumably is our goal. You'll end up with this:

    ```
    "Hidden"=dword:00000002
    ```

11. Next, paste in the key (in brackets) above the value. (In the case of our example, it was part of the FC output and can simply be left in.) You should end up with this:

    ```
    [HKEY_CURRENT_USER\Software\Microsoft\Windows\CurrentVersion\
        Explorer\Advanced]
    "Hidden"=dword:00000002
    ```

12. Lastly, add the text Windows Registry Editor Version 5.00 followed by a blank line at the beginning of the file (see "Edit a Registry patch," earlier

* MRU stands for Most Recently Used. Windows stores the most recent filenames typed into file dialog boxes; from this example, you'll notice several references to the filenames you used to save the Registry snapshots.

† For more information on section headers, see "Edit a Registry patch," earlier in this chapter, as well as "Using INI Files," later in this chapter (*.ini* files have a format similar to Registry patches).

in this chapter, for more information). The final result should look something like this:

```
Windows Registry Editor Version 5.00

[HKEY_CURRENT_USER\Software\Microsoft\Windows\CurrentVersion\
    Explorer\Advanced]
"Hidden"=dword:00000002
```

13. Save this as a new file called *User-final.reg*.

    If the settings you've changed have resulted in changes in the HKEY_LOCAL_MACHINE branch, simply repeat steps 9–12 for the *machine.txt* file as well.

14. If your setting resulted in changes in both HKEY_CURRENT_USER and HKEY_LOCAL_MACHINE, your last step would be to consolidate the two patches into one file. See "Protect Your File Types" in Chapter 4 for a practical example of how this is done. When consolidating, make sure you have only one instance of the Windows Registry Editor Version 5.00 line.

For some settings (such as the one in this example), you may want to make two patches: one to turn it on, and one to turn it off. Simply double-click the patch corresponding to the setting you desire.

You may notice that some changes involve the actual removal of a key or value, instead of simply the modification of an existing entry. See "Edit a Registry patch," later in this chapter for details on automating the deletion of Registry data.

This solution will help you find the appropriate keys and values associated with a particular Windows or application setting, and it can also help locate *hidden* settings (those that don't appear in dialog boxes). The setting in the previous example is located in a key that contains other settings, some of which aren't included in the Folder Options dialog box. Experiment with some of the more interesting sounding values, such as CascadePrinters and ShowSuperHidden.

There are some caveats to this approach, mostly that the File Compare utility will often pull out more differences than are relevant to the change you wish to make. It's important to look closely at each key in the resulting Registry patch to see if it's really applicable and necessary.

See Chapter 9 for a discussion on the Windows Script Host, which documents automating changes to the Registry that don't involve Registry patches.

It's always smart to create a corresponding *undo* Registry patch while you're using a solution like this. For example, because our Registry patch contains the differences in the *after* file, *user2.reg*, the corresponding *undo* patch would contain the corresponding lines in the *before* file, *user1.reg*. Applying the *undo* patch effectively returns the keys and values stored within to their state before the setting was changed. Obviously, an important caveat is that an undo patch for one computer won't necessarily be an effective undo for another computer.

Search the Registry Effectively

The Registry Editor has a simple search feature, allowing you to search through all the keys and values for text. Just select **Find** from the Registry Editor's **Edit** menu, type the desired text (Figure 3-6), and click **Find Next**.

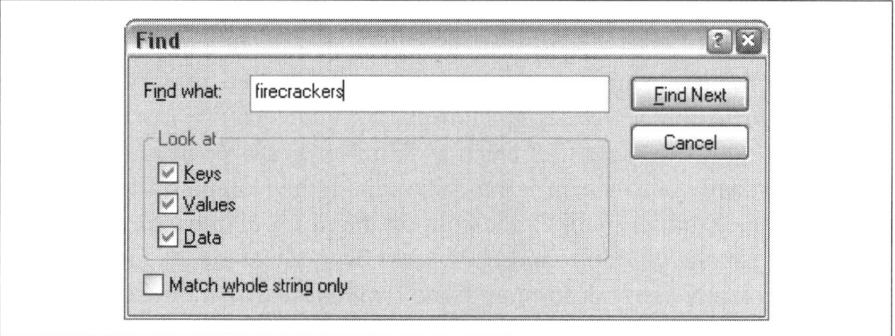

Figure 3-6. Use Registry Editor's Search feature to find text in key names, value names, and value data

Because the Registry can become quite large and have a wide variety of settings and information, it is important to learn to search effectively, so you don't miss anything or waste a lot of time wading through irrelevant results. Additionally, the Registry Editor doesn't have a search-and-replace feature, so doing something as simple as changing every occurrence of *c:\program files* to *d:\program files* can be a monumental chore. Here are some tips that may help:

- Make sure that all three options in the **Find** window's **Look at** section are checked, unless you know specifically that what you're looking for is solely a **Key**, **Value** (value name), or **Data** (value contents).

You'll also usually want the **Match whole string only** option turned off, unless you're searching for text that commonly appears in other words; searching for `handle` might otherwise trigger entries like `PersistentHandler` and `TeachAndLearn`.

- Many folder names in the Registry are stored in both long and short versions.* For example, say you want to move your *Program Files* folder from one drive to another. When you install Windows, any settings pertaining to this folder may be stored in the Registry as *c:\Program Files* or *c:\Progra~1*. Make sure you search for both.

  If you're searching the Registry for both `Program Files` and `Progra~1`, you may want to just search for `progra`, which will find both variations. Because this will stumble upon other instances of the word `program`, try limiting the results by placing a backslash (\) in front of it (e.g. `\progra`) to limit the search to only directory names beginning with those letters. A minute of preparation can save you an hour of searching.
- You may want to search the Registry for an interface element, such as a new item added to a context menu or text in a list in a dialog box. If the text contains an underlined character,† you'll need to add an ampersand (`&`) to the search string. For example, say you've installed a program that creates *.zip* files (such as WinZip, available from *http://www.winzip.com*), and the program has added the command **Add to Zip** (with the Z underlined) to the context menu for all files. You'll need to search for `add to &zip` to match the text properly; a search for `add to zip` will probably turn up nothing. Note also that text searches are *not* case-sensitive, so you don't have to worry about capitalization.
- Searching begins at the currently selected key. If you want to search the entire Registry, make sure the `My Computer` entry at the top of the Registry tree is highlighted before you begin. However, if you know the setting you want to change is in, for example, `HKEY_LOCAL_MACHINE`, you should highlight that key beforehand to reduce search time and eliminate irrelevant results.
- Although the Registry Editor has a search feature, it doesn't allow you to search and replace. If you have a branch of settings you wish to change (for example, if you've moved an application from one drive to another or want to, say, replace every occurrence of *notepad.exe* with

* See "Advanced NTFS Settings" in Chapter 5 for more information on short filename generation.

† Underlined letters in dialog box elements (buttons, menu items, etc.) are hints to the shortcut keys that can be used to activate them. However, by default in Windows XP, underlined letters are hidden in many applications until you press the **Alt** key. You can change this behavior by going to **Control Panel → Display → Appearance** tab **→ Effects**.

another application), you can use a Registry patch; see "Using Registry Patches" earlier in this chapter. Just create a patch of the branch in question and use your favorite text editor's search-and-replace feature to change the values in the patch. When you apply the patch, all the settings will be changed for you. Note that you should use this with caution, because you can screw up many settings unwittingly by searching and replacing common pieces of text.

If you want to use search and replace more often and the previous Registry patch tip isn't sufficient, you may want to try the Registry Agent tool, part of Creative Element Power Tools (*http://www.creativelement.com/powertools/*).

The Registry

Search and Replace Registry Data

The Registry Editor has no search-and-replace feature, and with good reason: a single poorly chosen replace operation could make Windows inoperable. But there are times when you do need to replace all occurrences of, say, a folder name like `c:\stuff\Cory` with another folder name like `d:\stuff\Henna`. Depending on the number of occurrences, such an operation could take hours.

Registry Agent (part of Creative Element Power Tools, available at http://www.creativelement.com/powertools) not only gives you an better way to search the Registry (search results are shown in a list, instead of one at a time), but supports search-and-replace operations as well. Here's how to replace all occurrences of `Microsoft` with `DaveSoft`:

Replacing the word `Microsoft` in your registry is a really bad idea. Don't try this at home. Now, ordinary searching with Registry Agent is totally harmless, but the Replace feature can be dangerous if you're not careful.

1. Open Registry Agent.
2. Type text to search (e.g. `Microsoft`), and click **Find Now**.
3. The results are shown in a list (Figure 3-7) with three columns. The left column shows the location (key) where the text was found; you can click it to open the Registry Editor at that location. The middle and right-hand columns show the value name and contents, respectively.
4. Select the **Replace** tab.
5. Place a checkmark next to the occurrences you wish to replace. Use the checkmark above the list to check or uncheck the entire list.

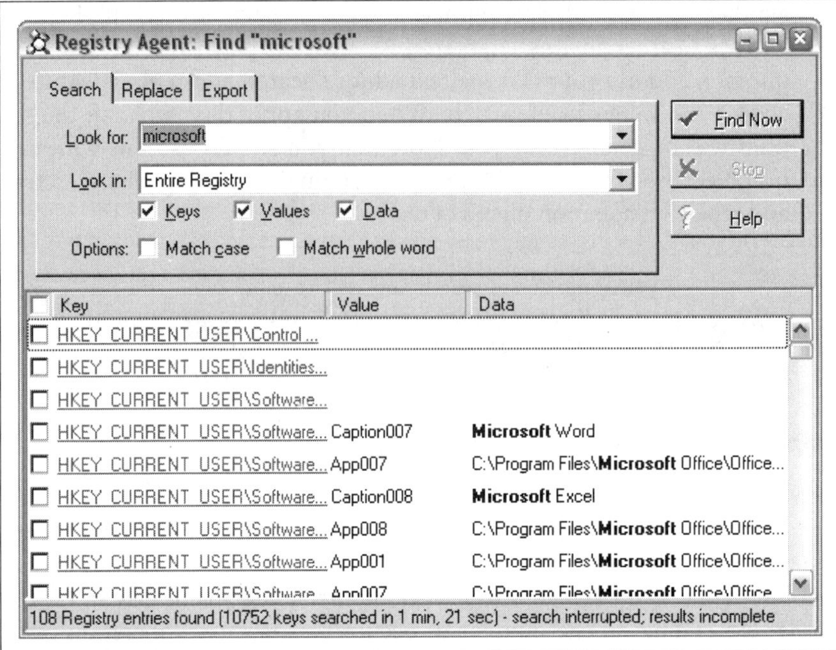

Figure 3-7. Use Registry Agent for a faster Registry search, as well as for search-and-replace operations

6. Type the new text (which will replace the old text) in the **With** field.

You don't have to replace the same text you searched. For instance, you can search for Microsoft and then do a search-and-replace within these results for different text. Type anything you like in the **Replace** field.

7. Choose what types of text you'd like to replace by checking or unchecking the **Keys**, **Values**, and **Data** options. Note that the **Keys** checkbox is grayed-out (disabled) by default; refer to the documentation to lift this restriction.

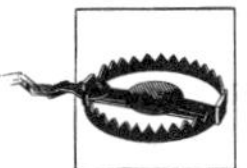

The Replace tool has no "undo" feature, which means that if you screw something up here, the only way to recover is to restore your Registry from a backup (discussed earlier in this chapter). You can also use the Export tab to export a Registry patch (see the next section) containing the selected values, but you shouldn't rely on this as a reliable backup.

8. Click the **Replace** button to perform the search-and-replace.

Even if you don't use the search-and-replace feature, Registry Agent serves as a pretty slick searching tool, and overcomes the annoying hunt-and-peck approach of the Registry Editor's search feature.

Using Registry Patches

In addition to editing the Registry with the Registry Editor (see earlier in this chapter), you can make changes by using Registry patches. A Registry patch is simply a text file with the *.reg* extension that contains one or more Registry keys or values. If you double-click on a *.reg* file, the patch is "applied" to the Registry, meaning that the contents of the patch are *merged* with the contents of the Registry. This tool is especially handy for backing up small portions of the Registry or distributing Registry settings to other computers.

For example, if a particular application stores its custom toolbar in the Registry, you can use a Registry patch to copy the toolbar to another computer, saving time that would otherwise be spent painstakingly configuring the 431 toolbar items on the new machine.

A Registry patch is also a handy way to back up Registry data, such as file types, which are constantly at risk of being changed by other applications (see "Protect Your File Types" in Chapter 4). More importantly, however, Registry patches can be used to back up portions of the Registry to safeguard them against modifications you're about to make, such as the modifications suggested throughout the rest of this book.

Create a Registry patch

1. Open the Registry Editor, and select a branch you wish to export.

   The branch can be anywhere from one of the top-level branches to a branch a dozen layers deep. Registry patches include not only the branch you select, but all of the values and subkeys in the branch. Don't select anything more than what you absolutely need.

2. Select **Export** from the **File** menu, type a filename, and press **OK**.

   All of the values and subkeys in the selected branch will then be stored in the patch file. Make sure the filename of the new Registry patch has the *.reg* extension.

Creating a Registry patch is the easy part; the hard part can be determining the Registry key to be exported in the first place. See "Finding the Right Registry Key" earlier in this chapter for details.

Once you've created the patch, you can modify it or apply it to your (or someone else's) system, as described in the following sections.

Edit a Registry patch

Since Registry patches are just plain text files, you can edit them with any plain-text editor, such as Notepad (*notepad.exe*). The contents of the Registry patch will look something like the text shown in Example 3-1.

Example 3-1. Contents of a Registry patch created from HKEY_CLASSES_ROOT\.txt

```
Windows Registry Editor Version 5.00

[HKEY_CLASSES_ROOT\.txt]
@="txtfile"
"PerceivedType"="text"
"Content Type"="text/plain"

[HKEY_CLASSES_ROOT\.txt\ShellNew]
"NullFile"=""
```

The first line, `Windows Registry Editor Version 5.00`, tells Windows that this file is a valid Registry patch; don't remove this line. The rest of the Registry patch is a series of key names and values.

The key names appear in brackets (`[...]`) and specify the full path of the key. The values contained within each key follow. The name of the value is given first, followed by an equals sign and then the data stored in each value. The value names and value data are always enclosed in quotation marks. A value name of `@` tells the Registry Editor to place the value data in the `(default)` value (as shown in the fourth line of the example).

Registry patches created in Windows 95, 98, or Me will have the line `REGEDIT4` at the top of the file. These patches can be imported into the Windows XP Registry without a problem (that is, not taking into account the settings contained therein). However, older versions of Windows may complain if you try to import Registry patches created in Windows XP. If you encounter this problem, just replace the header line with REGEDIT4.

If you are familiar with the particular information contained within the Registry patch you've just created, you can edit anything you wish and save the changes when you're done. Note that only making changes to a Registry patch doesn't mean anything; your changes won't take effect in the Registry until the Registry patch is applied (described in the next section).

There are several reasons why you might want to edit a Registry patch file:

Streamline a lot of edits

Modifying a large number of Registry values may turn out to be much easier with a text editor than with the Registry Editor, since you don't have to open—and then close—each individual value.

Keep in mind that if you change the name of a value (to the left of the equals sign), as opposed to the value contents (on the right side), you'll effectively be creating a new value. See the next section for details on how Registry contents are merged.

Search and replace

The Registry Editor has no search-and-replace function (for reasons that shouldn't need explaining). However, most text editors do, so you can quite easily search for and replace text when editing a Registry patch.

If you have a branch of settings you wish to change—for example, if you've moved an application from one drive to another—you can use a Registry patch. Just create a patch of the branch in question and use your favorite text editor's search-and-replace feature to change the values in the patch (e.g., replace all occurrences of *c:\big_program* with *e:\big_program*). When you apply the patch, all the settings will be changed for you.

Note that it's very easy to change more than you intended with a search-and-replace, so be careful. However, one of the benefits of Registry patches is that you can double-check your changes before they're applied to your Registry. Also, a second Registry patch can be used to easily restore the modified portion of the Registry if necessary. See "Search the Registry Effectively" earlier in this chapter for more tips.

If you want to use search and replace more often, you may want to try Registry Agent, described in "Search and Replace Registry Data."

Easily duplicate keys and branches

The Registry Editor provides no way to copy or move a key (such as using drag-drop).* If you create a Registry patch of a key, change the key name, and then reimport it, it will effectively duplicate the key. This can be a handy way to create new file types (described in Chapter 4).

Automate the deletion of Registry data

Lastly, there's really no way, using the Registry Editor, to create a patch that *deletes* a Registry key (think about it). However, you can modify a Registry patch to accomplish this feat.

* Trust me, this is a good thing. Keys and values are referenced by their location; change the location, and as far as Windows knows, the key is gone. The last thing you'd want to do is inadvertently hose your system by dragging an important key into oblivion.

To delete a key with a Registry Patch, place a minus sign *before* the key name, like this:

```
-[HKEY_CURRENT_USER\Control Panel\don't load]
```

If you delete a key, all of its values will also be deleted. However, a security feature present in Windows XP* prevents the removal of any key that currently has subkeys. This means that to remove an entire branch, you'll have to recursively delete all of the subkeys first, which is something typically only possible from within a programming language.

To delete a value with a Registry Patch (but leave the key untouched), place a minus sign *after* the equals sign, like this:

```
[HKEY_CURRENT_USER\Control Panel\don't load]
"desk.cpl"=-
```

Merging multiple patches

One of the advantages of Registry patches is that they enable you to change several Registry settings in a single step. However, sometimes those settings are located in different parts of the Registry, and since it isn't practical to export the entire Registry just to catch all of the applicable keys, you can quite easily merge two different Registry patches into a single file. See "Protect Your File Types" in Chapter 4 for a practical example.

Apply a Registry patch

You can apply a Registry patch at any time and to any computer. There are three ways to do this, but there is really no difference between them, at least as far as the final results are concerned. Do whatever is most convenient.

Solution 1: From Explorer

1. Double-click on a Registry patch file (with the *.reg* extension) in Explorer or on your desktop. It doesn't matter if the Registry Editor is running or not.
2. Answer **Yes** to the warning message that asks, "Are you sure you want to add the information in *c:\stuff\MyPatch.reg* to the Registry?"

   Immediately thereafter, you'll see the message, "Information in *MyPatch.reg* has been successfully entered into the Registry."

* This restriction is not present in Windows 9x/Me.

Solution 2: From within the Registry Editor

1. Select **Import** from the **File** menu, and select the patch you wish to import.
2. Click **OK** to merge the file. You won't be prompted to confirm that you actually do want to apply the patch (as with Solution 1), but you will receive the confirmation message that the patch was successful.

Solution 3: From the command line

1. Open a Command Prompt window (*cmd.exe*).
2. Using the `cd` command, as described in Chapter 10, navigate to the folder containing the Registry patch. Note that instead of changing the working directory, you can also simply specify the full path of the patch in the next step.
3. Assuming the Registry patch is named *MyPatch.reg*, type the following:

   ```
   regedit mypatch.reg
   ```

   You'll then receive the same "Are you sure?" message, as when double-clicking the Registry patch in solution 1. However, the advantage of using the command line is the ability to apply Registry patches from a WSH script or batch file, so the preferred method is to bypass the confirmation, like this:

   ```
   regedit /s mypatch.reg
   ```

   where the `/s` switch instructs the Registry Editor to import the patch silently (without the prompt).

If the Registry Editor is currently running and you are viewing a key that was modified by a patch that was just applied, RegEdit should refresh the display automatically to reflect the changes. If it doesn't, press the **F5** key or go to **View → Refresh**.

When you apply a Registry patch, you are *merging* the keys and values stored in a patch file with the Registry. Any keys in the applied patch *that don't already exist* will be added to the Registry. Pre-existing keys in the patch will be left alone. If a specific value already exists, the value will be changed to whatever is in the patch. However, any values already in an existing key that *aren't* in the Registry patch will remain. This means that if you create a patch, rename a key or value (different from changing its data), and then apply it, the original key or value will remain intact and you'll have a duplicate.

If you're creating a Registry patch on your computer for use on another, make sure any folder names or drive letters are corrected for the new computer. If, for example, a Registry patch created on one computer references *c:\my_folder\my_program.exe*, you'll need to make sure to change all occurrences of the text to *d:\her_folder\my_program.exe* to reflect any applicable differences. Using Expandable String values, as described earlier in this chapter, virtually eliminates this problem.

See Chapter 9 for a discussion on the Windows Script Host, which documents how to further automate changes to the Registry.

Using Registry patches on earlier versions of Windows

Many of the Registry patches you create and modify in Windows XP will be applicable in other versions of Windows. But there are two issues you'll need to address before you can use Registry patches on a computer running Windows 9x/Me:

Unicode versus ANSI
: Registry patches created in Windows XP and Windows 2000 are encoded as Unicode text, a format not supported by the Registry Editor in Windows 9x/Me. Unless you convert these files to ANSI or ASCII files, they'll just show up as jibberish in earlier versions of Windows.

The header
: As stated previously, the single-line header placed at the beginning of every Registry patch in Windows XP is `Windows Registry Editor Version 5.00`. If you change this to `REGEDIT4`, the Registry patch will be readable in Windows 9x/Me, as well as in Windows 2000/XP.

Here's a quick procedure to convert a Registry patch created in Windows XP so that it can be used in Windows 9x/Me. Note that this procedure won't stop Windows XP and Windows 2000 from recognizing the patches, which makes one wonder why Microsoft changed the format.

1. Open a newly created Registry patch file in Notepad (*notepad.exe*).
2. Remove the line that reads:

   ```
   Windows Registry Editor Version 5.00
   ```

   and replace it with the following:

   ```
   REGEDIT4
   ```

3. Go to **File → Save As**, and choose **ANSI** from the Encoding list at the bottom of the **Save As** dialog. Make sure the filename is correct, and click **Save** when you're done.

You can also save Registry patches for use in earlier versions of Windows right in the Registry Editor. Go to **File → Export**, and then choose **Win9x/NT 4 Registration Files** from the **Save as type** list.

Despite the different format, Registry patches are applied in the same way in all versions of Windows. Refer to the instructions earlier in this section for details.

Create an Interface for a Registry Setting

The whole point of accessing the Registry is to view and modify settings that are otherwise inaccessible in Explorer, the Control Panel, or the hundreds of dialogs boxes scattered throughout the operating system. However, there is a way to patch into the interface and add checkboxes and radio buttons that are linked to whatever Registry settings we want.

Start by going to **Control Panel → Folder Options → View** menu. At first glance, the **Advanced settings** list in this dialog box is presented in a somewhat awkward list format, apparently to accommodate the large number of options. However, the less-than-ideal presentation is actually designed to allow customization, permitting Microsoft (or you) to easily add or remove items from the list. See Figure 3-8 for an example of a customized version of this window.

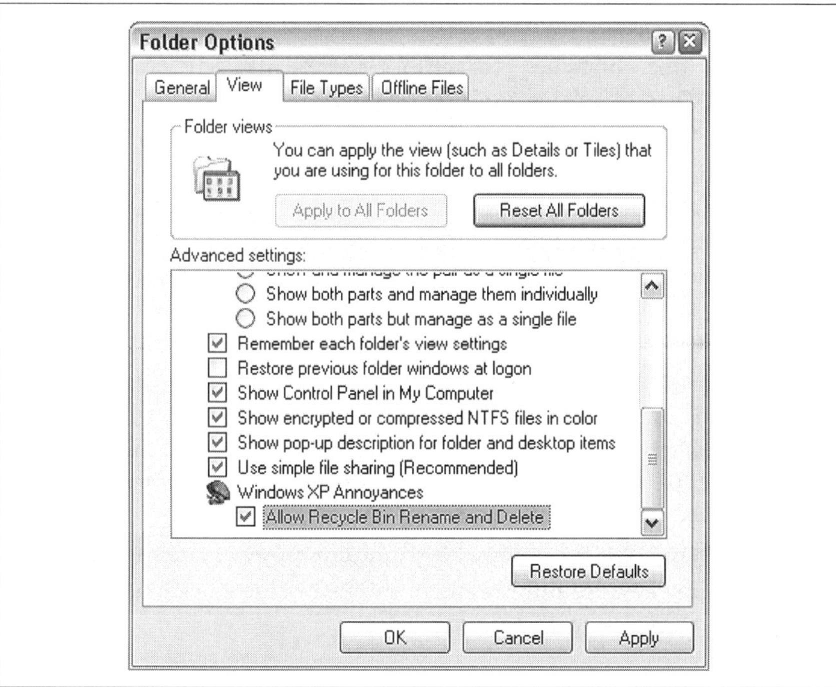

Figure 3-8. The Advanced Folder Options dialog box is a flexible, customizable list of Registry settings

Although the "customizability" of this dialog isn't necessarily intended for you to add an option for any Registry setting you want, whether it's related to Explorer or not, that's precisely what you can do with it, thanks to the following solution.

The idea of this solution is that you link up a checkbox or radio button to a value—any value you choose—in your Registry. This would, for example, allow you to make certain Registry changes accessible to yourself or others (such as users in a workgroup that you administer), reducing the need for them to mess around in the Registry. You can also remove any unwanted options that normally appear here but that you don't want easily changed.

The format is actually quite remarkable, because you don't have to be a programmer to utilize this feature. You can add new options to a certain portion of the Registry and then tie those options to other Registry settings. The downside is that the syntax requires that numerous parameters be typed, which can be cumbersome. The following procedure should allow you to make changes to existing settings, as well as add your own settings fairly easily:

1. Open the Registry Editor.
2. Expand the branches to: `HKEY_LOCAL_MACHINE\Software\Microsoft\Windows\CurrentVersion\Explorer\Advanced\Folder`.

   Notice that the actual hierarchy in the Folder Options window is reproduced here in the Registry, although the list items may appear in a different order than their corresponding Registry entries. This is because the captions in the Folder Options list aren't necessarily the same as the names of the corresponding Registry keys here, yet both collections are sorted alphabetically. For example, the **Remember each folder's view settings** option is represented by the `ClassicViewState` key in the Registry.
3. Take this opportunity to back up the entire branch by highlighting the `Advanced` key and selecting **Export** from the **File** menu. This way, you'll be able to easily restore the defaults without having to reinstall Windows.
4. At this point, you can remove any unwanted entries by deleting the corresponding keys from this branch; the `Text` value in each key should be enough to explain what each key is for.

5. To add a new item, start by simply creating a new key, keeping the hierarchy in mind—for example, are you adding a setting to the top level, or possibly a new setting to an existing group, or are you creating a new group for additional options?

   Name the key anything you want, although the more descriptive, the better.

6. The values inside each key determine the properties of the corresponding setting. For example, one value affects the caption, while another affects the default value. Feel free to fish around the existing keys for examples.

   To add a property, create a new value, name it appropriately (described later), double-click it, and then type the contents for the value. Table 3-2 lists the properties that affect the visual appearance of a specific item, and Table 3-3 lists the properties that affect what happens when a specific item is turned on or off in the Folder Options window.

Table 3-2. Visual properties of Folder Options items

Value name	Data type	Description of value contents
Type	String	This can be set to either `group`, `checkbox`, or `radio`, representing a folder, checkbox, or radio button, respectively. Checkboxes are square options and can either be either on or off. Radio buttons are round options that are linked to other radio buttons in the same folder, in that only one at a time can be selected (you can have multiple groups of radio buttons). And folders, of course, are used to organize the various other options. This parameter is required by all items.
Text	String	This is the actual caption of the option as it will appear in the dialog box. This can be as long as you want (better too descriptive than too vague), but the paradigm dictates that only the first word be capitalized and that there be no period. This parameter is required by all items.
Bitmap	String	This specifies the icon, used for folder items only. If omitted, it's a rather ugly bent arrow. The syntax[a] is `filename,index`, where `filename` is the full path and filename of the file containing the icon, and `index` is the icon number (starting with zero), if the file contains more than one icon. To specify the familiar yellow folder, type `%SystemRoot%\system32\Shell32.dll,4` here. This parameter is optional for all folders and has no effect on checkboxes and radio buttons.
HelpID	String	This is the filename and optionally the help context ID, pointing to the documentation for this item. If the user selects the item and presses the F1 key, this specifies the help note that will appear. The syntax is `filename#id`, where `filename` is the name of a *.hlp* or *.chm* file, and `id` is the numeric help context id (commonly used by programmers) of the topic you want to display. Omit `id` to simply show the index page of the specified help file. This parameter is optional.

[a] The Bitmap value uses the same syntax as the `DefaultIcon` property for file types, as documented in "Understanding File Types" in Chapter 4.

Table 3-3. Registry-related properties of Folder Options items

Value name	Datatype	Description of value contents
HKeyRoot	DWORD	This is an eight-digit number representing the root of the Registry path containing the target Registry setting. Use the *hexadecimal* number 80000000 for HKEY_CLASSES_ROOT, 80000001 for HKEY_CURRENT_USER, 80000002 for HKEY_LOCAL_MACHINE, 80000003 for HKEY_USERS, or 80000005 for HKEY_CURRENT_CONFIG. For some reason, it must be separated from the rest of the Registry path, specified in RegPath, later. This parameter is required for all checkbox and radio items.
RegPath	String	This is the path specifying the location of the target Registry setting, not including the root (see HKeyRoot, earlier). For example, for HKEY_CURRENT_USER\Software\Microsoft\Windows\CurrentVersion, you would only enter Software\Microsoft\Windows\CurrentVersion here. This parameter is required for all checkbox and radio items.
ValueName	String	This is the name of the target Registry value. This value is where the setting data is stored when the option is turned on or off in the Folder Options window. The key containing said value is specified by the RegPath and HKeyRoot parameters, listed earlier. This parameter is required by all checkbox and radio items.
CheckedValue	Should match target value data type	This holds the data to be stored in the target Registry value (specified by the RegPath and ValueName parameters earlier), when said option is turned *on*. If you're configuring an option to be used on both Windows 9x/Me and Windows XP/2000 systems, use both the CheckedValueW95 and CheckedValueNT parameters *instead of this value*. Otherwise, this parameter is required by all checkbox and radio items.
Checked-ValueW95	Should match target value data type	Use this instead of CheckedValue, above, if you're configuring an option to be used on both Windows 9x/Me and Windows XP/2000 systems. This value contains the data that will be applied if the system is running Windows 9x/Me. Used in conjunction with CheckedValueNT, below.
Checked-ValueNT	Should match target value data type	Use this instead of CheckedValue, above, if you're configuring an option to be used on both Windows 9x/Me and Windows XP/2000 systems. This value contains the data that will be applied if the system is running Windows XP, 2000, or NT. Used in conjunction with CheckedValueW95, later.
UnChecked-Value	Should match target value data type	This holds the data to be stored in the target Registry value, when said option is turned *off*. This value is optional; if omitted, it is assumed to be 0.
DefaultValue	Should match target value data type	This is the default value, used only if the target Registry value does not already exist. As soon as the option in the Folder Options window is turned on or off at least once, this parameter is ignored, and Windows instead reads the state of the target value, comparing it to CheckedValue and UnCheckedValue to determine if the option should appear checked or unchecked. This value is optional; if omitted, it is assumed to be 0.

The value type (String, Binary, DWORD) of the CheckedValue, UnCheckedValue, and DefaultValue parameters all depend on what the target value requires. For example, if the target value you're changing is a DWORD value, then all three of these parameters must also be DWORD values.

7. After you've created keys and entered the appropriate property values, your Registry should look something like Figure 3-9, and the resulting Folder Options dialog box should look like Figure 3-8. If Folder Options is open, you'll have to close it and reopen it for the changes to take effect.

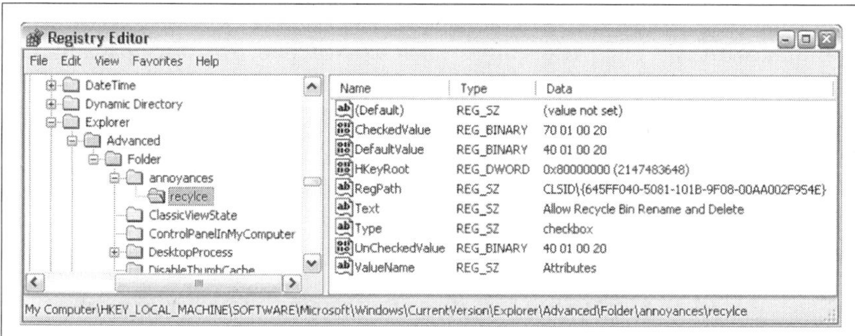

Figure 3-9. Settings that appear in the Advanced Folder Options list are configured in the Registry

If you try to add a setting using the previous procedure and it doesn't show up in Folder Options, most likely one or more required values are missing.

8. Close the Registry Editor when you're finished.

The examples shown in Figure 3-8 and Figure 3-9 show how another solution in this book (see the discussion of the Recycle Bin in "Cleaning Up Desktop Clutter" in Chapter 4) can be turned into an advanced Folder Options setting. Here, a single checkbox allows you to easily turn on and off the *Rename* and *Delete* commands in the Reeycle Bin's context menu.

When the Folder Options dialog box is first displayed, each option is set according to the current value of the corresponding settings. More specifically, the current data stored in each target value is compared with the corresponding `CheckedValue` and `UnCheckedValue`, and the option in the **Advanced settings** list is set accordingly. When the **OK** button is pressed in Folder Options, the settings in the Registry are then written using the same criteria.

To reproduce a setting elsewhere in the Windows interface or the interface of a third-party application, you'll first need to find the respective Registry setting; see "Finding the Right Registry Key," earlier in this chapter, for more information. Refer also to the section on Registry patches, which offers a very handy way to reproduce the customizations made here on any number of computers.

Using INI Files

If you've been using a Windows PC for any length of time, you've probably come across files with the *.ini* filename extension. Initialization files (or Configuration Settings, as they're known in any recent release of Windows) were used in the old days to store settings for applications, as well as Windows itself, before the Registry was implemented. INI files are simply text files (editable with any plain-text editor, such as Notepad) that are specially formatted to store such settings. Because INI files are limited in their maximum file size (64 KB) and are not as efficient as the Registry, application developers have been strongly encouraged to abandon INI files and instead store settings in the Registry. Since some applications still use INI files to store certain settings, it may become necessary to look for and change settings in INI files as well.

An example of an application that may still use an INI file today is an application installer. An INI file would allow a program to read and store settings without having to rely on the Registry; that way, the settings would be accessible regardless of the computer on which the program was run. INI files are also handy (for the same reason) for programs that run over a network. Windows also includes a few INI files, although they're generally used only to maintain compatibility with older applications.

To edit an INI file, just double-click it, and it will open in Notepad.* A typical INI file looks something like this:

```
[Episodes]
2F01=The Last Traction Hero
9F22=Spay Anything
4f12=Why do Fools fall in Lava?
7F09=Porch Pals

[Cities]
first=Brockway
second=Ogdenville
third=North Haverbrook
```

Section names are always enclosed in square brackets (`[...]`); the lines that follow are the settings contained in that section. A section continues until the next section begins or the file ends. Settings include a setting name, followed by an equals sign, and then the data assigned to that setting.

You'll notice that the structure of INI files is similar (but not identical) to that of Registry patches, discussed earlier in this chapter.

* To configure another text editor to be the default INI file editor, see the discussion of file types in Chapter 4.

Searching INI files for settings

In addition to searching the Registry, you may want to search all INI files for a particular setting:

1. Open a Search window (see Chapter 2).
2. Type `*.ini` in the **All or part of the file name** field, and type the text for which you want to search in the **A word or phrase in the file** field.
3. Double-click on any file in the search results to view it, and use your text editor's search feature to find the specific instance of text in the file.

Special case: System.ini and Win.ini

INI files can be found in a variety of places; some applications place their INI files in the application folder, while others store them in the Windows folder (the preferred location, recommended by Microsoft many years ago). Although it's becoming less common, some applications store their settings in the file, *Win.ini*, which is the INI-file equivalent of the `HKEY_USERS` branch of the Registry.

Right alongside *Win.ini* is the *System.ini* file, the INI-file equivalent of the `HKEY_LOCAL_MACHINE` Registry branch. Both of these files are still included in Windows XP, although it's primarily to maintain compatibility with such older applications that expect to find or store certain settings therein.

There's typically little interest anymore in either of these files. If you're familiar, for example, with the now-obsolete `Load=` and `Run=` lines in the `[Windows]` section of *Win.ini*, that functionality is taken care of by the *Startup* folder in the Start Menu, as well as several locations in the Registry (see Chapter 6 for details). Similarly, the `shell=` line of *System.ini*, which was used to specify an alternate Windows shell (replacing Program Manager in Windows 3.x or Explorer in Windows 95) is no longer supported at all in Windows XP.

CHAPTER 4

Tinkering Techniques

The most important part of software design is the interface. The interface is the only link we humans have with the machines we use—the better the interface, the better the link, and the more useful the machine will be. Because the Windows XP software has already been designed and written, the most we can hope to do is to tinker with it so that it works more like we think it should.

The first thing I do when I hit a roadblock or find a "feature" in Windows is jump into the Registry and try to fix it. The more I hack away at Windows's flaws, the easier it gets, and the leaner, cleaner, and less annoying Windows becomes. The solutions in this chapter illustrate this point.

The unfortunate methodology behind the design of the Windows interface is that it's supposed to be usable by the lowest common denominator: the person who has never seen Windows before. Don't get me wrong, one of the most important interface design considerations is its ability to be used by the uninitiated. But there are three main problems with this approach if not done correctly. One, such an interface can be inherently condescending. Two, no user is a beginner forever. Three, users are not all the same.

Many people don't realize that it is possible to have an elegant, simple interface that is easy and comfortable for beginners to use, yet is not limited in its usefulness as users gain experience. A dumbed-down interface is not the answer.

One of Windows's strong points is its flexibility. For example, the fact that you can reprogram almost any system object on the desktop to serve a different function, and this is one of the main reasons that Windows enjoys such a large market share. Although the variety of solutions presented here is a testament to the power and flexibility of Windows XP, I'd also like to note the need for such solutions in the first place.

This chapter takes advantage of the basic topics covered in Chapter 2—such as shortcuts, system objects, and some of Windows's more obscure settings—as well as usage of Registry, discussed in Chapter 3, to customize Windows beyond Microsoft's intentions. We'll start by clearing some of the clutter caused by the installation of Windows and move on to customizing whatever is left over to suit your needs.

Although most of these solutions target specific annoyances in the operating system, each one is used to illustrate broader concepts and methodology.

Now, we certainly don't expect every user to feel compelled to take all the advice in this book: not everyone is going to want to turn off Windows's built-in support for ZIP files nor disable the Windows Picture and Fax Viewer application. However, by excavating the Registry and many of the more obscure dialog boxes, you'll discover other things along the way that will assist you in resolving your own annoyances.

If you haven't reviewed Chapter 3, I suggest you do so at this point. It covers the Windows Registry and the Registry Editor, which are used extensively in many of the solutions in this and subsequent chapters.

Registry patches, discussed in Chapter 3, are great for backing up portions of the Registry and can be used to undo any changes you may decide to make here. Furthermore, once you've made a change you like, you can back it up with a Registry patch of its own, making it easy to restore it should it be overwritten by an application installer or Windows Update.

Customizing Your Desktop

The default configuration of Windows XP—including the way the desktop and Start Menu are configured and which optional Windows components are installed—was decided by a committee at Microsoft. The motivation was not so much ease of use as it was how to best showcase the features included in the new operating system. This criterion may be great for the marketing department at Microsoft, but it doesn't make for a very pleasant experience for the user.

The best place to start when customizing an interface is to throw out all the stuff you don't want, which will make much more room for the stuff you actually use. By not being forced to wade through dozens of icons or menu items to find the one you want, you can complete your work more easily and with less aggravation.

Cleaning Up Desktop Clutter

Not only does Windows XP sport fewer icons on the desktop, by default, than any preceding version of Windows, but the icons that have remained are actually easy to remove. The removal process, however, depends on the type of object you're trying to remove.

There are two types of icons that appear on the desktop (not including the taskbar or Start Menu). Those objects that are physical files or shortcuts to files are simply stored in your desktop folder (typically *\Documents and Settings\{username}\Desktop*); these items can be deleted, moved, renamed, etc. as easily as any other file on your hard disk. The Desktop Cleanup Wizard, an interactive program designed to help the truly lazy among us remove less frequently used file and shortcut desktop icons, can be found in **Control Panel** → **Display** → **Desktop** tab → **Customize Desktop** (shown in Figure 4-1).

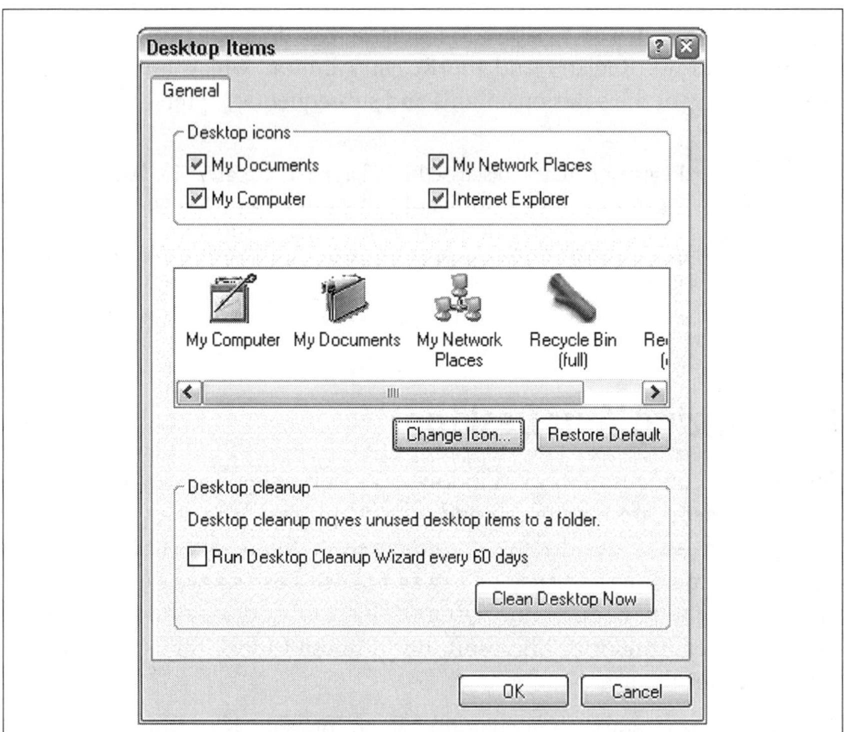

Figure 4-1. The Desktop Items window allows you to show or hide a few prominent desktop objects, as well as customize their icons

Other icons, such as the Recycle Bin and My Computer are *virtual objects*, in that they don't represent physical files on the hard disk, but rather are internal components of the *Explorer.exe* application. These icons are referenced in the Registry and can be removed by deleting the corresponding Registry keys (details can be found later in this section); the only exception is the Recycle Bin, which is discussed subsequently. The Internet Explorer and My Documents icons are also virtual objects, despite the fact that they appear to be functionally identical to shortcuts to the Internet Explorer application and My Documents folder.

You can remove or reinstate the My Documents, My Computer, My Network Places, and Internet Explorer icons by going to **Control Panel** → **Display** → **Desktop** tab → **Customize Desktop**. This displays the Desktop Items window, shown in Figure 4-1, where you can also change the icons for these objects. Additionally, you can rename any of these items (except for the Recycle Bin) as you would any ordinary file: by selecting and pressing **F2**, by right-clicking and selecting **Rename**, or by clicking twice (slowly) on the icon caption.

Special case: the Recycle Bin

Having the Recycle Bin icon on your desktop can be convenient, but because there are several other ways to delete an object (such as right-clicking and selecting **Delete** or highlighting an item and pressing the **Del** key), it really isn't necessary. Furthermore, there's a *Recycler* folder on every drive, which works just like the Recycle Bin desktop icon.

The *Recycler* folder, found on every hard disk and some removable volumes, is actually where the Recycle Bin stores files before they're actually deleted. Dragging items into these folders has the same effect as dragging them into the Recycle Bin icon. If you don't see it, you'll need to configure Explorer to show hidden files and folders (**Control Panel** → **Folder Options** → **View** tab).

The following solution allows you to modify the Registry data for the Recycle Bin object, making it easy to rename or delete it, as shown in Figure 4-2:

1. Open the Registry Editor (discussed in Chapter 3).
2. Expand the branches to `HKEY_CLASSES_ROOT\CLSID\{645FF040-5081-101B-9F08-00AA002F954E}\ShellFolder\`. You know you have the right Class ID key if its `(Default)` value is set to `Recycle Bin`. It may be easier to locate this key by searching for the first few characters of the Class ID or for the text `Recycle Bin`.

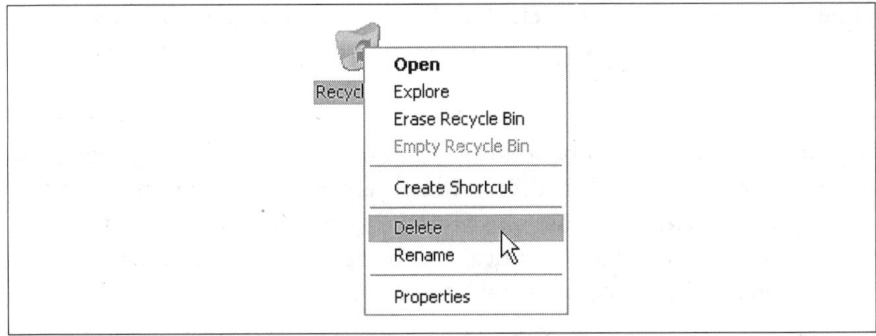

Figure 4-2. Adding the Delete option to the Recycle Bin's context menu

3. Double-click the `Attributes` value, and replace the contents with `70 01 00 20`. If you only want to add the **Rename** context menu item (without **Delete**), type `50 01 00 20` instead.

   Note that this is a binary value, and the input box may not behave like a normal text box; if you mess up, just click **Cancel** and try again.

4. Close the Registry Editor—the change should take effect immediately.
5. You now have the option of deleting the Recycle Bin at any time by right-clicking on it and selecting **Delete**, or renaming it just as you'd rename any ordinary file.

To restore your Recycle Bin to its default, removing the **Rename** and **Delete** options from its context menu, repeat the above process but instead enter an `Attributes` value of `40 01 00 20`. Note that this won't restore the Recycle Bin's original name, nor will it put it back on the desktop if it has been deleted (see the following topic for a solution).

If you delete the Recycle Bin, it's still possible to delete files and subsequently retrieve them. Any file or folder can always be deleted by right-clicking and selecting **Delete**, or by selecting and pressing the **Del** key. If you have the Recycle Bin configured to store recently deleted files, you can retrieve them by opening Explorer and navigating to *c:\Recycler*.* In that folder will be a folder for each user on the system, signified by a long numeric code (described in "Taming Recent Documents," later in this chapter); in most cases, there will be only one such folder here. Open the folder to view recently deleted files.

* If you don't see the *Recycler* folder, go to **Control Panel → Folder Options → View** tab, and make sure the **Show hidden files and folders** option is selected, and the **Hide protected operating system files** option is turned off.

Special Case: really stubborn icons

Once in a while, you'll encounter an icon on your desktop, most likely installed by an older application from Microsoft or another manufacturer, that you just can't get rid of using the solutions in the proceeding sections.

The easiest way to hide (or show) these icons is to use Microsoft's TweakUI (see Appendix A): just select the **Desktop** category and uncheck any desktop item you'd like to hide. If you don't have access to TweakUI, or just don't want to take the time to download and install it, the following procedure will do the same thing:

1. Open the Registry Editor (discussed in Chapter 3).
2. Expand the branches to: `HKEY_LOCAL_MACHINE\SOFTWARE\Micro-soft\Windows\CurrentVersion\explorer\Desktop\NameSpace\`.
3. The key itself will most likely be devoid of values, but it should have a few subkeys, which will be named something like `{645FF040-5081-101B-9F08-00AA002F954E}`. These codes are called Class IDs and point to other parts of the Registry that contain more information about them. Class IDs are stored in the `HKEY_CLASSES_ROOT\CLSID` branch and are discussed in Appendix D.
4. Start by clicking on a key and looking at the `(Default)` value to the right. It *should* contain a description of the item. If it doesn't, you can still find out what it is by right-clicking on the key name in the left pane, selecting **Rename**, then right-clicking on the text itself, and selecting **Copy**. This will copy the key name to the Clipboard. Then move to the top of the Registry tree (select **My Computer** at the root), and select **Find** from the **Edit** menu. Right-click on the **Find What** field, and select **Paste**. Click **Find Next** to search through the Registry for that key. When you find it, do a little digging in that key and its subkeys to find out what it's really for.
5. If one of the keys under the `...Namespace` branch turns out to match the item you're trying to get rid of, you can go ahead and delete the key.

   Now, deleting an item here is a little like deleting a shortcut in Explorer: it doesn't actually delete functionality from your system, it only removes the pointer to the information from the desktop namespace key. If you're worried that you might want it back some day, highlight the key, select **Export Registry File** from the **Registry** menu to back it up. See Chapter 3 for more information on Registry patches.
6. When you're done making changes, close the Registry Editor and refresh the desktop. See "Refresh the Desktop Without Restarting Windows" in Chapter 2 for more information.

Tinkering Techniques

Hide all desktop icons

To achieve a truly clean UI, you may wish to hide desktop icons altogether. This solution will disable the display of all icons on the desktop, including any files in your *Desktop* folder, as well as the virtual icons discussed in the previous sections. It doesn't involve the actual deletion of any data; it merely instructs Windows to leave the desktop blank. A benefit of this solution is that, unlike the previous solutions in this section, it has no effect on the desktop contents when viewed in Explorer:

1. Right-click an empty area of the desktop.
2. Select **Arrange Icons** and then turn off the **Show Desktop Icons** option.

If the Show Desktop Icons entry doesn't appear in your right-click menu (possible if you've upgraded a computer on which the "Active Desktop" feature found in some earlier versions of Windows was disabled on your system), here's an alternate solution:

1. Open the Registry Editor (discussed in Chapter 3).
2. Expand the branches to: `HKEY_CURRENT_USER\Software\Microsoft\Windows\CurrentVersion\Policies\Explorer`.
3. Double-click the `NoDesktop` value. If it's not there, select **New** from the **Edit** menu, and then select **Binary Value**; type `NoDesktop` for the name of the new value.
4. Replace the contents with `01 00 00 00`. If at any time you wish to restore the desktop icons, just delete the `NoDesktop` value or replace its contents with `00 00 00 00`.
5. Note that this is a binary value, and the input box may not behave like a normal text box; if you mess up, just choose **Cancel** and try again.
6. Click **OK** and close the Registry Editor. You'll have to log out and then log back in for the change to take effect.

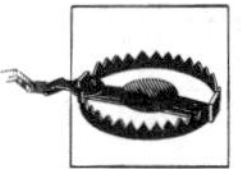

If you hide all icons on your desktop, it will no longer respond to right-clicks. To open the Display Properties dialog, you'll have to go through Control Panel.

Customizing My Computer and Other System Folders

The My Computer and My Documents icons on the desktop, as well as the respective windows they open, are both gateways to the files, folders, and drives in your computer. Both their appearance and behavior can be customized, as illustrated by the following solutions. Likewise, My Network Places is a gateway to the resources available on your network (discussed in Chapter 7) and can be similarly customized.

Renaming My Computer, My Documents, and My Network Places

As described earlier in this chapter, you can rename any of these items with the same technique you'd use to rename any other object: by selecting and pressing **F2**, by right-clicking and selecting **Rename**, or by clicking twice (slowly) on the icon caption.

Note that any new name you choose for either of these icons will also be used elsewhere in Windows where these objects are referenced. The exception is the folder to which the My Documents icon points; its name on your hard disk will not change when the icon is renamed.

Choosing icons for desktop objects

You can choose new desktop icons for these system objects by going to **Control Panel** → **Display** → **Desktop** tab → **Customize Desktop** (shown in Figure 4-1). See "Customize Drive and Folder Icons," later in this chapter, for more solutions.

Customize the contents of My Computer

The My Computer window, by default, contains links to all your drives, shortcuts to your *My Documents* and *Shared Documents* folders, icons for any installed scanners, and, optionally, an icon for Control Panel.* To add more system objects to the My Computer window and, consequently, to Explorer, follow these steps:

1. Open the Registry Editor (discussed in Chapter 3).
2. Expand the branches to `HKEY_LOCAL_MACHINE\Software\Microsoft\Windows\CurrentVersion\explorer\MyComputer\NameSpace`. Hint: create a Registry patch of this branch before continuing, in the event that you need to restore the default setup.
3. Under this branch, you should see one or more keys—each named for a different Class ID. For help in identifying unlabeled keys, see the "Special Case: Really stubborn icons" section.
4. To add a new key, select **New** from the **Edit** menu, and then select **Key**. You can then enter any Class ID for the name of the key, and the corresponding system object will be added to the My Computer folder. See Appendix D for a table of Class IDs, or copy and paste a Class ID from elsewhere in the Registry.

* To enable or disable the Control Panel icon in the My Computer folder, go to Control Panel → **Folder Options** → **View** tab.

5. Refresh the My Computer window to see your changes by pressing the **F5** key.

This solution does not work as you might expect for all system objects. For example, the My Network Places icon will behave erratically if placed in My Computer. You'll have to use a little trial and error to get the desired results.

You can remove any icon added in this way by deleting the corresponding Registry keys. You can also use TweakUI (see Appendix A); just expand the My Computer category and select Drives, and uncheck any drives you want hidden.

Customize the contents of My Network Places

You can add items (shortcuts, folders, etc.) to the My Network Places window by simply adding Windows Shortcuts to the *\Documents and Settings\{username}\Nethood* folder. For example, place shortcuts to frequently accessed network folders here. The process is similar to the way custom items are added to the Start Menu and the Send To menu.

Redirect the My Computer desktop icon

All of My Computer's default resources are also available in Explorer and the Start Menu, so you may prefer to connect another program to the My Computer desktop icon. For example, if you simply prefer Explorer's hierarchical tree view to My Computer's Macintosh-style, single-folder navigation, you can configure My Computer to launch Explorer:

1. Open the Registry Editor (discussed in Chapter 3).
2. Expand the Registry branches to: `HKEY_CLASSES_ROOT\CLSID\{20D04FE0-3AEA-1069-A2D8-08002B30309D}\shell`. You know you have the right Class ID key if its `(Default)` value is set to `My Computer`.
3. You'll see an existing key already in this branch named `find`, representing the **Search** command in the My Computer icon's context menu. Select **New** from the **Edit** menu, and then select **Key**. Type `Open` for the name of the new key, and press **Enter**.
4. Right-click the new `Open` key, select **New** again and then **Key**. Type `Command` for the name of this new key, and press **Enter**.
5. Click once on the new `Command` key, double-click the `(Default)` value in the right pane, type `explorer.exe` in the box, and press **Enter**. Your Registry Editor window should resemble Figure 4-3, except that I've also included some optional command-line parameters (discussed in "Force Explorer to Remember Its Own Settings" in Chapter 2). You can, of

course, replace explorer.exe with the full path and filename of any other program you'd rather use.

6. Next, navigate to HKEY_CLASSES_ROOT\CLSID\{20D04FE0-3AEA-1069-A2D8-08002B30309D}\shell, double-click the (default) value, and type open for its contents.
7. Close the Registry Editor when you're finished. Click on an empty area of the desktop, and press **F5** to refresh the desktop so that this change will take effect. Double-click the My Computer icon at any time to start the specified application.

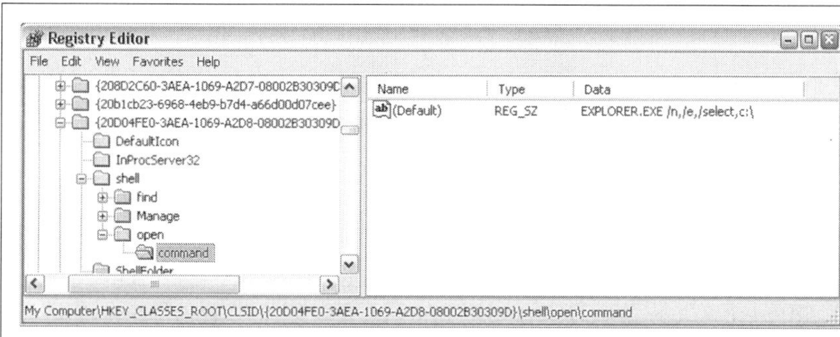

Figure 4-3. Use the Registry Editor to customize the behavior of the My Computer icon

Using this method, you can also add additional entries to My Computer's context menu; see "Customize Context Menus," later in this chapter for details.

Redirect the My Documents Desktop icon

Right-click the My Documents icon on your Desktop and select Properties. The Target tab, shown in Figure 4-4, allows you to choose any folder to be opened when the My Documents icon is double-clicked. You can also click **Move** to relocate the "official" My Documents folder, regardless of whether the My Documents icon points there or not.

Getting rid of the Shared Documents folder

The following procedure will remove the *Shared Documents* folder that shows up in Explorer and My Computer:

1. Open the Registry Editor (discussed in Chapter 3).
2. Expand the branches to: HKEY_LOCAL_MACHINE\SOFTWARE\Microsoft\Windows\CurrentVersion\Explorer\MyComputer\NameSpace\DelegateFolders.

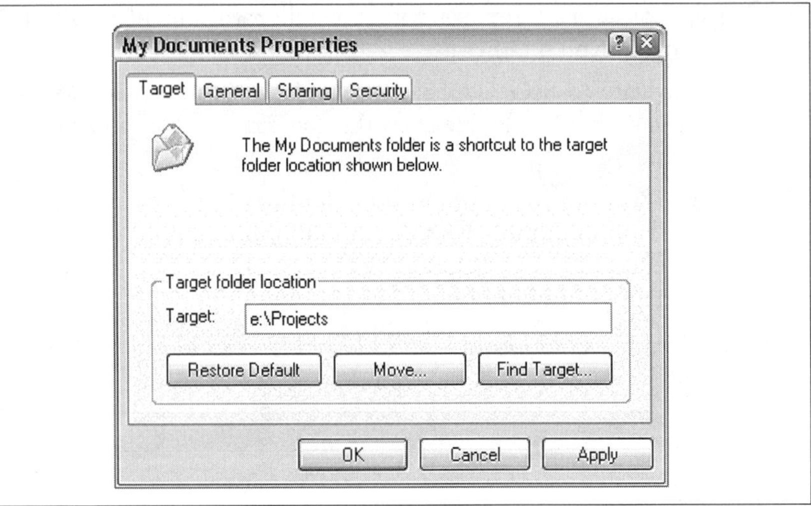

Figure 4-4. The Properties sheet of the My Documents icon allows you to easily change what happens when it's double-clicked

3. Under this branch, you should see several subkeys, each named for a different Class ID. Delete the one named `{59031a47-3f72-44a7-89c5-5595fe6b30ee}`.

   One of the other branches here, `{E211B736-43FD-11D1-9EFB-0000F8757FCD}`, is responsible for adding folders for each of your installed scanners and cameras to My Computer and Explorer. It can also be deleted, if desired.

4. Close the Registry Editor when you're done. The change will take effect immediately, but you may have to close and reopen any Explorer windows to force them to recognize the change.

Covering Your Tracks

In nearly every part of the interface, Windows keeps a history of your activity, from a drop-down list of typed commands in the Address Bar to the Recent Documents list in the Start Menu. The problem is there's no apparent way to control this record-keeping. Using the Registry and a number of tricks, it's possible to control some of these features and even wipe out the history at your whim.

Note that the drop-down list that appears in File-Save and File-Open dialogs when you type into the **File name** field is not actually a history of previously selected or typed files. Instead, it's an auto-complete mechanism that fills in the field as you type, using the names of the files in the current folder.

Taming Recent Documents

Every time you double-click a document in Explorer or on your desktop, Windows places a shortcut to the file in your *Recent Documents* folder. At any given time, you might have a few hundred shortcuts in there, effectively tracing your every action when sorted by date.

The contents of this folder are used to populate the **Recent Documents** menu in the Start Menu (just called **Documents** if the Classic Start Menu is used), as well as the handful of recent documents shown in the **File** menu of some applications (such as Microsoft Office 2002). The contents of the *Recent* folder are also accessible, by default, from the Places Bar shown in most file dialogs (discussed later in this chapter).

These solutions should help you tame the Recent Documents list.

Choose how many recent documents are shown in the Start Menu

Assuming you haven't disabled the *Recent* folder or hidden the **Documents** menu, as described later, you can control how many of the most recent document shortcuts are shown in the **Recent Documents**:

1. Open the Registry Editor (discussed in Chapter 3).
2. Navigate your way to `HKEY_CURRENT_USER\Software\Microsoft\Windows\CurrentVersion\Policies\Explorer`.
3. Create a new DWORD value (go to **Edit → New → DWORD Value**), and name the new value `MaxRecentDocs`.
4. Double-click the new value, select the **Decimal** option, and type the number of entries to show in the **Recent Documents** menu. The default is 15.
5. Close the Registry Editor when you're done. You'll have to log out and log back in for this change to take effect.

Clear out the Recent Documents folder

Since the contents of the *Recent* folder are just shortcuts, they can be safely and easily deleted on the fly:

1. To empty the Recent Documents list, just open Explorer and navigate to *\Documents and Settings\{username}\Recent*. This folder is hidden, so if you haven't done so already, you'll have to configure Explorer to show hidden files by going to **Control Panel → Folder Options → View** tab.
2. Select some or all (using **Ctrl-A**) of the shortcuts here and delete them. Keep in mind that these are only shortcuts, so deleting them won't put any of your data at risk. The change will take effect immediately.

Note that this solution will erase current shortcuts, but it won't prevent new ones from being created.

Turn off the Recent Documents menu in the Start Menu

It's possible to hide the **Recent Documents** menu altogether, although Microsoft hasn't made it too easy for you.

If you have TweakUI (see Appendix A), open the Explorer category and turn off the **Allow Recent Documents on Start Menu** option. If you don't have TweakUI, open the Registry Editor, navigate to `HKEY_CURRENT_USER\Software\Microsoft\Windows\CurrentVersion\Policies\Explorer`, and create a new binary value named `NoRecentDocsMenu`. Double-click `NoRecentDocsMenu` and enter `01 00 00 00` for its data.

Keep in mind that even if the **Recent Documents** menu is hidden, shortcuts to launched documents will still be created in the *Recent* folder. See the next solution for a way to prevent this from happening.

Permanently disable the Recent Documents folder

Although there is no way to actually disable the creation of shortcuts in the *Recent* folder, there is a way to short-circuit the feature so that newly created shortcuts are deleted immediately. We do this by instructing Windows to put the shortcuts right into the Recycle Bin; the only requirement is that you configure the Recycle Bin to delete files instead of storing them:

1. Open the Registry Editor (discussed in Chapter 3).
2. Expand the branches to `HKEY_CURRENT_USER\Software\Microsoft\Protected Storage System Provider`. Under this key, you should see a single subkey with a long string of numbers for its name, which will look something like this:

   ```
   S-1-5-21-1727987266-1036259444-725315541-500
   ```

   This code, which will be different on your system, represents the currently logged-in user (namely, you). Since Windows XP maintains a separate Recycle Bin for each user on your system, you'll need to reference this code in the following steps for this solution to work.
3. Highlight the numeric key, press **F2** to pretend you're renaming the key, and then press **Ctrl-C** to copy the key name to the clipboard. Lastly, press **Esc** to abort the renaming process.
4. Expand the branches to: `HKEY_CURRENT_USER\Software\Microsoft\Windows\CurrentVersion\Explorer\Shell Folders`.
5. To the right, you'll see a list of values representing custom user folders. Double-click the `Recent` value, and type the following:

   ```
   c:\recycler\
   ```

where *c:* is the drive on which your copy of Windows is installed. Then, press **Ctrl-V** to paste the key name from step 2 into the field, so it looks like this:

```
c:\recycler\S-1-5-21-1727987266-1036259444-725315541-500
```

Remember, your numeric code will be different than the one shown here. Click **OK** when you're done.

6. Next, navigate to: `HKEY_CURRENT_USER\Software\Microsoft\Windows\CurrentVersion\Explorer\User Shell Folders`, and repeat step 5 for this key as well.
7. Close the Registry Editor when you're done. You'll need to log out and then log back in for the change to take effect.
8. Lastly, if your Recycle Bin is set up to store deleted files, you'll have to configure it to erase them instead. Right-click the Recycle Bin desktop icon, and select **Properties**. Check the **Do not move files to the Recycle Bin** option, and click **OK**.

Test the setup by double-clicking a few documents on your Desktop or in Explorer. Then, open the *\Documents and Settings\{username}\Recent* folder and verify that it's still empty. Voila!

Thinning Out Explorer's New Menu

If you right-click on the desktop or an open folder (or open Explorer's **File** menu) and choose **New**, you will be presented with a special list of registered file types that can be created on the spot. Choose one, and Explorer will create a new, empty file with the appropriate extension in that location (although sometimes a special template file will be used instead; see "File Types: The Link Between Documents and Applications" in this chapter, for details).

This list is maintained by certain Registry entries, and since most of us will not need to create new Ami Pro documents on the fly, there is a way to remove these unwanted entries. Having an extra entry here and there is not necessarily a big deal, but it can be quite frustrating if you're forced to wade through a long list of file types every time you want to create a new file.

The following two solutions allow you to selectively remove unwanted entries from the **New** menu but won't prevent applications from adding entries, either when they're first installed or every time they're run.

Solution 1: Using the Registry Editor

1. Open the Registry Editor (discussed in Chapter 3).
2. Select **Find** from the **Edit** menu, type `ShellNew`, and press **OK**.
3. Every `ShellNew` key that is found will be a branch of a particular key named for a file extension (see "Understanding File Types" later in this chapter). If you don't want that file type in your **New** menu, delete the entire `ShellNew` branch.
4. Repeat this for every unwanted file type, and close the Registry Editor when finished. The changes will take effect immediately.

Solution 2: Using TweakUI

1. Open TweakUI (see Appendix A), and select the **Templates** category.
2. Uncheck any unwanted items, or click **Remove** for those items you're sure you never want to see again.

Note: If you investigate what TweakUI actually does to your registry when you turn off a template, you'll see that the `ShellNew` branch described in Solution 1 has simply been renamed `ShellNew-` (making it easy for you to reactivate it later). The corresponding key is only deleted if you click **Remove**.

Solution 3: Prevent recurring entries (advanced users only)

If either of the previous solutions is ineffective in removing a particularly stubborn entry, in that it keeps coming back every time you start the associated application, you still have one last resort. For example, some applications actually replace this entry every time they're started, completely ignoring your preferences. Two popular programs known for this annoying behavior are Adobe Photoshop 4.0 and 5.0 (they've fixed it in version 6.0 and later) and JASC's Paint Shop Pro 4.0 or later. The following solution works on both of these applications and should work on any other program that does this as well.

You'll need a good hex editor, such as UltraEdit-32 (*http://www.ultraedit.com/*), which we'll use to actually change the program executable.

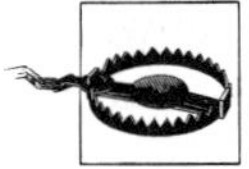

If this is done incorrectly, it can damage an application. But if you back up any files before altering them, you eliminate this possibility.

The following example assumes you're using UltraEdit-32 to fix this problem in Paint Shop Pro 4.0. Although the specifics may change for later versions of the application you're editing, or if you're using a different hex editor, the technique should still be applicable:

1. First, follow the instructions in the previous Solution 1 or Solution 2 to get rid of any existing entries.
2. Because Paint Shop Pro automatically adds the `ShellNew` branch (explained earlier in Solution 2) every time it starts, we'll start by assuming that the code responsible resides in the main executable, *Psp.exe*. Make sure that Paint Shop Pro is not running before you start messing around with its files.
3. Make a backup of the *Psp.exe* file in the Paint Shop Pro installation directory. See "Make a Duplicate of a File or Folder" in Chapter 2 for more information.
4. In UltraEdit-32, select **Open** from the **File** menu, and select *Psp.exe* from the Paint Shop Pro installation directory.
5. Because this editor is used to edit ASCII (plain text) files as well as binary (hex mode) files, make sure it's in hex mode (make sure the **Hex Edit** option is checked in the **Edit** menu).
6. Select **Find** from the **Search** menu, type `shellnew` in the **Find What** field, check the **Find ASCII** option, and click **Find Next**. When UltraEdit-32 finds the first occurrence of **ShellNew**, close the **Find** box and change the text so it reads `ShellNix`—a change that small (like the "ix") isn't likely to disrupt anything in the program, but it's enough to fool Explorer.

   If you can't find the **ShellNew** text in the application you're editing or if replacing it as described earlier doesn't do the trick, there are other places to look. For example, many programs have several *.DLL* files in the same directory. Use Explorer's **Find** feature to look through all the files in the application's directory for the text **ShellNew**. Repeat the previous steps in any file in which it's found.
7. Repeat the process for all additional occurrences of **ShellNew**. When you're finished, select **Save** from the **File** menu and close UltraEdit-32. The change should take effect the next time you start Paint Shop Pro.

Admittedly, Solution 3 is extreme, but sometimes the programmers have been so stubborn that it's your last resort. Also, if you get a hankering for some tinkering, learning the procedure for this type of customization can come in very handy.

Customize the Tray/Notification Area

The *tray* is the little box (usually in the lower-right corner of your screen, at the end of your taskbar) that, by default, contains the clock and the little speaker (plus a few other icons). Microsoft calls this space the "Notification

Area," because its intended use is to notify you of system status: when you're connected to the Internet, when your laptop's battery is low, etc. This area is also often referred to as the *System Tray* (or *systray*) for no compelling reason.

If you turn off the clock and remove all tray icons, the tray will disappear completely, providing more space for taskbar buttons. It will reappear when any tray icon is added.

Figure 4-5 shows a more-or-less typical tray. Odds are that you have more icons in your tray than you actually want or need. Whether that bothers you or not is anybody's guess. However, tray icons typically correspond to running programs, and it's usually a good idea to shut down running tasks you don't need, for the sake of both improved performance and increased system stability.

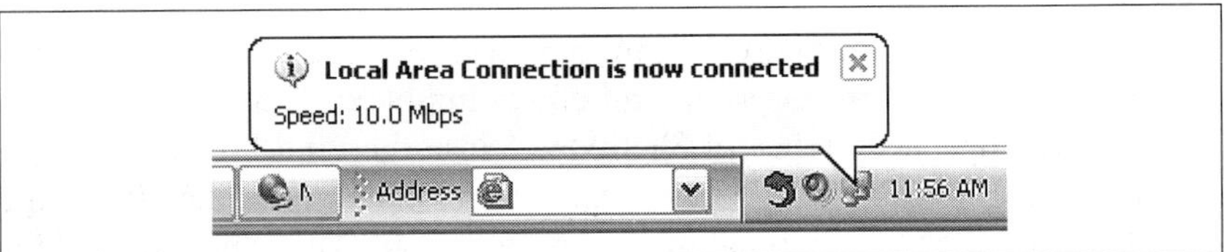

Figure 4-5. The tray contains several (usually too many) icons, as well as the clock

The problem is that there doesn't seem to be any sort of consistency or standards for items in the tray; some icons get double-clicked, some require a single right- or left-click, and some don't get clicked at all. Some items can be removed easily, some can be removed with a setting in some obscure dialog box, and some can't be removed at all. Here are some ways to get a little more control of the tray.

Remove common items from the tray

Volume control

To remove the yellow speaker icon (the volume control), right-click it and select **Adjust Audio Properties**, or go to **Control Panel → Sounds and Audio Devices** and turn off the **Show volume icon on the taskbar** option. If you remove the yellow speaker, you can still adjust the volume with the Volume Control utility (*sndvol32.exe*) included with Windows, as well as with the volume control on your speakers (if applicable).

Network connections

Each network connection configured on your system can have its own tray icon, showing at a glance when the particular connection is actually connected. This may be handy for dial-up or VPN connections but is probably unnecessary for connections that are always on, such as LAN and high-speed Internet connections. To turn off the tray icon for a particular connection, go to **Control Panel → Network Connections**, right-click the connection entry corresponding to the tray icon you wish to remove, and select **Properties**. Turn off the **Show icon in notification area when connected** option at the bottom of the **General** tab, and click **OK**. See Chapter 7 for more information on network connections.

Windows Messenger

By default, the Windows Messenger program is loaded automatically when Windows XP starts, even though the vast majority of users will never use this program. To let you know it's there, its icon appears in the tray. To get rid of the icon, you'll have to close the program; to get rid of the icon permanently, you'll have to instruct it not to load automatically:

a. Double-click the Messenger icon (which looks like two little people) or right-click it and select **Open**.

b. Note that the icon will have a red X over it if you haven't yet set up a Messenger profile. Don't worry; you don't have to set up a profile unless you want to use Messenger.

c. If a sign-up wizard appears, just click **Cancel**.

d. Go to **Tools → Options → Preferences** tab, and turn off both the **Run this program when Windows starts** and **Allow this program to run in the background** options.

e. Click **OK** and then close Windows Messenger when you're done.

See "Eliminate Unwanted Windows Components" in Chapter 5 for information explaining how to completely uninstall the Windows Messenger component from your system.

RealPlayer

Some earlier versions (prior to 9.0) of RealNetworks's *RealPlayer* utility (*http://www.real.com*) place a little blue icon in the tray when they're first installed. The program this icon represents doesn't do anything and can be removed without any adverse effects. (In fact, disabling this program will allow Windows to start a little more quickly next time.) To disable it, start Real Player and open the configuration dialog box. Disable the **Start Center** option, and click **OK** when you're done.

In more recent versions of RealPlayer (9.0 and later), the Start Center has been replaced with something called the *Message Center*, which is responsible for displaying advertisements and annoying update reminders from RealNetworks. To disable this silly accessory, start Real Player, go to **Tools → Preferences**, expand the **Automatic Services** category, select **Message Center**, and then click **Configure Message Center**. Turn off the **Check for new messages** and **Show Message Center icon in the System Tray** options, and then click **OK** when you're done.

Safely Remove Hardware
: This icon appears if you have certain types of removable media drives, such as memory card readers. Windows suggests that you use it to "stop" a device before ejecting its media, but very rarely is this step necessary. Unfortunately, there's no way to remove this icon—your only choice is to use the solution in the next topic, "Hide stubborn icons."

Windows Security Alerts
: Double-click the icon and then click **Change the way Security Center alerts me**. Turn off all the settings here and then click **OK**. See Chapter 7 for details.

Hide stubborn icons

A new feature in Windows XP is the ability to hide tray icons that otherwise can't be removed, decreasing clutter and increasing taskbar real estate. Here's how to do it:

1. Right-click an empty area of the taskbar and select **Properties** (or go to Control Panel → Taskbar and Start Menu).
2. Turn on the **Hide inactive icons** option and then click **Customize**. The Customize Notifications dialog, shown in Figure 4-6, will appear.
3. Windows keeps a history of every icon that has ever appeared in your tray, and they're all shown in this window. The first section, **Current Items**, lists the icons that currently appear in your tray; all others are shown in the **Past Items** section.
4. The options in this list are, unfortunately, not terribly intuitive. Start by selecting an entry in the list. A drop-down list then appears next to its title, from which there are three choices:

   Hide when inactive
   : This is the default for all icons and simply means that the icon is only shown when the application that owns it instructs Windows to display it.

   Always hide
   : Choose this to, not surprisingly, hide the icon.

   Always show
   : This option does absolutely nothing; it's no different than the **Hide when inactive** option. The only way to have an icon always appear

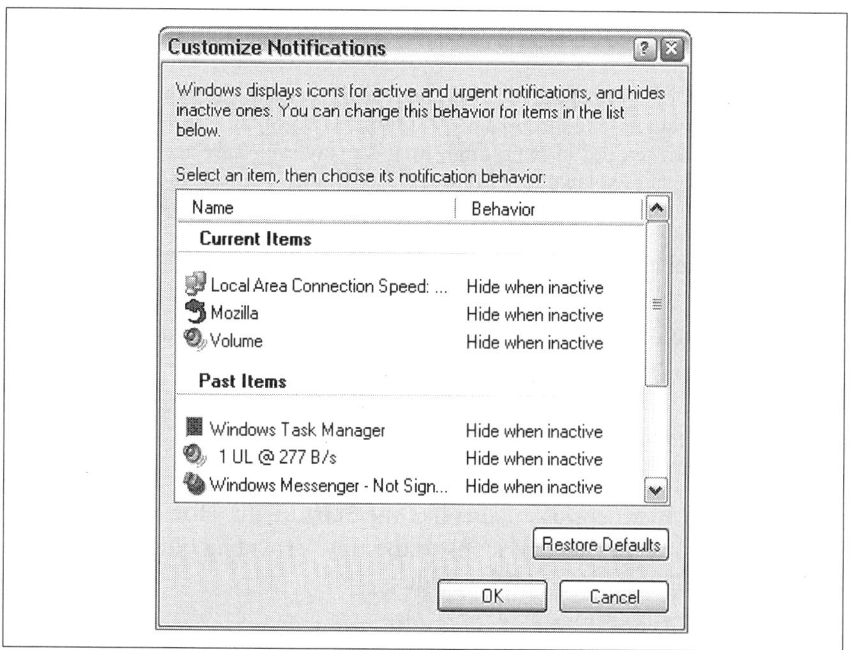

Figure 4-6. The Customize Notifications dialog allows you to hide tray icons that can't otherwise be disabled

is to configure your own, using the solution in the following topic, "Add your own programs to the tray."

5. When you're done, click **OK**, and then **OK** to close the Taskbar and Start Menu Properties window for your changes to take effect. (For some reason, the **Apply** button doesn't always work here, at least with regard to hidden or unhidden tray icons.)

If at least one active tray icon is hidden, it won't simply disappear. Instead, you'll see a little left-arrow button in its place at the edge of the tray. Click the button to temporarily expand the tray to show the "hidden" items. The tray automatically collapses when you move your mouse away, hiding the icons again. Unfortunately, the only way to simultaneously hide this button and hide the tray icons you don't want is to remove the tray completely (explained next).

Hide the tray completely

If all you're after is a clean taskbar, and you don't need access to any icons remaining in your tray, you can hide it completely:

1. Start the Group Policy Editor (**Start → Run** and then type `gpedit.msc`).
2. Navigate to the `User Configuration\Administrative Templates\Start Menu and Taskbar` branch.

3. Double-click the **Hide the notification area** setting on the right side.

Don't be afraid to experiment with some of the other settings in the Group Policy Editor. Most of the settings are written out in plain English, and many even have accompanying explanations. Among other things, you can hide certain elements of the Start Menu, customize the appearance of the Internet Explorer toolbars, and turn off some other annoying features.

4. Select **Enabled** and then click **OK**. You'll need to log out of Windows and then log back in for this change to take effect.

Add your own programs to the tray

The icons that appear in the Tray are placed by applications; this area is not really designed to accept user icons like the Start Menu. However, there is a way to add your own shortcut icons to the tray, providing quick buttons for a few commonly used programs or folders:

1. Obtain and install the Tray utility (download it from *http://www.annoyances.org/*).
2. Run *Tray.exe*, right-click on the new icon in the tray, and select **Help** for instructions.

File Types: The Link Between Documents and Applications

The term *file types* describes the collection of associations between documents and the applications that use them. The most apparent use of this feature is that, for example, Windows knows to run Notepad when you double-click on a text document in Explorer (proof that Windows XP is not truly object oriented).

True object-oriented design dictates that objects (in this case, files and folders) be aware of their own traits. This design is only mimicked in Windows XP. Instead of each file knowing which application is used to edit it, Windows determines how to handle a file based solely on the filename extension. This design has advantages and disadvantages, but Microsoft's decision to hide filename extensions, the basis for file associations, only makes the whole system more difficult to understand and master.

It all starts with file extensions, the letters (usually three) that follow the period in most filenames. For example, the extension of the file *Readme.txt* is *.txt*, signifying a plain-text file; the extension of *Resume.wpd* is *.wpd*, signifying a document created in WordPerfect. By default, Windows hides the extensions of registered file types in Explorer and on the desktop, but it's best to have them displayed.

File extensions not only allow you to easily determine what kind of file a certain file is (because icons are almost never descriptive enough), but also allow you to change Windows's perception of the type of a file by simply renaming the extension. Note that changing a file's extension doesn't actually change the contents or the format of the file, only how Windows interacts with it.

To display your file extensions, open **Folder Options** in Control Panel (or from Explorer's **Tools** menu), choose the **View** tab, and turn off the **Hide extensions for known file types** option. Click **OK** when you're done.

By hiding file extensions, Microsoft hoped to make Windows easier to use—a plan that backfired for several reasons. Because only the extensions of registered files are hidden, the extensions of files that aren't yet in the File Types database are still shown. What's even more confusing is that, when an application finally claims a certain file type, it can appear to the inexperienced user as though all of the old files of that type have been renamed. It also creates a "knowledge gap" between those who understand file types and those who don't; try telling someone whose computer still has hidden extensions to find *Readme.txt* in a directory full of files. Other problems have arisen, such as trying to differentiate *Excel.exe* and *Excel.xls* in Explorer when the extensions are hidden; one file is an application and the other is a document, but they may be otherwise indistinguishable.

Customize Context Menus

A *context menu* (sometimes called a *shortcut menu*) is the little menu that appears when you use the right mouse button to click on a file, folder, application titlebar, or nearly any other object on the screen. Most of the time, this menu includes a list of *actions* appropriate to the object you've clicked. In other words, the options available depend on the *context*.

The context menu for files, the most commonly used and customized context menu, depends upon the type of file selected, which is determined by the filename extension. For example, all text files (with the *.txt* extension) will have the same context menu, regardless of what they contain or which application was used to create them. (This is why Windows gives you a stern warning when you try to change a file's extension.)

In addition to the standard context menu items, such as **Copy**, **Paste**, **Delete**, **Rename**, and **Properties**, you'll usually see **Open**, **Print**, and **Print To** (at the top of the list), which represent customizable actions that can be performed with the selected file. Each of these actions is linked to an application: if you right-click on a *.txt* file and select **Open**, Windows will launch Notepad (by default) and instruct it to open the selected file. Customizing this association between the document type and the applications installed on your computer is what this section is about.

The *default* action—the action that is carried out when a file of a given type is double-clicked—appears in **bold** text in the context menu. If a file type is not registered with Windows, double-clicking on a file of that type will open the **Open With** dialog box, allowing you to choose an associated application on the spot. The exception to this occurs when a file type *has* been registered, yet has no actions associated with it (useful if you want to identify a file type, but not necessarily open it).* In this case, nothing will happen when the file is double-clicked.

The default action is also what can cause the most controversy. Say you have grown accustomed to double-clicking *.html* files on your hard disk and having them opened in Netscape Navigator (in other words, Netscape is the default application for that file type). One day, out of necessity or obligation or whatever, you install one of Microsoft's updates to Windows, which happens to contain a new version of Internet Explorer. Unless you're careful to choose the correct advanced options, suddenly, and without warning, all of your *.html* associations are changed, making Internet Explorer the default application.

Although the most obvious reason to customize a file's context menu is to control the default action, what makes context menus so useful is that you can assign as many different actions as you like to any given file type. In the case of *.html* files, for example, you could add an **Edit** action to open your favorite web page editor, a **View with Netscape** action, and a **View with Internet Explorer** action—all in addition to the default action.

It's possible to add, remove, or modify context menu items for nearly any file type. The File Types window, shown in Figure 4-7, is the only dedicated tool provided by Microsoft to manage file associations in Windows; it has been somewhat improved in Windows XP from previous versions. Some

* An example is the way DLL files are registered with Windows by default.

thought has been given to both experienced and novice users, although it still lacks the streamlining and advanced functionality such an important feature deserves.

Figure 4-7. The File Types tool has been significantly improved in Windows XP from previous versions, although it has some very annoying quirks

For the most flexibility in customizing context menus, you'll want to see how file associations are actually stored in the Registry, as described later in this chapter.

Use file types to add, remove, or edit context menus

1. Select **Folder Options** from Explorer's **View** menu (or double-click the Folder Options icon in Control Panel), and choose the **File Types** tab.

   The list shows all of the file types that have been configured on your system. You can sort the entries by filename extension or file-type description to make any given file type easier to find by clicking the respective column headers.*

Keep in mind that some file types may claim more than one extension. For example, the *.htm* and *.html* extensions are most likely associated with the same file type. If you are editing such a file type, it won't matter which extension you select. See "Link a filename extension to an existing file type" later in this chapter for more information.

2. Select a file type from the list, and click **Advanced**. Don't bother with the **Change** button; it only displays the more limited **Open With** dialog box, discussed in "Choose a file-type association on the fly," later in this section.

   If you see **Restore** here instead of **Advanced**, see "What to do when the Advanced button is missing," also later in this section.

3. The **Actions** list, shown in Figure 4-8, contains a list of the customizable context-menu items for the selected file type. Each one has a name and a command line (the application filename followed by command-line parameters, if applicable).

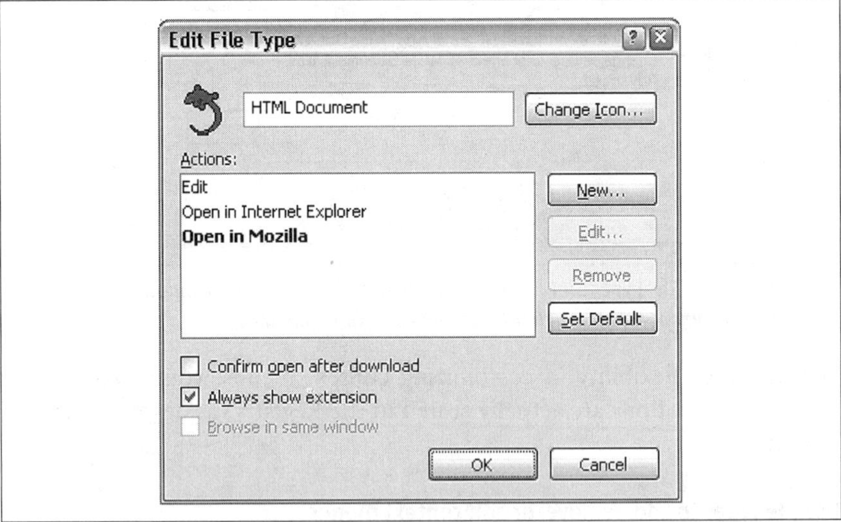

Figure 4-8. The Edit File Type window shows the customizable actions (each of which appears as a context-menu item) for any given file type

* The ability to sort the entries is a relatively new and sorely needed feature. In earlier versions of Windows (before Windows Me), finding file types in this window has been difficult: for example, the entry for the *.xls* extension was listed under "Microsoft Excel Spreadsheet," putting it alphabetically under "M" instead of "E" for Excel or "X" for XLS.

The bold item is the default action, also shown in bold at the top of the context menu. If there's no bold item, and therefore no default, double-clicking a file of that type will probably do nothing. The exception is that if one of the actions is named open, it will be the default whether or not it appears in bold.

To make *no action* the default, you'll have to delete the current default (bold) action. If you don't want to remove any actions, just add a new, temporary action, make it the default, and then delete it. You might wish to have only non-default actions for a file type if you want to prevent accidental activation.

The **Use DDE** option, if enabled, means that the action is intended to activate an already running instance of an application (if possible), rather than starting a new instance. DDE is a poorly documented yet important feature used by Windows to communicate with applications that are already open; for example, if you right-click one or more Microsoft Word Documents (*.doc* files) and select **Print** while Word is already running, Windows simply uses DDE to communicate with Word and instruct it to open the file.

4. Click **OK** when you're done. The changes should take effect immediately; your desktop and any open Explorer or single-folder windows should automatically refresh within a few seconds.

   In some cases, your changes will not take effect in any open Explorer windows. If, for example, you rename an existing file type or change its icon, and the old information still appears in file listings when you're done, just close the Explorer window and then reopen it to force it to utilize your new settings.

Link a filename extension to an existing file type

Sometimes two filename extensions share the same file type—that way, you don't have to go to the trouble of creating and modifying a separate set of actions for each extension. In cases where two file formats are similar enough to warrant file-type sharing, such as *.jpg* and *.jpeg* files, or even *.jpg* and *.gif* files, follow the upcoming steps.

To see a list of all the extensions owned by a given file type, sort the **Registered file types** list by file-type description by clicking on the respective column header. Note that it's possible for two *different* file types with a different set of actions to have the same description, which would unfortunately make then indistinguishable in this view.

1. In the File Types window (discussed earlier in this section), configure a single file type as desired (or simply locate an existing file type).

2. Click **New**, and type the filename extension *without the dot* (e.g., `txt`) in the **File Extension** field. If the extension is currently associated with another file type, that link will be broken then replaced with the one you choose here.
3. Click **Advanced >>** to show a second list of existing file types, and choose any desired file type to claim ownership of the new extension.

   If, instead, you want to create a new file type, either choose **<New>** or simply make no choice from the list. A new file type will be created and named for the extension; if you type `xyz`, the new file type will be named "XYZ File."
4. You can then proceed to edit the new entry. If you've linked the new extension with an existing file type, all that file type's properties (e.g., actions, icon, description) will appear in the new entry as well.

Choose a file-type association on the fly

If you have double-clicked on a file with an extension that has not yet been registered, you may have seen the dialog box shown in Figure 4-9, which is Windows's way of asking what to do with the selected file. Here, you have two choices:

Use the Web service to find the appropriate program
: This option jumps to a page at Microsoft's web site, which is used to look up the extension of the selected file to give you a clue as to what type of file it might be. See the "Microsoft Extension Finder" sidebar for details.

Select the program from a list
: In most cases, you'll want to use this option to choose an application you've already installed to open the document. The subsequent solution shows how to do this for file types that have already been registered.

This is the same box that appears if you open the File Types window, select a file type from the list, and click **Change**. To get this window for an already registered file type without having to open the File Types window first, follow these steps:

1. Right-click the document you wish to open and select **Open With**.*

   You can also right-click the file and select **Properties** to see which program is configured as the default for the type. You can then click **Change** to display the Open With dialog.

* Previous versions of Windows required that you hold the Shift key to display the **Open With** item, a step no longer necessary in Windows XP.

Microsoft Extension Finder

Microsoft has put together a simple "extension finder" web site, intended to provide more information about file types that Windows doesn't recognize. Unfortunately, it's only available through the interface for unregistered file types, but you can go directly to this URL to look up any filename extension:

> *http://shell.windows.com/fileassoc/0409/xml/redir.asp?Ext={your extension}*

where *{your extension}* is the filename extension (without the dot) that you wish to learn more about. For example, to find out about the *.sit* extension, you'd go to:

> *http://shell.windows.com/fileassoc/0409/xml/redir.asp?Ext=sit*

The resulting page typically includes a description of the file format and links to one or more applications that can be used to view or edit files of the requested type.

Tinkering Techniques

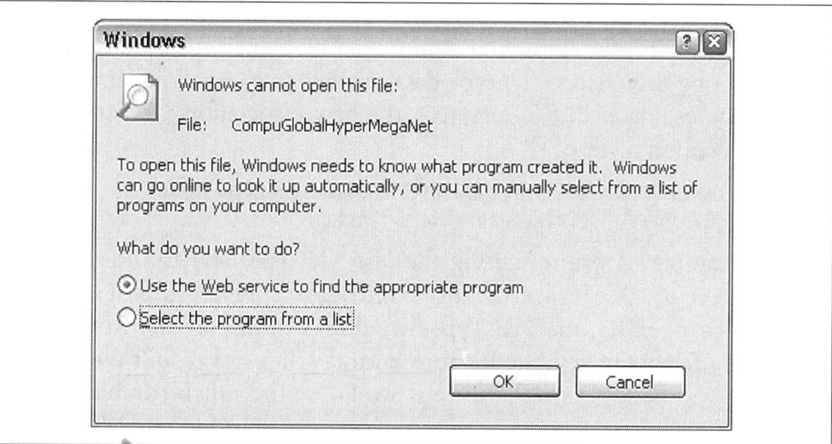

Figure 4-9. Double-click a file of an unknown type (unfamiliar filename extension), and Windows will display this dialog asking what to do

2. The Open With dialog appears, as shown in Figure 4-9. Choose an application from the list, or click **Browse** if the desired application is absent.

3. Click **Always use this program to open these files** to assign a new default action using the selected application. This option will be turned off by default, allowing you to choose an application without affecting your current associations. Unfortunately, there's no way to add a non-default context-menu item with this method.

This is a quick way to not only create new file types on the fly, but change an existing file type without having to return to the File Types window. It's important to realize, however, that when you change an *existing* file type's default action using this method, Windows XP considers the change to be tentative, and displays different controls the next time you view the file type. See the following topic, "What to do when the Advanced button is missing," for details.

What to do when the Advanced button is missing

Occasionally, the **Advanced** button in the File Types window will be replaced with a **Restore** button for a given file type. This is the result of a new built-in mechanism for restoring file types that have been overwritten with the "Choose a file-type association on the fly" procedure, explained earlier in this section. Unfortunately, this mechanism doesn't work very well and ends up causing more frustration than if it were not present at all.

The problem is that if the **Restore** button is present, there's no way to edit a file type without first completely reverting it to its earlier configuration.

The cause of this problem is the way file-type information is stored in the Registry when the default action is modified by using Open With—instead of overwriting the existing file-type data (explained in detail in "Understanding File Types," later in this chapter), the new association is written to this Registry location instead:

```
HKEY_CURRENT_USER\Software\Microsoft\Windows\CurrentVersion\
    Explorer\FileExts\{your file extension}
```

So, for example, if you're editing the *.asp* file type, and the Registry key, `HKEY_CURRENT_USER\Software\Microsoft\Windows\CurrentVersion\Explorer\FileExts\.asp`, exists, the File Types window will display the **Restore** button. If you delete the key, the **Restore** button will go away, but the new file-type data will be lost as well. Since it would be too much trouble to move the relevant Registry data to its more permanent location, there's unfortunately no practical way to get the **Advanced** button back without first reverting the file type. Let's hope Microsoft fixes this in the next version.

Understanding File Types

All active file-type associations are stored in the Registry. Understanding the structure of file-type data can be very helpful in not only fixing problems, but performing advanced techniques (illustrated later in this chapter). Examples include backing up your file types and modifying otherwise inaccessible file types, such as drives and folders.

The HKEY_CLASSES_ROOT branch of the Registry stores information on all your file types. File-extension keys (preceded by periods) are listed first on the tree, followed by the actual file-type keys.

The first Registry keys, named for file extensions, typically only contain pointers to other keys, which then describe the file types. For example, if you navigate to the key HKEY_CLASSES_ROOT\.txt (note that the period *is* included here), you'll notice that there's not a lot of information there. The important (and often sole) piece of information is the (default) value, which is set to the name of another key, located lower down the tree.* In the case of *.txt*, the (default) value contains only the text txtfile (see Figure 4-10). This, in effect, is a reference to HKEY_CLASSES_ROOT\txtfile, which is the key that contains the actual information for the file type, as shown in Figure 4-11.

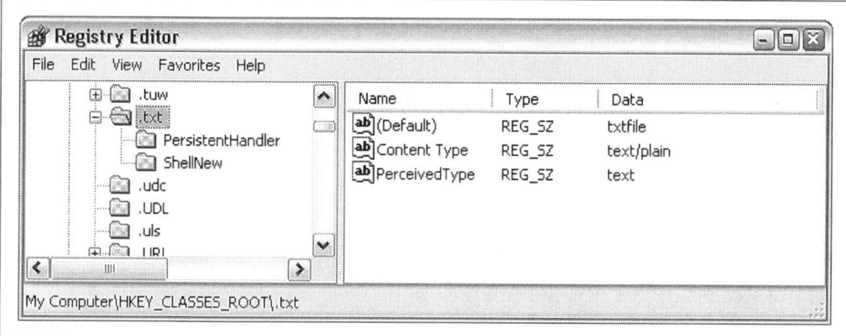

Figure 4-10. The Registry key named for the filename extension contains a pointer to another Registry key (see Figure 4-11)

All of the details of this file type are stored in the txtfile branch, such as the formal name shown in the **Type** column in Explorer (in this case, "Text File"), the icon used for all files of this type, and the applications used to open the file. Many different extension keys can point to this branch, so a single file type like txtfile can have many filename extensions associated with it. This architecture can make it a little tricky to understand the way file types are stored in the Registry, but it does afford a fairly flexible system of file associations.

The structures shown in Figure 4-10 and Figure 4-11 illustrate the two Registry branches that make up a typical file type. File types can be created by application installers, through changes made in the File Types window

* The reason the other keys appear lower down on the tree is merely due to alphabetical sorting.

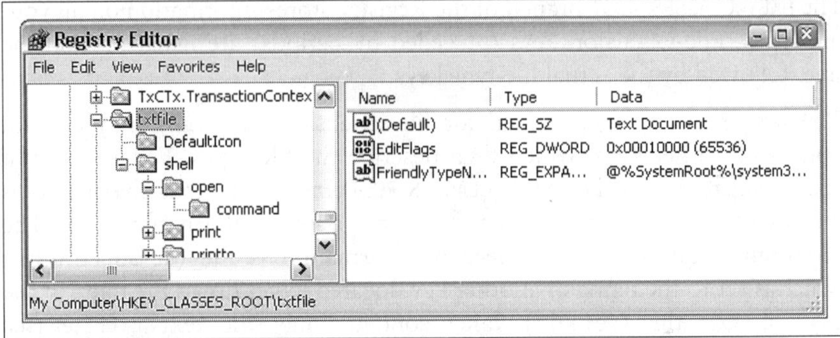

Figure 4-11. The second Registry key contains the file-type information; several file-extension keys can point to this key

(explained earlier in this section), or even manually by editing the Registry directly. A bunch of file types are also set up automatically when Windows is first installed.

First, a key is created that is named for each extension associated with the file type (usually only one, for starters).* The `(default)` value of this key contains the name of the file-type Registry key; it does not contain the full Registry path, however, nor does it contain the formal name of the file type (shown in Explorer). For example, put `txtfile` here and not `Text File`. The `Content Type` value shown in Figure 4-10 may appear for some file types, but it is not necessary for normal operation.

A key called `ShellNew` may also appear underneath the file-extension key. The existence of this key tells Windows to include the extension in Explorer's **New** menu (discussed earlier in this chapter), allowing the user to create a new, empty file of that type without having to open an application. The reason that the `ShellNew` key is located underneath the extension key and not the file-type key (discussed later in this section) is that a file type may have more than one extension, and Windows needs to know which extension to use when creating a new file. The `ShellNew` key is usually empty, although there may be a value called `FileName` that points to a template file, a file on your hard disk that Windows will use to create a new, blank document (stored, by default, in *\Documents and Settings\{username}\Templates*). In most cases, the `FileName` value is omitted, and Windows will create a zero-byte (empty) file with the appropriate extension.

Most of a file type's definition is located in the main file-type key, the name of which is specified in each of the extension keys listed earlier. In

* An example of a file type with two or more extensions is the HTML file type (used by web browsers), typically associated with *.html*, *.htm*, *.shtml*, and *.shtm* files.

Figure 4-11, the txtfile key contains the rest of the settings for the Text File file type. First of all, the (default) value in this key specifies the formal, aesthetic name of the file type—the text that appears in the **File Types** dialog box in Explorer and in the **Type** column in Explorer's **Details** view (e.g., "Text File").

If the value named AlwaysShowExt is present in this key, the extension for this file type will be displayed in Explorer, even if the user has elected to hide extensions for file types that are registered (a setting described at the beginning of this section). A related value, NeverShowExt, appears in a few file-type keys, such as those for Windows Shortcuts (*.lnk* files), Internet Shortcuts (*.url* files), and Explorer Commands (*.scf* files), and means that the extensions for these types are never shown, even if the user has elected to show all extensions. Simply delete the NeverShowExt value to instruct Explorer to show the filename extension for the corresponding file type.

You may also see a binary or DWORD value entitled EditFlags, which tells Windows what is allowed and what is not allowed in the File Types window. See Table 4-1 for some of the possible values and their meanings. Feel free to change or simply remove this value to allow changes to a particular File Type. Unfortunately, these restrictions only apply to the File Types window and don't prevent other applications from changing your file types.

Tinkering Techniques

Table 4-1. Some of the possible values for EditFlags and what they mean

EditFlags bit[a]	Meaning
00 00 00 00(or omitted)	No restrictions
01 00 00 00	Not shown in the File Types window at all
02 00 00 00	**Change** button disabled in File Types window
08 00 00 00	**Advanced** button disabled in File Types window
00 01 00 00	Can't change file type description in Edit File Type window
00 02 00 00	**Change Icon** button disabled in Edit File Type window
40 00 00 00	**Edit** button disabled in Edit File Type window
80 00 00 00	**Remove** button disabled in Edit File Type window

[a] EditFlags values can be summed to implement several restrictions; for example, an EditFlags value of 00 03 00 00 will disable the description field and **Change Icon** button in the Edit File Type window.

In the file-type key are three or four independent subkeys. DefaultIcon contains only the (default) value, set to the filename of the file containing the icon used for the file type. Icons are specified by filename and icon index, separated by a comma; for example, c:\windows\system32\shell32.dll,152 specifies the 153rd icon in the *shell32.dll* file. The file that is specified can be any *.ico* or *.bmp* file, as well as an *.exe* or *.dll* file containing one or more icons. To use the first icon in the file, omit the number or specify `0` (zero); use `1` (one) for the second icon, and so on. The easiest way to choose an icon is with the **File Types** dialog box in Explorer, which will allow you to browse and choose icons without typing or guesswork.

Internet Shortcuts don't launch applications directly; instead, they redirect the URL contained therein to Windows, which then delegates the task to an application suitable to the particular type of URL (e.g., web browser for http:// addresses, FTP client for ftp:// addresses, etc.). As part of this design, you won't be allowed to change the icon for Internet Shortcuts, even if you delete the `EditFlags` value (explained earlier in this chapter). To fix this, you'll have to delete the `IconHandler` key, located in the `shellex` branch, as well.

Most of the meat of the file type is stored in the `shell` key. Its subkeys define the actions, or what happens when a file of this type is double-clicked and which commands appear in the file type's context menu (explained earlier in this section). Underneath `shell` is a separate key for each command shown in the context menu; that is, when you right-click on a file of this type, these are the commands that will appear at the top of the list. Most file types have an *Open* command (with a key of the same name). You may also see *Edit*, *Print*, *PrintTo*, *Play*, and *View* here. You can add, remove, or change any of these commands you wish. In each one of *these* keys is a key called `command`. Each `command` key's `(default)` value is set to the application filename used to carry out the respective command. Figure 4-10 and Figure 4-11 illustrate this particular structure.

For example, if Notepad is associated with the *Open* command for text files, the contents of `HKEY_CLASSES_ROOT\txtfile\shell\open\command` will be:

```
Notepad.exe "%1"
```

Now, the `"%1"` (including the quotation marks) is very important—`%1` is where Windows substitutes the full path and filename of the clicked file, and the quotation marks are necessary in case there are any spaces in the filename of the clicked file. So, if you were to right-click on any file with the *.txt* extension (say, *c:\documents\my file.txt*) and select **Open** from the context menu that appears (see Figure 4-12), Windows would carry out the command:

```
Notepad "c:\documents\my file.txt"
```

which will launch Notepad and instruct it to open the document.

While there can be several available commands for any given file type, only one of the commands will ever appear in bold. This command is called the

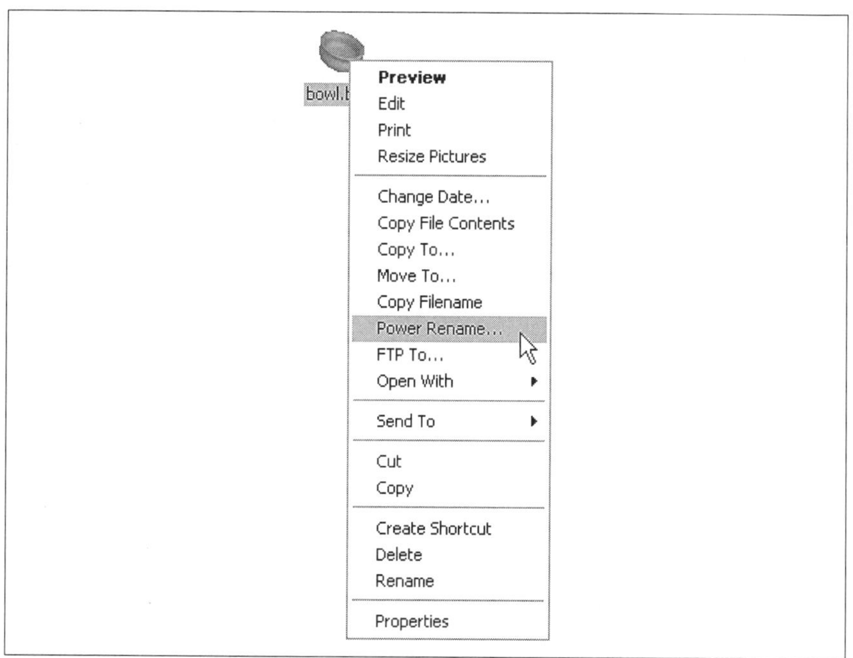

Figure 4-12. A context menu for the bitmap file type shows the default Preview option, as well as the extra Edit and Power Rename... options

default and is the one that Windows uses when you double-click on a file instead of right-clicking. Usually, *Open* is the default, but any existing command can be set as the default.* To make a different command the default, specify the name of the command in the `(default)` value of the `shell` key. For example, if a file type contains *Open*, *Edit*, and *Print*, and you type `edit` in `shell`'s `(default)` value, the *Edit* command will appear bold in the file type's context menu, and *Edit* will be the command carried out when you double-click the file. If the `(default)` value is empty, the *Open* command (if present) is assumed to be the default.

The `shellex` key contains references to *shell extensions*, programs designed to work especially with context menus. These are never shown in the File Types window but are nonetheless very important, and it can be very handy to be able to modify or remove them. For example, the **Power Rename** command shown in Figure 4-12 is a shell extension. Unless you're able to write and compile DLLs, however, you won't be able to create new `shellex`

* Note that although the word *open* is often spelled with all lower-case letters in the Registry, it still appears capitalized in the context menu. Windows will preserve the case of all other commands as you've typed them, but will automatically capitalize *Open*.

entries. However, you can remove some unwanted context menu commands and extra tabs in property sheets of certain file types by removing the corresponding shell extension keys here. I don't have to tell you that it's a good idea to back up any file-type key with a Registry patch before you make any changes.

You might also see a key named `CLSID` in various parts of file-type keys; these are merely pointers to registered application components. To find out what a particular entry means, copy the CLSID code to the clipboard (hit **F2** to rename, **Ctrl-C** to copy, and then **ESC** to abort the renaming process), and then search the Registry for other references to it.

Lastly, you may see a `ddeexec` key, which contains DDE commands and associated data. DDE, discussed earlier in this section, is used to communicate with running applications.

The next few solutions in this chapter illustrate some of the ways you can use the file-type Registry entries to accomplish things otherwise not possible.

Protect Your File Types

One of the most aggravating aspects of using Windows is when the settings you've spent time customizing are overwritten or simply forgotten. Sometimes this is the result of a bug, but often, and especially in the case of file types, there's more to it. Some software developers jury-rig an application so that it overwrites your file associations, either when it's first installed or, even worse, every time the program runs. That way, their program becomes the default whether you like it or not.

For some proprietary file types, such as Excel Files (*.xls*), this isn't much of a problem, because there really aren't any other programs that use these files. The impact is greater on more general file types, such as the large quantity of graphics formats (*.gif*, *.jpg*, *.tif*, *.bmp*, and *.png*), where there are literally hundreds of applications that use these files. It's not unusual for several of these applications to be installed simultaneously on a single system, all competing for the dubious distinction of being the default. Probably the most high-profile example of this competition is that between competing web browsers; not only are file associations in play, but URL associations as well. Every time you open an Internet Shortcut or click a web link in any application, the URL association is what's used to decide which web browser application to use.

Ideally, only you should be in the position to decide which program you use for each task. Unfortunately, it's essentially impossible to write-protect (prevent the overwriting of) any Registry settings—including file types—in Windows

XP. Although it's possible to set user permissions for various Registry keys (see Chapter 8), this only restricts access for programs run by *other users*.

Probably the most effective protection against overwriting file types is to back up the portions of the Registry that are at risk, allowing you to easily restore them should the need arise. This is accomplished with Registry patches; see "Using Registry Patches" in Chapter 3 before continuing.

The procedure outlined here would be a good one to follow, for example, before installing an application you believe might overwrite an existing file type. Repeat these steps for each file type you wish to protect:

1. Open the Registry Editor (discussed in Chapter 3).
2. Expand the `HKEY_CLASSES_ROOT\` branch, and locate the keys that you wish to protect.

   Any given file type is stored as one or more extension keys and a file-type key. For example, the extensions *.txt* and *.log* may both be linked to the `txtfile` file type. So, to save the entire file type, you'll need to save each of the following Registry branches:

   ```
   HKEY_CLASSES_ROOT\.txt
   HKEY_CLASSES_ROOT\.log
   HKEY_CLASSES_ROOT\txtfile
   ```

   If you only save the extension keys or the file-type key, the Registry patch will be incomplete. See "Understanding File Types," earlier in this chapter, for details on this structure.

   To see a list of all the extensions owned by a given file type, open the File Types window (see "Customize Context Menus" earlier in this chapter), and sort the **Registered file types** list by file-type description.
3. When you've highlighted a Registry key you want to export, select **Export Registry File** from the **Registry** menu and specify a filename for the patch. Because you'll be exporting at least two patches, don't worry too much about the filenames just yet. Just make sure not to export two branches to the same file, however, as one will simply overwrite the other.

   Also, don't try to export the entire `HKEY_CLASSES_ROOT` branch, because it contains much more information than we need for this purpose, and restoration of a patch will have unpredictable effects.
4. You can only export one key at a time, so start with one and repeat step 3 for each remaining key. Once you've exported all the keys you're interested in, close the Registry Editor.
5. You should have at least two Registry patches from this exercise, perhaps more. Because they're just plain text files, we can easily merge them together into a single file with Notepad. Choose one file to be the

main patch, and then cut and paste the contents of the other patches into it. The only editing you'll have to do is to remove the `Windows Registry Editor Version 5.00` line from all but the main patch, so that it only appears once—at the top of the file.

If you're exporting multiple complete file types, you might want to merge the individual patches into *several* separate Registry patches—one for each file type.

6. Whenever a particular file type that you've backed up becomes overwritten by an errant application, just double-click the patch you made to restore it.

   In most cases, when you apply a Registry patch, it will simply overwrite the information that's there with whatever is in the patch. However, since applying registry patches merges their information with anything that is already in the registry, there may be leftover context-menu items from any newly installed applications.

7. To apply the patch automatically whenever you start Windows, create a new Windows Shortcut in your *Startup* folder (usually *\Windows\Start Menu\Programs\Startup*), and type the following into the shortcut's command line:

   ```
   regedit /s "filename"
   ```

   where *`filename`* is the full path and filename of the Registry patch you wish to apply (e.g., *c:\filetypes\text.reg*); the quotation marks are included to accommodate any spaces in the file or folder names. Note the `/s` switch, which runs the Registry Editor in *silent* mode, skipping the two prompts that normally appear when Registry patches are applied.

Although there's unfortunately only so much you can do to prevent your file types from being overwritten, other workarounds do exist. Try adding a context-menu item for each program installed on your system, such as "Open with Notepad" and "Open with WordPerfect" for text files. That way, whatever the default is, you'll always have your preferred applications handy.

One sticking point you may encounter when trying to reconfigure file types is that some actions use Dynamic Data Exchange (DDE). DDE is a method of communication between applications, sometimes used by Windows to communicate with the applications it launches, and is discussed earlier in this section. If a particular file type for an application stops working for some reason, it could be that the DDE information has changed or been erased altogether. If this is the case, you'll usually have to reinstall the application to restore the DDE-enabled file types, because there's little standardization with DDE. Often, however, simply deactivating the **Use DDE** option in the **Editing action for type** window is enough to fix the problem.

Customize Context Menus for Drives, Folders, and Desktop Icons

Folders, drives, and desktop icons also have customizable context menus, but the File Types window (described earlier) has limitations on what can actually be changed. However, you can modify these context menus in the Registry. Refer to "Understanding File Types," earlier in this chapter, for more information on the Registry structure involved in this solution:

1. Open the Registry Editor (discussed in Chapter 3).
2. The Registry key you'll need to open depends on what object you're customizing:
   a. For folder context menus, expand the branches to `HKEY_CLASSES_ROOT\Directory\shell\`.
   b. For drive context menus (visible in Explorer and the My Computer window), expand the branches to `HKEY_CLASSES_ROOT\Drive\shell\`.
   c. For the context menus of any system objects, such as My Network Places, expand the branches to `HKEY_CLASSES_ROOT\CLSID\{`*`class id`*`}\shell\`, where {*class id*} matches one of the codes listed in Appendix D, including the braces.
3. Select **New** from the **Edit** menu, select **Key**, type the name of the new item you want added to the list, such as `Open` or `Edit`, and press **Enter**.
4. Highlight the new key, select **New** from the **Edit** menu, and then select **Key** again.
5. Type `command` for the name of this new key, and press **Enter**.
6. Double-click the `(Default)` value in the right pane, and type the full command line (path and filename of the application executable, followed by any applicable command-line parameters) you want associated with this entry.
7. Close the Registry Editor when you're finished. These changes should take effect immediately.

Print Out a Folder Listing

What would seem to be a simple function, the ability to print out a list of files in any given folder, does not exist in Windows XP. However, there is a way, using folder context menus, to add this functionality to Windows:

1. Open the Registry Editor (discussed in Chapter 3), and expand the branches to `HKEY_CLASSES_ROOT\Folder\shell`.
2. Select **New** from the **Edit** menu, select **Key**, and type `Print Contents` for the name of this new key.
3. Highlight the new `Print Contents` key, select **New** from the **Edit** menu, select **Key** again, and type `command` for the name of this new key.
4. Double-click the `(Default)` value in the right pane, and then type the following:

   ```
   cmd.exe /c dir "%1" > PRN
   ```

   This line launches the *cmd.exe* application (also known as the Command Prompt, discussed in Chapter 10) and then, using the `/c` parameter, instructs it to carry out the following command:

   ```
   dir "%1" > PRN
   ```

   which generates a folder listing* and sends it to the printer object (`PRN`). You can use any of the `dir` command's optional parameters to further customize the listing it generates. For example, to specify the desired sort order, change the above to the following:

   ```
   cmd.exe /c dir "%1" /o:xxx > PRN
   ```

   where *`xxx`* can be any or all of the following letters, in the order that you want the sorts to take place: `N` to sort by name, `E` by extension, `S` by size, `D` by date, `G` to group directories first, and `A` by last access date (earliest first). See Chapter 10 for more information on the `dir` command.
5. If you wish to send the folder listing to a text file in the folder, navigate to `HKEY_CLASSES_ROOT\Folder\shell\Save Contents\command` (create the missing keys just like in steps 2 and 3), and then type the following for the `command` key's `(Default)` value:

   ```
   cmd.exe /c dir %1 > "Folder Listing.txt"
   ```
6. Close the Registry Editor when you're done; the change will take effect immediately. Just right-click any folder and select **Print Contents** to send the contents of the selected folder to the default printer.

Creative Element Power Tools (available at *http://www.creativelement.com/powertools*) comes with several similar context-menu add-ons, allowing you to print or copy a folder's contents to the clipboard, among other things. See

* See the discussion of file types, earlier in this chapter, for an explanation of `"%1"` as it is used here.

Windows XP in a Nutshell (O'Reilly) for extensive coverage of batch files and DOS commands such as `dir`.

Turn File Icons into Thumbnail Previews

Windows tries to be as graphical as possible, which is sometimes its downfall. Case in point: when was the last time you found the icon for an application or associated document to be the least bit helpful in determining what was inside?

In Explorer, when you view a folder containing cursors (*.cur* files), animated cursors (*.ani* files), or icons (*.ico* files), their file icons are *previews* of their contents instead of simply generic icons for the application with which they're associated. Now, Windows has the capability to generate these types of thumbnail previews for other kinds of files as well, and a special feature in Windows XP takes it even further.

Solution 1: Icon previews for bitmap (.bmp) files

The advantage of this solution is that once the change has been made, it will be enabled automatically for all folders on your system. The disadvantages are that this solution works only for *.bmp* files, and the thumbnail previews will never be larger than the rest of your system icons (usually 32 × 32 pixels):

1. Open the Registry Editor discussed in Chapter 3.
2. Expand the branches to `HKEY_CLASSES_ROOT\Paint.Picture\DefaultIcon`.
3. Change the `(Default)` value to `%1`. If the *.bmp* file type is no longer associated with MS Paint, the correct Registry location will be somewhere other than in `Paint.Picture`. Try looking in the `(Default)` value of `HKEY_CLASSES_ROOT\.BMP` for the current file type (see "Understanding File Types," earlier in this chapter, for more information).
4. Close the Registry Editor and press **F5** to refresh any open windows to reread the icons for bitmap files. If it doesn't work right away, you might have to close any open Explorer windows and reopen them for the change to take effect.

To increase the size of icons, double-click the Display icon in Control Panel, choose the **Appearance** tab, and click **Advanced**. Select **Icon** from the **Item** menu, and type in a larger value for the size, such as `48` or `64`. Note that this will make all icons on your system (those on the desktop, and in the **Large Icons** display in Explorer) larger.

Solution 2: Use built-in icon previews for all graphic files

The advantages of this solution are that it works for more file types, including *.bmp*, *.jpg*, and *.gif* files, and that the previews can be larger than normal icons. The disadvantages include that the option needs to be enabled for each folder you view (you wouldn't want to set it as the default). Also, it's a pretty clumsy interface, and image files that it doesn't understand are shown simply with their standard file icons rather than being hidden. If you are viewing a folder containing more than just image files, the display is less than ideal.

Open Explorer and locate any folder that contains at least one graphic image file (*.jpg*, *.gif*, or *.bmp*). Select **Thumbnails** from the **View** menu (this option may not be available if you have Internet Explorer integration disabled—see Chapter 8). Select one of the other view modes (such as **Details** or **Large Icons**) to restore the display to normal.

If you've configured Explorer to display hidden files, you'll notice a new hidden file, *thumbs.db* (which contains the thumbnail data), in any folder you view. As long as this file is present, the folder's view will always be set to **Thumbnails**. If you delete this file, and then reopen the folder, it should revert back to the standard **Details** or **Large Icons** view.

To choose the size of Windows Explorer's thumbnail previews, start TweakUI (see Appendix A), expand the **Explorer** category, and select **Thumbnails**. Use the **Size (pixels)** value to choose the maximum width and height of your thumbnails (specify 32 to make them the same size as ordinary icons, for instance). You can also decrease the amount of memory Windows Explorer uses to display thumbnail previews by sliding the **Image Quality** slider all the way to **Low**.

If you need a better thumbnail preview, try a third-party application, such as ACDSee (*http://www.acdsee.com/*). It not only has a far superior thumbnail viewer, but is a much better and faster image viewer than XP's Windows Picture and Fax Viewer (discussed later in this chapter).

Disable the Automatic Display of Thumbnails in Certain Folders

One of the new marketing gimmicks Microsoft is using to promote Windows XP is that it is supposedly "task oriented," which means that the design elements are first and foremost designed to help accomplish tasks. Unfortunately, this is more lip service than anything else; most of the time, Windows XP tends to be more component-oriented than task oriented. What Microsoft is actually referring to is the added assumptions Windows makes, many of which are just plain wrong and end up simply annoying us.

For example, if you view certain folders (such as *My Pictures*) in Explorer or the File Open/Save dialog, its contents will be shown using the **Thumbnails** view instead of the standard **List** or **Details** views. Although you can manually switch the view each time you open the folder, there are several ways to turn it off.

Solution 1: Modify the assumptions made about a given folder

1. Right-click on any given folder icon, and select **Properties**.
2. Choose the **Customize** tab, and choose **Documents (for any file type)** from the list.
3. Click **OK** when you're done. You'll probably have to close the folder and reopen it for the change to take effect.

This feature should be available for every folder on your system except your system folders. Unfortunately, you can't customize system folders (such as *My Pictures*), so you'll have to settle for one of the remaining solutions.

Solution 2: Change the way thumbnails look (requires TweakUI)

1. Open TweakUI (see Appendix A).
2. Expand the **Explorer** category branch, and select **Thumbnails**.
3. Change the value of **Size** to 32.

Unfortunately, this won't disable the thumbnails, but it will make them the same size as standard icons. The result is a less cumbersome and easier-to-use interface, but it's not perfect. See the following solution if this isn't suitable.

Solution 3: Relocate your system folders

1. Open TweakUI (see Appendix A).
2. Expand the **My Computer** category branch, and select **Special Folders**.
3. Change the locations of the special folders (such as *My Pictures*) you wish to have point to different locations. This lifts the restriction noted in Solution 1.

While this returns the display of your folders to the standard icon view, it does cause any applications that default to your *My Pictures* folder (when using File Open/Save dialogs, for instance) to look in a different location, which means that you'll have to manually navigate to the desired folder each time. See "Customize the Places Bar," later in this chapter, for a further workaround.

Turn off the Windows Picture and Fax Viewer

The Windows Picture and Fax Viewer is set as the default image viewer for all sorts of file types in Windows XP. Unfortunately, choosing another program as the default in the File Types window (described earlier in this chapter) won't change this, and there's no option in the interface that can disable this component. It's a really stupid design, and it takes a Registry change to fix it:

1. Open the Registry Editor (discussed in Chapter 3).
2. Expand the branches to `HKEY_CLASSES_ROOT\SystemFileAssociations\image\ShellEx\ContextMenuHandlers`.
3. Delete the `ShellImagePreview` key.
4. Close the Registry Editor when you're done; the change will take effect immediately.

Cool Things You Can Do with Drives and Folders

Given the important role of folders in Windows, not only in their ability to store our personal data, but in the way they're used to organize the files that comprise the operating system, it should not be surprising that there are lots of cool things you can do with them. The next few solutions should illustrate the flexibility of Windows XP, and the lengths one can go to accomplish just about anything.

Customize Drive and Folder Icons

There may come a time when you may get a little sick of the generic icons used for drives and folders in My Computer and Explorer (personally, I'm not a big fan of the liberal use of yellow in the Windows XP interface). Now, you've probably figured out that you can create a shortcut to any drive or folder, choose a pretty icon, and place it on the desktop or in some other convenient location. Unfortunately, the icon you choose doesn't propagate to the target object. Here's how to make the change a little more universal.

Solution 1: Customize drive icons

Using the functionality built into Windows CD auto-insert notification feature—functionality that allows Windows to determine the name and icon of a CD as soon as it's inserted in the reader (see "Curb AutoPlay for CDs and DVDs" later in this chapter)—there's a simple way to customize the icons of all your drives:

1. Open a plain-text editor, such as Notepad.
2. Type the following:

   ```
   [autorun]
   icon=filename, number
   ```

   where *`filename`* is the name of the file containing the icon, and *`number`* is the index of the icon to use (leave *`number`* blank or specify `0` [zero] to use the first icon in the file, `1` for the second, and so on).
3. Save the file in the root directory of the hard disk, floppy, or removable drive you wish to customize, naming it *Autorun.inf*.
4. This change will take effect the next time the **My Computer** view is refreshed; with Explorer or the My Computer window open, press the **F5** key to refresh the display and read the new icons (Figure 4-13).

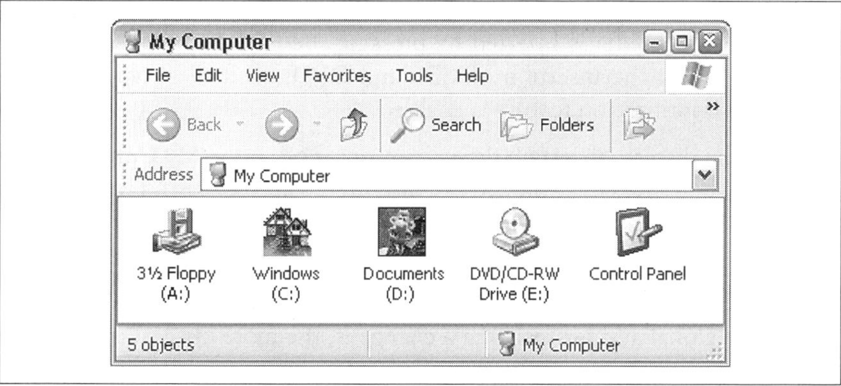

Figure 4-13. Make Explorer and My Computer less drab by customizing drive and folder icons

Solution 2: Customize individual folder icons

The icon for any individual folder can be customized to suit your taste:

1. Open a plain-text editor, such as Notepad.
2. Type the following:

   ```
   [.ShellClassInfo]
   IconFile=filename
   IconIndex=number
   ```

   where *`filename`* is the name of the file containing the icon, and *`number`* is the index of the icon to use; leave the `IconIndex` line out or specify `0` (zero) to use the first icon in the file, `1` for the second, and so on. Note the dot (`.`) in `[.ShellClassInfo]`.
3. Save the file directly in the folder you wish to customize, naming it *desktop.ini*.

4. Open a command-prompt window (*cmd.exe*), and type the following at the prompt:

   ```
   attrib +s foldername
   ```

   where *foldername* is the full path of the folder containing the *desktop.ini* file (i.e., *c:\docs*). This command turns on the **System** attribute for the folder (not the *desktop.ini* file), something you can't do in Explorer.

   Note that turning on the **System** attribute for a folder will have no adverse effect on your system, your data, or any other applications.

5. Close the Command Prompt window when you're done. You'll have to close and reopen the Explorer or single-folder window to see the change (pressing **F5** won't do it).

If you're customizing a drive icon for a removable drive (i.e., Zip, CD-R, floppies), you may need to refresh the My Computer or Explorer window every time the media is inserted by pressing the **F5** key, because Windows can only detect the insertion of CDs and DVDs, and then only when the auto-insert notification feature is enabled.

To turn the display of certain drive icons on or off in the My Computer window, open Drives in the **My Computer** category in TweakUI (see Appendix A).

Solution 3: Customize all folder icons

The more global and far-reaching a change is, the more likely it is to be difficult or impossible to accomplish without some serious tinkering in the Registry. An example are the icons used by some of the seemingly hard-coded objects in Windows, such as the icons used for ordinary, generic folders:

1. Open the Registry Editor (discussed in Chapter 3).
2. Expand the branches to `HKEY_CLASSES_ROOT\Folder\DefaultIcon` (you can also customize drive icons by going to `HKEY_CLASSES_ROOT\Drive\DefaultIcon`).
3. Double-click the `(Default)` value in the right pane. This value contains the full path* and filename of the file containing the icon, followed by a comma, and then a number specifying the index of the icon to use (0 being the first icon, 1 being the second, and so on). The file you use can be an icon file (**.ico*), a bitmap (**.bmp*), a *.dll* file, an application executable (**.exe*), or any other valid icon file.

* You can omit the full path if the file you wish to use is in the system path, as described in Chapter 6.

The default for folders is `%SystemRoot%\System32\shell32.dll,3`, and the default for drives is `%SystemRoot%\System32\shell32.dll,8`.

4. When you're done, close the Registry Editor. You may have to log out and then log back in for this change to take effect.

There's a bug in Windows Explorer that may prevent your custom icon from being used in certain circumstances. The icon will appear whenever you view folders on the desktop or in single-folder windows, but if you open an Explorer window directly (*explorer.exe*), the old yellow icons will still appear. The way around this is to right-click a folder icon and select **Explore**, which will display a true Explorer window (with the tree) using your custom icon.

Solution 4: Just about any system object

1. Open the Registry Editor discussed in Chapter 3.
2. Expand the Registry branches to: `HKEY_CLASSES_ROOT\CLSID\{class id}\DefaultIcon`, where `{class id}` is the Class ID of the object you wish to change. To find the class id of an object, do a search in the `HKEY_CLASSES_ROOT\CLSID\` branch for the formal name of the object (e.g., `Recycle Bin`).
3. Double-click the `(Default)` value in the right pane. The icon is specified here the same way it is for folders and drives (see the previous solution).
4. This change should take effect the next time you refresh the folder containing the object you've just customized. For example, press the **F5** key while the desktop is active to refresh any desktop icons.

Solution 5: Applications (.exe and .dll files)

For most people, all that will be necessary to change the icon for an application is to change the icon for the application's shortcut, usually found in the Start Menu or on the desktop. Just right-click the desired shortcut, click **Properties**, choose the **Shortcut** tab, and click **Change Icon**. But there is actually a way to change the icon resource embedded in any *.exe* or *.dll* file, using the following procedure:

1. Download and install Microangelo (*http://www.microangelo.us/*).
2. Start the Microangelo Librarian, and open the file you wish to change. All of the file's icons are shown in the window here. Just double-click an icon to edit it (the one shown in Explorer is typically the first one shown here).

3. When you're done in the editor, just select **Update Librarian** from the **File** menu, and select **File → Save** in the Librarian window to write the changes to disk.

Note that another way to change the icon used for a system object is to edit the icon directly in the *shell32.dll* file (found in *\Windows\System32*). However, since this file is in use while Windows is running, you'll need to edit a copy of the file, and then replace the original with the modified copy using the System Recovery Console, described in Chapter 6.

Mirror a Folder with Folder Shortcuts

Windows Shortcuts are tiny files that link to applications, documents, drives, folders, and some system objects. They're convenient in that they usually behave the same way as the objects to which they're linked when you double-click them or drag-drop other objects on them. If you drag a file into a folder's shortcut, for example, it's the same as dragging the file into the folder.

The inherent problem with Window Shortcuts is that they are files, and as such, have the same limitations as files. They are sorted in Explorer with the rest of the files; shortcuts to folders are not grouped with folders as you might expect. Furthermore, shortcuts to folders cannot be specified in a path. For example, if you were to create a shortcut to the folder *d:\Yokels\Cletus*, name the shortcut *Cletus*, and then place the shortcut in *c:\Brandine*, you wouldn't be able to reference files stored in *d:\Yokels\Cletus* by using the path *c:\Brandine\Cletus*.

Enter **Folder Shortcuts**, an undocumented feature in Windows XP.* Folder Shortcuts behave exactly like folders because they *are* folders. With a little tweaking, any empty folder can be turned into a Folder Shortcut, a mirror† of any other drive or folder on your system, on your network, or even on the Internet!

If you create a Folder Shortcut and then try to delete it, you *will* be deleting the target folder and all of its contents. Folder Shortcuts must be dismantled before they can be removed. Be sure to read the entire solution for details.

* Folder Shortcuts are also supported in Windows 2000 and Windows Me.

† Strictly speaking, a "mirror" of the folder would create *copies* of all the source folder's contents. A Folder Shortcut doesn't actually duplicate any data; it only makes the existing data accessible from two different locations.

Folder Shortcuts, once in place, are practically indistinguishable from the folders to which they link. If, revisiting the aforementioned example, you create a Folder Shortcut to *d:\Yokels\Cletus* and place it in *c:\Brandine*, then it will appear as though there's a folder called *Cletus* located in *c:\Brandine*; in other words, *c:\Brandine\Cletus* will be a valid path. (For those of you familiar with Unix, Folder Shortcuts are very similar to symbolic links.)

Why would you want to do this? Among other things, a Folder Shortcut can be used to trick Windows or an application into thinking that a folder contained on a different drive or computer is actually somewhere else. For example, you could replace your *My Documents* folder with a Folder Shortcut pointing to a folder on your network, allowing you to access the same group of files on any number of computers as easily as on the computer on which the files are actually stored. Or say you're using an older application that only permits its datafiles to be stored in a specific location. Using a Folder Shortcut, you can trick the application into storing them elsewhere.

Use the following solutions to create and manage folder shortcuts.

Tinkering Techniques

Create a Folder Shortcut

Here's how to make a Folder Shortcut to an existing folder on your hard disk or on your local network:

1. Choose an existing folder in Explorer—it can be located on any drive, including your network. Create a standard Windows Shortcut to that folder on your desktop, and name the new shortcut `target`. (The shortcut filename will actually be *target.lnk*, although the *.lnk* filename extension won't be visible in Explorer.)

The easiest way to create this shortcut is to drag-drop the folder icon using your right mouse button, and then select **Create Shortcut(s) Here** from the menu that appears. See "Copy or Move to a Specified Path" in Chapter 2 for more information on this process.

2. Next, make a new folder on your desktop; the name actually doesn't matter, but for sake of argument, I choose to call my example folder, *Dingus*.
3. To help protect a Folder Shortcut from accidental deletion, make the folder read-only: right-click the *Dingus* folder icon and select **Properties**. Turn on the **Read-only** option and click **OK**.
4. Drag-drop the `target` shortcut you made in Step 1 into the newly created folder.

5. Open a plain-text editor, such as Notepad, and type the following four lines:

   ```
   [.ShellClassInfo]
   CLSID2={0AFACED1-E828-11D1-9187-B532F1E9575D}
   Flags=2
   ConfirmFileOp=0
   ```

   Save this into the *Dingus* folder and name the file *desktop.ini*.

You may notice that the text in *desktop.ini* contains no specific information about *Dingus* or our target folder. This means that you only need to type this once; thereafter, you can use the same *desktop.ini* file again and again.

6. Open a Command Prompt window (*cmd.exe*), and change the active/working directory to the new *Dingus* folder. The easiest way to do this is to type `cd`, followed by a space, at the prompt. Drag-drop the *Dingus* folder onto the Command Prompt window, and the full path of the folder will be typed for you. It'll probably look something like this:

   ```
   cd c:\Documents and Settings\{username}\Desktop\dingus
   ```

   Then, just press **Enter**—this changes the active directory to the new *Dingus* folder. (See Chapter 10 for more information on the `cd` command.)
7. Next, type:

   ```
   attrib +h +s desktop.ini
   ```

   and then press **Enter**. This will turn on the **Hidden** and **System** attributes for the *desktop.ini* file, a task not possible from within Explorer. (See Chapter 10 for more information on the `attrib` command.)
8. Type `exit` and then press **Enter** when you're done with the Command Prompt.
9. If the new folder is open, close it now. The next time you open the folder, you'll see the contents of the target folder, rather than the two files, *desktop.ini* and *target*.

The new Folder Shortcut can now be copied or moved anywhere you like. For the sake of safety, you should take certain steps to mark this new folder as a Folder Shortcut. Although it will be described as a "Folder Shortcut" in Explorer's **Type** column, as well as in the folder's Properties dialog box, it will be otherwise indistinguishable from a standard folder. In addition to naming it something like *Shortcut to Dingus*, you can also customize the icon for the new Folder Shortcut in the same way as for a standard folder (described earlier in this chapter). If you don't choose an icon, the Folder Shortcut will assume the icon of the folder to which it's linked.

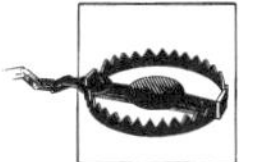

You should only use an empty folder to transform into a Folder Shortcut. If there are any objects stored in said folder (e.g. *Dingus*), they will become inaccessible in Windows when the folder becomes a Folder Shortcut; they will otherwise only be visible from the command prompt, or after you dismantle the Folder Shortcut, as explained next. There should be no adverse effect on the contents of either folder, however.

If you find the need to create Folder Shortcuts more easily, see "Mirror a Folder with Folder Shortcuts" in Chapter 9 for a Windows Script Host (WSH) script that automates this process.

A Folder Shortcut can also be used to mirror an FTP site, effectively allowing you to transfer files across the Internet using Explorer. See "Accessing an FTP Site in Explorer" in Chapter 7 for details.

Dismantle a Folder Shortcut

It's important to realize that once you create a Folder Shortcut, you should never try to delete it using traditional methods. If you try to delete a Folder Shortcut by dragging it into the Recycle Bin, for example, Windows will actually delete all the contents of the *target* folder! To remove a Folder Shortcut, you must first *dismantle* it. Because the command prompt doesn't recognize Folder Shortcuts, you can use it to delete the two files you created when you constructed the Folder Shortcut:

1. Open a Command Prompt window (*cmd.exe*), and change the active directory to the Folder Shortcut (not the target folder). See step 5 in the previous solution on how to do this with the `cd` command.
2. Type:

   ```
   attrib -h -s desktop.ini
   ```

   which will turn off the **Hidden** and **System** attributes for the *desktop.ini* file, a task not possible from within Explorer. Note that this is similar to the use of the attrib command in Step 6 in the previous solution, except that we're using minus signs (-) to turn off the attributes instead of plus signs (+).
3. Next, type the following two commands:

   ```
   del desktop.ini
   del target.lnk
   ```

4. Type exit when you're done. (See Chapter 10 for more details on the `CD`, `ATTRIB`, and `DEL` commands used here.)
5. If the new folder is open, close it now. The next time you open the folder, it should be empty, and can be safely deleted.

Customize the Places Bar

The Places Bar is the gray bar along the left edge of the File → Open and File-Save dialog boxes used by most applications in Windows XP. Like many of the dialog boxes and controls (pushbuttons, menus, etc.) in most applications, these file dialogs are a function provided by Windows, and are used for the following reasons:

- Application developers don't have to reinvent the wheel with their own file dialogs.
- Users get a common experience and don't have to learn a new interface for each application.
- Microsoft can add new features to file dialogs (like the Places Bar), which are immediately and automatically propagated to all applications that use the feature properly.

The Places Bar has a maximum of five buttons, each of which points to a different folder on your system. By default, these places are Desktop, My Documents, Favorites, My Computer, and Recycle Bin. If you don't see the Places Bar on your system, the feature may simply be disabled (as described in the following Solution 1) or the particular application you're using uses nonstandard or obsolete versions of the file dialogs.

There are three solutions that allow you to customize the Places Bar; the first works for most applications, but not Microsoft Office. Solutions 2 and 3 apply only to Microsoft Office XP and Office 2000, respectively. To customize all instances of the Places Bar, you may have to use all three solutions on your system. Note that Creative Element Power Tools (available at *http://www.creativelement.com/powertools*) allows you to customize the places bar for all applications simultaneously, including Office.

Solution 1: Places Bar for most applications

1. Start TweakUI (see Appendix A), and then open the Common Dialogs category.
2. Select **Custom places bar**, and then choose the desired system folders from each of the lists. Your selections will appear in the Places Bar in the same order as you choose them here. You can also type the full path of

any existing local or network folder here; the folder's actual name and icon will appear on the corresponding button.

You can also choose either **Show default places** or **Hide places bar** at this point, both of which should be self-explanatory.

3. Click **OK** when you're done. You'll have to close and reopen any currently open applications for the change to take effect.

Solution 2: Places Bar in Microsoft Office XP and later versions

The following works in Office XP (aka Office 2002 or Office 10.0) and later versions, and requires no Registry editing. However, it's somewhat limited; for more control, or if you're using Microsoft Office 2000, use Solution 3, explained next.

1. Open any Office application, and go to **File → Open**.
2. To add a new place to the Places Bar, navigate to the parent folder of the folder you would like to add (not to the folder itself) and highlight it in the window.
3. Click **Tools** (in the upper right) and select **Add to "My Places."**
4. To rearrange places, right-click any existing place icon in the Places Bar, and select **Move Up** or **Move Down**.
5. You can delete any custom places by right-clicking their icons on the bar and selecting **Remove**, but you won't be able to remove the standard Places Bar entries without editing the Registry, as described in Solution 3.

Tinkering Techniques

Solution 3: Places Bar in Microsoft Office 2000 and later versions

1. Close any open Microsoft Office applications.
2. Open the Registry Editor, discussed in Chapter 3.
3. If you have Office 2002 (also known as Office XP or Office 10), expand the branches to:

   ```
   HKEY_CURRENT_USER\Software\Microsoft\Office\10.0\Common\Open Find\Places
   ```

   If you have Office 2000 (also known as Office 9.0), expand the branches to:

   ```
   HKEY_CURRENT_USER\Software\Microsoft\Office\9.0\Common\Open Find\Places
   ```

   Either way, you should see two subkeys here: `StandardPlaces` and `UserDefinedPlaces`.
4. First, you'll have to disable the existing items; otherwise, your custom items won't be shown. This is done by adding a new value, not by deleting existing data. Don't worry if you want to keep one or more of the

defaults; it's easier in the long run to disable them all here and then re-create the five you want to keep.

One by one, highlight each key under the `StandardPlaces` key (e.g., `Desktop`, `Recent`), and select **New** and then **DWORD Value** from the **Edit** menu. Name the new value *`Show`*, and leave the value of `0` unchanged. Make sure the values you add are `DWORD` values; otherwise, this won't work.

5. Next, highlight the `UserDefinedPlaces` key and add five new keys. Name them `Place1`, `Place2`, `Place3`, `Place4`, and `Place5`. You can add more if you like (see Step 7).
6. In each of these new keys, you'll want to create the following values, filling in the appropriate information in each value:

   A String value called Name
   : This value contains the caption that will appear under this place (example: `Desktop`).

   A String value called Path
   : This value contains the full folder path for the place (for example: *c:\windows\desktop*).

   A `DWORD` value called Index
   : This value allows you to choose how your places are sorted. Enter `0` for the first place, `1` for the second, `2` for the third, and so on. The key names typed in the previous step (`Place1`, `Place2`, etc.) do not determine the sort order.
7. Even if you add more entries here, only the first five will be shown. To allow more than five buttons on the Places Bar, go back to `HKEY_CURRENT_USER\Software\Microsoft\Office\10.0\Common\Open Find\Places` (replace the `10.0` here with `9.0` if you're using Office 2000). Select **New** and then **DWORD Value** from the **Edit** menu. Name the new value `ItemSize`, and leave the value of `0` unchanged (regardless of the number of items you want to appear). Now, any additional keys you add using the above procedure will also appear in the file dialog.
8. After you've entered all the new places, open any Office application to try it out. This may require some trial and error to get it right.

   One of the things that makes this difficult is that Office tends to indiscriminately add new keys and values, which can clutter up what you're working on. If you've done it right, however, the seemingly random keys and values that appear will have no effect on what actually appears in the dialog boxes.

When you're done, you'll want to make a Registry patch to back up your settings, just in case a subsequent Office update overwrites them. See "Using Registry Patches" in Chapter 3 for more information.

Curb AutoPlay for CDs and DVDs

AutoPlay (also called Autorun) is a feature intended to make using CDs and other removable media easier for inexperienced Windows users, but more experienced users may end up simply being irritated by it. AutoPlay is responsible for starting an audio CD, data CD, or DVD the moment it is inserted into your drive. If you wish to insert a disk for browsing or any other purpose than playing it, you'll be forced to wait for Windows to load the AutoPlay application before you can close it and continue with your work.

What's worse is that even after all this has happened, the AutoPlay process starts over again if you double-click on the CD icon in your My Computer window—contrary, of course, to the normal folder window that one would expect to see. (You can get around this on a disk-by-disk basis by right-clicking on the disk icon and selecting **Open** or by using Explorer and navigating to the disk in the folder tree.)

The AutoPlay feature works by polling the CD or DVD drive every few seconds to see if a disk has been inserted. If Windows detects a disk that wasn't there a few seconds ago, it reads the label of the disk and looks for a file called *Autorun.inf* in the disk's root directory. *Autorun.inf* usually contains two pieces of information: a reference to an icon file (to display, along with the disk label, in My Computer and Explorer) and a reference to an AutoPlay application.* If an AutoPlay application is specified, Windows proceeds to run the program, which is usually a large, brightly colored window with links to the application's setup program, documentation, the manufacturer's web site and, hopefully, an Exit button. Otherwise, any of several predefined "player" applications may be launched, depending on the type of content detected on the disk. In addition to CDs and DVDs, the AutoPlay system also supports some removable media drives, such as digital-camera memory-card readers.

There are several different solutions available to control this feature in Windows, all of which perfectly illustrate the advantage of tweaking Windows to get around all its annoyances.

* See "Customize Drive and Folder Icons" earlier in this chapter for another solution that uses the *Autorun.inf* file.

Solution 1: Disable AutoPlay on the fly

If you hold down the **Shift** key when inserting the disk, the AutoPlay feature is bypassed (although it's not exactly graceful trying to insert a CD while holding down keys on the keyboard).

Depending on the speed of your drive, you may have to hold Shift for only a few seconds, or longer if it's slow. This feature can be especially aggravating if you hold **Shift** while inserting a disk, as well as for 5–6 seconds thereafter, only to have the AutoPlay application start when you let go of the **Shift** key.

Solution 2: Choose AutoPlay preferences on a per-content basis

This next solution allows you to choose what happens when Windows detects a newly inserted disk, based on the type of content the media contains. Note that this feature has bugs in it, and Windows doesn't always pay attention to your selection made here.

1. Right-click the drive icon for your CD drive, CD recorder, or DVD drive, select **Properties**, and choose the **AutoPlay** tab.
2. At the top of the dialog is a list of content types, allowing you to choose an AutoPlay action depending on the type of files on an inserted disk. Among the available content types are the following:
    - Music files (e.g., *mp3*, *wma*)
    - Pictures (e.g., *jpg*, *gif*, *tif*, *bmp*)
    - Video files (e.g., *avi*, *mpg*, *asf*)
    - Mixed content (used when no *Autorun.inf* file is found, and either no media files are found or more than one type of media files are detected)
    - Music CD
    - DVD movie (appears only for DVD players)
    - Blank CD* (appears only for CD/DVD recorders)

    You may have noticed that "Data CD" is absent from this list, meaning that this window won't allow you to modify AutoPlay behavior for CDs or DVDs containing an *Autorun.inf* file. Unfortunately, there's no way to modify or add to this list.
3. Select an entry in the content-type list, and then select an appropriate action to take. Each action is linked to an application, similar to File Type actions (discussed earlier in this chapter). Unlike the content

* Although it doesn't say it, "Blank CD" implies "Blank DVD" as well.

types, though, the actions *can* be customized, and the procedure to do so is explained in the next solution.

4. Click **OK** when you're done; the change will take effect the next time a disk is inserted in the drive. Note that you will have to repeat this for each of your removable media drives: CD, DVD, and memory-card readers included.

Solution 3: Selectively control AutoPlay actions, or disable it altogether

This next procedure adds more customizability to the AutoPlay feature, including a quicker way to disable AutoPlay than the previous solution, as well as a way to customize the list of actions in the **AutoPlay** tab of the drive-properties dialog. It also allows you to disable AutoPlay completely for a given drive (or drive type), including data CDs (something not possible with the previous solution).

1. Open TweakUI (see Appendix A), expand the **My Computer** category, and then expand **AutoPlay**. There are three subcategories here: **Drives**, **Types**, and **Handlers**.
2. Select **Drives** to selectively disable AutoPlay for individual drives. Any unchecked drive will not AutoPlay inserted media, regardless of content.
3. Select **Types** to more globally disable AutoPlay for CD and DVD drives and removable drives.
4. Lastly, the **Handlers** category allows you to customize the actions shown in the **AutoPlay** tab of the drive-properties dialog, as described in the previous solution.
5. TweakUI won't let you delete any of the predefined actions, but it will change the content types for which each is available. For example, you can choose whether or not the **Copy pictures to a folder on my computer action** is shown when you select **Video files** in the **AutoPlay** tab of the drive-properties dialog.

If you want to remove one of the predefined actions, you can do so in the Registry. Just go to `HKEY_LOCAL_MACHINE\SOFTWARE\Microsoft\Windows\CurrentVersion\Explorer\AutoplayHandlers\Handlers`, and delete the corresponding key there.

6. Click **Create** here to add a new action, which can subsequently be selected for any removable media drive, and nearly any content type. Figure 4-14 shows the Autoplay Handler dialog.

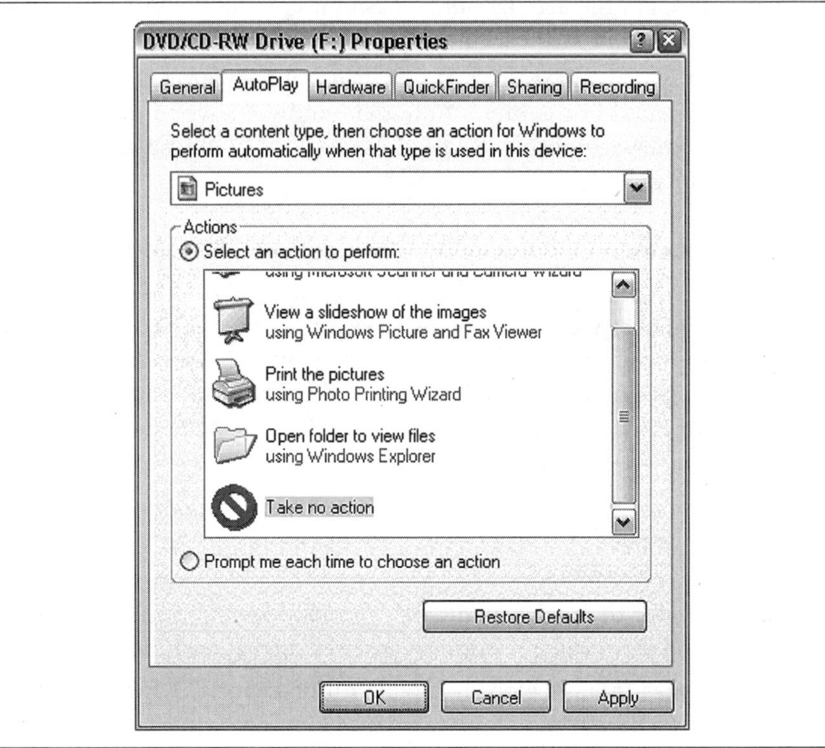

Figure 4-14. Use the Autoplay Handler dialog to add new handler applications to be automatically launched when certain types of removable media are inserted

7. The first two fields are decorative; the text you type for **<description>** and **<program name>** are merely the captions to be displayed next to the action. Click **Change Program** to choose an application executable (*.exe* file).

8. Lastly, the **Args** field, filled by default with `"%L"`, allows you to specify one or more command-line parameters. Whatever you type here should be supported by the application you've selected (more details may be available in the application's documentation).

   Similar to `%1`, discussed in the File Types section earlier in this chapter, `%L` represents the full path of the drive that was activated by the AutoPlay feature. The quotes are simply included for good measure, intended to allow for any spaces in the path name. For example, if you chose Windows Explorer (*explorer.exe*) as the program, and change **Args** to:

   ```
   /n, /e, "%L"
   ```

then Windows will execute the following command when, say, a CD is inserted in drive *g*:

```
\Windows\explorer.exe /n, /e, "g:"
```

9. Click **OK** and close TweakUI when you're done. To take advantage of any newly created AutoPlay actions, see Solution 2.

If you disable the AutoPlay feature for data CDs, the AutoPlay application on any given CD will, as you'd expect, not run automatically. Fortunately, it's easy to run the setup application or any other application on the CD manually. To do this, right-click on the drive icon in Explorer and select **AutoPlay**. Alternatively, you can open the root directory of the CD drive in Explorer: on most data CDs that contain software, you'll see something like *Setup.exe* or *Autorun.exe*. Double-click the file to run it. Sometimes, however, the AutoPlay application file is not obvious, in which case you can open the *Autorun.inf* file and look at the line that begins with `open=`. If you don't see an *Autorun.inf* file in the root directory of the CD, it doesn't support the AutoPlay feature and wouldn't have started on its own even if AutoPlay was still enabled.

Tinkering Techniques

Solution 4: Turn off CD polling

If you want a quick and dirty way to disable all AutoPlay functionality for CD and DVD drives, as well as the system that polls the drive every few seconds (as described at the beginning of this section), use the following solution.

1. Open the Registry Editor discussed in Chapter 3.
2. Expand the branches to `HKEY_LOCAL_MACHINE\SYSTEM\CurrentControlSet\Services\Cdrom`.
3. Double-click the `Autorun` value and type `0` for its value. If it's not there, create it by selecting **Edit → New → DWORD Value**, and typing `Autorun` for the name of the new value.
4. Close the Registry Editor when you're finished. You'll have to log out of Windows and then log back in for this change to take effect.

Note that with this solution, Windows will no longer be notified when you insert a new CD. To make sure the correct icon and title for the current CD are displayed in My Computer and Explorer, press **F5** to refresh the window.

CHAPTER 5

Maximizing Performance

Although your computer spends 99.9% of the time waiting for you to do something, the biggest concern is that other 0.1% of the time when eight seconds can seem like an eternity.

A common misconception is that—with all else being equal—a computer with a fast processor, say 3 GHz, will naturally be faster than a 2 GHz system, and the microprocessor industry wouldn't have it any other way. Sure that new system you're eyeing seems a whole lot faster than your year-old machine, but how much is due merely to the processor's clock speed and how much is determined by other factors?

Now, the increased processor speed is an obvious benefit in some specific circumstances, such as when you're performing intensive statistical calculations, using 3D modeling software, or playing particularly processor-intensive games. But in most cases, one's qualitative assessment of a computer's speed is based on its ability to respond immediately to mouse clicks and keystrokes, start applications quickly, open menus and dialog boxes without a delay, start up and shut down Windows quickly, and display graphics and animation smoothly. For the most part, all of these things depend far more upon correctly optimized software, the amount of installed memory, the speed of your hard drive, and the amount of free disk space than on mere processor power.

Probably the biggest drag on an older system's performance, and the primary reason it may seem so much slower than a new system (not to mention slower than it might have been only last year), is the glut of applications and drivers that have been installed. Any computer that has been around for a year or more will likely suffer a slowdown, the only remedy being either a thorough cleansing or a complete reinstall of the operating system (see "Reinstalling Windows XP" in Chapter 1).

Because financial limitations prevent most people from replacing all their hardware every three months (or whenever the proverbial ashtray gets full), most of this chapter is devoted to solutions that will help improve the performance of your existing system without spending a fortune on new gadgets. For example, the way Windows uses the swapfile (virtual memory) can be inefficient, and spending a few minutes fixing this bottleneck can result in performance increases all across the system.

Of course, this doesn't mean it never makes sense to upgrade, only that it's not always the best answer to a performance problem. Even if money were no object and you could simply buy a new computer or component without thinking twice, you'd still have to take the time to install and troubleshoot the new hardware and reconfigure your software.

Naturally, there is a certain point past which your computer is going to turn into a money and time pit. The older your system is, the less vigorously you should try to keep it alive. It's easy to calculate the point of diminishing returns: just compare the estimated cost of an upgrade (both the monetary cost and the amount of time you'll have to commit) with the cost of a new system (minus what you might get for selling or donating your old system). I stress this point a great deal, because I've seen it happen time and time again: people end up spending too much and getting too little in return. A simple hardware upgrade ends up taking days of troubleshooting and configuring, only to result in the discovery that yet something *else* needs to be replaced as well. Taking into account that whatever you end up with will still eventually need to be further upgraded to remain current, it is often more cost effective to replace the entire system and either sell or donate the old parts.

Trimming the Fat

In many ways, Windows XP is able to better take advantage of your hardware than Windows 9x/Me, but that doesn't mean it's configured for optimal performance right out of the box. Because all the software you run is dependent upon the operating system, tweaking Windows for better performance can result in performance gains across the board.

To start off, there are several easy settings that can have a substantial effect on Windows responsiveness. The next few sections explain these settings.

Tame Mindless Animation and Display Effects

Windows XP adds animation to almost every visual component of the operating system. While these affectations may be cute, they can easily make a 2 GHz computer perform as though it were an antiquated 386. Rather than watch your Start Menu crawl to its open position, you can configure your menus and list boxes to snap to position. You'll be surprised at how much faster and more responsive Windows will feel.

The settings that can affect performance are scattered throughout the interface, but the ones that control display effects are the ones that concern us here. Double-click the System icon in Control Panel, choose the **Advanced** tab, and click **Settings** in the Performance section. The **Visual Effects** tab, shown in Figure 5-1, contains sixteen settings, all explained later.

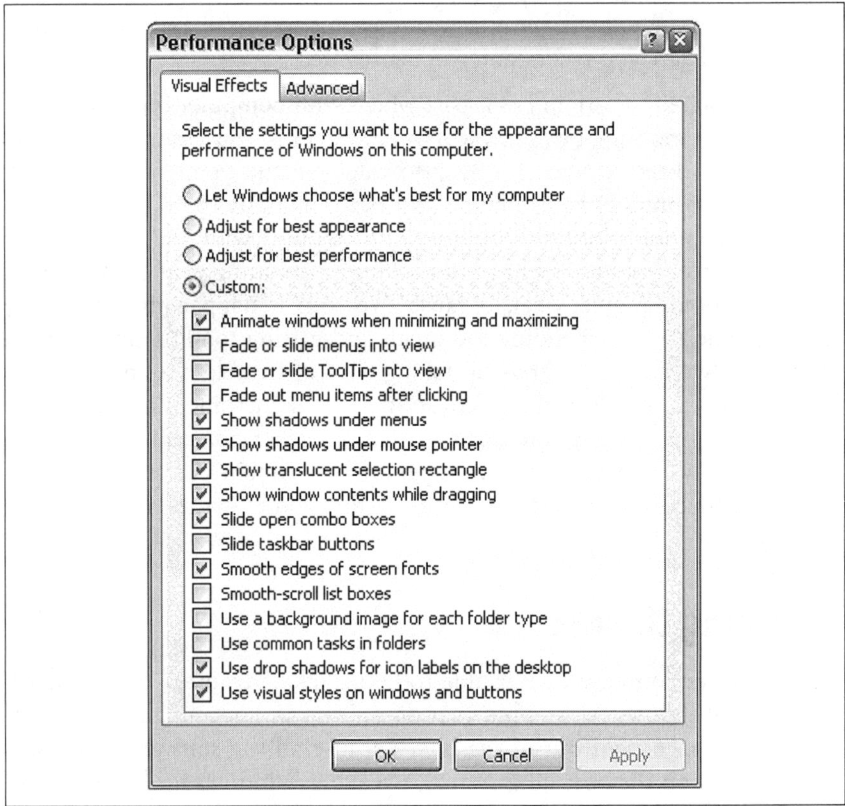

Figure 5-1. The Performance Options window is a good place to start when looking for Windows bottlenecks to eliminate

Unfortunately, the four selections above the list are rather misleading. For example, the **Let Windows choose what's best for my computer** option reverts all settings to their defaults, chosen by a marketing committee at Microsoft to best showcase their product's features. The **Adjust for best**

appearance option simply enables all features in the list, while the **Adjust for best performance** option just disables them.

Keep in mind that disabling some of these options will definitely improve Windows performance, while others may only be of benefit if you are using older video hardware.

Newer video cards (display adapters), especially better 3D-accelerated AGP cards, have built-in processors that handle drawing routines, such as shadows and translucent effects. If your video card is fast enough, these effects won't cause a performance hit. Other settings, such as animated menus, rely on time-based delays and slow down everyone's system, regardless of hardware.

Ultimately, the choice comes down to personal preference: some of these features are just plain annoying, and turning them off can be beneficial to your sanity. Others are actually kinda cool:

Animate windows when minimizing and maximizing

If enabled, this option causes windows to appear to shrink into their respective taskbar buttons when minimized, and expand to their full-size windows when restored or maximized. Although not as slick as the minimize/maximize animation in Apple's OS X, it can nonetheless give a quick clue as to where your window goes when it's minimized. If you see excessive flickering when you minimize or maximize, try turning this one off.

If you have both the **Auto-hide the taskbar** setting in Taskbar and Start Menu Properties and the **Show window contents while dragging** option (described later) enabled, turning off the **Animate windows** option will also disable the animation for the disappearing taskbar.

Fade or slide menus / ToolTips into view

This is the option that enables or disables animation shown when menus are opened. Turn this option off to have menus "snap" open.*

If you choose to keep menu animation, you can change the type of animation used by double-clicking on the Display icon in Control Panel, choosing the **Appearance** tab, and clicking **Effects**.

Show shadows under menus / mouse pointer

If you have a newer video card, disabling this option should have no discernible effect on performance.

* By default, there will still be a short delay before a menu is opened. See "Speed Up Menu Responsiveness," later in this chapter, for more information.

Show translucent selection rectangle

The translucent selection rectangle (referred to as a "rubber band" in Chapter 2) takes advantage of extended support for alpha channels in your display driver. Only those systems with older video cards will see a performance hit from this feature. With this option disabled, rubber bands appear as dotted rectangles.

Show window contents while dragging

Disable this option to show only window outlines when dragging and resizing windows. Unless you have a very old video card, you most likely won't see any difference in performance with this turned off. In fact, your system is likely to seem more responsive with this feature enabled, as windows will appear to respond immediately to dragging rather than responding only after you let go of the mouse button.

Slide open combo boxes

This option controls the animation of drop-down listboxes, similar to the fade or slide menus option described earlier.

Slide taskbar buttons

When a window is closed, its taskbar button disappears. If this option is enabled, the taskbar buttons to its right will slide to the left to close the gap. Since this animation doesn't cause any delays, you're unlikely to achieve any performance gains by disabling this option. However, I find the taskbar animation rather annoying and personally prefer to have this one turned off.

Smooth edges of screen fonts

Using a process called anti-aliasing, Windows fills in the jagged edges of larger text on the screen with gray pixels, making the edges appear "smooth." Turn this option off to slightly improve the speed at which larger fonts are drawn on the screen.

If you're using a flat-panel display (laptop or otherwise), you may find smoothed fonts more difficult to read. Instead of simply turning the option off, you may wish to try an alternate anti-aliasing method. Double-click the Display icon in Control Panel, choose the **Appearance** tab, and click **Effects** to choose between the **Standard** and **Clear Type** smoothing methods. Experiment with this setting to see which one looks best on your display.

Smooth-scroll list boxes

Just because standard listboxes don't "open" like menus and drop-down listboxes doesn't mean they're not animated. By default, when you scroll a listbox, its contents move slowly. Turn this option off to improve the responsiveness of listboxes.

Use a background image for each folder type

Turn this off to disable the background image shown in some system folders, such as Control Panel (category view only) and the *My Pictures* folder. These folders will not only open more quickly without the background images, but they'll be more readable as well.

Use common tasks in folders

The common task pane can also be disabled by opening Folder Options in Control Panel, and selecting **Use Windows classic folders**. Common tasks, described in more detail in Chapter 2, are the panes shown on the left of single-folder windows and contain links to related areas and features.

Use drop shadows for icon labels on the desktop

This option does more than simply enable or disable shadows for desktop icon captions. If you turn this option off, not only will the shadows disappear, but the background behind the text will no longer be transparent. Windows XP is the first version of Windows to offer this option. See Figure 5-2 for an illustration of this setting.

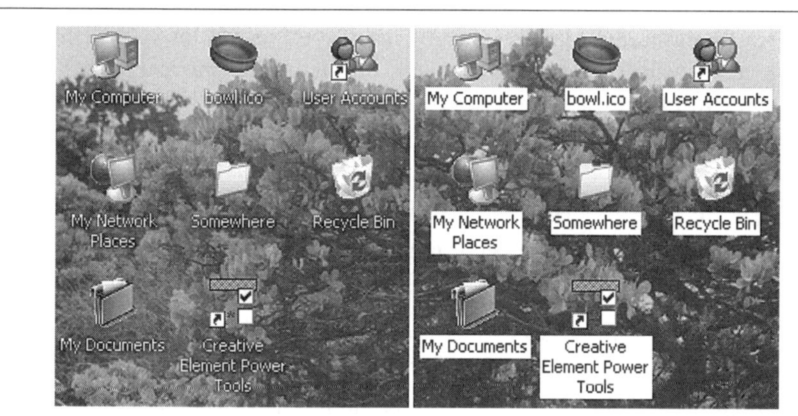

Figure 5-2. If you turn off shadows for desktop icon labels and you're using a background image, desktop icon labels will be shown over rectangles of the current background color

Use visual styles on windows and buttons

Turning this option off is essentially the same as choosing **Windows Classic style** from the **Windows and buttons** list in **Control Panel → Display → Appearance** tab. See "Dealing with Themes, Schemes, Styles, and Skins" in Chapter 2 for more information.

Other settings that affect your display performance can be found by going to **Control Panel → Display → Settings** tab → **Advanced**. The **Troubleshoot** tab has a couple of settings that allow you to disable some video functionality, useful to help isolate video driver problems. See also "Get the Most Out of Your Games, Speed-Wise" for more settings, including those that affect the Direct3D and OpenGL subsystems.

You'll find additional settings in TweakUI, although many are simply duplicates of the settings described above. See also Appendix A, for details on TweakUI and additional performance-related settings.

Speed Up Menu Responsiveness

In addition to turning off the menu animation, as described in the previous section, there's another setting that affects how responsive menus (including the Start Menu) are. By default, there's a half-second or so delay between the time you move the mouse over a menu item and the time the menu is opened. If you reduce this value, your menus will open much more quickly.

There's another feature that is incidentally affected by this setting. In all releases of Microsoft Windows since Windows 95, all menus "follow" the mouse, which allows you to navigate through menus without having to click repeatedly. The problem with this design is that it can be very difficult to navigate menus unless you're able to hold your mouse or other pointing device very steadily. Even the smallest unintentional move in the wrong direction can cause the menu you're using to disappear. This can be even more annoying to those with more sensitive pointing devices, such as touch pads, pens, and other digitizers. This behavior can be completely disabled by increasing the menu open delay to a sufficiently large value:

1. Open the Registry Editor (described in Chapter 3).
2. Expand the branches to `HKEY_CURRENT_USER\Control Panel\Desktop`.
3. Double-click the `MenuShowDelay` value. If it's not there, go to **Edit → New → String Value** and type `MenuShowDelay` for the name of the new value.
4. The numeric value you enter here is the number of milliseconds (thousandths of a second) Windows will wait before opening a menu. The default is `400` (a little less than half a second). Enter `0` (zero) here to eliminate the delay completely, or a very large value (65534 is the maximum) to disable the automatic opening of menus.
5. Click **OK** and close the Registry Editor when you're finished. You may have to log out and then log back in for this change to take effect.

This setting can also be changed in the **Mouse** category of TweakUI (see Appendix A) or in Creative Element Power Tools (available at *http://www.creativelement.com/powertools/*).

Speed Up System Startup

Several factors can impact the amount of time it takes for your computer to load Windows and display the desktop so you can start working. As you install software and add devices, Windows gets more and more bogged down. The most effective way to combat this is to routinely format your hard disk and reinstall the operating system and all applications. In fact, the computer on which I wrote this book was wiped clean before I began the project. Initially, I had upgraded a Windows 2000 system with XP, and it took 2–3 minutes to boot each time. After wiping it clean and reinstalling, the boot time dropped to about 45 seconds.

Unfortunately, reinstalling is a whole lot easier said than done, and is simply not practical for many of us. The following is a checklist of ways to more easily (although less substantially) reduce Windows boot time.

Add more memory

You should have a minimum of 256 MB of memory (RAM) to run Windows XP, but 384 MB to 512 MB is better. Many systems can accept up to 768MB or even 1 GB (1024 MB), although only users of graphic-intensive applications (such as Photoshop) are likely to benefit from that much memory.

Memory prices are always dropping, typically making it remarkably inexpensive to add more RAM to your system, and doing so will *significantly* improve performance across the board.

Maximizing Performance

Make more free disk space

You may not have sufficient free disk space for your swap (paging) file. Windows uses part of your hard disk to store portions of memory; the more disk space you devote to your swapfile, the easier it will be for Windows to store data there. See "Optimize Virtual Memory and Cache Settings" later in this chapter for more information.

The easiest way to create more free disk space is to delete the files on your hard disk that you no longer need. It's best to back up your system before deleting anything, or at least to rename (or move) files to see if they're being used before you get rid of them permanently. See "Increasing Disk Space (or What to Throw Away)," later in this chapter, for more information.

Lastly, a new hard disk will give you dramatically more disk space. A faster hard disk can also improve boot time. If you're on the fence about replacing that older drive, consider the performance boost of getting a larger, faster drive.

Clean out your Temp folder

Sometimes having too many files in your *\Windows\Temp* folder can not only slow Windows startup but, in extreme cases, can prevent Windows from loading at all. Windows and your applications use this folder to temporarily store data while you're working with documents. When those applications and documents are closed (or when the applications just crash), they often leave the temporary files behind, and they accumulate fast.

See "Mirror a Folder with Folder Shortcuts" in Chapter 4 for more information on the *Temp* folder, including a hint on automatically clearing out the *Temp* folder when Windows starts.

Thin out your fonts

If you have more than 600 fonts installed on your system, it may be negatively impacting the time it takes to load Windows. If you can survive without 400 different decorative fonts (especially if all you ever use is Times Roman), try temporarily removing them. If you periodically need a lot of fonts, you might want to invest in font-management software, such as Adobe Type Manager, which can remove and reinstall fonts in groups at the click of a button.

Tame antivirus software

Antivirus programs are typically configured to be run whenever you turn on your computer. These programs are always in memory, scanning programs as you open them and files as you download them. In some cases, this is overkill. For most users—especially those who take the proper precautions—getting a computer virus is about as likely as getting struck by lightning.

I certainly wouldn't recommend getting rid of all antivirus programs; just restrict their use to manually scanning your system when you want by disabling the automatic feature. You'll notice a faster startup for Windows and applications alike. See "Viruses, Malware, and Spyware" in Chapter 6 for details.

Eliminate autostart programs

Probably the most common thing that slows down the loading of Windows is all of the programs that are configured to load at boot time. Not only do they take a while to load, but they commonly eat up processor cycles while they're running. There are several places such programs are specified. Look carefully in each location, and feel free to remove anything you don't want running. See "Programs Run by Windows when It Starts" in Chapter 5 and "Eliminate Unwanted Windows Components" later in this chapter for details.

Nitpicking

Leaving removable media (such as memory cards and removable hard disks) connected when you boot up may add boot delays. This is reportedly fixed in Service Pack 2, but it's still good practice to remove all CDs, disks, and cards from your computer when you're not using them.

Some people recommend using Microsoft's free BootVis tool to analyze your system's boot time and make appropriate changes to speed things up. Although it has some snazzy graphs, it has not been proven to have any noticeable effect on your system's boot time. Of course, because of the interest in this tool, Microsoft has decided to remove it from their site (see *http://www.microsoft.com/whdc/system/sysperf/fastboot/bootvis.mspx*), although you will likely be able to find it elsewhere.

Another thing that can increase boot time is network adapters that aren't plugged in. Windows polls each active network connection on your system when you boot your system and quits as soon as a connection is confirmed. If Windows can't establish a connection, it waits as long as 30 seconds before it gives up and moves on. (You can tell that Windows is doing this when hard disk activity ceases and the activity lights on your network devices start to blink.) To solve this problem, open the Network Connections window (see Chapter 7), right-click on each network connection you're not using, and select **Disable**.

While you're at it, disable any other networking components you don't need, including unnecessary protocols and drivers. Also, disable drive-letter mapping (discussed in Chapter 8) unless you use those drive letters all the time.

Start Windows Instantly

You can optimize Windows all you want, possibly shaving ten to fifteen seconds off your boot time (see the last section), or you can approach the problem from a different angle. Most new computers, and nearly all laptops, have a functional *Stand by* mode, allowing you to shut down Windows quickly, and more importantly, start it back up in only a few seconds.

Start by going to Control Panel and opening Power Options. Choose the **Advanced** tab, and then choose **Stand by** from all available listboxes in your **Power buttons** section, as shown in Figure 5-3. Click **OK** when you're done.

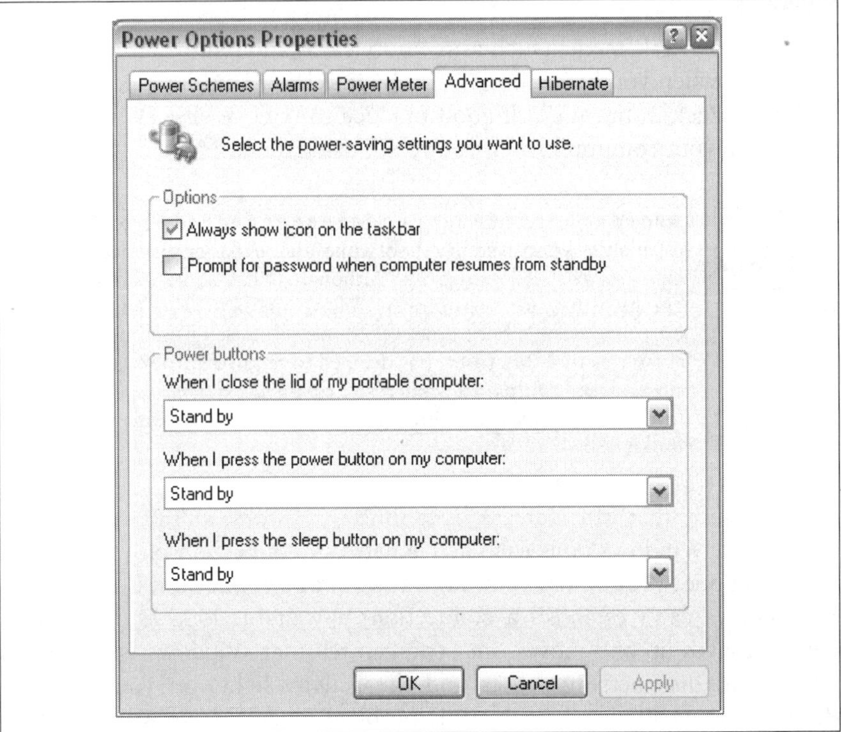

Figure 5-3. Make the Stand By mode more accessible to facilitate near-instant boots

If any of these options (or the entire **Advanced** tab) isn't available in your Power Options Properties window, then your computer's support for Advanced Power Management (APM) is likely disabled in your system's BIOS. See Appendix B for details on APM and APM-related settings, or jump to the next section for APM troubleshooting.

Then, while Windows is still running, press your computer's power switch (or, if it's a laptop, close its lid). Don't go through the normal shut down process via the Start Menu; just turn it off. Windows will briefly display a "Preparing to stand by..." message, and then your computer should shut itself off.

Now, press the power switch again. Your computer should power itself on, and the Windows desktop should appear in less than five seconds, allowing you to pick up where you left off. You can even leave applications open. The problem, of course, is when this doesn't work like it's supposed to, which, as it turns out, is most of the time.

Hibernate vs. Stand by

When you place a computer into Stand by mode, you're placing it into a "deep sleep" power-saving mode (known as the S3 sleep state), instead of actually turning it off. During Stand by, power to your system memory is maintained while power is cut to most of the rest of your system's hardware. This allows your computer to resume to the exact state it was in before it entered Stand by mode with a minimum of power consumption. Unfortunately, if power is cut completely, which can happen if you unplug your desktop system or remove the battery from your laptop, it will be equivalent to powering it off without going through the shutdown procedure, and you may lose data.

The other option is to have your computer enter *hibernation* mode (S4 sleep state), which saves an image of your system memory into a file on your hard disk (known as a *memory dump*) before power to the computer is completely shut off. The obvious benefit over Stand by mode is that the system memory isn't being kept alive with electricity, making it a better choice if you're shutting the computer down for the weekend. The downside is that writing to disk takes more time, as does reading the image file from disk when you wake up the system.

To enable hibernation mode, go to Control Panel → Power Options → **Hibernate** tab (Figure 5-4). Turn on the **Enable hibernation** option, and you'll see that the **disk space required to hibernate** is equal to the amount of installed RAM in your computer.

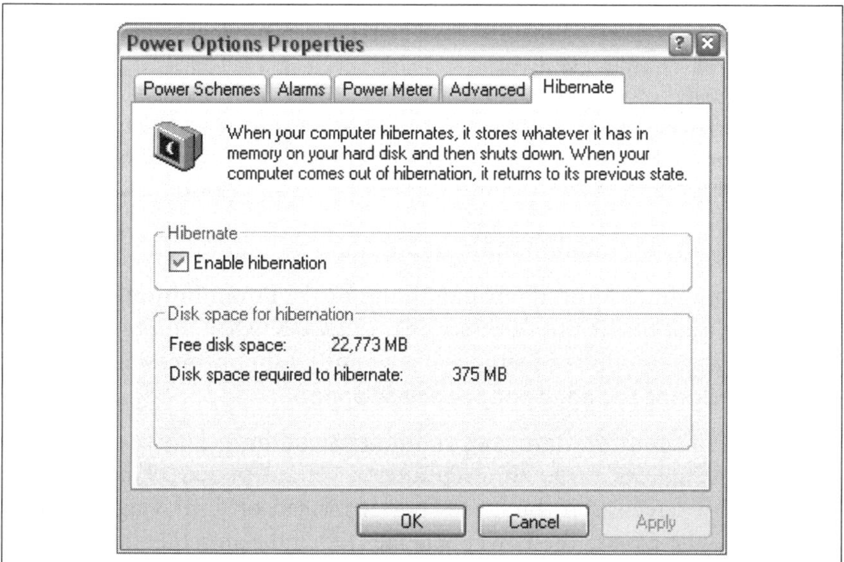

Figure 5-4. Use Hibernate instead of Stand by to enable more robust, yet slightly slower system boots

Other Ways to Wake Your Computer

You can use your computer's power switch to wake up your system from Stand by or Hibernate mode, but it may not be your only choice. Provided that your mouse and its respective driver supports it, you can wake up a sleeping system as though it were nothing but a screensaver. To configure your mouse to wake your system, follow these steps:

1. Open Device Manager (*devmgmt.msc*).
2. Expand the **Mice and other pointing devices** category, right-click the entry for your mouse, and select **Properties**.
3. Choose the **Power Management** tab, and turn on the **Allow this device to bring the computer out of standby** option. (If this Properties box doesn't have a **Power Management** tab, then your mouse driver doesn't support this feature.)
4. Click **OK** when you're done.

These other devices may also be capable of waking up your computer:

Network adapters
: Using the Wake-on-LAN protocol (sometimes called Remote Wake Up), you can wake a computer remotely over a network connection.

Modems
: Wake your computer every time your phone rings. Of course, this may be an annoyance you're trying to solve, rather than a feature you're trying to enable, but, nevertheless, now you know where it is.

IEEE 1394 (FireWire) devices
: Actually, you'll probably never have a reason to enable this option for FireWire controllers or devices, but the option can appear by mistake in some circumstances and can cause problems if it's enabled. Make sure it's turned off on your system.

Next, choose the **Advanced** tab and change all the **Power buttons** options to **Hibernate** (just like in the last section). Click **OK** when you're done. You can make your computer hibernate at any time by simply pressing the power switch (or closing the lid, if you're using a laptop).

Whether you choose to have your computer Stand by or Hibernate, you can configure Windows to go to sleep after a certain period of inactivity. It works like a screensaver, but saves power instead of displaying a cheerful animation. Just choose the **Power Schemes** tab of the aforementioned Power

Options properties dialog, and set the **System standby** (or **System hibernates**) option to a suitable amount of time (e.g., "After 30 mins").

You can also make your computer enter Stand by mode by selecting **Shut Down** (or **Turn Off Computer**) from the Start menu and then selecting **Stand by**. If you're using the classic log-off screen, you'll also see a **Hibernate** option in the list (assuming the option above has been enabled). But if you're using the default Welcome screen and the corresponding Turn Off Computer dialog (discussed in Chapter 8), you'll only see the **Stand by** option. Just press and hold the **Shift** key to temporarily switch the button to Hibernate, should you need it.

Troubleshooting Stand by and Hibernate modes

If you experience a problem with one of the sleep modes (Stand by or Hibernate), it's likely one of the following:

- Windows won't go to sleep at all; either nothing happens when you try to stand by, or the system just crashes in the middle of the process.
- Windows wakes up after going to sleep, or Windows simply boots normally instead of recovering your previous session.
- Some features stop working after waking from hibernation or Stand by, such as the Internet connection. (Hint: restart Windows to fix the problem.)
- Once Windows has been placed in Stand by or Hibernate mode and is then woken up, it's unable to go back to sleep.
- Some or all of the power-management features and settings discussed here are grayed-out (disabled) or missing.

Unfortunately, all of these problems are extremely common, mostly because of the sloppy and inconsistent support for Advanced Power Management (APM) and Advanced Configuration and Power Interface (ACPI) in the computer industry. The good news is that there are a few things you can do to help improve your computer's support for APM and ACPI, should you be experiencing any of the above problems:

Get a BIOS update

Check with the manufacturer of your computer system (or motherboard) for a BIOS update, the most likely fix (if available) for any power-management problems you might be having. See Appendix B for details.

Here's a little Microsoft-sponsored paradox for you: you'll know that your motherboard isn't fully APM-compliant if your Power Options dialog box has an APM tab. If the APM tab is present on your system, try turning on the **Enable Advanced Power Management support** option and then clicking **Apply**. (If there's no tab, then your computer does indeed support ACPI and APM, and you don't have to do anything.)

Look for incompatible hardware or drivers
: The second-most common cause of power-management problems is a hardware device or driver that isn't fully APM-compliant, meaning that it doesn't support S3 sleep mode or can't be woken up after entering this power-saving state. Video cards (display adapters) and many USB devices are common culprits; check with their respective manufacturers for firmware and driver updates (see Chapter 6). See the "Increase the USB Polling Interval" sidebar for another solution.

Make room for the hibernation file
: As explained earlier, the Hibernate feature creates an image file on your hard disk equal in size to the amount of installed memory. If you have 384 megabytes of RAM, then Windows will need 402,653,184 bytes of free space. This feature may not work reliably if you don't have enough disk space, or if there's excessive fragmentation, so try deleting some unnecessary files and running Disk Defragmenter (*dfrg.msc*, discussed later in this chapter) if your PC is having difficulty hibernating.

Turn off the Indexing Service
: If your hard disk won't turn off after a certain period of inactivity, Windows Indexing Service may be keeping them awake. See Microsoft Knowledge Base article 313300 (*http://support.microsoft.com/?id=313300*) for more information.

Use Sleeper
: Go to *http://www.passmark.com/products/sleeper.htm* and download the free PassMark Sleeper utility to help test your computer's ability to enter and recover from sleep and hibernation modes.

Keep in mind that you may never get your system to reliably go to sleep and wake up, but if you are able to get it working, it can be very convenient.

Speed Up System Shutdown

Theoretically, when you shut down Windows, your computer should be powered down in under fifteen seconds. The problem is that all of the cleanup that is done before Windows considers it "safe" to power the

Increase the USB Polling Interval

One of the things that can prevent your computer from entering its Stand by or Hibernate modes is Windows's support for USB. In order to detect newly connected USB devices, Windows polls your USB controller(s) once each millisecond by default. Unfortunately, this frequent polling may prevent your processor from believing that it is idle, a necessary condition before it can initiate any power-saving features.

The solution is to give your CPU a rest by increasing the interval between polls to the USB controller. Open the Registry Editor (see Chapter 3) and expand the branches to `HKEY_LOCAL_MACHINE\SYSTEM\CurrentControlSet\Control\Class\{36FC9E60-C465-11CF-8056-444553540000}`. You'll know you have the right key if its `(default)` value is "Universal Serial Bus controllers."

In this key, you'll find one or more numbered subkeys (e.g. `0000`, `0001`, `0002`), each of which represents a USB controller. Now, if you've ever upgraded the motherboard in your computer, you'll likely see a lot of subkeys here. Most represent controllers no longer installed on your system; only the last couple (with the highest numbers) are likely still active. To find out which ones are currently active, cross-reference the names (in the `DriverDesc` value) with the USB controllers that currently show up in Device Manager (*devmgmt.msc*). If in doubt, you can always repeat this procedure for all the subkeys displayed here.

Select a subkey for an active USB controller, and create a new DWORD value inside (**Edit → New → DWORD value**) called `IdleEnable`. Double-click the new value and set its data to `1`. (To undo this setting, just delete the `IdleEnable` value.) You'll need to restart Windows for this change to take effect.

Maximizing Performance

system down—including shutting down your open applications, stopping any running services, and writing any pending cache data to the disk—can sometimes delay the shutdown procedure.

In the course of using your computer, Windows sometimes postpones writing data to the disk to improve performance. This is called *write caching*, and as a consequence, Windows must take a few seconds before you shut down to make sure all data queued to be written is actually, physically written to the disk before power is lost. See the discussion of removable drives in Chapter 6 for a way to disable this feature.

The following solutions should help eliminate the sometimes-unnecessary delays that can accompany system shutdown.

Part 1: Reduce the hung application timeout

When shutting down, Windows attempts to stop all running tasks. If a task is not responding or refuses to shut down, there's a built-in delay before Windows will force the task to end. This delay is called the timeout, and it can be shortened if you're experiencing problems or unreasonable delays when shutting down your system:

1. Open the Registry Editor (described in Chapter 3).
2. Expand the branches to `HKEY_CURRENT_USER\Control Panel\Desktop`.
3. Double-click the `WaitToKillAppTimeout` value. This number controls the time to wait, in milliseconds, before unresponsive applications are forced to close. The default is `20000` (twenty seconds), but it can be decreased to any value; the minimum is 1 millisecond, although it's impractical to use any value smaller than about `2000` (two seconds) here.
4. Also in this key is the `HungAppTimeout` value, which does pretty much the same thing as `WaitToKillAppTimeout`; just enter the same number for both values.
5. Expand the branches to `HKEY_LOCAL_MACHINE\SYSTEM\CurrentControlSet\Control`.
6. Double-click the `WaitToKillServiceTimeout` value. This works the same as the `WaitToKillAppTimeout` value described above, except that it applies to services instead of applications. See Chapter 7 for more information on services.
7. Close the Registry Editor when you're done. You'll have to restart Windows for the change to take effect.

These values also affect the timeouts at times other than just shutting down, such as when you click **End Process** in the Windows Task Manager.

Part 2: Use the User Profile Hive Cleanup Service

Occasionally, Windows has trouble unloading the hive containing the HKEY_CURRENT_USER branch of the Registry (see Chapter 3). If your system appears to repeatedly take a long time to log out and shut down, download and install Microsoft's UPHClean utility. See Microsoft Knowledge Base article #837115 (*http://support.microsoft.com/default.aspx?scid=kb;en-us;837115*) for details.

Part 3: Have Windows power down your computer automatically

You may have noticed that some computers—especially laptops—are able to power themselves off when you choose **Shut Down** from the Start Menu, rather than displaying the "It's now safe to turn off your computer" screen. This is convenient and makes for faster shutdowns.

In order to configure your computer to behave this way, you'll need the following: if you're using a desktop (as opposed to a portable) computer, you must have an ATX-compliant case and motherboard. You can tell an ATX system from the power button; if it's a momentary pushbutton (that doesn't stay in when you press it), you've likely got an ATX case. The difference is that power switches in ATX systems send a "shut down" command to the motherboard, rather than simply cutting power. All new computers are ATX-compliant, as is any machine that is likely to be capable of running Windows XP.

Secondly, you must have Advanced Power Management (APM) enabled in your system BIOS. Enter your system BIOS setup screen when first starting your computer (usually by pressing the **Del** key), and make sure any options labeled "Advanced Power Management," "APM," or "APM-aware OS" are enabled. See Appendix B for more information on BIOS settings, and the previous section for more details on APM troubleshooting.

If these two conditions are met, Windows should automatically power down your system the next time you shut down.

Eliminate Unwanted Windows Components

Maximizing Performance

In addition to the settings and tweaks described elsewhere in this chapter, a common and effective technique for removing the bottlenecks in Windows is to eliminate the programs and Windows components you don't use.

Most optional Windows components can be removed by double-clicking on the Add or Remove Programs icon in Control Panel, clicking **Add/Remove Windows Components**, and unchecking any unwanted components. Single programs may not seem to make much of a difference, but they do add up. Note, however, that not all optional components are listed here. To add unlisted Windows components to your Control Panel, follow these steps:

1. Start Notepad (or your favorite plain-text editor), and open *\Windows\Inf\Sysoc.inf*.
2. The structure of this file is that of an *.ini* file, discussed in Chapter 3. The `[Components]` section lists the components shown in the Windows Components Wizard. Each entry in this section has this format:

   ```
   name=options
   ```

   where *`options`* is a list of parameters, separated by commas. The second to last parameter is the one that interests us. If it's empty (nothing between the surrounding commas), the corresponding entry will appear in the Windows Components Wizard. Otherwise, if the parameter is `hide`, the entry will not appear. To "unhide" the entry, simply delete the `hide` keyword. For example, the entry for Windows Messenger looks like this:

```
msmsgs=msgrocm.dll,OcEntry,msmsgs.inf,hide,7
```

To add Windows Messenger to the list, allowing you to remove the component, simply change the line so it reads:

```
msmsgs=msgrocm.dll,OcEntry,msmsgs.inf,,7
```

3. When you're done, save the file, and reopen the Windows Components Wizard to see the new entries.

Get the Most Out of Your Games, Speed-Wise

Dude, don't tell me only kids play games. I know you play Freecell more often than you check your email. The catch, of course, is that Freecell spends much more time waiting for you to move a card than it spends on any calculations. Speed is primarily a concern with the more processor-intensive games, such as 3D games or anything with full-screen animation.

Improving game performance, as with improving performance in any other application, involves removing software bottlenecks and upgrading hardware where necessary. However, games are unique in that they can benefit greatly from certain types of hardware, such as 3D accelerators and sound cards with digital signal processors. Games also suffer the most from background applications and out-of-date drivers. Here are some ways to improve performance in the more processor-intensive games:

- Most high-end games rely on DirectX, essentially a set of optimized video, sound, and game input drivers supported by Microsoft. Make sure you have the latest DirectX drivers by using the Windows Update feature (see Chapter 6) or going to *http://www.microsoft.com/directx/*.
- Many games are also optimized to work with specific types of video and sound hardware. For example, a particular game's setup screen might allow you to choose between Direct3D and OpenGL for the video output; sometimes you even need to choose a particular video chipset (e.g., nVidia GeForce4). Your 3D accelerator might support several standards, but a given game might run better using the DirectX drivers, and another game might prefer the OpenGL setting.
- The speed at which a video card can draw to your screen is somewhat dependent on the current color mode and resolution. If your games are running slowly, try reducing the color depth and resolution—either globally in Windows or in a particular game's setup screen (if it supports

it)—to increase the speed. It's funny, though—I've seen some games run smoother in 24-bit mode than 16-bit mode, even though in theory the extra colors should cause a performance hit. Better video cards will not show any performance hit when run at higher resolutions or color depths.

- Games are highly optimized for speed, which tends to make them finicky—a game might run beautifully with one video card but horribly with another. Check the documentation (manual, readme file, online FAQs) released by the game manufacturer for details that may affect you. Also look for updates to the game software that can fix performance issues, as well as add features and even new levels. Check the web sites of both the video card manufacturer and the game manufacturer for tips and patches.
- Most 3D accelerators and even some games allow you to modify or disable certain 3D features, such as 8-bit palletized textures, gamma adjustment, zbuffer, and bilinear filter. In most cases, you'll probably just end up leaving these alone. However, some games might have conflicts with some hardware, and fiddling with these settings may make one or more of your games run smoother. Game fan web sites and discussion boards are the best places to find recommended settings relating to particular games and hardware.
- Any unnecessary background applications should be disabled, either temporarily or permanently. Each program that runs invisibly or in your system tray takes precious CPU cycles away from the processor-intensive games and can make the difference between 20 frames per second and 30 frames per second. See "Speed Up System Startup" elsewhere in this chapter for details.
- If a game runs off a CD or DVD, the Windows Autorun feature, which continually polls the CD drive, can sometimes interrupt data transfer. Symptoms include hiccups in video clips and music and slow loading of levels. See "Curb AutoPlay for CDs and DVDs" in Chapter 4 for details. Note that old CD drives can also cause problems like this. Also, try gently rubbing the disk against a soft, clean cloth (or barring that, your shirt) to remove dust and fingerprints.
- If you're playing a network game, either on a local network or over the Internet, you can improve performance by optimizing your network settings. See Chapter 7 for details.
- Lastly, the performance of high-end games is extremely dependent on game hardware, such as 3D accelerators and sound cards. High-end video and sound cards not only will add features, but also will handle

many of the calculations themselves, freeing up your processor significantly. A good 3D accelerator does more than just make 3D performance acceptable at high resolutions; it can even make the renderings look better, too. Your gaming system will actually benefit much more from a fast 3D card than from a doubling of processor power. Likewise, a good sound card with 3D environmental audio and a good digital signal processor (DSP) can add background sounds that will bring any game alive, without eating up processor cycles. I'm not trying to sell you any hardware, but don't overlook the value of dedicated hardware if you're serious about gaming.

Hard Disk

Your hard disk is more than just a storage device; it's used to hold your operating system and to supplement your system's memory. The speed and health of your hard disk is a major factor in your computer's performance, not to mention its reliability and security. The following topics all deal with different aspects of your hard disk and how effectively Windows uses it.

Inevitably, the storage in your computer will need to be expanded, either to make room for a newer version of Windows, or to make room for all your stuff after installing Windows. Later in this section, you'll find tips on upgrading and repartitioning your hard disk, allowing you to keep your disk and its data in tip-top shape.

A Defragmentation Crash-Course

The best way to ensure maximum performance from your drive is to regularly (weekly or biweekly) defragment it (also called optimizing). Figure 5-5 shows how frequent use of the hard drive can cause files to become fragmented (broken up), which can slow access and retrieval of data on the drive, as well as increase the likelihood of lost data.

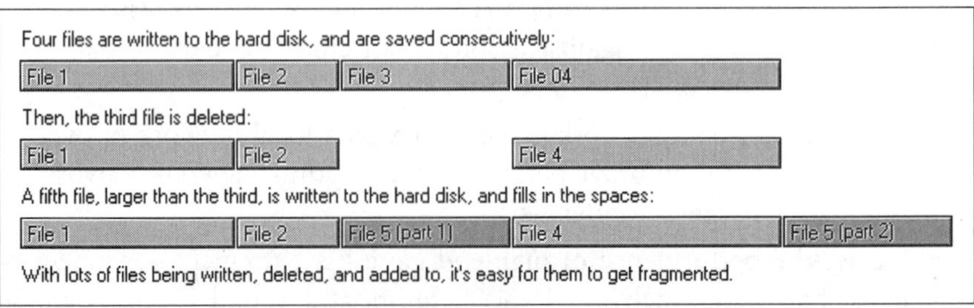

Four files are written to the hard disk, and are saved consecutively:
File 1
File 2
File 3
File 04
Then, the third file is deleted:
File 1
File 2
File 4
A fifth file, larger than the third, is written to the hard disk, and fills in the spaces:
File 1
File 2
File 5 (part 1)
File 4
File 5 (part 2)
With lots of files being written, deleted, and added to, it's easy for them to get fragmented.

Figure 5-5. File fragmentation on your hard disk can slow performance and decrease reliability

To defragment your drive, run the Disk Defragmenter (*dfrg.msc*), which rearranges the files on your hard disk to make them contiguous (not broken into pieces). It also defragments the free space, and optionally places the files you access more frequently (such as programs and recently modified documents) at the start of the drive and less frequently accessed files at the back of the drive.

If you find that Disk Defragmenter is having trouble completing its job, either continually restarting, or simply defragmenting your drive only partially, the culprit may be either of the following:

- To avoid corrupting data, Disk Defragmenter stops what it's doing and restarts whenever it detects that another process has written to the drive. To allow Disk Defragmenter to do its job, make sure to close all nonessential programs and background processes. Also, if necessary, disable the Disk Indexing service by right-clicking the drive icon in Windows Explorer, selecting **Properties**, and turning off the **Allow Indexing Service to index this disk for fast file searching** option.
- If the amount of free disk space is low (less than 15% of the size of the drive), Disk Defragmenter may refuse to run. You can force it to defragment your drive by opening a Command Prompt window (Chapter 10) and typing `defrag` *`c:`* `/F`, where *`c:`* is the drive letter of the hard drive you want to defragment. Better yet, delete some files (see "Increasing Disk Space (or What to Throw Away)") and try again.

If you're compulsive about disk defragmentation, superior alternatives to Disk Defragmenter include Norton Speed Disk (included with Norton Utilities, *http://www.symantec.com*) and Diskeeper (*http://www.executive.com/*).

Maximizing Performance

Enable automatic boot defragments

Here's a funny little setting in the Registry that seems as though it's supposed to instruct Windows to defragment your hard disk automatically each time it starts:

1. Open the Registry Editor (described in Chapter 3).
2. Expand the branches to `HKEY_LOCAL_MACHINE\SOFTWARE\Microsoft\Dfrg\BootOptimizeFunction`.
3. Double-click the `Enable` value, and type `Y` for its data (or type `N` to disable it).

The funny part is that this setting is probably already enabled on your system (it's enabled by default on most XP systems). Now, have you ever seen Windows run Disk Defragmenter at startup?

The reason you don't see it is because it isn't a full defragment. Instead, it's only a boot defragment, which only affects the files registered with the Windows Prefetch feature (see the "Keeping an Eye on Prefetch" sidebar) and listed in the *Layout.ini* file (not a standard INI file). You can perform this boot defragment at any time by opening a Command Prompt window (see Chapter 10) and typing `defrag c: -b`.

> **Keeping an Eye on Prefetch**
>
> Prefetch is a new feature, introduced in Windows XP, that stores specific data about the applications you run, in order to help them start faster. Prefetch is an algorithm that helps anticipate cache misses (times when Windows requests data that isn't stored in the disk cache), and stores that data on the hard disk for easy retrieval.
>
> This data is located in *\Windows\Prefetch*, and, as the theory goes, periodically clearing out the data in this folder (say, once a month) will improve performance. As new applications are subsequently started, new prefetch data will be created, which may mean slightly reduced performance at first. But with older entries gone, there will be less data to parse, and Windows should be able to locate the data it needs more quickly. Any performance gains you may see will be minor (if you see any at all), but those wishing to squeeze every last CPU cycle out of their computer will want to try this one.
>
> Note that deleting Prefetch data may increase boot time slightly, but only the next time you boot Windows. Each subsequent boot should proceed normally, since the prefetch data will already be present for the programs Windows loads when it boots.
>
> If you want to disable Prefetch, open your Registry Editor (Chapter 3), navigate to `HKEY_LOCAL_MACHINE\SYSTEM\CurrentControlSet\Control\Session Manager\Memory Management\PrefetchParameters`, and change the `EnablePrefetcher` value to `0`. (Other supported values: `1` to Prefetch applications only, `2` to Prefetch boot processes, and `3` to Prefetch both.)

Increasing Disk Space (or What to Throw Away)

Parkinson's law states that work expands so as to fill the time available for its completion. Along the same lines, it's safe to say that files will quickly expand to fill the amount of available disk space.

Low disk space doesn't just make it harder to store files, however; without ample room for virtual memory (discussed earlier in this chapter), Windows performance will slow to a crawl. Less disk space also increases file fragmentation, as Windows scrambles to find places to place the data; this, in turn, greatly lowers performance. Keeping a healthy amount of free disk space is vital to a well-performing system.

Additionally, removing drivers and applications that are no longer used clears more memory and processor cycles for your other applications, which can substantially improve overall system performance.

If your PC is low on disk space, try enabling NTFS compression.* Right-click any folder, select **Properties**, click **Advanced**, and turn on the **Compress contents to save disk space** option. Note that this can degrade performance slightly, so you'd be wise to only use it for data that you don't access or modify often.

Even before you install your first application, your hard disk is littered with files from the Windows installation that you most likely don't need. The standard installation of Windows XP puts about 10,000 files in more than 600 folders, consuming more than a gigabyte of disk space.

Whether you need a particular file can be subjective; the 2.5 MB of *.wav* files that one person might consider excessive might be valued by another. Naturally, it makes sense to be cautious when removing any files from your system. The removal of certain files can cause some applications, or even Windows itself, to stop functioning. It's always good practice to move any questionable files to a metaphorical purgatory folder before committing to their disposal. And I don't have to tell you that routinely backing up your entire hard disk (see Chapter 6) is very important. What follows are some tips to help you identify the more common files and folders that can be safely removed, as well as those that should be left alone.

Windows XP files that can be deleted

The following tips apply to files located in your Windows folder or a subfolder thereof. Select **Search** and then **For Files or Folders** from the Start Menu, type `c:\windows` in the **Look in** field (assuming Windows is installed on drive *c:*), and type the filename as described later in the **Search for files or folders named** field. For example, to search for all files with the *.tmp* filename extension, you would use the asterisk wildcard character, like this: `*.tmp`.

Note that this is only a guideline; I'm not instructing you to delete all of these files (okay, maybe I am a little). If you're in doubt about a specific file,

* This feature is only available on NTFS-formatted drives. See "Choosing the Right Filesystem," later in this chapter, for details. It's also mutually exclusive of the **Encrypt contents to secure data** option discussed in Chapter 8.

Disable Disk Cleanup

When your PC starts running out of disk space, Windows will prompt you to run the Disk Cleanup Wizard, which presents a list of some of the files you can delete to recover free disk space (the solutions in this book are much more comprehensive).

To disable this annoying warning, open the Registry Editor (see Chapter 3) and expand the branches to HKEY_CURRENT_USER\Software\Microsoft\Windows\CurrentVersion\Policies\Explorer. If it's not already there, create a new DWORD value (**Edit → New → DWORD value**) called `NoLowDiskSpaceChecks`. Double-click the new value and type `1` for its data. The change will take effect immediately.

see the "If in doubt" section that follows for details on finding out what's inside of most types of files. The following files are typically safe to delete:

- Any file with the filename extension: **.log*, **.old*, **.- - -*, **.bak*, and **.000*, **.001*, **.002*, and so on.
- Any files with the extensions **.bmp* (bitmap files), **.wav* (sound clips), and **.avi* (video clips). These can take up a great deal of space and are usually superfluous.
- In the Windows folder only, there are a ton of text files (**.txt*), which are essentially "Readme" and log files and can be safely deleted. Double-click any text file to view its contents.
- Any files or folders found in your *\Windows\Temp* folder. You won't be able to delete some files in this folder, because they will be in use by whatever applications you may have open. But applications in previous Windows sessions may not have deleted files there, and those types of files tend to accumulate very rapidly. It's not uncommon to find dozens of megabytes of useless files here. If you find files in your *Temp* folder that have a date and time *earlier* than the last time you started your computer, you can safely delete them. See "Mirror a Folder with Folder Shortcuts" in Chapter 4 for more information on the *Temp* folder.
- The following file dates are common to older versions of Windows (releases other than the American English editions may have different dates); some files with these dates may still be around if you've upgraded to Windows XP:

July 11, 1995, 9:50 AM	Windows 95
August 2, 1996, 1:30 AM	Windows NT Workstation 4.0

August 12, 1996, 3:50 PM	Windows 95 OSR2
May 11, 1998, 8:01 PM	Windows 98
April 23, 1999, 10:22 PM	Windows 98 Second Edition
December 7, 1999, 5:00 AM	Windows 2000 Professional
June 8, 2000, 5:00 PM	Windows Me

- See "Mirror a Folder with Folder Shortcuts" in Chapter 4 for more information on all the extra empty folders that Windows won't let you delete.

Files found elsewhere on your system

In addition to those files in your Windows folder, there are plenty of files elsewhere that you can consider deleting:

- There are some unnecessary files in the root directory of your boot drive (usually *c:*); these include files with the extensions **.txt*, **.prv*, **.log*, **.old*, and **.- - -*. Most files with the **.dos* extension (except for *Bootsect.dos*—see "Files NOT to delete" later in this chapter) are also safe to delete.
- Other files that can be deleted include *Mscreate.dir*, an absolutely useless, empty, hidden file created by older Microsoft application installers. There may be hundreds of these empty files on your hard disk.
- Folders named *~Mssetup.t*, *msdownld.tmp*, *WUTemp*, or something similar are temporary folders created when some applications or Windows updates are installed. They can all be removed, as long as you've restarted your computer since said installation took place.
- If you're trying to create more disk space, you can also delete application help files (**.hlp* and **.chm*) you may never need (as a last resort). Also, many applications include bitmaps (**.bmp*), sound clips (**.wav*), and video clips (**.avi*, **.mov*, and **.mpg*), which take up enormous amounts of disk space for virtually no reason. To view a video clip before deleting it, just double-click the file icon.

Files NOT to delete

In your travels, you may encounter some of the following files, all of which should be left alone:

- Any files in your root directory not mentioned earlier should be left alone. This includes *Bootsect.dos*, *Boot.ini*, *Ntldr*, and *Ntdetect.com*, all parts of the Boot Manager (discussed in Chapter 1). You may also see *Io.sys*, *Msdos.sys*, and *Command.com*, if you've set up a dual-boot system with Windows 9x/Me.

- Be extremely careful with anything in the *\Windows*, *\Windows\System*, and *\Windows\System32* folders, as these files may be vital Windows support files.
- Your Registry hive files, discussed in Chapter 3, should never be moved or deleted.
- Any files and folders in your *\Program Files* or *\Windows\MSAPPS* directories that have names like *Microsoft Shared* and *Common Files*. These files can be used by several applications simultaneously, which is why they haven't been placed in the folders of the applications that put them there.

If in doubt

Before you delete any questionable file, there are several things you can do to get a better idea of what the file contains:

- Start by double-clicking a suspicious file to open it in its default application. If you then see the **Open With** dialog box, it means the specific filename extension has not yet been registered. In that case, your best bet is to drag-drop the file into an open Notepad window.
- Right-click the file, and select **Properties**. If the file has a **Version** tab, it's likely an application, driver, DLL, or other support file. Choose it to view the manufacturer, copyright date, and possibly the application it accompanies.
- If you're not sure if something should be deleted but want to try anyway, move it to another directory first to see if everything works without it for a week or so. If all is clear, toss it.
- Check the file's **Last Accessed** date (right-click it, and select **Properties**). The more recent the date, the more likely it's still being used. For information on removing a particular application, contact the manufacturer of that application or refer to the application's documentation.

Special consideration: hidden files

Some files on your hard disk are hidden files—files that, by default, can't be seen in Explorer. To configure Explorer to show hidden files, go to **Control Panel → Folder Options → View** tab, and select the **Show hidden files and folders** option. All hidden files will become visible, but their icons will remain somewhat transparent.

Most hidden files have been hidden to protect them from deletion. If you see a hidden file, think twice before deleting it for this reason. On the other hand, some hidden files are truly unnecessary and are hidden only to reduce the clutter they would otherwise generate. An example is the temporary hidden file Microsoft Word creates alongside every open document.

To hide or unhide a file, right-click its icon and select **Properties**. Check or uncheck the **Hidden** option as desired, and click **OK**.*

Special consideration: System File Protection and System Restore

When I first installed Windows XP, I proceeded to delete the superfluous *Internet Connection Wizard* folder,† as I do whenever I install a new version of Windows. This time, I was in for a surprise—seconds after I deleted it, I saw it reappear as though Windows was telling me, "Just kidding!"

It turned out to be the System File Protection feature, which continually scans your system, replacing system files as it sees fit. Unfortunately, this approach creates several problems, not the least of which is the 12% of your hard drive's total capacity it consumes. See "Working with Restore Points" in Chapter 6 for more information on this feature, as well as on the related feature, System Restore.

If you do decide to disable System File Protection, you can then safely delete the Internet Connection Wizard.

Optimize Virtual Memory and Cache Settings

One of the most frustrating and irritating things about Windows is the way that it can seize up for several seconds with seemingly random, pointless disk activity. This is caused by the way that Windows handles disk virtual memory by default.

Normally, Windows loads drivers and applications into memory until it's full and then starts to use part of your hard disk to "swap" out information, freeing up more memory for higher-priority tasks. The file that Windows uses for this type of "virtual memory" is the paging file (aka swapfile), *pagefile.sys*, and is stored in the root folder of your hard disk.

Because your hard disk is so much slower than physical memory, the more Windows does this swapping, the slower your computer will be. Naturally, adding more memory will reduce Windows's appetite for virtual memory.

* The *Attrib* command in DOS is used to list the attributes of files (e.g., Hidden, Read-only), as well as to turn those attributes on or off. It's also the only way to turn on or off a file's System attribute. See Chapter 10 for details.

† Windows runs the Internet Connection Wizard once: the first time you try to access the Internet after installing Windows XP, regardless of whether you already have a dial-up Networking connection configured. In some cases, you'll see this useless wizard appear again and again.

But regardless of the amount of installed physical memory in your system, there are always things you can do to improve virtual memory performance.

Windows's defaults here are rather conservative and can fortunately be modified for better performance. It's important to realize, though, that some experimentation may be required to achieve the best configuration for your setup. Different hardware, software, and work habits require different settings; those with ample hard disks, for instance, can afford to devote more disk space to virtual memory, while others may simply wish to place a cap on the disk space Windows consumes.

Part 1: Virtual memory settings

One of the reasons the default settings yield such poor performance is that the swapfile grows and shrinks with use, quickly becoming very fragmented (as illustrated by Figure 5-5, earlier in this chapter). The first step is to eliminate this problem by setting a constant swapfile size.

Note that making the swapfile constant will also result in a more constant amount of free disk space. If your hard disk is getting full, consider this solution to restrict Windows from using up every bit of free space:

1. Double-click the System icon in the Control Panel, choose the **Advanced** tab, and click **Settings** in the **Performance** section. Choose the **Advanced** tab here, and then click **Change**. You'll see the Virtual Memory window, shown in Figure 5-6.
2. The virtual memory settings are set for each drive in your system independently. If you have only one drive, virtual memory will be enabled for that drive. If you have more than one drive, virtual memory will be enabled, by default, only on the drive on which Windows is installed.

   For each drive, you have three choices, all of which should be pretty self-explanatory. The total disk space for all drives is shown at the bottom of the window.

   Important: after you've made a change for any drive, click **Set** to commit the change before moving onto another drive or clicking **OK**.
3. To specify a constant size, select **Custom size**, and then type the same value for both **Initial size** and **Maximum size**.

   The size, specified in megabytes, is up to you. I typically use three times the amount of installed RAM (e.g., 1536 MB of virtual memory for 512 MB of physical memory), but you may wish to experiment with different sizes to find the one that works best for you.

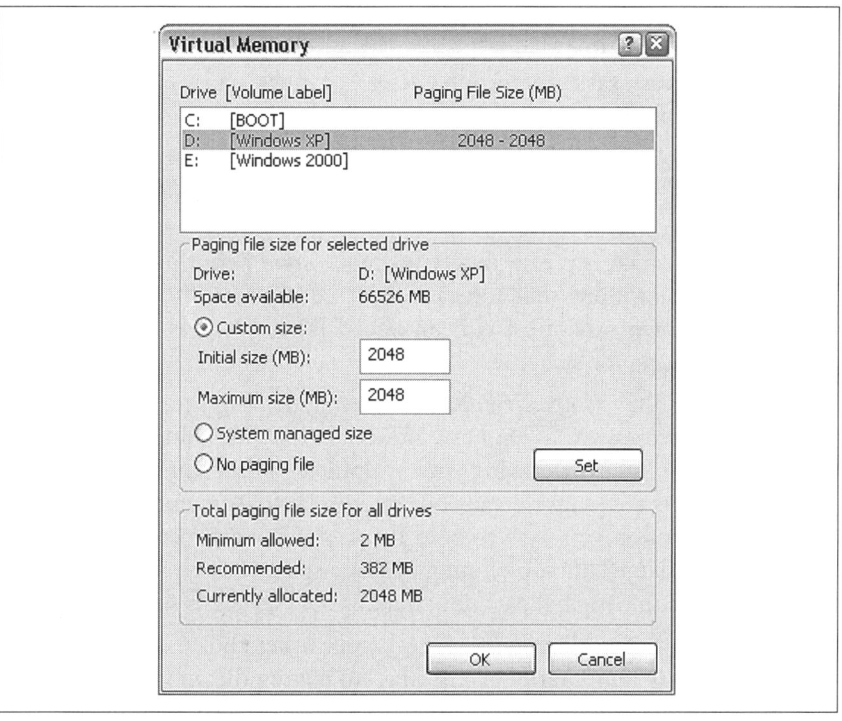

Figure 5-6. Change the way Windows handles virtual memory to improve overall system performance

Some users have had limited success disabling virtual memory altogether, although I wouldn't recommend it. The theory is that if there's enough physical memory installed, and virtual memory is completely disabled, Windows will access the hard disk much less often. It may be worth a try if you have at least 512 MB of physical memory, but you may find that certain programs won't run without at least some virtual memory. It's even possible that eliminating the swapfile will prevent Windows from loading altogether.

4. Press **OK** on each of the three open dialogs. If you have only resized your swapfile, you won't have to restart. However, if you've added (or removed) a swapfile on a different drive, Windows will prompt you to restart at this point.

Part 2: Defragment the paging file

Part 1 will eliminate the possibility of your swapfile becoming fragmented, but it won't defragment an already fragmented swapfile. You'll need to defragment it at least once for it to remain that way in the future. See Figure 5-5, earlier in this chapter, for details on file fragmentation. Note that this is not an easy task if you don't have the right tools. Here are several ways to accomplish this:

- If you have Norton Utilities (*http://www.symantec.com*), you'll be able to optimize the swapfile fairly easily using its Speed Disk utility. Speed Disk is also able to move your swapfile to the physical beginning of your partition, which can also theoretically improve performance. The Disk Defragmenter utility that comes with Windows XP (*dfrg.msc*) is actually a scaled-down version of Norton Speed Disk, but it is not capable of defragmenting the swapfile.
- If you don't have software capable of defragmenting your swapfile, there are two alternatives. If you have more than one partition or hard disk in your system, start by moving your swapfile to a different drive letter (see the previous section for details). Then, run Disk Defragmenter (*dfrg.msc*) on the partition you wish to hold the swapfile permanently, which will set aside a large chunk of contiguous free space. Lastly, move the swapfile back to the original partition, making sure its size is set constant.
- If you don't have a second partition, your other choice is to disable virtual memory temporarily by clicking **No paging file** and then **Set** in the Virtual Memory window (see Figure 5-6). After restarting Windows, run Disk Defragmenter (*dfrg.msc*) to set aside a large chunk of contiguous free space. When you're done, go back to the Virtual Memory window, and re-enable the paging file, making sure to set a constant size.

Note that if you have fewer than 256 MB of physical memory, there is a risk that Windows may not boot properly without a paging file. If this happens, you should be able to load Windows in Safe Mode and re-enable your swapfile. See "What to Do when Windows Won't Start" in Chapter 6 for details.

Part 3: Clear the paging file on shutdown

It's possible to have Windows delete your paging file whenever you shut down Windows. There are three reasons you might want to do this:

- If you have a multiboot system, as described in Chapter 10, each operating system on your computer will have its own virtual memory settings. If the paging file from one OS is present while the other is running, it may cause a conflict and will certainly waste a lot of disk space.
- If your paging file becomes corrupted or highly fragmented, Windows may load more slowly (or not at all). Deleting the paging file will force

Windows to re-create it the next time it starts, which may alleviate this problem.

- If you're concerned about the security of your data, it is theoretically possible for a hacker to extract sensitive information from your paging file.

Naturally, if you've gone through the steps to defragment your paging file, as described earlier in this topic, you probably won't want it to be deleted (lest it become fragmented when it is re-created).

Here's how to do it:

1. Open the Local Security Settings console (*secpol.msc*). See Chapter 7 for more information on the settings in this window.
2. Navigate to `Security Settings\Local Policies\Security Options`.
3. Double-click the **Shutdown: Clear virtual memory pagefile** entry on the right.
4. Select **Enabled** and then click **OK**. You'll need to restart Windows for the change to take effect.

Part 4: Advanced settings for the adventurous

Like virtual memory settings, disk cache settings in Windows XP aren't necessarily optimized for the best performance, but rather for the best compromise between performance and compatibility with older computers.

Each of these settings, as described here, will typically benefit only those with large amounts of physical memory (at least 384 MB). Those with less memory (under 256 MB) may not see any performance increase; in fact, some of these settings may actually degrade system performance if your system has too little RAM. Essentially, you'll want to experiment with different values until you find ones that work best for your system.

Entering incorrect values for some of these settings can render Windows inoperable. Make sure you have a recent backup before you continue, not only of your system, but of the specific Registry key discussed (using a Registry patch, explained in Chapter 3).

Start by opening the Registry Editor (described in Chapter 3) and expanding the branches to `HKEY_LOCAL_MACHINE\SYSTEM\CurrentControlSet\Control\Session Manager\Memory Management`. Some of the more interesting values in this key include the following:*

* If any of the keys listed here are not present, they can be added by going to **Edit → New → DWORD Value** and then typing the name exactly as shown.

`DisablePagingExecutive`

Values: `0` = disabled (default), `1` = enabled

Enabling this setting will prevent Windows from paging certain system processes to disk, which effectively will keep more of the operating system in the faster physical memory, which, in turn, will make Windows much more responsive.

`IoPageLockLimit`

Values: *varies*

This value, in bytes, specifies the maximum amount of memory that can be used for input/output operations. Since this setting deals with the transfer of data into and out of your computer, it will be of the biggest benefit to those running servers and those who use their network or Internet connections most heavily.

The default value is 512 KB (524,288 bytes), but increasing it should improve performance. This value is specified in bytes (not MB) and must be entered in Hexadecimal mode.* Recommended values, based on the amount of physical memory in your system, are shown in Table 5-1.

Table 5-1. Recommended values for the IoPageLockLimit setting

Amount of physical RAM	Recommended value	Maximum value
128 MB	4194304 bytes (4 MB)	physical RAM minus 16MB
256 MB	10485760 bytes (10 MB)	physical RAM minus 32MB
512 MB or more	41943040 bytes (40 MB)	physical RAM minus 64MB

`LargeSystemCache`

Values: `0` = standard (default), `1` = large

By default, Windows uses only 8 MB of memory for the filesystem cache. Enabling this option will allow Windows to use all but 4 MB of your computer's memory for the filesystem cache. This will improve Windows performance, but potentially at the expense of the performance of some of your more memory-intensive applications.

This option can also be changed by going to **Control Panel → System → Advanced** tab, clicking **Settings** in the **Performance** section, and then choosing the **Advanced** tab. The Memory usage section has two

* When editing DWORD Values in the Registry, you can choose the **Base** to use (**Hexadecimal** or **Decimal**). If you use the incorrect base, the value you type will have a different meaning. See Chapter 3 for details.

settings: **Programs** and **System cache**, which correspond to the `0` and `1` values here.

Other values in this key include `PagingFiles`, which is more easily set in the Virtual Memory window described in "Part 1: Virtual memory settings" and `ClearPageFileAtShutdown`, more easily set in the Local Security Settings console, as described in "Part 3: Clear the paging file on shutdown."

Choosing the Right Filesystem

The filesystem is the invisible mechanism on your hard disk that is responsible for keeping track of all the data stored on the drive. Think of the filesystem as a massive table of contents, matching up each filename with its corresponding data stored somewhere on the disk surface. Windows XP supports three different filesystem types:*

FAT (File Allocation Table, 16-bit)
: FAT is used for all drives under 512 MB, including floppy and ZIP disks. The largest drive supported by the FAT filesystem is 2GB, which is why older drives larger than 2GB were often divided into several partitions.

FAT32 (File Allocation Table, 32-bit)
: Designed to overcome the 2 GB partition limit of the FAT system, FAT32 is supported by newer operating systems. In addition to the support for larger drives, it also supports smaller file clusters (described later), so it's more efficient than FAT.

NTFS (NT Filesystem)
: NTFS was designed from the ground up to completely replace FAT/FAT32. It supports encryption, compression, and robust security,† and is typically more reliable than FAT/FAT32 as well.

If Windows XP is the only operating system on your computer, you should be using NTFS—no question. The only compelling reason to use another filesystem is if you have a dual-boot setup with an earlier version of Windows, in which case you'd need to choose a filesystem recognized by all operating systems on your computer. See the "Filesystems and Multiple Drives" sidebar for more information. Table 5-2 shows which filesystems are supported by recent versions of Microsoft Windows.

Maximizing Performance

* There's actually a fourth type, CDFS, used by CD-ROMs.

† The encryption and security features of NTFS are discussed in Chapter 7. NTFS compression is discussed in "Increasing Disk Space (or What to Throw Away)" earlier in this chapter.

Table 5-2. Filesystems supported by recent versions of Windows

	FAT	FAT32	NTFS
Windows XP	✓	✓	✓
Windows 2000	✓	✓	✓
Windows Me, 98, and 95 ORS2	✓	✓	
Windows NT 4.0	✓		✓
Windows 95	✓		

To find out which filesystem is currently being used by a particular drive, just right-click the drive in Explorer (or My Computer), and select **Properties**. Figure 5-7 shows the drive-properties window for an NTFS partition. You can also open the Disk Management utility (*diskmgmt.msc*) to see an overview of all of your drives.

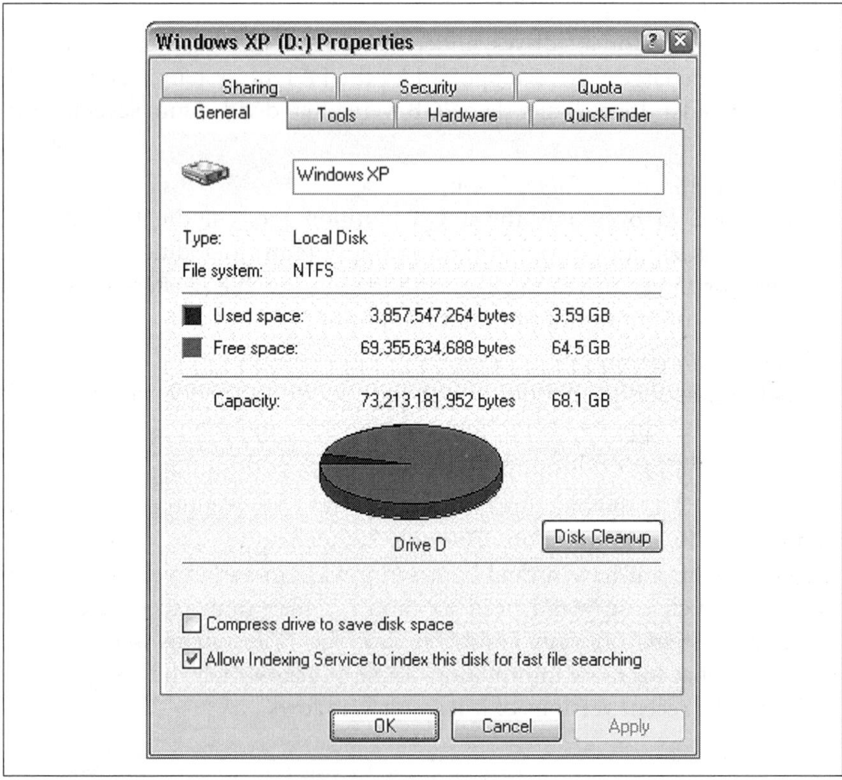

Figure 5-7. Use a drive's properties sheet to see which filesystem it's currently using

Note that some of the elements on the drive-properties window won't be present for non-NTFS drives, such the **Security** and **Quota** tabs and the **Compress drive** and **Allow Indexing** options.

Filesystems and Multiple Drives

If you have more than one drive on your system, whether they're separate physical drives or separate partitions of the same drive, they can have different filesystems. This is common on multiboot systems (discussed in Chapter 1), where each OS will reside on a different partition. Just keep in mind the filesystem compatibility shown in Table 5-2; if you have Windows 98 on a FAT32 partition and Windows XP on an NTFS partition, the XP partition will be invisible to the 98 installation but both drives will be visible and accessible from the XP installation.

Convert your drives to NTFS

If you're not using NTFS on your drive and you don't need to support FAT/FAT32 for compatibility with other operating systems, you can convert your drive to NTFS quite easily, and without harming your data. For example, if you've upgraded to Windows XP from Windows 9x/Me, and you didn't elect to convert your drive(s) to NTFS during setup, you are likely still using FAT32.

Windows XP comes with the FAT to NTFS Conversion Utility (*convert.exe*), which is used as follows. To convert drive *c:*, for example, just open a command-prompt window (*cmd.exe*) and type the following:

```
convert c: /fs:ntfs
```

The following options are also available for this utility:

`/v`
: Run in verbose mode (provide more information).

`/cvtarea:`*`filename`*
: Specifies a contiguous file, *`filename`*, in the root directory as the placeholder for NTFS system files.

`/nosecurity`
: Include this parameter if you want the initial security privileges for all files and folders on the newly converted volume to be set so the files and folders are accessible by everyone.

`/x`
: Forces the volume to dismount first, if necessary closing any opened files on the volume. Use this option if you're on the network and there's concern that other users may attempt to access the drive during the conversion process.

Note that this is a one-way conversion, at least when using the software included with Windows XP. If you need to convert an NTFS drive to FAT32 for some reason, you'll need a third-party utility such as PartitionMagic (*http://www.symantec.com/partitionmagic/*).

Understanding cluster sizes

Clusters are the smallest units into which a hard disk's space can be divided. A hard disk formatted with the traditional FAT system, found in Windows 95 and all previous versions of Windows and DOS, can have no more than 65,536 clusters on each drive or partition. This means that, the larger the hard disk, the larger the size of each cluster. The problem with large clusters is that they result in a lot of wasted disk space. Each cluster can store no more than a single file (or a part of a single file); if a file does not consume an entire cluster, the remaining space is wasted. For example, a 2 GB drive would have a cluster size of 32 KB; a 1 KB file on a disk with a 32 KB cluster size will consume 32 KB of disk space; a 33 KB file on the same drive will consume 64 KB of space, and so on. The extra 31 KB left over from the 33 KB file is called *slack space*, and it can't be used by any other files. With thousands of files (especially those tiny shortcuts littered throughout a Windows installation), the amount of wasted slack space on a sizeable hard disk can add up to hundreds of megabytes of wasted space.

The NTFS and FAT32 filesystems supported by more recent versions of Windows can handle over four billion clusters,* resulting in much smaller cluster sizes. The same 2 GB drive formatted with FAT32 or NTFS will have only a 4 KB cluster size. Figure 5-8 illustrates the slack space created by files stored on a traditional FAT system versus the same files stored on a FAT32 or NTFS drive.

You can see how much space is wasted by any given file by right-clicking on the file icon, selecting **Properties**, and comparing the **Size** value with the **Size on disk** value. The same works for multiple selected files and folders; highlight all the objects in your root directory to see the total amount of wasted space on your drive. To find the current cluster size of your drive, just open the properties sheet for a small file you know will only consume a single cluster (such as a Windows Shortcut); its **Size on disk** will be equal to the size of one cluster.

* Four billion clusters, at 4 KB each, results in a maximum partition size of 14.9 terabytes (15,259 GB) for FAT32 and NTFS volumes. Of course, if this drive were commercially available, its manufacturer would contend that 1 terabyte is equal to 1,000,000,000,000 bytes, and advertise the unit as a 16.4 TB (16,384 GB) drive.

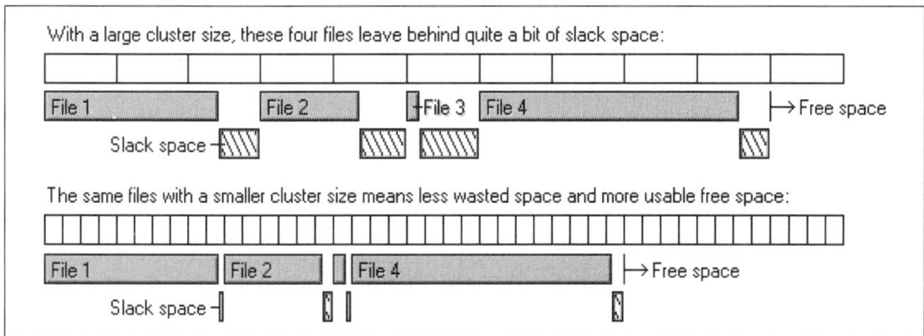

Figure 5-8. FAT32 stores files more efficiently by allowing smaller cluster sizes

So, what does this all mean? It means that if you convert a drive from FAT to FAT32, you will definitely reclaim some wasted space. But, since FAT32 and NTFS drives have the same cluster size (4 KB), there is no slack-space incentive to convert to NTFS. In fact, the extra features of NTFS (discussed earlier in this section) have slightly more overhead, and thus a conversion from FAT32 to NTFS will most likely result in slightly *less* overall free disk space.

Advanced NTFS Settings

As mentioned in the last section, the extra features of the NTFS filesystem come at a price: a small amount of disk space and performance overhead. The following settings allow you to fine-tune NTFS to squeeze the most performance out of your NTFS drive; experiment with these settings to find the configuration that works best for you.

Maximizing Performance

Note that these settings will have no effect for non-NTFS drives. See "Choosing the Right Filesystem," earlier in this chapter, for more information.

Start by opening the Registry Editor (described in Chapter 3), and expanding the branches to `HKEY_LOCAL_MACHINE\SYSTEM\CurrentControlSet\Control\Filesystem`. There are three values here that concern us:*

`NtfsDisable8dot3NameCreation`

Values: `0` = enabled (default), `1` = disabled

Early versions of Windows and DOS did not support long filenames, but rather allowed only eight-character filenames followed by three-letter filename extensions. Although Windows 95 and all subsequent versions of Windows eliminated this restriction,† an eight-dot-three version

* If any of the keys listed here are not present, they can be added by going to **Edit → New → DWORD Value**, and then typing the name exactly as shown.

† Long filenames can be practically as long as you like, and can, for example, include spaces.

of the filename was always generated to maintain compatibility with older applications. For example, the file, *A letter to Mom.wpd* would also be referenced as *alette~1.wpd*. If you don't use older 16-bit programs, either on your computer or on your network, you can disable Windows XP's creation of these 8.3 aliases by changing this value to `1` (the default is zero).

`NtfsDisableLastAccessUpdate`

Values: `0` = enabled (default), `1` = disabled

Windows keeps a record of the time and date every file and folder on your hard disk was created, as well as when it was last modified and last accessed. You can stop Windows from updating the "last accessed" date for folders every time they're opened by changing the value to `1` (the default is zero), which should improve drive performance. This setting has no effect on files.

`NtfsMftZoneReservation`

Values: `1` = small (default), `2` = medium, `3` = large, `4` = maximum

The core of the NTFS filesystem is the master file table (MFT), a comprehensive index of every file on the disk (including the MFT itself). Since disk defragmenters can't defragment the MFT (also known as *$mft*), Windows reserves a certain amount of extra space for it to grow, in an effort to reduce its eventual fragmentation. The more fragmented the MFT gets, the more it will hamper overall disk performance.*

You can determine the current size and fragmentation level of the MFT on any drive by opening Disk Defragmenter (*dfrg.msc*). Select a drive from the list, click **Analyze**, and then **View Report** (see Figure 5-9). The numbers relating to the MFT are shown at the end of the **Volume Information** report. Probably the most interesting statistic here, though, is **Percent MFT in use**. The higher the number, the less space the MFT has to grow (and it will).†

The `NtfsMftZoneReservation` setting allows you to increase the space reserved for the MFT. Although the default is 1, values of 2 or 3 are probably better for most systems with large hard disks; the maximum value of 4 is good for very large drives with a lot of small files. Specify too small of a value here, and the MFT will become fragmented more quickly as it grows; too large of a value, and it will consume (waste) too much disk space.

* See "A Defragmentation Crash Course," earlier in this chapter, for more information.

† For example, a 40 MB MFT file with 88 percent in use has 4.8 MB of empty space reserved for it, which means roughly 4,800 more files can be added to the volume before Windows increases the MFT, probably creating more fragments.

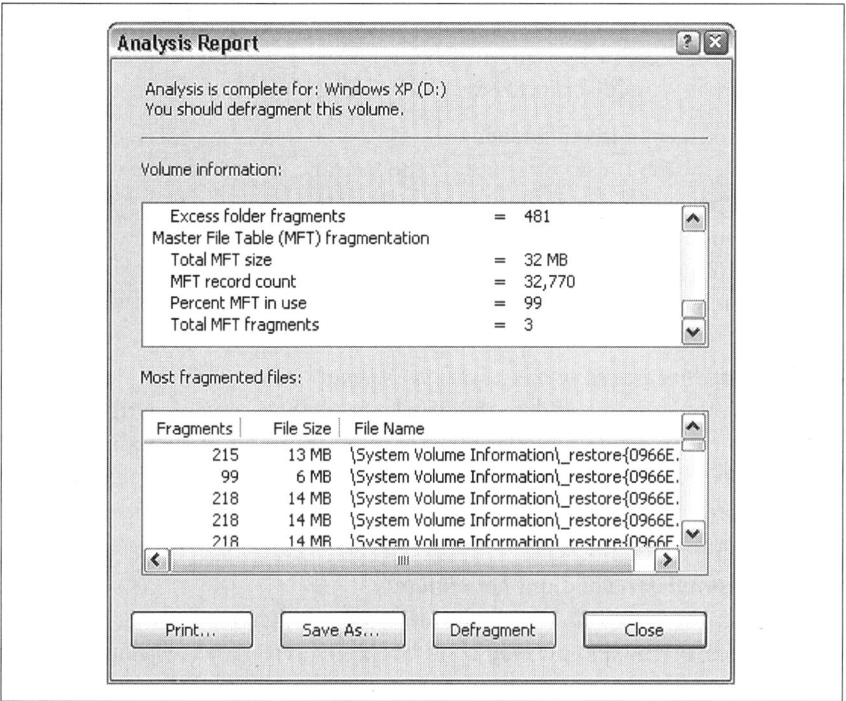

Figure 5-9. Find the size and fragmentation of the Master File Table (MFT) by viewing Disk Defragmenter's report for NTFS volumes

> The problem is that changing this setting will not result in any modification of the current MFT, but rather only influence its future growth. For this reason, the earlier this value is increased in the life of a disk, the better. Unfortunately, the only way to defragment or rebuild the MFT is to format the drive.

You'll need to restart Windows for any of these changes to take effect.

What to Look for in a New Hard Disk

The speed of your hard disk is a major factor of your system's overall performance. After all, the faster it's able to find data and transfer it to your system's bus, the faster Windows will load, the faster your virtual memory will be, and the faster you'll be able to copy files.

If you're thinking of upgrading your hard disk (see "Transfer Windows to Another Hard Disk or System" in Chapter 5), there are several measures of speed that you should scrutinize when choosing a drive:

Seek time (measured in milliseconds)
: The seek time (or access time) is the average length of time required to find a piece of information; lower times are faster. There are a few variants, such as *track-to-track* and *full stroke*, and there are often separate measurements for reading and writing data. But the *average* seek time is the one that is most often advertised; don't settle for anything slower than about 9 ms.

Transfer rate (measured in megabytes per second)
: This is the amount of data the drive can transfer to your motherboard's data bus in a second; higher transfer rates are faster. Although the maximum *burst* transfer rate is the one most often advertised (typically in the hundreds of megabytes per second), the maximum *sustained* transfer rate is probably the more important of the two.

RPM (measured in revolutions per minute)
: This is the speed at which the disk spins; higher numbers are faster. Cheaper drives spin at 5400 rpm, but don't settle for anything less than 7200 rpm. If you're serious about performance, look for a more expensive 10,000 rpm (10k) or 15,000 rpm (15k) drive.

Buffer (measured in megabytes)
: The buffer is memory (RAM) installed in the drive's circuitry, allowing it to accept data from your computer faster than it is able to physically write to the disk surface, and read data from the disk surface faster than it's able to transfer data to your computer. A larger buffer is better; don't settle for less than 8 megabytes.

Whether you're shopping for a new hard drive or just trying to determine if your existing drive is as fast as it should be, these measurements should give you enough to go on. If your drive seems excessively slow, you can either replace it or try some of these solutions:

- Add more RAM (see "Memory" earlier in this chapter).
- Get more free space. Either delete some files or replace your hard disk with a larger one (or add another drive). Regardless of the amount of RAM you have, Windows will still need a substantial amount of space for virtual memory and temporary files. If you run out of space, Windows will slow down and will be more likely to crash.
- Defragment your hard disk by running Disk Defragmenter (*dfrg.msc*).
- Put your hard disk on its own controller, so it isn't sharing the cable with any other drives. For instance, if your hard disk is connected to

your primary IDE controller, plug your CD/DVD drive into your secondary IDE controller.

Scan your system for spyware, discussed at the beginning of this chapter.

Transfer Windows to Another Hard Disk or System

With the release of an operating system as large and power-hungry as Windows XP, it shouldn't be surprising that many users need to upgrade their hard disks—or even their entire systems—just to accommodate the new version.

Either way, some or all of the files on the old hard disk will need to be transferred to the new hard disk, and this can be a difficult task. Sure, you can simply install Windows XP from scratch and then proceed to reinstall all your applications, configure all your settings, and rewrite all your documents, but that's not exactly the most practical solution. Besides, your Freecell statistics would be lost forever.

You can transfer the data from one drive to another (or one system to another) in several ways, explained in the following solutions. The one you choose depends on your available hardware and specific needs. If you just purchased a new hard disk, you need to prepare it by partitioning and formatting it before you continue. See "Working with Partitions," later in this chapter, for details.

Solution 1: Using a disk-cloning utility

The following procedure is probably the most pain-free solution of those in this section, at least in terms of the amount of interaction and work involved. However, you will need to crack open your case and fuss with cables (something you'll have to do anyway if you're only upgrading your hard disk, versus the entire system). Also, it requires that you purchase a third-party utility, although the aggravation and time it saves can offset the cost (even if you only use it this once). Note also that any data on the new hard disk will be lost as it is replaced with the data on the old disk:

1. Obtain a disk-cloning utility such as Norton Ghost (*http://www.symantec.com*).*

If you purchased the product online and have only the downloadable edition, you may have to create a bootable diskette as described in the documentation included with the product you're using.

* Now-defunct alternatives to Norton Ghost include the excellent DriveCopy and Drive Image utilities from PowerQuest (now Symantec). Although they're not commercially available anymore, if you can find XP-compliant versions of either tool (in your closet or perhaps on eBay), they're worth a try.

2. Connect both your old hard disk and your new hard disk to the same computer simultaneously. If you're upgrading to a new system, it usually doesn't matter which computer you use for this process. However, drive configurations in the following list are usually required by this type of utility (see the software's documentation for details):
   - If you're using IDE drives, the old hard disk should be connected as "master" and the new hard disk should be connected as "slave."
   - If you're using SCSI drives, configure the SCSI controller BIOS to boot off the old drive.
   - If you're using one IDE and one SCSI drive, the configuration shouldn't matter.
3. If your disk controller doesn't have enough free ports, just temporarily disconnect a CD drive or other storage device to make room for the new drive.
4. Insert the boot disk from the disk-cloning utility you're using and boot your computer. The program should start up and walk you through the rest of the process. Just be careful when choosing the "from" and "to" drives.

While this sounds complicated, it's actually quite fast, as data transfer between two hard disks on the same system is much faster than over a network or using removable media.

The particular procedure from this point forward depends on the type of disk-cloning utility you chose. There are typically two types:

- The more traditional disk-cloning programs simply copy all data on one drive, byte for byte, to another drive. Any partitions (discussed later in this chapter) are duplicated as well but are expanded proportionally. For example, if you have a 10 GB drive with two 5 GB partitions, and you transfer the data to a 60 GB drive, you'll end up with two 30 GB partitions (which can later be combined, if desired, with the solutions found later in this chapter).
- Newer "image" utilities take a slightly different approach. Instead of copying data between drives, these programs start by creating an *image* of the old drive, which is essentially a single, enormous file that contains every byte of data on the drive. The new drive is then reconstructed from the image.

This can be especially useful if you need to create several exact copies of a single drive, a common practice for network administrators who don't want to spend days individually configuring a bunch of otherwise identical computers.

The problem with this intermediate step is that you need somewhere to store this image file. If you're creating an image of a 10 GB drive with 8 GB of data on it, there will only be 2 GB of free space, which won't be enough to store an 8 GB image file. Since you won't be able to store the image file on the target (new) disk, you'll actually need a *third* hard disk to hold the image.

Solution 2: Use a backup device

If you have a tape drive or other large-capacity backup device, another thing you can do is back up your entire system and then restore it to the new drive. Here's how to do it:

1. Back up your entire system, making sure to include every file on your hard disk. See Chapter 6 for more information on backup devices and procedures.
2. If you're only upgrading your hard disk, shut down your computer, remove the old hard disk, and install the new hard disk. Then, install Windows using the "Installing on a New (Clean) System" procedure in Chapter 1.

   If you're upgrading to an entirely new machine, you'll need to install your backup device on the new system.
3. Install the backup software (the same as the one you used in Step 1) onto the new drive or new system.
4. Restore the files from the backup media onto the new drive, but make sure you restore the entire tree of files into a temporary folder, rather than into the root directory. For example, if your temporary folder is named *Old Hard Disk*, then the path to the restored *Documents and Settings* folder will actually be *\Old Hard Disk\Documents and Settings*. This prevents errors you may encounter trying to replace files and folders in use by the current installation of Windows.
5. When the restore process is complete, selectively (one-by-one) drag the old folders out of your *Old Hard Disk* folder and into the root directory of your new hard disk.

   In the cases of your Windows folders (such as the *\Windows*, *\Program Files*, and *\Documents and Settings* branches), you won't be able to drag them if they're replacing existing in-use folders. Instead, you have two options: either don't copy every folder (instead, only move selected files and folders) or use the following workaround.

Here are the optional additional steps to replace your Windows folders:

1. Start by renaming the three conflicting folders, all still located in the *Old Hard Disk* folder, as follows:
   - *Windows* becomes *oldwin*
   - *Program Files* becomes *oldprogs*
   - *Documents and Settings* becomes *olddocs*
2. Drag the three folders into your root directory, so they're right alongside the folders they're intended to replace.
3. Restart the computer and load the Windows Recovery Console (described later in this chapter).
4. After logging in, issue the commands in the following list:

   ```
   ren Windows newwin
   ren "Program Files" newprogs
   ren "Documents and Settings" newdocs
   ren oldwin Windows
   ren oldprogs "Program Files"
   ren olddocs "Documents and Settings"
   ```

   See Chapter 10 for more information on the `ren` command. Note the use of quotation marks to accommodate the folder names with spaces.
5. Restart your computer when you're done. The old installation of Windows will now be used to start your computer. If you're upgrading to an entirely new computer, Windows will detect a bunch of new hardware the first time it starts.

   The new, temporary Windows installation is now stored in the *newwin*, *newprogs*, and *newdocs* folders, which can be deleted or stored as you see fit.

Alternate Method of Shuffling Restored Files

While we're at it, another way to accomplish all of this is to divide your new drive into two partitions (as discussed later in this chapter). When installing the new copy of Windows, put it on the second partition (usually *D:*). Then, restore the backed-up files onto the first partition (usually *C:*). Since the restore process will replace the *boot.ini* file in the root directory of drive *C:* with the one from your backup, your computer will boot to the restored Windows installation on drive *C:* the next time you restart. You'll then be able to delete the extraneous, temporary second partition. (See "Set up a Dual-Boot System" in Chapter 1 for more information on the *boot.ini* file.)

Solution 3: Transferring data manually

Although the previous two solutions are preferred, since they allow you to move a great deal of data from one drive to another, they're also more involved than the following solution. If you don't really need to move everything from the old drive to the new one, but instead only wish to copy personal documents and perhaps some settings, consider the following tips:

- The File and Settings Transfer Wizard is included with Windows XP for the specific purpose of transferring files from one computer to another. Unfortunately, it doesn't work very well, and can even end up being more trouble than it's worth. Essentially, everything it does can be accomplished manually with a network connection or removable media storage device.
- Be careful when installing two drives in the same computer, as Windows XP has a tendency of permanently changing drive letters in a way that is difficult to undo. For example, if you have two drives, each known as *C:* in their respective computers, and you install both in the same computer, the secondary (or slave) drive will be changed so that it shows up as *D:*, so as not to conflict with the existing drive *C:* that has priority. If you then remove the drive and put it back in the original computer, it will still think of itself as drive *D:*, and may not boot because of it. For this reason, only put the "old" drive in this position, so you don't risk the "new" drive getting "re-lettered." See "Working with Partitions," later in this chapter, for more information on this paradox.
- If you have two separate computers, transferring the files over your network may be the best way to avoid the complexities of hooking up both drives to the same machine. Although the network connection will be slower, it's easier and less risky. See Chapter 7 for more information on networking.
- Since Windows XP won't let you copy certain system files that are in use, you won't be able to copy your Windows Installation simply by dragging and dropping files in Explorer, whether you're using a network connection or removable media drive. To do this, you'll have to use one of the first two solutions in this section. The alternative is to install Windows on the new drive and then find a way to be satisfied copying only some files.
- You can copy user profiles from one computer to another. User profiles are stored in the *Documents and Settings* folder, and include the Desktop, Start Menu, and many personal settings. However, you won't be able to overwrite the user profile in use by the currently logged-in user.

See "Backing Up the Registry" in Chapter 3 for more information user settings, and all of Chapter 7 for more information on user accounts.

- To copy selected settings, such as application toolbars and other personal preferences, you can use Registry patches, as described in Chapter 3.

Working with Partitions

Most hard disks are known by a single drive letter, usually *C:*. However, any hard disk can be divided into several drive letters, known as *partitions*.

For example, if you have an 240 GB hard disk, you may wish to have three 80 GB partitions, or perhaps a 100 GB partition and two 70 GB partitions. There are several reasons why you might want to do something like this:

Organization
: Use multiple partitions to further organize your files. For example, put Windows on one drive, work documents on another, games on another, and music and other media on yet another.

Isolation of system and data
: Partitions can be used to isolate your programs from your data. For example, place Windows on drive *C:*, your personal documents on drive *D:*, and use drive *E:* for your swapfile. This gives you the distinct advantage of being able to format your operating system partition and reinstall Windows without touching your personal data. (See Chapter 8 for help relocating personal folders, such as *My Documents*.)

Performance
: As illustrated in "A Defragmentation Crash Course," earlier in this chapter, your hard drive can become fragmented very quickly, which can decrease performance and increase the chances of data corruption. Because files cannot become fragmented across partition boundaries, splitting your drive into several partitions will isolate groups of files and thus help curb their fragmentation. Plus, in the event that a single partition becomes significantly fragmented, its smaller size will mean it can be defragmented in much less time.

Isolate your swapfile on its own partition to allow it to grow and shrink as needed, without becoming fragmented as it would if it shared a drive with other files. See "Optimize Virtual Memory and Cache Settings," earlier in this chapter, for details.

Dual-boot

To set up a dual-boot partition, described in Chapter 1, you'll want to create a separate partition for each operating system you wish to install.

Multiple users

If you have several users, you can isolate their personal data from the operating system by creating a separate partition for each user.

Web Server

If you're setting up a web server (or other type of network file server) or if you're participating in peer-to-peer file sharing, it's good practice to put the publicly accessible folders on their own partition. This not only helps to secure the operating system from unauthorized access, but allows the OS to be upgraded or replaced without disrupting the shared folders and programs.

Consolidation

If you're using an older computer that has been upgraded to Windows XP, your hard disk may have been partitioned to work around a limitation in the earlier version of Windows (described in "Choosing the Right Filesystem," earlier in this chapter). Using the tools discussed in this section, you can consolidate those drives into a single partition and possibly make more efficient use of your free space.

The Disk Management tool

Windows XP comes with an all-encompassing utility, Disk Management (*diskmgmt.msc*), which is used to view the partition table of any drive on your system, as well as create and delete partitions and even change the drive letters for existing drives.*

The main Disk Management window, as shown in Figure 5-10, is divided into two parts. You can change the arrangement of the panes in this window by going to **View → Top** or **View → Bottom**.

There are three possible views, each displaying some redundant and some unique information, but by default, only the Volume List and Graphical View are shown (in the top and bottom positions, respectively):

Volume List

Use this view to show a summary of all the currently mounted logical drives on your system. This includes all active partitions on all hard disks, as well as any media currently inserted into your removable drives

* Disk Management effectively replaces the FDISK utility, used in some earlier versions of Windows to prepare a hard disk before installing the operating system.

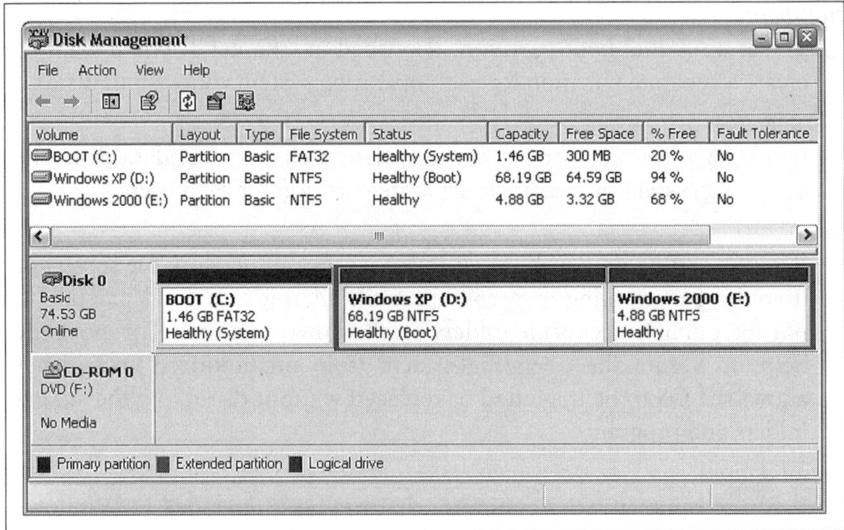

Figure 5-10. Open the Disk Management utility to add or remove partitions, shuffle drive letters, and even change the way volumes are mounted

(which include CD and DVD drives, memory card readers, and removable cartridge drives). Removable drives without media (e.g., an empty CD drive) will not show up here, as these volumes are not mounted. See the subsequent discussion for more information on mounting drives.

This view is called the Volume List because it lists volumes, not disks. The term *volume* is essentially another word for partition. A single disk can contain several volumes (such as the one shown in Figure 5-10), although most hard disks (and all CDs, for instance) only contain a single volume. The way that each volume is accessed in Explorer (usually with a drive letter) is determined by how the volume is mounted (explained below).

Graphical View

Probably the most useful view in Disk Management, the Graphical View lists a single entry for each physical drive in your system. Then, next to each device is shown all of the currently mounted volumes associated with the respective disk.

By default, the boxes representing multiple partitions (volumes) are not sized proportionally to their size (i.e., a 2 GB partition will appear to be roughly the same size as a 10 GB partition). To fix this, go to **View → Settings → Scaling** tab, and choose the **According to capacity, using linear scaling** option in both sections. You can also customize the colors used in the Graphical View by choosing the **Appearance** tab in this dialog.

Disk List

The Disk List is similar to the Graphical View but abandons the display of the volumes for each disk in favor of additional technical information about each disk. The only information displayed here that is not available in the Graphical View is the Device Type (e.g. IDE, SCSI, USB) and Partition Style.*

Hidden

Select this option to turn off the lower pane (it's not available for the upper pane), leaving the remaining selection to consume the entire window.

Press **F5** or go to **Action → Refresh** to refresh all views, necessary if you've inserted or removed a CD, for example. Use **Action → Rescan Disks** for a more thorough refresh.

Feel free to customize the view of this window, but be aware that Disk Management won't save your customization settings, unless you first create a custom console file, described as follows.

Customizing Disk Management

The Disk Management tool is actually what Microsoft calls a "snap-in" for the Microsoft Management Console (MMC) application.† Other snap-ins include Disk Defragmenter, Device Manager, and the Group Policy Editor. The *.msc* file you launched to open the Disk Management tool is not actually the program, but rather just a small *console* file, which contains only the settings for the current view. The following procedure not only shows how to create a new console file that you can customize in a way that be saved, but shows how to create custom console files for all sorts of purposes.

1. Open the Microsoft Management Console (*mmc.exe*). A new, blank "Console Root" window will appear in the MMC window.
2. Go to **File → Add/Remove Snap-in**, and then click **Add**.
3. Select **Disk Management** from the **Available Standalone Snap-ins** list, and then click **Add**.
4. Another window will appear, giving you a choice between **This Computer** and **The following computer**. Although it's possible to view the partition table to another computer using a network connection, you'll want to choose **This Computer** for the time being.

* For nearly all disks on a Windows system, the Partition Style will be MBR (Master Boot Record). The exception is GPT (GUID partition table) drives, used by Windows XP 64-Bit Edition.

† For more information on the Microsoft Management Console, as well as the available snap-ins, see *Windows XP in a Nutshell* (O'Reilly).

5. You can add other snap-ins at this point, or simply click **Close** when you're done. Finally, click **OK** to close the Add/Remove Snap-in window.
6. Highlight the Disk Management entry in the tree in the left pane, and then go to **View → Customize** and turn off the **Console tree** option to simplify this window. You won't want to hide the console tree if you added more than one snap-in in the previous step. Figure 5-11 shows a custom console file with a bunch of useful snap-ins, all accessible from the same window.

Figure 5-11. If you find yourself using Disk Management or other MMC snap-ins frequently, you can create your own custom console file to provide quicker access to your favorite tools

7. You can further customize this window as you see fit. When you're done customizing, go to **File → Save** to save your custom console view into a new *.msc* file.

The next time you use the Disk Management tool, just open your custom *.msc* file instead of the *diskmgmt.msc* file included with Windows XP.

Mounting volumes

As stated in the previous section, a hard disk can have one partition or many. Other types of storage devices, such as CD drives, only have single partitions. These partitions, regardless of the nature of the physical device on which they're located, are all recognized as *volumes* by the Disk Management tool and by Windows Explorer.

Mounting is the method by which a volume is made accessible to Explorer and all your applications. In most cases, each volume has its own drive

Alternatives to the Disk Management Tool

The Disk Management utility is not your only choice when it comes to repartitioning drives, but as far as the tools included with Windows XP are concerned, it's the best one.

One alternative is the DiskPart utility (*diskpart.exe*), a way of viewing, adding, and removing partitions from the command prompt. DiskPart is essentially the command-line equivalent to the Disk Management tool, although it has a few extra features (see "Resizing and moving partitions," later in this section). The biggest advantage to DiskPart is that it can also be run from the Windows Recovery Console, discussed later in this chapter. This allows you to modify your boot and system partitions, as well as work on your partition table when Windows XP won't start.

The other alternative is the disk partitioning tool built into Windows Setup. It's quick and simple, but it's only available while installing Windows XP. See "Installing the Operating System" in Chapter 1 for more information.

Finally, PartitionMagic (*http://www.symantec.com/partitionmagic/*) is a third-party utility, discussed in other parts of this chapter, that allows you to resize existing partitions on the fly, and without erasing the data they hold—something Disk Management can't do.

letter, such as *C:* or *D:*. But a volume can also be accessed through a folder on a different volume, called a mount point (NTFS only). Finally, there can be volumes on your system that aren't mounted at all, typically including volumes with filesystems[*] not recognized by Windows XP and volumes simply not currently in use. Such unmounted drives will be shown in the Disk Management window but won't appear in Windows Explorer.

You can change how any volume on your system is mounted,[†] except for the system volume (the one containing your boot files) and the boot volume (the one on which Windows is installed).[‡] This is one of the reasons I like to partition my disks into several partitions: so I can more easily make changes to

[*] See "Choosing the Right Filesystem" in for more information on filesystems. Examples of filesystems not supported by Windows XP include Linux and Unix partitions

[†] In some earlier versions of Windows, the drive letters of hard disks were controlled by DOS, but in Windows XP, you have much more control. See the "Designate Drive Letters" solution in any of my earlier *Annoyances* books for more information on the limitations involved in the assignment of drive letters in Windows 9x/Me systems.

[‡] Note that the naming of the boot and system volumes is counterintuitive. The DiskPart utility, described later in this section, can be used to operate on the boot and system volumes.

my *other* drives as needed. With all my data on the same volume as Windows, I would have very little flexibility in this area.

In most cases, changing how a volume is mounted involves changing the drive letter. The easiest way to start is to change the drive letter of a removable or CD drive, and since applications are typically not installed on removable drives, there shouldn't be any adverse effects. For example, Figure 5-10, shown earlier in this chapter, shows a system with a DVD drive set to *F:*, a recordable CD drive set to *R:*, and a digital camera memory card reader set to *X:* (drives *R:* and *X:* are not shown).

To change the drive letter of any volume on your system, start by right-clicking any volume in the Graphical View or Volume List, and select **Change Drive Letter and Paths**. The Change Drive Letter and Paths dialog, as shown in Figure 5-12, lists the mount points for the selected volume. A volume can have as many mount points as you like, but only one of them can be a drive letter. (A volume can also have no drive letter or even no mount points at all.)

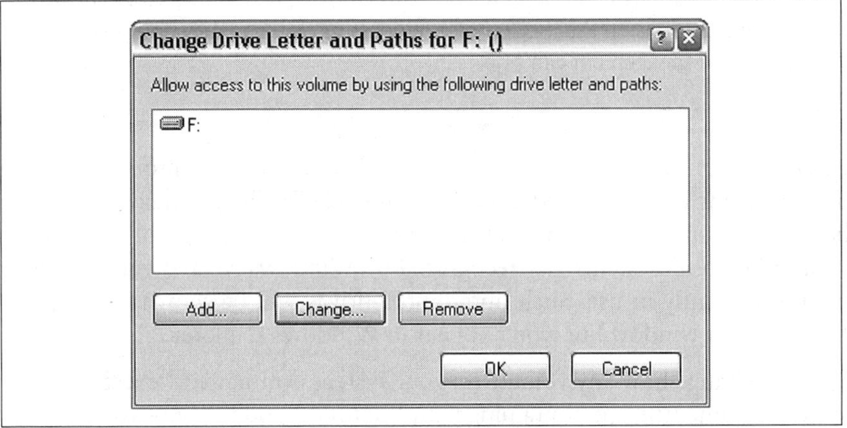

Figure 5-12. You can change the drive letter for any device, as well as as mount the volume as a folder on another drive, using the Change Drive Letter and Paths dialog

Click **Add** to display the Add Drive Letter or Path dialog. Here, you'll have two choices:

Assign the following drive letter
: Select this option and then choose an unused drive letter from the list to mount the drive using the selected letter. If the selected volume already has a drive letter, this option will be grayed out, and you'll have to select the drive letter in the previous dialog and select either **Change** or **Remove**.

The only roadblock you may encounter when trying to change a drive letter is when one or more applications are installed on the drive in question. You should still be able to change the drive letter, but said application(s) may no longer work on the newly lettered drive.

Mount in the following empty NTFS folder

This option is used to link up the volume with a folder on a different drive. For example, say the current volume already is using the drive letter *E:*. If you were to mount the volume in the folder *d:\backdoor*, then the contents of *E:* would be identical to the contents of *d:\backdoor*, and *e:\some folder* would be the same as *d:\backdoor\some folder*.

Any drive on your system can be mounted in this way, but the mount point (the target folder) must be on an NTFS drive (discussed in "Choosing the Right Filesystem," earlier in this chapter) and must be empty. You can even mount a CD in a folder on your desktop. You can view all of the drives mounted in folders by going to **View → Drive Paths**.

There are a few reasons why you might want to do this. For example, if your hard disk is running low on space, and you don't wish to take the time to replace it and transfer all your data over (as described in "Transfer Windows to Another Hard Disk or System," earlier in this chapter), you can install a new drive and mount it in, say, your *Documents and Settings* folder. That way, the role of storing all personal files will be assumed by the new drive, and the old drive should regain a great deal of disk space.

Features similar to this one include network-drive mapping, explained in Chapter 7, and Folder Shortcuts, explained in Chapter 4.

Maximizing Performance

Creating and deleting partitions

Every hard disk must be partitioned before it can be used, even if that disk is to have only a single partition.

During the installation process, explained at the beginning of this chapter, the disk-partitioning utility included with Setup allows you to partition the drive on which Windows is to be installed before the files are copied. From within Windows, the Disk Management tool is used to create and delete partitions. The following procedure shows how to create and delete partitions with Disk Management, although the methodology applies to either tool.

1. Open the Disk Management tool (*diskmgmt.msc*). Make sure the Graphical View, explained in the previous section, is visible.

2. Select the physical drive you wish to partition. Any existing partitions (volumes) for the current drive will be shown to the right. At this point, you can delete or add partitions, or change the drive letters (as explained previously).
3. To delete a partition, right-click the blue box representing the partition and select **Delete Partition** or **Delete Logical Drive**.

   This option will be grayed out if you're trying to delete the system volume (the one containing your boot files) or the boot volume (the one on which Windows is installed).*

If you delete a partition, all the data on that volume will be permanently lost. This happens immediately, and there is no undo. Data on other partitions of the same drive, however, won't be affected. If you wish to make a partition smaller or larger without erasing the data, see the "Resizing and moving partitions," which follows.

4. To create a new partition, right-click the green box representing the remaining free space on the drive, and select **New Partition** or **New Logical Drive**.
5. A wizard will appear, asking several questions about the new volume, including how much space to use, what kind of volume to create, and which filesystem to use.

   When choosing the size of the volume, you can specify any size you want, from only a few megabytes to the total amount of contiguous free space on the drive. As for the filesystem, you'll want to use the NTFS filesystem in most cases (see "Choosing the Right Filesystem" earlier in this chapter).

   The type of volume to create is probably the most confusing setting here. The three volume types,† as illustrated in Figure 5-13, are explained in the following list.

   Primary partition

   The first partition on a drive should always be a primary partition. If all your partitions are to be used by Windows, then there should never be more than one primary partition on a drive. The exception is when you're setting up a dual-boot system, as described later in

* Note the counterintuitive naming of the boot and system volumes. You can use the DiskPart utility, described later in this section, to operate on the boot and system volumes.

† There are actually other partition types, but such types are only available with dynamic disks, which are beyond the scope of this topic.

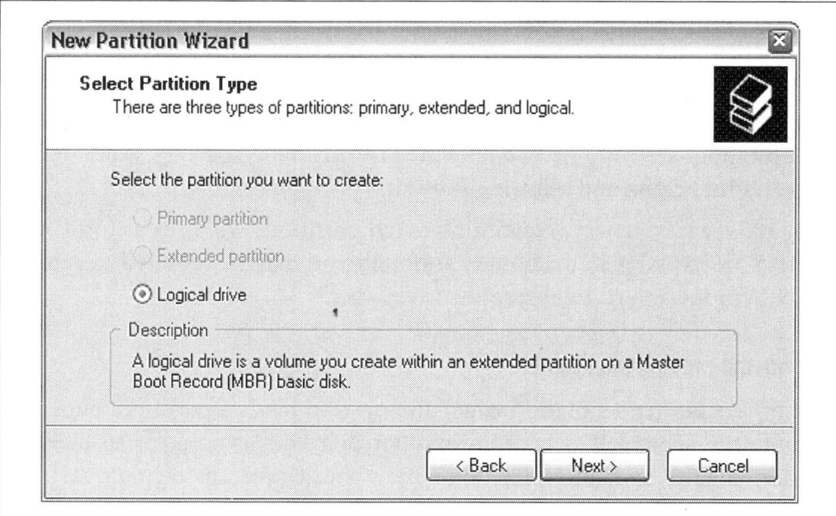

Figure 5-13. There are three basic types of partitions, each used under a specific circumstance

this chapter, where each non-Windows OS will need it's own primary partition. You can have up to four primary partitions on a drive, or up to three primary partitions and one extended partition.

If you have more than one drive, each drive should have one primary partition. Additional partitions should be defined as "logical drives."

Primary partitions are, by default, shown in dark blue.

Extended partition

The extended partition does not actually contain data; it only encapsulates the logical drives (below). A drive can contain only one extended partition.

The extended partition is, by default, shown in green, and only appears as a thick stripe surrounding any defined logical drives.

Logical drive

If you want more than one partition on a drive, the second, third, fourth, and so on, should all be defined as logical drives (since the first is a primary partition). You must define an extended partition before you can create any logical drives.

Logical drives are, by default, shown in light blue, and appear within the green box representing the extended partition.

For example, to create three 10 GB partitions on a 30 GB drive, you would create one 10 GB primary partition, followed by one 20 GB extended partition. Then, you'd create two 10 GB logical drives in the extended partition.

6. Disk Management will typically format new partitions as they're created (a required step if you wish to store data on them). However, you can format any volume (which will erase any data currently stored on it) by right-clicking and selecting **Format**.
7. In most cases, newly created or deleted partitions will appear (or disappear) in Explorer immediately, although you may be required to reboot for Windows to recognize some drive types.

Resizing and moving partitions

You may encounter a situation when you need to resize a partition, either to consume the space left over from another deleted partition, or to make a partition smaller to make room for a new one. Unfortunately, support for this type of partition manipulation is extremely limited with the tools included with Windows XP.

Now, the simplest way to resize a partition is to delete it and then create a new one. Unfortunately, this has the rather undesirable side effect of completely erasing any data stored on the volume.

There is, however, one case where you can resize a partition in Windows XP without erasing the data contained therein. Say you have three 10 GB partitions on a 30 GB drive (just like the example in the previous section). If you delete the third partition, it's possible to "extend" the second one so that it will consume the newly available free space. Note that a volume can only be extended to the "right"—using the paradigm employed by the Graphical View in the Disk Management tool. (If you haven't yet deleted the extraneous volume, do so now using Disk Management.):

1. Open a Command Prompt window (*cmd.exe*), and type `diskpart` at the prompt to start the DiskPart utility.*
2. At the `DISKPART>` prompt, type:

   ```
   list disk
   ```

   to display all the drives on your computer. Each disk will have a disk number, starting with 0 (zero). Unless you have only one drive, you'll have to tell DiskPart which drive you wish to modify. Do this by typing:

   ```
   select disk n
   ```

* For some reason, the "extend" feature is not available in the Disk Management tool, which is why we must use the other disk partitioning tool included with Windows XP, DiskPart.

where *n* represents the number of the disk you wish to modify. For example, type `select disk 0` to select the first disk.

3. Next, at the `DISKPART>` prompt, type:

```
list volume
```

to display all the volumes on the selected disk. Each volume will have a volume number, starting with 0 (zero). Even if you have only one volume on this drive, you'll have to tell DiskPart which volume to extend by typing:

```
select volume n
```

where *n* represents the number of the volume you wish to modify. For example, type `select volume 2`. Remember, there must be free space immediately *after* the selected volume for this to work (double-check this by using Disk Management's Graphical View).

Why It's Difficult to Resize Partitions

When it comes to resizing partitions, the disk partitioning tools in Windows XP are only able to make them larger, and then only in specific circumstances. But why the limitation?

The reason for this is fairly simple. Open Disk Defragmenter (*dfrg.msc*), select a volume with a lot of files on it, and click **Analyze**. You'll then see a map—labeled **Estimated disk usage before defragmentation**—showing how the files are physically distributed on the selected volume. Notice how they appear to be scattered throughout the volume from beginning to end (left to right, respectively)? Using Disk Defragmenter (see "A Defragmentation Crash Course") will reduce the scatter somewhat, but it's designed mainly to rearrange files to improve performance, rather than prepare a partition to be resized.

The process to "extend" a volume, explained in this section, simply involves moving the partition boundary to the right, and as long as it doesn't hit another partition (or the end of the drive), there should be no problem.

In order to make a partition smaller, however, Windows would have to rearrange the files so that sufficient free space is grouped into a single, contiguous block at the very end of the partition. That way, the partition boundary could be moved to the *left*, making the partition smaller, without losing any file data. Unfortunately, neither the Disk Management or DiskPart tools are capable of this advanced manipulation, which is why you'll need another tool, such as PartitionMagic, to accomplish this.

4. When you're ready, type

   ```
   extend
   ```

   to extend the volume. The `extend` command takes no options and displays no warning message or confirmation. The process begins immediately after pressing the Enter key and should take only a few seconds.
5. When it's done, type `exit` to quit the DiskPart utility, and then type `exit` again to close the Command Prompt window.

Unfortunately, resizing a partition in the opposite direction (i.e., shrinking a volume)—without erasing its data—is not supported by Disk Management or the DiskPart utility. For this, you'll need the PartitionMagic utility (available at *http://www.symantec.com/partitionmagic/*), which can not only expand and shrink partitions, but move them as well—all without erasing the data they contain. PartitionMagic can even be used to make changes to the system and boot volumes, something that neither Disk Management nor DiskPart will let you do.

System Hardware

Not every performance problem can be fixed from within Windows. Here are some things you can do to your hardware to improve performance.

Managing IRQ Priority

Most components directly attached to your motherboard, including PCI slots, IDE controllers, serial ports, the keyboard port, and even your motherboard's CMOS, have individual IRQs assigned to them. An IRQ, or interrupt request line, is a numbered hardware line over which a device can interrupt the normal flow of data to the processor, allowing the device to function. Windows XP allows you to prioritize one or more IRQs (which translate to one or more hardware devices), potentially improving the performance of those devices:

1. Start by opening the System Information utility (*msinfo32.exe*) and navigating to `System Summary\Hardware Resources\IRQs` to view the IRQs in use on your system.
2. Next, open the Registry Editor (see Chapter 3) and navigate to `HKEY_LOCAL_MACHINE\SYSTEM\CurrentControlSet\Control\PriorityControl`.
3. Create a new DWORD value in this key, and call it `IRQ#Priority`, where # is the IRQ of the device you wish to prioritize (e.g., `IRQ13Priority` for IRQ 13, which is your numeric processor).

4. Double-click the new value, and enter a number for its priority. Enter `1` for top priority, `2` for second, and so on. Make sure not to enter the same priority number for two entries, and keep it simple by experimenting with only one or two values at first. Some users have gotten good results prioritizing IRQ 8 (for the system CMOS) and the IRQ corresponding to the video card.
5. Close the Registry Editor and reboot your computer when you're done.

Overclock Your Processor

The processor is the highest-profile component (at least where marketing is concerned), as a fast processor often translates into a fast overall computer, especially with respect to games. But processors also become obsolete the fastest, and given how expensive they can be, it's often smart *not* to buy the fastest processor available.

Now, a processor's clock speed is just one of several factors upon which overall system speed is dependent. For example, jumping from a 1.5 GHz CPU to a 3 GHz unit will *not* double the speed of the computer. In fact, clock speed can be very misleading; a dual 800-Mhz system may outpace a 1 Ghz system, and a 1.4 GHz Pentium-III may outpace a 1.4 GHz Pentium-4. So keep this in mind when deciding how to spend your time and money on performance enhancements. That said, you may be able to squeeze a little more life out of your existing CPU at a fraction of the cost of a new one.

Maximizing Performance

Overclocking is the process of instructing your processor to run at a higher clock speed (MHz) than its rated speed.* For example, you may be able to overclock a 900 MHz chip to run at 950 MHz, or even faster. Supposedly, Intel and other chip makers have taken steps to prevent overclocking (theoretically prompting purchases of faster CPUs instead), but some motherboard manufacturers have found ways to do it anyway. Settings allowing you to overclock your CPU can be found in your BIOS setup (see Appendix B), assuming your motherboard supports it.

Now, over-overclocking a CPU (overclocking past the point where it's stable) can cause it to overheat and crash your PC frequently. The most important aspect of overclocking your system involves cooling; make sure you beef up your computer's internal cooling system if you plan on messing around with overclocking. (Obviously, your options will be limited here if you're using a laptop.)

* There's also the lesser-known practice of under-clocking a CPU. While this may seem silly, it's done to decrease power consumption and increase battery life on portable computers.

Increase your CPU's speed in stages, if possible; don't start off with the fastest setting, or you may end up with a fried processor and lightly singed eyebrows.

If you feel that your system isn't adequately cooled, don't be afraid to add more fans. Some fans connect directly to special plugs on your motherboard, and are activated when internal thermometers detect too high of a temperature; these do a good job of cooling your system without generating excessive noise. Fans that connect to your power supply's drive cables run all the time, and will make more noise, but will do a better job of cooling your system. Peltier cooling units (also known as thermoelectric heat pumps) will do a great job without making any noise, but they are expensive and a little hard to find.

CHAPTER 6

Troubleshooting

Most Windows users would probably consider the barrage of incomprehensible error messages and crashing to be the operating system's biggest annoyance, and I'd be the last one to argue with them. But the problems that plague our computers vary widely from simple features not working to massive data loss, with a whole range of annoying quirks in between.

No single resource could possibly document every bug and every error message produced by Windows and every possible combination of drivers and applications, and this chapter is no exception. Instead, the topics in this chapter use many of the more common problems to show you how to troubleshoot your Windows system by isolating the problem and then using the tools available to find a solution.

First off, if you remember only two pearls of wisdom from this chapter, let them be the following:

1. 99% of all computer problems are solved by pressing your computer's Reset button.
2. Insanity can be defined as repeating the same actions over and over again, expecting different results. (Or, worse, repeating the same actions over and over again, *knowing* that you'll never get different results.)

Naturally, a corollary to these principles is that resetting your computer repeatedly will get you nowhere. Herein lies the rub: what do you do during that remaining 1% of the time when restarting your computer doesn't help?

General Troubleshooting Techniques

Troubleshooting a computer involves more than just whining about it. One of the first things you need to do to solve a problem is to find the right words to describe the problem. You don't know how many people have come to me simply saying, "It doesn't work." I have to prod them to find what they did (or didn't do), whether or not they received an error message, if they saw smoke billowing out of one of their drives, or if the computer simply didn't do what they expected.

Like it or not, most problems are simply caused by poorly written software. As soon as you remove yourself (the user) as a potential cause of the problem, it makes it much easier to track down the real source of the problem and fix it.

Computer problems can come in many forms: error messages, crashes, lock-ups, unexpected results, and corrupted data. A crash is usually accompanied by a cryptic error message of some sort (General Protection Fault, Blue Screen of Death, etc.), followed by having the application—or the entire operating system—shut down abruptly. A lock-up is what happens when an application (or Windows) stops responding to the mouse and keyboard; sometimes you can recover from a lock-up (often by pressing **Ctrl-Alt-Del** or just waiting a few seconds), and sometimes you can't.

Much of this chapter focuses on some specific problems and their solutions, but most troubleshooting requires nothing more than a little reasoning. If you're looking for a chart of every conceivable error message and its cause, you're out of luck: such a thing simply doesn't exist. There are infinitely many combinations of computer systems, add-on devices, application software, and drivers; unfortunately, some of those combinations can be fraught with headaches. However, later in this chapter, you'll find a list of common BSoD (Blue Screen of Death) error messages, typically considered the most extreme you'll encounter.

The most important step—and usually the most difficult—in troubleshooting a computer system is to isolate the problem. Here are some questions to ask yourself when you're trying to isolate a problem:

Is this an isolated incident, or does this problem occur every time I perform some action?

As much as Microsoft will deny it, crashing is a fact of life on a Windows system, even when using Windows XP (although some users will swear up and down that their systems are "rock-solid").

An isolated incident is often just that, and, if nothing else, is a good reminder to save your work often. On the other hand, if a given error message or crash repeatedly occurs at the same time, in the same place, or as a result of the same mouse click, you need to be aware of that fact if you hope to solve the problem.

Did I install or remove any software or hardware around the time this problem started occurring?

Sudden changes in your computer's behavior are almost never spontaneous; if something suddenly stops working, you can bet that there was a discernible trigger.

Is the problem with a specific application or hardware device, or is Windows at fault?

You can rule out specific applications if the crash or another problem doesn't just occur in one program. You can rule out most hardware by removing or disabling the unnecessary devices attached to your system. And you can rule out Windows by installing a second copy of the operating system on a different drive, as described in Chapter 1.

Did I read the directions?

Unfortunately, a well-designed interface is still something not implemented by many software manufacturers these days, so if you're not getting the results you expect from your word processor, printer, scanner, mouse, web browser, or other hardware device or application, make sure that you have read the directions (and release notes) that accompany such products and that the product in question is installed properly. Also, software manufacturers frequently release updates and fixes, so it's always a good idea to check to see if you have the latest versions of all applications and drivers. See "Dealing with Drivers and Other Tales of Hardware Troubleshooting," later in this chapter, for details.

How likely is it that someone else has encountered the same problem I have?

This is often the most useful question to ask, because the odds are that someone else not only has encountered the same problem (anything from an annoying software quirk to a deafening application crash), but has already discovered a solution and written about it in some online forum. For example, there's a Windows XP discussion forum at *http://www.annoyances.org* for specifically this purpose!

Am I asking the right people?

If you just installed a new version of America Online and now your Internet connection doesn't work, you shouldn't be calling your plumber. On the other hand, nothing compares to trying to convince a technical support representative that the problem you're experiencing is actually *their* company's fault and *not* someone else's.

Am I using the latest version of the software or drivers for the product in question?

Most manufacturers routinely place software patches, updated drivers, and other fixes on their web sites. In many cases, the manufacturer has fixed the problem you're having and all that's left to do is download and install the new version.

The last tidbit of wisdom comes from years of experience. Some problems require hours and hours of fruitless troubleshooting and needless headaches. In some cases, it makes more sense to replace the product that's giving you trouble than to try to fix it. Keep that in mind when it's four o'clock in the morning, and Windows refuses to recognize your ninety-dollar scanner.

Where to Go from Here

More specific troubleshooting information can be found throughout this book:

Software issues
: The first part of this chapter is devoted to software troubleshooting, such as issues involving starting and shutting down Windows, error messages, and crashes.

Hardware issues
: See "Dealing with Drivers and Other Tales of Hardware Troubleshooting," later in this chapter, for topics such as hardware conflicts and Plug and Play issues. This is followed by "Fixing Device-Specific Problems," which covers each device in your system, one by one.

: See also Chapter 7 for help with troubleshooting a network or Internet connection.

Backups and data recovery
: In addition to isolating and solving problems, the other important aspect of troubleshooting involves data loss caused by those problems. See "Preventive Maintenance and Data Recovery," later in this chapter, for details on what do when a problem is bad enough to corrupt or erase important documents or other data, and how to protect yourself from this eventuality.

Specific Software Issues

Once you start peeking under the hood of Windows XP, you'll notice some of the tools that have been included to help the system run smoothly. Some of these tools actually work, but it's important to know which ones to use and which ones are simply gimmicks. A good example is System Restore, a feature intended to solve certain file-version conflicts automatically; its brute-force method often ends up causing more problems than it solves. See the discussion of System Restore later in this chapter for details.

Here are some software-specific issues that should help you solve most problems with Windows XP and the applications that run on it.

Patching Windows with Windows Update

If software manufacturers waited until their products were completely bug-free before releasing them, then we'd all still be using typewriters.

Windows XP has a fairly automated update system, wherein patches to the operating system that Microsoft considers to be important are made available on their web site and, by default, automatically downloaded and installed on your computer.

Just open Internet Explorer (other web browsers won't work) and visit *http://www.windowsupdate.com* (or go to **Tools → Windows Update**) to load the Windows Update program. Click **Scan for updates** to compile a list of the updates you haven't yet installed from which you can selectively download those updates you want or need.

This is a fairly straightforward procedure, and one you should do regularly. Here are a few tips to improve your experience with this tool:

Disable automatic Windows Update

Depending on your settings, Windows XP may routinely activate the Windows Update feature to scan for and download updates to Windows XP automatically. If you have a fast Internet connection and usually don't remember to check for updates yourself, you'll probably want this feature turned on. However, if you already check for updates and would rather not have Windows interrupt you while you work, you'll probably want to disable automatic updating by going to **Control Panel → System → Automatic Updates**.

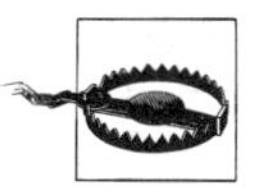

Even if you've enabled full automatic updating, Windows XP may only install critical updates. It's a good idea to check with Windows Update manually to make sure the updates you want are installed.

See the "Block Service Pack 2" sidebar for a way to take advantage of automatic updates without automatically updating Microsoft's Service Packs.

Block Service Pack 2

Microsoft distributes its service packs through the Windows Update service. This means that if you have the Automatic Updates feature enabled, your system may download and install SP2 (or a subsequent Service Pack) without your knowledge or express permission. This can cause serious problems, both in the installation process itself and in the subsequent use of the new version of Windows.

(Service Pack 1, released in 2001, gained an unfavorable reputation for the fact that this 250+ megabyte update was automatically installed on many Windows XP systems, whether or not your computer had sufficient free disk space.)

Fortunately, there's a way to block Windows Update, at least temporarily, from installing Service Pack 2 on your system:

1. Open the Registry Editor (described in Chapter 3).
2. Expand the branches to `HKEY_LOCAL_MACHINE\Software\Policies\Microsoft\Windows`.
3. If it's not already there, add a new subkey to this branch (**Edit → New → Key**) and name it `WindowsUpdate`.
4. Open the new `WindowsUpdate` key.
5. Add a new DWORD value (**Edit → New → DWORD Value**) and name it `DoNotAllowXPSP2`.
6. Double-click the new `DoNotAllowXPSP2` value and type `1` for its data. Click **OK** and close the Registry Editor when you're done.

Now, here's the catch: Microsoft will only respect this setting until April 12, 2005. After that time, Windows XP SP2 will be "delivered" (as Microsoft puts it) to all Windows XP and Windows XP Service Pack 1 systems.

In order to block Service Pack 2 *permanently*, you'll have to disable the Automatic Updates feature, and then subsequently only install updates by manually visiting the Windows Update web site.

Dealing with missing files

During the installation of updates, Windows may occasionally inform you that it can't find one or more files. This, of course, is a bug in the installer, but the workaround is easy. Open a Search window (see "Fix the Search Tool" in Chapter 2), and type the name of the specified file in the **All or part of the file name** field. If the file is already on your hard disk, it will show up in the search results; just type the full path of the folder containing the file into the **Copy files from** field, and click **OK** (or **Retry**). In most cases, such files will already be on your system, typically in the *\Windows\System32* and *\Windows\System32\drivers* folders.

Whether or not to install Driver Updates

For the most part, it's a good idea to install all of the updates in the **Critical Updates** and **Windows XP** categories, but use your judgment when installing items in the **Driver Updates** category. The drivers recommended in here (typically only for devices already using a Microsoft drivers) may be older than the ones you're using, or may even be inappropriate for your hardware. If Windows Update is recommending a driver update, check with the manufacturer of the corresponding device and install their latest driver instead.

Managing Windows Updates for a large number of computers

If you're a system administrator and are responsible for a large number of Windows XP machines, you may not want your users to have access to Windows Update. Otherwise, you may have to deal with increased network traffic whenever a new update becomes available, and you may have to clean up the mess left behind by a bad update.

The solution lies in Microsoft's Software Update Services (SUS), a system by which administrators can deploy critical updates to their Windows XP and Windows 2000–based systems. More information on SUS can be found at *http://www.microsoft.com/windows2000/windowsupdate/sus/*.

One other way to prevent your users from accessing the Windows Update site is to set up firewall rules to restrict access to the server. You can also set up the *hosts* file on each computer to redirect any requests to *www.windowsupdate.com* and *windowsupdate.microsoft.com* to a different location, as described in "Managing the Nameserver (DNS) Cache" in Chapter 7.

Download updates for installation on other computers

If you have more than one XP machine to update, you may not want to download the same updates again and again. Start by loading Windows Update, as described earlier. Then, click **Personalize Windows Update** on the left side and turn on the **Display the link to the Windows Update Catalog under See Also** option. Finally, click **Windows Update Catalog** (which should now appear to your left) to enter the catalog and selectively download self-installing updates.

What to Do when Windows Won't Start

Unfortunately, Windows's inability to start is a common problem, usually occurring without an error message or any obvious way to resolve it. Sometimes you'll just get a black screen after the startup logo, or your computer may even restart itself instead of displaying the desktop. Of the many causes of this problem, many deal with hardware drivers, conflicts, or file corruption—all of which are discussed elsewhere in this chapter.

In previous versions of Windows, up until Windows 98, one could start a DOS session before loading Windows, which was a gateway to several effective troubleshooting techniques. In Windows XP, this lifeline is gone, but, fortunately, there are several other tools in place to take up the slack:

Windows Recovery Console
: The Windows Recovery Console, discussed later in this chapter, is a way to repair your operating system or boot manager. It also lets you delete or replace system files, something not possible from within Windows. Use the WRC when Windows won't start at all.

Safe Mode with Command Prompt
: The Safe Mode with Command Prompt, explained in "How to Delete or Replace In-Use Files" in Chapter 2, is somewhat of a hybrid of the Windows Recovery Console and a standard Command Prompt window. (It's also described later.) Use it to effect minor repairs when the Windows Recovery Console is overkill.

In either case, you'll get a Command Prompt interface that allows you to copy, move, rename, or delete files, as well as start certain programs. The specific steps you take depend on what you're trying to accomplish.

If you don't know where to start, you'll probably want to scan your hard disk for errors, since corrupted files can prevent Windows from loading. See "Check Your Drive for Errors with Chkdsk," later in this chapter, for details.

The other choice you have, instead of using one of these Command Prompt variants, is to use one of Windows's built-in troubleshooting startup modes. Press the **F8** key when Windows begins to load (or during the Boot Manager menu, if you're using a dual-boot system, as described in Chapter 1). You'll see a menu with the following choices:

Safe Mode (also with Networking support or Command Prompt)
: This forces Windows to start up in a hobbled, semifunctional mode, useful for troubleshooting or removing software or hardware drivers that otherwise prevent Windows from booting normally.

Enable Boot Logging
: This starts Windows normally, except that a log of every step is recorded into the *ntbtlog.txt* file, located in your *\Windows* folder. If Windows won't start, all you need to do is attempt to start Windows with the **Enable Boot Logging** option at least once. Then, boot Windows into Safe mode (or Safe mode with Command Prompt) and read

the log with your favorite text editor (or Notepad). The last entry in the log is most likely the cause of the problem.

Enable VGA Mode
: Start Windows normally, but in 640×480 mode at 16 colors. This is useful for troubleshooting bad video drivers or incorrect video settings by allowing you to boot Windows with the most compatible display mode available.

Last Known Good Configuration
: This starts Windows with the last set of drivers and Registry settings known to work. Use this if a recent Registry Change or hardware installation has caused a problem that prevents Windows from starting.

Directory Services Restore Mode
: Used only if your computer is a Windows NT domain controller.

Debugging Mode
: This option, typically of no use to end-users, sends debug information to your serial port to be recorded by another computer.

Start Windows Normally
: Use this self-explanatory option to continue booting Windows normally, as though you never displayed the **F8** menu.

Lastly, you should look for error messages, both fleeting ones that quickly disappear, and ones displayed when the Windows startup procedure comes to a screeching halt. See the next section for details.

Error Messages During Startup

You may have seen a strange message when loading Windows, either during the display of the Windows logo screen or after the taskbar appears. Many different things can cause this, but there are a few common culprits. If you're having trouble starting Windows, see "Where to Go from Here" earlier in this chapter.

A driver won't load
: When Windows starts, it loads all of the installed drivers into memory. A driver may refuse to load if the device for which it's designed isn't functioning or turned on, if there's a hardware conflict, if the driver itself isn't installed properly, or if the driver file is misconfigured or corrupted in some way. If you remove a device, make sure to take out the driver file as well—even if it isn't generating an error message, it could be taking up memory. See "Dealing with Drivers and Other Tales of Hardware Troubleshooting" later in this chapter.

A program can't be found

After Windows loads itself and all of its drivers, it loads any programs configured to load at startup. These include screen savers, scheduling utilities, Palm HotSync software, all those icons that appear in your notification area (tray), and any other programs you may have placed in your *Startup* folder or that may be been configured to load automatically in the system Registry. If you removed an application, for example, and Windows continues to attempt to load one of its components at startup, you'll have to remove the reference manually. See "Programs Run by Windows when It Starts" later in this chapter, for details.

A file is corrupt or missing

If one of Windows's own files won't load and you're sure it isn't a third-party driver or application, you may actually have to reinstall Windows to alleviate the problem. I'll take this opportunity to remind you to back up frequently.

An error message of this sort will usually include a filename. To help isolate the problem, write down the filename when you see the error message, and then try searching your hard disk for the reported file, as well as looking for places where the file may be *referenced* (see "Programs Run by Windows when It Starts" later in this chapter for details). If you don't know what the error means exactly, you should definitely do both; a lot can be learned by finding how and where Windows is trying to load a program. However, if you know that the file or files are no longer on your system, you can proceed simply to remove the reference.

Conversely, if you know the file *is* still on your system and you want to get it working again, you'll probably need to reinstall whatever component or application it came with in order to fix the problem. Once you've located a particular file, it may not be obvious to which program it belongs. You can usually get a good clue by right-clicking on the file, selecting **Properties**, and choosing the **Version** tab.

Please wait while Windows updates your configuration files

This isn't an error but rather a message you may see occasionally when Windows is starting. It simply means that Windows is copying certain files that it couldn't otherwise copy while Windows was loaded, most often as a result of software being installed during the last Windows session. For example, if a program you install needs to replace an old DLL in your *\Windows\System32* folder with a newer version, but the DLL is in use and can't be overwritten, the program's setup utility will simply instruct Windows to do it automatically the next time it's restarted. The mechanism responsible is discussed in the discussion of the *Wininit.ini* file in "How to Delete or Replace In-Use Files" in Chapter 2.

If the name of a driver, service, or application is specified in the error message, there are three places you can look for more information:

- In the startup log, *ntbtlog.txt*, located in your *\Windows* folder. See "What to Do when Windows Won't Start," earlier in this chapter, for details.
- In the Event Viewer (*eventvwr.msc*); open the **System** branch, and then sort the listing by clicking the **Source** column header.
- In one of the places Windows looks for startup programs, discussed in the next section.

Silence the error messages altogether

Obviously, the best way to deal with a startup message is to fix the cause. But if you can't locate the problem (or if you just don't want to bother), you can suppress many of the messages completely:

1. Open the Registry Editor (discussed in Chapter 3).
2. Expand the branches to: `HKEY_LOCAL_MACHINE\SYSTEM\CurrentControlSet\Control\Windows`.
3. Create a new value by going to **Edit → New → DWORD Value**, and type `NoPopupsOnBoot` for the name of the new value.
4. Double-click the new `NoPopupsOnBoot` value, enter `1` for the **Value data**, and click **OK**.

Note that this solution treats the symptoms rather than the underlying problem and, in doing so, may mean you might miss an important error message later on.

Troubleshooting

Programs Run by Windows when It Starts

Any driver or program that Windows loads when it boots will be listed in at least one of the following places. Access to these locations is useful not only for adding your own startup programs, but eliminating ones that are either causing problems or are simply unnecessary and slowing down the boot process.

The Startup folder
: Your *Startup* folder (usually *\Documents and Settings\{username}\Start Menu\Startup*) contains shortcuts for all the standard programs you wish to load every time Windows starts. You should routinely look for—and eliminate—shortcuts to outdated or unwanted programs. If you're not sure of the application with which the shortcut is associated, right-click it, select **Properties**, and then click **Find Target**.

The Registry

There are several places in the Registry (see Chapter 3) in which startup programs are specified. Such programs are specified here for several reasons: to prevent tinkering, for more flexibility, or—in the case of viruses, Trojan horses, and spyware—to hide from plain view.

These keys contain startup programs for the current user:

```
HKEY_CURRENT_USER\SOFTWARE\Microsoft\Windows\CurrentVersion\Run
HKEY_CURRENT_USER\SOFTWARE\Microsoft\Windows\CurrentVersion\RunOnce
```

These keys contain startup programs for all users:

```
HKEY_LOCAL_MACHINE\SOFTWARE\Microsoft\Windows\CurrentVersion\Run
HKEY_LOCAL_MACHINE\SOFTWARE\Microsoft\Windows\CurrentVersion\RunOnce
```

The naming of the keys should be self-explanatory. Programs referenced in either of the `Run` keys listed above are run every time Windows starts. Likewise, an entry referenced in one of the `RunOnce` keys is run only once and then removed from the key.

Services

The Services window (*services.msc*) lists dozens of programs especially designed to run in the background in Windows XP. The advantage of services is that they remain active, even when no user is currently logged in. That way, for example, your web server can continue to serve web pages when the Welcome screen (or Log On dialog) is shown.

By default, some services are configured to start automatically with Windows and others are not; such information is found in the **Startup Type** column. Double-click any service and change the **Startup type** option to **Automatic** to have it start with Windows, or **Manual** to disable it.

However, changing the **Startup type** for a service won't load (start) or unload (stop) the service. Use the **Start** and **Stop** buttons on the toolbar of the Services window, or double-click a service and click **Start** or **Stop**. For an example, see the discussion of Universal Plug and Play in "Closing Back Doors in Windows XP" in Chapter 7.

The WIN.INI file

Although it's uncommon, you may occasionally see a program referenced at the top of the *WIN.INI* file, on the lines that start with `LOAD=` or `RUN=`. See "Using INI Files" in Chapter 3 for details on the structure of files of this type.

Although you may want to disable or eliminate unwanted startup programs in an effort to solve a problem or just improve system performance, you should not blindly disable any program you don't immediately recognize. Keep in mind that some of the startup programs referenced in the Registry and some of the services configured to start automatically are there for a reason, and are required for Windows XP to function. See "Programs Commonly Running in the Background," later in this chapter, for a list of programs you should not close with the Task Manager.

In many cases, it should be obvious what a particular startup program is for. If not, try these steps:

1. Search your system for the filename(s) specified. Once you find it, right-click it, select **Properties**, and choose the **Version** tab. The manufacturer name, and sometimes the product name, will be listed here. If there's no **Version** tab, it means the file has no version information, which may suggest that it's a virus or some form of malware (see the next section).
2. Search Google (*http://www.google.com*) for the filename. In nearly all cases, you'll find a web site that describes what it's for and, in the case of malware, how to remove it.

Among Google's search results, you'll likely encounter some sites that specialize in cataloging startup programs, both benign and malicious, commonly found on Windows systems. Two of the best are *http://www.processlibrary.com/* and *http://www.2-spyware.com/files.php*, both of which allow you to search their databases by filename.

3. If you have a hunch it doesn't belong, try temporarily relocating it.

   If it's a shortcut in your Startup folder, move the shortcut to a temporary folder rather than deleting it, allowing easy retrieval if it turns out to be necessary. Likewise, for entries in your Registry, create a Registry patch (see Chapter 3) of the entire Registry key in question before removing the questionable entry. If anything goes wrong, you can reapply the Registry patch to restore the setting.
4. Restart your system, and look for abnormalities (as well as normalities). If all is well, you can probably discard the removed entries.

Viruses, Malware, and Spyware

Malware, or *mal*icious soft*ware*, is a class of software specifically designed to wreak havoc on a computer. Malware includes such nasty entities as viruses, Trojan horses, worms, and spyware.

If you're experiencing frequent crashing, nonsensical error messages, pop-up advertisements (other than when surfing the Web), or slower-than-normal performance, the culprit may be one of the following types of malware (as opposed to a feature authored by Microsoft):

Viruses

A virus is a program or piece of code that "infects" other software by embedding a copy of itself in one or more executable files. When the software runs, so does the embedded virus, thus propagating the "infection." Viruses can replicate themselves, and some (known as polymorphic viruses) can even change their virus signatures each time to avoid detection by antivirus software.

Unlike worms, viruses cannot infect other computers without assistance from people (aka you), a topic discussed in detail in the next section. One particular type of virus, a Trojan Horse, spreads itself by masquerading as a benign application (as opposed to *infecting* an otherwise valid file), such as a screensaver or even a virus removal tool.

Worms

A worm* is a special type of virus that can infect a computer without any help from its user, typically through a network or Internet connection. Worms can replicate themselves like ordinary viruses, but do not spread by infecting programs or documents. A common example is the *W32.Blaster.Worm*, which exploited a bug in Windows (eventually fixed as part of update #824146), causing it to restart repeatedly or simply seize up.

Spyware, adware, and rootkits

Spyware is a little different than the aforementioned viruses and worms, in that its intent is not necessarily to hobble a computer or destroy data, but rather something much more insidious. Spyware is designed to install itself transparently on your system, spy on you, and then send the data it collects back to an Internet server. This is sometimes done to collect information about you, but most often to serve as a conduit for pop-up advertisements (known as adware).

* The term *worm* is said to have its roots in J.R.R. Tolkien, who described dragons in Middle Earth that were powerful enough to lay waste to entire regions. Two such dragons (Scatha and Glaurung) were known as "the Great Worms." The *Great Worm*, a virus written by Robert T. Morris in 1988, was particularly devastating, mostly because of a bug in its own code. *Source: Jargon File 4.2.0.*

Rootkits are a particularly dangerous class of spyware, designed to hide their presence from conventional spyware-detection tools, typically by integrating themselves with the operating system kernel. Rootkit removel often requires formatting the hard disk. Visit *http://www.rootkit.com* for news of the latest rootkit threats.

Aside from the ethical implications, spyware can be particularly troublesome because it's typically very poorly written and, as a result, ends up causing error messages, performance slowdowns, and seemingly random crashes. Plus, it uses your computer's CPU cycles and Internet connection bandwidth to accomplish its goals, leaving fewer resources available for the applications you actually want to use.

Now, it's often difficult to tell one type of malicious program from another, and in some ways, it doesn't matter. But if you understand how these programs work—how they get into your computer and what they do once they've taken root—you can eliminate them and keep them from ever coming back.

How malware spreads

Once they've infected a system, viruses and the like can be very difficult to remove. For that reason, your best defense against them is to prevent them from infecting your computer in the first place.

The most useful tool you can use to keep malware off your computer is your cerebral cortex. Just as malware is written to exploit vulnerabilities in computer systems, the *distribution* of malware exploits the stupidity of users.

Malware is typically spread in the following ways:

Email attachments

One of the most common ways viruses make their way into computers is through spam. Attachments are embedded in these junk email messages, sent by the millions to every email address in existence, which unsuspecting recipients click, open, and execute. But how can people be that dumb, you may ask? Well, consider the filename of a typical Trojan horse:

kittens playing with yarn.jpg   .scr

Since Windows, by default, has its filename extensions hidden (see "File Types: The Link Between Documents and Applications" in Chapter 4), most people wouldn't see that this is an *.scr* (screensaver) file and not a photo of kittens. (The long space in the filename ensures that it won't be easy to spot, even if extensions are visible.) And since most spam

Troubleshooting

filters and antivirus programs block *.exe* files, but not *.scr* files (which are just renamed *.exe* files, by the way), this innocuous looking file is more than likely to spawn a nasty virus on someone's computer.

So, how do you protect yourself from these? First, don't open email attachments you weren't expecting, and manually scan everything else with an up-to-date virus scanner (discussed later in this section). Note that you may also want to employ a spam filter to throw away most of these messages before they reach your in-box. (If you're worried about valid messages being deleted as well, use a filter that only marks suspected spam instead of deleting it, such as SpamPal, available at *http://www.spampal.org/*.)

Peer-to-peer (P2P) file sharing

Napster started the P2P file-sharing craze, but file sharing goes far beyond the trading of harmless music files. It's estimated that 40% of the files available on these P2P networks contain viruses, Trojan horses, and other unwelcome guests, but these aren't even the biggest cause of concern.

In order to facilitate the exchange of files, these P2P programs open network ports (Chapter 7) and create gaping holes in your computer's firewall, any of which can be exploited by a variety of worms and intruders. And since people typically leave these programs running all the time (whether they intend to or not), these security holes are constantly open for business.

But wait...there's more! If the constant threat of viruses and Trojan horses isn't enough, many P2P programs come with a broad assortment of spyware and adware, intentionally installed on your system along with the applications themselves. Kazaa, one of the most popular file-sharing clients, is also the biggest perpetrator of this, and the likely culprit if your system has become infected with spyware. (Note that other products like Morpheus, BearShare, Imesh, and Limewire do this too, just in case you were thinking there was a completely "safe" alternative.)

There are some spyware-free P2P file-sharing programs out there, although it's a bit of a mixed bag at best. For instance, a group of hackers have released a stripped-down version of the spyware-ridden Kazaa, called Kazaa Lite (*http://www.klitesite.com*), and there are so-called "lite" versions of other applications as well. But if you want a non-hacked P2P client, try WinMX (*http://www.winmx.com*) or Shareaza (*http://www.shareaza.com*), both of which are free and completely spyware-free. Be warned, however, that even without the spyware, P2P software will nonetheless compromise the security of your system.

Infected files

Viruses don't just invade your computer and wreak havoc; they replicate themselves and bury copies of themselves in other files. This means that once your computer has been infected, the virus is likely sitting dormant in any of the applications and even personal documents stored on your hard disk. This not only means that you may be spreading the virus each time you email documents to others, but that others may be unwittingly sharing viruses with you.

As part of a virus's objective to duplicate and distribute itself, many hijack your email program and use it to send infected files to everyone in your address book. In nearly all cases, these viruses are designed to work with the email software most people have on their systems, namely Microsoft Outlook and Outlook Express. If you want to significantly hobble your computer's susceptibility to this type of attack, you'd be wise to use *any other* email software, such as Eudora (*http://www.eudora.com*).

One of the most common types of viruses utilizes *macros*, small scripts (programming code) embedded in documents. By some estimates, roughly 3 of every 4 viruses is actually a macro written for Microsoft Word or Excel. These macros are executed automatically when the documents that contain them are opened, at which point they attach themselves to the global template so that they can infect every document you subsequently open and save. Both Word and Excel have security features that restrict this feature, but these measures are clumsy and most people disable them so they can work on the rest of their documents. In other words, don't rely on the virus protection built into Microsoft Office to eliminate the threat of these types of viruses.

Web sites

It may sound like the rantings of a conspiracy theorist, but even the act of visiting some web sites can infect your system with spyware and adware. Not that it can happen transparently, but many people simply don't recognize the red flags even when they're staring them in the face. Specifically, these are the "add-ins" employed by some web sites that provide custom cursors, interactive menus, and other eye candy. While loading a web page, you may see a message asking you if it's okay to install some ActiveX gadget "necessary" to view the page (e.g. Comet Cursor); here, the answer is simple: no.

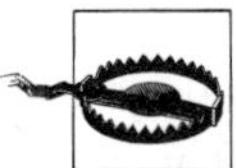

Just as many viruses are written to exploit Microsoft Outlook, most spyware and adware is designed to exploit Microsoft Internet Explorer. By merely switching to a different browser, such as Netscape, Mozilla, or Firefox, you can eliminate the threat posted by many of these nasty programs. Plus, Netscape and Mozilla (both of which are free) have built-in features that disable pop-up ads and some of the more malicious (or just annoying) JavaScript features.

Network and Internet connections

Finally, your network connection (both to your LAN and to the Internet) can serve as a conduit for a *worm*, the special kind of virus that doesn't need your help to infect your system. Obviously, the most effective way to protect your system is to unplug it from the network, but a slightly more realistic solution is to use a firewall. Windows XP comes with a built-in firewall (significantly improved in Service Pack 2), although a router will provide much better protection. See Chapter 7 for details.

Protecting and cleaning your computer

The most popular and typically the most effective way to rid your computer of malware is to use dedicated antivirus software and antispyware software. (At the time of this writing, no single product claims to do both.) These programs rely on their own internal databases of known viruses, worms, Trojans, spyware, and adware, and as such must be updated regularly (daily or weekly) to be able to detect and eliminate the latest threats.

Windows XP doesn't come with any antivirus or antispyware software, but Windows XP Service Pack 2 does includes the Security Center utility (found in Control Panel, and shown in Figure 6-1), which can interface with newer third-party software designed to do so.

As stated above, you'll need to provide your own antivirus software. Keep in mind that not all antivirus programs are created equal; visit *http://www.software-antivirus.com* for in-depth reviews and *http://www.av-test.org* for independent antivirus testing. Among the more popular antivirus products are:

Kaspersky Antivirus Personal (http://www.kaspersky.com)

Very highly-regarded solution with an excellent detection record

McAfee VirusScan (http://www.mcafee.com)

Trusted and well-established all-around virus scanner with an intuitive interface and few limitations

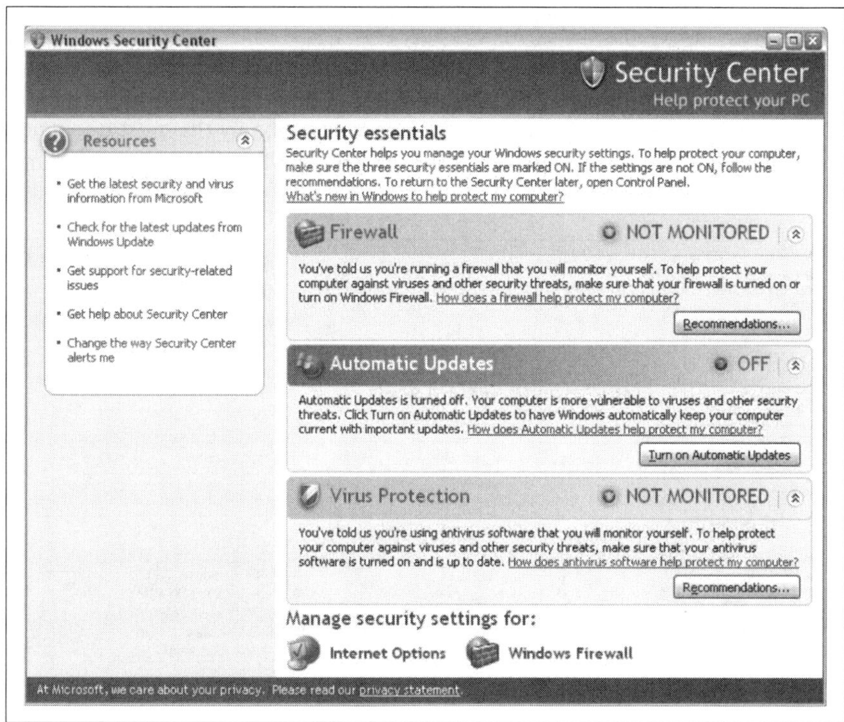

Figure 6-1. New in Service Pack 2, the Security Center serves as a central interface for Windows Update, Windows's own built-in firewall, and whatever antivirus software you provide

Panda Anti-Virus Titanium & Platinum (http://www.pandasecurity.com)
: Lesser-known but capable antivirus software

Symantec Norton AntiVirus (http://www.symantec.com)
: Mediocre, slow antivirus program with a well-known name; beware expensive subscription plan to keep virus definitions updated

AntiVir (http://www.free-av.com)
: Freeware, with frequent updates but only average detection rates

Avast Home Edition (http://www.asw.cz)
: Freeware, with slick interface and good feature set

AVG (http://free.grisoft.com)
: Freeware, a popular yet poor-performing antivirus solution

Antispyware software is a newer phenomenon and, as a result, there are fewer offerings. However, they do their job well and complete their scans in only a few minutes (compared with the hours it takes to scan all your files for viruses). The top antispyware products include:

Ad-Aware Personal Edition (http://www.lavasoft.de)
: Ad-Aware (Figure 6-2), along with Spybot, is probably the most frequently suggested solution to spyware problems on the Annoyances.org forums, for good reason. The personal edition is free, very slick, and works well.

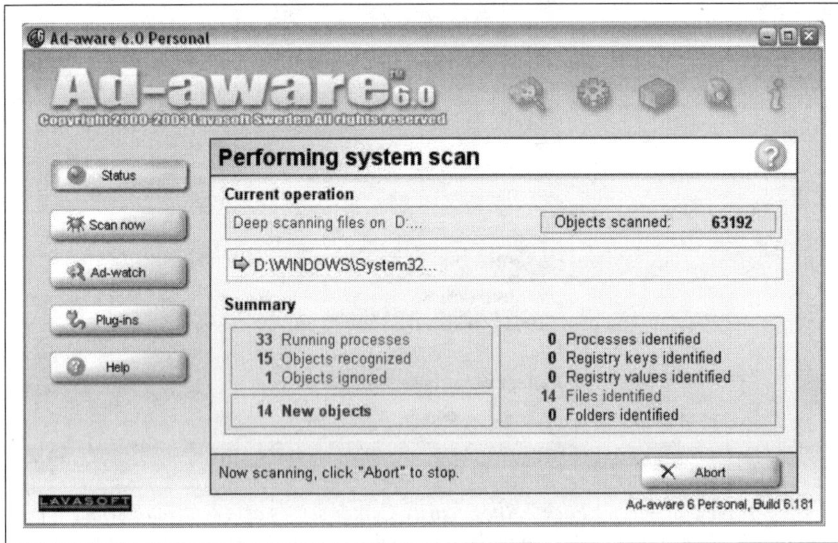

Figure 6-2. Use Lavasoft's Ad-Aware to rid your system for all sorts of spyware and adware

When using Ad-Aware, make sure you click **Check for updates now** before running a scan. Also, to turn off the awful, jarring sound Ad-Aware plays when it has found spyware, click the gear icon to open the settings window, click the **Tweak** button, open the **Misc Settings** category, and turn off the **Play sound if scan produced a result** option.

Spybot - Search & Destroy (http://www.spybot.info)
: When used along with Ad-Aware, this free software can be counted on to remove virtually all types of spyware and adware from your computer. While both Ad-Aware and Spybot remove tracking cookies (used to deliver ads in web pages) from Internet Explorer, only Spybot supports Mozilla and Firefox as well.

HijackThis (http://www.spychecker.com/program/hijackthis.html)
: Use this tool to generate a report listing all the browser add-ons and startup programs installed on your system. You can then either

scrutinize the report yourself or send the resulting HijackThis Log to someone else for their help.

Spy Sweeper (http://www.webroot.com)
: This highly-regarded antispyware tool, while not free like the first two, is still a welcome addition to any spyware-fighter's toolbox.

Rootkit Revealer (http://www.sysinternals.com/ntw2k/freeware/rootkitreveal.shtml)
: This bleeding-edge tool detects installed persistent rootkits.

So, armed with proper antivirus and antispyware software, there are four things you should do to protect your computer from malware:

1. Place a router between your computer and your Internet connection, as described in Chapter 7.
2. Scan your system for viruses regularly, and don't rely entirely on your antivirus program's auto-protect feature (see the next section). Run a full system scan at least every two weeks.
3. Scan your system for spyware regularly, at least once or twice a month. Do it more often if you download and install a lot of software.
4. Use your head! See the previous section for ways malware spreads and the next section for some of the things you can do to reduce your exposure to viruses, spyware, adware, and other malware.

Malware is constantly evolving, perpetually taking on new forms and exploiting new vulnerabilities. To keep tabs on the latest threats, check out Counterexploitation (*http://www.cexx.org/*) and the Adware Report (*http://www.adwarereport.com/*). And don't forget to keep your antivirus and antispyware software updated.

The perils of auto-protect

Antivirus software is a double-edged sword. Sure, viruses can be a genuine threat, and for many of us, antivirus software is an essential safeguard. But antivirus software can also be real pain in the neck.

The most basic, innocuous function of an antivirus program is to scan files on demand. When you start a virus scanner and tell it to scan a file or a disk full of files, you're performing a useful task. The problem is that most of us don't remember or want to take the time to routinely perform scans, so we rely on the so-called "auto-protect" feature, where the virus scanner runs all the time. This can cause several problems:

- Loading the auto-protect software at Windows startup can increase boot time; also, because each and every application (and document) you open must first be scanned, load times can increase. In addition, a virus scanner that's always running consumes memory and processor cycles, even though you're not likely to spend most of your time downloading new and potentially hazardous files for it to scan.

- If the antivirus software or virus definitions become corrupted, the application auto-scanner may prevent any application on your system from loading, including the antivirus software itself, making it impossible to rectify the situation without serious headaches. (Yes, this actually happens.)
- Some antivirus auto-protect features include web browser and email plug-ins, which scan all files downloaded and received as attachments, respectively. In addition to the performance hit, these plug-ins sometimes don't work properly, inadvertently causing all sorts of problems with the applications you use to open these files.
- The constant barrage of virus warning messages can be annoying, to say the least. For instance, if your antivirus software automatically scans your incoming email, you may be forced to click through a dozen of these messages warning you of virus-laden attachments, even though your spam filter will likely delete them before you even see them.
- Lastly, and most importantly, having the auto-protect feature installed can give you a false sense of security, reducing the chances that you'll take the precautions listed elsewhere in this section and increasing the likelihood that your computer will become infected. Even if you are diligent about scanning files manually, no antivirus program is foolproof—and certainly is no substitute for common sense.

Now, if you take the proper precautions, your exposure to viruses will be minimal, and you will have very little need for the auto-protect feature of your antivirus software. Naturally, whether you disable your antivirus software's auto-protect feature is up to you. If you keep the following practices in mind, regardless of the status of your antivirus autoprotect software, you should effectively eliminate your computer's susceptibility to viruses:

- If you don't download any documents or applications from the Internet, if you're not connected to a local network, if you have a firewalled connection to the Internet, and the only type of software you install is off-the-shelf commercial products, your odds of getting a virus are pretty much zero.
- Viruses can only reside in certain types of files, including application (*.exe*) files, document files made in applications that use macros (such as Microsoft Word), Windows script files (*.vbs*), and some types of application support files (*.dll*, *.vbx*, *.vxd*, etc.). And because ZIP files (described in Chapter 2) can contain any of the aforementioned files, they're also susceptible.

Conventional wisdom holds that plain-text email messages, text files (*.txt*), image files (*.jpg*, *.gif*, *.bmp*, etc.), video clips (*.mpg*, *.avi*, etc.) and most other types of files are benign in that they simply are not capable of being virus carriers. However, things aren't always as they seem. Case in point: a new type of threat discovered in September 2004 involves certain JPG files and a flaw in Internet Explorer (and most other Microsoft products) that can exploited.* Fortunately, the bug has been fixed in Service Pack 2, but it's not likely to be the last.

- Actually, it is possible to embed small amounts of binary data into image files, which means, theoretically, that an image could contain a virus. However, such data would have to be manually extracted before it could be executed; a virus embedded in an image file would never be able to spontaneously infect your system.
- Don't *ever* open email attachments sent to you from people you don't know, especially if they are Word documents or *.exe* files. If someone sends you an attachment and you wish to open it, scan it manually before opening it. Most antivirus software adds a context-menu item to all files (see "File Types: The Link Between Documents and Applications" in Chapter 4), allowing you to scan any given file by right-clicking on it and selecting **Scan for Viruses** (or something similar).
- Note that there are some types of viruses that will hijack a user's address book (typically MS Outlook users only) and automatically send an infected email to everyone that person has ever emailed. This means that you may get a virus in an email attachment from someone you know, but it will have a nonsensical filename and a generic, poorly written message body, like "*I send you this file in order to have your advice.*" If you get an email from someone you know, and it doesn't look like something that person would send you, it likely wasn't sent intentionally, and should be deleted. The worst thing that could happen if you're wrong is that the sender will just have to send it again.

If you're on a network, your computer is only as secure as the least secure computer on the network. If it's a home network, make sure everyone who uses machines on that network understands the previous concepts. If it's a corporate network, there's no accounting for the stupidity of your coworkers, so you may choose to leave the auto-protect feature of antivirus software in place.

* For more information, search Google for *Exploit-MS04-028* or *Bloodhound.Exploit.13*.

Check Your Drive for Errors with Chkdsk

The Chkdsk utility (*chkdsk.exe*, pronounced "check disk") is used to scan your hard disk for errors and optionally fix any that are found. To run Chkdsk, open a Command Prompt window (*cmd.exe*) by going to **Start → Run** and typing `cmd`, and then type `chkdsk` at the prompt and press **Enter**.

Chkdsk can also be run from either the Windows Recovery Console (discussed later in this chapter) or the Safe Mode with Command Prompt (discussed in "How to Delete or Replace In-Use Files" in Chapter 2, respectively).

When you run Chkdsk without any options, you'll get a report that looks something like this:

```
The type of the file system is NTFS.
Volume label is SHOEBOX.

WARNING!  F parameter not specified.
Running CHKDSK in read-only mode.

CHKDSK is verifying files (stage 1 of 3)...
File verification completed.
CHKDSK is verifying indexes (stage 2 of 3)...
Index verification completed.
CHKDSK is verifying security descriptors (stage 3 of 3)...
Security descriptor verification completed.

  87406395 KB total disk space.
  26569944 KB in 42010 files.
     23844 KB in 896 indexes.
         0 KB in bad sectors.
    114839 KB in use by the system.
     65536 KB occupied by the log file.
  60632232 KB available on disk.

      4096 bytes in each allocation unit.
   4351598 total allocation units on disk.
    176942 allocation units available on disk.
```

If any errors are found, such errors will be listed in the report along with the statistics in the example above. However, unlike the Scandisk utility found in some earlier versions of Windows, Chkdsk doesn't make any changes to your drive (repairs or otherwise) unless you specifically request them. As suggested by the "F parameter" warning in the report, you'll need to type `chkdsk /f` to effect any necessary repairs on the drive.

The /f parameter is not available in the Windows Recovery Console; instead, you'll need to use the more powerful /r option to effect repairs, as described below. The other exception when Chkdsk is run from the WRC is that it won't usually scan for errors unless you include the /p option (which has no meaning outside the WRC).

The following terms describe most of the different types of problems that Chkdsk might report:

Lost clusters
: Lost clusters are pieces of data that are no longer associated with any existing files.

Bad sectors
: Bad sectors are actually physical flaws on the disk surface. Use the /r option, below, to attempt to recover data stored on bad sectors. Note that recovery of such data is not guaranteed (unless you have a backup somewhere). Typical symptoms of bad sectors include seeing gibberish when you view the contents of a directory, or your computer crashing or freezing every time you attempt to access a certain file.

Cross-linked files
: If a single piece of data has been claimed by two or more files, those files are said to be *cross-linked*.

Invalid file dates or times
: Chkdsk also scans for file dates and times that it considers "invalid," such as missing dates or those before January 1st, 1980.

By default, Chkdsk will only scan the current drive (shown in the prompt—`C:>` for drive *C:*). To scan a different drive, include the drive letter as one of the command-line options, like this: `chkdsk d: /f`.

The other important options available to Chkdsk are the following:

`/r`
: The `/r` parameter is essentially the same as `/f`, except that it also scans for—and recovers data from—bad sectors, as described earlier. When using Chkdsk from within the Windows Recovery Console, the `/f` option is not available, which means the `/r` option is your only choice if you need to effect repairs.

`/x`
: Include this option to force the volume to dismount before scanning the drive; otherwise, Windows will have to schedule the drive to be scanned

during the next boot. This has the effect of temporarily disconnecting the drive from Explorer and all other programs, and closing any open files stored on the drive. The `/x` parameter implies the `/f` option; the `/x` option is not available in the Windows Recovery Console.

Additionally, the `/i` and `/c` options, which are applicable only on NTFS volumes, are used to skip certain checks in order to reduce the amount of time required to scan the disk. There is typically very little reason to use either of these options. Finally, you can run Chkdsk on a specific file (or group of files), but only on FAT or FAT32 disks (not NTFS drives). This is used to check a single file or a specific group of files for fragmentation, subsequently fixed by Disk Defragmenter (*dfrg.msc*).

To run Chkdsk from Explorer, right-click any drive, select **Properties**, choose the **Tools** tab, and click **Check Now**. Here, the **Automatically fix file system errors** option corresponds to the `/f` parameter, and the **Scan for and attempt recovery of bad sectors** option corresponds to the `/r` parameter.

Special case: dirty drives and automatic Chkdsk

When a volume is marked "dirty," Windows scans it with Chkdsk automatically during the boot process. A drive can become dirty if it's in use when Windows crashes or if Chkdsk schedules a scan when you attempt to check a disk that is in use. A drive not considered dirty is marked "clean."

The Fsutil (*Fsutil.exe*) utility is used to manage dirty drives. Open a Command Prompt window (*cmd.exe*) and type `fsutil` (without any arguments) to display a list of commands that can be used with Fsutil. As you might expect, the `dirty` command is the one that concerns us here. Here's how it works:

To see if drive *G:* is currently marked as dirty, type:

```
fsutil dirty query g:
```

To mark drive *H:* as dirty, so it will be scanned by Chkdsk the next time Windows starts, type:

```
fsutil dirty set h:
```

Note that Fsutil has been found to be unreliable when used on FAT or FAT32 drives, so you may only wish to use it on NTFS disks.

Another utility, Chkntfs, is used to choose whether or not Windows runs Chkdsk automatically at Windows startup. (It is not used to check NTFS drives, as its name implies, however.) Here's how it works:

To display a dirty/clean report about any drive (say, drive *G:*), type:

```
chkntfs g:
```

To *exclude* drive *H:* from being checked when Windows starts (which is not the default), type:

```
chkntfs /x h:
```

To *include* (un-exclude) drive *H:* in the drives to be checked when Windows starts, type:

```
chkntfs /c h:
```

To force Windows to check drive *H:* the next time Windows starts, type:

```
chkntfs /c h:
fsutil dirty set h:
```

To include all drives on your system, thereby restoring the defaults, type:

```
chkntfs /d
```

Finally, when Windows detects a dirty drive, it starts a timed countdown (10 seconds by default), allowing you to skip Chkdsk by pressing a key. To change the duration of this countdown to, say, five seconds, type:

```
chkntfs /t:5
```

The Registry location of the timeout setting is stored in the `AutoChkTimeOut` value in the `HKEY_LOCAL_MACHINE\SYSTEM\CurrentControlSet\Control\Session Manager` key.

You'll have to restart Windows for any of these changes to take effect.

Error Messages and Crashing Applications

There are basically two different types of error messages:

- An error that tells you that you've done something wrong, such as trying to delete or rename an file that is being used by an open application.

  Obviously, the best way to alleviate these problems is to stop doing things wrong. But, of course, what's "wrong" is often a matter of interpretation, so in this case, it typically makes more sense to simply talk about making the resulting error messages less annoying (for example, by turning off the sounds associated with them), or making them go away altogether (by making liberal use of the **Don't show this again** options that sometimes appear).

- An error that is the result of an application crash, hardware error, or problem with Windows's configuration.

  Such errors are the subject of this section and many of the topics in this chapter. These errors can range from a single error message appearing and then disappearing with no discernible aftereffects, to the more severe Blue Screen of Death (BSoD) errors, discussed later in this chapter.

Now, it's important to realize that error messages of both types are essentially canned responses to predetermined criteria, and any given error message may be used in a variety of instances. This means that error messages are typically verbose, yet rarely helpful. And software developers are rarely English majors.

For example, a message might report that a program has crashed or isn't able to load, but the actual problem may be something completely unrelated to what the message is reporting. For example, you may see a "file not found" error when trying to start an application, if, perhaps, one of the support files has the incorrect file permissions (explained in Chapter 8).

Using Compatibility Mode

If you find that you're having trouble with a specific application, you can try running it in Compatibility Mode.

Right-click any *.exe* file (or a shortcut to any *.exe* file), select **Properties**, and choose the **Compatibility** tab. The display settings allow you to limit the screen resolution and color depth, and disable visual themes, if they appear to be causing a problem.

However, the real meat is the **Run this program in compatibility mode for** list, from which you can choose Windows 95, Windows 98/Me, Windows NT 4.0 w/SP5, or Windows 2000. This is useful if the program you're trying to run was specifically designed for an earlier version of Windows, and either refuses to run on Windows XP or simply doesn't work as well as it did in earlier versions of the operating system.

This also applies when installing applications. Some application installers are designed only to allow installation on certain versions of Windows, even though the application, once installed, will actually work on Windows XP. Just enable Compatibility Mode for the installer executable (usually *setup.exe* or *install.exe*) to fool it into thinking you're installing on an earlier version of Windows.

Error messages resulting from application crashes

Sometimes, a problem is severe enough to cause an application to close immediately. Fortunately, Windows XP isolates applications from one another, and from the operating system itself, which means that a single application crash is much less likely to bring down the entire system.*

When an application crashes, Windows will close it and then, by default, display an error message explaining what happened. Naturally, as you'd expect, this error message doesn't really explain what happened, but rather only informs you that *something* happened.

Often, this type of error is accompanied by lists of numbers (accessible by clicking **Details**), although these numbers will never be the least bit helpful for most users. Now, don't be fooled: the Details view also often lists a specific executable, blaming it for the problem. However, this doesn't necessarily mean that the program listed *actually* caused the problem; it only means that it crashed as a result of the problem.

When you see one of these errors, the first thing to do is determine if any action is necessary. You should expect this to happen occasionally, due to the complexity of today's software, but if it happens more frequently than, say, once a day, it could be the sign of a more serious problem. See if you can reliably reproduce the problem. If it seems to be application- or device-specific, where the same action in a program or the repeated use of a certain device causes the crash, then you've found the culprit.

If the occurrences instead appear to be random and not associated with any piece of hardware or software, there are some remaining possibilities. Errors in your system's memory and on your hard disk can cause these problems as well. To diagnose and repair problems on your hard disk, see "Check Your Drive for Errors with Chkdsk," earlier in this chapter, or see "Dealing with Drivers and Other Tales of Hardware Troubleshooting," later in this chapter, for help with misbehaving devices.

Not only will Windows XP usually display an error message when a program crashes, but will ask you if you wish to report the problem to Microsoft. If you actually believe that Microsoft will use the data you send them to fix bugs in Windows, I have some beachfront property in Wyoming to sell you.

Fortunately, not only can you turn off error reporting, you can disable the error messages entirely. Here's how to control this behavior:

1. Open **Control Panel → System**, and choose the **Advanced** tab
2. Click **Error Reporting**, and select the **Disable error reporting** option.

* This is one of the advantages of Windows XP/2000 over its DOS-based predecessors, such as Windows 9x/Me. See "Exploring Basic Explorer Settings" in Chapter 2 for an option to isolate separate instances of Windows Explorer from one another.

3. To also turn off the error messages associated with application crashes, turn off the **But notify me when critical errors occur** option.

   If you turn off these error messages, and a program subsequently crashes, its window will simply disappear. It may be a little disconcerting at first to see programs spontaneously vanish, but you'll quickly grow to appreciate the fact that Windows will no longer add insult to injury by hassling you with unnecessary error messages.
4. Click **OK** and then **OK** again when you're done; the change will take effect immediately.

Details on Blue Screen of Death (BSoD) errors, as well as how to stop Windows from restarting immediately after one occurs, can be found later in this chapter.

Closing Hung Applications

Not all programs that crash are closed automatically by Windows. Such applications are said to be "hung," "frozen," or "locked up."

When an application hangs, you have two choices. First, you can wait patiently to see if the application is simply busy and will eventually start responding again. This actually is the case more often than you'd expect, even on very fast computers. For example, if you're using a CD burner, the program may stop responding for up to a minute while it waits for your hardware to respond.

The other choice is to take matters into your own hands and close hung applications yourself. There are two ways to do this:

Solution 1: Close the program window

Although the program will not respond normally, Windows will typically still allow you to move or close the window of a hung application. Just click the small [X] button on the application toolbar, or right-click the taskbar button corresponding to the hung application, and select **Close**.

Solution 2: Use the Windows Task Manager

The Windows Task Manager (*taskmgr.exe*) allows you to close any running process, which includes any visible application or even any program running invisibly in the background.

To start the Task Manager, right-click an empty area of the taskbar, and select **Task Manager**. Or press **Shift-Ctrl-ESC** to open the Task Manager more quickly.*

To close any program, choose the **Processes** tab, select the application in the list, and click **End Process**. To make it easier to find a particular program, click the **Image Name** column header to sort the programs alphabetically.

See the next section, "Programs Commonly Running in the Background," for a list of programs you should not close with the Task Manager.

Special case: Change the "Not Responding" timeout

Windows XP waits a predetermined amount of time before it considers an application to be hung ("Not Responding," in Microsoft vernacular). To change this timeout, follow these steps:

1. Open the Registry Editor (discussed in Chapter 3).
2. Expand the branches to `HKEY_CURRENT_USER\Control Panel\Desktop`.
3. Double-click the `HungAppTimeout` value in the right pane, and enter the number of milliseconds for the timeout. For example, type `4000` to set the timeout to 4 seconds.
4. Click **OK**, and then close the Registry Editor when you're done; you'll have to restart your computer for the change to take effect.

Special case: Choose how Windows closes hung applications when you shut down

Windows XP attempts to close all running programs, services, and other background processes before it shuts down. If it encounters an application that does not appear to be responding, it will wait a predetermined amount of time, and then it will force the program to close. You can change this behavior with the following procedure:

1. Open the Registry Editor (discussed in Chapter 3).
2. Expand the branches to `HKEY_CURRENT_USER\Control Panel\Desktop`.
3. Double-click the `AutoEndTasks` value in the right pane, and enter 1 (one) to automatically end tasks or 0 (zero) to prompt before ending tasks.
4. Double-click the `WaitToKillAppTimeout` value, and enter the number of milliseconds for the timeout. For example, type `7000` to set the timeout

* You can also press **Ctrl-Alt-Del** to open the Task Manager if you've enabled the Welcome screen, as described in Chapter 8. If the Welcome screen is disabled, you can press **Ctrl-Alt-Del** to display the Windows Security dialog, at which point you can click the **Task Manager** to launch it.

to 7 seconds. (This setting is also discussed in "Speed Up System Shutdown" in Chapter 5.)

5. Click **OK**, and then close the Registry Editor when you're done; you'll have to restart your computer for the change to take effect.

Programs Commonly Running in the Background

Windows is basically just a collection of components, and at any given time, some of those components may be loaded into memory and listed as running processes in Task Manager (discussed in the previous topic).

As you might expect, the programs required by one system won't necessarily be the same as those required by another. Table 6-1 lists the those items commonly found on most Windows XP systems.

Table 6-1. Processes you should expect to find running on your system

Process	Description
csrss.exe	Called the Client Server Runtime Process, *csrss.exe* is an essential Windows component, as it handles the user-mode portion of the Win32 subsystem. It is also a common target for viruses, so if this process appears to be consuming a lot of CPU cycles on your system, you should update and run your antivirus software.
explorer.exe	This is simply Windows Explorer, which is responsible for your Desktop and Start Menu. If this program crashes or is closed, Windows will usually start it again automatically. If you see more than one instance of *explorer.exe*, it means that each folder window is being launched as a separate process (see "Exploring Basic Explorer Settings" in Chapter 2 for details).
lsass.exe	This is the Local Security Authority subsystem, responsible for authenticating users on your system.
rundll32.exe	This program, the purpose of which is to launch a function in a DLL as though it were a separate program, is used for about a million different things in Windows.
services.exe	This is the Windows NT Service Control Manager; it works similarly to *svchost.exe*, below. The difference is that *services.exe* runs services that are processes, and *svchost.exe* runs services that are DLLs.
smss.exe	Called the "Windows NT Session Manager," *smss.exe* is an essential Windows component. Among other things, it runs programs listed in the `HKEY_LOCAL_MACHINE\SYSTEM\CurrentControlSet\Control\Session Manager` key in the Registry.
spoolsv.exe	This handles printing and print spooling (queuing).
svchost.exe	The application responsible for launching most services (listed in *services.msc*). See the "What is Svchost" sidebar for details. See also *services.exe*, above.
System	The System process, an essential Windows component.
System Idle Process	The "idle" process is a 16k loop, used to occupy all CPU cycles not consumed by other running processes. The higher the number in the CPU column (99% being the maximum), the less your processor is being used by the currently running programs.

Table 6-1. Processes you should expect to find running on your system (continued)

Process	Description
winlogon.exe	This process manages security-related user interactions, such as logon and logoff requests, locking or unlocking the machine, changing the password, and the remote registry service.
wmiprvse.exe	This is responsible for WMI (Windows Management Instrumentation) support in Windows XP, also known as WBEM. Like *csrss.exe*, above, *wmiprvse.exe* is a common target for viruses, so if this process appears to be consuming a lot of CPU cycles on your system, you should update and run your antivirus software.

Naturally, you shouldn't interfere with the components Windows requires to operate while you're looking for errant programs or programs you can get along without. And just because something isn't listed here doesn't mean it isn't required by your system, so use caution when ending a process with which you're not familiar.

What Is Svchost?

Svchost.exe and *services.exe* are the programs responsible for launching the processes associated with the behind-the-scenes programs controlled by the Services window (*services.msc*).

A single instance of *Svchost.exe* may be responsible for a single service or several. You should never interfere with any instances of *svchost.exe* or *services.exe* you might see listed in Task Manager. Instead, use the Services window (*services.msc*) to start or stop a service or choose whether or not a service is started automatically when Windows starts.

If you're using Windows XP Professional edition, you can use the TaskList utility (*tasklist.exe*) to see which services are handled by any given instance of *svchost.exe*. Just open a Command Prompt window (*cmd.exe*) and type:

```
tasklist /svc
```

Then, match up the numbers in the PID column of TaskList's output with those in the **PID** column of Task Manager's **Processes** tab.

If you're not familiar with a particular program that is running, there's a relatively easy way to learn more about it. First, right-click the associated *.exe* file (easily located with the Search tool), and select **Properties**. Choose the **Version** tab, and look under the various resources listed in this dialog; typically, the most useful information will be listed under the **Company** and **Product Name** entries. If no **Version** tab is present, it means the file has no version information, and you'll have to use other means to find out what the file is for. For example, if the file is located in a particular application directory, odds are it belongs to that application. Often, you can learn quite a bit by simply searching the Web for the name of the file.

What to Do when Windows Won't Shut Down

Most of the problems that prevent Windows from shutting down properly have to do with power management and faulty drivers, although there are plenty of other causes to consider. The following solutions should help fix most shutdown problems.

Part 1: Power management issues

Start by checking out the solutions in "Speed Up System Shutdown" in Chapter 5, which explain the power management settings that can affect shutdown performance, as well as the problems associated with such settings.

Power management settings in Windows XP can be set by going to **Control Panel → Power Options**. For example, if there's a tab named **APM**, it means Windows correctly identifies your motherboard's APM (Advanced Power Management) support. Choose the APM tab and make sure the **Enable Advanced Power Management Support** option is enabled.

If the aforementioned **APM** tab is not present, though, you'll need to check your computer's BIOS setup (see Appendix B) and make sure that APM (Advanced Power Management) or ACPI (Advanced Configuration and Power Interface) support is enabled. You'll also need to make sure you're using the correct HAL (Hardware Abstraction Layer) for your computer.

Next, check these two power-management-related settings in the Registry:

1. Open the Registry Editor (discussed in Chapter 3).
2. Expand the branches to `HKEY_CURRENT_USER\Software\Microsoft\Windows\CurrentVersion\Explorer`.
3. Double-click the `CleanShutdown` value. The default is `0` (zero) for this value, but you can change it to `1` (one) if you're experiencing shutdown problems, such as your system restarting instead of shutting down.
4. Click **OK**, and then expand the branches to `HKEY_LOCAL_MACHINE\SOFTWARE\Microsoft\Windows NT\CurrentVersion\Winlogon`. (Note the use of the `Windows NT` branch here, as opposed to the more common `Windows` branch).

5. Double-click the `PowerdownAfterShutdown` value in the right pane, and enter `1` (one) to have Windows power down your computer or `0` (zero) to disable this feature.
6. Click **OK**, and then close the Registry Editor when you're done; you'll have to restart your computer for the change to take effect.

Finally, the following steps have been known to work on some computers:

1. Open the Device Manager (*devmgmt.msc*).
2. Select **Show Hidden Devices** from the **View** menu. (See "Show Hidden Devices in Device Manager," later in this chapter, for details.)
3. If an entry named **APM/NT Legacy Node** appears in the **System devices** category, and there's a red ✗ over its icon, right-click it and select **Enable**. (If the entry isn't there, then this solution doesn't apply to you.)
4. Close the Device Manager when you're done.

Part 2: Look for shutdown scripts

If you have a shutdown script configured, it may be preventing Windows from shutting down properly.

1. Open the Group Policy window (*gpedit.msc*).
2. Expand the branches to `Computer Configuration\Windows Settings\Scripts (Startup/Shutdown)`.
3. Double-click the `Shutdown` entry in the right-hand pane to show the Shutdown Properties dialog. If there are any entries in the list, make a note of them (in case you need to re-establish them), and then remove them.
4. Click **OK** and close the Group Policy window when you're done.

Part 3: Virtual memory problems

There's a setting in Windows XP that forces the swapfile (paging file) to be cleared when you shut down, which can cause problems on some systems. To disable this, try the following:

1. Open the Group Policy window (*gpedit.msc*).
2. Expand the branches to `Computer Configuration\Windows Settings\Security Settings\Local Policies\Security Options`.
3. Double-click the `Shutdown: Clear virtual memory page` entry in the right-hand pane, and select **Disabled**.
4. Click **OK** and close the Group Policy window when you're done.

See "Optimize Virtual Memory and Cache Settings" in Chapter 5 for more information on virtual memory and your computer's swapfile.

Part 4: Other causes

Some other things that can cause Windows XP shutdown problems:

- Antivirus software has been known to prevent Windows from shutting down; see "Programs Run by Windows when It Starts," earlier in this chapter, for more information.
- If shutting down results in a Blue Screen of Death (BSoD), see the discussion of the "Blue Screen of Death" later in this chapter.
- See "Closing Hung Applications," earlier in this chapter, for solutions concerning the way Windows XP automatically shuts down running programs and processes during shut down.
- Make sure you have the latest XP updates from Microsoft; see "Patching Windows with Windows Update," earlier in this chapter, for details.
- If you have a desktop computer with at least one network card, try moving the card to a different slot.
- Your power supply could be to blame; see the discussion of power supplies later in this chapter for tips.
- If Windows is allowed to shut down your USB controller to save power, it may prevent Windows from shutting down. See "USB Controllers and Devices," later in this chapter, for details.

Here are some examples of popular products whose early drivers were notorious for causing shutdown problems, fixed, in all cases, by updates available at the manufacturers' web sites:

Adaptec/Roxio Easy CD Creator
: *http://www.roxio.com*

nVidia-based video cards (nVidia Driver Helper Service)
: *http://www.nvidia.com*

Sound Blaster Live! (Devldr32.exe)
: *http://www.creaf.com*

Blue Screen of Death

The Blue Screen of Death (BSoD) is aptly named. It's blue, it fills the screen, and it means death for whatever you were working on before it appeared. Microsoft refers to BSoD errors as "Stop Messages," a euphemism for the types of crashes that are serious enough to bring down the entire system.

A single error is no cause for concern. Only if an error happens a few times, or repeatedly, do you need to pursue any of the solutions listed here.

By default, Windows restarts your computer as soon as the BSoD appears, leaving almost no time to read the error message before it vanishes. To change this, go to **Control Panel → System → Advanced** tab, click **Settings** in the **Startup and Recovery** section, and turn off the **Automatically restart** option. (See below for more information on the **Write debugging information** options.)

However, turning off the **Automatically restart** option may not really be necessary. Every time you get a BSoD, Windows logs the error, although not in the standard Event Log (*eventvwr.msc*) as you might expect. Instead, a single *.wdl* (WatchDog Log) file is created in the *\Windows\LogFiles\Watchdog* folder for each crash. Just open the most recently dated file in your favorite text editor (or Notepad) to view details of the crash and some related information.

In addition to the *.wdl* file created for each crash, a *.dmp* file is created in the *\Windows\Minidump* folder. These files are known as memory dumps and contain some (or all) of the information in your computer's memory when the crash occurred. Typically only developers will be able to make use of this information, but it might be worth investigating if you're trying to solve a problem. To read the *.dmp* files, open a Command Prompt window (*cmd.exe*) and type `dumpchk` *`filename`*, where *`filename`* is the full path and filename of the *.dmp* file. To control how much information is written to the *.dmp* files, or to disable *.dmp* file creation altogether, return to the aforementioned Startup and Recovery Settings window.

Alphabetical List of BSoD Errors

There are a whole bunch of possible BSoD messages, probably more than 100. However, only about 20 happen frequently enough that they might imply that an actual problem exists. More than likely, you've seen at least one of the following stop messages on your own system:

Attempted Write To Readonly Memory (stop code 0X000000BE)
: A faulty driver or service is typically responsible for this error, as is outdated firmware. If the name of a file or service is specified, try uninstalling the software (or rolling back the driver if it's an upgrade).

Bad Pool Caller (stop code 0X000000C2)
: Causes and remedies are similar to "Attempted Write To Readonly Memory," above. Additionally, this error might also be the result of a defective hardware device.

  If you encounter this message while upgrading to Windows XP (see Chapter 1), it may mean that one or more devices in your system are not compatible with XP. Try disconnecting unnecessary devices, or at least look for updated drivers and firmware. Also, disable any antivirus software you may have running.

Data Bus Error (stop code 0X0000002E)

This can be caused by defective memory (see "Fixing Device-Specific Problems" later in this chapter), including system RAM, the Level 2 cache, or even the memory on your video card. Other causes of this error include serious hard disk corruption, buggy hardware drivers, or physical damage to the motherboard.

Driver IRQL Not Less Or Equal (stop code 0X000000D1)

Drivers programmed to access improper hardware addresses typically cause this error. Causes and remedies are similar to "Attempted Write To Readonly Memory," earlier.

Driver Power State Failure (stop code 0X0000009F)

This error is caused by an incompatibility between your computer's power management and one or more installed drivers or services, typically when the computer enters the "hibernate" state (discussed at length in Chapter 5). If the name of a file or service is specified, try uninstalling the software (or rolling back the driver if it's an upgrade). Or try disabling Windows support for power management.

Driver Unloaded Without Cancelling Pending Operations (stop code 0X000000CE)

Causes and remedies are similar to "Attempted Write To Readonly Memory," earlier in this section.

Driver Used Excessive PTEs (stop code 0X000000D8)

Causes and remedies are similar to "No More System PTEs," later in this section.

Hardware Interrupt Storm (stop code 0X000000F2)

This error occurs when a hardware device (such as a USB or SCSI controller) fails to release an IRQ, a condition typically caused by a buggy driver or firmware. This error can also appear if two devices are incorrectly assigned the same IRQ (discussed later in this chapter).

Inaccessible Boot Device (stop code 0X0000007B)

You may see this error during Windows startup if Windows cannot read data from the system or boot partitions (described in Chapter 1). Faulty disk controller drivers are often to blame, but this problem can also be caused by hard disk errors, or even a corrupted *boot.ini* file (also described in Chapter 1).

If all is well with your drivers and your drive and you haven't been messing with the *boot.ini* file (such as while installing multiple operating systems), check your system BIOS settings (described in Appendix B).

If you encounter this message while upgrading to Windows XP (see Chapter 1), it may mean that one or more devices in your system are not compatible with XP. Try disconnecting unnecessary devices, or at least look for updated drivers and firmware. Also, disable any antivirus software you may have running.

Kernel Data Inpage Error (stop code 0X0000007A)
: This error implies a problem with virtual memory (discussed in Chapter 5), often that Windows wasn't able to read data from—or write data to—the swapfile. Possible causes include bad sectors, a virus, improper SCSI termination, bad memory, or physical damage to the motherboard.

Kernel Stack Inpage Error (stop code 0X00000077)
: Causes and remedies are similar to "Kernel Data Inpage Error," earlier in this section.

Kmode Exception Not Handled (stop code 0X0000001E)
: A faulty driver or service is sometimes responsible for this error, as are memory and IRQ conflicts and faulty firmware. If the name of a file or service is specified, try uninstalling the software (or rolling back the driver if it's an upgrade).

  If the *Win32k.sys* file is mentioned in the message, the cause may be third-party remote control software (discussed in Chapter 7).

  This error can also be caused if you run out of disk space while installing an application or if you run out of memory while using a buggy application with a memory leak. Developers may wish to use the *poolmon.exe* utility to help isolate the problem, as described in Microsoft Knowledge Base article Q177415.

Mismatched Hal (stop code 0X00000079)
: The currently installed Hardware Abstraction Layer (HAL) must match the type of computer on which Windows XP is installed, or you may see this error. For example, if you use a HAL intended for a dual-processor system on a single-processor motherboard, Windows may not start. The best way to correct problems with the HAL is to reinstall Windows XP.

  This error can also be caused by out-of-date *Ntoskrnl.exe* or *Hal.dll* files, so if you've recently attempted to repair these files on your system, look for backups of the original versions.

No More System PTEs (stop code 0X0000003F)
: Page Table Entries (PTEs) are used to map RAM as it is divided into page frames by the Virtual Memory Manager (VMM). This error usually means that Windows has run out of PTEs.

Aside from the usual assortment of faulty drivers and services that can cause all sorts of problems, this error can also occur if you're using multiple monitors.

If you find that you're experiencing this error often, you can increase Windows's allocation of PTEs with this procedure:

a. Open the Registry Editor (discussed in Chapter 3).

b. Expand the Registry branches to `HKEY_LOCAL_MACHINE\SYSTEM\CurrentControlSet\Control\Session Manager\Memory Management`

c. Double-click the `PagedPoolSize` value, enter `0` for its value data, and click **OK**.

d. Next, double-click the `SystemPages` value. If you're using multiple monitors, enter a value of `36000` here. Otherwise, enter `40000` if you have 128MB of system RAM or less, or `110000` if you have more than 128MB of RAM.

e. Click **OK** and then close the Registry Editor when you're done. The change will take effect when you restart Windows.

NTFS File System (stop code 0X00000024)

This is caused by an problem reported by *Ntfs.sys*, the driver responsible for reading and writing NTFS volumes (see Chapter 5). If you're using the FAT32 filesystem, you may see a similar message (with stop code 0X00000023).

Causes include a faulty IDE or SCSI controller, improper SCSI termination, an overly aggressive virus scanner, or errors on the disk (try testing it with Chkdsk). See the discussion of SCSI controllers in "Fixing Device-Specific Problems," later in this chapter.

To investigate further, open the Event Viewer (*eventvwr.msc*) and look for error messages related to **SCSI** or **FASTFAT** (in the **System** category), or **Autochk** (in the **Application** category).

Page Fault In Nonpaged Area (stop code 0X00000050)

Causes and remedies are similar to "Attempted Write To Readonly Memory," earlier in this section.

Status Image Checksum Mismatch (stop code 0Xc0000221)

Possible causes for this error include a damaged swapfile (see the discussion of virtual memory in Chapter 5) or a corrupted driver. See "Attempted Write To Readonly Memory," earlier in this section, for additional causes and remedies.

Status System Process Terminated (stop code 0Xc000021A)

This error indicates a problem with either *Winlogon.exe* or the Client Server Runtime Subsystem (CSRSS). It can also be caused if a user with administrator privileges has modified the permissions (see Chapter 8) of certain system files such that Windows cannot read them. In order to fix the problem, you'll have to install a second copy of Windows XP (see "Setting up a Dual-Boot System" in Chapter 1) and then repair the file permissions from there.

Thread Stuck In Device Driver (stop code 0X000000EA)

Also known as the infamous "infinite loop" problem, this nasty bug has about a hundred different causes. What's actually happening is that your video driver has essentially entered an infinite loop because your video adapter has locked up. Microsoft has posted a solution on their web site that involves disabling certain aspects of video acceleration, but I've never encountered an instance where this worked. Instead, try the following:

- Try upgrading your computer's power supply. A power supply of poor quality or insufficient wattage will be unable to provide adequate power to all your computer's components and may result in a "brownout" of sorts in your system. Note that newer, more power-hungry video adapters are *more* susceptible to this problem. See the discussions of power supplies later in this chapter.
- Make sure you have the latest driver for your video card. If you already have the latest driver, try "rolling back" to an older driver to see if that solves the problem.
- Make sure you have the latest driver for your sound card, if applicable. Also, make sure your sound card is not in a slot immediately adjacent to your video card.
- Make sure your video card is properly seated in its AGP or PCI slot. If it's a PCI card, try moving it to a different slot.
- Inspect your video card and motherboard for physical damage.
- Try messing with some of your system's BIOS settings, especially those concerning your AGP slot or video subsystem, as described in Appendix B. For example, if your AGP slot is set to 2x mode and your video adapter only supports 1x AGP mode, then you'll want to change the setting accordingly.
- Make sure your computer—and your video card—are adequately cooled. Overheating can cause the chipset on your video card to lock up.
- Check with the manufacturer of your motherboard for newer drivers for your motherboard chipset.

  For example, the "infinite loop" problem is common among motherboards with VIA chipsets and nVidia-based video cards. Visit the

VIA web site (*http://www.viaarena.com/?PageID=64*) for updated drivers and additional solutions.

- Try replacing your system's driver for the Processor-to-AGP Controller. Open Device Manager (*devmgmt.msc*), expand the **System devices** branch, and double-click the entry corresponding to your Processor-to-AGP Controller. Choose the **Driver** tab, and click **Update Driver** to choose a new driver. Unless you can get a newer driver from the manufacturer of your motherboard chipset, try installing the generic "PCI standard PCI-to-PCI bridge" driver shown in the Hardware Update Wizard.
- If your motherboard has an on-board Ethernet adapter, try disabling the "PXE Resume/Remote Wake Up" option in your system BIOS (see Appendix B).
- If you're using a dual-processor motherboard, Windows XP is probably loading a HAL (Hardware Abstraction Layer) for a MPS (Multiple Processor System). Such HALs support the I/O APIC (Advanced Programmable Interrupt Controller), a method of accommodating more than 15 IRQs in a single system. Unfortunately, APIC can cause problems with AGP-based video cards. Try changing your HAL to "Standard PC" to see if that solves the problem.

Unexpected Kernel Mode Trap (stop code 0X0000007F)
: Typical causes of this error include defective memory, physical damage to the motherboard, and excessive processor heat due to overclocking (running the CPU faster than its specified clock speed).

Unmountable Boot Volume (stop code 0X000000ED)
: This means that Windows was unable to mount the boot volume, which, if you have more than one drive, is the drive containing Windows (see Chapter 1 for more information on the boot and system volumes). This can be caused by using the wrong cable with a high-throughput IDE controller (more than 33 MB/second); try an 80-pin cable instead of the standard 40-pin cable. See also "Inaccessible Boot Device," earlier in this section.

Dealing with Drivers and Other Tales of Hardware Troubleshooting

A driver is the software that allows your computer—and all of its applications—to work with a hardware device, such as a printer or video adapter. That way, for example, each word processor doesn't need to be preprogrammed with the details of all available printers (like in the early days of

PCs). Instead, Windows manages a central database of drivers, silently directing the communication between all your applications and whatever drivers are required to complete the task at hand.

Let's get one thing straight before we begin: if it ain't broke, don't fix it. Many problems are actually caused by people looking for problems to solve. For example, installing a new driver just for the sake of having the "latest and greatest" version on your system may introduce new bugs or uncover some bizarre incompatibility. This doesn't mean that updating your drivers isn't a good idea, but you'll typically only want to do this if something isn't working or performing at its best.

Problems arise when a driver is buggy or outdated, or when one of the files that comprise a driver is missing or corrupted. Outdated drivers designed either for a previous version of Windows or a previous version of the device can create problems. Additionally, manufacturers must continually update their drivers to fix incompatibilities and bugs that surface after the product is released. It's usually a good idea to make sure you have the latest drivers installed in your system when troubleshooting a problem. Furthermore, newer drivers sometimes offer improved performance, added features and settings, better stability and reliability, and better compatibility with other software and drivers installed in your system.

The other thing to be aware of is that some drivers may just not be the correct ones for your system. For example, when installing Windows, the setup routine may have incorrectly detected your video card or monitor and hence installed the wrong driver (or even a *generic* driver). A common symptom of this is if Windows does not allow you to display as many colors or use as high a resolution as the card supports. Make sure that Device Manager (*devmgmt.msc*) lists the actual devices, by name, that you have installed in your system.

Device drivers worth investigating include those for your video card, monitor, sound card, modem, printer, network adapter, scanner, SCSI controller, camera, backup device, and any other devices you may have. If you're not sure of the exact manufacturer or model number of a device installed inside your computer, take off the cover of your computer and look, or refer to the invoice or documentation that came with your system. However, most hard disks, floppy drives, CD-ROM drives, keyboards, mice, power supplies, memory, and CPU chips don't need special drivers (except in special circumstances).

Looking for a Driver

Windows XP comes with a huge assortment of drivers for hardware available at the time of its release, but as time passes, more third-party devices are released, requiring drivers of their own. Most hardware comes packaged with instructions and a driver disk; if in doubt, read the manual. If, on the other hand, you acquired a peripheral without the driver or manual, both of these are almost always available from the manufacturer's web site.

When you connect a device for which Windows has a driver, Windows will automatically install the driver when it first detects the device. However, you may wish to find out if Windows comes with a driver for a specific piece of hardware before you try to install it (or even before you purchase it). Here's how to do it:

1. Start the Add Hardware Wizard by going to **Control Panel → Add Hardware**, and click **Next** on the first page.
2. The wizard begins by scanning your system for any newly attached Plug and Play devices. If one or more devices are found, the appropriate drivers are located and installed. This same process happens every time Windows is started. If no new devices are found, you'll be asked if the device has been connected to the system. If you choose **No**, the wizard quits.
3. The next step, assuming you selected **Yes** on the previous page, displays a list of all of your existing devices. If you select one of the devices and click **Next**, the wizard will quit. So, scroll to the bottom of the list, select **Add a new hardware device**, and click **Next**.
4. Your next choice is between having Windows search for and install your new hardware or having Windows present a list from which you can manually select a driver. Only choose the first option, **Search for and install...**, if you don't already have a driver. Otherwise, choose the second option, **Install the hardware...**, and click **Next**.
5. Chose the category of the device, or just select **Show All Devices** if you're feeling lazy, and click **Next**.
6. This next page, shown in Figure 6-3, is essentially a list of every hardware device driver included with Windows XP. Choose a manufacturer from the list on the left, and then the specific model number from the list on the right.

If the driver you seek is not listed and you don't see a driver for a similar device that may be used, you'll have to obtain a driver from the manufacturer.

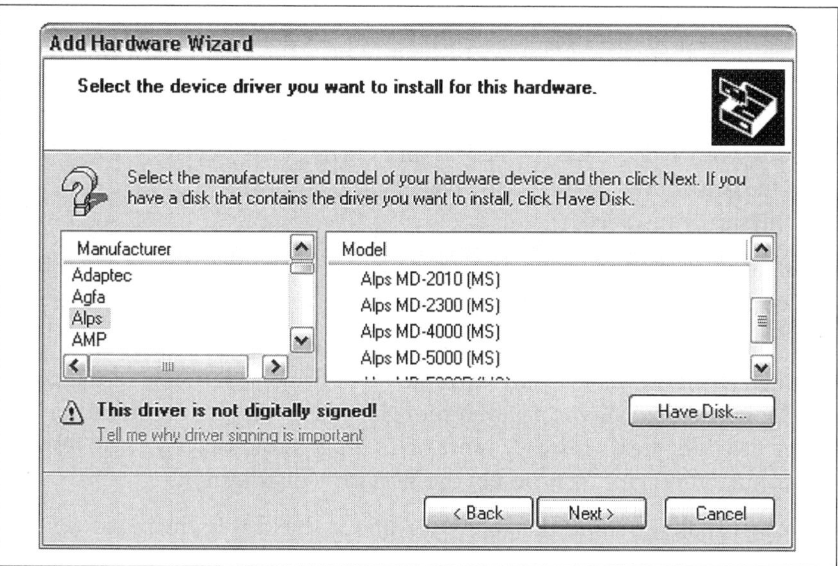

Figure 6-3. Use the Add Hardware Wizard to list the devices that Windows supports out of the box

If you find yourself in the unenviable position of searching for support for an unsupported product, you may find help at *http://driverguide.com*. In addition to drivers for older products, you'll find tips from others who have tried (successfully or otherwise) to get the same hardware working with Windows XP. You can also often find older versions of drivers and other software at *http://oldversion.com*—handy if the latest release of a program causes more problems than it solves.

Updating and Verifying Drivers

Assuming you've already installed a driver for a given device, the next hurdle is to see how recent it is and, if necessary, to update it. Although many drivers will never need to be updated manually, you may need to do just that to solve some hardware problems.

Video drivers are notoriously buggy, especially the ones that come with newly released video cards. (Drivers are often rushed to completion to coincide with the release of a video adapter.) If you're experiencing problems with windows not updating their displays properly, frequent system crashes, odd mouse-cursor behavior, or any number of other seemingly unexplainable glitches, a buggy video driver is a likely culprit. In addition, video drivers are very complex and can always benefit from additional tweaking.

If a specific piece of hardware is already installed and the driver has already been chosen, there are two ways to figure out if the correct driver is being used. First of all, the name used to identify the device in Device Manager (*devmgmt.msc*) is a good clue. For example, if under the Display Adapter category, your video card is listed as an "NVIDIA GeForce3 Ti 200," then that's the driver that's being used, even if that's not really the video card you have physically installed.

However, there's more to the driver than just the name; to find the date and revision number of the driver, double-click on the device in Device Manager and choose the **Driver** tab.

Although Windows does come with plenty of drivers, very few of them are actually written by Microsoft, even though "Microsoft" may be listed in the **Driver Provider** field. Instead, most are simply submitted by their respective manufacturers for inclusion in the Windows distribution.

You can usually assume the following about the drivers included on the Windows CD (versus those that come with your hardware devices):

- The drivers included with Windows are usually fairly stable.
- The dates are usually consistent with the release of Windows, not with the historical release of the manufacturers' drivers.
- The version numbers are usually consistent with the version numbers of the manufacturers' drivers.
- Any special features or extras present in the manufacturers' version of the drivers have been left out. For example, many aftermarket display drivers include better performance, support for more colors and higher resolutions, and other goodies.

An easy (but certainly not foolproof) way to tell if you're using the driver that came with Windows is to look at the driver date—it should be July 1, 2002 (if you're using the initial release of Windows XP). If not, it probably came from another source, such as a driver disk, from the Web, from Windows Update, or from a previous installation of Windows. Drivers with newer dates are usually—but not always—more recent, but the date alone is not a reliable indicator.

More importantly, the **Driver Version** shows the official revision number of the driver; you can also click **Driver Details** to see the versions of the individual components of the driver.

To change the driver for the selected device, either to install a newer version or to replace it with a driver for a different device, click **Update Driver**. This opens the Hardware Update Wizard, which allows you to specify the location of the new driver to install. However, you may wish to consult the documentation (if any) that comes with your device, because not all drivers can be installed in this way.

Watch out for driver installer inconsistencies

Note that some drivers have their own installation programs, to be used either before or after the device has been attached, while other drivers require that they be installed at the moment the hardware is automatically detected by Windows. If the driver has no install program and you aren't asked to locate the driver when you first start Windows, you can almost always update the driver by using the **Update Driver** feature explained here.

If in doubt, check the driver's documentation (usually in a *readme.txt* file or on the manufacturer's web site). Not many manufacturers follow the standards closely, which can be very frustrating. As a last resort, try removing the driver from Device Manager, which will allow the hardware to be re-detected and its driver reinstalled the next time Windows is started.

The importance of .inf files

A common scenario involves downloading a zipped driver from the Web, unzipping it to a separate folder on your hard disk, and then using the Hardware Update Wizard to instruct Windows to load the driver from the folder. Windows will accept a folder containing any valid driver, which is detected by the presence of an appropriate *.inf* file. Actually, all the drivers already installed on your system have a corresponding *.inf* file in the *\Windows\INF* folder.

The *.inf* file is the heart of each Windows driver. Sometimes it contains all the necessary device information (most modems only require this single file), and other times it contains information and links to other files (*.dll* and *.vxd* files) that do the actual work of the driver. Unfortunately, each device is different—don't expect a set of tricks that worked for one driver to necessarily work for another.

Troubleshooting

Handling Misbehaving Drivers

Never install or upgrade more than one new device at once. By installing one driver at a time, you can easily spot any potential new problems, as well as recognize when an existing problem has been solved. Wait for Windows to restart (if applicable) and try starting an application or two. If you install several new drivers at once, you'll have a hard time trying to find where you went wrong.

Supporting Unsupported Hardware

You may be disappointed to discover either that a manufacturer of a discontinued product has stopped supporting the product or has just gone out of business. If this happens, you may be out of luck and forced to replace the device if it isn't supported in your version of Windows; see Chapter 5 for more information on upgrading your system.

There is a way out, however. Many products—such as video cards, modems, and SCSI controllers—use similar components that are widely supported by the industry. For example, many video cards use controller chips manufactured by a single company; by looking at your video card, you should be able to determine which variety of chipset it uses (look for the brand and model number). Even if the manufacturer of your video card has gone out of business, there may be other video cards that use the same chipset and, therefore, may use the same driver.

Note that an indicator of a good manufacturer is one that makes drivers freely available for all their products, even discontinued ones. If they are supporting yesterday's products today, they'll be likely supporting your product tomorrow.

When you install a driver, Windows first copies the various driver files to a handful of different folders. The Registry is then updated with the driver filenames, the specific resources used by the device (interrupt request lines [IRQs], I/O addresses, etc.), and any special hardware-specific settings. One problem, typically common with older devices, is that the special settings can be incorrect, and no amount of fiddling with them can straighten out a misbehaving device.

This often happens with network cards and SCSI adapters; either the device doesn't function at all, Windows doesn't recognize the device's resources correctly, or an attempt to use the device hangs the system. The solution is simply to reinstall the driver. The best way to go about this is to locate and select the device in **Device Manager** (*devmgmt.msc*) and click **Remove**. Then close **Device Manager** and restart your computer.

The next time Windows starts, it will redetect the hardware and reinstall the corresponding driver, the purpose of which becomes evident when you discover that the settings for the driver have been reverted to their defaults.

More drastic measures include removing all the actual driver files from the hard disk before allowing Windows to install new ones. Because all drivers are different, however, there are no standard files to remove. More conscientious developers will either provide an uninstall utility for their drivers, or at least provide a list of the supported files so you can find them easily. If in doubt, visit the manufacturer's web site and wade through the miles of FAQs, looking for some assistance.

My last piece of advice is to put a copy of the latest drivers for all of your devices on a recordable CD or other removable drive for easy access the next time you need them. You'll be glad you did when you realize that you can't download the right driver for your network adapter if said network adapter has stopped working and is responsible for your Internet connection.

Interpreting Device Manager Errors

From time to time, Device Manager will report a problem with one of your devices by marking it with a yellow exclamation mark (!) or a red ✗. Double-click the device name, and you'll likely see one of the following errors (based on Microsoft Knowledge Base Article 310123):

This device is not configured correctly. (Code 1)
: This is a driver problem; click Update Driver to install a new driver.

Windows could not load the driver for this device... (Code 2)
: Again, try installing a new driver. If that doesn't work, contact the manufacturer of your motherboard for a BIOS update.

The driver for this device may be bad, or your system may be running low on memory or other resources. (Code 3)
: Try removing the device (right-click and select **Uninstall**), restarting Windows, and then reinstalling the driver.

This device is not working properly because one of its drivers may be bad, or your registry may be bad. (Code 4)
: Of course, try updating the drivers. (Laughably, Microsoft suggests running *Scanregw.exe*, a program designed for Windows Me and not included in Windows XP, to fix this error.) If a new driver doesn't fix the problem, try the solution for Code 3, above.

The driver for this device requested a resource that Windows does not know how to handle. (Code 5)
: Remove the device (right-click and select **Uninstall**) and then run the Add New Hardware wizard from Control Panel.

Another device is using the resources this device needs. (Code 6)
: You'll see this error if you've installed a device that doesn't support Plug and Play. See "Resolving Hardware Conflicts" later in this Chapter.

The drivers for this device need to be reinstalled. (Code 7)
: Click Update Driver to reinstall the drivers. Duh.

This device is not working properly because Windows cannot load... (Code 8)

This may indicate a missing or damaged *.inf* file, described in "Updating and Verifying Drivers" earlier in this chapter, which may make it difficult to reinstall the driver for this device. If the Reinstall Device button doesn't work (or isn't there) and installing drivers provided by the manufacturer fails, you may have to run Windows setup again.

This device is not working properly because the BIOS in your computer is reporting the resources for the device incorrectly. (Code 9)

This indicates a problem with your motherboard's support for ACPI power management (discussed in Chapter 5). Contact the manufacturer of your motherboard for a BIOS update. Next, try removing the device (right-click and select **Uninstall**) and then restarting Windows.

This device is either not present, not working properly, or does not have all the drivers installed. (Code 10)

If the device is a PCI or ISA card inserted in your computer, make sure it's firmly seated in its slot. Otherwise, make sure it's plugged in and powered up. If it's an external device, try turning it off and then on again. Then, of course, try removing the drivers (right-click and select **Uninstall**) and then run the Add New Hardware wizard from Control Panel.

Windows stopped responding while attempting to start this device, and therefore will never attempt to start this device again. (Code 11)

Windows may disable devices that prevent it from loading. To re-enable this device, right-click the device name and select **Uninstall**, and then restart Windows.

This device cannot find any free {type} resources to use. (Code 12)

See the solution for error code 6.

This device is either not present, not working properly, or does not have all the drivers installed. (Code 13)

See the solution for error code 10.

This device cannot work properly until you restart your computer. (Code 14)

Do I need to tell you what to do here?

This device is causing a resource conflict. (Code 15)

See the solution for error code 10.

Windows could not identify all the resources this device uses. (Code 16)

Right-click the device, select **Properties**, and then choose the **Resources** tab. You may have to fill in some information provided by your hardware documentation. See also the solution for error code 10.

The driver information file {name} is telling this child device to use a resource that the parent device does not have or recognize. (Code 17)

You'll need to obtain and install newer drivers for this device.

The drivers for this device need to be reinstalled. (Code 18)

See the solution for error code 7.

Your registry may be bad. (Code 19)

This extremely helpful message will appear if there is any corrupt data in your Registry pertaining to this device. Note that if you restart Windows, it may revert to an earlier copy of your Registry, which you may or may not want to happen. See Chapter 3 for help with backing up your Registry.

Windows could not load one of the drivers for this device. (Code 20)

The driver you're using is likely designed for an earlier version of Windows; contact the manufacturer of the device for a driver written for Windows XP.

Windows is removing this device. (Code 21)

This temporary message will appear immediately after you've attempted to uninstall a device. Close the Properties window, wait a minute or two, and then try again. If it doesn't go away, try restarting Windows.

This device is disabled. (Code 22, version 1)

This means you've manually disabled the device by right-clicking and selecting **Disable**. Click **Enable Device** to re-enable the device. If you can't enable the device, try removing it (right-click and select **Uninstall**) and then restarting Windows

This device is not started. (Code 22, version 2)

Some devices can be stopped, either manually or via its drivers. Click **Start Device** to re-enable the device. If this persists, look for updated drivers and see if the device has any power management features you can disable.

This display adapter is functioning correctly. (Code 23)

Despite the fact that the message states the device is functioning correctly, there's obviously a problem. This typically occurs in systems with two display adapters (video cards), wherein one doesn't fully support being installed in a system with two display adapters. Try updating the drivers for both cards and look for an updated BIOS for either card.

This device is either not present, not working properly, or does not have all the drivers installed. (Code 24)

See the solution for error code 10.

Windows is in the process of setting up this device. (Code 25 and Code 26)
You'll see this if Windows is waiting until the next time it starts to complete the installation of the drivers for this device. Restart Windows to use the device. Note that you may have to restart twice. If that doesn't help, remove the device (right-click and select **Uninstall**), restart Windows one more time, and then try again.

Windows can't specify the resources for this device. (Code 27)
See the solution for error code 16.

The drivers for this device are not installed (Code 28).
Click Reinstall Driver to install the drivers currently on your system, or obtain new drivers from the manufacturer of the device.

This device is disabled because the BIOS for the device did not give it any resources. (Code 29)
This message appears for devices on your motherboard—such as onboard hard disk controllers, network adapters, or video adapters—that have been disabled in your computer's BIOS setup. See Appendix B for more information. (Note that this error may also appear for the device's *firmware* if it's not on your motherboard; in this case, refer to the hardware documentation.)

This device is using an Interrupt Request (IRQ) resource that is in use by another device and cannot be shared. (Code 30)
See the solution for error code 10.

This device is not working properly because {device} is not working properly. (Code 31)
This means that the device is dependent on another device. For instance, this message may appear for a joystick (game) port that is physically installed on a sound card that is having problems. To fix this error, troubleshoot the hardware on which this device is dependent.

Windows cannot install the drivers for this device because it cannot access the drive or network location that has the setup files on it. (Code 32)
First, restart your computer. If that doesn't fix the problem, copy the relevant drivers directly to your hard disk and try installing them again.

This device isn't responding to its driver. (Code 33)
This may indicate a problem with the hardware, or simply a bad driver. Start by removing the device (right-click and select **Uninstall**), restarting Windows, and then reinstalling the drivers. If that doesn't help, you may have a dead device on your hands.

Currently, this hardware device is not connected to the computer. (Code 45)
This message will appear for any hidden, or *ghosted*, device, described in "Show Hidden Devices in Device Manager" later in this chapter. This

means the driver is installed, but the hardware has been physically disconnected or removed.

Working with Restore Points

The System Restore feature is used to roll back your computer's configuration to an earlier state, with the intention of undoing a potentially harmful change.

For the most part, System Restore runs invisibly in the background, routinely backing up drivers, important system files, and certain Registry settings. The idea is that at some point, you may wish to roll back your computer's configuration to a time before things started going wrong. This can be very handy, especially if you frequently install new hardware or applications.

The problem is that System Restore can indiscriminately replace files on your PC with potentially earlier versions, reset Registry preferences, and, in some cases, uninstall software. While the intention is to solve problems without requiring user interaction, it can inadvertently cause other, more serious problems. If you suspect that a particular application is causing a problem, your best bet is to uninstall that single application rather than to attempt a System Restore. In other words, use System Restore as a last-ditch effort to return your system to a state of normalcy.

Furthermore, System Restore, when enabled, uses up to 12% of your computer's hard disk space; on a 80 GB hard drive, that means that nearly 10 GB are devoted to a feature that typically needs no more than a few hundred megabytes.

To configure System Restore, go to **Control Panel → System → System Restore** tab. Here, you can turn off the feature, change the amount of disk space that is used (on a per-drive basis), and view the status of the System Restore service.

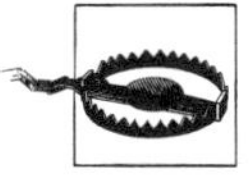

If you decrease the disk space made available to System Restore, you may be reducing the number of available "restore points," theoretically reducing the effectiveness of this tool.

Start the System Restore application (*\Windows\System32\restore\rstrui.exe*) if you wish to restore an earlier configuration or create a new restore point. Restore Points are "snapshots" of your system: packages containing important files and settings, created at regular intervals. To roll back your computer's configuration, simply choose a date during which a restore point was created. You can also create a restore point at any time to "lock in" today's configuration.

Restore points are stored in the hidden *System Volume Information* folder on your drive (if you have more than one drive, there will be one such folder on each drive). However, these folders will be inaccessible in Explorer, even if you've configured Explorer to show hidden files. (You can use the Command Prompt, *cmd.exe*, to view these files.)

To delete all restore points, just disable the System Restore feature by turning on the **Turn off System Restore on all drives** option and clicking **OK**. You can then re-enable System Restore if desired. It can become necessary to delete your restore points if System Restore is preventing you from upgrading (or downgrading) one or more of your drivers.

Understanding Version Control

One of the cornerstones of the Windows architecture is the use of Dynamic Link Libraries (*.dll* files), which are encapsulated application components that can be shared by several—sometimes all—Windows applications.

Naturally, in the life cycle of an application or operating system, DLLs are constantly updated with bug fixes and new functionality. When you install an application, all of the most recent *.dll* files are installed along with it, at least in theory. The problem arises when one errant application overwrites a newer version of a DLL with an older (or just different) version. This problem has been partially addressed by the System Restore feature, discussed in the previous section, but it's not perfect.

Although each *.dll* file has a "last modified" date stamp (like any other file), what Windows relies on is actually the version information stored inside the file. In theory, this works quite well. However, older applications don't always follow the rules, and newer applications sometimes come with shared files that introduce new bugs. And, because the *.dll* files that come with Windows are used by the majority of applications (as opposed to a *.dll* used by only a single program), Microsoft DLLs are under the most scrutiny.

To determine the version of any file, right-click on it in Explorer and click **Properties**. You should see a **Version** tab (if not, the file you've chosen is either corrupted or simply doesn't contain any version information). This tab displays the version of the file, some copyright information, usually the name of the manufacturer, and a short description of the file. Just shuffle through the items in the **Item name** list to see the various clues.

File types that usually contain version information include *.dll* files, *.exe* files, *.drv* files, *.vxd* files, and *.ocx* files.

Usually, newer versions of *.dll* files are just that; they serve the same purpose as the original version, but add more functionality, include bug fixes, or improve performance. In some isolated situations, a certain *.dll* file can be replaced with a completely different file, with which all it has in common is the filename.

Firmware: Software for Your Hardware

User-upgradable firmware is a feature found in many modern devices. Firmware is software stored in the device itself, used to control most hardware functions. Although it's not possible to, say, increase a hard disk's capacity by upgrading its firmware, it is possible to improve performance of an adapter or storage device, as well as solve some compatibility problems that may have been discovered after the product shipped.

The beauty of firmware is that if you purchase a peripheral and the manufacturer subsequently improves the product, you can simply update the firmware to upgrade the product. While user-upgradable firmware can increase the initial cost of a product slightly, such an increase is dramatically outweighed by the money the manufacturer can save by not having users send in equipment to be updated. Naturally, user-upgradable firmware also is a boon to the end user, who can make simple updates in a matter of minutes without having to send in the product or even open up the device.

Devices that commonly have user-upgradable firmware include modems, CD/DVD recorders, removable drives, tape drives, motherboards (in the form of an upgradable BIOS), SCSI controllers, and network adapters, hubs, and routers.

Some older devices allow you to change the firmware by upgrading a chip. It's not as convenient as software-upgradable firmware, but it's better than tossing the whole thing in the trash.

Resolving Hardware Conflicts

Most hardware and software problems are caused by incompatibilities or conflicts, where two or more components simply don't work together—even though they may work perfectly well on their own.

A conflict occurs when two devices try to use the same resource, such as an IRQ or memory address; other conflicts can happen between two drivers as well. The telltale signs of a conflict include one or more devices not working, one or more devices not showing up in Device Manager, or your system crashing every time one or more devices are used. Now, as Plug and Play (PnP) technology slowly improves in the number of devices that it supports, the problem of hardware conflicts diminishes; but conflicts will continue to be a thorn in our sides for quite some time to come.

Each installed device can use one, several, or, occasionally, no resources. An expansion card, such as a sound card or modem, usually uses a single IRQ, a single I/O address range, and sometimes a direct memory access (DMA) address. Other devices—such as memory addresses, SCSI IDs, integrated drive electronics (IDE) channels, and serial and parallel ports—can consume more than one of each, as well as other resources.

If two or more devices try to use the same resource, problems can occur that range from slow performance to system crashes. Most older, pre-PnP devices (called *legacy* devices) allow you to configure which resources they use by setting appropriate jumpers or switches on the devices themselves. Nearly all devices made since 1995 allow their settings to be changed with software, and thereby automatically changed by a PnP-compliant operating system like Windows XP.

Note that some devices—such as pointing devices, scanners, cameras, and printers, which connect to your computer's external ports—don't technically use any resources of their own; however, the ports to which they're connected do use resources. You can usually change the resources used by any given device (ports included). The trick is to configure all of your devices to use different resources so that no conflicts occur. All devices are different; refer to the documentation included with each device, or contact the manufacturer for specific configuration instructions and possible conflict warnings.

To determine which resources are available in your system, as well as which devices are using the rest of the resources, open System Information (*msinfo32.exe*) and expand the **Hardware Resources** branch.

Be aware that some devices *can* share resources. For example, your communication ports share IRQs (COM1 and COM3 both use IRQ 4, and COM2 and COM4 both use IRQ 3). And most PCI slots can share IRQs, which only occasionally causes problems.

If you discover a conflict, start by either removing or reconfiguring one of the devices involved. You may be required to reconfigure several devices, delegating resources around until all the conflicts are resolved. Again, the method used to change the resources used by a particular device depends upon the device itself. You should be able to see all the resources used by a given device by double-clicking it in Device Manager and choosing the **Resources** tab. Figure 6-4 shows the **Resources** tab of a common SCSI controller.

Figure 6-4. The Resources tab of a device's Properties sheet shows the hardware resources currently in use by the device

Tips for installing new hardware

If you're installing more than one device, do so one at a time; it's much easier to isolate problems when you know which device has caused them. You should expect installation of Plug and Play devices to be quick, automatic, and painless—at least in theory. However, many devices, while able to configure themselves automatically, may not be able to adapt entirely to your system. Be prepared to reconfigure or even remove some of your existing devices to make room for new ones.

If you're trying to get an existing device to work, try removing one of the conflicting pieces of hardware to see if the conflict is resolved. Just because two devices are conflicting doesn't mean that they are intrinsically faulty. It's possible a third, errant device could cause two other devices to occupy improper resources and therefore conflict with each other or simply not function.

If removing a device solves a problem, you've probably found the conflict. If not, try removing all devices from the system and then reconnect them one by one until the problem reappears. Although it may sound like a pain in the neck to remove all the devices from your system, it really is the easiest and most surefire way to find the cause of a problem like this. Because there are so many different combinations of resource settings, it can be a laborious task to resolve conflicts.

The Trials and Tribulations of Plug and Play

Most internal peripherals (cards, drives, etc.), as well as some external devices (printers, scanners, etc.), will be automatically detected when Windows boots up. Ideally, Windows should notify you that the new device has been identified and give you the option of using the driver that comes with Windows (if available) or providing the driver on your own (either with a diskette or a folder on your hard disk). Windows should then load the driver, configure the device, and restart with no ill effects.

The problem is when the new device either doesn't work or causes something else to stop working. Even the newest devices can sometimes cause conflicts, although with the passage of time, the PnP-compliance of most new devices has generally improved. To aid in troubleshooting conflicts where PnP devices are involved, it's important to realize first exactly what Plug and Play technology is. PnP-compliant devices must have the following characteristics:

- The device must have a *signature* that is returned when Windows asks for it. Windows then looks up this signature in its driver database and either finds a driver that matches it or asks you to insert a disk with a compatible driver. If a driver is not required or a suitable driver is not found, no driver will be loaded for the device.
- All configurable resources (applicable primarily to internal devices) of the device must be software-adjustable, meaning it is not necessary to physically set jumpers or switches on the hardware to reconfigure it. This doesn't mean, however, that the device can't come with jumpers; some cards let you disable their Plug and Play features and set resources manually—sometimes a *very* handy feature.
- The driver, if supplied, must be capable of instructing Windows which resources the device can occupy (if any) and must be able to receive instructions from Windows and reconfigure the card accordingly. That way, Windows can read all the possible configurations from all the drivers and then reconfigure each one so that there are no conflicts.

You can see, then, how dependent PnP devices are on their drivers and why a buggy driver can cause problems with the entire system, regardless of how PnP-compliant all the components in your system are. One bug commonly found in some drivers is that they are unable to configure the corresponding device reliably. For example, say a sound card requires a single IRQ and is capable of being set to IRQ 5, 7, 9, 10, or 11, but the driver is incorrectly programmed to also accept IRQ 13. When Windows attempts to shuffle all the devices around, it may then ask the sound card to occupy IRQ 13; because this is impossible, it will remain at its previous setting (or at no setting at all), most likely causing a conflict with another device (say, a modem or parallel port). In this scenario, a tiny bug in a single driver has caused two separate devices to stop functioning.

Now, it's also possible that Windows will be unable to find a mutually agreeable configuration for all installed devices—even if one does exist—which means that Windows will simply boot with one or more conflicts. I've encountered this scenario when trying to install an additional IDE controller in a system otherwise full and completely out of resources. In most cases, Windows won't even tell you that PnP has failed. This is where you have to take matters into your own hands: learn to recognize the symptoms (crashing, hanging, slow performance) and know how to look for conflicts. See "Resolving Hardware Conflicts," earlier in this chapter, for details.

One of the loopholes that you can take advantage of is the way that Plug and Play systems assign resources (IRQs in particular) to PCI devices. Your BIOS will assign a different IRQ to each PCI *slot*, rather than having each device try to grab an IRQ for its own; this ensures that PCI cards don't conflict. The funny thing about PnP BIOSes and Windows XP is that, occasionally, some IRQs are neglected. If you have a full system and find yourself running out of IRQs, this can be a real problem. The good news is that you can enter your system's BIOS setup (see the next section) and manually assign an IRQ to each PCI slot, often even specifying previously ignored IRQs, such as IRQs 12, 14, and 15.* This will then leave spaces open (usually lower IRQs), which other devices in your system can then occupy.

Finally, a common problem with Plug and Play is its occasional propensity to detect devices that have already been configured. For example, after you've hooked up a printer, installed the drivers, and even used it successfully, Windows may inform you that it has detected a new printer the next time you boot. The cause of this is almost always an incorrect initial installation (that is, contrary to the manufacturer's recommended installation procedure); for example, you may have connected your printer after Windows had started. The best course of action is to remove the drivers for the device

* Note that IRQs 12, 14, and 15 aren't always available and sometimes can be occupied by other motherboard components or non-PCI devices. In most cases, trial and error is the best approach to take.

(usually through Device Manager), reboot, and allow Windows to detect and set up the printer automatically. Naturally, you should check the printer's documentation for any abnormalities of the installation process.

Special case: Stop Plug and Play from detecting devices

One of the problems with Plug and Play is its tendency to detect and load drivers for devices you don't want to use. Although there is no way to prevent the Windows Plug and Play feature from detecting and installing drivers for some devices, you can disable most devices that may be causing conflicts. The best use for this is in conjunction with multiple hardware profiles, where you might want to disable a device in one profile, yet enable it in another. (See "Using Multiple Hardware Configurations" later in this chapter for more information.)

To disable a device and prevent Windows from detecting it again, right-click it in Device Manager (*devmgmt.msc*), and select **Disable**. A red ✗ will then appear over the device's icon to signify that it has been disabled. You can later re-enable the device by right-clicking and selecting **Enable**.

Show Hidden Devices in Device Manager

By default, Device Manager doesn't show devices that aren't connected to your computer, even if the drivers for those devices are installed and loaded. But why would you want to do this?

First of all, when you disconnect or remove a device from your system without first right-clicking its entry in Device Manager and selecting **Uninstall**, its driver will remain installed on your system. The only way to remove it is to either reattach the device or show hidden devices.

If the device is preventing you from starting Windows, showing hidden devices will be the only way to uninstall the driver, possibly allowing you to subsequently reinstall it to get it working.

Plus, even when a device isn't connected, some of its drivers may still be loaded and causing conflicts with other devices. Merely disconnecting a device may not be sufficient to fix the problem.

Now, in Device Manager, you can select **Show hidden devices** from the **View** menu, but all this will add to the listing are non–Plug and Play devices. To have Device Manager show *all* hidden devices, follow these steps:

1. Open System Properties in Control Panel (or right-click the My Computer icon and select **Properties**).
2. Choose the **Advanced** tab and then click Environment Variables.
3. In the lower **System variables** section, click New.
4. Type `devmgr_show_nonpresent_devices` for the **Variable name**, and enter `1` for the **Variable value**. Click **OK** when you're done, and click **OK** to close System Properties.
5. If Device Manager is open, close it and reopen it.
6. In Device Manager, select **Show hidden devices** from the **View** menu.

Hidden devices (sometimes called *ghosted* devices) will appear in Device Manager with grayed-out icons. Other than the fact that they represent non-present hardware, these hidden entries should behave normally, in that you can uninstall them, change their properties, or update their drivers.

Using Multiple Hardware Configurations

In many cases, solving a problem with a computer simply means finding the correct configuration. It's unfortunately not unusual to spend hours shuffling around the various devices in your system in an effort to resolve all the conflicts, or even just to get it all to fit in the box at the same time.

Sometimes, if you can't come to an acceptable resolution, you may have to set up multiple configurations, just to get everything to work. Start by going to **Control Panel** → **System** → **Hardware** tab → **Hardware Profiles**.

By default, you'll see only one entry here: **Profile 1 (Current)**. Any settings made in Device Manager will be saved under this profile.

To create a new profile, just click **Copy**, and then make the desired changes in Device Manager.

If you have more than one profile, you'll be prompted to choose one every time Windows starts. To disable this prompt without eliminating any hardware profiles, first choose a profile to be your default. Then, highlight one of the *other* profiles, click **Properties**, turn off the **Always include this profile as an option when Windows starts** option, and click **OK**. Repeat this for all profiles except your default, and the only one left will be the one used automatically the next time Windows starts.

Which Slots to Use for Internal Devices

Theoretically, the slot in which you install a particular expansion card shouldn't matter; they're all supposed to be the same. In practice, however, this isn't necessarily true. (Naturally, this doesn't apply to laptops.)

Most modern computers come with a handful of PCI slots, one AGP slot, and occasionally one or two ISA slots for compatibility with older devices. PCI slots are usually numbered right on the board or at least in the manual; if you can't determine the numbers for your slots, assume the first is on the far left (when viewed from the front of your computer), and the last is closest to the processor and keyboard port.

Here are a few tips to help you put internal cards in the most suitable locations inside your computer:

- If you're using an AGP video adapter, avoid placing your sound card in the PCI slot immediately adjacent to it, usually slot 5. Also, avoid putting any card in slot 1 (furthest from the AGP slot).
- If your motherboard has a built-in SCSI controller or Ethernet (LAN) adapter, then these integrated devices may share resources (IRQs, etc.) with one or more of your PCI slots (typically slots 4 and 5; see your manual for details). You should avoid placing cards in these slots, if possible.
- Cooling is important for your cards as well as your motherboard. By spreading your cards as far apart as possible, you allow air to move more easily between them. Cooling is most important for your video adapter, so make sure that no other cards or stray cables are impeding the flow of air around it.
- Place your sound card in PCI slot 2, which is typically assigned to IRQ 5 (commonly used by sound cards).
- Place your modem, if you have one, in PCI slot 4, typically assigned to IRQ 9 or 10.
- The rest of your cards can be stuck in whatever slots are left over.

Fixing Device-Specific Problems

More often than not, problems are unique to a particular type of component. For example, modems often suffer similar types of problems, and not necessarily the same as those that affect other types of hardware. The following guidelines should help you solve most component-specific problems (as opposed to general lockups or application error messages).

A non-functioning component can be a great excuse for an upgrade, especially considering the amount of time and money involved in getting your old hardware to work properly. Consider the fact that a new device may work better or may be faster than the component it replaces, often at half the cost.

Video Cards (Display Adapters)

Most likely, without the correct video driver installed, you still should be able to use Windows at a bare-minimum resolution of 640×480 with an 8-bit color depth (256 colors); this is a standard mode supported by all video adapters and is Windows's default display mode. If you can display this mode but no others, odds are you don't have the proper drivers installed. In fact, nearly all video card problems are caused by faulty or incorrect video drivers.

Whether or not you're currently experiencing problems with your video, you can often significantly improve your video card's performance—and possibly the stability of your entire system—by installing the latest drivers available from the manufacturer of your video card. Such optimized drivers can increase speed, offer higher resolutions with more colors, give you more control over advanced settings, yield superior performance in games (discussed in Chapter 5), and offer better stability than the plain-vanilla drivers that come with Windows (likely the ones you're using now).

Most modern video cards are based upon a certain chipset (controller), usually identifiable by the large, square chip in the center of the card itself. (Obviously, the chipset will be nearly impossible to identify in a laptop, at least without the manual or original invoice within reach.) If the chip is covered with a sticker or cooling fan, you should be able to remove it to see what's printed on the chip surface. Common chipset manufacturers include nVidia, ATI, and 3D Labs. In many cases, Windows will be able to detect the type of chip even if it can't determine the specific make and model of the card. If you can determine the type of chipset your video adapter uses, you should be able to use either a generic video driver made for that chipset (typically available at the chipset manufacturer's web site), as well as a driver for another card that uses the same chipset.

If you know you are using the correct video driver but can't use all of the resolutions it supports, make sure Windows is identifying your monitor correctly (see the next topic).

If you're experiencing general video problems, such as display corruption, crashing, or poor performance, try disabling some features of your video driver. Such settings are typically found in **Control Panel** → **Display** tab → **Settings** → **Advanced**. Other settings that can affect your display's stability and performance are located in **Control Panel** → **System** → **Advanced** → **Performance** → **Settings** → **Custom**, discussed in Chapter 5.

Understanding Color Depth

Have you ever noticed that photos appear excessively grainy or contain ugly bands or streaks where a smooth sky or gradient should appear? Do all the colors on your screen become distorted when new images or web pages are displayed? These problems are symptoms of an *adaptive palette*. When your display is set to 256 colors, it means that there can never be more than 256 individual colors in use at any given time. Because 256 isn't nearly enough to represent all the colors in the spectrum, Windows simply chooses the best 256 colors each time you display an image. The more images displayed, the more horrendous it can look.

However, since 65,536 colors (16-bit mode, or 2^{16} colors; sometimes called *High Color*) is sufficient to display photographic images (as are the even-better 24- and 32-bit modes), the palette is fixed and does not have to *adapt* to what is on the screen. This gives a richer, faster display; web pages, games, and photos look better; and you don't have to put up with the bother of a constantly changing palette.

To set the color depth, double-click the Display icon in Control Panel, and choose the **Settings** tab. Move the **Screen resolution** slider to the right to increase your display's resolution (more dots equals more screen real estate, but smaller screen elements). To the right is a drop-down list labeled **Color quality**, with all of the color depth settings your video card supports. Select the highest color quality setting your video hardware supports (at least **Medium (16-bit)**).

Note, as you adjust your color depth, that Windows may automatically adjust other settings depending on your card's capabilities, especially if you're using an older video card. The amount of memory on your video card dictates the maximum color depth and resolution you can use. The memory required by a particular setting is calculated by multiplying the *horizontal size* times the *vertical size* times the *bytes per pixel*. If you're in 32-bit color mode, then each pixel will require 32 bits, or 4 bytes (there are 8 bits to a byte). At a resolution of 1600 × 1024, that's 1600 × 1024 × 4 bytes/pixel, or 6.25 MB. Therefore, a video card with 8 MB of memory will be able to handle the display setting, but a card with only 4 MB will not. The card's refresh rate (explained in this section) can also limit the maximum resolution and color depth. Most newer cards easily exceed these restrictions, so the case may be moot.

In most cases, you should choose the highest color depth your system supports at whatever resolution you're currently using. However, since higher color depths may cause your applications to run a little more slowly and eat up more system memory (at least on slower systems), you may wish to drop down to 16-bit color if you're experiencing any video slowdowns.

If you're trying to use Windows XP's support of multiple monitors, you need to be aware of a few things. Your system BIOS (see Appendix B) chooses which video card is your *primary* adapter (marked with a **1** in Display Properties) and which card is your secondary adapter (marked **2**). Some motherboards allow you to choose, and some do not. If yours doesn't, you may have to physically swap their positions in your computer if you want to make the *other* card the primary adapter. Because your primary video card does *not* need to support multiple adapters explicitly, although the secondary card *does*, you may have to swap them to get multiple-monitor support to work at all. One problem you may encounter is trying to negotiate one PCI card and one AGP card; if your motherboard's BIOS initiates PCI before AGP, your AGP card probably will never be the primary card. In this case, you'll either have to make do with what you've got or replace both cards with a single AGP adapter that can drive two monitors.

Monitors

If Windows knows what type of monitor you're using, it can determine which resolutions and color depths it's able to support. In Windows XP, monitors have drivers, although they do little more than inform Windows of the monitor's capabilities. Plug and Play monitors allow Windows to automatically identify them, though you may still have to supply a driver when prompted. To see if your monitor is properly identified, go to **Control Panel** → **Display** → **Settings** tab → **Advanced** → **Monitor** tab (see Figure 6-5).

Don't be alarmed if it says only "Plug and Play Monitor" here, although you can always replace the generic driver with one for your specific monitor (if it's available from the manufacturer) to possibly get support for more video modes.

Troubleshooting

One of the lesser-known settings that can affect your display quality is the refresh rate (also under the **Monitor** tab), although the setting is less important when you're using a flat-panel display (and is practically meaningless for digital flat-panels). Although the maximum refresh rate is not dependent on the amount of your card's memory, you may have to lower your resolution to achieve a higher refresh rate, especially for older video cards. Windows should theoretically automatically adjust your refresh rate to the highest setting your card supports, but this is not always the case. If you notice that your display appears to be flickering, especially under florescent lights, you'll need to raise your refresh rate, either by adjusting the refresh rate setting directly or by lowering your resolution or color depth. Consequently, if you hear a slight *whine* from your monitor, it actually means your

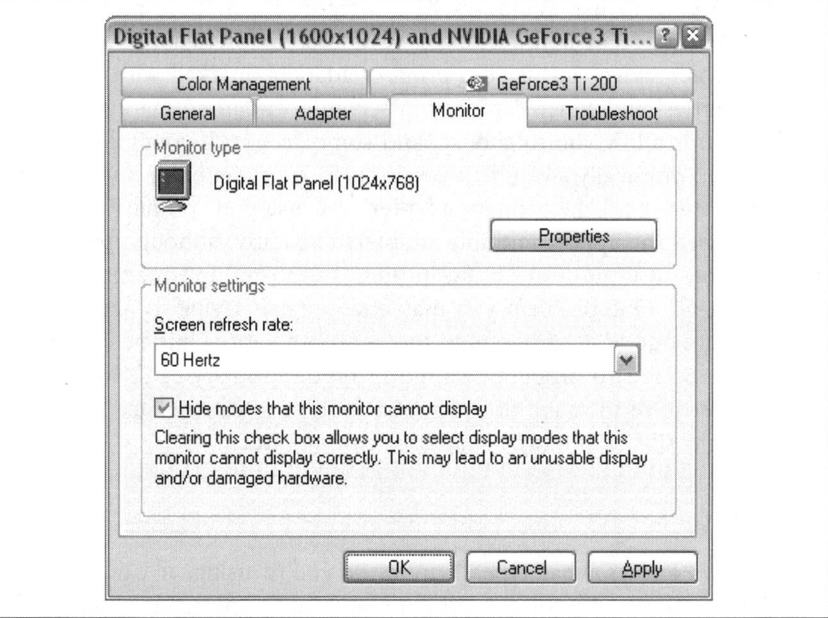

Figure 6-5. Change your display driver and adjust your video refresh rate to solve some video problems

refresh rate is too *high*. The minimum refresh rate you should tolerate is 72 Hz. People with corrective lenses seem to be more sensitive and might require a higher setting to be comfortable. Most cards available today support refresh rates of 75 Hz and higher, so this is usually not a problem. To change the refresh rate, go to **Control Panel** → **Display** → **Settings** tab → **Advanced** → **Monitor** tab. If your display driver supports it, you can adjust your refresh rate with the **Screen refresh rate** setting. If the setting is not there, you'll either need to obtain a more recent video driver, reduce your resolution or color depth, or get yourself a better video card.

If the colors displayed on your monitor look washed out or too saturated, try playing with your monitor's contrast and brightness controls. Calibrate your monitor so that black appears dark black and not washed-out gray, and everything else should pretty much fall into place. (The easiest way to do this is to open a Command Prompt window, discussed in Chapter 10, and press **Alt-Enter** to switch to full-screen mode.) Try turning the contrast control all the way up and the brightness control somewhere between its minimum and middle positions. Some better monitors also have color temperature and gamma adjustments; don't be afraid to mess around with these to fine-tune your display.

If the colors on your screen don't match those produced by your color printer, consider using a *colorimeter* to measure the way your monitor displays colors. This *color correction* allows your graphics software (such as Adobe Photoshop) to adjust your monitor so that your images are displayed more accurately.

For problems using multiple monitors, see the discussion of video cards earlier in this section.

Motherboards

Motherboards can be finicky, but most problems are indeed caused by the components on the board, such as processors, memory, add-on cards, and the power supply, all discussed elsewhere in this section. Here are some motherboard-specific troubleshooting tips.

It's possible that a problem you're experiencing is caused by nothing more than a misconfiguration in your motherboard's BIOS setup; see Appendix B for details.

Your motherboard's chipset is responsible for coordinating the flow of data between your processor, memory, and PCI/AGP bus. Chipset manufacturers (commonly including Intel, VIA, and Serverworks) sometimes have newer drivers for some of the system devices upon which Windows depends; it's a good idea to look for such drivers if you're experiencing crashing or other problems.

Some motherboards support two (or more) processors, which use symmetric multiprocessing (SMP) to boost performance. Unlike Windows 9x/Me, Windows XP fully supports SMP, and is able to work with the motherboard's chipset to distribute processing load among the CPUs. For instance, one CPU handles the foreground process while the other handles the background processes, making Windows XP extraordinarily responsive on a multiprocessor machine. Or, if a program crashes and eats up all your CPU cycles on a single-processor system, your computer hangs; on a multiprocessor system, the other CPU just takes over and you can safely shut down the errant task or even continue working. The problem is that multiprocessor motherboards require special chipsets that typically have much less industry support than their single-CPU cousins, making them especially finicky and troublesome when it comes to add-ons (like high-performance video cards). If you're having trouble getting a multi-CPU system to work, check with the manufacturer for a list of approved hardware. See *http://www.2cpu.com* for more information on SMP.

Check with the manufacturer of the motherboard to see if newer firmware (see "Firmware: Software for Your Hardware," earlier in this chapter) for your motherboard is available; newer motherboards allow you to update the BIOS by simply downloading and running a small program.

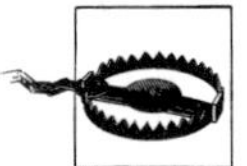

Upgrading your BIOS firmware can solve some problems, but you should only do so if absolutely necessary. Never install a BIOS not specifically written for your exact motherboard. A mistake can fry your motherboard and your warranty, leading to another, rather expensive, solution: replacement.

Even the newest motherboards come with jumpers. If you're trying to solve a nasty problem, it's best to go through the "setup" portion of your motherboard's manual and verify that each jumper is set correctly.

Finally, all motherboards have built-in hard-disk controllers, serial, parallel, and USB ports. Many boards also have integrated SCSI controllers, network adapters, video cards, and sound cards, all of which can save money and open up additional PCI slots for other devices. Problems arise when these devices conflict with other hardware in your system; for instance, if you install a video card, make sure you disable the on-board video if applicable. See "Which Slots to Use for Internal Devices," earlier in this chapter, for other ways to avoid conflicts.

Processors

There's really nothing you can do to diagnose a bad CPU chip (recognizable by frequent system crashes or your machine's inability to boot up at alll) other than to simply replace it. If you have a dual-processor motherboard, you're fortunate in that you can remove only one of the processors to see if that solves the problem.

Otherwise, your best bet may be to take your motherboard, complete with CPU and memory, to your local mom-and-pop computer store, ask them to test it for you, and replace components as needed.

Improper or inadequate cooling is the main cause of a malfunctioning processor (e.g., your computer will crash if the CPU gets too hot), so make sure those fans are firmly attached, free of excessive dust, and running smoothly. See "Overclock Your Processor" in Chapter 5 for CPU cooling tips.

Memory

Bad memory can manifest itself in anything from frequent error messages and crashes to your system simply not starting. Errors in your computer's memory (RAM) aren't always consistent, either; they can be intermittent and can get worse over time.

Any modern computer will use memory modules, but don't be fooled into thinking there's a well-established standard. Older machines use EDO or FPM SIMMs, newer ones use PC100 or PC133 DIMMs, and the newest machines, at the time of this writing, use RDRAM. Within each of these categories are different speeds, capacities, and even standards.

Problems due to using the wrong kind of memory are not uncommon, especially in generic and noncommercially built machines. To find out the type of memory you should use, consult the documentation that accompanies your computer or motherboard. If you have no such literature, check the web site of the computer or motherboard manufacturer and find out for sure before you just jam something in there. Odds are your friend's old memory modules will not only not work in your system, but may also potentially cause permanent damage.

The first thing you should do is pull out each memory module and make sure there isn't any dust or other obstruction between the pins and your motherboard (use a dry tissue or lens cleaning paper; don't use any liquids or solvents). Look for broken or bent sockets, metal filings or other obstructions, and, of course, any smoke or burn marks. Make sure all your modules are seated properly; they should snap into place and should be level and firm (don't break them testing their firmness, of course).

If all that is in order, there are three ways to determine if your RAM is actually faulty. The first way is to use a software testing program capable of checking physical memory. Use the program to run a continual test of your RAM and have it repeat the test many times, perhaps overnight. The problem with testing your RAM with any type of software is that not only are they not 100% reliable, but once you've found a problem, you need to follow the next method *anyway* to find and replace the faulty module.

The second method requires a friendly, patient, and helpful person at a small computer store—a rare commodity these days, especially with the popularity of the large, faceless mega-super computer marts filled with inexperienced technicians. Look for a local mom-and-pop store, and see if they have a memory-testing device. These devices are too expensive for the average user, but most people who sell computer memory should have one. Take all your memory modules in and ask them to check them for you. Not only is this test very reliable, but they'll be able to instantly match whatever memory you need, at least in theory. Hopefully they won't charge you for this service, especially because they'll likely be selling you a replacement.

The third method of finding and replacing bad memory is to go to your local computer store and just buy more. It may only be necessary to buy a single additional module, because most likely only one module in your system is actually faulty (make sure you get the right kind). Next, systematically replace each module in your computer with the one you've just acquired, and test the system by turning it on. If the problem seems to be resolved, you've most likely found the culprit—throw it out immediately. If the system still crashes, try replacing the *next* module with the new one, and repeat the process. If you replace all the memory in your system and the problem persists, there may be more than one faulty memory module, or the problem may lie elsewhere, such as a bad CPU or motherboard (or you may even find that you're not using the correct memory in the first place).

To eliminate the possibility of a given problem being caused by a device other than your memory, remove all unnecessary devices (internal and external) from your system before testing your memory.

You can, of course, also take this opportunity to add more memory to your system (possibly replacing all your existing modules). Adding memory is one of the best ways to improve overall system performance; see the "How to Buy Memory" sidebar for more information.

USB Controllers and Devices

USB is the answer to most of the headaches caused by serial (COM) ports, parallel (printer) ports, keyboard and mouse ports, and, in some circumstances, SCSI ports. USB is fully PnP-compliant, so not only should a USB controller not give you any trouble, neither should any USB devices (at least in theory). In fact, if you're having trouble with a device that connects to a serial or parallel port or if you've simply run out of free ports, get an inexpensive serial-to-USB or parallel-to-USB adapter, and plug your "vintage" device into it.

Although most computers only come with one or two USB plugs, the USB system can handle up to 128 devices; if you've run out of plugs, a USB hub will expand your USB bus easily. Note that hubs can cause problems for some devices (such as uninterruptible power supplies) that may not support being plugged into a hub. Some hubs have their own power supplies,

How to Buy Memory

There are no two ways about it: the more memory, the better (at least up to a point). Adding more memory to a computer will almost always result in better performance, and will help reduce crashes as well. Windows loads drivers, applications, and documents into memory until it's full; once there's no more memory available, Windows starts pulling large chunks of information out of memory and storing them on your hard disk to make room for the applications that need memory more urgently. Because your hard disk is substantially slower than memory, this "swapping" noticeably slows down your system. The more memory you have, the less frequently Windows will use your hard disk in this way and the faster your system will be. (See "Optimize Virtual Memory and Cache Settings" in Chapter 5 for more information on this mechanism.)

The nice thing about memory is that it is a cheap and easy way to improve performance. When Windows 3.x was first released, 32 MB of RAM cost around a thousand dollars. The same quantity of memory (of a faster variety) when Windows XP was released cost less than a ticket to the movies.

The type of memory you should get depends solely on what your motherboard demands—refer to the documentation that came with your motherboard or computer system for details. There are different brands of memory out there, and some are simply known for better reliability and stability. Some motherboards require more expensive varieties (and some even demand certain brands), so do your research before you buy.

That simply leaves one thing to think about: quantity. In short, get as much memory as you can afford. Like everything else, though, there is a point of diminishing returns. 384 MB is probably the lowest amount you should tolerate on a Windows XP system. Depending on how you use your computer, 512 MB or 768 MB might be enough for more uses, whether it's doing light work in Photoshop or playing streaming audio over the Net. But if you get into something like heavy-duty digital-video editing, you'd need even more memory.

Lastly, memory comes in individual modules, which are inserted into slots on your motherboard. The higher the capacity of each module, the fewer you'll need; the fewer modules you use, the more slots you'll leave open for a future upgrade. Sometimes, however, lower-capacity modules can be a better deal (costing fewer dollars per megabyte).

necessary to provide adequate power to devices that get their power from the USB bus, so check the hub power if you're experiencing problems with any of the devices plugged into it.

If you need more USB ports, but your devices won't tolerate a hub, consider adding a USB card with 4 more ports.

If can't get Windows to recognize your USB controller or any USB devices attached to it, try entering your computer's BIOS setup program (see Appendix B) and look for USB settings. Usually, it's simply a matter of enabling the USB hardware already in your system.

Most systems also have a BIOS setting for USB "legacy" support; enable this feature only if you have a USB mouse or keyboard and you need to use them in an environment that doesn't support USB, such as DOS, Unix, or an earlier version of Windows.

USB power management issues

Power management is a common cause of USB problems; if Windows is able to shut down your USB controller to save power, it sometimes won't be able to power it back up again, which will prevent some USB devices (especially scanners) from working. To prevent Windows from "managing" power to your USB controller or devices, follow these steps:

1. Open Device Manager (*devmgmt.msc*).
2. Expand the **Universal Serial Bus controllers** branch.
3. Double-click the **USB Root Hub** device, and choose the **Power Management** tab.
4. Turn off the **Allow the computer to turn off this device to save power** option, and click **OK** when you're done.

What about FireWire?

FireWire, or IEEE-1394, is an alternative to USB, favored for more data-intensive applications because of its speed (though USB 2.0 is now roughly on par). FireWire devices are typically more expensive and less common than USB devices, and can sometimes be a little finicky, but are otherwise fairly straightforward. If you're having trouble getting a FireWire device to work, it's almost certainly the fault of the device's driver software. The controller itself shouldn't need any troubleshooting, especially if it's built in. But cheaper add-on FireWire controllers have been known to be problematic, so if all else fails, try replacing your FireWire controller.

Hard Disks

These drives almost never need special drivers, unless they use some proprietary interface (such as external drives hooked up to a parallel, USB, or FireWire port). Windows will support virtually all IDE drives right out of the box, as well as most SCSI controllers and devices.

To get Windows to recognize an IDE hard disk connected to your system, you'll need to do three things:

- Specify whether your IDE hard disk is a "slave" or "master" by setting the appropriate jumper.* Your system likely has two IDE controllers (*primary* and *secondary*), each of which has its own IDE cable. Each controller is capable of controlling two IDE drives (one *master* and one *slave*), so unless you install extra controllers, your system will be able to support a maximum of four IDE drives: a *primary master*, a *primary slave*, a *secondary master*, and a *secondary slave*. If your system won't recognize a drive, it's likely a jumper conflict (i.e., two drives set as the *master* on the *primary* controller). Remember, your IDE hard disk must peacefully coexist with any other IDE drives (e.g., CD/DVD drives, ZIP drives, tape drives).
- In your system BIOS screen, enable the IDE controller to which the drive is connected (see Appendix B) and set the drive type. In nearly all cases, the drive type should be set to "auto-detect." At this point, your BIOS may confirm that it recognizes your drive by displaying its size right in the BIOS setup screen. All drives recognized by your BIOS will also be listed when you first boot your system, just before the beep. (Press ESC to see all BIOS messages if you only see a corporate logo when you first boot your system.)
- A brand-new hard disk must be partitioned, as described in "Working with Partitions" in Chapter 5, and formatted with a filesystem Windows XP can understand, as explained in "Choosing the Right Filesystem," also in Chapter 5.

Occasionally, a system will be in bad enough shape that it won't even boot. Although it's possible that the hard disk has crashed and is unrecoverable, it's just as likely that the motherboard or hard-disk controller has died. In this case, your best bet at recovering the data on that drive is to connect the drive to another functioning system and attempt to access the data there. See

* Most IDE drives have an "auto" or "cable select" jumper setting as well. If you're having trouble getting your computer to recognize any of your drives with these settings, your best bet is to use only the "slave" and "master" settings for all drives.

"Preventive Maintenance and Data Recovery" later in this chapter for related information.

If you're building or maintaining a critical system, you'll be wise to consider the possibility that your hard disk may fail. RAID, or Redundant Array of Inexpensive Disks, allows you to have two or more drives with exactly the same data on them. The redundancy is for fault tolerance, allowing the computer to continue working even if one drive bursts into flames.

IDE Controllers

Most hard drives available today are the IDE/ATA /Ultra DMA type; the controllers for these drives are almost always built into the motherboard. If your motherboard develops a problem with the controller, you should be able to disable the controller and obtain a separate controller for a few bucks.

The most common problem, though, is with IDE cables. The cheap cables that come with most computers can develop flaws, causing symptoms ranging from occasional errors to Windows not being able to recognize a drive at all.

SCSI Controllers

Most SCSI controllers are either supported by Windows out of the box or have native Windows drivers you can use (which either come with the card or are available from the manufacturer's web site). For the most part, all SCSI controllers are fairly well supported, with recent drivers nearly always available. If you're experiencing a SCSI problem, you should first check to see if newer drivers for your card are available.

If you're unable to find drivers for your SCSI card, you may still be able to use it in Windows if you can find a driver for *another* card that uses the same SCSI controller chip (sometimes called a miniport driver). For example, you may have a sound card that has a built-in SCSI controller intended for your CD drive. If that SCSI controller chip just happens to be made by Adaptec, for example, you should be able to use a driver for the corresponding Adaptec product that runs off the same chip.

Next to drivers, the two most common problems with SCSI controllers and the devices that attach to them are bad cables and incorrect termination. When diagnosing any SCSI problems, it's best to have replacements handy for your SCSI cable(s), so you can easily swap them to help isolate the problem. The use of improper or non-SCSI adapters and connectors is also a common culprit; for example, you can't use a standard SCSI-III cable to connect Ultra160 SCSI devices.

The art of SCSI is in the cabling. You may experience slow performance with your SCSI devices if your SCSI termination is incorrect or if your SCSI chain (the length of all your SCSI cables added up) is more than the recommended maximum for your adapter type. For standard SCSI (10–20 MB/sec), the chain should be no longer than 3.0 meters (9.8 feet); for Ultra SCSI (20–40 MB/sec), the maximum chain length is 1.5 meters (4.9 feet); for Low Voltage Differential (LVD) Ultra2 and Ultra160 (80–160 MB/sec) SCSI chains, the chain should be no more than 12 meters (39.2 feet).

As for termination, a SCSI chain (the long string of devices connected by cables) won't work properly unless it's correctly terminated. By either using the built-in termination on your SCSI controller and SCSI devices or attaching standalone terminators, make sure that both ends of the chain (but nothing in the middle) are terminated. Active terminators are best and are absolutely required for Ultra160 and Ultra320 SCSI buses.

The SCSI card itself should be terminated (or its self-termination feature be turned on), unless you have both internal and external devices, in which case only the devices at the end of each side should be terminated.

All SCSI controllers also have a built-in BIOS, and most have a corresponding setup page (accessible when your computer boots) that let you configure a bunch of different SCSI parameters. Each SCSI device attached to your SCSI controller may have different requirements, so check the documentation that came with your devices and make sure the SCSI controller's settings (max data rate, sync-negotiation, termination power, etc.) match the requirements of *each* specific device.

For problems with specific devices connected to SCSI controllers—such as CD drives, scanners, hard disks, and removable drives—refer to the corresponding topics elsewhere in this section.

CD and DVD Drives, Recordable and Otherwise

Most CD drives don't need special drivers. In fact, if you plug in a CD drive and then start up Windows, it should detect it and display an icon for it in My Computer automatically. If your drive isn't detected, first check the controller. Most CD-ROMs connect to your IDE or SCSI controller; if your drive isn't recognized, most likely the controller isn't working or you don't have the right drivers for your controller installed, as mentioned earlier.

Common causes of problems include dirt and dust, not only in the drive but on the discs as well. A can of compressed air is a good solution to this problem, as is a clean shirt,* against which you can rub the occasional dirty disc.

Most CD drives are cheap and easily replaceable; if yours is giving you any trouble, throw it out and get a new one. Most of the more annoying problems with these drives involve CD and DVD *writers*, and those are a little more difficult to solve. Here are a few tips:

- Most CD burning problems are caused by poor-quality media. If your recorder won't recognize any of your blank discs, try a different brand. Verbatim and 3M are both known for producing reliable CD media; avoid the no-name bargains like the plague.
- Bad media can also be responsible for poor-quality audio CDs. If you hear cracks and pops that weren't present in the source audio, or if the sound quality appears to degrade over time, then the media is probably to blame.
- Watch out for incompatible media. Blank CDs rated for 12x drives may be unreliable when burned with 24x drives, even if you're only burning at a speed of 12x. (Some people reported problems burning 24x discs on 12x drives, although in theory, this shouldn't be a problem. Likewise, don't try to use a DVD+R disc in a recorder that only supports DVD-R media.
- So-called *combo* drives, which are both DVD readers and CD writers, tend to be less reliable and more picky about the types of media they like. If you're having continuing trouble with a combo drive, consider replacing it with a dedicated CD writer and separate DVD reader. Better yet, upgrade to a fullblown DVD+/-R writer, and burn both CDs and DVDs.
- A buffer overrun occurs when your recorder's buffer (the memory in your recorder used to temporarily store data to be burned to the CD) is full. This happens when the recorder is unable to write to the CD for some reason. Look for updates to your CD burning software (see below) and try different media if this keeps happening.
- A buffer underrun occrurs when your computer can't supply data to the recorder as quickly as it needs it. This is more common on older, slower computers and older CD burners with smaller data buffers. If this happens to you, close all nonessential applications (any of which can slow down your computer) and try again. Note that newer recorders have larger buffers to prevent this from happening, as well as features to recover otherwise-ruined discs if it ever does happen again.

* Or better yet, a clean, dry, lint-free cloth. Strictly speaking, you should gently rub a disc from the center outward (along the radii), but if you just want to use a dirty dishrag, I won't tell anyone.

If you continue to get this error, try different media or a different recorder, and make sure the drive containing the source data is able to deliver it quickly enough for your CD burner. For instance, if you're having trouble copying data from CD to CD, try copying the data to your hard drive first.

As long as your burner and burner software support Burn-Proof (Sanyo's "Buffer Under RuN-Proof" technology), you should never ruin another disc as a result of a buffer under-run. For instance, Easy CD Creator and Nero Burning Rom, versions 4.02 and 5.0, respectively, and later versions, reportedly support this feature. See *http://www.roxio.com/en/support/recorders/burnproof.html* for details.

- Don't forget the software! Windows XP's built-in support for CD burning is rudimentary at best, so if you can't get it to work, give a third-party solution a try. Nero Burning ROM (*http://www.nero.com/*) and Easy Media Creator (*http://www.roxio.com/*) are both good choices.

Tape Drives

The best thing you can do to keep a tape drive running smoothly and reliably is to keep it clean. Dust and dirt translate into poor performance, lost data, or even an early death. Some (but not all) tape drives require that you use cleaning tapes on a regular basis; consult with your drive's documentation for details.

Most tape devices require proprietary drivers from their manufacturers, mostly because there is currently no "standard" driver for them. The common exception is SCSI; all you should need to do is plug in your SCSI tape drive and make sure the drivers for the SCSI *controller* are installed and working. The backup program you use will then come with generic drivers for SCSI tape drives (as does the backup software that comes with Windows XP).

See "Preventive Maintenance and Data Recovery," later in this chapter, for more information on backup software.

Flash Cards and Other Removable Drives

Removable drives are as varied as the problems you're likely to have with them. As with other hardware, the first step in troubleshooting these drives is to make sure the drivers are correct and up-to-date.

If you're using a USB flash card reader, and you've eliminated the possibility of a problem with the USB controller or cable, then the culprit is likely the flash media itself. If you're having trouble reading from or writing to a flash card, try formatting it, not with Windows but with the camera, MP3 player, or PDA with which it's used. The most common cause of problems with flash cards is an incorrect or unsupported filesystem (e.g., a card formatted as FAT32 in a camera that can only read FAT). See Chapter 5 for more information on filesystems.

One important option that is available for some removable media drives, such as digital camera memory card readers, is write caching. Write caching, typically disabled by default in Windows XP, can improve performance by waiting until your computer is in an idle state before physically writing data to the drive. While write caching is always enabled for hard disks, it's not always advisable for removable drives because the media can be ejected when there's still data waiting to be written, which can mean lost data. Open Device Manager (*devmgmt.msc*), right-click the drive, and choose the **Policies** tab (if the tab isn't there, this option isn't available for the selected drive). The **Optimize for quick removal** option disables write caching, and the **Optimize for performance** option enables it. While the second option will improve performance, it should only be used for drives and readers with electronic (not mechanical) eject buttons; such drives will be capable of requesting that any pending data be written before the media is actually ejected, thereby preventing any lost data.

Modems

If you're having trouble with an analog modem that is 32 Kbps or slower, throw it out immediately. You can get a brand new 56 Kbps modem for less money than it would cost in long-distance support calls to find drivers for the old one. If you only use your modem to connect to the Internet, consider a malfunctioning modem an excuse to get DSL or cable Internet.

Settings for your modem can be found in Device Manager (*devmgmt.msc*); just open the **Modems** category, and double-click your modem to view its Properties sheet. The more interesting settings are as follows:

- The Speaker volume (in the **Modem** tab) is obviously self-explanatory. But not all modems respond to this setting. Furthermore, some modems use your PC speaker, which is controlled by the Volume Control (*sndvol32.exe*).
- The Maximum Port Speed (in the **Modem** tab) is the speed of the COM port used by your modem, not by the modem itself. Set it to **115200** in all cases. The COM port used by the modem is hidden in the Advanced

Settings dialog; go to **Advanced** tab → **Advanced Port Settings**. While you're here, set the FIFO (First In, First Out) buffers; push both sliders all the way to the right.

- The diagnostics tab provides information you can use to determine the model and capabilities of your modem. The upper field contains the Hardware ID, which is your modem's Plug and Play signature (explained in "The Trials and Tribulations of Plug and Play," earlier in this chapter). The lower field (assuming you've pressed **Query Modem**) contains the results of several AT commands sent to it.
- The initialization string (required by some modems) is specified in the **Extra initialization commands** field under the **Advanced** tab. If you don't have an initialization string, leave this field blank.
- Finally, like other devices, the modem's driver and resources can be configured in the **Driver** and **Resources** tabs, respectively.

Getting the right driver for your modem

Windows might simply recognize your modem as a "standard modem" if it can't autodetect the make and model, even though a driver for your modem may be included with Windows. Although the "standard modem" driver isn't ideal, you can often get by with it in a pinch.

A driver made especially for your modem will usually yield the best performance and reliability, but if it's not available, you can sometimes use a driver for another product by the same manufacturer, as long as it's rated the same speed (e.g., 56 K).

If Windows doesn't identify your modem or if it identifies it as an "unknown device," there are two possibilities that could cause this problem. First, your modem could be a proprietary model (always something to avoid, although often inevitable in laptops), which you simply won't be able to use without a manufacturer-supplied driver. Second, the serial port to which your modem is connected may be misconfigured or conflicting with another serial port in your system; see the discussion of serial ports in Appendix B for a solution.

Occasionally, a functioning modem can stop working temporarily. Modems constantly receive commands from your computer, so it's possible for the modem to become confused if it is sent a garbled or incomplete command. The easiest way to correct a confused modem is to turn it off and then on again. If the modem is an internal model, you'll need to *completely* power down your computer and then turn it on again; simply pressing the reset button or restarting Windows may not be sufficient.

If you know the software is installed and configured correctly, there are external factors that can either prevent modems from working or slow their performance. Start by removing all other electronic devices from the phone line, including answering machines, fax machines, autodialers, and standard telephone handsets. Any of these can actually interfere with the modem, preventing it from detecting the dial tone or causing it to hang up prematurely. Other factors include bad phone cables and wall sockets; try replacing your old phone cord with a brand new one, just long enough to reach the wall jack. A noisy phone line can also cause slow performance and frequent disconnects; contact the phone company to investigate.

If you have a DSL adapter or cable modem, these techniques most likely won't apply, because neither of these are technically modems; see Chapter 7 for help troubleshooting network and Internet connections.

Diagnosing slow or unreliable modem connections

The most common cause for slow connection speeds is a noisy phone line. Noise can corrupt the data being transferred; if your modem gets corrupted data, the data must be sent again. If 15% of the data needs to be resent, it will take 15% longer to transfer any given file. Start by connecting a telephone handset to the phone line or to the jack labeled "phone" on the back of your modem, and make a normal call. If you hear any crackling or interference, it means the line is very noisy (you may not be able to hear low-to-moderate noise, however). If you suspect line noise, try replacing the phone cord or even the entire wall jack. Note that the phone cord shouldn't be any longer than is absolutely necessary.

Also, make sure there isn't anything else connected to the line, especially between the computer and the wall. That is, any answering machines, fax machines, and telephones should be plugged into the back of your modem (the jack labeled "phone"), and your modem should be plugged *directly* into the wall. These devices can interfere with transmission since the signal must pass through them in order to reach your computer.

Network Interface Cards (NICs)

In most cases, Windows will detect your network adapter and install the correct drivers for it automatically. However, there are so many different types and manufacturers of network cards, and so many of those are completely proprietary that you may be out of luck if you can't obtain drivers made specifically for yours.

Isolating networking problems can be especially difficult, because you're not dealing with a standalone device. If your printer stops working, you know immediately where the problem is, but if your network stops working, it could be your card, the network cable, the hub, your colleague's network card, your network drivers, your colleague's network drivers, or any number of other things. See Chapter 7 for detailed network troubleshooting assistance.

Because there are no "generic" or "standard" network drivers, if you can't find a driver for your network adapter, or if it has stopped working, just throw it out. Brand-new Ethernet adapters are ridiculously cheap and most likely superior to the antique you'd be replacing.

If you're having problems with your network card in a desktop computer, try moving it to a diffrerent slot. If you're dealing with a network adapter built into your motherboard or laptop, check your BIOS (see Appendix B) for applicable settings, and contact your motherboard or laptop manufacturer for the latest drivers.

Wireless NICs and Routers

Everything that applies to network cards, discussed in the previous topic, applies to wireless network cards as well. However, there's a peculiarity that affects both wireless NICs and wireless routers alike, and it has to do with the fact that most manufacturers of wireless equipment rush their products to market before they're ready.

For this reason, the first thing you should do when you set up any wireless equipment, as well as the instant you start experiencing problems, is to download and install the most recent version of the firmware available (discussed earlier in this chapter). Not only will this likely fix connection and performance problems, but it will sometimes provide more features and interface improvements (where applicable).

Sound Cards

It seems that the better sound card technology gets, the more troublesome these devices are.

In the old days, troubleshooting a sound card involved only eliminating conflicts by finding an IRQ that wasn't used by another device in your system. All modern sound cards are now Plug and Play, which leaves only the driver and its physical placement in your system to contend with.

If you're having problems, such as crashing when you try to play sound, or if you only suspect that your sound card is causing other, seemingly unrelated problems with your system, start by moving it to a different slot. See "Which Slots to Use for Internal Devices," earlier in this chapter, for tips.

Many sound cards come with extra drivers that offer support for older DOS games. Unless you specically need these, it's best to remove them entirely. Sound drivers intended for Windows XP will be different than those written for earlier versions of Windows, so make sure you have your manufacturer's latest drivers installed. If you can't get Windows XP–specific drivers, it may be time for a new sound card.

If you're getting poor sound quality in games, make sure you have the latest version of Microsoft's DirectX layer (available at *http://www.microsoft.com/directx*). To solve game-specific problems, check the game developer's web site for suggested settings and workarounds; see "Get the Most Out of Your Games, Speed-Wise" in Chapter 5 for more tips.

Printers

Whether you're using USB or an older parallel cable, bad cables are a frequent cause of problems. If Windows is having trouble recognizing your printer, or it seems to be printing too slowly, try replacing the cable.

Although USB doesn't have a practical limit on distance, parallel cables do. Some parallel-based printers won't function if they're too far away from your computer, so try a shorter cable. Remove any switching boxes, printer-sharing devices, and extraneous connectors unless they're absolutely necessary. If your parallel port is built into your motherboard (as most are), you should go to your system BIOS setup screen (see "Motherboards" topic earlier in this chapter) to make sure your parallel port is configured for its optimal setting (usually ECP). Refer to Appendix B for details.

If you must keep your printer some distance from your computer, consider using a network print server, which allows you to connect your printer directly to your LAN (see Chapter 7). Note that this isn't the same as sharing a printer with others over your network, a task explained in Chapter 8.

If you're experiencing poor printing speed or frequent errors with a USB printer, try eliminating any USB hubs, if applicable. See the discussion of USB controllers earlier in this chapter.

As with most other peripherals, getting the right drivers is essential. Now, Windows can print plain text (without fonts or graphics) on nearly any printer without knowing what kind of printer you have. If you don't have a driver made especially for your model, you still may be able to substitute another printer's driver. For example, if you have a Hewlett Packard 700-series inkjet printer, you might be able to get it to work with drivers for HP's 600 series.

A problem that plagues many printers is that the drivers provided by the printer manufacturer try to do too much and, as a result, bog down your system (and your printing) with extraneous programs and dialog boxes. If Windows XP supports your printer out of the box, consider abandoning the fancy drivers that came with your printer in favor of the plain-vanilla ones Microsoft provides.

Also, since many printers are compatible with Hewlett Packard's PCL printer control language (PCL3, PCL5, etc.), you may be able to use the driver for the classic Hewlett Packard Laserjet Series II (for older laser printers) or the Hewlett Packard Deskjet (for older inkjet printers). If you have a Postscript laser printer, you should be able to use the driver for one of the Apple LaserWriter varieties.

Aside from drivers and cabling, common printer problems involve incorrect paper: use laser paper for laser printers and inkjet paper for inkjet printers—avoid the "multipurpose" junk. Also, the ink cartridges in inkjet printers are usually cheaply made and therefore are one of the first things to fail; simply installing a new ink cartridge will fix many printing problems.

Scanners and Cameras

Scanners not only require the appropriate drivers to function in Windows, but special scanning software as well; as with tape drives, the software and hardware are typically sold as a pair. If you can't find a driver or software that specifically supports your scanner, you're probably out of luck. However, because many companies simply repackage scanners made by other manufacturers, you may be able to obtain a driver from the original equipment manufacturer (OEM) of the stuff under the hood.

As for cameras, because there are so many different kinds, probably the only productive discussion involves how they connect to your computer. Modern digital cameras either connect through a serial port, a USB port, or a FireWire port; any communication problems will probably be addressed by fixing the ports (or adapters, where applicable) themselves.

Scanners commonly are connected through USB ports but can also plug into parallel and SCSI ports; an older scanner may connect to a proprietary controller card. See "Printers" for help with parallel ports, "SCSI Controllers" for help with SCSI, and "USB Controllers and Devices" for help with USB, all earlier in this section.

Keyboards

Most keyboards are exceptionally cheap and flimsy, a fact that has its pros and cons. On the plus side, if something goes wrong, the keyboard will be easy and inexpensive to replace. However, cheapness has its price, and a cheap keyboard typically won't last that long.

Double-click the Keyboard icon in Control Panel to adjust the various settings of your keyboard. Moving the **Repeat Rate** slider all the way to the right will do wonders to make your computer seem faster, especially when scrolling through a long document or moving the cursor through a lot of text. The **Repeat Delay** is different, though—just adjust this to your liking, and test the setting in the box below.

Sticky or dirty keys can slow things down when you're typing; you can pull your keys off one by one and remove whatever is caught underneath. Some people have actually been successful cleaning the entire keyboard by immersing it in plain water (unplugged, of course) and reconnecting it when completely dry. Another suggestion is to lay out a piece of newspaper, invert the keyboard, and give it a good spanking to dislodge dust, food, and any small critters that might be living inside.

Ergonomics

Keep in mind that most keyboards haven't been effectively designed for use with the human hand, no matter what Microsoft says in trying to market their "Natural" keyboard; true ergonomic keyboards are adjustable, not just shaped funny. True ergonomic keyboards are now getting more affordable and more popular. Some of the more radical designs have split, movable keypads, curved to fit the motion and shape of your hands, and reduce the distance your wrists and fingers have to travel to press the keys. Try one before buying, though: they aren't for everyone.

Your best defense in reducing hand and back strain is to position your keyboard (and yourself, if you have an adjustable chair) so that your elbows are at the same level (distance from the floor) as your hands and your arms are well supported. And if your chair tilts forward, it may induce a more comfortable sitting and typing position.

Another way to reduce typing strain is to just not use your keyboard at all. Products like Dragon NaturallySpeaking (*http://www.dragonsys.com*) and IBM ViaVoice (*http://www.ibm.com*) support so-called "natural-speech" dictation, which allow you to speak comfortably into a microphone and dictate as you would to a human assistant or inhuman tape recorder, often at much higher speeds than are possible with hand entry. These can be quite effective but, like everything else, aren't for everyone. Some of the material in this book was actually dictated with such software (fry two guest witch cent ounces).

A wrist rest may be comfortable, but they sometimes put too much pressure on the median nerves in your wrists. If you're experiencing wrist pain or numbness, try eliminating the wrist rest for a day or two, or simply move it so that it supports your palms instead of your wrists. If you're experiencing any pain or numbness in your hands, wrists, arms, back, or neck, drop this book immediately and talk with a physician. In short, take repetitive stress injuries seriously.

The Num Lock, Scroll Lock, and Caps Lock keys

Ever since IBM introduced the "enhanced" 101-key keyboard with two sets of cursor keys back in 1984, the **Num Lock** key on most keyboards is turned on by default, nudging people to use the standard cursor keys rather than the numeric keypad to control the cursor. This may seem an inconsequential setting, but it affects a basic function of the primary input device, the keyboard, and can therefore be quite important. Some of us prefer the numeric keypad, and therefore prefer **NumLock** to be turned off; others prefer the opposite.

In most cases, you can choose the default (on or off) in your computer's BIOS setup, as described in Appendix B. However, this doesn't always work, and Windows may override the setting. To override Windows, and choose the default setting for your Num Lock, Scroll Lock, and Caps Lock keys, follow these steps:

1. Open the Registry Editor (discussed in Chapter 3).
2. Expand the branches to `HKEY_CURRENT_USER\Control Panel\Keyboard`.
3. Double-click the `InitialKeyboardIndicators` string value, and replace its data with a number between `0` (zero) and `7`. The number is the sum of

up to three values: `1` to turn on Caps Lock, `2` to turn on Num Lock, or `4` to turn on Scroll Lock. Here is a summary of the possible values:

Value	Caps Lock	Num Lock	Scroll Lock
0			
1	✗		
2		✗	
3	✗	✗	
4			✗
5	✗		✗
6		✗	✗
7	✗	✗	✗

4. Click **OK** when you're done.
5. Expand the branches to `HKEY_USERS\.Default\Control Panel\Keyboard`, and enter the same value.
6. Close the Registry Editor when you're done.

Mice and Other Pointing Devices

If you have any software that came with your mouse (such as "Intellipoint" for Microsoft mice and "Mouseware" for Logitech mice), it's probably unnecessary and just taking up memory and disk space. Unless you need the advanced features, such as programming a third mouse button, you probably should remove said software, because Windows supports nearly all mice out of the box.

If you work in a dusty or otherwise filthy environment, consider replacing that old mechanical mouse with a shiny new "optical" mouse with no moving parts to clean.

Double-click the Mouse icon in Control Panel to adjust the sensitivity of your mouse. You can also adjust the double-click speed and turn on "pointer-trails" to increase visibility on laptop displays. The mouse is a primary method of input, and fine-tuning these settings can go a long way toward improving your relationship with your mouse.

One of the most common problems with mice is the pain they can cause in your wrist and hand, due to the unnatural position in which they force your hand to rest. A stylus (pen) will afford a more natural and comfortable position, not to mention more precise control over the pointer on your screen.

You can get a pressure sensitive, cordless, battery-less stylus and a tablet for under a hundred bucks—more than a mouse, but worth it if you use Photoshop or other graphics software. My advice: try a tablet before you invest in another rodent.

Power Supplies

Don't overlook the power supply! Every time I encounter a problem that seems to have no reasonable explanation, the culprit has been the power supply. I'm beginning to think it's a conspiracy.

Say, all of a sudden, one of your storage devices (hard disk, tape drive, etc.) starts malfunctioning, either sporadically or completely. You try removing and reinstalling the drivers (if any), you replace all the cables, and you take out all the other devices. You may even completely replace the device with a brand new one—and it still doesn't work. Odds are your power supply needs to be replaced.

Your computer's power supply powers all of your internal devices, as well as some of your external ones (i.e., the keyboard, the mouse, and most USB devices). If your power supply isn't able to provide adequate power to all your hardware, one or more of those devices will suffer.

The power supplies found in most computers are extremely cheap, a fact that ends up being the cause of most power supply problems. This means that it doesn't make too much sense to replace one cheap unit with another cheap unit, even if the replacement has a higher wattage rating.

Power supplies are rated by the amount of power they can provide (in watts); most computers come with 200–300W supplies, but many power users end up needing 350–400W. The problem with power ratings, however, is that most of those cheap power supplies don't hold up under the load. A cheap 400W unit may drop under 300W when you start connecting devices, but better supplies can supply more than enough power for even the most demanding systems, and will continue to provide reliable operations for years to come. A well-made power supply will also be heavy and have multiple fans, as well as being a bit more expensive than the 20-dollar landfill fodder lining most store shelves.

Possible exceptions are portable computers, which may not have user-replaceable power supplies. However, the need for increased power is generally only applicable to a desktop system that can accommodate several additional internal devices, so the matter is pretty much moot.

Preventive Maintenance and Data Recovery

Face it: some sort of data loss is inevitable. Whether it's a single lost file or a dead hard disk—whether it's tomorrow or twelve years from now—it will happen. On that happy note, there is plenty you can do about it.

First and foremost, there's no better method of disaster recovery than having a good backup copy of all your data. Any stolen or damaged hardware is easily replaced, but the data stored on your hard disk is not. Unfortunately, hindsight is 20/20, and if you didn't back up, there's not much you can do about it after the fact; even if your computer equipment is insured with Lloyds of London, once your data is gone, it's gone. So, we'll begin our discussion with some preventive maintenance before covering any disaster recovery techniques.

Quick, On-the-Fly Backups

In its simplest form, a backup is a copy of your data. Now, a full system backup, as described later in the next topic, is obviously valuable, but often too involved of a procedure to practice often enough to be entirely effective.

While you might perform a full backup once a week or once a month, you can do a quick backup of your most important files several times a day. No special software or hardware is required, and, best of all, it will only take a few seconds.

The following two solutions are remarkably simple, but the idea is sound, and if you make a habit of making these quick, on-the-fly backups, it will save you hours of work.

Solution 1: Simple copy

The next time you've put a few hours into a document, open the folder in Explorer, and make a duplicate of the file by dragging it to another part of the same folder with the right mouse button and selecting **Copy Here**. See "Make a Duplicate of a File or Folder" in Chapter 2 for more information on this function.

Then, if you screw up a file you're working on, if it gets accidentally deleted, or if it gets corrupted by a system crash, you'll have a fresh backup right in the same folder.

Solution 2: Simple ZIP

If you've followed the advice in "A Crash Course on File Organization" in Chapter 2, your files will be organized by project rather than application.

At the end of the day (or even several times a day), just right-click the folder of a project on which you've been working, select **Send To**, and then select **Compressed (zipped) Folder**. A new *.zip* file containing compressed versions of all of its contents will appear next to the folder in a few seconds.

If you then need to retreive a file from the backed-up folder, just double-click the new *.zip* file.

If you've disabled Windows XP's built-in support for ZIP files, and have instead installed a third-party utility, such as WinZip (*http://www.winzip.com*), the procedure may be slightly different. In the case of WinZip, all you'd have to do is right-click the folder and select **Add to *foldername*.zip**.

See "Working with ZIP Files" in Chapter 2 for more information on this mechanism.

Back Up Your Entire System

There are more ways to back up your data than to store it in the first place. The sole purpose of a backup is to have a duplicate of every single piece of data on your hard disk that can be easily retrieved in the event of a catastrophe (or even just an accidental deletion). Imagine if your computer were stolen and you had to restore a backup to a brand-new computer. Could you do it? If the answer is no, you're not backed up.

You need to be able to complete a backup easily and often, to store the backup in a safe place, away from the computer, and to retrieve all your data at any time without incident. If it's too difficult or time-consuming, odds are you won't do it—so make it easy for yourself.

A bare-minimum backup could be little more than a single CD or floppy diskette with your last three or four important documents on it. It's better than nothing, and it does protect your most recent work, but what about your email, your web browser bookmarks, and the documents you wrote six years ago?

I know what you're thinking, because I've heard it a thousand times: *nothing on my computer is really that important, so it's really not worth the time to back up*. Okay, assume that's true—how long would it take you to reinstall

Windows and all your applications, install all your drivers, reconfigure all your hardware, and customize all your toolbars? If you have a full backup of your system, the answer is not only "not long," but "no problemo" as well.

Ideally, you should be able to back up your entire hard disk on a single piece of media. We won't even entertain the idea of floppies, so think about investing in a dedicated backup solution. The hardware you use should be fully supported by Windows XP, and the backup media (tapes, cartridges, or disks) should be cheap, reliable, and readily available, and you should be able to use them over and over again.

The backup solution that is appropriate for you depends on your work habits and your available funds. Tape drives, optical drives, removable cartridges, and recordable CDs are all getting cheaper, and manufacturers are competing for your business.

While removable cartridge drives (Iomega Zip drives, recordable or rewritable CDs, and even recordable DVDs) are great for quickly archiving data (long-term storage of important documents or projects), they still aren't as appropriate as tape drives for repeatedly backing up entire systems and restoring them in the event of a disaster. Removable drives and CDs use random access, meaning that you can simply open Explorer and read or write to any file on the media immediately. This may be convenient in the short run, but this convenience comes at a price: the media used for these types of backups can be quite expensive (per megabyte) and, more importantly, the backup procedures for random-access drives can be more labor-intensive than for tape drives.

Tape backup drives are still the most cost-effective, reliable, and convenient method for backing up and recovering your system after a disaster. The most obvious caveat is that tape drives use sequential access, rather than random access, meaning that they require special backup software and tend to be slower than comparably priced removables, especially when used for restoring single files. However, remember their key advantage: you can easily and painlessly duplicate the contents of your *entire* system on *one* piece of removable media and restore some or all of that data just as easily.

Although tape backup software may seem awkward on the surface, it's designed to allow you to perform a backup in a single step and without user intervention. Good backup software will also make restoring easy; the best programs keep catalogs of your backups, allowing you to find a single, previously backed-up file and get it back quickly and painlessly.

Now, many manufacturers of the various competing products and technologies market their products as backup devices, which isn't necessarily accurate. Basically, you need to find the system that works best for you and fits in your budget. Do some research before investing in any one technology, and make sure it truly suits your needs for a backup device.

Try this: add the cost of the drive you're considering with the media required to store the *entire* contents of your hard drive *twice*, and compare it with other solutions. Table 6-2 shows six example technologies and the estimated costs associated with each, at the time of this writing, to back up a 30 GB hard drive. These show that initial bargains are rarely good deals.

Table 6-2. A comparison of the actual costs associated with different types of backup hardware

Technology	Cost of drive	Cost of single cartridge	Capacity of single cartridge	Cartridges per 30 GB backup	Cost of drive and media for two backups
Rewritable CD drive	$100	30 cents	700 MB	43 = $13	$126
Removable Hard Disk	$250	*n/a*	200 GB	*n/a*	$250
Recordable DVD drive	$300	$1	4.7 GB	7 = $7	$314
AIT tape drive	$325	$40	70 GB	1 = $40	$405
DDS4 (4mm) tape drive	$400	$15	40 GB	1= $15	$430
Zip drive (750)	$80	$10	750 MB	41 = $410	$900
Floppies	*n/a*	$0.20	1.4 MB	21,429 = $4,286	$8,572

Naturally, the prices and capabilities of the various technologies will change as quickly as the weather, but the methodology is always the same. Aside from the price, the most important figure to look at is the "Cartridges per 30GB backup"; if it's more than one, it means you're going to have to sit and swap cartridges during each backup. If it's that difficult, odds are you'll never do it.

Do your research, and it will save you time and money in the long run, not to mention that extra peace of mind.

Installing Microsoft Backup

Some sort of backup software has been included with every version of Windows since Windows 3.1 more than a decade ago.

Microsoft Backup (*ntbackup.exe*), a scaled-down version of the now-defunct, yet excellent Backup Exec Desktop by Veritas (*http://www.veritas.com*), is installed by default in Windows XP Professional edition, but not in Windows XP Home edition. The implication that backing up is a feature required only by "professional" users and network administrators is one of the reasons nobody backs up their data.

Backup is not available in **Control Panel → Add or Remove Programs**; instead, you'll need to install it manually from the Windows XP CD:

1. Insert your Windows XP installation CD, and close the annoying welcome screen that appears if you haven't disabled CD AutoPlay, as described in Chapter 4.
2. Open Explorer and navigate to *\valueadd\msft\ntbackup*.
3. Double-click the *Ntbackup.msi* file to install the software (or right-click the file and select **Install**).
4. When installation is complete, a new **Backup** entry will appear in your Start Menu, in **All Programs → Accessories → System Tools**. Or, you can launch it by going to **Start → Run** and typing `ntbackup`.

When Backup first starts, you'll get the cumbersome Backup Wizard. To get out of the wizard and use the more straightforward main window, turn off the **Always start in wizard mode** option, and then click **Cancel**. Then, start Backup again, and choose the **Backup** tab to get started.

Although this is a good program, it does lack some of the capabilities of the full-featured software, such as a catalog of all backed-up files, a dedicated scheduler, and support for additional hardware. Catalogs, for example, keep track of all your backups, allowing you to choose a single file to be restored and have the software tell you which tape to insert.

Microsoft Backup supports backing up to a hard disk, floppy, or tape drive, but it can't back up to CD, despite Windows XP's built-in support for CD writers. To get around this, select **File** from the **Backup Destination** listbox, and Backup will store your data in a file on your hard disk. Then, use your CD or DVD writer software to burn the single file to disc.

Because most backup devices come with some sort of dedicated backup software, you may never need Microsoft Backup. Since most backup software is pretty awful, however, you should try all the alternatives available to you before committing to a single solution.

Tips for a Better Backup

The following tips should help ensure you will never be without adequate data protection, whether you've already invested in a backup solution or not.

Keep it simple
: The problem with backups is that most people don't do them. A few minutes every couple of weeks is all it takes, and it can save many, many

hours in the long run. A good time to do a backup is just before lunch, just before you go home (if the computer is at work), or just before you go to bed (if the computer is at home). You can also schedule your backup to occur automatically and repeatedly at any time, although you'll need to leave your computer on for that to work.

Do it after-hours
: Don't do a backup while you're working on the computer. Your backup program will not be able to reliably back up any files that are in use, and your system will be slower and more likely to crash if you are doing too many things at once.

Use at least two cartridges
: Maintain at least two sets of backups, alternating media each time you back up. If you back up to tape, for example, use the tape "A" for the first backup, tape "B" for the second backup, and then use tape "A" again. That way, if one of the tapes develops a problem or your backup is interrupted, you'll still have an intact, fairly recent backup.

Name your tapes correctly
: Most backup programs allow you to specify a name for the media the first time you use them (or whenever you *initialize* the media), which allows the cataloging feature to tell you on which cartridge a certain file resides.

Make sure each of your tapes or cartridges has a unique name that matches the tape's handwritten label, which will ensure that your software identifies each tape the same way you do. Call your tapes something like "Backup A" and "Backup B," or "Kearney," "Jimbo," and "Nelson." But don't use dates, and don't use the same name for two different cartridges.

Keep your cartridges off-site
: Your backups should not be kept near your computer, and especially not *inside* the computer. If your computer is stolen or if there's a fire, your backups would go with it. Keeping one of the backups (see alternating backups earlier in this list) somewhere off-premises is a really good idea.* And if you make your living off a computer, you might consider keeping a backup in a safe deposit box.

* Some people keep an extra backup cartridge in their car, which can be handy if you want to keep it off premises, yet still accessible if you need it in a pinch. This is fine, as long as you don't park in the sun, and as long as you don't care if you car gets stolen (from a data privacy point of view).

Lock 'em up

Remember that your tape will typically contain a copy of every file on your system, including sensitive data. Even if you protect your data with passwords and encryption (see Chapter 8), anyone could have access to your data if you leave a backup tape sitting right in the drive or in a nearby unlocked drawer. While you're at it, you may wish to employ your backup software's security features, such as password-protecting your backups.

Back up the System State

Most backup utilities designed especially for Windows XP give you the option of backing up your "System State," which is essentially a euphemism for the files that make up your Registry (see Chapter 3). You should always take advantage of this feature; without a valid Registry backup, all those backed-up applications won't do you any good.

Forget floppies

Don't back up to floppies if you can avoid it. Floppies are *much* more likely to fail than your hard disk, although it's marginally better than no backup at all. Floppies should only be used to transfer information from one computer to another, and then only if there's no network connection between them and you don't have a CD writer.

Back up your backup software

Make sure you have a copy of your backup software handy at all times. If you can't install your backup software, you won't be able to access your backups.

Automate your backups

Configure your system for unattended backups. Ideally, you should only have to insert a single cartridge and click "Go" to complete a backup. Don't put up with lower-capacity backup devices that require you to swap cartridges in order to do a single backup. Additionally, most backup software has options to bypass any confirmation screens; by taking advantage of them, you eliminate the possibility of starting a backup before you go home and coming to work the next day only to see the message, "Overwrite the data on tape?"

Don't bother with incremental backups

Most backup software allows you to do a full-system backup and then supplement it with incremental backups that only store the files that have changed since the last backup. This may mean that you can do some backups in less time, but it also means that you'll have to restore each of those backups when recovering from a disaster—one full backup and ten incremental backups adds up to eleven restores. More importantly, incremental backups require that the original full backup be intact. If something happens to that one backup, all subsequent incremental backups will be rendered completely useless.

Prepare for the worst
: Throughout this book, you'll find tips to help you prepare for a catastrophe, such as a hard disk crash or virus attack. For example, Chapter 10 explains how to repair a Windows installation and even create a boot diskette so you can start Windows even if something goes wrong. If you take the time to prepare for these problems now, rather than after they happen, you won't have to say "I should've..."

Test your system
: Don't wait until it's too late to find that the restore process doesn't work or requires a step you hadn't considered. Just do a simple trial backup of a single folder or group of files. Then, try to restore the backup to a different drive or folder. Only after you've successfully and completely retrieved a backup can you truly consider your data safe.

Recovering Your System After a Crash

The purpose of backing up is to give you the opportunity to restore your system to its original state if something unforeseen should happen to your hard disk, whether it be theft, fire, malfunction, or just user error. You'd be surprised at how many people back up their system without having any idea how to restore it later should the need arise. The backup doesn't do you any good if you can't get at your files later, so it's important to take steps to make sure you can restore your system *from scratch* if necessary.

The most important consideration is that the software you use to restore your files be the same one you used to back them up. This means installing Windows and then installing your backup software before you can even begin the restoration process.

Now, reinstalling Windows doesn't necessarily mean that you lose your Windows preferences and must reinstall all your applications. All you need to do is to reinstall Windows (as well as the software and drivers for your backup device, if necessary) to a state sufficient only to run your backup software. You'll also want to install this temporary version of Windows in a different folder name than what was used previously. See Chapter 1 for issues concerning installing and repairing Windows, as well as setting up a dual-boot system for the purposes of this solution. You may also need the Windows Recovery Console, discussed at the end of this chapter, to help recover a broken system.

Protecting Your Hardware

Although this section focuses mostly on backups, you shouldn't neglect your hardware. All hardware is sensitive to heat, light, dust, and shock. Don't block any vents on your computer or your monitor, and routinely vacuum all around to remove dust (too much dust can cause your components to overheat and your disk drives to fail).

For desktop computers, make sure you have at least one functioning fan in your computer's power supply (preferably two), one mounted directly on top of your processor and one mounted on the main chip on your video card; an additional fan in front won't hurt, either. If you can't hear your computer, odds are it isn't being adequately cooled. Make sure that air can flow freely inside from the front of the computer to the back; look for a mass of cables blocking the passage of air. Overheated components can cause system crashes, slow performance, and data loss.

If your computer and every external peripheral are connected to a surge protector, the possibility of damage by an electrical surge is virtually eliminated. Many surge protectors also allow you to run your phone cables through them, protecting them from phone line surges that can damage your modem. And if you live in an area susceptible to blackouts or brownouts, you might consider an uninterruptible power supply (UPS), which will eliminate the problem of lost data due to lost power. (Naturally, your battery-powered laptop has a UPS built in.)

Make sure all your cables are tied neatly behind the computer so pins and plugs don't get broken and plugs don't become loose; pets love to chew on cables, pulling them out and otherwise mangling them. And tighten all those cable thumbscrews.

Keep floppies, tapes, and other magnetic cartridges away from your monitor and speakers; they're just big magnets that can turn disks into coasters in no time. And sit up straight—no slouching!

Create a Boot Disk

Long gone are the days when an entire operating system can be fit on a single floppy diskette. Actually, many would argue that the floppy drive is essentially obsolete, with no real purpose in a modern computer, at least as long as there a network connection or CD writer is available to transfer files. However, from time to time, a floppy can still prove useful.

In some earlier versions of Windows (e.g., Windows 9x/Me), there was a built-in feature for making a bootable floppy, but it only installed a few files on a blank disk that essentially allowed you to boot into DOS and then start or repair the Windows installation on your hard disk. Being able to boot off a floppy also meant that you could access your files if Windows wouldn't start at all.

Now, if you have a bootable floppy made on a Windows 9x/Me system, you can use it to boot any modern system, even if it is running Windows XP. However, if your hard disk uses the NTFS filesystem (discussed in Chapter 5), you won't be able to access your hard drive from the DOS floppy (since NTFS isn't supported in those versions of Windows). And even if you're still using the FAT32 filesystem, which will be readable from a Windows 9x/Me boot disk, you won't be able to start Windows XP or effect any substantial repairs from such a floppy.

Essentially, if you've become accustomed to being able to boot to DOS in earlier versions of Windows, you'll have to adjust your strategy, but that doesn't mean you'll have to live without any safety net at all. There are several ways in Windows XP to fill the holes left by the absence of DOS:

Running old programs
: One reason to use a boot disk in the early days was to run old DOS software that refused to operate from within Windows. Although this is no longer practical in Windows XP, you can run any such software in "compatibility mode" (discussed earlier in this chapter). Another way to access old software that won't run in Windows XP is to set up a dual-boot system, discussed in Chapter 1.

Repairing Windows
: The best way to repair a Windows installation that won't start is to use the Windows Recovery Console, covered later in this chapter.

Installing Windows
: Since Windows XP comes on a bootable CD (see Chapter 1), you don't need a floppy to install it.

Accessing files
: If you can't start Windows, and attempts to repair it have failed, you'll still need to access your personal files. Installing Windows XP in a second directory is probably your best bet here. See "Setting up a dual-boot system" in Chapter 1 for instructions.

Now that I've effectively talked you out of creating a bootable floppy in Windows XP, I'll show you two ways to do it.

Make a Windows XP boot disk

Follow these steps to make a boot diskette that will load the copy of Windows XP on your hard disk. Use this when your hard disk won't boot by itself, but Windows appears to be undamaged. Use the Windows Recovery Console (see the next section) to repair the problem.

1. Obtain a blank diskette, and insert it into your floppy drive. Floppies can typically be found behind file cabinets, under coffee cups, and at the bottom of "junk" drawers.
2. If you haven't done so already, you'll need to configure Explorer to show your hidden and system files. Go to **Control Panel → Folder Options → View** tab, and select **Show hidden files and folders**. Next, turn off the **Hide protected operating system files** option, and click **OK** when you're done.
3. Open Windows Explorer, and navigate to the root directory of your boot drive (usually *C:*).
4. Copy the following three files from this folder to your floppy (usually *A:*): *ntdetect.com*, *ntldr*, and *boot.ini*.*
5. Close Explorer and eject the floppy when you're done.

This bootable floppy won't get you to a command prompt, as you might expect. If you need access to a non-Windows command prompt, you have two options: use the Windows Recovery Console (see the next section), or create a Windows 9x boot disk.

Make a DOS boot disk

Here's how to make a diskette—from within Windows XP—that will boot you into DOS, just like the old days:

1. Insert a diskette into your floppy drive.
2. Open Windows Explorer, right-click your floppy drive icon, and select **Format**.
3. Turn on the **Create an MS-DOS startup disk** option and click **Start**.
4. Wait.

When you're done, you'll have a disk that will boot into the last version of MS-DOS ever released by Microsoft: Windows Millenium (also known as Windows Me).

* See "Setting up a dual-boot system" in Chapter 1 for details on the *boot.ini* file.

This can be really handy if you're trying to resurrect an older computer running Windows 9x/Me, but it will be of minimal use in Windows XP. Even if you were to boot a Windows XP system with this disk, you most likely wouldn't be able to see any of its drives, because Windows Me isn't compatible with NTFS volumes. See "Choosing the Right Filesystem" in Chapter 5 for more information.

If you need another specific version of DOS (e.g., Windows 98 Second Edition, Windows 95, MS-DOS 3.3), go to *http://www.bootdisk.com/* and download the specific disk image you need.

Using the Windows Recovery Console

The Windows Recovery Console (WRC) is a tool included with Windows XP, used to repair the operating system when it won't start, as well as perform some other tasks not otherwise possible from within Windows.

For those accustomed to being able to boot into DOS to effect repairs in some earlier versions of Windows, the WRC is the Windows XP equivalent; see "Create a Boot Disk," earlier in this chapter, for more information.

The Windows Recovery Console allows you to do the following:

- Repair certain parts of a Windows XP installation, including the filesystem boot sector, the Master Boot Record (MBR), and the Boot Manager configuration
- Copy, rename, delete, or replace operating system files—or any "in-use" files for that matter—that otherwise can't be modified while Windows is running.
- Enable or disable services or devices for the next time Windows is started.
- Create and format hard drive partitions (discussed in Chapter 5).

The whole point of the Windows Recovery Console is that it can be started when Windows isn't running. To get into the WRC, start by booting up off the Windows CD, as described in "Installing Windows XP" in Chapter 1. After Setup loads all of its drivers, press **R** to start the Windows Recovery Console.

Recovery Console as a Boot Option

You can install the Recovery Console on your hard disk so that you can get to it without having to boot off the CD. Given how useful the WRC can be in a jam, you may want to do this now as a preventative measure, especially if you're unable to reliably boot from a CD. And if you use the Recovery Console frequently, you'll be able to start it more quickly if it's installed on your hard disk.

To install the WRC, go to **Start → Run** and type the following:

```
d:\i386\winnt32.exe /cmdcons
```

where *d:* is the drive letter of your CD drive. This adds the Recovery Console to your Boot Manager menu (see "Setting up a dual-boot system" in Chapter 1), giving you the option to start it every time your computer boots.

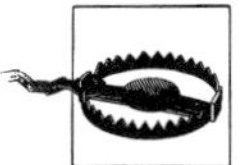

For security purposes, the Recovery Console has been intentionally hobbled to prevent access to most of the folders on your hard disk. Before you find yourself in the inevitible position of not being able to get into Windows, you should take this opportunity to lift these restrictions. Start the Local Security Settings editor (*secpol.msc*), and navigate to **\Security Settings\Local Policies\Security Options** in the tree. Double-click the **Recovery Console: Allow floppy copy and access to all drives and all folders** entry, click **Enabled**, and then click **Ok**.

Regardless of how the WRC is started, you'll be greeted with the following friendly welcome message:

```
Windows NT(TM) Boot Console Command Interpreter.

WARNING:
This is a limited function command prompt intended only as a system
recovery utility for advanced users. Using this utility incorrectly can
cause serious system-wide problems that may require you to reinstall
Windows to correct them.

Type 'exit' to leave the command prompt and reboot the system.

1: C:\WINDOWS
2: D:\WINDOWS
3: E:\WINNT

Which Windows installation would you like to logon to (enter to abort)?
```

Naturally, the operating systems installed on your system (and thus the options available to you) may be different. In most cases, choose `1` here; if you have more than one Windows installation, choose the one you wish to repair, and log in using your Administrator password.

If you've forgotten your Administrator password (set when Windows XP was installed), WRC won't let you in. You'll have three tries before WRC reboots your system. If this is the case, and Windows won't start, your best bet is to try one of the other repair options described in "Reinstalling Windows XP" in Chapter 1.

Once you've logged in, the WRC looks and feels like the Windows XP Command Prompt (see Chapter 10). However, it's important to realize that it's not exactly the same: for example, you can execute some of the standard DOS commands (albeit in a more limited fashion), but you won't be able to launch DOS or Windows programs.

Windows Recovery Console commands

The following DOS commands, documented in Chapter 10, can be used in the Windows Recovery Console: `attrib`, `cd`, `cls`, `copy`, `del`, `dir`, `exit`, `md`, `more`, `ren`, `rd`, `set`, and `type`. In addition, you'll be able to use the `chkdsk` utility discussed earlier in this chapter, the DiskPart utility discussed in "Working with Partitions," earlier in this chapter, as well as the `expand`, `format`, and `net` utilities.*

The following special commands are available in the Windows Recovery Console:

`batch` *`filename`* [*`outputfile`*]
: Executes a batch file, where *`filename`* is the name of the batch file to run, and *`outputfile`* is the name of an optional file into which the output from the job is stored. Note that you can't execute batch files simply by typing the filename, as you can in the real Command Prompt; see the discussion of batch files in Chapter 10.

`bootcfg` */`command`*
: Starts the Boot Manager configuration and recovery tool. This tool is used to view, edit, and rebuild the *boot.ini* file, discussed in "Setting up a Dual-Boot System" in Chapter 1. The *`command`* can be any of the following:

  `add`
  : Adds a new entry to the *boot.ini* file.

  `copy`
  : Creates a backup of the *boot.ini* configuration file.

* These commands are documented in detail in *Windows XP in a Nutshell* (O'Reilly).

Troubleshooting

`default`
: Sets the default boot entry.

`disableredirect`
: Disables redirection instigated by the `redirect` command.

`list`
: Displays the entries currently specified in *boot.ini*.

`rebuild`
: Lists all of the Windows installations and rebuilds the boot menu by selectively adding entries. Note that it's a good idea to use `bootcfg /copy` to create a backup of *boot.ini* before using `rebuild`.

`redirect [`*`port baudrate`*` | useBiosSettings]`
: Enables redirection of the boot loader output to the specified serial *`port`*, using the specified *`baudrate`*. Alternately, specify `bootcfg /redirect useBiosSettings` to use the default COM port settings in the system BIOS (see Appendix B).

`scan`
: Scans your hard disk for all Windows installations and displays a list of the results. This list is not dependent on the contents of the *boot.ini* file, but rather on the actual operating systems found on the system. The `rebuild` command incorporates the `scan` function.

`disable [`*`service`*` | `*`device_driver`*`]`
: Disables a system service or a device driver for the next time Windows starts. See `enable`, next, for details.

`enable `*`service`*` | `*`device_driver`*` [`*`startup_type`*`]`
: Starts or enables a system service or a device driver for the next time Windows starts. Use the `listsvc` command to list the names of all available services and device drivers. The *`startup_type`* option can be `SERVICE_BOOT_START`, `SERVICE_SYSTEM_START`, `SERVICE_AUTO_START`, or `SERVICE_DEMAND_START`.

`fixboot [`*`drive`*`]`
: Writes a new partition boot sector onto the specified partition, where *`drive`* is the drive letter. In most cases, you can omit *`drive`* to use the current partition. Use this command to fix the partition boot sector if it has been damaged, typically by a virus or the installation of another operating system.

`fixmbr [`*`device`*`]`
: Repairs the master boot record of the specified disk. Use the `map` command to display the entries for *`device`*. In most cases, you can omit *`device`* to use the default boot device, upon which your primary operating system is installed. Use this if the boot record has been damaged,

typically by a virus or the installation of another operating system. See "Creating a Dual-Boot System" for a practical example of this command.

`listsvc`
: Lists the services and drivers available on the computer, for use with the `enable` and `disable` commands.

`logon`
: Logs on to another Windows XP/2000 installation (assuming you have more than one) without having to reboot and re-enter the Recovery Console. Naturally, you'll need the administrator password for any such installation.

`map`
: Displays the drive-letter mappings for use with the `fixmbr` command.

`systemroot`
: Changes the current directory (like the `cd` command explained in Chapter 10) to the "systemroot" directory of the operating system to which you are currently logged on (usually *c:\windows*).

Lifting Recovery Console restrictions

By default, the `attrib`, `copy`, `del`, `dir`, and `ren` commands don't support wildcards (* and ?) when used in the Windows Recovery Console. While this is a safety feature intended to prevent unintentional damage to the system, it can be frustrating (to say the least) when you actually need to get something done. To lift this restriction, type:

```
set AllowWildcards = true
```

Make sure to include spaces before and after the equals sign whenever using the `set` command (e.g., "`AllowWildcards = true`" instead of "`AllowWildcards=true`"); otherwise, you'll get an error as well as a little insight into precisely how dense some Microsoft developers can be.

Another restriction is one placed on the `cd` command, where WRC will only allow you to change to certain directories. To fix this, type:

```
set AllowAllPaths = true
```

To enable access to the floppy drive, type:

```
set AllowRemovableMedia = true
```

Finally, to turn off the prompt that appears when you try to replace a file with the `copy` command, type

```
set NoCopyPrompt = true
```

Unfortunately, these are only temporary settings and are lost as soon as the system is restarted. For more information, see the set command in Chapter 10.

If you haven't already enabled the **Allow floppy copy and access to all drives and all folders** option from within Windows (as described in the beginning of this section), you may encounter a "Set command is currently disabled" error. This, unfortunately, can only be fixed by returning to Windows, thus becoming somewhat of a Catch-22 if your computer currently won't boot. Probably the best solution is to install a second copy of Windows XP into a different directory (see Chapter 1), and effect your repairs from there.

CHAPTER 7

Networking and Going Wireless

A network is the interconnection of two or more computers, facilitating the exchange of information between them. Networking—whether it's between two computers in the same room or among hundreds of millions of machines around the globe—can open a host of possibilities not feasible on a standalone system.

Connect your computer to the Internet to exchange email and files with others around the world, use video and audio conferencing software, surf the Web, and even host your own web site. Connect the computers in your home or office to exchange files, share printers, play networked games, and share an Internet connection. Nearly everything you need to do these things is present in a basic installation of Windows XP, with the exception of a clear and easy way to set them up without compromising the security of your system.

Connecting your computer to a network exposes its vulnerabilities to any number of different types of attacks, all of which can be avoided or prevented. See "Securing Your System on a Network," later in this chapter, for details. See Chapter 6 for details on dealing with spyware and viruses, and see Chapter 8 for user security.

Use the solutions in this chapter to set up a network, overcome the hurdles and annoyances of Windows support for networking, and do more with your network than you ever thought possible.

Getting Started with Networking

There are several different kinds of networks, each with their own limitations and advantages. A simple "peer-to-peer" workgroup can comprise as few as two computers connected with a single cable or pair of wireless adapters. This is ideal in a home office or small business setting, where individual systems can be linked together with minimal effort and configured to *share* resources. A shared folder, for example, is merely a standard folder residing on a single computer, made accessible to any other computer on the network through Windows Explorer as though it were actually on each computer's hard disk.

Larger organizations typically deploy networks based on the *client/server* topology. Client/server networks are different from peer-to-peer networks not so much in technology employed as in the roles the different computers play. For example, one computer on the network, which might be running Unix or Windows, takes on the role of the mail server, while another is configured to handle such tasks as printing, storage of data and applications, backup, and user authentication. The rest of the computers—the clients—are used to retrieve email from the mail server, send print jobs to the print server, and store data on the file server.

A seemingly different kind of connection, usually involving a measly telephone line or a more modern high-speed broadband connection, allows access to the Internet from a single PC. Again, this is more of a matter of the roles the different computers play than the actual technology involved in establishing the connection.

It can get more complicated, say, if you want to connect a workgroup to the Internet or create a workgroup *across* the Internet. Both of these tasks involve the combination of several different technologies, the results of which can be very interesting and are all discussed later in this chapter.

Windows supports most types of networking out of the box, but the actual process involved in setting up a given form of networking can be quite confusing, and troubleshooting a network can drive you nuts.

Terminology Primer

To start building a network, you should understand a few basic networking concepts:

The distinction between local and remote resources

A *local resource* (such as a directory or printer) is one that resides on or is physically connected to your computer. Conversely, a *remote resource* is one that resides on another computer connected to yours over a network. For example, a particular web page on *http://www.annoyances.org*

is a remote file, but an HTML file on your own hard disk is a local file. And a printer connected to your PC's USB port is a local printer, while one that is wired to another computer on your network is a remote printer. (And naturally, what's local to you may be remote to someone else.) In some cases, local and remote resources may appear indistinguishable on the surface, but details concerning how each is accessed and configured may be different. And, as they say, the devil is in the details.

LAN versus WAN

LAN stands for Local Area Network, a designation typically referring to a network contained in a single room or building. A peer-to-peer workgroup is an example of a LAN.

Likewise, WAN stands for Wide Area Network, or a network formed by connecting computers over large distances. The Internet is an example of a WAN.

Ethernet

Ethernet is the technology upon which the vast majority of local area networks is built. A standard Ethernet connection is capable of transferring data at a maximum of 10 Mbps (see Bandwidth), and a Fast Ethernet connection can transfer data at 100 Mbps. A device capable of communicating at both speeds is typically labelled "10/100."

Most modern Windows computers come with Ethernet adapters (also called NICs, or Network Interface Cards) preinstalled; for older computers, NICs are cheap and commonly available.

WiFi

WiFi is a trendy shorthand term for wireless networking based on the 802.11b standard, which allows data to be transferred at a maximum of 11 Mbps (real-world speeds tend to be closer 3.5–4.5 Mbps, however). The newer 802.11g standard is much faster (54 Mbps), backward-compatible with 802.11b, and only marginally more expensive than its slower cousin. (WiFi is now used to describe both standards.) Windows XP Service Pack 2 improves Windows built-in support for WiFi dramatically, as discussed throughout the rest of this chapter.

Almost everything in this book that applies to wired networks also applies to wireless connections. See the wireless section later in this chapter for a bunch of wireless-only tips and tricks.

Bluetooth is a different wireless networking standard, incompatible with WiFi. It's an inexpensive, low-power technology and is commonly used in high-end cell phones, handheld PDAs, and some laptops (typically via a USB Bluetooth *dongle*). For instance, you can use a Bluetooth headset with a Bluetooth-enabled cell phone, and dispense with the cumbersome cord. Or, you can surf the web with your Bluetooth-enabled handheld PC connected to the Internet wirelessly via your Bluetooth phone. There are even tiny remote-controlled toy cars that you can drive with your Bluetooth phone (truly illustrating the noble role of technology in our lives).

Bandwidth

Bandwidth is the capacity of a network connection to move information (the size of the pipe, so to speak). Bandwidth is measured in Kbps (kilobits per second) for slow connections, such as analog dialup Internet connections; Mbps (megabits per second) for fast connections such as DSL, cable, or Ethernet LAN connections; and Gbps (gigabits per second) for the kinds of connections used by huge corporations and Internet providers.

Bandwidth can be shared. If a network connection is capable of transferring data at, say, 1.5 Mbps, and two users are simultaneously downloading large files, each will only have roughly 0.75 Mbps (or 768 Kbps) of bandwidth at their disposal.

Ethernet-based local networks can support transfer rates at either 10 Mbps or up to 100 Mbps. High-speed T1, DSL, and cable modem connections typically transfer data up to 1.0 to 1.5 Mbps, while the fastest analog modems communicate at a glacial 56 Kbps, or 0.056 Mbps.

To translate a bandwidth measurement into more practical terms, you'll need to convert bits to bytes. There are eight bits to a byte, so you can determine the theoretical maximum data-transfer rate of a connection by simply dividing by 8. For example, a 384 Kbps connection transfers 384 / 8 = 48 kilobytes of data per second, which should allow you to transfer a 1 megabyte file in a little more than 20 seconds. However, there is more going on than just data transfer (such as error correction), so actual performance will always be slower than the theoretical maximum.

Protocols

A protocol is the language, so to speak, that your computer uses to communicate with other computers on the network. A network is built by installing hardware and configuring various network protocols, most of which are named with cryptic acronyms.

TCP/IP

TCP/IP is a protocol, or more accurately, a collection of protocols, used in all Internet communications and by most modern LANs. For those of you excited by acronyms, the TCP/IP specification includes TCP (Transmission Control Protocol), IP (Internet Protocol), UDP (User Datagram Protocol), and ICMP (Internet Control Message Protocol).

The amazing thing about TCP/IP, and the reason that it serves as the foundation of every connection to the Internet, is that data is broken up into *packets* before it's sent on its way. The packets travel to their destination independently, possibly arriving in a different order than the one in which they were sent. The receiving computer then reassembles the packets (in the correct order) into data.

TCP Ports

TCP/IP data moves into and out of your computer through *ports*, which are opened by the software that use your network connection. For example, your email program uses port 25 to send mail (using the SMTP protocol) and port 110 for retrieving email (using the POP3 protocol). Other commonly used ports are listed in Appendix C.

> Windows XP typically has more ports "open" than you probably need, meaning that it's vulnerable to spyware, pop-ups, viruses, intruders, and other annoyances. See "Securing Your System on a Network," later in this chapter, for the solution.

IP addresses

An IP address is a set of four numbers (e.g., `207.46.230.218`) that corresponds to a single computer or device on a TCP/IP network. Each element of the address can range from 0 to 255, providing 256^4 or nearly 4.3 billion possible combinations. On the Internet, dedicated machines called domain name servers are used to translate named hosts, such as *www.microsoft.com*, to their respective numerical IP addresses and back again.

No two computers on a single network can have the same IP address, but a single computer can have multiple IP addresses (one for each network to which it's connected).

To connect two different networks to each other, while still maintaining two separate sets of IP addresses, you'll need either a *bridge* or a *router*. Provided that you install two network adapters in your PC, Windows XP can act as a bridge; just highlight two connections in your Network Connections window (discussed later in this chapter), and select

Bridge Connections from the **Advanced** menu. A router, on the other hand, is a physical device you can use to connect your LAN to the Internet; since it acts as an effective firewall, though, it's a good idea even if you have only one PC.

Firewalls, and why you need one

A firewall can be used to restrict unauthorized access to your system from intruders, close backdoors opened by viruses and other malicious applications, and eliminate wasted bandwidth by blocking certain types of network traffic.

A firewall is a layer of protection that permits or denies network communication based on a predefined set of rules. These rules are typically based on the TCP port through which the data is sent, the IP address from which the data originated, and the IP address to which the data is destined.

The problem is that an improperly configured firewall can cause more problems than it ends up preventing. Windows XP includes a rudimentary firewall feature, described later in this chapter, but software-based firewalls simply don't work as well as hardware firewalls, such as routers.

Switches, access points, and routers

A switch allows you to connect more than two computers together—using cables—to form a local network (Figure 7-1). (Note that a *hub* does pretty much the same thing as a switch, but much less efficiently.) Without a hub or switch, the most you could do is connect two computers to each other with a *crossover* cable (discussed later in this chapter).

A wireless access point is essentially a switch (or a hub) for a wireless network, allowing you to connect multiple computers wirelessly. Without an access point, you could only connect two computers wirelessly in "ad hoc" mode (more on wireless access points later in this chapter).

Finally, a router is a device that connects two networks, and *routes* traffic between them. For example, a router can connect a peer-to-peer workgroup to the Internet, allowing you to share an Internet connection with all the computers in your office (see "Sharing an Internet Connection," later in this chapter, for details). Most routers also double as switches, just as *wireless routers* double as wireless access points. Plus, any modern router (wireless or otherwise) will have a built-in firewall (typically superior to a software firewall that runs on your computer), so you can basically get everything you need in one inexpensive package.

Now, this book only touches the surface of a large and complex topic, but it should help you get a handle on the drivers, hardware, and workarounds required to set up some of the more common types of networks quickly and painlessly. Maybe, once all the frustrations are whisked away, you might even have some fun.

Planning Your Network

There are many types of networks and nearly limitless combinations of networking technologies, but for the purposes of this chapter, most situations can be covered by considering two basic types of network setups: *workgroups* and *Internet connections*. Strictly speaking, there isn't a lot of difference between these two, at least as far as Windows XP is concerned. The distinction is made primarily to help you plan the topology of your networking environment.

Drawing a diagram of the physical layout of the computers and devices on your network can help you visualize the topology and plan the cables, routers, antennas, and aspirin you'll need to complete the job.

Wiring can vary in complexity and cost, depending on your needs, budget, and the layout of your office. (See the "Cabling Tips" sidebar for additional help.) For example, if you have two or more desktop computers in the same room, wiring is a simple matter of adding a switch (or hub) and one category-5 *patch* cable for each machine, as shown in Figure 7-1.

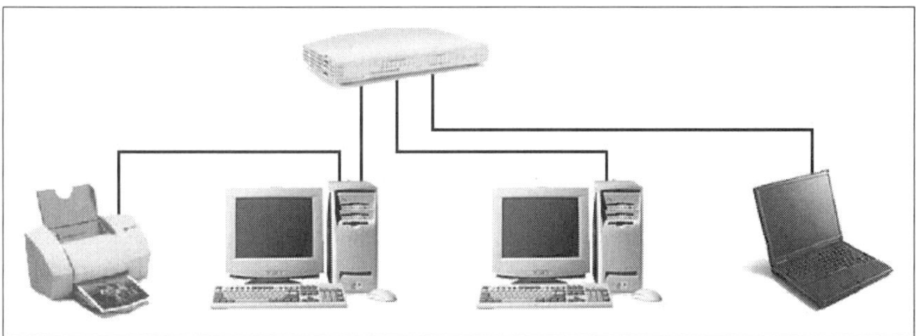

Figure 7-1. An example of a peer-to-peer network (LAN) comprised of three computers connected with a switch (or hub); the printer is connected to one of the computers, which shares it with the others

If you only have two computers, you can eliminate the hub and simply connect them with an inexpensive category-5 *crossover* cable, as shown in Figure 7-2. Total cost: $3.99.

Of course, thanks to wireless technology (e.g., WiFi or 802.11), the whole concept of wiring a network can be considered optional. However, there are a few drawbacks. First of all, wireless equipment is more expensive than simple cabling, and the technology can be temperamental, resulting in a lot of frustration until you get it working.

Figure 7-2. A quick-and-dirty hubless workgroup; given its limitations, however, it's best suited as a temporary solution

Cabling Tips

Within a second or two of connecting both ends of a network cable, the corresponding lights on your hardware should light up. Lights should be visible right on the network adapter, whether it's in the back of your desktop computer or in the side of your laptop. If you are using a laptop and your network adapter requires a dongle, the light may be on the adapter or on end of the dongle. (Note that some devices use multicolor LEDs that light green if the connection is correct, and red if it's wrong.)

Connect all your cables while your hub/switch and any other equipment is turned on and Windows is running. That way, you'll see the corresponding indicator lights go on, indicating that the hub, switch, router, or Ethernet adapter has detected the new connection. Note that the lights only confirm the cabling is correct; they won't tell you if the drivers and protocols are correctly installed.

Use only category-5 (Cat-5) *patch* cables, except for a few specific situations that require category-5 *crossover* cables. Use a crossover cable to connect two computers directly (without a hub, switch, or router), or to connect multiple hubs/switches to one another. In some cases where a DSL/cable modem connects directly to a computer with a patch cable, a crossover cable may be required to connect either of these devices to a hub or switch (consult the documentation to be sure). Either way, if the lights go on, you're using the right kind of cable.

When measuring for cables, always add several extra feet to each cable; too long is better than too short. Also, bad cables are not uncommon, so have a few extras around in case any of those lights don't light up.

Shop around when looking for cables. Most of the huge mega-computer stores charge too much for cables; you can often find longer, better cables at a fraction of the price (sans the fancy packaging) by shopping at smaller mom-and-pop computer stores.

Finally, if your cables are to pass through walls, you may want to install category-5 wall jacks for the tidiest appearance. Note that these accessories can be expensive and cumbersome to wire properly, and are typically unnecessary for all but the most compulsive neatness freaks among us.

Wireless networking is not as fast as wired Ethernet. Wireless data is transferred at a maximum throughput of 11 Mbps (or 54 Mbps for "wireless-G" connections), and this speed decreases rapidly as reception worsens. Fast Ethernet connections allow data to be transferred at 100 Mbps, reception notwithstanding. While the speed difference won't matter for an Internet connection (typical broadband is only about 0.5–1.5 Mbps), an Ethernet connection will allow you to transfer files between computers in your workgroup in half the time.

The most compelling reasons to use a wireless LAN are portability, distance, and convenience. A wireless LAN adapter in your laptop would mean, for example, that you could have Internet access anywhere in your house or office, and without having to hassle with wires. (Naturally, your mileage will vary with any interference or natural obstacles present in your environment). Distance is an issue, for instance, when you'd otherwise have to extend a wire from one end of a building to another, drilling holes in walls and such. Of course, distance also degrades wireless signals, but this can be dealt with by adding aftermarket antennas or a repeater (also called a "range expander"). Figure 7-3 shows a typical wireless network with four computers (three PCs and one PDA).

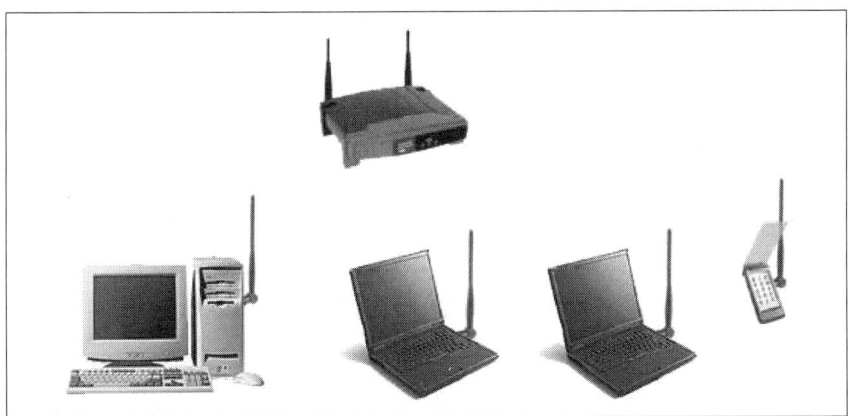

Figure 7-3. A wireless router acts as both a wireless access point and a switch, allowing you to connect any number of computers (and even WiFi-enabled PDAs) to form a wireless LAN (WiFi antennas are typically internal, and are shown here only for illustrative purposes)

It's also important to realize that you don't have to commit solely to one technology or another. For instance, you can mix and match wireless and wired networks, which may mean only purchasing wireless equipment for laptops, or those computers that would otherwise be very difficult to wire. Figure 7-4 shows a simple peer-to-peer network with two wired desktop computers and a wireless connection to a laptop.

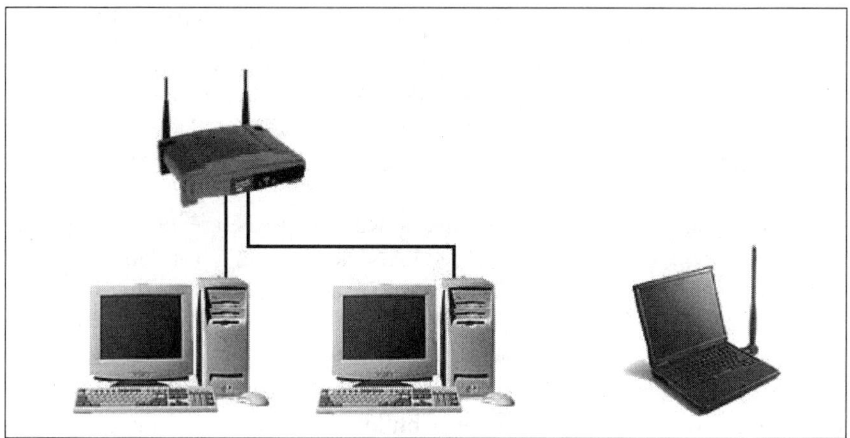

Figure 7-4. You can mix and match wired and wireless devices with a wireless router; these three computers are on the same network, despite the different means of connection

There's one crucial aspect of wireless networking that simply doesn't exist on a wired network: *intruders*. By default, most wireless routers have no security features enabled, meaning that any WiFi-enabled computer within range can connect to your workgroup and use your Internet connection. See "Set Up a Wireless Router" and "Sniff Out WiFi Networks," both later in this chapter, for help securing your wireless network and connecting to someone else's unsecured wireless network, respectively.

Adding Internet to the Mix

When including an Internet connection, you have several choices. The old-school approach, illustrated in Figure 7-5, involves a single computer connected directly to the Internet (via broadband, dial-up, or whatever). The aforementioned PC then serves as a *gateway* (thanks to Internet Connection Sharing, discussed later in this chapter) and shares the Internet connection with the other computers on the LAN.

There are several downsides to Internet Connection Sharing. For one, it can be temperamental and frustrating to set up. Performance and security leave a lot to be desired, and it tends to be slow. Also, one computer (the gateway) must always be on for the others to have Internet access, and that computer must have two network adapters.

The preferred method is to use a wireless router, as shown in Figure 7-6.

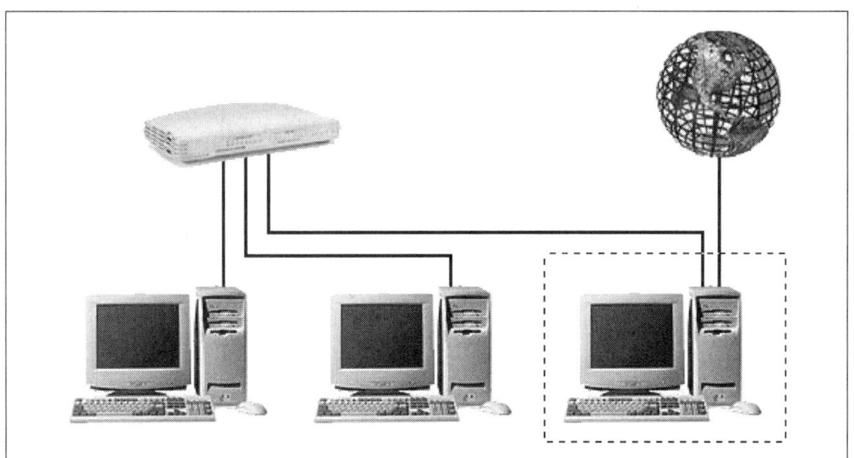

Figure 7-5. A simple workgroup with three computers, one of which has a shared Internet connection (see the next section, "Configuring Network Connections," for the significance of the dotted rectangle)

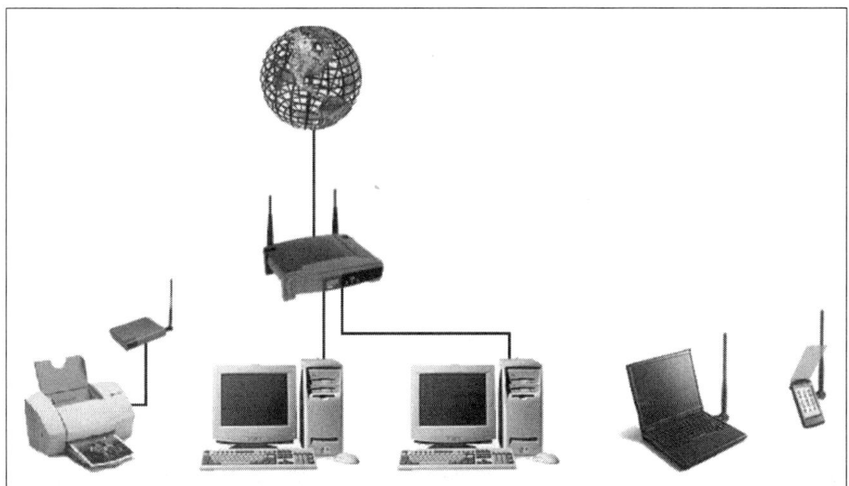

Figure 7-6. A wireless router makes it easy to share an Internet connection and offers better security than the old-school gateway approach—note the wireless print server

The router is a sole unit (the little box with two antennas in Figure 7-6) that plays a whole bunch of valuable roles on your network:

A switch, through which a local network (LAN) consisting of wired and wireless computers is built.

A wireless access point, connecting any number of wireless PCs, handhelds, and other devices to your LAN.

A router, bridging your local network to the Internet, thus providing Internet access to all the computers on your LAN. Plus, if you're using a broadband connection that requires a username and password (e.g., PPPoE), the router will log in automatically for you, and keep you logged in.

A DHCP server, which automatically assigns IP addresses to computers in your local network (typically starting with 192.168.1.2, where 192.168.1.1 is the router itself), allowing them to peacefully coexist on your network.

A firewall, preventing any and all communication from the outside world, except that which you specifically allow. (This is done through your router's port-forwarding feature.)

A print server, to which you can connect a USB or parallel-port printer, and print from any computer (without sharing).

Historically, the print server tended to be the proverbial straw that broke the proverbial camel's back, in that such all-in-one devices tended to be unreliable. Some people have had great success with routers with built-in print servers, while others haven't been so lucky. For this reason, you may wish to use a standalone (or even wireless) print server, separate from your router.

Routeres are discussed throughout the rest of this chapter. If you don't yet have one, do yourself a favor and pick one up. They're cheap and, as shown here, do quite a lot. Even if you only have a single PC (no network), the firewall feature of a router provides excellent security, far better protection than Windows XP's built-in firewall (even the one that comes with Service Pack 2).

Configuring Network Connections

The Network Connections window, shown in Figure 7-7, is the central interface you use to configure the networking features in Windows XP. Go to **Control Panel → Network Connections** or right-click the My Network Places icon and select **Properties** to open the Network Connections Window.

If you haven't done so already, select **Details** from the **View** menu to see all the pertinent information at once. Then, simplify the listing by going to **View → Arrange Icons by** and turn off the **Show in Groups** option.

If you don't see Network Setup Wizard or New Connection Wizard here, you're probably viewing Network Connections from Windows Explorer (with the folder-tree pane). To fix the problem, go to **Tools → Folder Options → General** tab, select **Use Windows classic folders**, and click OK.

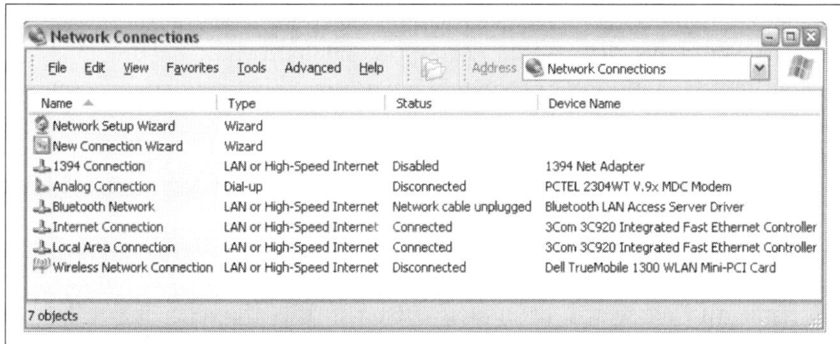

Figure 7-7. The Network Connections window, shown here with the default common tasks pane, is where you configure and manipulate all network resources in Windows XP

As its name implies, Network Connections lists all of the networking connections configured on your computer. In the rather-full example window in Figure 7-7, there are two wired Ethernet connections, one WiFi wireless connection, one analog (dial-up) connection, a IEEE-1394 (Firewire) connection, and a Bluetooth wireless connection. The computer that owns these connections is illustrated in Figure 7-5 earlier in this chapter, the one encapsulated by the dotted rectangle. This rectangle, called a *control volume*, shows the scope of Windows XP's awareness of its role in your network.

Windows doesn't care how many computers are on your network, whether your network is wired or wireless, or even what kind of broadband Internet connection you have. The only thing you need to worry about in the context of this window is the individual connections attached to your PC.

Part 1: Adding new connections

A connection icon for each network adapter (NIC) installed in your system should appear automatically in your Network Connections window. Install a new network adapter, and—assuming it has been properly set up—it will show up there as well.

Additionally, you might have one or more connection icons for any *virtual* connections, such as dial-up connections (for your analog or ISDN modem), PPPoE connections (for broadband connections requiring a login), and VPN (Virtual Private Networking) connections. You can add a new virtual connection by double-clicking **New Connection Wizard**, or, if you if you have the common tasks pane enabled, by clicking **Create a new connection**. You can also go to **Start → Run**, type `icwconn1`, and click **OK**.

The New Connection Wizard is fairly self-explanatory, but what may not be obvious is that you cannot use it to add a new hard-wired connection.

Instead, as mentioned above, such connections are added automatically as soon as Windows detects the corresponding hardware. If you're having trouble getting Windows to recognize a hard-wired network connection, see Chapter 6.

The four options on the first page of New Connection Wizard are:

Connect to the Internet
: You'll only need this option to add a dial-up Internet connection or to configure PPPoE (used by DSL or cable connections that require a username and password, as discussed later in this chapter). If you have a high-speed connection with a static IP address (including many DSL or cable connections), you won't need this wizard.

  The next page has three choices, the second of which, **Set up my connection manually**, will be the appropriate choice in most cases. The first option is basically only for those who wish to sign up for MSN (Microsoft's online service), and the third simply starts the setup program on whatever CD is inserted in your drive.

Connect to the network at my workplace
: This option is only used to set up a remote connection to a business network, either through a dial-up connection or through VPN (Virtual Private Networking). See "Virtual Private Networking," later in this chapter, for details.

Set up a home or small office network
: This simply closes the New Connection Wizard and starts the Network Setup Wizard, discussed in the next section.

Set up an advanced connection
: The last entry here is used to set up other types of connections, such as PC-to-PC connections using a serial or parallel cable, and setting up your computer as a VPN host (discussed later in this chapter).

After creating a new connection, rename it so that it is easier to distinguish from any other connections you may have. To make other changes to the new connection, right-click it and select **Properties**, as described next

Any network connection that can be added with the New Connection Wizard can be copied by right-clicking and selecting **Create copy**. Create a copy of a dial-up connection, for example, to set up two similar connection profiles without having to enter all the information twice. Copies are also handy for creating backups of connections so that you can experiment with different settings without losing a working profile. Note that if you only want to add alternate phone numbers, you can right-click the connection, select **Properties**, and click **Alternates**.

Part 2: Working with connection properties

The Network Connections window lists all hardware and software connections currently configured on your computer. And if you're using the Details view, as shown in Figure 7-7, you'll also see such pertinent information as the type of connection, whether or not it is enabled and connected, the name of the hardware device to which it corresponds, and a few other useful tidbits.

Right-click any connection icon and then select **Properties** to view the settings for the particular connection. This is where most of your network settings will be configured. A typical connection properties sheet is shown in Figure 7-8.

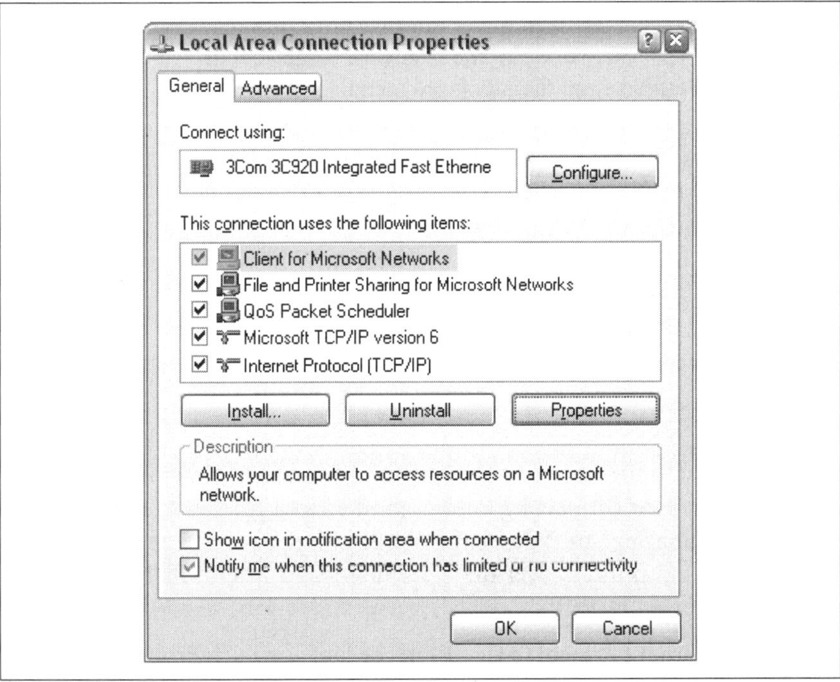

Figure 7-8. Right-click a connection and select Properties to view and modify the settings for the connection

If you've configured your Start Menu to "expand" Network Connections (**Control Panel → Taskbar and Start Menu → Start Menu** tab → **Customize**), you can also right-click the menu items right in your Network Connections menu and select **Properties**.

Depending on the type of connection you're viewing, the tabs that appear across the top of the dialog will vary. In addition, tabs by the same name will have different meanings for different connections, which can make things even more confusing. For example, for LAN or high-speed Internet connections, the list of the currently installed services and protocols is shown in the middle of the **General** tab page, but it appears in the **Networking** tab for any dial-up or broadband connections. Fortunately, the list itself is the same in all situations, and that's what matters. Figure 7-8 shows the entries installed for a typical network connection.

Prioritizing Network Connections and Services

There's a little-known setting you can play with that may improve performance on your network. In the Network Connections window, select **Advanced Settings** from the **Advanced** menu.

The **Adapters and Bindings** tab allows you to prioritize your network connections. Use the up and down arrow buttons to the right of the upper list on this page to move the connection you use most to the top of the list.

Likewise, the **Provider Order** tab allows you to prioritize your network services. In most cases, you'll want the **Microsoft Windows Network** entry to appear at the top of the list (although it typically won't be there by default), but you can prioritize any service you wish here.

Click **OK** when you're done; the change will take effect immediately.

Among the usual suspects here are **Client for Microsoft Networks**, an essential component for connecting your computer to a Microsoft network, **File and Printer Sharing for Microsoft Windows**, the service responsible for sharing files and printers over the aforementioned Microsoft Network, and **Internet Protocol (TCP/IP)**.

Highlight **Internet Protocol (TCP/IP)** in the list, and click **Properties** to view the TCP/IP Properties window shown in Figure 7-9. This dialog is used, among other things, to either specify the IP address for static IP connections or to instruct Windows to accept whatever IP address it is assigned.

All network connections that use the TCP/IP protocol (explained at the beginning of this chapter) have an IP address, including your Internet connection and any connections to your local workgroup. However, it's not always necessary to actually set an IP address. Use the following tips to help you determine whether or not you need to set the IP address for a particular connection, as well as which IP address you should use should the need arise.

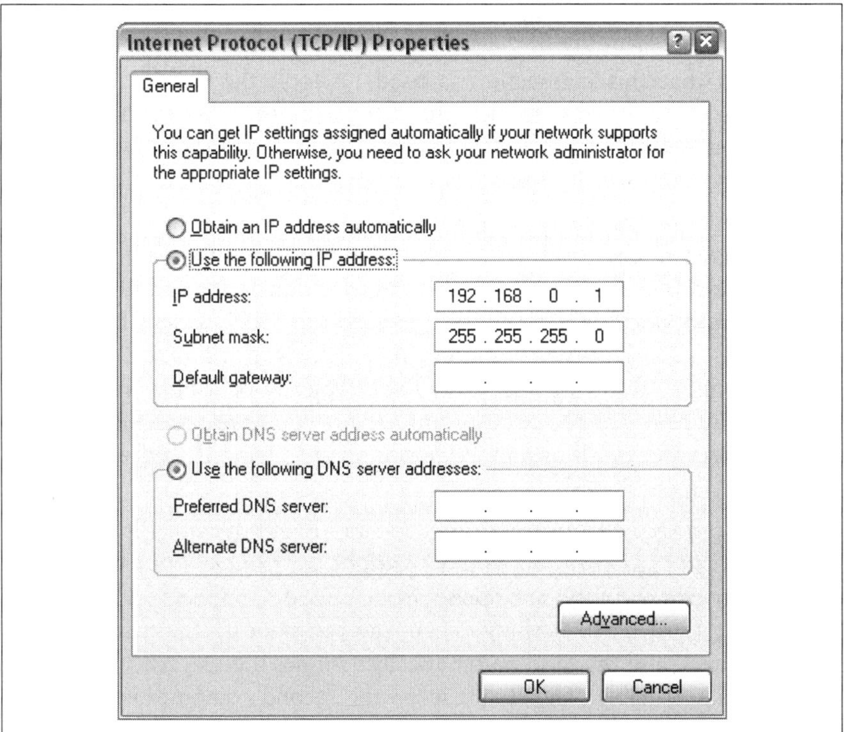

Figure 7-9. The properties sheet for the TCP/IP protocol allows you to set the IP address, DNS server addresses, and other settings required by some connections

No two computers on the same network should have the same IP address. This applies to two computers on your local network and two computers on the Internet on opposite ends of the planet.

Internet connection

If your Internet connection has a dynamic (changing) IP address, select the **Obtain an IP address automatically** option and leave the rest of the fields blank. These fields typically apply to dial-up connections, as well as DSL and cable connections that require a login with a username and password (see the discussion of PPPoE, later in this chapter).

In some cases, Windows will be able to detect the IP address and other settings for Internet connections that have static IP addresses. If Windows cannot auto-detect your settings, you'll have to enter the IP address, subnet mask, gateway, and nameserver addresses, as provided by your Internet service provider.

Workgroup (LAN) connection

In the example in Figure 7-9, the IP address is set to `192.168.0.1`, which implies that this connection is used to hook the computer up to a Microsoft workgroup. In fact, the entire `192.168.0.xxx` subnet—which includes `192.168.0.1`, `192.168.0.2`, `192.168.0.3`, and so on—is typically used by Windows to form its workgroups.

It's up to you whether or not the computers in your local workgroup have fixed IP addresses. If you leave these fields blank, you'll be relying on your router or switch to automatically assign an unused IP address to your computer each time it's powered on. If you specify fixed IP addresses for all of the computers in your LAN, it will take a little bit of extra initial effort, but the reward will typically be a more reliable and responsive peer-to-peer workgroup. Unless you have a specific reason to do otherwise, you'll usually be better off specifying IP addresses for all the PCs in your LAN.

It's also possible to mix and match static-IP and dynamic-IP computers on the same network, but you'd be asking for trouble. For example, say you have three computers, one set to `192.168.0.1`, one set to `192.168.0.2`, and the third set to nothing. Then, say you boot up the first and third computers, and the third automatically assumes the `192.168.0.2` address, since it's available. The result: when the second computer is eventually booted, it will be unable to join the network since its fixed IP address will have already been taken.

It's possible for a computer to have more than one IP address. For example, the right-most computer in Figure 7-5 has two connections: one for the workgroup and one for the Internet connection. Each connection will have its own IP address, either specified in the TCP/IP properties window or assigned automatically.

Windows 95/98/Me computers can have trouble connecting to XP machines in the same network, although, in theory, they're supposed to be compatible with one another. If this happens, try specifying static IP addresses for all computers in your LAN, and then make sure that no computers are using the obsolete NetBEUI protocol.

Also of interest in the connection-properties windows is the **Advanced** tab, used to enable Internet Connection Sharing and Windows XP's built-in firewall feature, both described later in this chapter.

The **Authentication** tab, found in the properties windows of LAN or high-speed Internet connections, is used only for wireless networks, despite the rather ubiquitous-sounding name. (This has nothing to do with user authentication, which is discussed in Chapter 8.) Likewise, the **Security** tab, found in dial-up and broadband connections, is used only to control how the username and password are transmitted across the connection, and is not related to any actual security features in Windows XP.

Part 3: Connection status and other ways to manipulate network connections

By default, all hard-wired network connections (also known as LAN or high-speed Internet connections) are enabled when Windows starts, and are connected (if possible).

Dial-up and broadband (including PPPoE) connections, on the other hand, need to be manually connected before they will function. Simply double-click (or right-click and select **Connect**) to initiate a manual connection. And when you're done, right-click the entry and select **Disconnect**.

Double-click any *connected* connection to view its Status window, shown in Figure 7-10. Among the items of interest are **Duration**, which shows how long the connection has been active, and **Activity**, which shows how much data has been sent and received (in packets). The size of each packet depends on your MTU setting (discussed later in this chapter), but this value is usually in the neighborhood of 1500 bytes. So, this example Status window shows that 484 packets (roughly 726 kb) have been sent and 371 packets (roughly 557 kb) have been received.

If you're working with a wireless connection, the Status window will also show the strength of the connection signal (up to five little green bars), plus the **View Wireless Networks** button. See the Wireless section of this chapter for more information on the Choose a Wireless Network window.

All connections, by default, have an icon that appears in the notification area (tray) when they're connected; double-click this icon to view the Status window, or right-click the icon for other options. To enable or disable the tray icon for *any* type of connection, right-click the connection in the Network Connections window, select **Properties**, and change the **Show icon in notification area when connected option** (located under the **General** tab) as needed.

LAN or high-speed Internet connections can be enabled or disabled by right-clicking their icons and selecting **Enable** or **Disable**, respectively. (You can also double-click a connection and click **Enable** or **Disable** in its Status window.) Disabling devices in this way is the same as disabling them from Device Manager and has the same effect as physically uninstalling them from your computer.

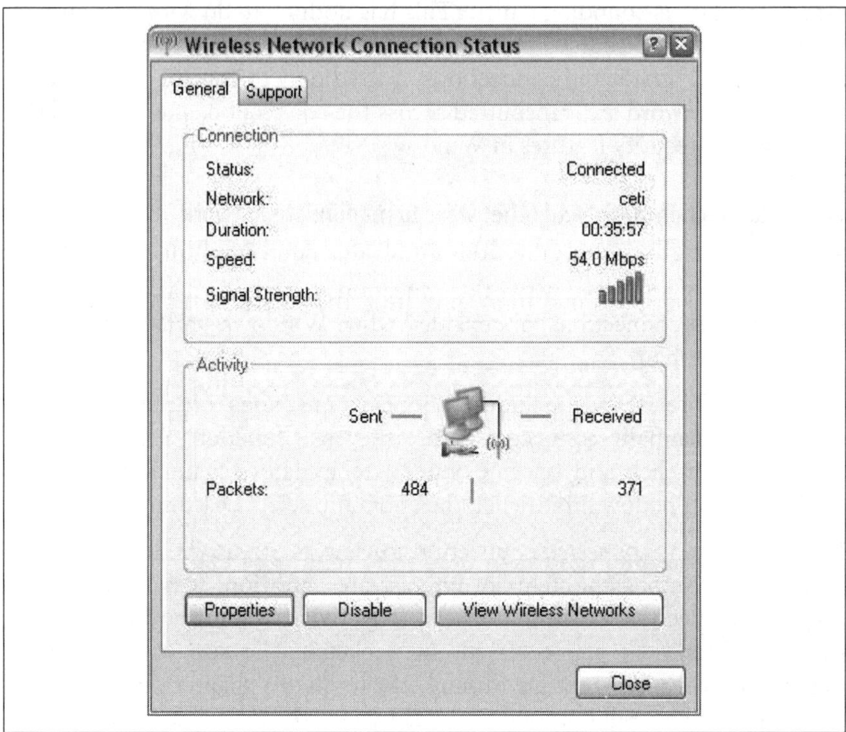

Figure 7-10. Double-click a connection icon in the Network Connections window or system tray to view its connection status

In addition to **Properties**, **Enable/Disable**, and **Connect/Disconnect**, there are other items available on some connection icons' context menus, depending on the connection type:

Repair
: The **Repair** command reinstalls the drivers associated with the connection. If a connection does not appear to be working, try disabling it and then re-enabling it (or disconnecting and then reconnecting, if applicable). If that doesn't work, you can try using the **Repair** feature, but the odds that it will do anything useful are fairly remote.

Set as Default Connection/Cancel as Default Connection
: This option is available only for dial-up and broadband (PPPoE) connections, and is used to decide which connection is "dialed" when Windows needs to automatically connect to the Internet. Go to **Control Panel → Internet Options → Connections** tab to configure this feature. A black checkmark in a circle will appear over the connection icon for any connection that is set as the default.

Bridge Connections

Simply put, a network bridge allows data to be transferred between two (or more) different networks. In effect, a bridge turns your computer into a router of sorts, but with the advantage of allowing you to combine two otherwise incompatible networks. Windows XP supports only one bridge at any given time, but a single bridge can contain as many different connections as you want. Most users will have absolutely no use for this feature. To initiate a network bridge, select at least two connection icons, right-click, and select **Bridge Connections** (or go to **Advanced → Bridge Connections**) to create a network bridge between the connections.

View Available Wireless Networks

This opens the Choose a Wireless Network window; see the Wireless section of this chapter for more information.

That about does it for the Network Connections window. You can use the tools in this window to build and configure your network, as described throughout the rest of this chapter.

Build a Workgroup (Local Area Network)

As explained earlier in this chapter, Windows is really only concerned with the connections directly attached to the computer, so building a network or connecting a computer to the Internet essentially involves hooking things up and then configuring the connections in the Network Connections window for each computer involved.

Building a Peer-to-Peer Workgroup

A peer-to-peer workgroup is comprised of two or more computers and the necessary networking hardware to connect them. Or, in broader terms, you'll need:

- At least two computers, each presumably running Windows XP. Naturally, you can connect an XP system to one running any other networkable operating system (Windows 9x/Me, Windows NT/2000, Mac, Linux, FreeBSD, BeOS, Unix, etc.), but for the purposes of this book, we'll assume both machines are running Windows XP.
- At least one Ethernet adapter installed in each computer. NICs are cheap and readily available, and are even built into most modern systems (anything capable of running XP, anyway).

If you're not sure what to get, just purchase a standard, Plug and Play 10/100 Ethernet adapter with an RJ45 connector (or an 802.11b/g-compliant card if you're going wireless). If you have a desktop system, get a PCI card; if you have a laptop, get a CardBus adapter. USB-to-Ethernet adapters are also available, and while they're easier to install (you don't have to take your desktop apart), they tend to be slower and more temperamental than the aforementioned types.

- Lastly, you'll need a hub (or switch) and two category-5 *patch* Ethernet cables. Alternately, you can use just a single category-5 *crossover* Ethernet cable and skip the hub, but this will limit your network to only two computers. Figure 7-1 shows a workgroup of four computers connected to a hub (or switch), and Figure 7-2 shows a simpler, hubless LAN with only two systems. An alternative to the cables and hub is wireless equipment, discussed in "Planning Your Network," earlier this chapter.

Once you have all of the components, you can begin with the following procedure. Naturally, different types of hardware will require a modified procedure, but the methodology is the same.

1. Plan your network by drawing a quick diagram similar to the ones shown in the figures in this chapter.
2. Install a network adapter in each computer, according to the instructions that accompany your hardware.

   A connection icon labeled Local Area Connection should appear in your Network Connections window for each installed adapter. See "Configuring Network Connections," earlier in this chapter, for details on working with these connections, checking their status, and so on. If the icons don't show up, make sure Windows recognizes your network cards in Device Manager, as explained in Chapter 6, and doesn't report any problems with the devices.
3. Next, hook up your cables (unless, of course, you're using wireless equipment). Nearly all network adapters, hubs, and switches have lights next to their RJ45 ports. When a cable is properly plugged in to both ends, the lights goes on. If the lights don't go on, you're either using the wrong type of cable, you've plugged the cable into the wrong port, or the cable is defective. Until the lights are lit, don't go any further. Hint: Use a different color cable for each computer to make troubleshooting easier. See the discussion of cabling, earlier in this chapter, for more information on the types of cables you'll need.
4. Go to **Control Panel → System**, choose the **Computer Name** tab, and click **Network ID** to run the Network Identification Wizard.

5. Click **Next** on the first page, choose **This computer is for home use and not part of a business network** and click **Next**, and then click **Finish**.
6. Next, click **Change** to open the Computer Name Changes window, as shown in Figure 7-11, and enter something for both the **Computer name** and **Workgroup**. The name you give to your workgroup should be the same for all computers on your local network, but the *computer name* (like the IP address) must be different for each computer.

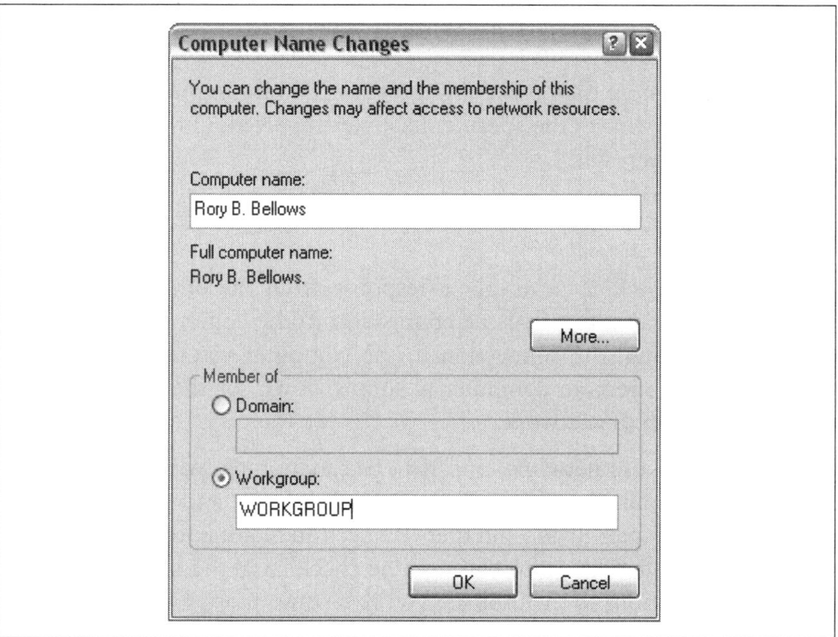

Figure 7-11. You'll need to open the Computer Name Changes dialog to identify your computer on your network

7. Click **OK** when you're done; if Windows informs you that you need to restart your computer, do so now. Repeat steps 4–6 for the other computers on your network.
8. Your connection should now be active. Double-click the LAN or high-speed icon corresponding to the connection to your workgroup to display that connection's Status window, from where you can determine the IP address of your computer. See "Configuring Network Connections," earlier this chapter, for an explanation of IP addresses, as well as how—and when—to set them manually.
9. The quickest way to test your connection is to use the Ping utility, which essentially sends small packets of information to another computer on your network and reports on its success (if any).

Go to **Start → Run**, and type ping *address*, where *address* is the IP address of the *other* computer—the one to which you're trying to connect. For example, to ping 192.168.0.1 from the computer at 192.168.0.2, you would type:

```
ping 192.168.0.1
```

If the network is working, the Ping transaction will be successful, and you'll get a result that looks like this:

```
Pinging 192.168.0.1 with 32 bytes of data:
Reply from 192.168.0.1: bytes=32 time=24ms TTL=53
Reply from 192.168.0.1: bytes=32 time=16ms TTL=53
```

If you have more than two computers, you'll want to ping them all since the test only covers the specific machines involved. On the other hand, if you get this result:

```
Pinging 192.168.0.1 with 32 bytes of data:
Request timed out.
Request timed out.
```

it means that Ping never got a response from the other computer. A failed ping can mean that the connection to the computer you're using is not working, the connection to the computer you're pinging is not working, the remote computer is simply down, or there's some other problem with the network.

If, at this point, your network appears to be functioning, you can proceed to set up the various services you need, such as file and printer sharing (described in Chapter 8) and Internet Connection Sharing (described later in this chapter). Otherwise, look through the checklist in the following section for possible solutions to the problem you're having.

Troubleshooting Your Workgroup

The following tips should help you get around most of the common hurdles you'll encounter when setting up a LAN:

- Heed the advice at the beginning of Chapter 6: restarting your computer will fix 99% of all problems. This is never more true than when diagnosing a networking problem.
- Run the Network Setup Wizard, as described in "The Network Setup Wizard" sidebar. While this step isn't always required, it does occasionally fix errant settings that otherwise would prevent a network from working properly.
- Try replacing one or more of the cables, especially if they're old or their connectors are worn.

- Make sure the appropriate lights are lit. See "Planning your Network" earlier in this chapter for a description of the way lights work on network devices.

The Network Setup Wizard

The Network Setup Wizard is an optional tool you can use to configure your connections to work with your particular network setup. Start it by double-clicking the **Network Setup Wizard** icon in your Network Connections window, or by clicking **Set up a home or small office network** (if the Tasks pane is visible).

The first page of the Network Setup Wizard explains that the wizard will set up a network for you, help you set up Internet connection sharing, install a firewall, and share files and printers. In fact, it will do none of these things; rather, it will simply ensure that some of the necessary protocols are installed and properly configured for the type of network to which you are connecting your computer.

In most cases, the Network Setup Wizard is not needed. However, if you're running into trouble configuring your network, it can't hurt to try it and see if it catches something you may have forgotten. Just answer the questions the best you can, and don't be afraid to choose **Other** on the **Select a connection method** page if the first two don't apply to your setup.

Note that if the Network Setup Wizard prompts you to create a setup disk for use on other computers, choose **Just finish the wizard**, as it will be of no use.

When you transfer data across a network connection, each network card and the hub (if you have one) should have an "activity" light that flashes. Some devices have separate lights for receiving and transmitting data, while others have only a single light for all incoming and outgoing communication. Activity lights tend to flash intermittently and irregularly; if they flash very regularly or not at all, it could be a sign of a problem with one of the devices.

- Windows XP is designed to implement most changes you make to your network settings without restarting. However, if you encounter problems, try restarting one or all of your machines to force them to recognize a newly configured network.
- Make sure no two computers on your network are attempting to use the same Computer name or IP address.

- Make sure you have the latest drivers for your NIC (network adapter); check with the manufacturer for details. Note that hubs, routers, and switches typically don't require any special drivers, but most have firmware that may need to be updated to fix bugs or support the latest hardware and features. See Chapter 6 for more information on firmware.
- Right-click the connection icon in the Network Connections window corresponding to your Ethernet adapter, and select **Repair**. Note that this feature essentially reinstalls drivers, but doesn't necessarily investigate other sources of problems. It's worth trying if all else fails, but don't expect any magic.
- Some problems are caused by improper hardware settings, usually attributed to the network card itself. Open Device Manager (discussed in Chapter 6), double-click the icon for your Ethernet adapter, and choose the **Advanced** tab. Choose a property in the list on the left and configure the selected property on the right. Try not to fuss with any settings you don't understand.

  If you're using an older network card that has more than one type of connector (commonly called a combo card), only one connector will be in use at any given time. The Windows default for the setting that governs this may be "autodetect," which may impair performance or even cause the device to stop working. Change this option so that it matches the connector you're using: for example, choose "coaxial" for round, 10base-2 cables and RJ-45 for the more common 10base-T cables.

  Another commonly misconfigured setting is the choice between full-duplex, half-duplex, and autodetection. Full-duplex is a connection where information can flow in both directions simultaneously; half-duplex only allows unidirectional communication. The wrong setting can cause a network connection to malfunction or just operate very slowly, especially with older adapters. Try experimenting with different settings.
- If the Ping test described in the previous section is successful, then your network is working. Other problems you may be having, such as not being able to "see" other computers in Explorer, are not necessarily the result of a network problem that can be solved here. For more information on shared resources, see Chapter 8.

Connect to the Internet

Although connecting to the Internet is really not any different than connecting to a workgroup, at least as far as Windows is concerned, you'll typically encounter different types of problems. Use these procedures to connect your computer (or your workgroup) to the Internet.

Connection Types

The procedure to initiate an Internet connection varies with the type of connection you wish to establish:

- DSL, cable, T1, or other high-speed connection with a static IP address (no username and password)
- DSL, cable, or other high-speed connection via PPPoE (username and password required)
- Connection provided by a router or another computer via Internet Connection Sharing
- Dial-up connection, including analog modems over standard phone lines

If your connection doesn't fit neatly into one of the above categories, your setup may still be similar to one of the following sections anyway. Otherwise, you'll need to contact your service provider for specific instructions and software for Windows XP. Details on each of these connection types are as follows.

DSL, cable, or other high-speed connection with a static IP address

High-speed connections with static IP addresses are probably the easiest of the aforementioned connections to set up in Windows XP.

A static IP address means you have the same IP address on the Internet every time you start your computer. If you're not sure if you have such a connection, check to see if your connection requires a username and password to log on; if so, you most likely have a PPPoE connection, described in the next section. Otherwise, proceed with these steps:

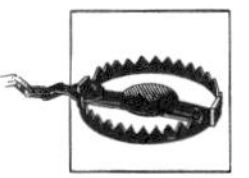

If you're using a router, don't use this procedure. Instead, enter your connection's IP address directly into your router's setup page (explained later in this chapter). Then, use the procedure later in this section to set up each workstation.

1. Connect your network adapter directly to the device that supplies your Internet connection, whether it's connected to a DSL adapter, a cable modem, or an Ethernet outlet in your wall. (If you're connecting to a router, see the section on routers later in this chapter.)

2. Open the Network Connections window, locate the connection icon corresponding to the network adapter plugged in to your Internet connection, and rename it "Internet Connection." Then, right-click the newly named Internet Connection icon and select **Properties**.
3. Under the **General** tab, make sure only the following entries are enabled (checked):
   - **Client for Microsoft Networks**
   - **Internet Protocol (TCP/IP)**

   If there are any other entries enabled here, clear their checkmarks.
4. Highlight Internet Protocol (TCP/IP) and click **Properties**. Click the **Use the following IP address** option and enter the IP address, subnet mask, default gateway, and preferred (primary) DNS server and alternate (secondary) DNS server addresses provided by your Internet service provider.
5. Click **OK**, and then click **OK** again; the change should take effect immediately. Test your connection by loading a web page or using Ping (as described in the previous section).

If, after completing these steps, Windows ever prompts you to connect to the Internet, go to **Control Panel → Internet Options → Connections** tab, and select the **Never dial a connection** option.

DSL, cable, or other high-speed connection via PPPoE

PPPoE is used to establish temporary, dynamic-IP Internet connections over high-speed broadband lines. If your Internet connection has a dynamic IP address, it means your Internet service provider assigns you a different IP address every time you connect to the Internet. The PPPoE (Point-to-Point Protocol over Ethernet) protocol facilitates this connection by sending your username and password to your provider.

If your ISP provides special software that connects to the Internet (such as Efficient Networks's truly awful NTS Enternet 300 software or RASPPPoE), you can abandon it in favor of Windows XP's built-in support for PPPoE, explained here.

One of the differences between this type of connection and the static IP connection discussed in the previous section is that PPPoE connections must be initiated every time you start Windows or every time you wish to use the Internet, which is somewhat like using old-fashioned dial-up connections (discussed in a subsequent section). Such connections are automatically disconnected when you shut down Windows.

If you have a PPPoE connection and you're using a router to share your Internet connection (explained later in this section), don't use this procedure. Instead, you'll need to enter your username and password into your router's configuration screen, as described in "Set Up a Wireless Router" later in this chapter.

Here's how to set up a PPPoE connection in Windows XP:

1. If you have PPPoE software (such as Enternet 300) installed, remove it from your system now. This is typically accomplished by going to **Control Panel → Add or Remove Programs**. Refer to the documentation that came with said software for details.
2. Open the Network Connection Wizard, as explained in "Configuring Network Connections," earlier in this chapter.
3. Click **Next** to skip the introductory page, choose the **Connect to the Internet** option, and then click **Next** again.
4. Choose the **Set up my connection manually** option, and click **Next**.
5. Choose the **Connect using a broadband connection that requires a user name and password** option, and click **Next**.
6. Type a name for this connection, and click **Next**. A good choice is the name of your ISP, or just "DSL" or "cable."
7. Enter your username and password, choose the desired options underneath (if you're not sure, turn them all on), and click **Next**.
8. Click **Finish** to complete the wizard.
9. To start the connection, double-click the icon you just created in the Network Connections folder. If you elected to create a desktop shortcut in the wizard, double-click the desktop icon.
10. By default, a Connect dialog will appear at this point. Click **Connect** to initiate the connection.

Here are some tips for working with PPPoE connections.

- To skip the Connect dialog, right-click the connection and select **Properties** (or click the **Properties** in the Connect window itself), choose the **Options** tab, and turn off the **Prompt for name and password, certificate, etc.** option.
- To have Windows connect automatically whenever the connection is needed, first right-click the connection icon and select **Set as Default Connection**. Then, go to **Control Panel → Internet Options → Connections** tab, and select the **Always dial my default connection** option.

- To have Windows connect automatically when you first start your computer, place a shortcut to the connection in your *Startup* folder. You'll also need to make sure that the **Prompt for name and password, certificate, etc.** option is turned off, as described earlier.
- If you need to make several similar PPPoE connections, you can save time by right-clicking the connection you just created and selecting **Create Copy**. Then, right-click the newly copied connection and select **Properties** to modify it.
- If you're having trouble getting your new PPPoE connection to work, check your DSL or cable modem first to see if the correct lights are lit (refer to your documentation). Sometimes, turning off the adapter, waiting several minutes, and then turning it back on solves the problem.
- If you're using PPPoE in conjunction with Internet Connection Sharing, discussed later in this chapter, and you've found that some web pages won't load on the client computers, see "Fix Your Shared Internet Connection with a New MTU," later in this chapter.

Connection provided by a router or another computer via Internet Connection Sharing

If you're using Internet Connection Sharing, described later in this chapter, the setup for the clients (all the computers on your network, other than the one with the physical Internet connection) is a snap. This procedure is also appropriate if you're using a router to share an Internet connection.

This procedure assumes you've already set up the aforementioned shared Internet connection (facilitated by either ICS or a router), as well as a properly functioning peer-to-peer workgroup, as described in "Building a Peer-to-Peer Workgroup," earlier in this chapter.

Follow these steps to connect a computer to an existing shared Internet connection:

1. Open the Network Connections window, right-click the connection icon corresponding to the network adapter plugged into your workgroup, and select **Properties**.
2. Under the **General** tab, make sure that at least the following entries are enabled (checked):
   - **Client for Microsoft Networks**
   - **Internet Protocol (TCP/IP)**

   Any other protocols and services enabled here should be left alone, as they may be needed for other purposes.

3. Highlight **Internet Protocol (TCP/IP)** and click **Properties**.
4. If you're not using fixed IP addresses on your LAN (which will be the most common case), select both the **Obtain an IP address automatically** and **Obtain DNS server address automatically** options, and click **OK**. Skip the next two steps, and proceed directly to step 7.
5. Otherwise, if you've set up your network with fixed IP addresses such as `192.168.0.1`, `192.168.0.2`, and so on (explained in "Planning Your Network," earlier in this chapter), select the **Use the following IP address** option and enter the IP address you wish to assign the machine. (Note that most routers use the `192.168.1.x` subnet instead of `192.168.0.x`.) Remember, this is the IP address of your computer *in your workgroup*, not the IP address of your Internet connection.
6. Type `255.255.255.0` for the subnet mask.
7. For the gateway, type the IP address of the computer hosting the shared Internet connection. If you're using a router to share your Internet connection, type the IP address of the router (refer to the instructions that came with the router for possible exceptions).
8. Lastly, type the Preferred (primary) DNS server and Alternate (secondary) DNS server addresses provided by your Internet service provider. Click **OK** when you're done.
9. Click **OK**, and then click **OK** again; the change should take effect immediately. Test your connection by loading a web page or using Ping (as described earlier in this chapter).
10. If the connection doesn't work at this point, open the Network Setup Wizard, as described in "The Network Setup Wizard" sidebar, earlier in this chapter. Click **Next** on the first two pages, and choose the **This computer connects to the Internet through another computer** and click **Next** on the third page. Depending on your network configuration, the remaining pages will vary here; answer the questions the best you can and complete the wizard.
11. If you're able to view some web sites but not others, and you're connecting to a shared Internet connection facilitated by PPPoE (described in the previous section), you may have to change the MTU setting. See "Fix Your Shared Internet Connection with a New MTU," later in this chapter.

Dial-up connection, including analog modems over standard phone lines

Of the connection types listed here, dial-up is the least expensive and probably still the most common. All you need is an ordinary analog modem, a standard telephone line, and a dial-up account with an Internet service provider. You can have as many dial-up connections configured at one time as you like, especially useful if you travel; just repeat these steps for each subsequent connection.

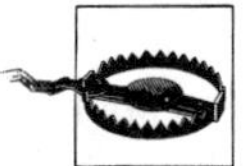

If you're using America Online, MSN, or some other proprietary service, these instructions may not apply to you. Contact your service provider for setup instructions for Windows XP.

1. Open the Network Connection Wizard, as explained in "Configuring Network Connections," earlier in this chapter.
2. Click **Next** to skip the introductory page, choose the **Connect to the Internet** option, and then click **Next** again.
3. Choose the **Set up my connection manually** option, and click **Next**.
4. Choose the **Connect using a dial-up modem** option, and click **Next**.
5. Type a name for this connection and click **Next**. A good choice is the name of your ISP, or just "Analog." If you're setting up multiple dial-up connections, choose descriptive names, such as "On the road" and "At home."
6. Enter the phone number for the connection, obtained by your service provider, and click **Next**.

   If your ISP provides two or more phone numbers, you have the option of creating multiple connections (one for each phone number), or creating a single connection that cycles through a list of phone numbers until a connection is established. If you choose the latter, you'll have the opportunity to enter additional phone numbers for the connection at the end of the procedure.
7. Enter your username and password, choose the desired options underneath (if you're not sure, turn them all on), and click **Next**.
8. Click **Finish** to complete the wizard.
9. To start the connection, double-click the icon you just created in the Network Connections folder. If you elected to create a desktop shortcut in the wizard, double-click the desktop icon.
10. By default, a Connect dialog will appear at this point. Click **Dial** to initiate the connection.

Here are some tips for working with Dial-up connections.

- To skip the Connect dialog, right-click the connection and select **Properties** (or click the **Properties** in the Connect window itself), choose the **Options** tab, and turn off the **Prompt for name and password, certificate, etc.** option.

- To have Windows connect automatically whenever the connection is needed, first right-click the connection icon and select **Set as Default Connection**. Then, go to **Control Panel → Internet Options → Connections** tab, and select the **Always dial my default connection** option.
- To have Windows connect automatically when you first start your computer, place a shortcut to the connection in your *Startup* folder. You'll also need to make sure that the **Prompt for name and password, certificate, etc.** option is turned off, as described above.
- If you need to make several similar dial-up connections, you can save time by right-clicking the connection you just created and selecting **Create Copy**. Then, right-click the newly copied connection and select **Properties** to modify it.
- To enter additional phone numbers for this connection (as opposed to making several separate connections), right-click the new connection icon, select **Properties**, choose the **General** tab, and click **Alternates**. Use the up and down arrow buttons to the right to change the priority of each phone number entered; numbers appearing higher on the list will be dialed first. Make sure to turn on the **If number fails, try next number** option.

Sharing an Internet Connection

Naturally, it doesn't make much sense to invest in a separate Internet connection for each computer in your home or office. Instead, you can use one of several different methods to share a single Internet connection among many separate computers.

The first solution utilizes the Internet Connection Sharing feature built into Windows XP. If you used the ICS feature found in Windows 98 Second Edition or Windows Me, you'll find that the system in XP makes a lot more sense and is much easier to set up. The advantage to ICS is that it is free; no additional software or hardware is required, but it does have its limitations. Alternatives to ICS are discussed subsequently.

Setting up Internet Connection Sharing

ICS is a system by which a single computer with an Internet connection acts as a gateway, allowing all other computers in the workgroup to use its connection to access the Internet. The computer that is connected directly to the Internet is called the *host*; all the other computers are called *clients*.

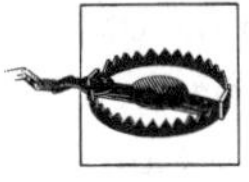

If you're using Windows XP Home Edition, you can share your Internet connection with a maximum of five other computers. If you're using Windows XP Professional, that limit is increased to 10.

In order to get ICS to work, you'll need the following:

- At least two computers, each with an Ethernet adapter properly installed and functioning. ICS can be used with both conventional and wireless networks.

  It is assumed you've already set up your local network, as described in "Building a Peer-to-Peer Workgroup," earlier in this chapter. Your Internet connection can be shared with as many clients as your LAN will support.
- One of the computers must have an Internet connection properly set up, as described in "Connect to the Internet," earlier in this chapter.

You do not need a special type of Internet connection, nor do you need to pay your Internet service provider extra fees to use Internet Connection Sharing. The whole point of ICS is to take a connection intended for a single computer and share it with several other machines.

- There is no minimum connection speed, but you should keep in mind that when two users are downloading using the shared connection simultaneously (the worst-case scenario), each user will experience half of the original performance. In other words, you probably don't want to bother sharing a 14.4 Kbps analog modem connection; see the discussion of "Bandwidth" at the beginning of this chapter, and "Test Your Throughput," later in this chapter, for more information.
- If you're sharing a DSL, cable modem, or other high-speed, Ethernet-based Internet connection, the computer with the Internet connection must have two Ethernet cards installed. See Figure 7-5 for a diagram of this setup.

If your Internet connection is accessed through a router or you've allocated multiple IP addresses, you don't need Internet Connection Sharing; see "Alternatives to Internet Connection Sharing," later in this chapter, for details.

The first step in setting up ICS is to configure the host, the computer with the Internet connection that will be shared:

1. Open the Network Connections window. If you haven't already done so, select **Details** from the **View** menu.
2. Here, you should have at least two connections listed: one for your Internet connection, and one for the Ethernet adapter connected to your LAN. If they're not there, your network is not ready. See the tips above for what you need, and try again.

For clarity, I recommend renaming the two connections to "Internet Connection" and "Local Area Connection," respectively, as illustrated in Figure 7-7.

3. Right-click the connection icon corresponding to your Internet connection, and select **Properties**. In most cases, it will be the Ethernet adapter connected to your Internet connection device.

   However, if you're using a DSL or cable connection that requires a login with a username or password, the icon to use is the broadband connection icon corresponding to your PPPoE connection. See "Connect to the Internet," earlier in this chapter, for further instructions.
4. Choose the **Advanced** tab, and turn on the **Allow other network users to connect through this computer's Internet connection** option, as shown in Figure 7-12.

   (For more information on the Firewall option shown here, see "Using the Windows Security Center," later in this chapter.)
5. Click **OK** when you're done. Verify that Internet Connection Sharing is enabled; it should say "Enabled, Shared" in the **Type** column of the Network Connections window, as shown in the example in Figure 7-7.
6. That's it! The change will take effect immediately. Verify that the Internet connection still works on the host by attempting to open a web page. If the Internet connection doesn't work on the host, it *definitely* won't work on any of the clients.

The next step is to configure each of the client computers to use the shared connection. The only requirements of the client machines are that they are running an operating system that supports networking and that their network connections are properly set up. The clients can be running Windows 2000, Windows Me, Windows 9x, Windows NT, Windows 3.x for Workgroups, or even Mac OS, Unix, Linux, or FreeBSD.

See "Connect to the Internet," earlier in this chapter, and follow the instructions in "Connection provided by a router or another computer via Internet Connection Sharing." Do this for each "client" machine on your network. While the instructions are specific to Windows XP, the settings explained

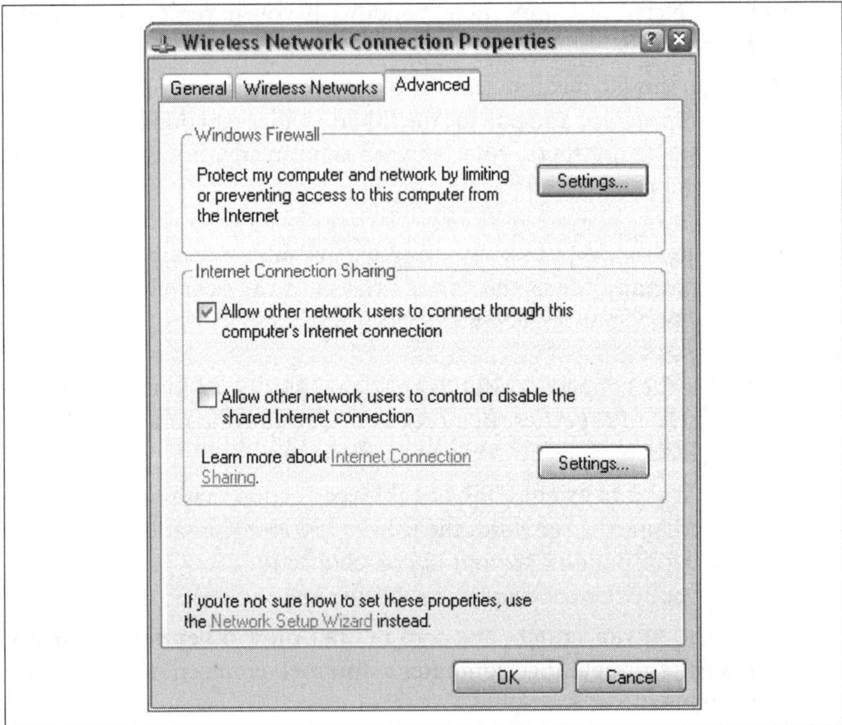

Figure 7-12. Any Internet connection can be shared with other computers in your workgroup

therein can be adapted to any OS; refer to your operating system's documentation for more information.

Troubleshooting Internet Connection Sharing

Here are some tips that should help you fix the problems you might encounter with ICS:

- If the Internet is accessible by one client machine, it should work for them all. If none of the clients work, the problem is most likely with the host; if some of the clients work and others don't, it's a problem with clients that don't work.
- ICS works over existing network connections, so those connections must be functioning before ICS will operate. Refer to "Building a Peer-to-Peer Workgroup," earlier in this chapter, for further troubleshooting details.
- Check to see if you have any firewall software installed on the host or clients that might be interfering with the connection. The Windows Firewall included with XP SP2 (discussed later in this chapter) won't interfere with ICS, however.

- The IP address of the host on the workgroup *must* be set to `192.168.0.1`, or ICS won't work. Among other things, this means that no other computers can be using that address. If you can't get ICS to work with the default Windows XP configuration, try assigning a fixed IP address to each of your clients, as described in "Configuring Network Connections," earlier in this chapter.
- If you're experiencing poor performance, it's important to realize that whatever bandwidth is available though a given Internet connection will be shared among all of the computers actively using the connection. The worst-case scenario is when two or more users simultaneously download large amounts of data; in this case, they would each receive only a portion of the total connection bandwidth. Bandwidth sharing is dynamic, though, so most of the time you shouldn't notice much of a decrease in speed.
- If you're using special connection software for use with your DSL or cable (such as Efficient Networks's NTS Enternet 300 software), it's best to remove it and use Windows XP's built-in support for PPPoE (described earlier in this chapter).
- If you're using PPPoE and find that you can access some web sites but not others from the client machines, see "Fix Your Shared Internet Connection with a New MTU," later in this chapter.

Alternatives to Internet Connection Sharing

The Internet Connection Sharing feature built into Windows XP has its limitations. For example, the host computer must be on and connected to the Internet for the other computers to have Internet access. If this "host" computer crashes or is shut down, Internet access will be cut off for the whole workgroup. This may be a small price to pay, considering that ICS is free, simple, and pretty convenient, but if you don't want your network's Internet connection to rely on any single computer, you may wish to consider the following alternatives to see if they make sense for you:

Use a router

A router works similarly to a hub or switch, both discussed at the beginning of this chapter, except that it will also be capable of sharing a single Internet connection with all members of your workgroup (and without the arbitrary 5- or 10-computer limits imposed by XP). Routers have added advantages, such as built-in firewalls and wireless access points; see "Planning Your Network" earlier in this chapter for details. Figure 7-13 illustrates a workgroup connected to the Internet with a wireless router.

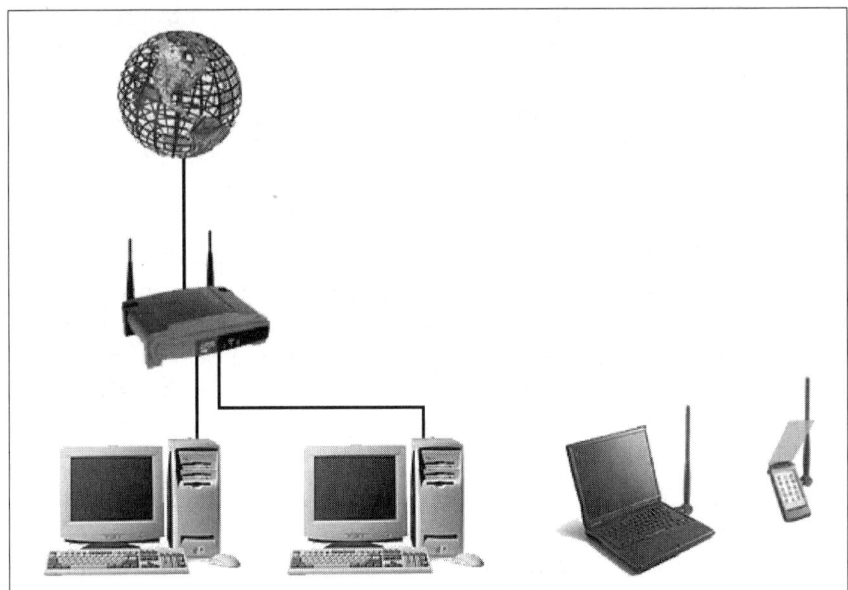

Figure 7-13. Instead of connecting a single computer to the Internet and then sharing the connection, a router allows you to plug an Internet connection directly into your LAN, providing Internet access to all your PCs, whether wired or wireless

Just plug your broadband modem into the WAN or Internet port in the back of the router, and then plug your PCs into any of the numbered ports (or connect them wirelessly, if applicable).

Avoid installing the software that comes with your router, as it will be almost certainly unnecessary. Instead, open a web browser and go to 192.168.1.1 (or whatever IP address your router uses by default), and complete your setup there. See the Wireless section later in this chapter for more information, including some important security precautions.

Refer to the documentation that comes with the router for basic setup instructions, and see the "Connection provided by a router or another computer via Internet Connection Sharing" section, earlier in this chapter, for instructions on connecting a Windows XP system to a router.

If you're shopping for a router, get one with wireless support, even if you don't need it. Wireless-G (802.11g) is faster than Wireless-B (802.11b), only marginally more expensive, and backwards-compatible, so there's little reason to go with the slower standard. Avoid routers that only work with specific Internet connections (e.g., DSL, cable), and instead get one that will work with any connection type.

Use multiple IP addresses

Some ISPs may provide, at extra cost, multiple IP addresses, with the specific intent that Internet access be provided for more than one computer. Since each computer has its own true IP address, there's no need for any "sharing" software or hardware. Instead, your hub or switch is plugged directly into your Internet device (DSL, cable, T1, or whatever), and each computer will effectively have its own Internet connection.

Refer to the instructions in the "DSL, cable, or other high-speed connection with a static IP address" section, earlier in this chapter, to set up each of your computers to access the Internet.

The advantages of multiple IP addresses over ICS or using a router, as described earlier, is that the setup is very easy, and no additional hardware or software is required. The downside is that Internet connections with multiple IP addresses are often much more expensive (in noncorporate environments, that is) than standard Internet connections, and provide no additional security. In fact, the added monthly cost will most likely exceed the one-time cost of a router very quickly.

Fix Your Shared Internet Connection with a New MTU

There are some circumstances when a shared Internet connection doesn't quite work as it's supposed to. The problem, where some web pages load and some do not, typically affects client computers that access a shared Internet connection facilitated by PPPoE.

Although all web sites will be accessible on the host computer, certain web sites will never load successfully from any of the client machines. If you don't know what "hosts" or "clients" are with regard to Internet Connection Sharing, you'll want to review the previous section before you proceed. Also, see "DSL, cable, or other high-speed connection via PPPoE," earlier in this chapter for more information on PPPoE connections. Note that this applies to Windows XP's built-in PPPoE support, as well as PPPoE provided by third-party software and even some routers.

The following solution is intended to fix this specific problem.

1. Sit down in front of one of your client machines, and type the following:

   ```
   PING -f -l 1500 192.168.0.1
   ```

   This assumes that `192.168.0.1` is the IP address of the host computer (or router); substitute the correct address if it's different. If you don't know the IP address of the host computer, open a Command Prompt window (*cmd.exe*) on the host, and type `ipconfig` at the prompt. (If a router is providing your Internet connection, consult the router documentation for details on obtaining its IP address.)

2. You'll probably get an error message indicating that it must be fragmented. (If not, then this solution doesn't apply to you.) Next, type the following:

   ```
   ping -f -l 1492 192.168.0.1
   ```

   If that results in the same error message, try this instead:

   ```
   ping -f -l 1480 192.168.0.1
   ```

   If you still get an error, try:

   ```
   ping -f -l 1454 192.168.0.1
   ```

   The numbers in each of these examples (`1500`, `1492`, `1480`, and `1454`) are values for the MTU (Maximum Transmission Unit). Continue issuing this command with lower and lower MTU numbers until you get normal ping responses instead of an error message. The highest MTU value that does not result in an error is the correct one for your network. It's not unheard of for an MTU as low as 576 to be required, although Microsoft recommends no value smaller than 1400 for Windows XP.

3. Once you've found an MTU that works for you, open the Registry Editor (see Chapter 3) on the *client* machine.

4. Expand the branches to `HKEY_LOCAL_MACHINE\SYSTEM\CurrentControlSet\Services\Tcpip\Parameters\Interfaces`.

   There should be several subkeys under the `Interfaces` key; most likely, you'll find three. View each key's contents, and find the one that corresponds to your primary network adapter; it will be the one with more values than the other two, and will have an `IP address` value set to the IP address of the machine.

5. Once you've found the correct subkey, create a new DWORD value in it by selecting **New** and then **DWORD Value** from the **Edit** menu. Name the value `MTU`.

6. Double-click the new value, choose the **Decimal** option, type the MTU value you earlier in this procedure, and click **OK**.

7. Close the Registry Editor when you're done; you'll need to restart Windows for this change take effect.

8. Repeat steps 3–7 for each client machine on your network (but not the host).

In most cases, this should solve the problem. However, on some systems, you may need to set the MTU in another registry location as well. If you've found that a lower MTU value is what you need, but the above procedure didn't work, try this as well:

1. Navigate to `HKEY_LOCAL_MACHINE\System\CurrentControlSet\Services\Ndiswan\Parameters\Protocols\0`. If any keys in this Registry path aren't there, just create them by going to **Edit → New → Key**.
2. Once you're in the key, create a new DWORD value called `ProtocolType` and give it a **Decimal** value of `2048`.
3. Then, create a new DWORD value called `PPPProtocolType` and give it a **Decimal** value of `33`.
4. Finally, create a new DWORD value called `ProtocolMTU` and give it a **Decimal** value of the MTU you determined above.
5. Close the Registry Editor and restart your system when you're done.

Test Your Throughput

Throughput is the practical measurement of bandwidth: the quantity of data you can transmit over a connection in a given period of time.

Now, most types of connections are classified for their bandwidth (discussed at the beginning of this chapter); a good ol' 33.6 Kbps modem is so-named because at its best, it can transmit and receive 33,600 bits per second. Because there are eight bits to the byte, this connection would give us a theoretical throughput of 4.1 kilobytes per second.

In reality, however, you're not likely to see a throughput any faster than about 3.6 kilobytes per second with the connection in this example. That's a difference of about 14%; a file that you would expect to take a minute to download will actually take about 70 seconds. The reason for this discrepancy is that there are other things that get transferred along with your data; error correction and lost packets because of noise on the line can make the actual throughput lower as well. Unfortunately, most of the factors that affect the actual throughput are beyond our control.

Broadband connections, such as DSL, cable, and T1, are also rated similarly and suffer the same throttling effect, but generally these connections are fast enough that the discrepancy isn't really that noticeable.

Among the factors within our control are the hardware and software we use and various settings and conditions in which we work. So it is often advantageous to test the throughput under different conditions and with different equipment so that you can achieve the best performance.

The simplest way to measure the throughput is to transfer a compressed binary file (such as a large *.jpg* or *.zip* file) from your computer to another location and then back again, recording the time it takes to complete the

Throttling Quality of Service

The Quality of Service (QoS) Packet Scheduler is a service included with Windows XP Professional that, when connected to a QoS-enabled network, reserves about 20% of your bandwidth for certain applications. Since this could mean that a rather large amount of your precious bandwidth is being wasted, you may wish to throttle or disable it. *Note that this does not apply to Windows XP Home Edition or any computer connected to a network that does not use the QoS service.*

1. You must be logged into the Administrator account (see Chapter 8).
2. Open the Group Policy Editor (*gpedit.msc*, available in Windows XP Professional only).
3. Expand the branches to `Computer Configuration\Administrative Templates\Network\QOS Packet Scheduler`.
4. Double-click the **Limit reservable bandwidth** entry in the right pane, and choose the **Setting** tab.
5. Select **Enabled**, and change the **Bandwidth limit (%)** value to `0` (or whatever value you prefer).
6. Click **OK** and close the Group Policy Editor when you're done. You'll need to restart Windows for the change to take effect.

Note that disabling the QoS Packet Scheduler (by unchecking the **QoS Packet Scheduler** option in **General** tab of the Properties sheet for your network connection) won't accomplish this.

transfer each way. Just divide the file size by the transfer time to get the throughput, typically in kilobytes per second.

Note that we test the "upload" as well as the "download" speed. Many types of connections are asymmetrical; 56 K modems, for example, download at around 53.2 Kbps, but upload at only 33.6 Kbps. Likewise, a midrange DSL connection might be rated at 768 Kbps download and 128 Kbps upload. Note also that you wouldn't want to use ASCII files (such as plain-text files and web pages) to test the throughput, because compression will yield uncharacteristic results.

Average throughputs for common connection speeds are shown in Table 7-1.

Table 7-1. Ideal download/upload throughputs for various connection speeds

Connection method	Ideal throughput (KB per sec)
14.4 Kbps modem	1.6 download, 1.6 upload
28.8 Kbps modem	3.2 download, 3.2 upload

Table 7-1. Ideal download/upload throughputs for various connection speeds (continued)

Connection method	Ideal throughput (KB per sec)
33.6 Kbps modem	3.6 download, 3.6 upload
56 Kbps modem	5.4 download, 3.6 upload
ISDN (dual channel, 128 Kbps)	14 download, 14 upload
Cable Modem (~800 Kbps synchronous)	84 download, 84 upload
DSL (asynchronous 1.2 Mbps/384 Kbps)	128 download, 42 upload
T1, fast DSL (1.5 Mbps)	160 download, 160 upload

Note that you shouldn't fret if your throughput doesn't exactly match the values in the table—they're only examples. If you find that you're getting substantially slower performance, however, you should test your equipment and cabling and see if there's any software that could be interfering with the connection. For example, a noisy phone line is the most common cause of poor performance of a dial-up connection. For DSL or cable, try turning off your modem for a minute or two and then turning it back on.

Another way to test the actual bandwidth of your connection is to visit one of the many bandwidth-testing web sites:

- *http://bandwidthplace.com/speedtest/*
- *http://www.dslreports.com/stest*

In addition to calculating your bandwidth and reporting the results, these services typically ask for your zip code and connection type to compile statistics on typical connection speeds in your area.

See Chapter 5 for solutions on improving overall system performance, some of which will also have a noticeable impact on your connection speed.

Stuff You Can Do with a Network

Now that you've get your network functioning, it's time to start taking advantage of the features it provides. In this section:

- Virtual Private Networking
- Accessing an FTP Site in Explorer
- Controlling Another Computer Remotely
- Managing the Nameserver Cache

See the section, "Go Wireless," for some cool things you can do with a wireless network.

Do Download Accelerators Really Work?

There are a number of "download accelerator" software products available, all of which promise to speed up the transfer of files downloaded to your computer. As you might have guessed, none of them are actually capable of increasing the bandwidth or throughput of your Internet connection. Rather, they employ download *managers* that compensate for inefficiencies in the download process.

These programs work by downloading a file in pieces, via multiple concurrent download streams (not unlike the TCP/IP protocol that powers the transfer explained at the beginning of this chapter). While two concurrent downloads would each be allotted half the bandwidth normally consumed by a single download, this boundary only applies when your Internet connection is the bottleneck. So, in theory, a download manager *may* improve your download speed if the *other* computer's connection is slower than yours.

Any speed advantage you notice may be offset by the annoying and cumbersome interfaces these programs add to the mix, but in the end, the convenience afforded by some of these programs' extra features may make them worth the hassle.

Here are a few recommended download managers:

- Fresh Download (freeware, *http://www.freshdevices.com*)
- Download Express (freeware, *http://www.metaproducts.com*)
- Free Download Manager (freeware, *http://www.freedownloadmanager.org*)
- Download Accelerator Plus (*http://www.speedbit.com*)

Be aware that some download accelerators contain spyware (see Chapter 6), so use caution when trying an unproven product.

Some programs also can resume aborted downloads, find alternative servers from which to download your files, and schedule downloads for off-peak times. At the time of this writing, however, there was no "perfect" download manager, or even one that I'd necessarily recommend over using no manager at all. But if you're so inclined, you'll probably it find worth the time experimenting with these tools, if only to get some of the aforementioned special features.

Virtual Private Networking

Virtual Private Networking (VPN) is a system whereby a workgroup of two or more computers can be connected by an Internet connection rather than a physical cable. In theory, VPN provides the security and privacy of a closed environment, without the astronomical cost of a private wide-area network.

The technology used in Virtual Private Networking—either the Point-to-Point Tunneling Protocol (PPTP) or the Layer Two Tunneling Protocol (L2TP)—allows you to create a private "tunnel" across your Internet connection. With a VPN, you can accomplish tasks previously available only over a LAN, such as file and printer sharing, user authentication, and even networked gaming. Figure 7-14 illustrates a typical scenario with a tunnel connecting a single computer to a remote workgroup.

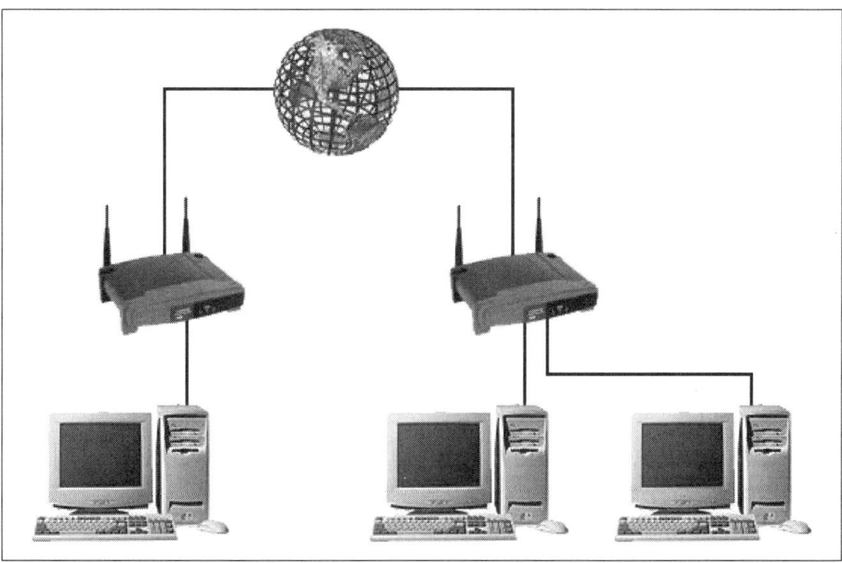

Figure 7-14. Form a virtual private workgroup through a tunnel across the Internet

Networking

Before you can set up VPN, you need a *tunnel server*. If you're connecting to a large company, the VPN administrator will provide the necessary settings (and software, if necessary) to establish a connection. If, however, you're building your own VPN, follow these instructions.

The following process briefly shows how to set up a simple VPN workgroup. Select one of the following procedures, depending on the operating system you're using for the tunnel server: Part 1a for Windows XP, Part 1b for Windows 2000, or Part 1c for Windows NT. Then, Part 2 shows you how to configure a Windows XP machine as a VPN client.

Part 1a: Set up the tunnel server (Windows XP Professional only)

Here are instructions on setting up a tunnel server in Windows XP Professional:

1. Log in as the Administrator.
2. Open the Network Connections window, and double-click **New Connection Wizard** (or click **Create a new connection** in the task pane to the left).
3. Click **Next** when you see the introductory page.
4. Select **Set up an advanced connection** and click **Next**.
5. Select **Accept incoming connections** and click **Next**.
6. The next page asks you to select devices you want to use for incoming connections. Don't select anything here; just click **Next** to skip this step.
7. Select **Allow virtual private connections** and click **Next**.
8. You'll then be presented with a list of configured users. Place a checkmark next to each username to whom you wish to grant VPN access, and click **Next**.
9. The next step allows you to choose which services, clients, and protocols are allowed with incoming VPN connections. These are the same components you'd use when building a workgroup (see "Building a Peer-to-Peer Workgroup," earlier in this chapter, for details). Highlight **Internet Protocol (TCP/IP)** and click **Properties**.
10. Turn on the **Allow callers to access my local area network** option, and then specify how you'd like to assign IP addresses to incoming connections, as shown in Figure 7-15.
11. Click **OK** and then **Next** when you're done.
12. Click **Finish** to complete the wizard.

If you're using a router on the server end, you'll need to set up Port Forwarding to route VPN traffic to the IP address for your tunnel server. VPN over PPTP uses port 1723, and IPSec uses 500, 50, and 51. If you're using Windows XP's built-in firewall (described later in this chapter), you'll probably need to enter these exceptions there as well. See Appendix C for more information on TCP/IP Ports.

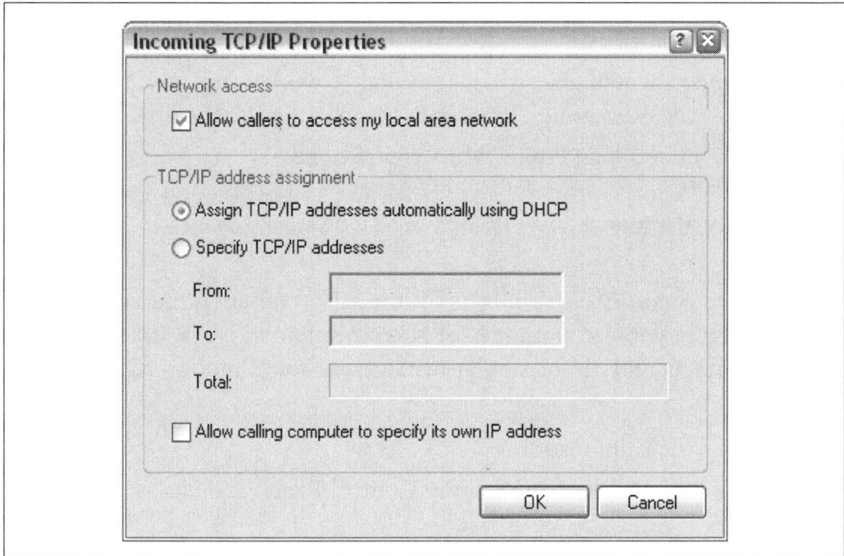

Figure 7-15. Windows XP, when set to accept incoming VPN connections, can act as a DHCP server and assign IP addresses to remote computers automatically; you can optionally assign a range of addresses here

Part 1b: Set up the tunnel server (Windows 2000 Server/Advanced Server only)

Here are instructions on setting up a tunnel server in Windows 2000, required before you can initiate a VPN connection with a Windows XP client. See parts 1a and 1c for similar instructions for WIndows XP and NT 4.0, respectively.

1. Log in as the Administrator.
2. Double-click the **Network and Dial-Up Connections** icon in Control Panel, and then double-click the **Make New Connection** icon. Note that all of the settings in this cumbersome wizard can be adjusted later by double-clicking on the **Incoming Connections** icon you're creating.
3. Click **Next**, select **Accept incoming connections**, and click **Next** again.
4. Place a checkmark next to the network adapter that you use to accept incoming VPN connections, and click **Next**.
5. Select **Allow virtual private connections**, and click **Next**.
6. You'll then be presented with a list of configured users—place a checkmark next to each username to whom you wish to grant VPN access, and click **Next**.

7. The next step allows you to choose which services, clients, and protocols are allowed with incoming VPN connections. These are the same components you'd use when building a workgroup (see "Building a Peer-to-Peer Workgroup," earlier in this chapter, for details).
8. Click **Next** and then **Finish** when you're done.

Part 1c: Set up the tunnel server (Windows NT 4.0 Server/Advanced Server only)

Here are instructions on setting up a tunnel server in Windows NT 4.0, required before you can initiate a VPN connection with a Windows XP client. See parts 1a and 1b for similar instructions for Windows XP and 2000, respectively.

1. Log in as the Administrator.
2. Double-click the Network icon in Control Panel, and choose the **Protocols** tab.
3. Click **Add**, select **Point To Point Tunneling Protocol** from the list, and click **OK**. When asked how many simultaneous VPNs you want the server to support, choose a nice, big, healthy number, and click **OK**.
4. Next, you'll need to add one or more the VPN devices to Remote Access Service (RAS): choose the **Services** tab and select **Remote Access Service**.
5. Click **Properties**, and then click **Add**.
6. From the **RAS Capable Devices** list, select a VPN device, and click **OK**. Once all the VPN devices have been added, select a VPN port, and click **Configure**. Check the **Receive calls only** option, and click **OK**.

   Repeat this step for each VPN device you've selected. You'll have to restart Windows NT when you're done.

Part 2: Set up the VPN client (Windows XP)

Although there only needs to be one VPN tunnel server, you can have as many clients as you like (that is, until you reach the limit specified in the tunnel server's configuration). Here's how to set up a Windows XP machine as a VPN client:

1. Open the New Connection Wizard, as described in "Configuring Network Connections," earlier in this chapter.
2. Click **Next** on the first page. Select **Connect to the network at my workplace** on the second page, and then click **Next**.
3. Choose **Virtual Private Network connection**, and click **Next**.

4. Next, choose a name for the new connection (it can be anything you want), type it into the **Company Name** field, and click **Next**.
5. Since VPN relies on an existing Internet connection, you have the option at this point of automatically connecting to the Internet before initiating this VPN connection. If you're using a high-speed Internet connection that is always on, choose **Do not dial the initial connection** here. If, however, you're using a PPPoE connection or analog dial-up connection that must be dialed to connect (as described in "Connect to the Internet," earlier in this chapter), choose **Automatically dial this initial connection** and then select the desired connection from the list. Click **Next** when you're done.
6. The next page is where you specify the network name or IP address of the tunnel server to which you want to connect. If you didn't set up the tunnel server yourself, you'll have to obtain the address from your network administrator.
7. Click **Next** and then **Finish** when you're done.
8. To initiate a VPN connection, double-click the new VPN connection icon, enter your username and password, and click **Connect**. As soon as you're connected, you should have access to the additional resources shared on the remote network; see Chapter 8 for details on accessing remote resources.

If you're using a router on the client side, you'll most likely need to turn on the IPSec option in your router's setup to get VPN to work. Refer to your router's documentation for details.

Note that in previous versions of Windows, it was necessary to "join" a domain (by going to **Control Panel → System → Computer Name** tab → **Change**) before you could connect to it with VPN. In most cases in Windows XP, this is no longer necessary; check with your system administrator for details.

For additional tips for working with VPN connections, such as how to bypass the Connect dialog, see "DSL, cable, or other high-speed connection via PPPoE" in the "Connect to the Internet" section, earlier in this chapter.

Accessing an FTP Site in Explorer

For years, FTP has been the quickest and most efficient way to move files from one machine to another across the Internet. Whether you're downloading drivers from a manufacturer's FTP site or uploading HTML files to a web server, FTP is often the preferred transfer method.

To access an FTP server, either to upload or download, you need an FTP application. Windows XP actually comes with three such applications:

- FTP, a traditional, command-line-based FTP client (*ftp.exe*)
- Internet Explorer (*iexplore.exe*)—or any web browser, for that matter—supports downloading files from FTP servers. Just go to an address like this: *ftp://ftp.mozilla.org/pub/mozilla.org/firefox/releases/* to view the contents of the specified directory or download the specified file, as the case may be.
- Windows Explorer* (*explorer.exe*) allows you to view any web site as though it were just another folder and is explained in the rest of this section.

Here are three different ways to hook up to an FTP site in Explorer:

Solution 1: Open a temporary FTP folder

This procedure is the quick-and-dirty way to open an FTP folder in Explorer:

1. Open Windows Explorer (*explorer.exe*).
2. If the Address Bar is not currently visible, go to **View → Toolbars → Address Bar**.
3. Type an address into the Address Bar, like this:

   ```
   ftp://host.com
   ```

   where *`host.com`* is the name of the FTP server. Note the syntax, similar to web page addresses. Press **Enter** to log in.

   Since you're not specifying a username or password here, Explorer assumes you want anonymous access (see the "Understanding Anonymous FTP" sidebar). If the specified server does not provide anonymous access, you'll see an error like this:

   ```
   Windows cannot access this folder...User anonymous unknown.
   ```

4. If you do indeed have an account on the server, select **Login As** from the **File** menu, type your username and password, and then click **Log On**.

* Microsoft and others might contend that Windows Explorer and Internet Explorer are actually the same program. Personally, I find this to be a matter of semantics (one could argue that all Windows applications are the same program, for they all share DLLs). For the purposes of this solution, and since both applications have distinctly different interfaces, it makes more sense to think of them as distinct and separate applications.

Understanding Anonymous FTP

If you have a personal account on the server to which you're connecting, you'll need to specify your username and password in order to gain access to your personal files.

However, many FTP servers also provide "anonymous" access to a special, public folder; to log in to this public folder, you just type anonymous for the username and an email address (or nothing) for the password. When you use a web browser to download from an FTP server, as described earlier, it's usually done through an anonymous account.

Note that not all hosts are FTP servers, and not all FTP servers allow anonymous access.

See the next solution for a way to specify the username and (optionally) the password right in the address so that you don't have to deal with the Log On As dialog.

5. As soon as you're logged in, you'll see a standard folder and file listing. You can rename, drag-drop, and even delete files and folders, just as though they were on your own hard disk.

   The connection will remain active as long as you use it, but will likely become disconnected if left idle for more than a few minutes. It will also be disconnected when you shut down Windows, but it won't be automatically connected when Windows starts.

6. When you're done, you can make an Internet Shortcut to this location, using the same method as you would for a web page. However, if Internet Explorer is not your default FTP client (see "File Types: The Link Between Documents and Applications" in Chapter 4), it won't work as expected. See the next solution for a more robust and permanent way to hook up an FTP site to Explorer.

Solution 2: Create a more permanent "place" in My Network Places

If you'd like to set up a more permanent FTP connection to use again and again, follow these steps:

1. Open My Network Places by double-clicking the icon on your desktop or by navigating to it in Explorer.

2. If you have the common-tasks pane enabled (**Tools → Folder Options → General** tab), click **Add a network place** in the **Network Tasks** box.

   Otherwise, simply double-click the Add Network Place icon.

3. When the Add Network Place Wizard appears, click **Next** to skip the intro page.
4. On the second page, you'll be given a choice of service providers. Make sure you select **Choose another network location** here, and click **Next**.
5. Next, you'll be prompted for the **Internet or network address** of the FTP server. If you're connecting to an anonymous FTP site, type:

   ```
   ftp://host.com
   ```

   where *host.com* is the address (or IP address) of the FTP server (see Solution 1, earlier). Or, if you want to log in to a personal FTP account, type:

   ```
   ftp://username@host.com
   ```

   Finally, if you want to log in to a personal FTP account, but do not wish to be prompted for a password, you can specify it here, like this:

   ```
   ftp://username:password@host.com
   ```

   Click **Next** when you're done.
6. If you didn't specify a username in the address you typed in the previous step, you'll be prompted for one now. Turn off the **Log on anonymously** option if you wish to specify a username now; otherwise, leave it enabled and click **Next**.
7. On the last page, you'll be asked to type a name for this connection, which will also be name of the folder as it appears in Explorer. The name can be anything you want, but it has to conform to Windows file-naming rules (e.g., no slashes, double-quotation marks, etc.).
8. Click **Next** and then **Finish** to create the connection.
9. If successful, you'll see the new entry in your My Network Places folder. Just open it to connect to the FTP site.

Windows provides no simple mechanism of changing the location or other properties of an FTP folder, which means that you'll have to delete and re-create an FTP folder in order to modify it. See Solution 3, next, for a workaround.

10. The connection created in this solution is simply a folder or, more precisely, a Folder Shortcut (discussed later), located in your *\Documents and Settings\{username}\NetHood* folder. If you'd prefer that the FTP folder be located elsewhere, open Explorer and move the folder to another location on your hard disk.

Solution 3: Another way to create an FTP folder

The functionality that allows you to link up a folder to an FTP site, as explained in Solution 2 earlier, is essentially that of Folder Shortcuts, as seen in "Mirror a Folder with Folder Shortcuts" in Chapter 4. This next solution has essentially the same result, but shows how to create such a folder manually. This can be useful, for example, when the Add Network Place wizard (which can be unreliable) doesn't work. It also lets you modify the location of an FTP folder without having to delete and re-create it. Finally, it can be used in conjunction with a WSH script to automate the creation of FTP folders.

1. Start by following the instructions for making a Folder Shortcut in "Mirror a Folder with Folder Shortcuts" in Chapter 4. (You can also use the example WSH script in "Mirror a Folder with Folder Shortcuts" in Chapter 9, although it will have to be altered slightly to accommodate FTP shortcuts.)
2. When it comes time to make the shortcut to a folder, though, make an Internet Shortcut to an FTP site instead. Open your favorite web browser—any web browser capable of making Internet Shortcuts will do—and type the URL address of any valid FTP server, as explained in either of the previous solutions in this topic.
3. Once the page loads successfully, create an Internet Shortcut, and name it *target*.

   Because Internet Shortcuts use the extension *.url* (which is not visible) and we need the extension to be *.lnk* (also not visible), we must rename the file. And because Windows will not let you change the filename extension when the extension isn't visible, you'll need to do it from the Command Prompt.
4. Open a Command Prompt window (*cmd.exe*), and type the following:

   ```
   cd foldername
   ```

   where *foldername* is the full path of the folder containing the target shortcut.

   Hint: to save typing, type only `cd`, followed by a space, and then drag-drop the folder icon (or even the shortcut itself) right onto the Command Prompt window, and the full path will be typed for you. (If you dragged the shortcut, you'll have to remove the shortcut filename, *target.url*, before you press **Enter**.)
5. Then, use the `ren` command to rename the file, like this:

   ```
   ren target.url target.lnk
   ```
6. Leave the prompt window open, if needed, for the rest of the solution in "Mirror a Folder with Folder Shortcuts" in Chapter 4.

Notes

- Regardless of the solution you use, the resulting FTP connection will remain active as long as you use it, but will likely become disconnected if left idle for more than a few minutes. It will also be disconnected when you shut down Windows. In either case, Windows will automatically reconnect as soon as you attempt to use the folder. Note that there's no way to manually disconnect an FTP folder (unless you delete it).
- You can access files contained in an FTP folder (created in either Solution 2 or Solution 3) from any 32-bit Windows application, and even save files there as well.
- Create a standard Windows shortcut to a subfolder of an FTP folder (created in either Solution 2 or Solution 3), and place it in your *Send To* folder (typically *\Documents and Settings\{username}\SendTo*). That way, you can right-click one or more files or folders, and use the **Send To** menu to quickly copy the selected items to the FTP location.
- The FTP protocol does not use encryption or any other method of security, which not only means that your data will not be transferred securely, but your username and password will also not be encrypted when you log in. More secure alternatives include Web Folders, described next; Virtual Private Networking, described earlier in this chapter; or a program that supports SCP (Secure Copy Protocol).
- Windows also supports a protocol called Web Folders, which works very similarly to the FTP folders feature described here. Although Web Folders also support encryption, very few servers support the WebDAV (Web Distributed Authoring and Versioning) protocol, which means you'll most likely want to stick with FTP or SCP (see Table 7-2).
- There are other programs you can use for transferring files (FTP and otherwise), any of which may be more or less convenient than Explorer, depending on your needs. See Table 7-2 for a list of alternatives.

Table 7-2. These programs can be used instead of Windows built-in support for FTP

Product	Notes
Creative Element Power Tools *http://www.creativelement.com*	Comes with a context-menu add-on that allows you to right-click any number of files, select **FTP To**, and quickly transfer them to a custom FTP location.
WS_FTP *http://www.ipswitch.com*	Although it's a rather old-school implementation of FTP, it's side-by-side layout can be extremely convenient for those who use FTP frequently.
SSH Secure Shell for Workstations *http://www.ssh.com*	A secure terminal (replacement for Telnet), which also comes with an SCP (secure copy) client.
WinSCP *http://winscp.vse.cz*	An implementation of SCP, it uses a convenient side-by-side layout similar to WS_FTP.

Controlling Another Computer Remotely (Just Like in the Movies)

A network is good for much more than simply transferring data. Although Windows does let you transfer files to and from other computers in Explorer (see Chapter 8), it's a far cry from actually sitting in front of the remote computer.

One of the severe limitations of the Windows platform is that only one user is allowed to operate the computer at any given time. Unix, on the other hand, allows many simultaneous remote users (even in addition to a user sitting right at the workstation), each with their own graphical X-Windows terminal connection.

Enter the new Remote Desktop feature in Windows XP. Although it still does not allow more than one simultaneous user per machine, it does allow you to view the desktop of another Windows XP computer on your network or over the Internet, just as though you were sitting in front of it.

There are almost limitless uses to this technology; a few examples include:

- Do you travel frequently, yet prefer to use a desktop (nonportable) computer at home? Rather than duplicating all your programs, documents, and settings on a laptop, or trying to carry all your files and programs with you to use on someone else's computer, just use Remote Desktop to connect to your home computer from the road, and check your email, fax, etc., as though you were sitting at your own desk.
- Do you need to access your work documents and programs while you're at home, or access your home documents and programs while you're at work? Use Remote Desktop to bridge the link and stop worrying about carrying so much stuff back and forth to work every day.
- Are you the person family members and friends call with their computer problems? Instead of spending hours on the phone, trying to explain to them how to fix their computers, just connect with Remote Desktop and fix the problem yourself in minutes.
- Do you administer several computers in different locations? Rather than having to go to the other side of the building (or the other side of the state) to access a computer, use Remote Desktop and get it done in half the time.
- Are you a software developer? If you need to test your software on different operating systems or platforms, it simply isn't practical to use a

multiboot computer;* you'll just spend all your time rebooting. Instead, set up a second (or even third) computer with the necessary test environments, and then control them remotely right from your development machine.

Well, now that this chapter has essentially become a commercial for Remote Desktop, here are some of the disadvantages. First of all, while both Windows XP Home and Professional editions can be Remote Desktop "servers," only XP Professional can be used as a "client" to access remote computers. And although you can use Remote Desktop with some previous versions of Windows, you'll need a different program (like VNC, discussed later in this chapter) to remotely access Mac and Unix machines.

You'll also need a relatively fast connection to use remote control software like Remote Desktop, since a lot of data is transferred to update the screen image. For example, a direct Ethernet (LAN) connection will provide nearly instantaneous response rates, while a DSL or cable connection will be a little more sluggish. Don't even bother using Remote Destop over an analog (dial-up) connection, though.

Overall, the technology included with Windows XP is pretty good. It's not entirely new, however; the same feature, called *Terminal Services*, is included in Windows 2000. It's also not your only choice; see the discussion of alternatives at the end of this section for more information.

Here's how to use the Remote Desktop feature built into Windows XP.

Part 1: Enable the Remote Desktop server

Allowing others to connect to a computer with Remote Desktop is easy. Use the following steps to set up your own computer to be accessed remotely, or you can read them over the phone to the owner of a computer you wish to access remotely.

1. Go to **Control Panel → System → Remote** tab.
2. Turn on the **Allow users to connect remotely to this computer** option.
3. By default, all users currently configured on the machine can connect to it remotely. If you wish to restrict access to only certain users, click **Select Remote Users**. See Chapter 8 for more information on user accounts.
4. Also available in this window is the **Remote Assistance** option; see the "Using Remote Assistance" sidebar for details.

* See Chapter 1 for information on setting up more than one operating system on a single PC.

Using Remote Assistance

The Remote Assistance feature is optional, but can make it easier for less experienced users to transmit the required information to the person who will be accessing their computer remotely, including the IP address and user account.

Turn on the **Allow Remote Assistance invitations to be sent from this computer** option, and then click the **Remote Assistance** link in this window to open the Remote Assistance dialog (or launch `rcimlby -launchra`). Here, you have the option of using Windows Messenger (MSN or .NET passport account required) or your default email program (set in **Control Panel → Internet Options → Programs** tab) to send the invitation. In most cases, email will be the best choice. When asked to type a personal message, just leave it blank. The final option is to choose a special password for the person connecting to your computer, useful if you don't want to give them your normal password.

Since these "invitations" can be a security hazard, there are two safeguards in place to automatically disable the feature after a specified amount of time. In the **Remote** tab of the System Properties dialog, click **Advanced** to disable the feature completely after a few days. Plus, when sending an invitation, you can configure it to expire only an hour or two after being sent.

5. Click **OK** when you're done.

If you're using a router and you're connecting across an Internet connection, you'll have to set up your router's port-forwarding feature to permit this service. This allows your router to "route" incoming signals (from port 3389) to the IP address of the computer of your choice. If you're using Windows XP's built-in firewall, you'll need to include an exception for port 3389 there as well. See Appendix C for more information on TCP/IP Ports.

Part 2: Connect to a remote computer

Once you've set up a machine to accept remote connections, follow these steps on the *client* side to connect to that computer remotely:

1. Start Remote Desktop Connection (*mstsc.exe*).
2. The default Remote Desktop Connection dialog is very simple, with only a single field. This typically will not be adequate, however, so click **Options** to display the full dialog, shown in Figure 7-16.

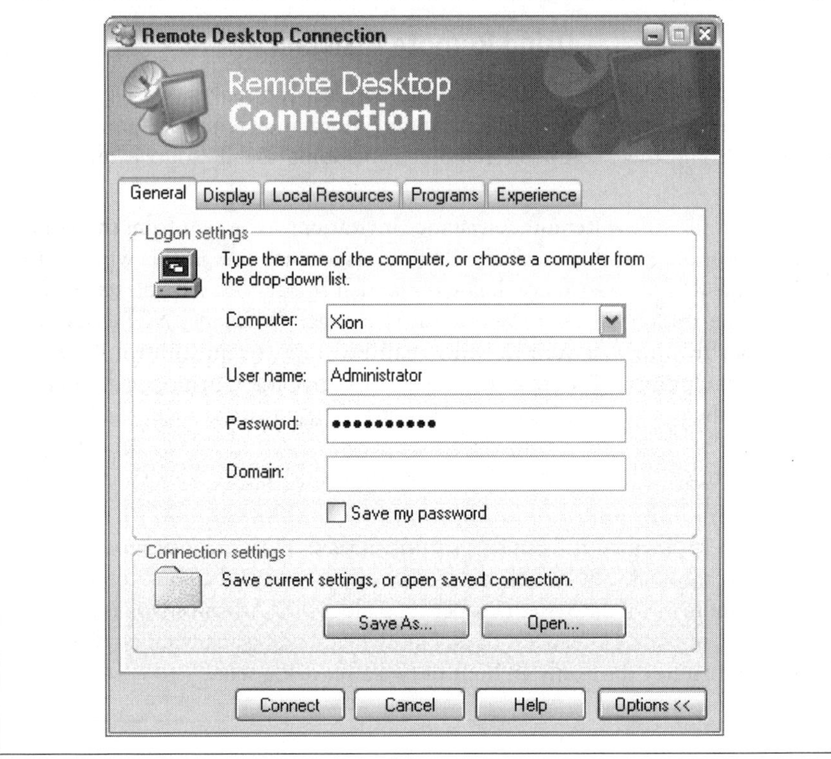

Figure 7-16. Use Remote Desktop Connection to initiate a connection to another computer and view and interact with its desktop as though you were sitting in front of it

3. If you're connecting to another computer in your workgroup, type the name of the computer in the **Computer** field, or if you're connecting to another computer on the Internet, type its IP address here.
4. Next, type the **User name** and **Password** of a valid user account on the remote computer. The **Domain** field is only used if you're connecting to a computer in a Windows NT/2000 domain; leave it blank otherwise.
5. If you're connecting to someone else's computer, you'll have to get their IP address, plus the username and password of an account on their computer (see Chapter 8).

The easiest way to get someone else's IP address is to ask them to visit *http://www.annoyances.org/ip*, and then have them read aloud the numbers on the page or email them to you. This is usually easier (and more foolproof) than other methods, such as using the Network Connections window or typing `ipconfig` at the Command Prompt.

Finally, you can have the remote user send you an invitation using Remote Assistance, described in the "Using Remote Assistance" sidebar. When you receive your invitation via email, it will come with a file attachment, *rcBuddy.MsRcIncident*, which you can double-click to initiate a connection to the sender's computer.

6. The rest of the options in this dialog are optional. The settings in the **Display** and **Experience** tabs deal with performance issues, and the **Programs** tab lets you start programs on the remote computer automatically. The **Local Resources** tab has similar options, plus a **Local devices** section, which lets you share remote drives, printers, and even serial ports.
7. If you plan on reconnecting to the remote computer at a later time, click **Save As** to create an *.rdp* file with all the information in this dialog. You can subsequently double-click the file to initiate a connection, or right-click and select **Edit** to modify its properties.

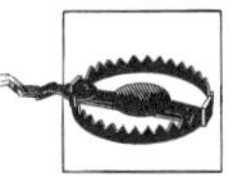

Keep in mind that many users' Internet connections use dynamic-IP addresses, explained earlier in this chapter, which would mean that saving someone's IP address would be pointless.

8. Click **Connect** to initiate a connection to the remote computer. If all is well, a window will appear with an image of the desktop of the remote computer. You can interact with this desktop by pointing, clicking, and dragging, just as if you were sitting in front of it.
9. Simply close the window or go to **Start → Disconnect** (in the Remote Desktop window, not in your own Start Menu) to close the connection.

Notes

Since Windows can only have one user logged in at a time, as mentioned at the beginning of this section, the user currently logged in to the remote computer will be automatically logged out to make way for the remote connection. This poses a significant problem if you wish to use the remote computer with its owner watching. VNC, described below, overcomes this limitation.

The Telnet service (enabled through *services.fmsc*) does allow multiple users to log on to a single Windows XP machine simultaneously. But since Telnet is little more than a Command Prompt window accessed remotely (via *telnet.exe*), it doesn't allow you to control any Windowed applications.

As suggested in the final step, above, a new item will appear in the remote computer's Start Menu, **Disconnect**. This takes the place of the **Shut Down** (or **Turn off Computer**) command normally found here. A consequence of this is that there's no obvious way to shut down a remote computer; this is obviously done intentionally, since a shut-down computer will not accept remote connections. To shut down a remote computer, open a Command Prompt window (*cmd.exe*) on the remote machine, and type:

```
shutdown -s -t 5
```

where 5 is the number of seconds to wait before shutting down; specify `0` here to shut down immediately.

It's helpful to have the resolution of the remote desktop lower than the resolution of the local desktop. That way, you'll be able to see the entire remote desktop and still be able to use the local computer's desktop. For example, if you're using a computer with a display resolution of 1280×1024, set the remote desktop to no more than 1024×768. Use the **Display** tab of the Remote Desktop Connection dialog to set the desktop size; note that this setting will have no effect on the remote computer's normal desktop size.

As nice as it would be to drag files into (and out of) the Remote Desktop window to transfer them, the Remote Desktop feature doesn't include any provision for transferring files. Instead, you'll need to use more traditional means of transferring files. If the remote computer is on your own LAN, you can drag and drop files right in Windows Explorer, as described in Chapter 8. Otherwise, if you're connected to the remote computer over the Internet, you'll either need to set up VPN to mimic a workgroup (described earlier in this chapter) or use FTP.

Alternatives to Remote Desktop Connection

Remote Desktop Connection is not your only choice when it comes to controlling a computer remotely. Since it's built into Windows XP, though, it's obviously a very convenient and cost-effective solution; if you want more flexibility or if you want to control (or be controlled by) a PC running a different operating system, you may wish to use a different program.

Although there are several commercial alternatives available, one of the best is a free program called VNC, available from *http://www.realvnc.com/*. Among other things, VNC has the advantage of a very small "viewer" executable. That is, the client software, used on the remote system to access the host, is only a single file, small enough to fit on a floppy. This makes it easy to carry it around with you and run it on any machine you come across with an Internet connection.

One of the drawbacks of Windows's Remote Desktop feature is that the person whose computer is being controlled won't be able to see their own desktop during a Remote Desktop session. VNC, on the other hand, runs transparently on the host computer, so that both people can see and interact with the same desktop simultaneously.

VNC also works on any version of Windows, Macintosh, UNIX, Linux, or FreeBSD, in addition to good ol' Windows XP. Someone has even made a Palm-based client (*http://www.btinternet.com/~harakan/PalmVNC/*), allowing you to control a remote computer from an Internet-enabled handheld device!

Otherwise, the system requirements are basically the same as Remote Desktop, described earlier in this section. You'll still need the remote computer's IP address, and some way of logging in to the remote computer. VNC has its own user-authentication system, while others such as pcAnywhere (*http://www.symantec.com*) use existing Windows user accounts.

Windows XP's Remote Desktop feature, when enabled, will remain enabled even if the computer is restarted. But third-party programs must be specifically configured to start automatically with Windows, in case the computer crashes or the power goes out. If the software you're using has an option to be started as a "service" (accessible in *services.msc*), you'd be wise to use it rather than adding it to your Start Menu's *Startup* folder. (VNC has such an option.)

If you run into a problem getting Remote Desktop or VNC working through a firewall, proxy, or router, or you simply need to get a connection up and running fast, you have another option. GoToMyPC (*http://www.gotomypc.com*) is a web-based service that tends to work when the others fail. Short sessions are free; longer sessions require a paid subscription.

Managing the Nameserver (DNS) Cache

As mentioned a few times elsewhere in this chapter, a nameserver is a machine that translates IP addresses to domain names and back again. For example, when you type *http://www.oreilly.com* into your web browser's address bar, Windows sends a request to your service provider's nameserver, and the nameserver responds with something like `209.204.146.22`, allowing your browser to contact the web server directly and download the requested page.

Each time such a DNS (Domain Naming System) lookup is performed, the information is stored in the DNS cache so Windows doesn't have to query the nameserver every time you access a page on that site. The DNS cache is emptied when you shut down Windows.

The following solutions allow you to change the way Windows interacts with its DNS cache, and will affect all applications that access the Internet (not just your web browser).

Part 1: Increase the size of the DNS cache

A larger DNS cache will mean fewer trips to the nameserver, and faster overall performance:

1. Open the Registry Editor (see Chapter 3).
2. Expand the branches to `HKEY_LOCAL_MACHINE\SYSTEM\CurrentControlSet\Services\Dnscache\Parameters`.
3. Add the following four DWORD values by going to **Edit → New → DWORD Value**. Then, enter the numeric values specified by double-clicking and selecting the **Decimal** option:
    - `CacheHashTableBucketSize`, set to `1`
    - `CacheHashTableSize`, set to `384`
    - `MaxCacheEntryTtlLimit`, set to `64000`
    - `MaxSOACacheEntryTtlLimit`, set to `301`

   Remember, these are **Decimal** values (not **Hexadecimal** values).
4. Close the Registry Editor when you're done. You'll have to restart Windows for this change to take effect.

Part 2: Add a permanent entry to the DNS cache

When you add a permanent entry to the DNS cache, it will always override the information provided by the nameserver. Here are a few reasons why you might want to do this:

- If a nameserver gives the wrong address for a domain or provides no information at all, you can still access the domain if it's listed as a permanent entry.
- A permanent entry with intentionally incorrect information will block requests sent to the corresponding servers. This can be an effective way to prevent some web sites from tracking you, stop some "spyware" software from recording your personal information, and even stop some pop-up ads when you visit web pages. A list of known "tracking" hosts can be downloaded from *http://www.accs-net.com/hosts/*.

- If you frequently access a particular server, and you know its IP address isn't likely to change anytime soon, you can add a permanent entry to eliminate the initial delay as Windows looks it up. For example, add an entry for your mail server to decrease the time it takes to check your email.
- If you frequently visit a remote server without a domain name (accessing it only by its IP address), you configure a custom domain name, for your use only, to be used as a kind of "shortcut" to the server.

Providing incorrect information here can prevent you from accessing certain remote servers. Use care when modifying the permanent DNS entry table. Coincidentally, some malware (see Chapter 6) adds entries to your DNS cache, such that you'll be intentionally redirected to the wrong server when you try to visit some web sites.

Here's how to create and modify the list of permanent DNS entries:

1. Open Explorer, and navigate to the *\windows\system32\drivers\etc* folder.
2. Look for a file called *hosts* (no filename extension). If it's not there, create it by going to **File → New → Text Document**, and typing `hosts` for the filename.
3. The *hosts* file is just a plain-text file; open it in your favorite text editor (or Notepad).
4. A standard entry looks like this:

   ```
   207.46.230.218    www.microsoft.com
   ```

   The first part is the IP address, and the second part (separated by a tab or several spaces) is the domain name.

   Keep in mind that variations, such as *www.microsoft.com* and *microsoft.com*, aren't necessarily the same server, and represent different DNS entries. You'll need to add a separate *hosts* entry for each variation if you want to access them all, like this:

   ```
   207.46.230.218    www.microsoft.com
   207.46.230.218    microsoft.com
   ```

   Using this syntax, add an entry for each domain you wish to hard-code into Windows's DNS table. Note that these addresses affect your machine only; other machines, such as those in your workgroup or others on the Internet, will not be affected.

5. You may also see some lines that begin with the # character. These are comments, and are ignored by Windows.
6. Save the *hosts* file when you're done. The change should take effect immediately.

The next time you type one of the web addresses listed in your *hosts* file, Windows will use the IP address you've specified instead of contacting the DNS server.

Go Wireless

If you're on a wireless network and you're *not* using Windows XP Service Pack 2, it means you're still suffering with the weak WiFi support built into the original release of Windows XP. Go ahead and upgrade to SP2 now; don't worry, I'll wait.

{Sounds of fingers tapping and whistling off-key.}

Got it? Good. The solutions in this section show you how to set up a simple wireless network and connect that network to the Internet, as well as connect your wireless devices to other people's wireless networks, and prevent others from sneaking on to *your* network. All of this is possible without wires, and the most amazing thing is that it actually works.

If you want to do a whole lot more with your wireless network, check out *Wireless Hacks* (O'Reilly). Among other things, it shows you how to extend the range of your wireless network from a few yards to several *miles* with homemade antennas. Very cool.

Set Up a Wireless Router

If you've read other solutions in this chapter, you've probably seen routers mentioned several times (if not, drop back to "Planning Your Network" to read up).

A router allows you to connect your computer (or your workgroup) to the Internet, while simultaneously protecting you with its built-in firewall. A wireless router does the same thing, but it also adds a wireless access point, allowing you to connect any number of WiFi devices to each other and to the Internet.

A typical WiFi setup is shown in Figure 7-3 (see, no wires), but you'll probably want something closer to the setup shown in Figure 7-6, in which a wireless router provides Internet access to all your computers. Here's how to set this up and configure the security measures that *should have* been enabled out of the box:

1. Plug your DSL or cable modem (or whatever broadband connection you're using) into your router's WAN or Internet port.
2. Plug one or more computers into the numbered ports on your router. Or, if you want to connect wirelessly, see "Sniff Out WiFi Networks" later in this chapter.
3. Dispense with the software that comes with your router. Instead, open a web browser on one of the computers and type the IP address of your router into the address bar. In most cases, this is `192.168.1.1`, but your router may be different; refer to your router's documentation for details. (You may also need to log in with a username and password at this point.)
4. Assuming your connection to your router is working, your router's setup page will look something like the one in Figure 7-17. Of course, your router's setup page will probably look different, but most of the same settings will still be there.

> If you can't connect to your router, the most likely cause is that your computer is not on the same subnet as the router. The first three numbers of your computer's IP address must mach the first three numbers of your router's IP address, but the fourth number must be different. For instance, if your router is at `192.168.0.5`, then the example here won't work; change the IP address of your computer to somethjng like `192.168.1.17` to connect to the router. Of course, you can try the Obtain an IP address automatically in your TCP/IP settings as described in "Configuring Network Connections" earlier in this chapter, but this doesn't always work.

5. Choose your connection type from the list. If your Internet connection requires a username and password, select **PPPoE**. If your ISP has provided an IP address for your connection, select **Static IP**. Otherwise, choose **Automatic Configuration - DHCP**.
6. If you've selected **PPPoE** or **Static IP**, you'll probably need to enter the IP addresses of your ISP's DNS servers (your ISP should provide these numbers for you).
7. Click **Apply** or **Save Settings** at the bottom of the page when you're done.
8. At this point, you should have Internet access; go ahead and test it by opening a second browser window (**Ctrl-N**) and visiting any web site.

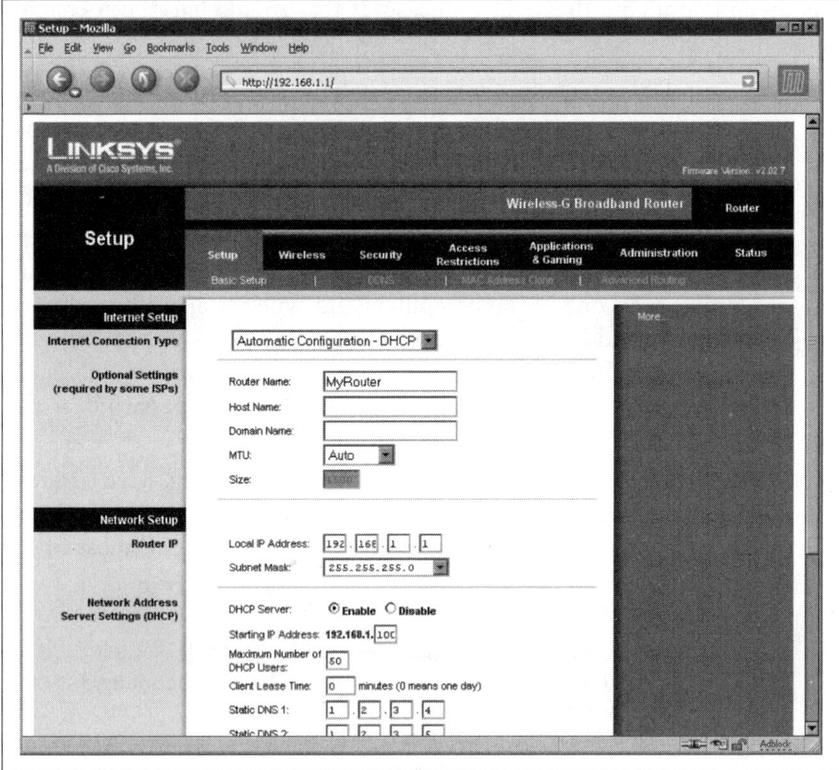

Figure 7-17. Most routers use a web-based setup, meaning that you can configure your router from any computer, running on any platform, as long as it has a web browser

9. Next, go to your router's wireless setup page. This is either a link in the main menu or a tab across the top of the page, as shown in Figure 7-18.
10. Choose a new name (SSID) for your wireless network, and turn off the **Wireless SSID Broadcast** option.

Your SSID is the backdoor into your wireless network. If you broadcast your SSID, anyone with an SSID sniffer will be able to find it in a matter of seconds (see "Sniff Out WiFi Networks" later in this chapter), and connect to your network. The same danger exists if you use your router's default; probably a million people around the globe are using the SSID "linksys," which makes it a good guess for anyone trying to gain access to your network.

11. Next, you'll want to set up encryption for the best wireless security. This page will either be accessible through a button on the current page

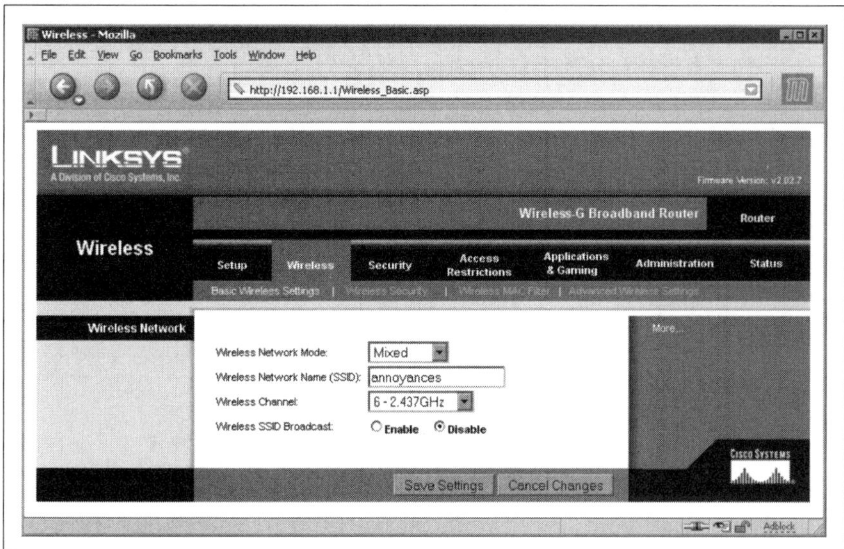

Figure 7-18. Use your router's wireless setup page to configure the security settings for your wireless network

entitled WEP or Encryption, or (in the case of the example in Figure 7-18), a separate tab. Make sure to click **Apply** or **Save Settings** on this page first, if needed.

WEP, or Wireless Encryption Protocol, prevents anyone from connecting to or spying on your wireless network unless they have your WEP key. Figure 7-19 shows a typical WEP setup page.

12. Choose **WEP** for the security mode (if available), and then choose the highest WEP encryption level supported by your router (here, it's 128-bit). Higher levels provide better protection, but also mean longer (and harder to type) WEP keys.
13. Some routers allow you to choose a *passphrase*, a word on which the WEP keys are based. Although Windows XP doesn't support the passphrase, some third-party devices do. In the example shown in Figure 7-19, I typed annoyances and clicked **Generate** to create the 26-digit WEP keys.
14. Once you commit this change, you'll need to enter one of the keys that appear here into each computer that connects to your wireless network, so take this opportunity to record the key *before* you save changes.

    Highlight the first key (**Key 1**), and press Ctrl-C to copy it to the clipboard. Then, open your favorite text editor (e.g., Notepad), and press Ctrl-V to paste it into a new, empty document. Save the file on your

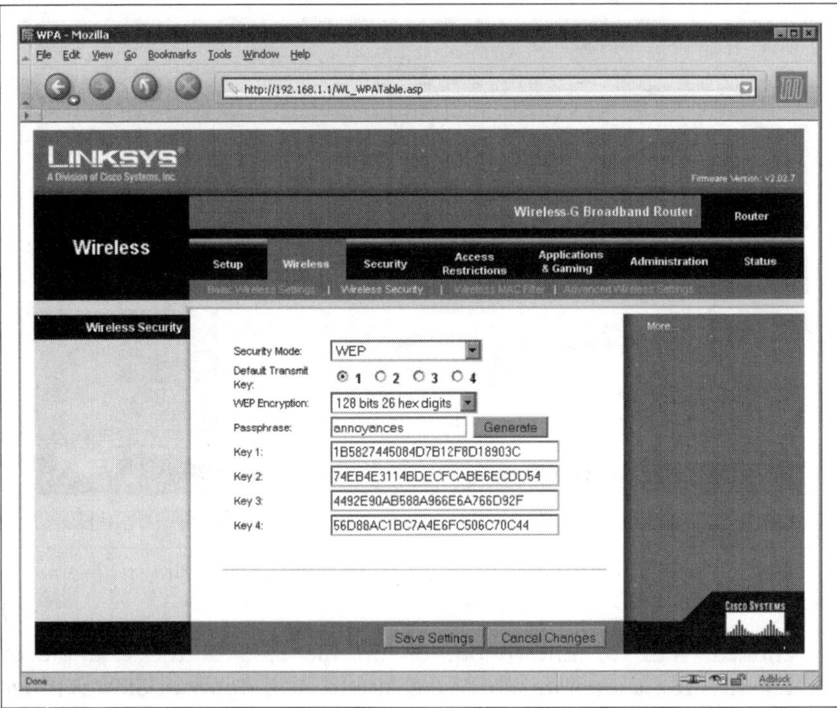

Figure 7-19. Configure your wireless router's WEP settings to prevent others from connecting to your wireless network without your permission

desktop; this will allow you to easily paste it into various dialog boxes later on, which is easier than having to type it.

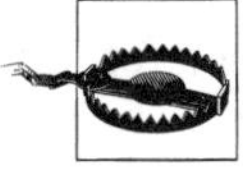

> If you enable WEP for your wireless network, but you subsequently can't connect to it wirelessly, it most likely means that you've gotten the WEP key wrong. To fix the problem, you'll have to either connect to it with a cable and change the settings or, as a final resort, reset the router as described in your router's documentation.

15. Click **Apply** or **Save Settings** at the bottom of the page when you're done.

See the next section, "Sniff Out WiFi Networks," for help connecting your computer to your (or someone else's) wireless network. See "Add Wireless Support to Any Device," later in this chapter, for ways to take advantage of your new wireless network. See the "Router Placement 101" sidebar for ways to improve reception (and thus performance of your wireless network).

Router Placement 101

The tiny WiFi transceiver in your laptop should be capable of picking up any wireless network within about 100 feet. If indoors, this typically includes no more than about 2 or 3 walls, and perhaps one floor or ceiling. But the placement of your wireless router and the arrangement of natural obstactles near it will have a significant effect on the strength and range of your WiFi signal.

Assuming you're using a setup like the one pictured in Figure 7-6, your router will need to be within spitting distance of your DSL or cable modem. But provided that the cable from your modem to your router is long enough, you should have a little leeway here.

Your router should be out in the open; don't put it under your desk, in a drawer, or behind a metal file cabinet. If you're feeding more than one computer, it should be placed in a central location, if possible. Use the signal strength indicator (Figure 7-10) to test various configurations. Consider cabling stationary computers so that you can optimize the placement of the router for your portable ones.

Both the 802.11b and 802.11g standards operate over the 2.4Ghz band, which is also inhabited by cordless phones and microwave ovens. (The black sheep of the family, 802.11a solves this problem by using the 5Ghz band, but its short range and limited compatibility make it an unpopular choice.) This means that you'll get better results if you move the router away from any cordless phone base stations, televisions, radios, or TV dinners.

If, after adjusting the placement of your router, you still need more range that it seems to be able to provide, consider either a repeater (range extender) or an aftermarket antenna.

Sniff Out WiFi Networks

Probably the most significant change in SP2 is the substantial improvement of the WiFi support built into Windows XP. The centerpiece of these improvements is the "Choose a wireless network" window shown in Figure 7-20.

A WiFi sniffer is a program (or device) that scans for and lists the WiFi networks within range. This is where the Broadcast SSID setting discussed in the previous section, "Set Up a Wireless Router," comes into play. If you're broadcasting your SSID, any sniffer within range will see it.

In the Network Connections window, double-click an unconnected Wireless connection to open the "Choose a wireless network" window. (You can also right-click the icon in your system tray or Network Connections window and select **View Available Wireless Networks**.) Windows XP will

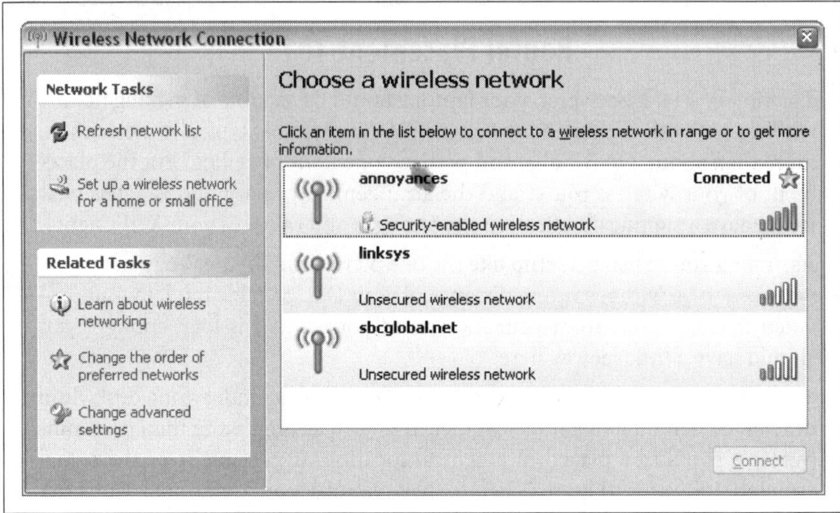

Figure 7-20. The WiFi sniffer in Windows XP SP2 lets you connect to any available WiFi network

automatically perform a scan and display the results; in all, it should take less than 5 seconds. Click **Refresh network list** to repeat the scan.

To connect to a network in the list, highlight it and click **Connect**. If no security is in effect, Windows will establish a connection without any further ado. But if there's any WEP encryption, you'll be asked to type a WEP key. Note the little padlock next to the first network listed in the dialog box in Figure 7-20, which tells you that the only network with encryption is annoyances; you'll be able to connect to the other networks without any special permission or additional information.

Sniffing hidden networks

But what if you've turned off the SSID broadcast feature, as described in "Set Up a Wireless Router" earlier in this chapter? If your network doesn't show up in the list, simply click **Set up a wireless network for a home or small office** (on the left side of the "Choose a wireless network" window shown in Figure 7-20). This will start the Wireless Network Setup Wizard (which is also accessible through My Network Places).

Click **Next** and then type your network's SSID in the **Network name (SSID)** field, as shown in Figure 7-21.

If you've enabled WEP encryption, select **Manually assign a network key** and click **Next**. On the next page, type (or paste) your WEP key into the **Network key** field.

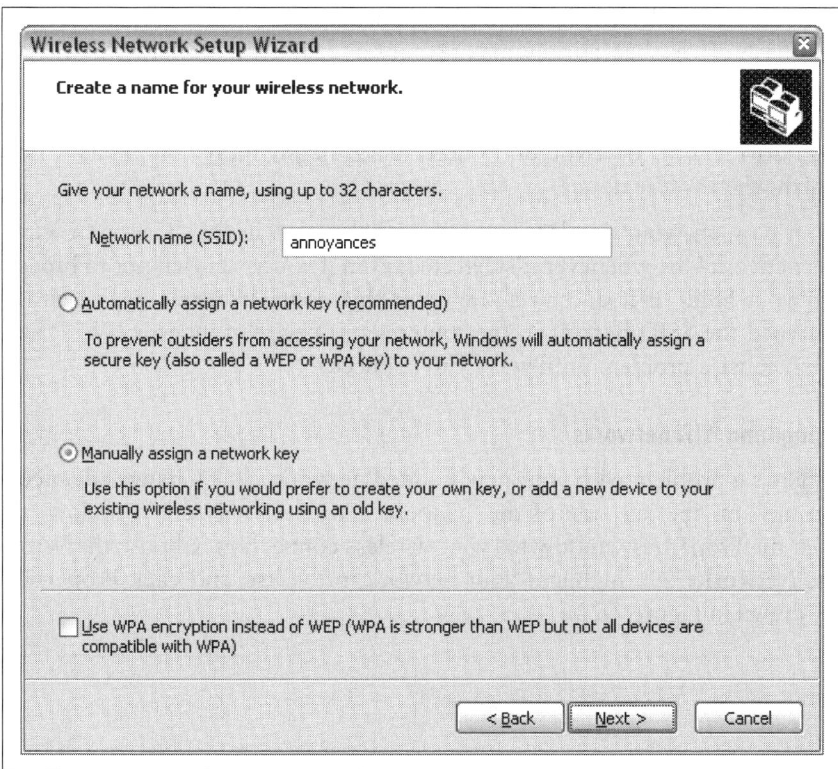

Figure 7-21. You'll need to run the Wireless Network Setup Wizard to connect to your wireless network if you've opted not to broadcast your SSID

As illustrated in Figure 7-19, many routers allow you to set more than one key; unless you have specific reason to do otherwise, just use the first one (**Key 1**) in Windows XP.

The length of the key you type is shown to the right of the field. If you're using 64-bit encryption, the key will be 10 characters long (or 5 if you're not typing hex codes); if you're using 128-bit encryption, the key will be 26 characters long (or 13 if you're not typing hex codes).

Unless you enjoy typing incomprehensible hex codes, turn off the **Hide characters as I type** option. Then, highlight the text in the **Network key** field, press **Ctrl-C** to copy it to the clipboard, click in the **Confirm network key** field, and press **Ctrl-V** to paste a copy of the key. If you stored your WEP in a text file, as suggested in "Set Up a Wireless Router," you can paste it into both boxes here, and avoid the tedious typing altogether.

Networking

Click **Next**. You'll then be given the opportunity to save your settings on a USB flash drive, theoretically making subsequent setups easier; why there's no option to save to a CD writer, floppy drive, or simply a file on your desktop is a mystery. Select **Set up a network manually** if you don't have a USB flash drive handy, or if you don't need to set up any more computers. Click **Finish** when you're done.

From now on, your wireless network will show up in the "Choose a wireless network" list whenever it's detected, even if you've chosen not to broadcast your SSID. If it doesn't show up at this point, it means you've either mistyped the SSID here or in the router setup page (an incorrect WEP key won't cause a problem until you try to connect.)

Configuring WiFi networks

If there's a problem with your newly added network, click **Change advanced settings** (on the left side of the "Choose a wireless network" window) to open the Properties window for your wireless connection. Choose the **Wireless Networks** tab, highlight your network in the list, and click **Properties** (as shown in Figure 7-22).

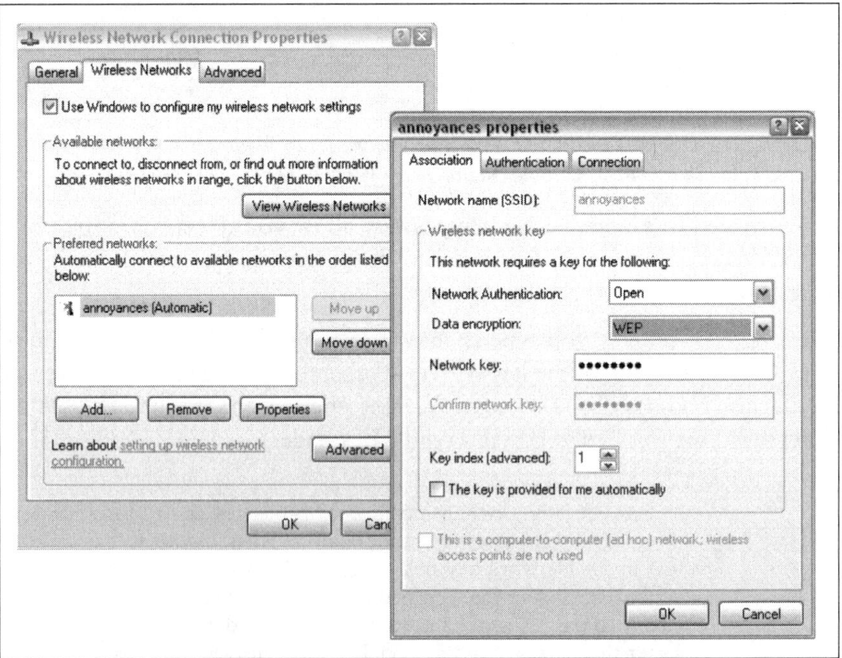

Figure 7-22. You may have to fiddle with XP's WiFi settings to get it to connect to secure WiFi networks

Here, you'll have a second chance to enter your WEP key, but you won't have the luxury of being able to see the characters as you type them (as in the Wireless Network Setup Wizard). The easiest way to deal with this is to open Notepad, type (or paste) your key there, and then copy (**Ctrl-C**) and paste (**Ctrl-V**) it into both the **Network key** and **Confirm network key** fields.

While you're here, choose the **Connection** tab. The **Connect when this network is in range** option (it's on by default) determines whether or not Windows XP will automatically connect to this network when it's available. In most cases, you'll want to leave this option checked.

Now, if you're in the enviable position of having access to more than one WiFi network regularly, and wish to have Windows connect automatically to more than one network, you can prioritize them. Just return to the **Wireless Networks** tab (Figure 7-22), highlight a network, and click **Move up** or **Move down**.

Click **OK** to save your settings when you're done. If all is well, Windows should reattempt the wireless connection automatically. If it doesn't, you'll need to return to the "Choose a wireless network" window (Figure 7-20), highlight the network, and click **Connect**.

See the next section, "Connect to a Public Wireless Network," for ways to protect your computer when using someone else's Internet connection.

Troubleshooting

WiFi tends to be temperamental, not to mention annoying and tear-your-hair-out frustrating. Among the things that can make it difficult to connect to a wireless access point, these are the most common:

Drivers and firmware
: If you ever have any trouble with your wireless router, visit the manufacturer's web site and see if there's newer firmware available for it. Likewise, make sure you're using the latest drivers for your WiFi PCI and PC Card adapters.

WiFi settings
: Make sure both your router and your other equipment are communicating on the same channel (channel 6, 2.437 Ghz, is the typical default) and are using the same SSID.

Encryption

Are you using encryption, as described in "Set Up a Wireless Router"? If so, you'll need to make sure that the Windows encryption settings exactly match those in your router's setup page. Check the security mode (e.g., WEP or WPA), the encryption level (40-bit, 64-bit, or 128-bit), and the WEP keys (use **Key 1** unless you have reason to do otherwise). If all else fails, try disabling encryption all around to see if it works at all. Then, add one security feature at a time.

Speed

Are you using an 802.11g router? If so, you can probably set it to operate only at 802.11b speeds, only at 802.11g speeds, or both. Note that if you select "G-only," no older 802.11b equipment will be able to connect to it.

Reception, Interference, and Performance

Your wireless network relies on good reception to achieve reliable performance. See the "Router Placement 101" sidebar, earlier in this chapter, for ways to improve reception.

Other WiFi sniffers

Since one of the biggest advantages of wireless networking is portability, it should stand to reason that you should be able to connect to your wireless network with something you can hold in the palm of your hand.

To that end, a number of handheld computers now come with WiFi support. Figure 7-23 shows the WiFi sniffer that comes with some Palm OS–powered handheld computers, allowing you to identify and connect to any available WiFi network.

A handheld sniffer can be a very valuable tool when setting up a wireless network. Among other things, you can test the range of your wireless router with a handheld sniffer more easily than by lugging around a laptop or desktop PC, allowing you to subsequently adjust the placement of your router for optimal range.

Connect to a Public Wireless Network

The point of wireless networking is not necessarily to do away with a few feet of cables, but to make a network do things it could never do before. For instance, if you have a portable computer equipped with wireless, you should be able to walk into any airport, coffee shop, hotel, or college dormitory and connect to the Internet in a matter of seconds. In more populated areas, it's

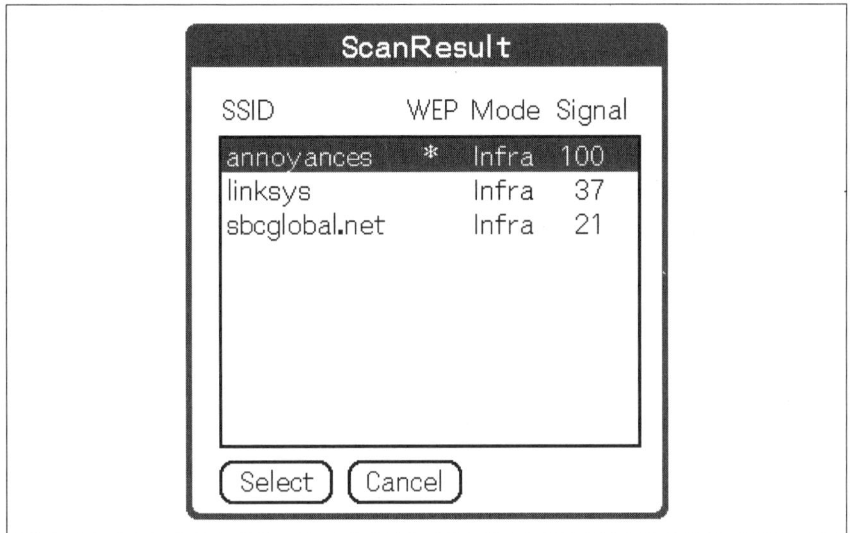

Figure 7-23. The WiFi sniffer on a Palm OS–powered handheld PDA shows the same wireless SSIDs as Windows XP's built-in WiFi sniffer

not uncommon to walk down the street and have your pick of WiFi networks. (See the "The Ethics of WiFi" sidebar for an extra consideration.)

As described in "Sniff Out WiFi Networks" earlier in this chapter, you can connect to any unsecured wireless network that Windows XP's built-in WiFi sniffer is able to detect. (The exceptions, of course, are those networks requiring a paid subscription or account access, but that's a different story.) This applies to networks you encounter while you're on the road, as well as those that are in range of your home or office.

The problem is that by connecting to these networks, you're exposing your computer to the full array of viruses, hackers, and other dangers present on any network.* The solution is to take action to protect your computer (or workgroup), and the necessary steps depend on the scenario.

Scenario 1: Single-serving Internet

Say you've just sat yourself down at a sidewalk cafe, and pulled out your laptop. (This scenario also applies to hotel rooms, airports, and coffee shops.) You boot up Windows, open the "Choose a wireless network" window as described in "Sniff Out WiFi Networks, find a local network, and

Networking

* This may be reason enough to keep strangers out of your own WiFi network; see "Set Up a Wireless Router," earlier in this chapter, for help securing your network.

> ### The Ethics of WiFi
>
> Once you get the technical details out of the way, the one remaining hurdle when considering using someone else's Internet connection is a question of ethics. There are countless personal wireless networks around the globe, and most of them, you'll find, are unsecured. This means that you can literally walk down the street in a populated area and probably find a working wireless Internet connection before you reach the end of the block. Some will have been left open intentionally, but most will be unsecured merely because their owners don't have the benefit of the "Set Up a Wireless Router" procedure detailed earlier in this chapter.
>
> Now, just because you can connect to these networks, does it mean you should? Are you taking advantage of someone else's ignorance by breaking into their private network, or are you simply making use of a public resource that you'd be equally eager to share?
>
> I'm not about to try to solve this dilemma in these few pages; I only wish to raise the question, and to suggest that if you do ever decide to utilize someone else's wireless network, do not do any harm. Think about your impact, both on the bandwidth of the foreign network and the privacy of those who operate it. And then tread lightly.

connect for approximately 20 minutes to check your email. When you're done, you'll likely never use this network again.

Now, if you typically use your laptop from behind a wireless router at home (as described in "Set Up a Wireless Router" earlier in this chapter), you'll want to take some extra steps to secure your computer *before* you connect elsewhere. Since you won't have your router with you on the road, and thus won't have any dedicated firewall hardware, you'll want to employ the built-in Windows Firewall software (or a third-party firewall solution), as described in "Using the Windows Security Center" later in this chapter. This will provide minimal protection, insufficient for the long haul.

Scenario 2: The long haul

Say you just moved into an apartment complex (or have a small business in an office building) that provides free wireless Internet. Naturally, you would never want to connect your computer or workgroup to this wireless free-for-all without some sort of reliable, long-term firewall solution. Now, since this is not your own private Internet connection, you can't just plug in a router to facilitate your firewall. But you can add another device, a wireless bridge, in order to build an "island" of sorts, in a sea otherwise filled with danger.

Figure 7-24 shows a sample setup involving a wireless bridge and a router. The two dotted rectangles represent the scope of the two different WiFi networks in effect: your own private, encrypted wireless network is shown on the right, and the public network is illustrated on the left. (Your bridge and router actually form a tiny, third network, complete with its own set of IP addresses separate from those in either of the two wireless networks.)

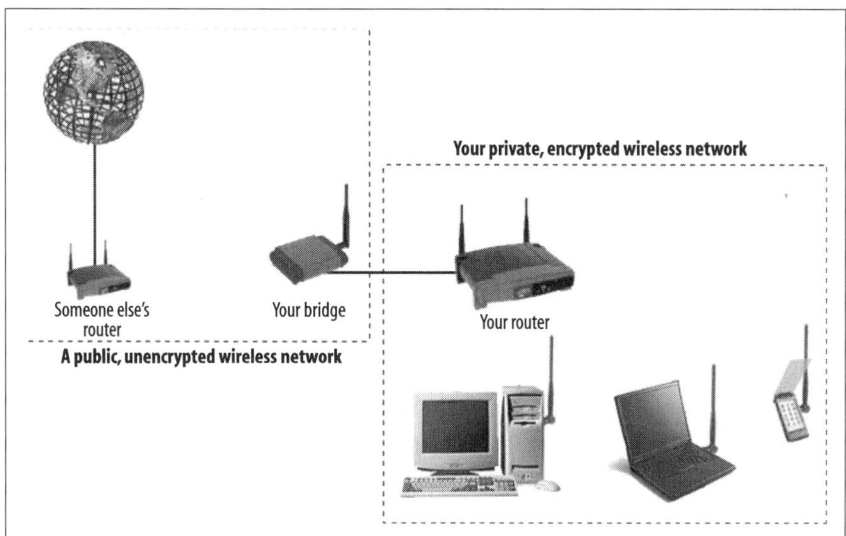

Figure 7-24. Use a wireless bridge in conjunction with a wireless router to protect your workgroup when connecting to a public Internet connection

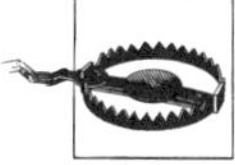

This can be tricky to set up, and may require some trial and error to get it right. Depending on your specific hardware and your needs, you may need to adjust this procedure somewhat. For the simplest setup, make sure your bridge and router are manufactured by the same company.

Here's how you set it up:

1. Use the "Choose a wireless network" window as described in "Sniff Out WiFi Networks to find the name (SSID) of the wireless network to which you'd like to connect. Connect to the network temporarily to confirm that it actually works.
2. Obtain a wireless bridge, and follow the procedure laid out in its documentation to set it up with the aforementioned public wireless network. (This typically involves plugging it directly into your PC or one of the numbered ports of your router.) While you're here, obtain the IP address of your bridge; it'll be something like `192.168.1.1` or `192.168.0.1`.

3. When you're done setting up the bridge, connect it directly to the WAN port of your wireless router. (This is the port into which you'd normally plug a DSL or cable modem.)
4. Connect your PC to your router and use a web browser to open up your router's setup page, as described in "Set Up a Wireless Router," earlier in this chapter.
5. Configure your wireless router so that it has a **Connection Type** of **Static IP**. (Refer to your router's documentation for the specific details on this and the next few settings.)
6. In the router setup, set the **Gateway** address to the IP address of your bridge that you obtained in step 2.
7. Then, set the IP address of the Internet connection (as the router sees it) to a fictitious IP address in the same *subnet* as your bridge. This means that the *first three numbers* of both IP addresses should be the same, but the fourth should be different. That is, if your router is located at `192.168.1.1`, then you could set the IP address of your Internet connection to something like `192.168.1.2` or `192.168.1.73`.
8. Finally, set the DNS server addresses in your router setup to the IP addresses of your Internet Service Provider's DNS servers.

If you don't know what Internet Service Provider you're using, connect your PC directly to the wireless network in question. Open a web browser, type *http://annoyances.org/ip* in the address bar, and press **Enter**; this will show the IP address of your Internet connection. Then, open a Command Prompt window (see Chapter 10) and type `nslookup` *`ip_address`*, where *`ip_address`* is the set of four numbers reported by Annoyances.org. This should give you the name of your ISP, plus some extra stuff. So, you might see something like `dsl456.eastcoast.superisp.net`, which means your ISP is "`superisp.net`." Then, it's only a matter of visiting their web site and determining their DNS server addresses from their online documentation!

9. Complete the setup of your router as explained in "Set Up a Wireless Router," earlier in this chapter, and make sure to enable WEP encryption and any other security settings at your disposal.

This should do it. The bridge funnels the public Internet connection into your router, and your router funnels it to the computers in your workgroup. The router acts like a firewall, provided that you connect all your computers directly to your personal WiFi network, and not the public, unsecured one.

Among other things, your bridge/router combination will serve as a repeater (aka range extender), and should boost the signal strength and might even improve performance over connecting directly.

Add Wireless Support to Any Device

As soon as you have your wireless network up and running, you'll probably be inclined to do away with as many cables as you can. This feeling is normal; there's no need to seek psychiatric help or psychic guidance.

There are ways to add support for wireless networking to nearly any computer or device, further illustrating what you can do with a wireless network:

Desktop computer
: Add a wireless PCI card just as you would an Ethernet NIC (network interface card). When shopping for a WiFi NIC, look for a card with an adjustable, external antenna (versus merely a nub.) Another alternative is a USB-based WiFi adapter, which will be easier to install, but probably at the expense of some performance.

Laptop computer
: WiFi PC Cards (PCMCIA adapters) have been available for some time, but if you have a modern laptop, you most likely have a better choice. For about the same price as the aforementioned PC Card, an *internal* Mini-PCI adapter will typically offer better range (thanks to the internal antenna that is likely already present in your laptop), without the clumsy protrusion of a PC Card. (See the "Handheld PDA" entry below for information on using Bluetooth with your laptop.) Another solution can be found in the "Quick and Dirty WiFi Piggyback" sidebar.

Printer
: Although you can connect a printer to a WiFi-equipped PC and share it with the rest of your network (as explained in Chapter 8), a better choice is to connect your printer directly to your wireless network. Among other things, this means you don't have to connect any cables to your laptop to print a document,* and you have the option of placing the printer in a more convenient location. To do this, you'll need a wireless print server, either a standalone unit or one integrated with your wireless router. Then, simply install the software that comes with your

Networking

* A number of years ago, printer manufacturers started including infrared ports on some printers, allowing laptops with infrared port to print to them wirelessly. This was never much of a success, which probably explains why it's now nearly impossible to find a laptop (or printer, for that matter) with an infrared port.

Quick and Dirty WiFi Piggyback

Let's say a friend visits your home or office and wants to check her email with her laptop. What do you do if you want to connect this laptop (or any desktop PC for that matter) to your wireless network *temporarily*, without having to purchase and install any costly additional hardware?

Assume you have a sample wireless network like the ones illustrated in Figure 7-3 and Figure 7-4. Now, you can, of course, plug any computer (provided that it has an Ethernet port) directly into your wireless router with an ordinary category-5 patch cable, and give it instant access to the Internet. But what if the computer doesn't have an Ethernet port? Or what if the router isn't in a convenient location?

Fortunately, any Windows PC can act as a gateway, funneling Internet access to any computer to which it is physically connected using Windows XP's built-in Internet Connection Sharing feature (discussed earlier in this chapter). All you need to do is connect this new laptop directly to your own desktop or laptop PC, and this typically requires only a single cable.

If said laptop has an Ethernet port, and your PC has an unused Ethernet port (likely if you're on a *wireless* network), just connect the two computers with a category-5 crossover cable, and you've got yourself something like the wired network shown in Figure 7-5. (If both computers have FireWire ports, you can also create an impromptu network with a simple FireWire cable.) Just activate Internet Connection Sharing on your PC, and the guest PC will have Internet access.

If you're in a pinch, you can also network the two computers with an old-school *null-modem* (LapLink) cable, which uses only serial ports. To do this, open the New Connection Wizard on both computers (see "Configuring Network Connections" earlier in this chapter), select **Set up an advanced connection**, then select **Connect directly to another computer**, and then complete the wizard as instructed by Windows.

Not that you'd want to use this as a long-term solution, but it works great and takes only a few minutes and a $4.00 cable.

print server to create a virtual printer port on your PC, to which your printer's drivers connect and send documents.

TiVo

One of the biggest hassles of using a Digital Video Recorder (DVR) is that you need to connect it to a phone line so that it can download the latest program data. If you have a newer DVR (such as Series-2 TiVo) that comes with built-in networking support, you can use a USB-based

WiFi adapter and finally cut the cord. If you have an older Series-1 TiVo, you'll need to add a TurboNet card (available at *http://www.9thtee.com/*) and then connect that to an external WiFi bridge. Alternatively, you can use a AirNet card (also available at *http://www.9thtee.com/*) along with a PCMCIA 802.11b adapter you provide, but its range will be more limited than the aforementioned bridge. See *TiVo Hacks* (O'Reilly) for more ways to modify your TiVo.

Video Game Console
: Own a Playstation2, XBox, or other network-capable video game console? Just plug a wireless bridge (sometimes called a wireless game adapter) into your console's Ethernet port, and play head-to-head games without the network cables stretched across your living room.

Handheld PDA
: As introduced in the beginning of this chapter, there are two prevailing wireless technologies: WiFi and Bluetooth. While some handhelds come with built-in WiFi, a larger percentage support Bluetooth (and only a select few play for both teams). Although only WiFi-equipped handhelds can connect to the WiFi networks discussed throughout this chapter, you'll need Bluetooth support if you want to connect to the Internet with your Bluetooth-equipped cell phone. (The same goes for laptops; get an inexpensive Bluetooth USB dongle to connect your Windows PC to your cell phone wirelessly and surf the web from the park or even the train!)

  Now, some higher-end PDAs come with WiFi or Bluetooth support built in, while others have special expansion cards that provide connectivity. You can get a WiFi SecureDigital (SD) card or a Bluetooth SD card that will fit in many PalmOS and PocketPC handhelds, but if you only have one SD slot, you'll have to remove your memory card. If you need the wireless support, you may prefer to replace your PDA with one that has WiFi or Bluetooth (or both) built in, and do away with the awkward protrusion of the expansion card.

Digital camera
: Some high-end digital cameras now have WiFi options, allowing you to send your photos to the hard disk of a nearby computer wirelessly, either in batches or immediately after you take them. Unfortunately, this only works in the studio (as opposed to outdoors), where you'd be in range of your wireless router. At the time of this writing, there are no wireless cards you can conveniently insert in place of your digital film, but it shouldn't be long.

Video camera (webcam)

Get a WiFi-enabled Internet video camera, and place it anywhere within range of your network. Then, use your PC to view a live video feed wirelessly. Or, use it in its server mode, and let anyone in the world see how much coffee is left in your coffee pot. (See Chapter 9 for a simple WSH script that works with webcams.)

Home stereo

Several companies sell WiFi music players that connect your MP3 collection on your computer to your component stereo system and allow you to hear your music on something better than the tinny computer speakers you're likely using now.

Car stereo

At the time of this writing, a WiFi-enabled MP3 player in your car is only vaporware, but keep your eyes open. Soon, manufacturers promise us, you'll be able to send digital music to your car wirelessly. I can't wait for my car stereo to catch an airborne virus.

There's virtually no limit to the number of devices you can make wireless, provided that they support some form of networking already. If all else fails, a wireless bridge, as illustrated in "Connect to a Public Wireless Network," earlier in this chapter, should allow you to connect just about anything to your wireless network.

Securing Your System on a Network

Security is a very real concern for any computer connected to a network or the Internet. There are three main categories of security threats:

A deliberate, targeted attack through your network connection

Ironically, this is the type of attack most people fear, even though realistically, it is the least likely to occur, at least where home and small office networks are concerned. It's possible for a so-called hacker to obtain access to your computer, either through your Internet connection or from another computer on your local network; it's just not terribly likely that such a hacker will bother.

An automated invasion by a virus, worm, Trojan horse, or robot

A virus is simply a computer program that is designed to duplicate itself with the purpose of infecting as many computers as possible. If your computer is infected by a virus, it may use your network connection to infect other computers; likewise, if another computer on your network is infected, your computer is vulnerable to infection. The same goes for Internet connections, although the method of transport in this case is typically an infected email message. (See Chapter 6 for complete coverage of viruses, worms, trojan horses, and spyware.)

There also exist so-called robots, programs that are designed to scan large groups of IP addresses, looking for vulnerabilities. The motive for such a program can be anything from exploitation of credit card numbers or other sensitive information to the hijack of computers for the purpose of distributing spam, viruses, or extreme right-wing propaganda.

Finally, a Trojan horse is a program that works somewhat like a virus, except that its specific purpose is to create vulnerabilities in your computer that can subsequently be exploited by a hacker or robot. For example, a program might open a port on your computer (see Appendix C) and then communicate with a remote system to announce its presence.

A deliberate attack by a person sitting at your computer

A person who sits down at your computer can easily gain access to sensitive information, including your documents, email, and even various passwords stored by your web browser. An intruder can be anyone, from the jerk who has just stolen your laptop to a coworker casually walking by your unattended desk. Naturally, it's up to you to determine the actual likelihood of such a threat and to take the appropriate measures (such as password-protecting your screen saver). Several examples are discussed in Chapter 8.

Defending your computer (and your network) against these attacks essentially involves fixing the vulnerabilities they exploit, as described in the next section.

See "Connect to a Public Wireless Network," earlier in this chapter, for ways to protect your computer and your workgroup if you're using someone else's Internet connection.

Closing Back Doors in Windows XP

Windows XP includes several features that will enable you to implement a reasonable level of security without purchasing additional software or hardware. Unfortunately, none of these features are properly configured by default.

The following steps will help you close some of these "back doors:"

- By default, the file-sharing service is enabled for Internet connections, but in most cases, there's no reason for this. Open the Network

Connections window, right-click the icon corresponding to your Internet connection, and select Properties. In the **General** tab, clear the checkmark next to the **File and Printer Sharing for Microsoft Networks** entry, and then click **OK**. If you have more than one Internet connection icon, repeat this procedure for each of the others. Make sure to leave it enabled for the connection to your workgroup (if applicable).

- One of the main reasons to set up a workgroup is to share files and printers with other computers. But it's wise to share only those folders that need to be shared, and disable sharing for all others.

  A feature called Simple File Sharing, which could allow anyone, anywhere, to access your personal files without your knowledge, is turned on by default in Windows XP. Go to **Control Panel → Folder Options → View** tab, and turn *off* the **Use simple file sharing** option.

  Details on sharing resources can be found in Chapter 8.

- Another feature, called Universal Plug and Play (UPnP), can open additional vulnerabilities on your system. UPnP would more aptly be called *Network Plug and Play*, since it only deals with network devices. UPnP is a collection of standards that allow such devices to announce their presence to UPnP servers on your network, much in the same way as your PnP sound card announces its presence to Windows when you boot your system.

  Windows XP supports UPnP out of the box, which, on the surface, sounds like a good idea. However, UPnP is a service that most users don't need, and unless you specifically need to connect to a UPnP device on your network, you should disable UPnP on your system *immediately*. Leaving a service like UPnP running unnecessarily exposes your system to several security threats.

  To disable UPnP, open the Services window (*services.msc*). Find the **SSDP Discovery Service** in the list and double-click it. Click **Stop** to stop the service, and change the **Startup type** to **Disabled** to prevent it from loading the next time Windows starts. Click **OK** and then do the same for the **Universal Plug and Play Device Host**. Close the Services window when you're done.

- The Remote Desktop feature, described in "Controlling Another Computer Remotely (Just Like in the Movies)," earlier in this chapter, is enabled by default in Windows XP. Unless you specifically need this feature, it should be disabled. Go to **Control Panel → System → Remote** tab, and turn off both of the options in this window.

- Make sure each and every user account on your system has a unique password. Even though you may not be concerned about security between users, unprotected accounts can be exploited by an attack over a network. See Chapter 8 for more information on user accounts.

- Set up a firewall, as described in the next section, to further protect your computer by strictly controlling network traffic into and out of your computer.
- Finally, look for vulnerabilities in your system by scanning for open ports, as explained at the end of this chapter.

Using the Windows Security Center

Next to the new wireless support highlighted in "Sniff Out WiFi Networks" earlier in this chapter, one of the biggest changes in Windows XP Service Pack 2 is the addition of the Windows Security Center, shown in Figure 7-25. You can get to the Security Center from the Windows Control Panel.

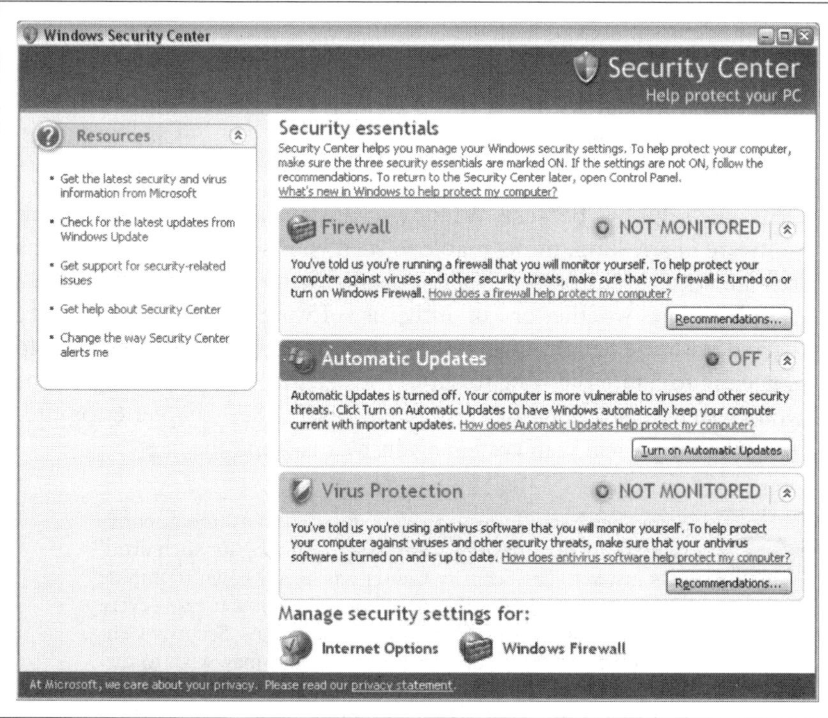

Figure 7-25. The new Security Center that comes with Service Pack 2 goes a long way to make Windows appear safer (not that it does anything to actually improve security...)

The Windows Security Center, unfortunately, is big on appearances and short on functionality. In fact, it's dangerous in that it may lull users into a false sense of security (it's effectively a placebo). The Security Center does nothing more than report the status of these three so-called "security essentials":

Firewall
: The Windows Firewall, discussed in the next section, is the firewall software built into Windows XP SP2. If you're already using firewall software, or are relying on a router to protect your network, click **Recommendations** and then turn on the **I have a firewall solution that I'll monitor myself** option. Click **OK**, and the firewall status will change to NOT MONITORED.

Automatic Updates
: The Automatic Updates feature is responsible for periodically contacting Microsoft to see if new Windows updates are available. In its most automated setting, Windows downloads and installs so-called "high priority" updates automatically. (Others, falling under the "optional" and "hardware" categories, will only be installed if you do so manually.) You can configure this setting by going to **Control Panel → System → Automatic Updates** tab. See "Patching Windows with Windows Update" in Chapter 6 for more information.

Virus Protection
: This one's funny, because Windows XP doesn't come with antivirus software of any kind, nor is it able to scan your system and confirm that any antivirus software is actually installed and functioning! Rather, it simply reports whether or not antivirus software has been properly registered with the Security Center. (And of course, it won't take long for someone to figure out how to spoof the Security Center and report that your system is protected when it actually isn't.) See Chapter 6 for effective ways to protect your system against viruses and the like.

Some newer antivirus software may support the Security Center, but you may not want to start hunting for such products just yet. The Security Center has been known to initiate virus scans unnecessarily, including—for some users—every time Windows starts. Even if you already have Security Center–aware antivirus software installed, you may wish to disable monitoring for this reason. Click **Recommendations** and then turn on the **I have a antivirus program that I'll monitor myself** option. Click **OK**, and the antivirus status will change to NOT MONITORED. See the "Disable the Security Center" sidebar for another solution.

Disable the Security Center

If you find that the Security Center is hassling you with unnecessary scans and warning messages, your only resort may be to disable it completely. Here's how to do it:

1. Open the Services window (*services.msc*).
2. Locate **Security Center** in the list, double click it, and change the **Startup type** to **Disabled**.
3. Click **OK** and close the Services window when you're done.

Note that this doesn't actually disable the firewall, antivirus, or automatic updates features you may have employed—only the "monitoring" effects of the Windows Security Center.

So, if you really want to protect your system, you'll basically ignore the Security Center and scrutinize each of these "essentials" individually. See the next section, for instance, for help setting up the Windows Firewall.

Setting up the Windows Firewall

A firewall is a layer of protection that permits or denies network communication based on a predefined set of rules. These rules restrict communication so that only certain applications are permitted to use your network connection. This effectively closes backdoors to your computer that otherwise might be exploited by viruses, hackers, and other malicious applications.

The Windows Firewall is the firewall software built into Windows XP Service Pack 2. It replaces the nearly worthless Internet Connection Firewall (ICF) found in earlier versions of Windows XP; while it's better than its predecessor, it's not nearly as effective as a router. See "Planning Your Network" and "Set Up a Wireless Router," both earlier in this chapter, for more information on routers.

The Windows Firewall only blocks incoming data, not outgoing data. This means that, by default, it will not allow you to host an FTP server, but it won't hinder your ability to connect to other, remote FTP servers. See "Alternatives to the Windows Firewall," later in this chapter, for other solutions that may provide better protection.

To illustrate the difference between the security offered by the Windows Firewall and that afforded by a router, consider Figure 7-26.

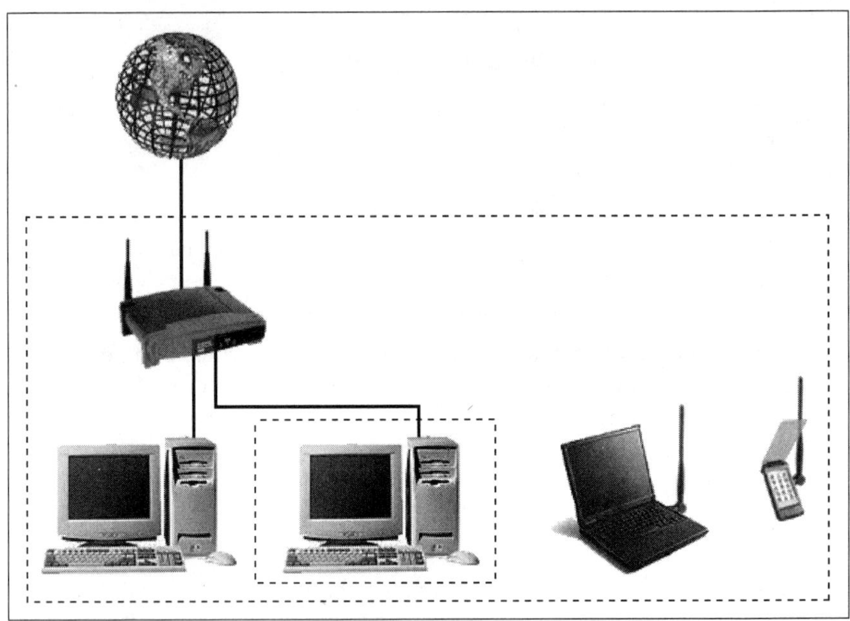

Figure 7-26. The larger dotted box shows the scope of protection offered by a router; the smaller box shows the scope of the Windows Firewall

The larger dotted rectangle shows what's protected by your router's firewall, and the smaller rectangle shows what's protected by Windows. In addition to the larger scope of the router's protection, it's also much less likely to be compromised than a software-based solution like the Windows Firewall.

Now, assuming you've bought the previous argument, you might think that more firewall is better, that using Windows Firewall along with a router will protect your system better than a router alone. The problem with this approach is that, again referring to Figure 7-26, the Windows Firewall isolates your PC somewhat from the other computers in your workgroup. This causes real problems when you try to share files across your workgroup, among other things.

Now, there is the chance that another computer in your workgroup can become infected with a virus (presumably through someone else's carelessness) and then infect yours if you're not using the Windows Firewall. Naturally, you'll need to assess the risk of such an attack and decide for yourself if enabling the Windows Firewall is worth the hassle.

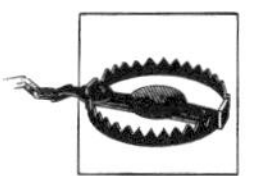

If you're not using a router or other firewall solution, the Windows Firewall is better than nothing. For instance, you'll definitely want to employ a firewall to protect you if you're "roaming" on a portable computer and connecting to an unknown or public wireless connection.

Should you decide to use the Windows Firewall, here's how to enable it:

1. Open the Network Connections window.
2. If you haven't already done so, select **Details** from the **View** menu; this will allow you to see which connections are firewalled (and which aren't) at a glance.
3. Right-click the connection icon corresponding to your Internet connection, and select **Properties**. In most cases, it will be the Ethernet or wireless adapter connected to your Internet adapter or router.

If you're using a DSL or cable connection that requires a login with a username or password, the icon to use is the broadband connection icon corresponding to your PPPoE connection. See "DSL, cable, or other high-speed connection via PPPoE," earlier in this chapter, for further instructions.

4. Choose the **Advanced** tab, and click the **Settings** button in the **Windows Firewall** section. The Windows Firewall window is shown in Figure 7-27.
5. Click **On** to enable the Windows Firewall, or **Off** to disable it.
6. By default, Windows will apply the firewall to all network connections as soon as you enable it for any single connection. Since it's unlikely that this is what you want, choose the **Advanced** tab and remove the checkmarks next to the connections you don't need to protect. For instance, turn off the firewall for your **1394 Connection** (Firewire), unless you want Windows to block data from your FireWire camcorder.
7. Windows XP does not log communication blocked by its firewall, unless you specifically request it to do so. To enable firewall logging, choose the **Advanced** tab, click **Settings** in the **Security Logging** section, and turn on the **Log dropped packets** option. The log is simply a text file that can be opened in your favorite text editor (or Notepad); by default, it's stored in *\Windows\pfirewall.log*.
8. Click **OK,** and then **OK** again when you're done. The change will take effect immediately (or at least after a several-second delay).

Figure 7-27. The new Windows Firewall included in Service Pack 2 has a simpler interface and is more configurable than its predecessor, the Internet Connection Firewall

Verify that Internet Connection Sharing is enabled; it should say "Enabled, Firewalled" or "Enabled, Shared, Firewalled" in the **Type** column of the Network Connections window.

The real test, however, is to see if the Windows Firewall has broken anything. Verify that your Internet connection still works by attempting to open a web page.

Poking holes in the firewall

As you use your computer, you may find that a particular network program or task no longer works properly after enabling the Windows Firewall (or after installing SP2). For example, you may lose your ability to access shared files and folders (as described in Chapter 8) when the firewall is activated. Or, if you use the Internet Time feature (**Control Panel → Date and Time → Internet Time** tab), you may find that it won't work from behind the firewall.

When Service Pack 2 was initially released, it got a bad rap for breaking many different kinds of network-sensitive applications. In reality, this was simply due to the firewall doing what it was designed to do, combined with the fact that it has different exceptions than its predecessor, the Internet Connection Firewall.

If you suspect that the Windows Firewall is preventing an application from working, verify that the firewall is actually causing the problem by temporarily disabling it (as described in the previous section) and then trying the task again.

Assuming the firewall is indeed the culprit, you can add a new rule to permit the program to communicate over your Internet connection.

1. Open the Network Connections window.
2. Right-click the connection icon corresponding to your Internet connection, select **Properties**, and choose the **Exceptions** tab.
3. There will likely be a few entries already present in your Programs and Services list, shown in Figure 7-28.

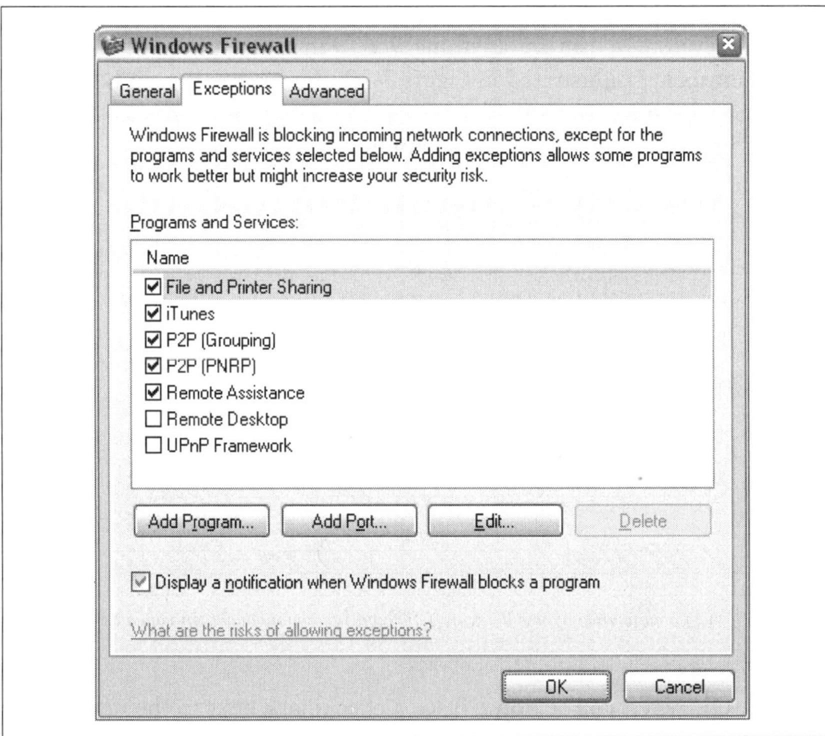

Figure 7-28. The Exceptions tab lists the programs and services permitted to receive data through all your network connections

Networking

This dialog can be a little misleading. Placing a checkmark next to an entry here won't turn on the service, but rather only lift the firewall's restriction for that service. Open the Services window (*services.msc*) to actually enable or disable services like the FTP server or Telnet server on your system.

4. At this point, you can modify an existing exception by highlighting it and clicking **Edit**, but you're here to add a new exception, so click one of the **Add** buttons:

   Add Program

   Use this to give a specific application free rein over your Internet connection. This is the easiest way to fix an application that has been broken by the Windows Firewall's restrictions. Just select an application from the list, or click **Browse** to choose one anywhere on your hard disk.

   Add Port

   Click **Add Port** to create a new rule based on a TCP/IP port. Use this to permit incoming data based on the *type* of data, as opposed to the application that uses the data. Type a **Name** for the new exception (it can be anything you want) and then specify a **Port number**, as illustrated in Figure 7-29. For instance, type `123` here to get the Internet Time feature to work. See Appendix C for more information on TCP/IP port numbers.

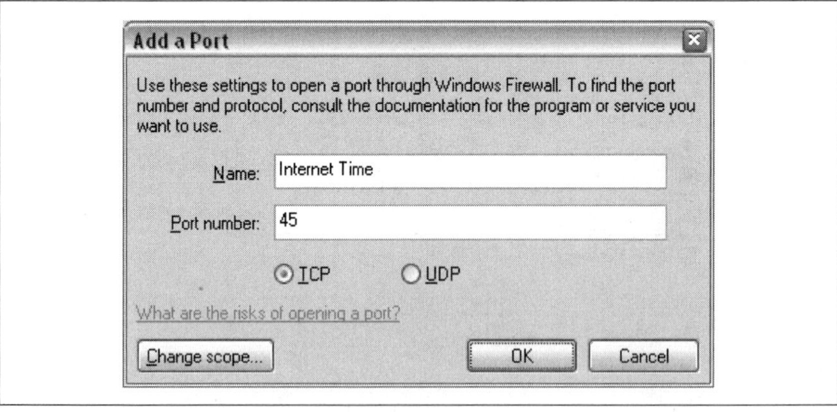

Figure 7-29. Add a new rule to the Windows Firewall to permit certain types of incoming data

5. Click **OK** when you're done. Place a checkmark next to the new exception to activate it, or clear the checkmark at any time to ignore it.

6. Click **OK** to close the Windows Firewall window, and then click **OK** to close the properties window.

The new exception will take effect as soon as all the windows are closed, at which point you can test the new exception. You may have to experiment with different firewall rules until your software or service works properly.

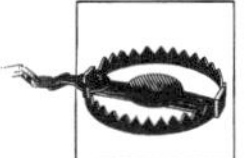

The Windows Firewall in SP2 only maintains one list of exceptions. This means that if you have more than one network connection, you won't be able to enable some services for one connection while blocking those same services for another connection. This is yet another reason that you shouldn't rely solely on the Windows Firewall to protect your computer.

Alternatives to the Windows Firewall

Strictly speaking, the Windows Firewall is pretty feeble. For example, it's only capable of blocking incoming communication; it won't block any communication originating from your computer, which means it may not protect you (or the other computers on your network) from viruses and Trojan horses (described in Chapter 6). It's also incapable of allowing incoming data from some remote computers while restricting data from others, which means that in order to enable a service, such as file sharing (explained in "Poking holes in the firewall," earlier), for one computer, you'll have to enable it for any and every computer that has access to your PC.

Probably the best firewall available, at least one that's reasonably affordable, is that built into an ordinary router, described in "Planning Your Network" and "Set Up a Wireless Router," earlier in this chapter. In addition to protecting your Windows XP machine, however, a router will also protect all the computers on your network from a single interface, which means that you don't have to install and configure a firewall on each computer individually.

There are also third-party firewall software products available for Windows XP, all of which promise to do a better job protecting your PC than the Windows Firewall.

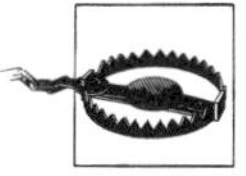

Be careful, however, when installing and configuring a third-party firewall solution, including the ones discussed here. Overly strict firewall rules may break some software on your system. Worse yet, overly lenient rules may not protect your computer adequately and give you a false sense of security.

Here are a few third-party firewall solutions, most of which have free versions available:

Agnitum Outpost. *http://www.agnitum.com*

Kerio Personal Firewall. *http://www.kerio.com*

Norton Personal Firewall. *http://www.symantec.com*

Sygate Personal Firewall. *http://soho.sygate.com*

Tiny Firewall. *http://www.tinysoftware.com*

No matter which firewall solution you choose, however, you'll most likely still need to take the time to configure custom rules using a similar procedure to the one described earlier in this section. For example, a common problem when installing an incorrectly configured firewall is that images will stop appearing in web pages, a situation that can be remedied by massaging the firewall's settings.

If you're currently using another firewall solution, such as firewall software or a firewall-enabled router, you'll probably want to disable the Windows Firewall. Although some people claim to have successfully used the Windows Firewall in conjunction with one of the third-party firewalls listed here, you're essentially asking for trouble if you do so.

Scan Your System for Open Ports

Each open network port on your computer is a potential security vulnerability, and Windows XP's tendency to leave more ports open than it needs is a common cause for concern (even with XP Service Pack 2). Fortunately, there's a way to scan your computer for open ports so you know which holes to patch.

Start by opening a Command Prompt window (*cmd.exe*). Then, run the Active Connections utility by typing:

```
netstat /a /o
```

The `/a` option is included so that all open ports are shown. Without it, only ports participating in active connections would appear. The `/o` option instructs the Active Connections utility to show the owning process of each port (explained below). The report will be displayed in the Command Prompt window, and will look something like this:

```
Active Connections

Proto  Local Address     Foreign Address            State         PID
TCP    annoy:pop3        localhost:4219             TIME_WAIT       0
TCP    annoy:3613        javascript-of-unknown:0    LISTENING    1100
```

```
TCP    annoy:3613      localhost:3614      ESTABLISHED    1100
TCP    annoy:3614      localhost:3613      ESTABLISHED    1100
UDP    annoy:1035      *:*                                1588
UDP    annoy:1036      *:*                                1588
UDP    annoy:1037      *:*                                1588
UDP    annoy:1038      *:*                                1588
UDP    annoy:1039      *:*                                1588
```

The width of the Command Prompt window is typically limited to 80 characters, causing some pretty ugly word wrapping. To send the report to a text file (say, *report.txt*) for easier viewing, type `netstat /a /o > report.txt` at the prompt.

The Active Connections utility displays information in these five columns:

`Proto`
: This will either be TCP or UDP, representing the protocol being used, as explained in Appendix C.

`Local Address`
: This column has two components, separated by a colon. The first part is the computer name, which will typically be the name of your computer. The second part will be either a port number or the name of a service. See Appendix C for help deciphering the port numbers that appear here (and in the `Foreign Address` column).

`Foreign Address`
: For active connections, this will be the name or IP address of the remote machine, followed by a colon, and then the port number being used. For inactive connections (showing only the open ports), you'll typically see only `*:*`.

`State`
: This shows the state of the connection (TCP ports only). For example, for server processes, you'll usually see `LISTENING` here, signifying that the process has opened the port and is waiting for an incoming connection.

For connections originating from your computer, such as a web browser downloading a page or an active Telnet session, you'll see `ESTABLISHED` here.

`PID`
: This is the Process Identifier of the application or service that is responsible for opening the port.

To find out more, open Task Manager (launch *taskmgr.exe* or right-click an empty area of your taskbar and select **Task Manager**), and choose the **Processes** tab. If you don't see a column labelled **PID**, go to **View → Select Columns**, turn on the **PID (Process Identifier)** option, and click **OK**. Finally, turn on the **Show processes from all users** option at the bottom of the Windows Task Manager window.

You can then sort the listing by PID by clicking the **PID** column header. The program filename is shown in the **Image Name** column.

This means that you can use the Active Connections utility in conjunction with the Windows Task Manager, as described here, to look up the program responsible for opening any network port on your computer.

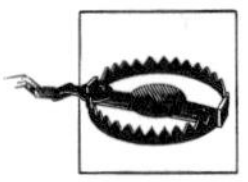

Don't be alarmed if you see a lot of open ports. Just make sure you thoroughly track down each one, making sure it doesn't pose a security threat.

You may see *svchost.exe* listed in the Windows Task Manager, and reported by the Active Connections utility as being responsible for one or more open ports. This program is merely used to start the services listed in the Services window (*services.msc*). For an example of a service that is running by default, but should be disabled for security reasons, see the discussion of Universal Plug and Play in "Closing Back Doors in Windows XP," earlier in this chapter.

Using an external port scanner

If you're using a firewall, such as the Windows Firewall feature built into Windows XP SP2 (discussed in the previous section), it should block communication to most of the currently open ports, even though they're listed by the Active Connections utility.

For this reason, you may prefer to use an external port scanner, a program that can connect to your computer through its Internet connection to check for all open ports, and do it more aggressively than the Active Connections utility. Here are some utilities that you can run from your own computer:

Nmap Security Scanner. *http://www.insecure.org*

AATools Port Scanner. *http://www.glocksoft.com/port_scanner.htm*

Furthermore, these web sites will allow you to perform port scans right from your web browser:

Sygate Security Scan. *http://scan.sygatetech.com*

PC Flank. *http://www.pcflank.com*

Among other things, you can use these services to test the effectiveness of your firewall. If a port scanner cannot detect any open ports, cannot determine your computer name, and cannot detect any running services, then you're in pretty good shape!

CHAPTER 8

User Accounts and Administration

User accounts have a much more prominent role in Windows XP than they've had in any previous version of Windows. Microsoft faced an interesting challenge with the release of this product, in that support for multiple users is typically a feature of server-type operating systems, and is often seen as a feature used only by network administrators. Since Windows XP is supposed to be a robust, networkable operating system, healthy support for multiple user accounts is a must.

But Windows XP is also intended to be suitable for so-called "home" users, who typically have little or no interest in user accounts, administration, or security. Whether or not Microsoft found an appropriate balance between the high level of interuser security administrators demand, and the streamlining and simplicity that single users expect, is really a matter of perspective.

Support for multiple users is built into Windows XP from the ground up, which is one of the advantages of the Windows NT/2000/XP platform over the older (and now-defunct) DOS-based platform used by Windows 9x/Me. (See Chapter 1 for more information.)

On its simplest level, multiple user accounts can be used to allow each member of a household—or each employee in an office—to have his or her own set of documents, display settings, application settings, Start Menu programs, and even Desktop icons.

But proper use of user accounts can also protect your computer from unauthorized intruders, whether they are sitting at your keyboard or connecting remotely from thousands of miles away. Having separate user accounts for each person allows them to protect their personal and sensitive documents from other users on the machine, as well as from other computers in a workgroup.

The solutions in this chapter not only show you how to set up and manage user accounts, but use them in conjunction with file and folder sharing to strike the balance between security and convenience that works best for you.

Managing Users

There are actually three different User Accounts dialogs in Windows XP, each with a different design and "intended audience," so to speak. The problem is that each window has a few options not found in the other, so no single window can be used exclusively to handle all tasks.

User Accounts

The primary user accounts interface, accessible by going to **Control Panel → User Accounts** and shown in Figure 8-1, is the one that most users see. It's large, friendly, and, unfortunately, somewhat cumbersome. But, given the "administrator" stigma behind user accounts, it's not surprising that Microsoft has gone to great lengths (some feel too far) to make this window less intimidating and easier to use than its counterparts in earlier versions of Windows.

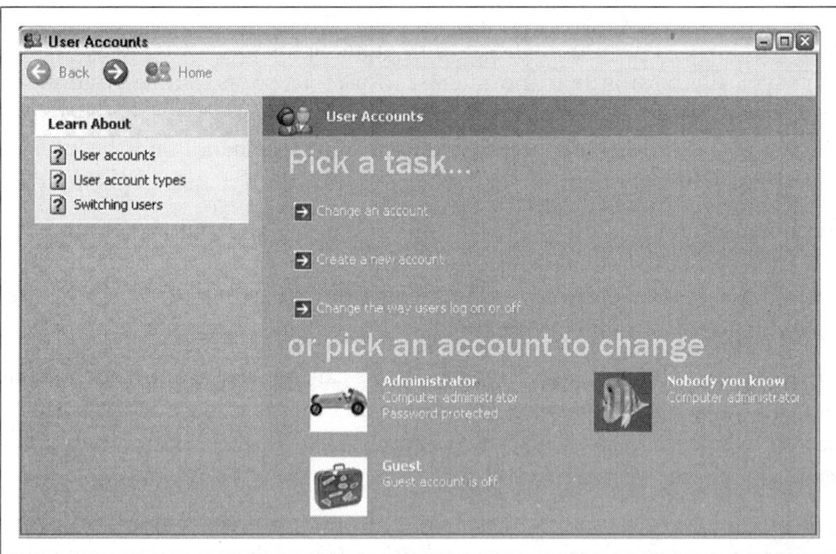

Figure 8-1. You can add, delete, or modify user accounts in the User Accounts dialog, but not much else

Adding, customizing, and removing user accounts is extremely easy and, for the most part, self-explanatory in this window, and that is admirable. But sometimes you'll need one of the alternate dialogs, listed below, to accomplish some of the more advanced tasks, such as managing groups and configuring Windows to log in a password-protected account automatically.

> ## Avoiding .NET Passport Accounts
>
> Littered throughout the operating system are various links and tie-ins to Microsoft's .NET online service. It seems as though no matter where you turn, there's another button that suggests that you need to sign up for a .NET "passport" in order to use the feature.
>
> The point is to try to make .NET passports seem as ubiquitous as the *My Documents* folder, so that customers will feel more comfortable using the service. That way, Microsoft can try to push its MSN online service and much-hyped .NET technology onto other companies, so that soon, any web site you visit and every program you start will require a .NET passport password.
>
> Fortunately, we haven't reached that stage yet. In fact, the only component in Windows XP that absolutely requires a .NET passport is Windows Messenger. In all other cases, signing up for MSN or .NET is purely optional, despite what the instructions in the dialog may suggest.

Note that this window is the only place you can choose a user's picture, shown in both the login dialog and at the top of the new-style Start Menu (see "Massaging the Start Menu" in Chapter 2). The primary User Accounts dialog is also the only place you can choose between the Welcome Screen and the standard Login screen, as discussed in "Use the Traditional Log On Dialog Instead of the Welcome Screen," later in this chapter.

User Accounts 2

Some additional settings, discussed later in this chapter, can be changed only with the alternate User Accounts window, which, incidentally, is identical to the one found in Windows 2000. To open the old-style User Accounts dialog, select **Run** from the Start Menu, type `control userpasswords2`, and click **OK**. This dialog is shown in Figure 8-2.

Like the primary User Accounts window, you can add new users, as well as rename or remove existing accounts. But here, you have more control over a user's permissions and restrictions. You can access accounts that would otherwise be hidden in the User Accounts window, such as the Administrator account (see "Logging in as the Administrator," later in this chapter) and the IUSR account used by the IIS web server. See

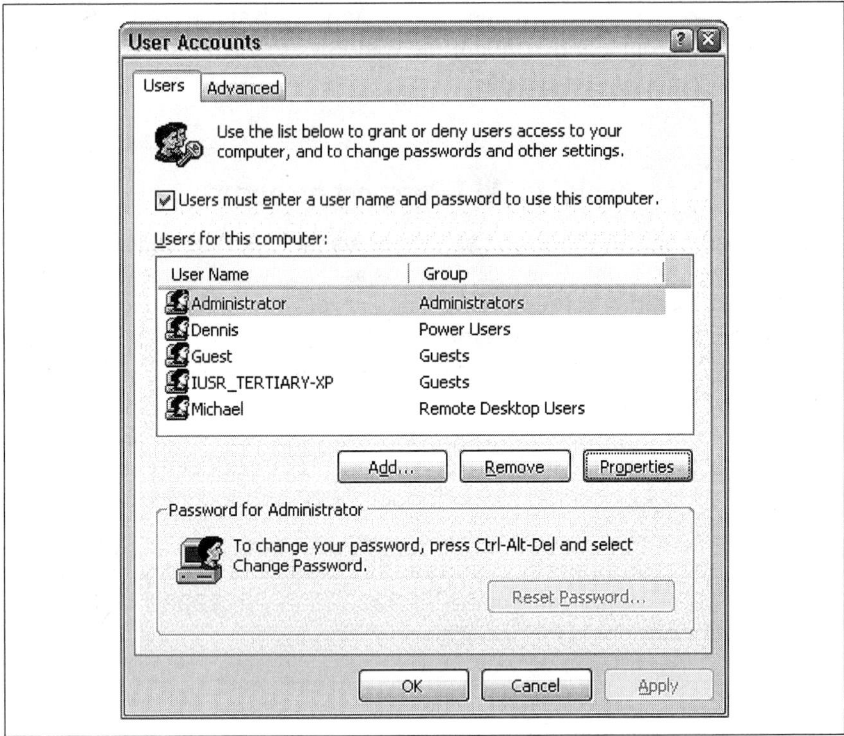

Figure 8-2. The "other" User Accounts dialog can do many things otherwise impossible in the standard User Accounts window

"Use the Traditional Log On Dialog Instead of the Welcome Screen," also later in this chapter, for another use of this dialog.

Local Users and Groups

The third way to manage user accounts in Windows is to use the Local Users and Groups policy editor (*lusrmgr.msc*), shown in Figure 8-3. The Local Users and Groups window (LUaG) is actually a Microsoft Management Console (mmc.exe) snap-in, like the Disk Management utility (see Chapter 5), and therefore can be accessed remotely if necessary. Figure 8-3 shows the LUaG dialog in all its glory.

LUaG is where you'll want to go to manage groups, set the automatic expiration of passwords, and change the location of a user's home directory. Just double-click any entry in the **Users** or **Groups** categories to change their properties. Or, right-click in an empty area of the right pane to add a new user or group.

Groups can be useful when you have a bunch of users. For example, say you wish to make a folder accessible to several users (as described later

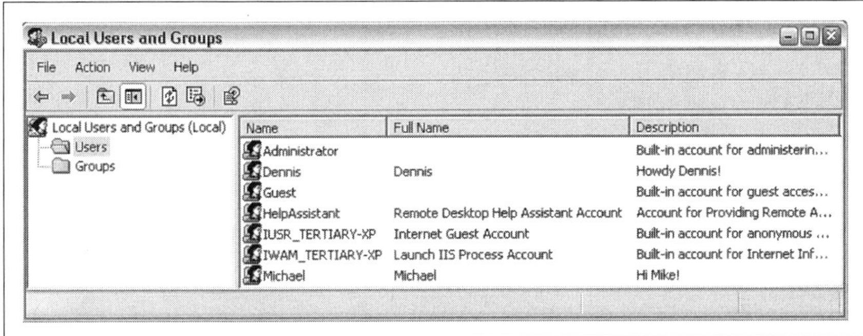

Figure 8-3. The Local Users and Groups window gives you the most control over user accounts, but at the expense of a rather sparse and intimidating Registry Editor-like interface

in this chapter); instead of having to specify each one individually, all you would need to do is specify the group. Note that once the group has been set up here, you can use the User Accounts 2 dialog to assign new or existing members to that group.

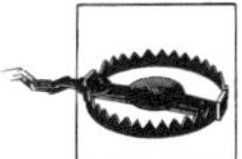

Use the alternate User Accounts dialog and the Local Users and Groups window with caution, as both allow you to disable all accounts with administrator privileges. If this happens, the computer will be completely inaccessible by any administrator, and you'll probably have to reinstall just to log in.

What can be confusing is finding the right place to accomplish a specific task regarding user accounts. Table 8-1 shows a bunch of different tasks and where to go to accomplish them.

Table 8-1. The various places user-account tasks can be performed

Task	User Accounts	User Accounts 2	Local Users and Groups
Add groups			✓
Add users	✓	✓	✓
Assign a user to a group		✓	✓
Assign a user to multiple groups			✓
Change a user's description		✓	✓
Change a user's home folder			✓
Change a user's password	✓	✓	
Change a user's picture	✓		
Choose a logon script			✓

Table 8-1. The various places user-account tasks can be performed (continued)

Task	User Accounts	User Accounts 2	Local Users and Groups
Disable a user or group account			✓
Manage network passwords	✓	✓	
Modify groups			✓
Prevent forgotten passwords	✓		
Remove almost any user	✓	✓	✓
Remove any user		✓	✓
Rename a user	✓	✓	✓
Require Ctrl-Alt-Del to log on		✓	
Set password expiration			✓
Turn off login window		✓	
Turn off welcome screen	✓		
Use Fast User Switching	✓		
View members of groups			✓

For the most part, adding, removing, and modifying user accounts is a fairly self-explanatory process, so I won't go into every excruciating detail here. Here are some tips for working with user accounts:

- Press **Ctrl-Alt-Del** and then click **Change Password** to change your own password. This is the only way to change the password of an account when you're not an administrator.
- If you have a lot of users coming and going, use the Local Users and Groups window to have passwords automatically expire. This not only forces users to change their own passwords regularly, but automatically blocks users who haven't logged in a while.

Permissions and Security

Setting the permissions for a file or folder allows you to permit access to some users while restricting access to others.

Before you start messing with permissions, you'll need to turn off Simple File Sharing. Go to **Control Panel → Folder Options → View** tab, and turn off the **Use simple file sharing** option. Click **OK** when you're done.

Note that permissions can only be used on files and folders stored on NTFS volumes (see the discussion of NTFS in Chapter 5).

Security Identifiers (SIDs)

Every user on your machine has a unique Security Identifier (SID), which is used in conjunction with most of the features discussed in this chapter, such as permissions and encryption, as well as some of the solutions in other chapters in this book. For example, your personal settings in the Registry (Chapter 3) are stored in a branch that looks something like this:

```
HKEY_USERS\S-1-5-21-1727987266-1036259444-725315541-500
```

The numeric portion is your SID, and is composed of the following elements:

```
S-r-i-sa-xxxxxxxxxx-yyyyyyyyy-zzzzzzzzz-uid
```

where `S` stands for security identifier, *`r`* is the revision level and is always set to `1`, *`i`* is the identifier authority, and *`sa-xxxxxxxxxx-yyyyyyyyy-zzzzzzzzz`*, is the sub-authority. Finally, *`uid`* is the user id.

For example, the identifier authority (*`i`*) can tell you something about the type of user to which an SID corresponds:

- `S-1-0`... is an unknown group or a group with no members
- `S-1-1`... is the "world" group that includes all users
- `S-1-2`... a local user logged into "terminal"
- `S-1-3`... is the creator of an object (file, folder, etc.)
- `S-1-4`... is a non-unique user identifier
- `S-1-5`... a standard user account

Aside from some of the solutions that use SIDs, they can be an issue if you clone your machine, at which time you may have to change your SID. Microsoft's System Preparation Tool (SysPrep) can be used to do this.

Setting Permissions for an Object

By default, everyone on your computer has access to every file on your hard disk. In order to restrict access, you'll have to change the permissions for your folders, files, and drives that contain more sensitive data. It gets a little confusing when you realize that there are two different Permissions windows for any given object (file, folder, printer, etc.).

Object permissions

Right-click any file, folder, drive, or printer, select **Properties**, and choose the **Security** tab to view or change the permissions for the selected object(s). These settings affect how the object is accessed by users on your machine.

Share permissions

Right-click any file, folder, drive, or printer, select **Properties**, choose the **Sharing** tab, and click **Permissions** to view or change the share permissions for the selected object(s). These settings affect how the object is accessed by users on other machines on your network. Note that the **Permissions** button will only be available for objects currently shared on your network. See "Sharing Printers," later in this chapter, for more information on sharing resources.

You can also right-click any Registry key in the Registry Editor (see Chapter 3) and select **Permissions** to restrict or permit viewing and/or modification of the key by the users on your machine.

Fortunately, all Permissions windows look and work the same; the only difference is their scope. Figure 8-4 shows a typical Permissions window.

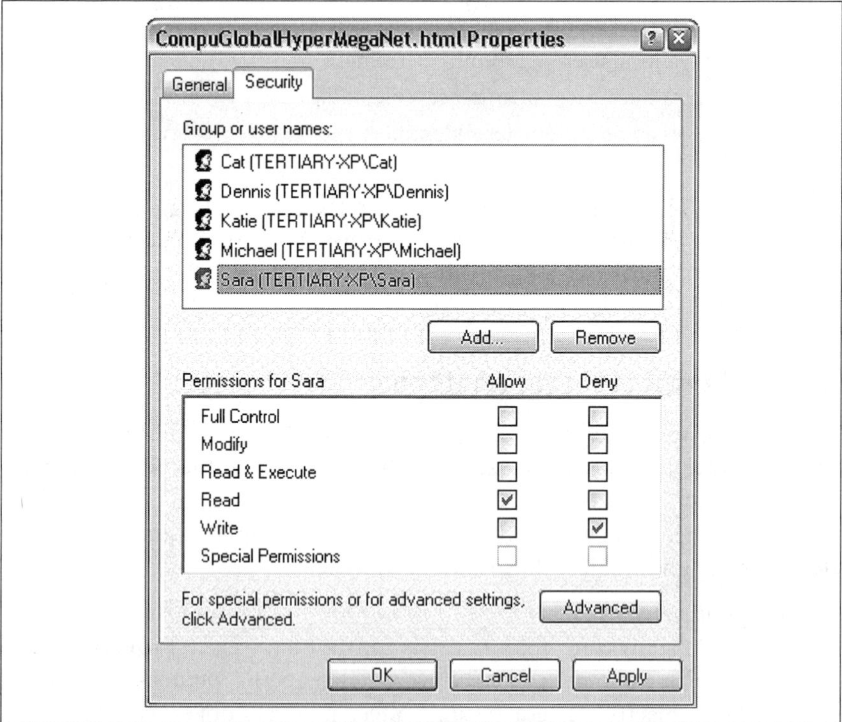

Figure 8-4. The standard Permissions window allows you to permit or deny access to other users on your computer or in your workgroup

Typically, a single entry, "Everyone," will appear at the top of the list. In the example in Figure 8-4, only five single users are shown here. Any user not in the list will not be allowed to view or modify the object.

Select any user in the list, and then use the checkboxes in the list below to modify the permissions for that user. In this example, the user named Sara is allowed to read the selected file, but not allowed to write to it. Although this window only shows the permissions for one user or group at a time, you can click **Advanced** to see a better overview, as shown in Figure 8-5.

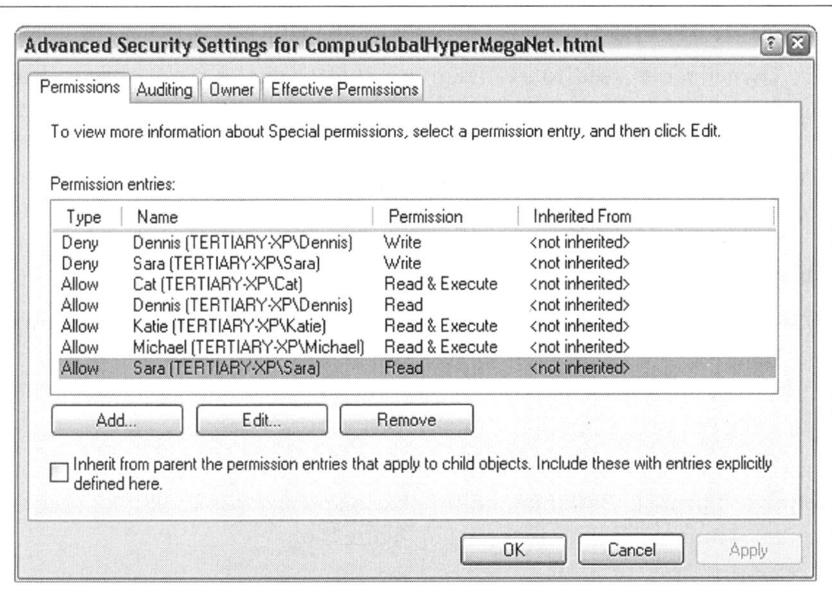

Figure 8-5. Open the Advanced Security Settings window to see all users and permissions for an object at once

In some cases, when you attempt to remove or modify permissions in the standard Permissions window (Figure 8-4), Windows will complain about the fact that the object is inheriting permissions. The reason is the **Inherit from parent** option in the Advanced Security Settings dialog (Figure 8-5).

Inheritance and other advanced options

Inheritance can be confusing at first, but it does save time in the long run. Essentially, if you set the permissions of a folder, those permissions will propagate to all of the files and subfolders contained therein (although Windows will usually ask you whether or not you want this to happen). When the permissions for a *parent* folder propagate to a *child* folder or file, that child object is said to *inherit* the permissions of its parent folder. Furthermore, these permissions are locked, at least until you turn off the aforementioned **Inherit from parent** option.

The **Auditing** tab in the Advanced Security Settings window allows you to log access activity relating to the selected object. Before Auditing will work, you'll need to set up an Auditing policy by opening the Group Policy window (*gpedit.msc*). Then, navigate to `Computer Configuration\Windows Settings\Security Settings\Local Policies\Audit Policy`. Then, open the Event Viewer (*eventvwr.msc*) to view the corresponding logs. Note that settings in the **Auditing** tab obey inheritance like Permissions, discussed earlier.

The **Owner** tab is used to assume ownership of one or more objects. I use this option most when I have a dual-boot system (see Chapter 1), and I have to access files that were placed on the hard disk by the other operating system. In most cases, Windows won't let you access such files until you "take ownership" using the **Owner** tab of this window.

Adding new users to the Permissions window

Typically, a single entry, "Everyone," will appear at the top of the **Group or user names** list in the Permissions window. More than likely, though, you'll want to eliminate the "Everyone" entry and add only those users and groups to which you need to specifically grant access.

Start by deleting any unwanted users by selecting them and clicking **Remove**. Then, click **Add** to add new users and groups. The Select Users or Groups window appears, as shown in Figure 8-6.

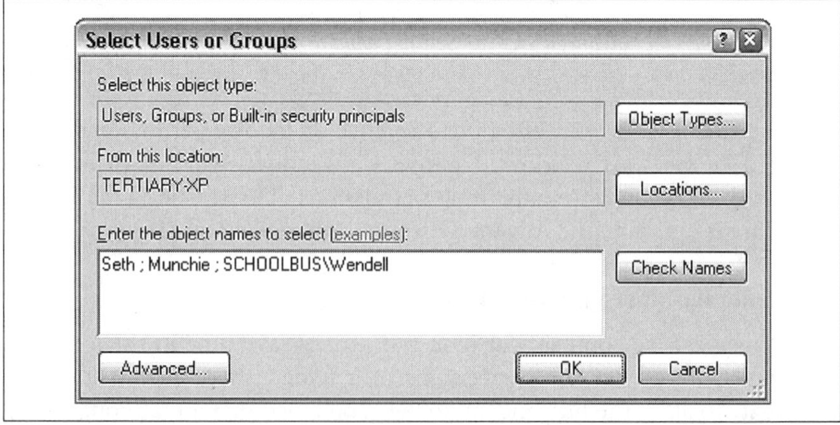

Figure 8-6. New users and groups are added to a Permissions list with this rather confusing dialog

Most users visiting this dialog for the first time will expect a list of the users on their machine; unfortunately, such a list isn't here. Instead, you'll have to type the name(s) of the users and groups you wish to add in the **Enter the object names to select** field. If you enter more than one user, simply separate them with semicolons.

In the example in Figure 8-6, you'll notice that the third entry, `SCHOOLBUS\Wendell`, is unlike the others. While "Seth" and "Munchie" are users on the machine (or in the domain to which the machine belongs), the third entry shows how a user on a different machine is specified; in this case, the user "Wendell" on the computer `SCHOOLBUS` is to be added.

So, why aren't user and group names listed here? The reason is that this dialog has been designed to accommodate a single computer with two users, as well as a company-wide network with thousands of users, and everything in between. Naturally, you can always open the User Accounts window to look up the users on the local machine. Or, if you're part of a Windows domain, you can click **Advanced** to search for users on your network.

When you click **OK**, Windows will verify the user and group names you've entered and, if all is well, will add them to the Permissions window. You can also click **Check Names** here to verify your entries without closing the window.

When a new user has been added to the Permissions window (Figure 8-4), highlight the user or group name, and selectively click the checkmarks in the **Allow** or **Deny** columns. Note that **Deny** entries take precedence over **Allow** entries.

Depending on the type of object you've selected, you may see any number of different types of entries here, such as **Full Control**, **Read**, **Write**, and **Modify**. After playing with the checkmarks, you'll notice that there is quite a bit of redundancy in this list; for example, **Modify** is an umbrella term that includes **Read & Execute**, **Read**, and **Write**.

For more control over permissions, click **Advanced** to show the Advanced Security Settings window (Figure 8-5), select the user, and click **Edit**. The Permission Entry window, shown in Figure 8-7, will allow you to fine-tune permissions and allow only those permissions that are absolutely necessary for the object.

When you're done choosing permissions, click **OK**. If you're modifying the permissions for a folder, Windows may or may not prompt you to have your changes propagated to all subfolders and files.

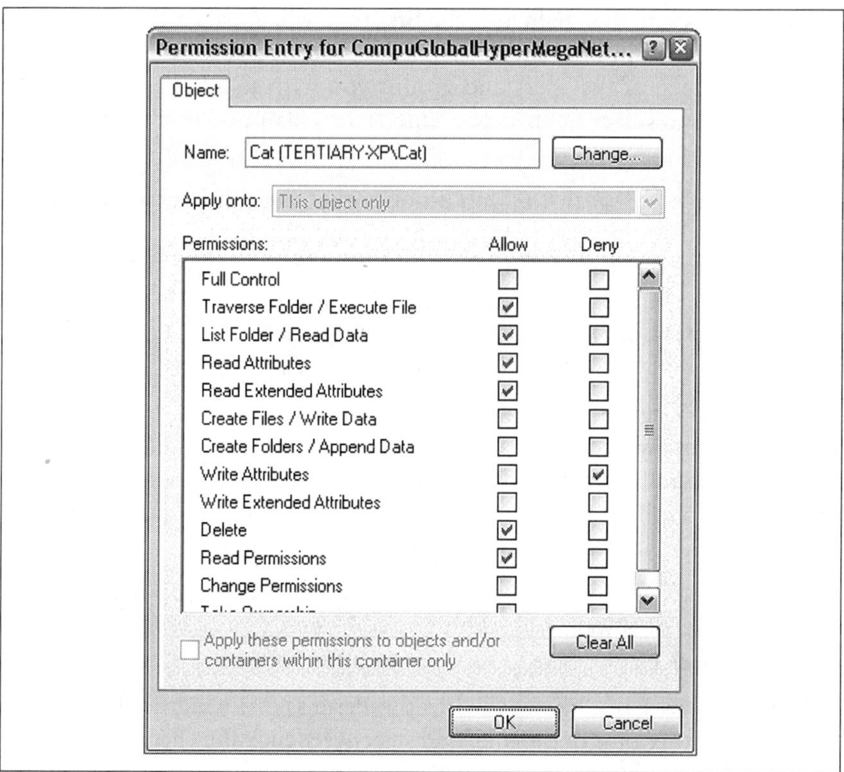

Figure 8-7. The Permission Entry window lets you fine-tune permissions

Notes

- In most cases, you'll want to set permissions to protect your files and folders from unauthorized access. But some permissions are necessary to get some programs to work.

  For example, if you're writing a CGI or ASP program for the IIS web server (see Chapter 9), you'll need to set the permissions of your files to give the Internet Guest Account full access. The Internet Guest Account user account name is based on the machine name: for a system named SERVER, you'd enter `SERVER\IUSR_SERVER` into the Select Users or Groups dialog (Figure 8-6).
- For better security, Windows XP Professional supports encryption, a feature used in conjunction with permissions. See "Protecting Your Files with Encryption," later in this chapter, for details.
- Permissions protect files from other user accounts only. If you walk away from your computer while it's logged in to your account, for

example, someone else sitting down at your computer will have full access to all your files, regardless of permissions or even encryption.

Protecting Your Files with Encryption

Encryption effectively adds another layer of protection for your especially sensitive data, ensuring that a file can only be viewed by its creator. If any other user—even someone with administrator privileges—attempts to view the file, they will see only gibberish.

When a file is marked for encryption, the encryption and decryption of the file are handled by Windows invisibly in the background when its creator writes and views the file, respectively. The problem is that Windows XP's on-the-fly encryption can be somewhat unpredictable, and security is one place where you don't want there to be any guesswork.

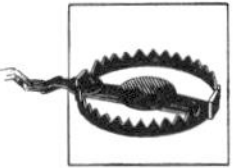

Encryption is a feature of the NTFS filesystem (discussed in "Choosing the Right Filesystem" in Chapter 5) and is not available with any other filesystem. This means that if you copy an encrypted file onto, say, a floppy disk, CD, or other removable media, the file will become unencrypted, since none of these drives support NTFS.

Here's how to encrypt a file:

1. Right-click one or more files in Explorer and select **Properties.**
2. Click **Advanced** in the **General** tab.
3. Turn on the **Encrypt contents to secure data** option, click **OK**, and click **OK** again.

See "Add Encrypt/Decrypt commands to context menus," later in this section, for a quicker way to encrypt and decrypt files.

4. If you encrypt a folder that contains files or other folders, Windows will ask you whether or not you want those contents to be encrypted as well. In most cases, you'll want to answer **Yes**. If you decline, the folder's current contents will remain unencrypted, but newly created files will be encrypted. See "The ins and outs of folder encryption," later, for details.

After a file has been encrypted, you can continue to use it normally. You'll never have to manually decrypt an encrypted file in order to view it.

Encrypting a file may not guarantee that it remains encrypted forever. For example, some applications, when editing and saving files, will delete the original file and then re-create it in the same place. If the application is unaware of the encryption, then it will be lost. The workaround is to encrypt the folder containing the file, rather than the file itself.

If you change the ownership of a file, as described in "Setting Permissions for an Object," earlier in this chapter, and the file is encrypted, the encryption will remain active for the *original* owner and creator of the file, even though that user no longer technically "owns" the file.

Since all users need to access files in certain folders, such as the *\Windows* and *\Windows\System* folders, Windows won't let you encrypt system files in system folders or the root directories of any drives.

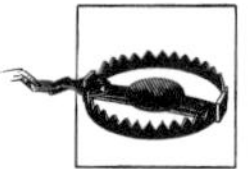

Compression, another feature of the NTFS filesystem, reduces the amount of space consumed by a file or folder. The rules that apply to compression are the same as those that apply to encryption. Note that you cannot simultaneously use encryption and compression on any object; turn on one option in the Properties window, and the other will be turned off. See "Increasing Disk Space (or What to Throw Away)" in Chapter 5 for more information.

Highlighting encrypted files

Windows Explorer has an option to visually differentiate encrypted files, which can be very handy, especially if you're just getting started with encryption. Start by going to **Control Panel → Folder Options → View** tab, and turn on the **Show encrypted or compressed NTFS files in color** option. Click **OK** when you're done.

By default, encrypted files appear in green, and compressed files appear in blue (except for icons on the Desktop). Note that files can't be simultaneously compressed and encrypted (as mentioned in the previous section), so you'll never see any turquoise files. If you wish to change these colors, open TweakUI (see Appendix A), and select **Colors** in the **Explorer** category.

Allowing others to view encrypted files

By default, only you can access your own encrypted files. The easiest way to allow other users on your machine (or network) to view one of your encrypted files is to unencrypt it. A more elegant (and safer) solution is to modify the file's permissions:

1. Right-click one or more files, and select **Properties**.
2. Click **Advanced** (under the **General** tab), and then click **Details**.

The Details button will be disabled (grayed out) if the **Encrypt contents to secure data** option is turned off. Of course, you can turn it on, but you won't be able to click **Details** until you've clicked **OK**, then **Apply**, and then **Advanced** again.

3. Click **Add** to select a user who can view your encrypted files, as shown in Figure 8-8. Note that the Expiration Date shown here represents the date the user's security certificate expires, and has nothing to do with the permissions you're setting up.

   Now, only those users who have security certificates installed on your machine will appear in this list. This means that there's no way to add users on other machines who don't already have accounts on your computer. To add a user from another machine, first create a user account, and then have that user encrypt at least one file on your computer.

4. Click OK when you're done.

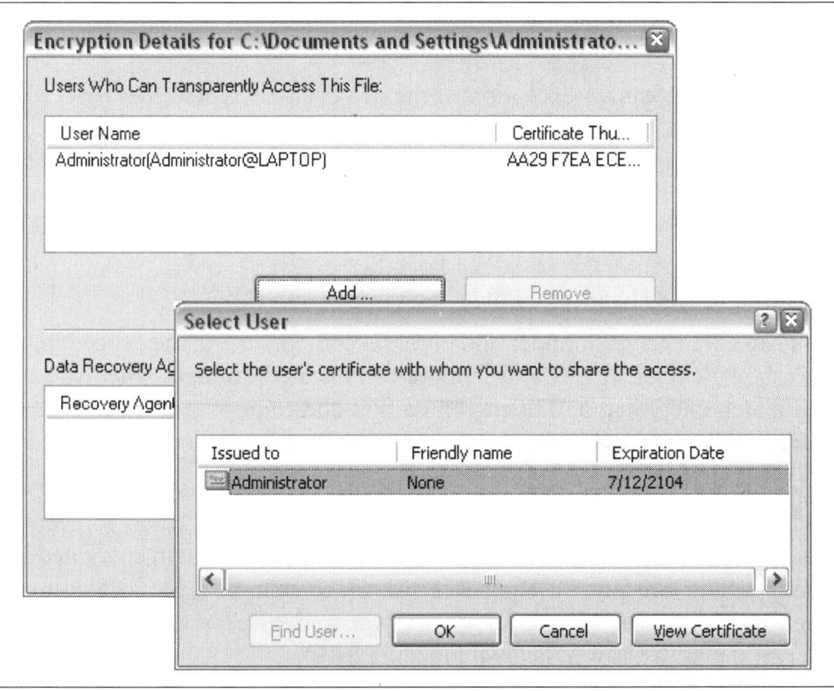

Figure 8-8. Use the Encryption Details dialog to choose other users who can view your encrypted files

User Accounts

So, how do you view someone else's encrypted files *without* their permission? (This is an important question to ask if you care about the security of your data.) If you try to view someone's encrypted files, you'll get an "Access is Denied" error message, as shown in Figure 8-9.

Figure 8-9. Try to access someone else's encrypted file, and you'll get this error

First of all, not even administrators can view files encrypted by other users. However, an administrator can change any user's password, and then subsequently log in to that user's account and view (or unencrypt) any of his protected files. This means that your files won't be totally secure unless you're the only administrator on the machine.

There is a little-known exception: if the owner of encrypted files deletes his or her encryption keys, neither the user nor any administrator will be able to read the encrypted files until the key is reinstalled. See "Using the NTFS Encryption Utility and working with keys," later in this chapter, for more information.

The ins and outs of folder encryption

You can also encrypt a folder and all of its contents using the procedure for files shown earlier. It gets a little more complicated, though, when you mix and match encrypted and unencrypted files and folders, and it can be difficult to predict what will happen to the contents of the folders.

Now, if a file contained in an encrypted folder is moved into an *unencrypted* folder, the file will become unencrypted. The exception is when you've specifically encrypted a single file; in this case, the file will remain encrypted, no matter where you put it. Whenever you try to encrypt a file located in an unencrypted folder, Windows warns you and gives you the option to encrypt the folder as well (shown in Figure 8-10).

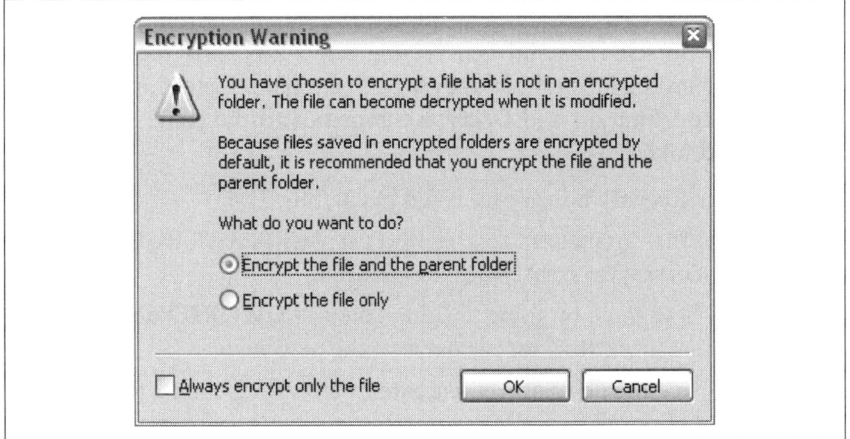

Figure 8-10. Windows displays this warning if you encrypt a file located in an unencrypted folder

Be especially careful here, as the default is to encrypt the containing (parent) folder in addition to the selected file, which can be counterintuitive. Check the **Always encrypt only the file** option to prevent this from happening in the future.

If you ever inadvertently encrypt your desktop (by encrypting an item on your desktop, and then accepting the default in this box), the only way to unencrypt it is to open Windows Explorer and unencrypt the source desktop folder (usually *\Documents and Settings\{username}\Desktop*).

Moving encrypted files around is complicated, too. If an unencrypted file is placed in an encrypted folder, the file will become encrypted. The catch is when one user has encrypted a folder and another user places a file in that folder; in this case, the file is encrypted for the *creator of the file*, which means that the owner of the folder, the one who originally implemented the encryption, will not be able to read it.

On the other hand, if the user places a file in a folder, and a different user comes along and encrypts the folder, only the user who implemented the encryption will be able to subsequently read the file, even though the file is technically owned by a different user.

Add Encrypt/Decrypt commands to context menus

If you find yourself frequently encrypting and decrypting files, having to repeatedly open the Properties window can be a pain. Instead, use this next solution to add **Encrypt** and **Decrypt** commands to the context menus for every file and folder.

1. Open the Registry Editor (discussed in Chapter 3).
2. Expand the branches to: `HKEY_LOCAL_MACHINE\SOFTWARE\Microsoft\Windows\CurrentVersion\Explorer\Advanced`.
3. Create a new value by going to **Edit → New → DWORD Value**, and type `EncryptionContextMenu` for the name of the new value.
4. Double-click the new `EncryptionContextMenu` value, enter `1` for the **Value data**, and click **OK**.
5. Close the Registry Editor when you're done. The change will take effect immediately.
6. To use this new trick, right-click any unencrypted file in Explorer or on your Desktop, and select **Encrypt**. Or right-click an already-encrypted file, and select **Decrypt**.

If at least one of the selected items is a folder, you'll have the option of encrypting only the folder or all the folders contained therein. If encrypting any individual files, you'll also be asked if you wish to encrypt only the file or the parent folder as well.

Using the NTFS Encryption Utility and working with keys

The NTFS Encryption Utility (*cipher.exe*) is the command-line equivalent of the **Encrypt contents to secure data** option discussed earlier, but it adds several powerful features not normally available through Explorer. Note that the NTFS Encryption Utility is included with Windows XP Professional only.

Open a Command Prompt window (*cmd.exe*) and type `cipher` without any arguments to display the encryption status for all the files in the current folder. (Use the `cd` command discussed in Chapter 10 to change to a different working folder.) Encrypted files will be marked with an `E`; all others will marked with a `U`.

To encrypt a file, type `cipher /e` *`filename`*, where *`filename`* is the name of the file or folder (include the full path if it's in a different folder). Likewise, type `cipher /d` *`filename`* to turn off encryption for the item. These functions are no different than using Explorer to control encryption, except that they have the advantage of being able to be executed from scripts (see Chapter 9) or batch files (see Chapter 10). Type `cipher /?` for more options.

The real meat, however, is in cipher's ability to work with cryptographic keys.* Windows XP's encryption system employs symmetric key cryptography, which uses the same key to encrypt and decrypt data. Windows generates a unique key for each user, so that no user can decrypt another user's data.

So, what happens if your computer crashes, and you need to retrieve your encrypted data? As long as you've backed up your encryption key, it's not a problem. At the command prompt, type the following:

```
cipher /r:filename
```

where *`filename`* is the prefix of the output filename (the filename without its extension). Cipher ask for a password, and then generate two separate files based on the specified filename. For example, if you type `cipher /r:julius`, you'll end up with two files:

julius.pfx
: This file contains the EFS (Encrypting File System) recovery agent key and certificate. Store this file in a safe place. If you ever need to retrieve the key, such as if your system crashes and you need access to encrypted data, just reimport the *.pfx* file by double-clicking it in Explorer.

`julius.cer`
: This file contains the EFS recovery agent certificate only (without the key). Double-click this file to open it in an official Certificate window, and optionally install it in another system. Open the Certificates window (*certmgr.msc*) to manage your installed certificates. Note that certificates are also used by Internet Explorer to communicate with secure web sites.

You can also generate a new key at any time by typing `cipher /k` (without any other options). Then, type `cipher /u` to update the encrypted files on your system with the new key.

Securing free space

Normally, when a file is deleted, only the file's entry in the filesystem table is deleted; the actual data contained in the file remains in the folder until it is overwritten with another file.

Cipher allows you to *wipe* a folder, which means that it goes back and cleans out any recently deleted files, overwriting the leftover data with random bits.

* The classic example of cryptographic keys is how Julius Caesar encoded messages to his allies. Each letter in the message was shifted by three: A became D, B became E, C became F, and so on. Only someone who knew to shift the letters *back* by three could decode the messages. Cryptographic keys work the same way, except they're much more complicated.

This effectively makes it impossible to subsequently recover deleted data with an "undelete" utility. Think of the wipe feature as a virtual paper shredder.

To wipe a folder, type `cipher /w:`*`foldername`*, where *`foldername`* is the full path of the folder to wipe. Note that the `/w` option does not harm existing data, nor does it affect any files currently stored in the Recycle Bin. It also works on unencrypted folders and encrypted folders alike.

Set up cipher to wipe folders containing sensitive data at regular intervals (or when Windows starts) to automatically protect deleted data. See Chapter 9 for information on the Scheduled Tasks feature and WSH scripts, both of which can be used to automate cipher.

Logon Options

Here's the dilemma: you've set up multiple user accounts on a machine, and you've gone the extra mile to ensure that your data is properly protected by configuring permissions and employing encryption. Now you find Windows so locked down that you can't do anything without having to enter a password first. Fortunately, you can customize the logon process to suit your needs and tolerance for cumbersome logon procedures.

Use the Traditional Log On Dialog Instead of the Welcome Screen

The new, friendly Welcome screen is the default interface used when logging on to Windows XP.

The traditional Log On dialog forces you to type both the username and password of a user account to log in. Since a list of active users is not shown, it's more secure than the default Welcome screen. Here's how to switch:

1. Open the User Accounts window in Control Panel.
2. Click **Change the way users log on or off**.
3. Turn off the **Use the Welcome screen** option, and click **Apply Options**.
4. This change will take effect the next time you log off or restart your computer.

When you switch from the Welcome screen to the Log On screen, several other aspects of the Windows interface will be affected. Table 8-2 shows the differences between these two options of this deceptively simple setting.

Table 8-2. How disabling the Welcome screen affects other features in Windows

	Welcome screen	Log On screen
Look and feel of Shut Down dialog:	Large, friendly, colorful buttons for **Stand By**,[a] **Turn Off**, and **Restart**	A simple drop-down list, like the Shut Down dialog found in earlier versions of Windows
Start Menu command to shut down:	**Turn Off Computer**	**Shut Down**
What happens when you press **Ctrl-Alt-Del**:	Opens Task Manager; security features shown in **Shut Down** menu (except for **Change Password**)	Opens the Windows Security dialog, from where you can log off, shut down, start Task Manager, change your password, or lock the computer
Access to hidden user accounts:	No access to hidden users	Log in to any user account by typing user name

[a] Hold the Shift key to display a **Hibernate** button instead of **Stand By** on the Welcome screen.

Customize the Welcome Screen

Although you can easily customize the look and feel of your own account, it's not so easy to customize the Welcome screen. The following solutions allow you change a few things about the Welcome screen. Note that these solutions have no affect on the Log On screen (discussed in the next section).

Choose new pictures for users

When a new account is created in Windows XP, a picture is chosen at random from a collection including a Monopoly racecar, a soccer ball, a butterfly, and others. Here's how to change the picture for any account:

1. Open the User Accounts window in Control Panel, and then choose an account to modify in the list below.
2. Click **Change my picture**.
3. Choose a picture from the collection, or click **Browse** for more pictures to choose your own image. Windows supports *.bmp*, *.jpg*, *.gif*, and *.png* image files.

   Note that the image you choose here will also be the one that appears at the top of the Start Menu (not applicable if you're using the Classic Start Menu).
4. Click **Change picture** when you're done. The new picture(s) will show up the next time you log off or restart Windows.

Create a new Welcome screen

Although changing the little picture for each user (as described earlier) is quite easy, it's an entirely different matter to customize the actual Welcome screen. The screen is embedded in a Windows *.exe* files, which means you'll need to extract the components of the screen to customize them.

1. Open Explorer, and navigate to your *\Windows\System32* folder.
2. Place a copy of the file *logonui.exe* somewhere convenient, such as on your Desktop or in your *My Documents* folder. Then, make another copy of the file, to be used as a backup in case something goes wrong.
3. Download and install the free Resource Hacker utility (available at *http://www.annoyances.org/*). Resource Hacker allows you to modify the bitmaps embedded in certain types of files, including *.exe* and *.dll* files, and is also used in a few solutions in Chapter 2.
4. Start Resource Hacker, and drag-drop the newly created copy of *logonui.exe* onto the Resource Hacker window to open it (or use **File → Open**).
5. Expand the Bitmap branch to show the various images used on the Welcome page. For example, bitmap `100` is the blue gradient background, bitmap `125` is the horizontal line that appears above and below, and bitmaps `123` and `127` both contain the Windows logo.

   Optional: you can export any of these bitmaps to *.bmp* files by selecting them in the tree, and then going to **Action → Save [Bitmap : ### : ###]**. Do this if you wish to modify the existing images rather than (or in addition to) creating your own.
6. Create new images—or modify images you've extracted—to your heart's content. Save your images as *.bmp* files.

Try to make your replacement images the same size (width × height) as the default images in this file. If you need to change the size of an image, you'll need a working knowledge of XML. See Step 10, below, for the additional modifications you'll need to make if your images have different sizes than the ones they're replacing.

7. When you're ready, go to **Action → Replace Bitmap**. Highlight an entry in the **Select bitmap to replace** list, then click **Open file with new bitmap**, and then locate the *.bmp* file you've created or modified.

   Repeat this for all the images you wish to replace.
8. Next, to customize any of the text shown in the Welcome screen, such as "To begin, click your user name," open the `String Table` branch, and choose one of the five categories shown. When you've found the text you want to change, just click in the right pane and start typing.

It's important that you keep the formatting of the text intact. For example, quotation marks, commas, and curly braces are used to separate and organize strings. Make sure you don't mess them up.

Here are some tips for modifying the text strings here:

- To include a line break, type `\n`.
- To include a double-quotation mark, type `\"` (necessary, since a quotation mark without the slash will be interpreted as the closing quotes that mark the end of the string).
- To insert the username of the selected user, type `%s`.
- Some of the strings have names of fonts; as you might expect, you can modify these to change the fonts used in the Welcome screen.

9. When you're done typing, click the **Compile Script** button.
10. The last component that can be modified is the actual layout of the Welcome page. This can be found in the `UIFILE\1000` branch. The beginning of the text in this branch is blank, but if you scroll down (in the right-hand pane), you'll see the content. This, essentially, is an XML file, and unless you are familiar with XML (similar to HTML), you won't want to touch it.

    However, you may need to modify one or more of the entries here if any of your new bitmaps have different dimensions than the ones they're replacing. Start by locating the `<element...>` tag that corresponds to the image you wish to resize; for image 100, for example, it will be the one that has this attribute:

    ```
    content=rcbmp(100,0,0,219rp,207rp,1,0)
    ```

    Here, the first number is the image number, and the numbers ending in "rp" are the dimensions.
11. When you're done editing, go to **File → Save** to save your changes.

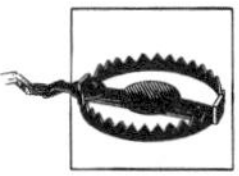

If you are wise, you will take this opportunity to make sure you have a safe backup of the original *logonui.exe* before you replace it. That way, if the modified version is corrupted in any way, you'll be able to repair your system without having to reinstall.

12. The last step is to replace the in-use version of *logonui.exe* with the one you've just modified. You should be able to just drag the modified version right into your *\Windows\System32* folder, replacing the one that's there.

If Windows complains that the file is in use and can't be replaced, you'll have to follow the steps outlined in "How to Delete or Replace In-Use Files" in Chapter 2.

13. The new logo should appear the next time you start Windows. If, for some reason, the Welcome screen is corrupted or won't load at all, the problem is most likely caused by a corrupt *logonui.exe* file. This can be repaired by using the instructions in the previous step to replace the modified version with the original version you backed up—you did back it up, didn't you?

See "Customize the Windows Startup Logo" in Chapter 2 for a related solution.

Turn off the mail notification

By default, Windows will display the number of unread messages underneath each name on the Welcome screen, but only if you're using Outlook or Outlook Express to retrieve your email. To turn off this notification, follow this procedure:

1. Open the Registry Editor (discussed in Chapter 3).
2. Expand the branches to `HKEY_CURRENT_USER\Software\Microsoft\Windows\CurrentVersion\UnreadMail`.
3. Double-click the `MessageExpiryDays` value in this key.

   If it's not there, go to **Edit → New → DWORD Value**, and type `MessageExpiryDays` for the name of the new value.
4. Type `0` for its value data, click **OK**, and then close the Registry Editor when you're done. You'll have to log off and then log back on for the change to take effect.

Instead of disabling the feature, you can merely adjust how far back Windows will "look" for unread messages, if you like. For example, change the `MessageExpiryDays` value to `5` to ignore any unread messages more than five days old. The default is `3`.

This feature has been known to stop working if two or more email accounts have been configured in Outlook for a single user account.

Customize the Log On Screen

Although you can easily customize the look and feel of your own account, it's not so easy to customize the Log On screen. The following solutions allow you to customize various aspects of this window and the desktop that appears in the background. Note that these solutions have no affect on the Welcome screen (discussed in the previous section).

Customize the appearance of the Log On dialog and the desktop background

Follow these steps to customize the colors used by the Log On dialog, as well as the colors and (optionally) the wallpaper of the desktop that appears behind it:

1. Open the Registry Editor (discussed in Chapter 3).
2. Expand the branches to `HKEY_USERS\.DEFAULT\Control Panel\Colors`.
3. Each of the values in this key represents the color of a different screen element. Each value has three numbers—the red, green, and blue values, respectively—that indicate the color of the corresponding object.

   For example, double-click the `Background` value and type `255 0 128` (note the spaces between the numbers) to have a hot-pink background behind the Log On dialog.

   To determine the RGB values for your favorite colors, open a Color dialog by going to **Control Panel** → **Display** → **Appearance** tab → **Advanced** → **Color 1** → **Other**.
4. While you're here, you can also turn on the ClearType feature for the Log On screen. ClearType helps make text more readable on laptop and flat-panel displays. Double-click the `FontSmoothingType` value and change its value data to `2` to enable ClearType. A setting of one (`1`) will enable standard font smoothing, and a setting of zero (`0`) will turn it off entirely.
5. If you wish to use wallpaper on the Log On desktop instead of a solid color, expand the branches to `HKEY_USERS\.DEFAULT\Control Panel\Desktop`. Double-click the `Wallpaper` value, and type the full path and filename of a *.bmp* or *.jpg* file to use as the wallpaper. To tile the wallpaper, set the `TileWallpaper` value to `1`, or to stretch the wallpaper, set the `WallpaperStyle` value to `2`.
6. Close the Registry Editor when you're done. The change will take effect the next time you log off or restart Windows.

Hide the last-typed username

By default, the username of the previously logged-in user is shown in the Log On screen. To disable this, follow these steps:

1. Open the Registry Editor (discussed in Chapter 3).
2. Expand the branches to `HKEY_LOCAL_MACHINE\SOFTWARE\Microsoft\Windows NT\CurrentVersion\Winlogon`. (Note the `Windows NT` branch here, as opposed to the more common `Windows` branch).

3. Create a new string value here by going to **Edit → New → String Value**, and type `DontDisplayLastUserName` for the name of the new value. If the value exists, it may be a `DWORD` value. Either value type is supported here.
4. Double-click the new value, type `1` for its value data, and click **OK**.

Note that hiding the last-typed username will disable the automatic login, described in the next section, "Logging on Automatically."

Customize the logon message (Log On screen only)

The following solution allows you to place your own message above the **User name** and **Password** fields in the Log On dialog:

1. Open the Registry Editor (discussed in Chapter 3).
2. Expand the branches to `HKEY_LOCAL_MACHINE\SOFTWARE\Microsoft\Windows NT\CurrentVersion\Winlogon`. (Note the `Windows NT` branch here, as opposed to the more common `Windows` branch).
3. Create a new string value here by going to **Edit → New → String Value**, and type `LogonPrompt` for the name of the new value.
4. Double-click the new value, type the message you'd like to appear, and click **OK**.

Logging on Automatically

Depending on your settings, you may or may not see the Welcome screen or the Log On to Windows dialog when Windows first starts. For example, if your computer only has one user account (in addition to the Administrator account, discussed in previous solution), and you haven't specified a password for that account, Windows will log you in automatically.

But it's never a good idea to have any accounts on your system set up without passwords, not so much because someone could break into your computer while sitting at your desk, but because if you're connected to a network or the Internet, an account—any account—without a password is a big security hole. See "Closing Back Doors in Windows XP" in Chapter 7 for more information.

The problem with setting up a password, however, is that Windows will then prompt you for the password every time you turn on your computer, which can be a pain if you're the only person who uses the machine. Fortunately, there is a rather easy way to password-protect your computer and not be bothered with the Log On screen.

1. Open the alternate User Accounts window (described at the beginning of this chapter) by going to **Start** → **Run**, typing `control userpasswords2`, and clicking **OK**.
2. Select the username from the list that you'd like to be your primary login, and then turn off the **Users must enter a username and password to use this computer** option.
3. The Automatically Log On dialog will appear, prompting you to enter (and confirm) the password for the selected user.
4. Click **OK** when you're done. The change will take effect the next time you restart your computer.

Note that this solution will not disable your ability to log out and then log into another user account (see below). Furthermore, logging out and then logging back in will not disable the automatic login; the next time you restart Windows, you'll be logged in automatically to the user account you specified.

Prevent users from bypassing the automatic login

Automatic logins are also good for machines you wish to use in public environments (typically called "kiosks"), but you'll want to take steps to ensure that visitors can't log in as more privileged users. There are two ways for a user to skip the automatic login and log into another user account:

- Hold the **Shift** key while Windows is logging in.
- Once Windows has logged in, log out by selecting **Log Off** from the Start Menu or pressing Ctrl-Alt-Del and selecting **Log Off**.

This next solution eliminates both of these back doors:

1. Open the Registry Editor (discussed in Chapter 3).
2. Expand the branches to `HKEY_LOCAL_MACHINE\SOFTWARE\Microsoft\Windows NT\CurrentVersion\Winlogon`. (Note the `Windows NT` branch here, as opposed to the more common `Windows` branch).
3. Create a new string value here by going to **Edit** → **New** → **String Value**, and name the new value `IgnoreShiftOverride`. Double-click the new value, type `1` for its value data, and click **OK**. (This disables the **Shift** key during the automatic login.)
4. Create a new DWORD value here by going to **Edit** → **New** → **DWORD Value**, and name the new value `ForceAutoLogon`. Double-click the new value, type `1` for its value data, and click **OK**. (This automatically logs back in if the user tries to log out.)

5. Close the Registry Editor when you're done. The change will take effect immediately.

To remove either or both of these restrictions, just delete the corresponding registry values.

Limit automatic logins

It's possible to limit the automatic login feature, so that the Log On dialog (or Welcome screen) reappears after a specified number of boots:

1. Open the Registry Editor (discussed in Chapter 3).
2. Expand the branches to `HKEY_LOCAL_MACHINE\SOFTWARE\Microsoft\Windows NT\CurrentVersion\Winlogon`. (Note the `Windows NT` branch here, as opposed to the more common `Windows` branch).
3. Create a new DWORD value here by going to **Edit → New → DWORD Value**.
4. Type `AutoLogonCount` for the name of the new value.
5. Double-click the new `AutoLogonCount` value, and type the number of system boots for which you'd like the automatic login to remain active.

Every successive time Windows starts, it will decrease this value by one. When the value is zero, the username and password entered at the beginning of this topic are forgotten, and the `AutoLogonCount` value is removed.

Logging in as the Administrator

When you first install Windows XP, Setup walks you through the process of setting up two separate user accounts. First, you're asked to choose an Administrator password, which is used for an actual account called "Administrator." Setup then requires you to enter the name of at least one user that will be using the computer; that second username is what is used to subsequently log you into Windows XP.

Although the second user has administrator privileges, it's not the true Administrator account, which is occasionally required for advanced solutions. What makes things more difficult is that the Administrator account is hidden from the Welcome screen and the User Accounts window. If you wish to log into the Administrator account, either to complete some solution or just to use it as your primary login, you should follow these instructions:

1. Get to the traditional Log On dialog, which requires you to type a username rather than simply clicking it. Not only is this window more secure than the Welcome screen, it's the only way to get to the Administrator account. There are two ways to open the Log On dialog:
    a. If you're currently logged in, select **Log Off** from the Start Menu. When the Welcome screen appears, press **Ctrl-Alt-Del** twice.
    b. To make the traditional Log On dialog your default, see "Customize the Welcome Screen," earlier in this chapter.
2. When the old-style Log On to Windows dialog appears, type `Administrator` into the **User name** field, and your administrator password into the Password field.
3. If, after logging in as the Administrator, you wish to delete the secondary account created during Setup, use the alternate User Accounts window by launching `control userpasswords2`, as described at the beginning of this chapter.

Notes

- Despite the fact that the Administrator account is hidden by default, it's perfectly acceptable to use it as your primary login. You may wish to do this simply if you've gotten tired of seeing your name in huge, blazing letters in the Start Menu.
- If you wish to use the Administrator account as your primary login, but don't wish to enter the password every time you turn on your computer, see the previous solution, "Logging on Automatically."
- After you log in to the Administrator account a few times, it will start showing up on the Welcome screen, at which point you can re-enable the **Use the Welcome screen** option if you so desire.

Hiding User Accounts

By default, several user accounts are hidden from the User Accounts window and the Welcome screen. Although you can access these accounts using the alternate User Accounts dialog as well as the Local Users and Groups window (both described at the beginning of this chapter), you can also simply unhide these accounts. Naturally, you can also hide additional accounts with this procedure.

1. Open the Registry Editor (discussed in Chapter 3).
2. Expand the branches to `HKEY_LOCAL_MACHINE\SOFTWARE\Microsoft\Windows NT\CurrentVersion\Winlogon\SpecialAccounts\UserList`. (Note

User Accounts

the `Windows NT` branch here, as opposed to the more common `Windows` branch).

3. In this key, there's a DWORD value named for each hidden user. To unhide a user account, simply delete a corresponding value here.
4. To hide a user, start by creating a new DWORD value by going to **Edit → New → DWORD Value**. Name the new value after the user you wish to hide.
5. Setting any of these values to zero (`0`) will hide the corresponding accounts from both the standard User Accounts window and the alternate User Accounts window, enabling access only through the Local Users and Groups window.

   However, if a value is set to `65536` (hex `10000`), it will only be hidden from the User Accounts window, allowing access through either the alternate User Accounts dialog or Local Users and Groups.
6. Close the Registry Editor when you're done. The change should take effect the next time any of the user-account dialogs are opened.

Prevent Users from Shutting Down

Among the restrictions you may want to impose on others who use your computer is one on shutting down Windows. For instance, if you're logging in remotely, as described in "Controlling Another Computer Remotely (Just Like in the Movies)" in Chapter 7, you'll want to make sure that your PC is always on. Or, if you're setting up a system to be used by the public, you won't want to allow anyone to shut down or reboot the system in an effort to compromise it. Here's how to do it:

1. Open the Registry Editor (discussed in Chapter 3).
2. Expand the branches to `HKEY_CURRENT_USER\Software\Microsoft\Windows\CurrentVersion\Policies\Explorer`.
3. Create a new DWORD value (**Edit → New → DWORD value**), and name it `NoClose`.
4. Double-click the new value and type `1` for its data.
5. Close the Registry Editor when you're done. You'll need to restart Windows for this change to take effect.

Keep in mind that this isn't a bulletproof solution. For instance, anyone will be able to shut down windows by pressing **Ctrl-Alt-Del** and clicking **Shut Down** there. Also, someone with ready access to your computer's on/off switch, reset button, or power cord will be able to circumvent this restriction. At the very least, though, it'll provide some reasonable assurance that your PC will remain powered on.

Working with User Folders

Every user account on your system has its own profile (home) folder, stored, by default, in the *\Documents and Settings* folder. In this folder are such special user folders as *Desktop*, *Send To*, *Start Menu*, *My Documents*, and *Application Data*, among others. Files placed in the *Desktop* folder appear as icons on the user's desktop, shortcuts placed in the *Start Menu* folder appear as Start menu items, and so on. This arrangement lets each user have her own Desktop, Start Menu, etc.

There's also an *All Users* folder, used, for example, to store icons that appear on all users' Desktops. Likewise, the *Default User* folder is a template of sorts, containing files and settings copied for each newly created user. All in all, the use of these folders is pretty self-explanatory.

See "Backing Up the Registry" in Chapter 3 for more information on the *NTUSER.DAT* file found in each user folder.

Modifying folder locations

You can change the default locations for any user's special folders, but the process is different for different folder types:

Home folder
: To change the location of any user's home folder, start the Local Users and Groups window (*lusrmgr.msc*, described at the beginning of this chapter). Open the **Users** category, double-click a user, and choose the **Profile** tab.

Documents, Send To, etc.
: To change the location of any system folder in a user's home folder, such as the *My Documents* folder or the *Send To* folder, you must be logged in as that user. Start TweakUI (see Appendix A), open the **My Computer** category branch, select **Special Folders**, and choose the folder to relocate from the **Folder** list. Note that this only changes the place that Windows looks for the associated files; you'll have to create the folder and place the appropriate files in it yourself.

  For folders not listed in TweakUI, you'll need to edit the Registry. Most user folders are specified in these two Registry keys:

```
HKEY_CURRENT_USER\Software\Microsoft\Windows\CurrentVersion\
   Explorer\Shell Folders
HKEY_CURRENT_USER\Software\Microsoft\Windows\CurrentVersion\
   Explorer\User Shell Folders
```

User Accounts

One of the exceptions is the *Application Data* folder, which is defined by the DefaultDir value in:

```
HKEY_CURRENT_USER\Software\Microsoft\Windows\CurrentVersion\
   ProfileReconciliation\AppData.
```

You'll need to log out and then log back in for any these changes to take effect.

Program Files

The *Program Files* and *Common Files* folders (shared by all users) are both defined in:

```
HKEY_LOCAL_MACHINE\SOFTWARE\Microsoft\Windows\CurrentVersion
```

For *Program Files*, you'll need to change both the ProgramFilesDir and ProgramFilesPath values; for *Common Files*, just change the CommonFilesDir value.

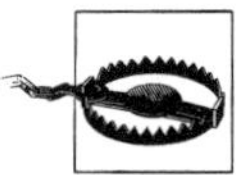

When relocating system folders, keep in mind that there can be hundreds of references to them throughout the Registry, especially *Program Files* and *Common Files*. You'll probably need to use a program like Registry Search and Replace (available at *http://www.annoyances.org*) to easily get them all.

Consolidating user folders

To effectively *remove* a user's system folder, the best thing to do is simply to consolidate it with another system folder. After specifying the new location, as described earlier, just drag-drop the contents of one into the other, and then restart Windows.

The benefits of doing this are substantial. For example, Windows XP comes with the *My Documents* folder, which helps to enforce a valuable strategy for keeping track of personal documents by providing a single root for all documents, regardless of the application that created them (see "A Crash Course on File Organization" in Chapter 2 for details). The problem is that this design is seriously undermined by the existence of other system folders with similar uses, such as *My Pictures*, *Favorites*, *Personal*, *Received Files*, and *My Files*.* Consolidating all of these system folders so that they all point to the same place, such as *c:\Documents* or *c:\Projects*, causes several positive

* *My Files* is the counterpart to *My Documents* that is used by some older versions of WordPerfect and other non-Microsoft application suites. The *Personal* folder was used by Microsoft Office 95, but not so much in subsequent releases. Depending on which programs you've installed or have used in the past, these folders may or may not appear on your system.

things to happen. Not only does it provide a common root for all personal documents, making your stuff much easier to find and keep track of, it also allows you to open any document quickly by using the **Favorites** menu in the Start Menu.

Sharing Files and Printers

One of the main reasons you might want to set up a workgroup between two or more computers in your home or office is to share files and printers between them, eliminating the need to "walk" a disk from one computer to another.

Once you've established a working network connection with another Windows computer, as described in Chapter 7, you can start sharing resources on your computer so that they can be accessed by other computers on the network.

A shared folder, for example, would allow anyone on your network to read and (optionally) write files to it, as though the folder were on their own hard disks. This effectively eliminates the need for multiple versions of documents on which more than one person is collaborating, since any number of people can open and edit the same document (sometimes even simultaneously). The primary limitation is that the computer hosting the file must be turned on for anyone to access it.

A printer physically connected to your computer can be shared on your network so any computer can print to it. Note that this is not the same as a network printer, which is connected directly to your network (and not through a computer).

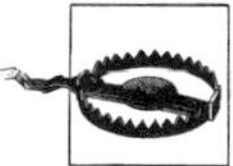

Whenever you share a folder, you are essentially opening a "back door" to your computer, allowing access to potentially sensitive data. It's important to keep security in mind at all times, especially if you're connected to the Internet. Otherwise, you may be unwittingly exposing your personal data to intruders looking for anything they can use and abuse. Furthermore, an insecure system is more vulnerable to viruses, Trojan horses, and other malicious programs. This doesn't mean that you shouldn't use file sharing, just that you'll want to use common sense if security is important to you.

Sharing Folders

Sharing resources is easy, but you'll need to disable the Simple File Sharing feature before you proceed. Go to **Control Panel → Folder Options → View** tab, and turn off the **Use simple file sharing** option. Click **OK** when you're done.

To share a folder with others on your network, simply right-click its icon and select **Sharing and Security** (or select **Properties** and choose the **Sharing** tab). Figure 8-11 shows a sharing window for a user's *Desktop* folder (sharing printers is discussed later).

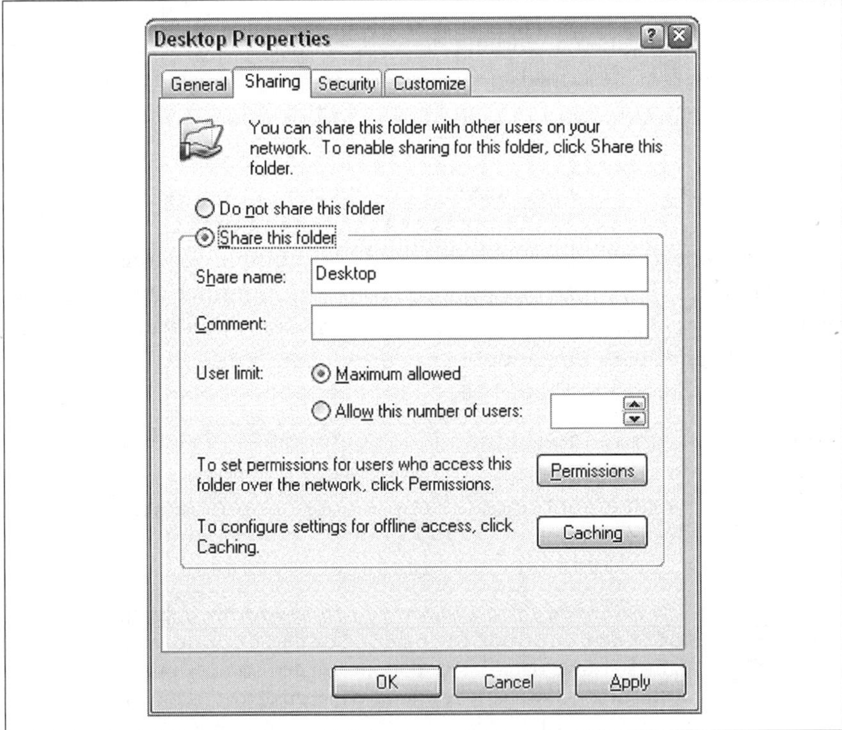

Figure 8-11. Use the Sharing tab of a folder's Properties window to control how it's accessed by other computers on a network

Select the **Share this folder** option to start sharing the selected folder and all of its contents. The **Share name** is the name under which the folder will be accessed from other computers; although the name can be anything, it usually makes sense to use the default, which is identical to the local name of the object.

A drive can be shared as easily as any folder. However, if you're trying to share a drive and you're using Windows XP Professional, you'll see that the drive will already appear to be shared. This is called an Administrative Share, and although it cannot be disabled, it is fairly harmless (as long as you've properly set up passwords for all your accounts as described earlier in this chapter). If you want to proceed to share a drive, you'll have to first click **New Share** at the bottom of the dialog. Make any desired changes in the New Share dialog or leave the default settings, and click **OK** when you're done. The new share name you've typed, as well as the default share (such as *D$*), will both appear in a drop-down list. Select either share to subsequently modify its settings.

As soon as you've chosen the desired sharing options, click **OK** to begin sharing the folder or drive (and all of its contents) over your network. When a folder or drive is shared, a small hand appears over its icon in Explorer.

The aforementioned Administrative Share illustrates an interesting, undocumented feature of share naming. If you place a dollar sign ($) at the end of a share name, it will be hidden when viewed from all remote computers. The only way, then, to access the share would be to type its address into Explorer's Address Bar.

Accessing Shared Resources Remotely

As soon as a folder or drive has been shared, it can be accessed from another computer. Here's how to access a remote folder:

1. Open the *My Network Places* folder in Explorer, or double-click the My Network Places icon on the Desktop.
2. Expand the branches to *Entire Network\Microsoft Windows Network*.
3. A branch for each workgroup detected by your computer will appear in the *Microsoft Windows Network* folder. For most smaller workgroups, you'll only see a single entry here, corresponding to the workgroup name entered in **Control Panel** → **System** → **Computer Name** tab → **Change**. If all computers in your LAN belong to the same workgroup, they'll all be listed under the corresponding workgroup folder here.

   Open any computer listed here to view the shared resources on that computer. In addition to any folders intentionally shared using the process earlier, you'll also see a *Printers and Faxes* folder and a *Scheduled Tasks* folder.

If you're looking for a particular computer or workgroup, and it's not shown here, try pressing **F5** to refresh the view. If that doesn't work, use the Search tool to look for the computer.

4. Every user who wishes to access data on a remote computer (that is, through a local network or VPN connection), must have a user account on the computer. For example, if you're logged in to a computer as "Mel," you'll only be able to access resources on other computers that also have an account called "Mel" *and* that have the same corresponding password. If you have two Windows XP machines, one with a "Mel" account and one with a "Mel" and a "Bob" account, a user logged in as "Bob" will only be able to access resources on the second machine.

   To restrict access to users, beyond simply removing their accounts, click **Permissions** in the **Sharing** tab of the object's Properties window. Note that although this Permissions window looks and works identically to the one discussed earlier in this chapter, the permissions set here only apply to those that access the object remotely, while standard, local permissions only apply to local users that access the object from the same machine.

5. Continue to navigate the tree and open folders as desired. Files and folders can be dragged and dropped, documents opened, etc., as though they were stored on your own hard disk.

The full path to a network resource (called a UNC path, for Universal Naming Convention) works like a standard folder path, but looks a little different.

For example, on a computer called "Luke," you might have a folder called *Sideshow*, stored in a folder called *Obscure References*, stored on drive *C:*. The *Sideshow* folder would then be referenced by this local path:

c:\Obscure References\Sideshow

But the same folder, when accessed from another computer, would be referenced by this UNC path:

\\Luke\Sideshow

What this shows is that only the *Sideshow* folder is actually shared. If, instead, the *Obscure References* folder were shared, the UNC path to the same *Sideshow* folder would look like this:

\\Luke\Obscure References\Sideshow

In neither of the above UNC examples does a reference to drive *C:* appear. This is because we're only sharing the folder instead of the whole drive. If drive *C:* were shared, the UNC path to *Sideshow* would look like this:

\\Luke\c\Obscure References\Sideshow

Note the absence of the expected colon after *c* in this path.

As stated earlier in this section, you'll typically want to limit the scope of your shared folders—that is, only share those folders you specifically want shared. In the final example, above, an entire drive is shared, which means that any file in any folder can be accessed by simply navigating. Naturally, employing permissions and encryption, both described earlier in this chapter, will further safeguard your data and the system on which it's stored.

Mapping Drives

In most cases, you'll want to access remote folders through the *My Network Places* folder, as described elsewhere in this section. However, there's another system in place in Windows XP, included mostly as a holdover from years past.

In Explorer, go to **Tools → Select Map Network Drive** to map a remote folder to a virtual drive letter on the local system. For example, choose an unused drive letter from the **Drive** list, such as *N:*, and then specify the UNC path to an existing network folder, such as *\\Luke\Sideshow*. Turn on the **Reconnect at logon** option if you want Windows to re-establish the mapped drive every time you start Windows. Click **Finish** when you're done.

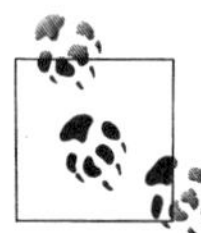

Alternatively, you can use Windows Explorer to navigate to the remote folder in My Network Places, right-click the folder, and then select **Map Network Drive**. Note that the **Map Network Drive** option will only appear for folders highlighted in the folder tree (the left pane).

A new drive will appear in Explorer, and its contents will mirror the remote folder you've selected. This is useful mostly for compatibility with older applications that don't support UNC paths, so that you can "fool" them into thinking that they're accessing only local folders.

The other reason one might want to map a drive is to provide quick access to a remote folder. However, it's typically just as easy (and often more useful) to create a Windows Shortcut to a remote folder for this purpose.

Sharing Printers

As soon as you share a printer, anyone on your workgroup can print to it.

Using the same procedure as sharing folders, described above, you can share almost any printer. Go to **Control Panel → Printers and Faxes**, right-click the printer you wish to share, and select **Sharing**. You'll notice that the Sharing window for printers, shown in Figure 8-12, is much simpler than its counterpart for folders. Select the **Share this printer** option, choose a share name, and then click **OK** to begin sharing the printer.

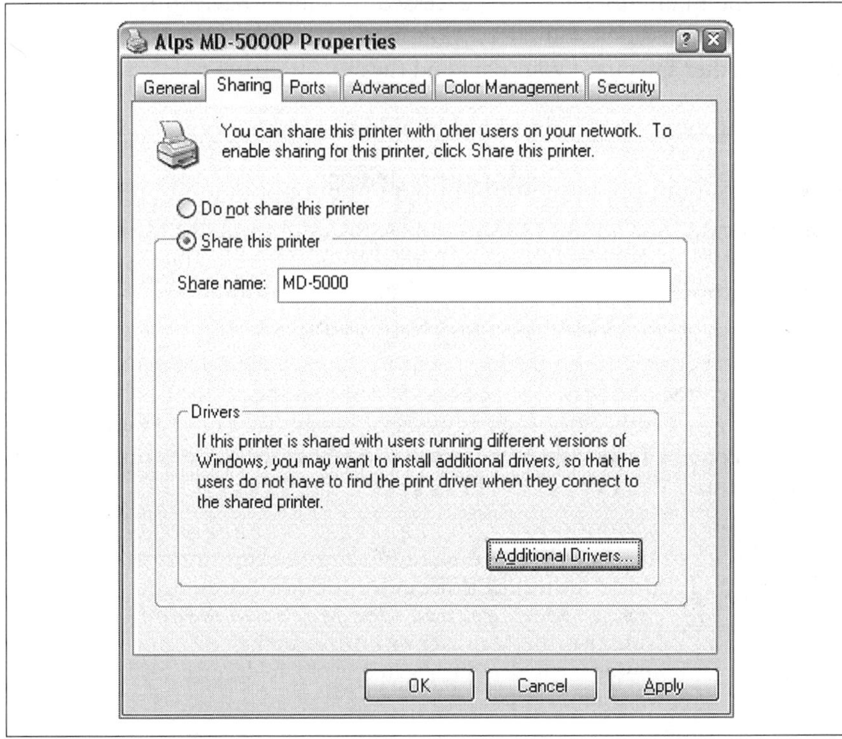

Figure 8-12. You can share a printer in much the same way as sharing a folder

Unlike folders, however, a shared printer must be installed on each remote computer before it can be accessed. Here's how to install a remote printer from a computer other than the one to which it's physically connected.

1. Open **Control Panel → Printers and Faxes**.
2. Double-click the Add Printer icon (or, if you have common tasks enabled, click **Add a printer** in the **Printer Tasks** pane).
3. Click **Next** on the first page, select **A network printer, or a printer attached to another computer** on the second page, and then click **Next**.
4. On the next page, leave the default setting of **Browse for printer** selected, and click **Next**.
5. On the next page, you'll see a nonstandard collapsible tree, from which you'll need to navigate to the remote printer you wish to install.

Navigation is a little different here than in Explorer; instead of the usual plus signs, you'll have to double-click branches to expand them. When you've found the printer, highlight it and click **Next**.

If the printer does not appear under the computer to which it's attached, either the printer has not yet been shared, the computer to which the printer is attached is not turned on, or the printer's driver does not support network sharing.

Some printers can't be shared over a network, which is usually a limitation of the printer's driver. Most printer manufacturers will make networkable drivers available for their printers, but some will intentionally disable this feature, especially for their less-expensive printers. In this case, your only recourse would either be to purchase a separate print-server device, or simply replace the printer.

6. Click **Finish** to complete the wizard.

   In most cases, Windows will simply copy the driver files from the host computer and install them automatically. But if the computer on which you're installing the printer is not running Windows XP, you may have to locate different drivers. You can eliminate this step by clicking **Additional Drivers** in the Sharing window (Figure 8-12) of the host computer and preparing versions of the printer's drivers for other operating systems, such as Windows 9x/Me.
7. Assuming all goes well, an icon for the new printer will appear in the Printers and Faxes window, and you'll be able to print to that printer from any Windows application. You'll need to repeat these steps for each computer from which you need to print to the new printer.

Note that the host computer, the one to which the printer is physically attached, must be turned on and connected to the workgroup in order to allow other computers to print. You can overcome this limitation by using a print-server device, which connects most types of printers directly to your network.

Stop Sharing Scheduled Tasks

As explained earlier in this section, you can access the shared printers and folders—as well as access the Scheduled Tasks folder—of any other computer in your workgroup. The problem is that sharing Scheduled Tasks slows network browsing considerably. Use this solution on each computer in your workgroup to stop the sharing of Scheduled Tasks and increase your network performance:

1. Open the Registry Editor (discussed in Chapter 3).
2. Expand the branches to `HKEY_LOCAL_MACHINE\SOFTWARE\Microsoft\Windows\CurrentVersion\Explorer\RemoteComputer\NameSpace`.
3. Under this key, there will be at least two keys named for Class IDs. The `(default)` value inside each key will tell you what the key is for. Find the key for "Scheduled Tasks" (it will be `{D6277990-4C6A-11CF-8D87-00AA0060F5BF}`), and delete it.
4. Close the Registry Editor when you're done.

The change will take effect immediately, and you'll notice that Windows is now much more responsive when browsing shared folders.

CHAPTER 9

Scripting and Automation

One of the ways to improve your experience with Windows XP is to reduce the time it takes to perform repetitive tasks, whether that involves backing up important files once a week, or generating custom web pages once every three seconds. Scripting, a form of very simple programming, is well suited to quick-and-dirty tasks, such as simple file operations, managing network connections, and even starting several programs with a single click of a button.

Scripts are plain-text files that can be written and executed without a special development environment and don't require a compiler—just use your favorite text editor, or Notepad. (Simply put, a compiler is a program that translates editable program source code into application executables, such as *.exe* and *.dll* files. Scripts are interpreted rather than compiled, which means that another program reads and executes the commands in the script, line by line.)

Windows comes with two forms of scripting: the Windows Script Host (WSH) and batch files. Both technologies have their strengths and limitations. Batch files are somewhat simpler to write, but WSH scripts are much more flexible and powerful and offer better user interaction. WSH scripts are Windows-based, and can take advantage of Windows services, such as printing, networking, and Registry access. DOS batch files can be run on any PC made after 1982, regardless of the version of Windows being used, but WSH scripts run only on Windows 98/Me, Windows 2000, and Windows XP. (Windows 95 and Windows NT 4.0 can also run WSH scripts, but only after installing Microsoft's freely available WSH add-on.)

The Windows Script Host is the engine behind the execution of scripts. Rather than being a tangible, interactive application like Notepad or Internet Explorer, WSH is simply an extensible collection of support files. The beauty of the Windows Script Host (yes, I said beauty in regard to a Microsoft product) is that it is language-independent, meaning that it will work with any modern scripting language. It has built-in support for JavaScript and VBScript, but it can be extended (with third-party add-ons) to use almost any other language, such as Perl and Python. This extensibility is a welcome change from Microsoft's usual narrow support of only its own proprietary technologies.

VBScript is based on another Microsoft programming language, Visual Basic (VB), which, in turn, is loosely based on Beginner's All-purpose Symbolic Instruction Code (BASIC). If you're at all familiar with BASIC, taught in grade school since the seventies, the basics of VBScript won't be much of a challenge. VBScript will be used primarily in this chapter because it's easy to learn; it supports easy access to the features we need, like Registry access and file operations; and its cousin, VB, is one of the most widely used programming environments in the world.

So where does the Windows Script Host end and the VBScript language begin? From the point of view of the end user, WSH is started when you double-click on a script file, at which point it automatically chooses an appropriate language interpreter based upon the script filename extension. From the point of view of the developer, WSH provides special functionality to all languages through the use of objects (see "Object References" later in this chapter); that way, each WSH-supported language needn't bother including functionality for advanced functions, such as Registry access and filesystem operations.

The primary goals of this chapter are to provide an orientation for using the Windows Script Host and to show useful problem-solving applications that illustrate the power and flexibility of WSH.

Building a Script with VBScript

A script is simply a list of commands that are placed one after another and stored in a text file. Script commands are like building blocks: the more commands and programming techniques you learn, the broader your palette will be for making useful scripts. Some of the simpler building blocks will be used in this section of the chapter to illustrate the way scripts are built. Advanced users may prefer to skip to subsequent sections, which cover more advanced topics.

To run a script, just double-click on the script file icon; you'll probably never need to run the Scripting Host program (*wscript.exe*) directly.

There are actually two script interpreters (engines) included with Windows XP. *WScript.exe* is a native Windows interpreter and is used in most cases. *CScript.exe* is a console interpreter, which is used when you want the script output to be sent to the console (Command Prompt). You can use *CScript.exe* at any time by right-clicking a script file and selecting **Open with Command Prompt**.

When the Scripting Host runs the script, the commands are executed in order, one by one. You can leave Notepad open to make changes and additions while you test the script (big screens are especially handy for this sort of thing).

You can quickly open an existing script file for editing by right-clicking on it and selecting **Edit**. This will, by default, open Notepad, although you might want to associate the Edit action for *.vbs* files with a more powerful text editor (see "Protect Your File Types" in Chapter 4).

The process of putting a script together essentially involves typing commands and then running the scripts to test them. In the following topics, we'll cover the background concepts necessary to complete many tasks with scripts:

- Using variables to store and manipulate information
- Asking for and displaying information with the *InputBox* and *MsgBox* commands
- Creating interactive scripts with conditional statements
- Using loops to repeat a series of commands
- Making building blocks with subroutines and functions
- Extending scripts with object references

Using Variables to Store and Manipulate Information

The use of variables is essential when some interaction is required by a script. A variable can be assigned a value, which is subsequently used or simply recalled later in the script. For example, the following two commands:

```
MyName = "joe user"
MyShoeSize = 12
```

assign two different variables to two different values. The first variable, *MyName*, is assigned a text string, while the second, *MyShoeSize*, is assigned a numeric value. You can also assign variables to values in terms of other variables:

```
MyIQ = MyShoeSize + 7
```

This statement, when placed after the two preceding lines, will result in the variable *MyIQ* having a value of 19 (12 plus 7). When a variable name appears on the left side of an equals sign, its value is being manipulated. When it appears on the right side of an equals sign or within some other command, its value is simply being read. You can carry out more complex mathematical operations using various combinations of parentheses and the standard operators (+, -, *, /, and ^ for addition, subtraction, multiplication, division, and exponentiation, respectively).

Giving Your Scripts an Interface with the InputBox and MsgBox Commands

Some scripts are ideally suited to run in the background and perform a sequence of tasks, and then simply exit when those tasks are complete. Others require some sort of user interaction, either in the form of asking the user for input or informing the user when something has gone wrong. For example, this command:

```
MyName = InputBox("Please enter your name.")
```

will display a prompt on the screen when the script is run, asking for some text to be typed. When you enter some text and click **OK**, the script places the text you've typed into the variable *MyName* and continues on to the next command.

Now, collecting and rearranging information does no good without the ability to spit out a result. The versatile `MsgBox` function allows you to display a simple message, as follows:

```
MsgBox "Hello, Hello Again."
```

Combining the principles we've covered so far, consider the following code:

```
MyAge = InputBox("Please type your age.")
NewAge = MyAge + 5
MsgBox "In 5 years, you will be " & NewAge & "."
```

The first line does two things: it first asks the user to type something, and then assigns the typed text to the variable *MyAge*. The second line creates a new variable, *NewAge*, assigns the user's input to it, and adds five. Note the lack of any error checking in this example: if the user enters something other than a number, this code will cause a WSH error, and the script will end early. The third line then uses the `&` operator to concatenate (glue together) a text string and the *NewAge* variable and displays the result in a message box. Notice that plain text is always enclosed in quotation marks, but variables are not. If we were to enclose the *NewAge* variable in quotation marks, the script would simply print out the text `NewAge` instead of whatever value is stored in the variable.

The `MsgBox` statement can also be used like this:

```
Response = MsgBox("Here's My Message", 17, "Message Title")
```

which allows it to be used for not only displaying a message, but recording the response as well. The `17` is the sum of a few different values, which specify the options used to customize the message box. Figure 9-1 shows two sample message boxes, each with different buttons and icons.

Figure 9-1. Various options can be combined to produce a variety of message boxes

To choose the buttons that are displayed by the `MsgBox` function, specify:

`0` for OK
`1` for OK & Cancel
`2` for Abort, Retry, & Ignore
`3` for Yes, No, & Cancel
`4` for Yes & No
`5` for Retry & Cancel

To choose the icon that is displayed, specify:

`16` for a red "X" (error)
`32` for a question mark (query)
`48` for an exclamation mark (warning)
`64` for a blue "I" (information)

Additionally, you can add:

`256` to give the second button the focus (dotted lines)
`512` to give the third button the focus
`4096` to make the message box "system modal" (i.e., all applications are suspended until the user responds to the message box)

So, to have a message box with the **Yes** and **No** buttons, to have the question mark icon, and to have **No** be the default, you would specify a value of `4 + 32 + 256 = 292`. The two message boxes in Figure 9-1 have values of `17` (that's **OK**, **Cancel**, and the "X" icon) and `292`, respectively. Note that it's good practice *not* to add the values together (like I did in the first example with 17), but rather to leave them separated, like this:

```
Response = MsgBox("Here's My Message", 16 + 1, "Message Title")
```

This way, it's easier to understand and modify later on.

When the user responds to the message box, the *Response* variable will be set to:

1 if the user clicked OK
2 for Cancel
3 for Abort
4 for Retry
5 for Ignore
6 for Yes
7 for No

The next step is to write code that can perform different functions based on this recorded response. See the subsequent "Creating Interactive Scripts with Conditional Statements" topic for details on using the results from a MsgBox statement to determine what happens next in a script.

Creating Interactive Scripts with Conditional Statements

Conditional statements allow you to redirect the flow depending on a condition you determine, such as the value of a variable. Take, for example, the following script:

```
Response = MsgBox("Do you want to continue?", 32 + 4, "Next Step")
If Response = 7 Then WScript.Quit
MsgBox "You asked for it..."
```

The first statement uses the MsgBox function, described in the previous topic, to ask a question. The value of 32 + 4 specifies **Yes** and **No** buttons, as well as the question mark icon. If the user chooses **Yes**, the value of the *Response* variable is set to 6; if **No** is chosen, *Response* is set to 7.

The next statement uses the vital If...Then structure to test the value of the *Response* variable. If it's equal to 7 (meaning the user clicked **No**), then the script exits immediately (using the WScript.Quit statement). Otherwise, script execution continues to the next command.

Here's another example using a slightly more complex version of the If statement:

```
MyShoeSize = InputBox("Please type your shoe size.")
MyIQ = InputBox("Please type your IQ.")
```

```
If MyShoeSize > MyIQ Then
  MsgBox "You need to read more."
Else
  MsgBox "You need larger shoes."
End If
```

One of the nice things about VBScript is that most of the commands are in plain English; you should be able to follow the flow of the program by just reading through the commands. Before you run the previous script, try to predict what will happen for different values entered at each of the two `InputBox` statements.

This script uses the `If...Then` structure to redirect output depending on the two values entered at runtime (when the script is actually being executed). It should be evident that the first message is displayed if the value of *MyShoeSize* is larger than the value of *MyIQ*. In all other cases (including when both values are equal), the second message is displayed. Note also the use of `End If`, which is required if the `If...Then` structure spans more than one line, as it does in this example.

The `If...Then` structure can have as many elements as you need. For example:

```
Crashes = InputBox("How many times a day does Windows crash?")
If Crashes <= 3 Then
  MsgBox "You lucky sod..."
ElseIf Crashes = 4 or Crashes = 5 Then
  MsgBox "The national average: good for you!"
Else
  MsgBox "Take two aspirin and call me in the morning."
End If
```

accommodates three different ranges of answers to the question posed by the first line of code (thanks to the `ElseIf` line). Note also the use of `or` on the fourth line; you can also use the `and` operator, or a combination of the two, in your scripts. Use parentheses to group conditions in more complex statements.

Using Loops, Using Loops, Using Loops

Another useful structure is the `For...Next` loop, allowing you to repeat a series of commands a specified number of times:

```
SomeNumber = InputBox("How many lumps do you want?")
TotalLumps = ""
For i = 1 To SomeNumber
  TotalLumps = TotalLumps & "lump "
Next

Rem -- The next line displays the result --
MsgBox TotalLumps
```

The `For...Next` loop repeats everything between the two statements while incrementing the value of the variable *i* with each iteration, ending the loop when *i* equals the value of the variable *SomeNumber*. Each time we go through the loop, another "lump" is added to our variable, *TotalLumps*. When the loop is finished, the contents of the *TotalLumps* variable are displayed.

Notice the use of the concatenation operator (`&`) in the middle of the loop, which adds a new lump to the variable. Those new to programming might be put off by the fact that we have the *TotalLumps* variable on both sides of the equals sign.* This works because the scripting host evaluates everything on the right side of the equals sign (adds it all up) and then assigns it to the variable on the left side.

Note also the `TotalLumps=""` statement before the `For...Next` loop; this empties the variable before we start adding stuff to it. Otherwise, whatever might be assigned to that variable before the loop would still be kept around—something we didn't anticipate or want. It's good programming practice to prepare for as many different situations as can be imagined.

Also good practice is the use of spaces, indentations, and remarks to make the code easier to read without affecting the execution of the script. The `Rem` command (shown earlier) is used to include remarks (comments that are ignored when the script is run), allowing you to label any part of the script with pertinent information. In place of the `Rem` command, you can also use a single apostrophe (`'`), which has the advantage of being used on the same line as another command.

As you write these scripts, think about the formatting as you would in writing a word-processor document; scripts that are easier to read are easier to debug and easier to come back to six months later.

Making Building Blocks with Subroutines and Functions

A subroutine allows you to encapsulate a bit of code inside a single command, making it easy to repeat that command as many different times as you want, just as if it were a built-in command in VBScript. Simply include the entire subroutine anywhere in a script, and then type the name of the subroutine elsewhere in the script to execute the subroutine.

* In traditional algebra, we couldn't have a statement like this; it would be like saying x=x+1, which has no solution. However, this is not an equation; it's a instruction that you want carried out. Besides, you're supposed to have forgotten algebra years ago.

A function is essentially the same thing as a subroutine, except that it has a result, called a return value. Both subroutines and functions accept input variables, listed in parentheses after their respective Sub and Function statements.

To those who are familiar with macros in a word processor, subroutines are similar. In fact, Microsoft Word, Excel, and Access (in Office 95 and later) save their macros as VB subroutines.

Consider Example 9-1, which compares the contents of two text files. At the heart of this example are the two structures at the end of the script, although their specific position in the script is not important. WSH separates all subroutines and functions before executing the script; they won't be executed unless they're called, and the variables used therein are unrelated to variables used elsewhere in the main script. Whenever it encounters the name of a subroutine or function in the script body, it executes it as though it were a separate script. Try to follow the execution of the script, command by command.

Example 9-1. Using functions and subroutines

```
Filename1 = InputBox("Enter the first filename")
Filename2 = InputBox("Enter the second filename")

If Not FileExists(Filename1) Then
  MsgBox Filename1 & " does not exist."
ElseIf Not FileExists(Filename2) Then
  MsgBox Filename2 & " does not exist."
Else
  Call RunProgram("command /c fc " & filename1 & _
              " " & filename2 & " > c:\temp.txt", True)
  Call RunProgram("notepad c:\temp.txt", False)
End If

Function FileExists(Filename)
  Set FileObject = CreateObject("Scripting.FileSystemObject")
  FileExists = FileObject.FileExists(Filename)
End Function

Sub RunProgram(Filename, Wait)
  Set WshShell = WScript.CreateObject("WScript.Shell")
  RetVal = WshShell.Run(Filename, Wait)
End Sub
```

One of the most important aspects of both subroutines and functions is that they can accept one or more input variables, called *parameters* or *arguments*. The parameters that a subroutine accepts are listed in parentheses after the subroutine definition and are separated with commas (if there are more than one). Then, using the Call statement, the values you wish to pass to the subroutine (which are placed in the parameter variables when the script is run) are listed in parentheses.

This way, the same subroutine or function can be called repeatedly, each time with one or more different variables. Functions (such as `FileExists` in this example) can also return a single variable (usually dependent on the outcome of some operation).

The first structure defines the `FileExists` function (discussed later in this chapter), which is passed a filename and returns a value of *True* (-1) if the file exists and *False* (0) if it does not. The `FileExists` function is called twice, once for each filename entered when the script is run (*Filename1* and *Filename2*). The `If...Then` structures (see "Creating Interactive Scripts with Conditional Statements" earlier in this chapter) first call the function, then redirect the flow based on the result of the function.

The second structure defines the `RunProgam` subroutine, also called from the script two times. `RunProgram` simply runs the program filename passed to it; because it's a subroutine and not a function, there is no return value. In theory, you could use functions exclusively, and simply ignore the return values of those functions that don't use them; the benefit of subroutines, though, is that you don't have to think about handling a return value at all.

In `FileExists` and `RunProgram`, *Filename* is a variable (shown in parentheses) in which passed data is placed so that it can be used inside the subroutine or function. It's considered a local variable; that is, it has no value outside of the subroutine or function.

The most important consequence of this design—the separation of the code into subroutines and functions—is that it makes it easy to reuse portions of code. Experienced programmers will intentionally separate code into useful subroutines that can be copied and pasted to other scripts. Just think of programming as building something out of Lego™ blocks; the smaller the blocks, the more versatile they become.

It's worth mentioning that, in the case of subroutines, the `Call` statement is not strictly necessary. For example, the line:

```
Call RunProgram("notepad c:\temp.txt", False)
```

is equivalent to:

```
RunProgram "notepad c:\temp.txt", False
```

Note that in removing the `Call` keyword, I've also had to remove the parentheses around the arguments. Personally, I like using the `call` command, as it makes references to my custom subroutines more distinct and easier to find, but others might prefer the simpler form.

The solutions in the subsequent topics are presented as either subroutines or functions. I've used subroutines for code that performs an action, such as copying a file or writing information to the Registry. When a result is expected, such as reading information from the Registry or finding the date of a file, a function is used instead.

You should be able to place these subroutines and functions directly into your scripts and call them with a single command. It's up to you to put the pieces together to accomplish whatever tasks you have in mind. Feel free, also, to alter these routines to suit your needs.

Object References

There are some operations that can be performed with the Windows Script Host regardless of the language being used. These operations, such as accessing the filesystem, are made possible by extending the language with objects. For the time being, we can consider an object to be simply a context that is referred to when carrying out certain commands.

Admittedly, this can make carrying out some tasks rather difficult and convoluted, but it is necessary given the modular architecture of WSH. For example, many scripts will require a line similar to the following (using VBScript syntax in this case):

```
Set WshShell = WScript.CreateObject("WScript.Shell")
```

which creates and initializes the `WshShell` object. `WshShell` is not a visible object like a file or other component of Windows, but rather a required reference used to accomplish many tasks with WSH, such as running programs, creating Windows shortcuts, and retrieving system information.

If you're unfamiliar with object references, your best bet is to simply type them as shown and worry about how they actually work when you're more comfortable with the language. The subsequent topics include many solutions that take advantage of objects, such as `WScript.Shell`, which has many uses, and `Scripting.FileSystemObject`, used for accessing files, folders, and drives.

Running Applications from Scripts

This code is used to run a program, which can be a DOS program, a Windows application, an Internet or *mailto* URL, or anything else you might normally type in the Start Menu's **Run** command or Explorer's Address Bar. Place this subroutine in your scripts:

```
Sub RunProgram(Filename, Wait)
  Set WshShell = WScript.CreateObject("WScript.Shell")
```

```
    RetVal = WshShell.Run(Filename, Wait)
End Sub
```

and call the routine like this:

```
Call RunProgram("c:\windows\notepad.exe", True)
```

You can replace True with False if you don't want to wait for the program to finish before the next script command is executed.

Accessing the Registry from Scripts

The following code is used to write, read, and delete information in the Registry. Include the following three routines in your script:

```
Sub RegistryWrite(KeyName, ValueName, ValueData, ValueType)
  ValueType = UCase(ValueType)
  If ValueType <> "REG_DWORD" and ValueType <> "REG_BINARY" Then _
                                        ValueType = "REG_SZ"
  Set WshShell = WScript.CreateObject("WScript.Shell")
  WshShell.RegWrite KeyName & "\" & ValueName, ValueData, ValueType
End Sub

Function RegistryRead(KeyName, ValueName)
  Set WshShell = WScript.CreateObject("WScript.Shell")
  RegistryRead = WSHShell.RegRead(KeyName & "\" & ValueName)
End Function

Sub RegistryDelete(KeyName, ValueName)
  Set WshShell = WScript.CreateObject("WScript.Shell")
  WshShell.RegWrite KeyName & "\" & ValueName, ""
  WshShell.RegDelete KeyName & "\" & ValueName
End Sub
```

Using these three routines, you can accomplish nearly all Registry tasks. To create a Registry key, type this (note that all HKEY... roots must appear in uppercase):

```
Call RegistryWrite("HKEY_LOCAL_MACHINE\Software\My Key", "", "", "")
```

To assign data to a Registry value:

```
Call RegistryWrite("HKEY_LOCAL_MACHINE\Software\My Key", "My Value", _
                                        "Some Data", "")
```

Leave "*My Value*" blank to set the (default) value. To read the data stored in a given value:

```
Variable = RegistryRead("HKEY_LOCAL_MACHINE\Software\My Key", "My Value")
```

Leave "*My Value*" blank to read the (default) value. To delete a key:

```
Call RegistryDelete("HKEY_LOCAL_MACHINE\Software\My Key", "")
```

To delete a value:

```
Call RegistryDelete("HKEY_LOCAL_MACHINE\Software\My Key", "My Value")
```

To delete the (default) value in a key, we just set the value to nothing:

```
Call RegistryWrite("HKEY_LOCAL_MACHINE\Software\My Key", "", "", "")
```

You'll notice that, in the RegistryDelete subroutine, there's a RegWrite statement. This is necessary to ensure that the key or value that you're trying to delete actually exists. If you *don't* include this statement and try to delete a nonexistent key or value from the Registry, the Windows Script Host will give an error to the effect that "The system cannot find the file specified." (A helpful Microsoft error message, as always.) This way, the subroutine will create the key or value entry to be deleted if it doesn't already exist.

As part of a security/safety feature present in Windows XP (and Windows 2000), you won't be able to delete a key that contains subkeys (this is not true of Windows 9x/Me) using the RegistryDelete routine. See "Using Registry Patches" in Chapter 3 for a workaround using Registry patch files.

See Chapter 3 for more information on Registry keys and values.

Manipulating Files from Scripts

One of the myths surrounding the Windows Script Host, and VBScript in particular, is that there's no provision for accessing the filesystem (copying, deleting, and writing to files). This assumption is based on the fact that VBScript, when used in web pages, is not permitted to access the filesystem for security reasons.

The following routines, all of which rely on the FileSystemObject object, should allow you to script most necessary file operations. The names I've chosen for these functions and subroutines are based on what they act upon and what they're used for; for example, the FolderCopy subroutine is used to copy a folder, and the FileCopy subroutine is used to copy a file.

The following two functions return properties of drives—whether a specific drive letter exists and how much free space a specified drive has, respectively:

```
Function DriveExists(DriveLetter)
  Set FileObject = CreateObject("Scripting.FileSystemObject")
  DriveExists = FileObject.DriveExists(DriveLetter)
End Function

Function DriveFreeSpace(DriveLetter)
  If Left(DriveLetter,1) <> ":" Then DriveLetter = DriveLetter & ":"
  Set FileObject = CreateObject("Scripting.FileSystemObject")
```

```
  Set DriveHandle = _
              FileObject.GetDrive(FileObject.GetDriveName(DriveLetter))
  DriveFreeSpace = DriveHandle.FreeSpace
End Function
```

These next seven subroutines and functions are used to manipulate folders. The functions are used to retrieve information about a folder, and the subroutines are used to perform actions on a folder. The arguments should all be full folder names (e.g., "*D:\Documents and Settings\All Users\Desktop*"). Note that the FolderSize function returns the combined size of all the contents of a folder, including all subfolders, and may take a few seconds to return a result for large folders. You may want to use the FolderExists function before any others to prevent errors:

```
Sub FolderCopy(Source, Destination)
  Set FileObject = CreateObject("Scripting.FileSystemObject")
  FileObject.CopyFolder Source, Destination
End Sub

Function FolderCreate(Foldername)
  Set FileObject = CreateObject("Scripting.FileSystemObject")
  Set Result = FileObject.CreateFolder(FolderName)
  If Result.Path = "" Then
    FolderCreate = False   'failure
  Else
    FolderCreate = True    'success
  End If
End Function

Sub FolderDelete(Foldername)
  Set FileObject = CreateObject("Scripting.FileSystemObject")
  FileObject.DeleteFolder(Foldername)
End Sub

Function FolderExists(Foldername)
  Set FileObject = CreateObject("Scripting.FileSystemObject")
  FolderExists = FileObject.FolderExists(Foldername)
End Function

Sub FolderMove(Source, Destination)
  Set FileObject = CreateObject("Scripting.FileSystemObject")
  FileObject.MoveFolder Source, Destination
End Sub

Function FolderSize(Foldername)
  Set FileObject = CreateObject("Scripting.FileSystemObject")
  Set FolderHandle = FileObject.GetFolder(Foldername)
  FolderSize = FolderHandle.Size
End Function

Function FolderParent(Foldername)
  Set FileObject = CreateObject("Scripting.FileSystemObject")
```

```
  FolderParent = FileObject.GetParentFolderName(Foldername)
End Function
```

These next seven subroutines and functions are used to manipulate files, and are similar to their folder counterparts listed above. And likewise, the functions are used to retrieve information about a file, and the subroutines are used to perform actions on a file. The arguments should all be fully qualified filenames (e.g., "*c:\windows\notepad.exe*"). You may want to use the `FileExists` function before any others to prevent errors:

```
Sub FileCopy(Source, Destination)
  Set FileObject = CreateObject("Scripting.FileSystemObject")
  FileObject.CopyFile Source, Destination
End Sub

Function FileDate(Filename)
  Set FileObject = CreateObject("Scripting.FileSystemObject")
  Set FileHandle = FileObject.GetFile(Filename)
  GetFileDate = FileHandle.DateCreated
End Function

Sub FileDelete(Filename)
  Set FileObject = CreateObject("Scripting.FileSystemObject")
  FileObject.DeleteFile(Filename)
End Sub

Function FileExists(Filename)
  Set FileObject = CreateObject("Scripting.FileSystemObject")
  FileExists = FileObject.FileExists(Filename)
End Function

Function FileExtension(Filename)
  Set FileObject = CreateObject("Scripting.FileSystemObject")
  GetFileExtension = FileObject.GetExtensionName(Filename)
End Function

Sub FileMove(Source, Destination)
  Set FileObject = CreateObject("Scripting.FileSystemObject")
  FileObject.MoveFile Source, Destination
End Sub

Function FileSize(Filename)
  Set FileObject = CreateObject("Scripting.FileSystemObject")
  Set FileHandle = FileObject.GetFile(Filename)
  FileSize = FileHandle.Size
End Function
```

These next two functions can be used on either files or folders and allow you to retrieve and set file attributes (Archive, Read-Only, System, and Hidden, respectively).

File attributes are specified numerically: Read-Only = 1, Hidden = 2, System = 4, and Archive = 32. So, to set the Hidden and System attributes for a file, the Attrib parameter would be set to 6 (or 2+4). To read a file's attributes, the same constants are used, but only individually. For example, to see if a file had, say, the System attribute turned on, you would use this statement: `If GetAttributes("c:\somefile.txt",4) = True Then Msgbox "This is a system File."`:

```
Function GetAttributes(Filename, Attrib)
  Set FileObject = CreateObject("Scripting.FileSystemObject")
  Set FileHandle = FileObject.GetFile(Filename)
  If FileHandle.Attributes And Attrib Then
    GetAttributes = True
  Else
    GetAttributes = False
  End If
End Function

Sub SetAttributes(Filename, Attrib)
  Set FileObject = CreateObject("Scripting.FileSystemObject")
  Set FileHandle = FileObject.GetFile(Filename)
  FileHandle.Attributes = Attrib
End Sub
```

The following four functions are used to obtain the locations of special Windows folders, or, in the case of GetTempFilename, to generate a new filename in the current user's *Temp* folder. (Rather than simply returning the location of the *Temp* folder, the GetTempFilename function returns the full path of a newly generated temporary filename. The corresponding file is guaranteed not to exist, so you can use it for the purposes of temporary storage without fear of conflicting with another open application.)

So, for example, to get the full path of the current user's *Desktop* folder, you would use GetSpecialFolder("Desktop"). The folders accessible with this function include *AllUsersDesktop*, *AllUsersStartMenu*, *AllUsersPrograms*, *AllUsersStartup*, *Desktop*, *Favorites*, *Fonts*, *MyDocuments*, *NetHood*, *PrintHood*, *Programs*, *Recent*, *SendTo*, *StartMenu*, *Startup*, and *Templates*. (See "Wacky Script Ideas" later in this chapter for several examples using these functions.):

```
Function GetSpecialFolder(Foldername)
  set WshShell = WScript.CreateObject("WScript.Shell")
  GetSpecialFolder = WshShell.SpecialFolders(Foldername)
End Function

Function GetSystemFolder( )
  Set FileObject = CreateObject("Scripting.FileSystemObject")
  GetSystemFolder = FileObject.GetSpecialFolder(1) & "\"
End Function
```

```
Function GetTempFilename()
  Set FileObject = CreateObject("Scripting.FileSystemObject")
  GetTempFile = FileObject.GetSpecialFolder(2) & "\" _
              & FileObject.GetTempName
End Function

Function GetWindowsFolder()
  Set FileObject = CreateObject("Scripting.FileSystemObject")
  GetWindowsFolder = FileObject.GetSpecialFolder(0) & "\"
End Function
```

While the previous functions and subroutines are used to manipulate files, the following two are used to manipulate the *contents* of files. The `ReadFromFile` function will transfer the contents of any file into a variable (naturally, this is most useful with plain-text files). Likewise, the `WriteToFile` subroutine will transfer the contents of a variable (called *Text*) into a file. If the file doesn't exist, it will be created; if the file already exists, the text will be appended to the end of the file:

```
Function ReadFromFile(Filename)
  Const ForReading = 1, ForWriting = 2, ForAppending = 8
  Set FileObject = CreateObject("Scripting.FileSystemObject")
  Set FileHandle = FileObject.OpenTextFile(Filename, ForReading)
  Buffer=""
  Do Until FileHandle.AtEndOfStream
    Buffer = Buffer & FileHandle.ReadLine & vbCrLf
  Loop
  FileHandle.Close
  ReadFromFile = Buffer
End Function

Sub WriteToFile(Filename, Text)
  Const ForReading = 1, ForWriting = 2, ForAppending = 8
  Set FileObject = CreateObject("Scripting.FileSystemObject")
  If FileObject.FileExists(Filename) Then
    Set FileHandle = FileObject.OpenTextFile(Filename, _
                                             ForAppending)
    FileHandle.Write vbCrLf
  Else
    Set FileHandle = FileObject.CreateTextFile(Filename)
  End If
  FileHandle.Write Text
  FileHandle.Close
End Sub
```

The use of all of the "file operations" subroutines and functions listed earlier should be fairly self-explanatory, and they all work similarly. For example, the `FolderExists` function and the `FileExists` function are both nearly identical, except that `FolderExists` checks for the existence of a folder, while `FileExists` checks for the existence of a single file. See the "Rename Files with Search and Replace" script at the end of this chapter for an example of these functions and subroutines in action.

Creating Windows Shortcuts and Internet Shortcuts in Scripts

Include the following subroutine in your script to allow easy creation of Internet Shortcuts (**.url*) and Windows Shortcuts (**.lnk*):

```
Sub Shortcut(LinkFile, CommandLine)
  Set WshShell = WScript.CreateObject("WScript.Shell")
  If LCase(Right(LinkFile, 4)) <> ".lnk" And _
         LCase(Right(LinkFile, 4)) <>".url" Then _
         LinkFile = LinkFile & ".LNK"
  Set ShortcutHandle = WshShell.CreateShortcut(LinkFile)
  ShortcutHandle.TargetPath = CommandLine
  ShortcutHandle.Save
End Sub
```

To create a shortcut to a program or file, use the following statement:

```
Call Shortcut("C:\Documents and Settings\All Users\SendTo\Notepad.lnk", _
              "Notepad.exe")
```

To create a shortcut to an Internet address:

```
Call Shortcut("D:\Prjects\Important\Annoyances.url", _
              "http://www.annoyances.org/")
```

If the first parameter, `LinkFile`, ends in *.lnk* (case doesn't matter), the `Shortcut` subroutine will automatically create a standard Windows shortcut; if LinkFile ends in *.url*, however, an Internet Shortcut file will be created. Note the `If...Then` structure in the routine, which automatically adds the *.lnk* filename extension if no proper extension is found.

The `LCase` function, which transforms the contents of any variable to lowercase, is vital here, and completely compensates for *.URL*, *.url*, *.Url*, and any other case mismatch in the specified filename.

If you specify a nonexistent folder in the path for the new shortcut file, an "Unspecified Error" will occur. You may want to use the `FolderExists` function, detailed in the "Manipulating Files from Scripts" topic earlier in this chapter, to supplement this routine and eliminate the possibility of this error.

Networking with Scripts

VBScript has a few limited networking functions built in that can be used for mapping network drives and connecting to network printers. For advanced network functionality (such as communication and network traffic monitoring), you'll have to look into a different scripting language. For more information on networking, see Chapter 7.

The following routines provide access to some of the more useful network-related functions in VBScript.

The following function checks a given drive letter to see if it has already been mapped. It returns True (-1) if the drive letter has been mapped, False (0) if it hasn't:

```
Function AlreadyMapped(DriveLetter)
  Set WshShell = WScript.CreateObject("WScript.Shell")
  Set WshNetwork = WScript.CreateObject("WScript.Network")
  Set AllDrives = WshNetwork.EnumNetworkDrives( )

  If Left(DriveLetter,1) <> ":" then DriveLetter = DriveLetter & ":"
  ConnectedFlag = False
  For i = 0 To AllDrives.Count - 1 Step 2
    If AllDrives.Item(i) = UCase(DriveLetter) Then ConnectedFlag = True
  Next

  AlreadyMapped = ConnectedFlag
End Function
```

This subroutine maps a drive letter to any valid remote path:

```
Sub MapNetDrive(DriveLetter, RemotePath)
  Set WshShell = WScript.CreateObject("WScript.Shell")
  Set WshNetwork = WScript.CreateObject("WScript.Network")
  WShNetwork.MapNetworkDrive DriveLetter, RemotePath
End Sub
```

This subroutine maps an unused printer port (e.g., LPT3) to any valid remote network printer:

```
Sub MapNetPrinter(Port, RemotePath)
  Set WshShell = WScript.CreateObject("WScript.Shell")
  Set WshNetwork = WScript.CreateObject("WScript.Network")
  WshNetwork.AddPrinterConnection Port, RemotePath
End Sub
```

This subroutine removes the mapping for a previously mapped drive letter:

```
Sub UnMapNetDrive(DriveLetter)
  Set WshShell = WScript.CreateObject("WScript.Shell")
  Set WshNetwork = WScript.CreateObject("WScript.Network")
  WShNetwork.RemoveNetworkDrive DriveLetter
End Sub
```

This subroutine removes the mapping for a previously mapped network printer:

```
Sub UnMapNetPrinter(Port)
  Set WshShell = WScript.CreateObject("WScript.Shell")
  Set WshNetwork = WScript.CreateObject("WScript.Network")
```

```
  WshNetwork.RemovePrinterConnection Port
End Sub
```

The following script serves as an example using these subroutines. It's used to map a network drive if it's not already mapped or to disconnect a currently mapped drive. The previous routines are required.

```
DriveLetter = "N:"
RemotePath = "\\server\c"

If AlreadyMapped(DriveLetter) then
  Call UnMapNetDrive(DriveLetter)
  Msgbox "Drive " & DriveLetter & " disconnected."
Else
  Call MapNetDrive(DriveLetter, RemotePath)
  Msgbox "Drive " & DriveLetter & " connected."
End if
```

This script requires no user interaction once it has been executed and displays only a single confirmation message when it's done. The first two lines contain the drive letter and network path to be mapped together. Then, the `AlreadyMapped` function is used to determine if the drive mapping already exists. The script then maps or disconnects the drive, depending on what's needed.

Manipulating Internet Explorer from Scripts

Because VBScript owes its existence, in part, to Internet Explorer (IE), it seems only fair that there would be some integration between WSH and IE. The key is the Internet Explorer *object* and the properties and methods associated with it.

Note that the code in this section is not presented as a subroutine, mostly because all of the subsequent statements that reference the `IEObject` object (such as `IEObject.Document.Write`) would fail if the initial `Set` statement were isolated in its own routine.

Begin with the following lines in your script, which start the Internet Explorer application, initialize an object to reference, and open a blank IE window:

```
Set IEObject = CreateObject("InternetExplorer.Application")
If Err.number <> 0 Then
  MsgBox "There was a problem starting Internet Explorer."
  wScript.Quit
End If
IEObject.Left = 75
IEObject.Top = 75
IEObject.Width = 400
```

```
IEObject.Height = 300
IEObject.Menubar = 0
IEObject.Toolbar = 0
IEObject.Navigate "About:Blank"
IEObject.Visible=1
Do while IEObject.Busy
  Rem -- wait for window to open --
Loop
```

Note the error checking at the beginning, which quits if there's a problem loading Internet Explorer. The subsequent commands customize the window to our needs. The `Left`, `Top`, `Width`, and `Height` properties are all in pixels; for the `MenuBar` and `Toolbar` properties, `0` means hidden and `1` means visible. Lastly, the `Navigate` property specifies the URL to load; in this case, we specify `About:Blank` to show a blank page.

Once the `IEObject.Visible=1` command is issued, the window appears, and the real fun begins. (Okay, maybe fun is too strong of a word.) The following lines send HTML code to the active IE window, and form a simple web page:

```
IEObject.Document.Write "<html>"
IEObject.Document.Write "<h1>Hello World</h1>"
IEObject.Document.Write "<p>"
IEObject.Document.Write "<i>Aren't we sick of that phrase yet?</i>"
IEObject.Document.Write "</html>"
```

This has nearly limitless possibilities, not the least of which is a more elegant way to display information than the `MsgBox` command, a much more sophisticated way of gathering information than the `InputBox` command (using fill-out forms), and a way to display an ongoing log of a script's activities without interrupting script flow. To clear the page at any time, simply issue another `IEObject.Navigate "About:Blank"` command.

Note that the IE window stays open after the script completes; use the `IEObject.Quit` command to close the window during script execution.

Using Command-Line Parameters in Scripts

A command-line parameter is a bit of text specified after the filename of a script when it is executed from a command prompt (see the following examples). The function used to convert a single command-line parameter into a variable is the following:

```
Function CommandLine(Number)
  Set Arguments = WScript.Arguments
  If Number <= Arguments.Count Then
    CommandLine = Arguments(Number - 1)
  Else
```

```
      CommandLine = ""
    End If
  End Function
```

For example, to display the second command-line parameter passed to a script, issue the following statement:

```
MsgBox CommandLine(2)
```

Although the command line may seem to be an antiquated concept, it's still very much a part of Windows. When you double-click on a *.vbs* file, for example, Windows actually executes the following command:

```
wscript.exe filename.vbs
```

where *filename.vbs* (the file that was double-clicked) is the command-line parameter for *wscript.exe*, telling it which script to run. Scripts also accept command-line parameters, which is accomplished like this:

```
wscript.exe filename.vbs param1 param2
```

The two additional parameters,* *param1* and *param2*, are both passed to the script as command-line parameters, and can be retrieved during runtime by referencing `CommandLine(1)` and `CommandLine(2)`, respectively.

One of the most common uses of command-line parameters in scripts is to accept filenames, and there are two circumstances when this is most useful:

- When you drag one or more items onto the script file icon. Note that this didn't work in earlier versions of Windows, as scripts were considered to be documents instead of programs.
- When you place the script in your *Send To* folder; then, right-click one or more items in Explorer, select **Send To**, and then select the name of the script. You can also place the a shortcut to the script in your *Send To* folder, which eliminates the *.vbs* filename extension that would otherwise appear in the **Send To** menu.

In either case, the script is executed, and the names of the input file(s) are accessible as command-line parameters, one for each filename. The following script shows the names of all files and folders drag-dropped on the script icon:

```
Report = ""
Set Arguments = WScript.Arguments
For i = 1 to Arguments.Count
  Report = Report + Arguments(i - 1) + vbCrLf
Next
Msgbox Report
```

* You can have as many or as few parameters as you like.

The script starts off by clearing the Report variable, and then borrows some code from the CommandLine function listed earlier* to initialize the Arguments object and determine the number of dropped files. Next, a For...Next structure is used to run through the arguments, adding each one to the Report variable, followed by a linefeed (using vbCrLf, a handy built-in constant containing carriage-return and linefeed characters). Note that the Arguments array is zero-based (the first item is Arguments(0), the second is Arguments(1), and so on), so we need to include the (i - 1) part to compensate. Lastly, a Msgbox command is used to display the list of dropped files.

Managing Services with Scripts

Windows XP Services, such as the IIS web server service, the FTP daemon service, or the Remote Desktop service, can be managed with the Services window (*services.msc*). Rudimentary service control is also possible with WSH scripts. The following routine allows you to start and stop any service, or just see if a service is running:

```
Function Service(ServiceName, Action)
  Const SERVICE_STOPPED = 1
  Const SERVICE_RUNNING = 4
  Set WshShell = WScript.CreateObject("WScript.Shell")
  Set EnvObject = WshShell.Environment("PROCESS")
  ComputerName = EnvObject("COMPUTERNAME")
  Set ComputerObject = GetObject("WinNT://" & ComputerName & ",computer")
  Set ServiceObject  = ComputerObject.GetObject("Service",ServiceName)
  If Action = 1 and ServiceObject.Status = SERVICE_STOPPED Then
    ServiceObject.Start
  ElseIf Action = 2 and ServiceObject.Status = SERVICE_RUNNING Then
    ServiceObject.Stop
  End If
  If ServiceObject.Status = SERVICE_RUNNING Then
    Service = True
  Else
    Service = False
  End If
End Function
```

This general-purpose routine accepts two parameters: ServiceName and Action. ServiceName is a single word that represents the service you wish to start, stop, or query, and Action is just a number, representing what you want the routine to do. To find the service name for a given service, open the Services window (*services.msc*) and double-click the service in question. The service name is listed at the top of the **General** tab; for example, the

* It's actually possible to use the CommandLine function itself here instead, but doing so would make the script more cumbersome. And exactly who are you going to impress with a cumbersome script?

service name for the IIS service is IISADMIN, the name for the FTP service is MSFTPSVC, and the name for the Remote Desktop (aka Terminal Services, discussed in Chapter 7) service is TermService.

So, to start the FTP service, you would type:

```
Result = Service("MSFTPSVC", 1)
```

or, to stop the service, you would type:

```
Result = Service("MSFTPSVC", 2)
```

Either way, the function returns True (-1) if your action resulted in the service being started, or False (0) if your action resulted in the service being stopped. To simply query the service, without starting or stopping it, specify any other number for Action, like this:

```
Result = Service("MSFTPSVC", 0)
```

Including this routine in your script allows you to start and stop a service with a single click (rather than having to wade through the Services window). Or, using these script routines in conjunction with Scheduled Tasks (explained later in "Automating Scripts with Scheduled Tasks"), for example, you could schedule your web server service to operate only during certain hours of the day.

Writing CGI Scripts for a Web Server

WSH scripts have the potential to produce simple, yet quite capable CGI (Common Gateway Interface) applications for use with web servers: programs that are run by web-server software to generate dynamic web content. For example, CGI programs can be used to process data entered in web-based fill-out forms or to read data from files and produce web content on the fly. Although a full discussion of web-server implementation and CGI programming is beyond the scope of this book, there are some extra steps and additional commands necessary to write CGI programs with WSH scripts.

The first step is to set up your web server software to execute WSH scripts. There is a variety of different web-server software packages (such as IIS, included with Windows XP, and Apache, freely available at *http://www.apache.org*), and naturally the configuration varies with each package. The following procedure shows how to set up IIS and configure it to execute WSH scripts as CGI programs.

1. If IIS is not currently installed, go to Add or Remove Programs in Control Panel, and click **Add/Remove Windows Components**. Highlight **Internet Information Services (IIS)** from the list, and click **Details**. Place a checkmark next to **Common Files**, **Internet Information Services Snap-In**, **World Wide Web Service**, and any other components you want installed. Click **OK** and then click **Next** to complete the wizard.
2. Start the IIS Snap-In (*\Windows\system32\inetsrv\iis.msc*), and then expand the branches to `Internet Information Services\My Computer\Web Sites\Default Web Site`. The files and folders that make up your web site are shown here (note that your setup may be different).
3. Scripts to be executed cannot be placed in ordinary folders; otherwise, the web server will simply display their contents instead of running them. So, they must be placed in a virtual directory with executable permissions; if you've already set up such a folder, you can continue to the next step. Otherwise, go to **Action → New → Virtual Directory**, and follow the prompts. The **Alias** option is the folder name that appears in the URL when referencing the script from a browser (described subsequently), and the **Directory** option is the full path of the physical folder on your hard disk containing your script. Finally, when asked about **Access Permissions**, make sure to turn on the **Execute** option.
4. Once you have a virtual directory configured, right-click the folder, click **Properties**, choose the **Virtual Directory** tab, and then click **Configuration**.

For a CGI program to work, its output must be sent to the "console," a text-based display which works like the Command Prompt. For this reason, the *CScript.exe* script interpreter (engine), mentioned earlier in this chapter, must be used instead of the standard *WScript.exe* Windows-based interpreter.

5. Click **Add**, and type the following:

   ```
   c:\windows\system32\cscript.exe "%s" "%s"
   ```

   in the **Executable** field (change the path to match your system, if necessary), and type `.vbs` in the **Extension** field (make sure to include the dot).

   Naturally, the filename extension will be different for JavaScript or Perl script files. Or, if you like, you can even make up a new filename extension for use with your VBScript CGI scripts (such as *.vbsc* or *.vbcgi*), as long as what you type doesn't conflict with another entry in the list.

6. The **All Verbs**, **Script engine**, and **Check that file exists** options should all be selected. Click **OK**, and then **OK** again when you're done.

The next step is to write a CGI script and place it in your executable folder. CGI scripts can use any of the commands and routines discussed elsewhere in this chapter, except, of course, for those that create dialog windows, such as `MsgBox` and `InputBox`.

The key to a CGI script, though, is the `WScript.Echo` command, which is used to send your text output to the web server. Here's an example of a simple four-line script that generates a basic HTML-formatted* web page:

```
WScript.Echo "<html>"
WScript.Echo "<body>"
WScript.Echo "<h1>Here Comes the Metric System!</h1>"
WScript.Echo "<body></html>"
```

To run the script, first save it in the executable folder you configured earlier. If the IISAdmin service is not currently running, start it now (via *Services.msc*). Then, open a web browser, and type this URL into the address bar:

```
http://localhost/foldername/script.vbs
```

where *`foldername`* is the `Alias` you chose for the executable folder, and *`script.vbs`* is the filename of the script. If all goes well, you should see our message, "Here Comes the Metric System!" right in the browser window. If it doesn't work, check the permissions of the script file and executable folder (right-click, select **Properties**, and choose the **Security** tab). See Chapter 8 for more information on user accounts, ownership, and file permissions.

Since we are talking about a web server, you can just as easily call the script from a remote computer, as long as you're connected to a network or to the Internet, and you know the IP address or URL of your machine (visit *http://www.annoyances.org/ip* to find out your computer's IP address). For example, if your IP address is `207.46.230.218`, you'd simply type `http://207.46.230.218/foldername/script.vbs`.

Naturally, you'll probably want to generate dynamic (rather than static) content with your CGI script. Here's a script that displays the current date and time in the browser window:

```
WScript.Echo "<html><body>"
WScript.Echo "Today's date is: " & Date
WScript.Echo "and the current time is: " & Time
WScript.Echo "<body></html>"
```

* A discussion of HTML (Hypertext Markup Language) is beyond the scope of this book, but there are many adequate HTML references on the web.

For those familiar with writing CGI programs, you may be confused by the handling of any HTTP headers you include in your WSH CGI scripts. Although the CGI specification requires that a CGI program produce its own HTTP headers (such as "`Content-type: text/html`"), IIS 5.x automatically generates the headers, based on the type of content it *thinks* you're sending (`text/html` for HTML or `text/plain` for plain text, for example). This not only means that any headers you include (with `WScript.Echo`) will simply appear as part of the generated page, but that there's no way to include your own headers.

If you need to obtain the value of a browser environment variable in your script, include this function:

```
Function Environment(EnviroName)
  Set WshShell = Wscript.CreateObject("Wscript.Shell")
  Set EnvHandle = WshShell.Environment("Process")
  Environment = EnvHandle(EnviroName)
End Function
```

For example, you can display the user's web browser version with this short script:

```
WScript.Echo "Your browser's signature is:"
WScript.Echo Environment("HTTP_USER_AGENT")
```

Some other useful environment variables include *QUERY_STRING* (for retrieving form input or any text after a question mark in the URL) and *HTTP_COOKIE* (for reading HTTP cookies).

You can, of course, use other routines in your CGI scripts. For example, here's a script that displays the contents of a text file, using the `ReadFromFile` function (see "Manipulating Files from Scripts" earlier in this chapter):

```
OrderNum = "234323"
WScript.Echo "Here is your order (number " & OrderNum & "):"
WScript.Echo "<p>"
WScript.Echo "<img src=""/pictures/smiley.jpg""><br>"
WScript.Echo ReadFromFile("d:\data\orders\" & OrderNum & ".txt")
```

Note the use of Hypertext Markup Language (HTML) to include an image in the output. Although many HTML tags require quotation marks, adding a quotation mark in the middle of a line would cause WSH to confuse it with the beginning and trailing quotes. To tell VBScript to treat a quotation mark as a character to print, just put two of them together (as shown on the "smiley" line).

Development Tips

As you develop WSH scripts, you'll quickly discover that you'll need more than just ephemeral knowledge of the commands and references to complete most tasks. Windows is a complex system, and your scripts don't exist in a vacuum. The rest of the solutions and examples in this chapter will help you write scripts that operate in the broader context of the fully functioning Windows XP environment.

Deciphering Script Errors

One of the general disadvantages of scripts is that they are typically created with a plain-text editor, rather than a rich debugging environment used with many more sophisticated programming languages (see "Finding a Better Editor" later in this chapter). Because Notepad isn't specifically designed to understand VBScript, it can't offer any assistance with syntax (grammar) or errors while you're editing. Therefore, you must wait until you run the script to see if there are any problems. If WSH encounters an error, it will display a message similar to that shown in Figure 9-2.

Figure 9-2. The Windows Script Host displays a message like this whenever it encounters an error

Surprisingly, this sparse message box actually provides enough information to resolve most problems. Naturally, the first field, **Script**, shows the script filename in which the error occurred. This is especially useful if the script was run from a scheduled task or from your Startup folder, and you might not otherwise know which script caused the error.

The **Line** field shows on which exact line of your script the error occurred and includes blank lines and remarks. Likewise, the **Char** field shows the *column* of the first character of the cause of the error, including any indent.

If you're using Notepad, select **Status Bar** from the **View** menu to display the line number (**Ln**) and column (**Col**) at which the insertion point (text cursor) is resting. Or, select **Go To** from Notepad's **Edit** menu to quickly jump to any line. Better yet, switch to a better text editor (discussed later in this chapter) that has line numbering and other handy debugging tools.

The **Source** field describes—more than anything else—what the WSH engine was doing when it encountered the error. A *compilation error* occurs when WSH is first reading the file and making sure all of the commands are correctly entered; you'll see this if you forgot a parenthesis or quotation mark, misspelled a command, or left out some other important keyword. A *Microsoft VBScript runtime error*, on the other hand, is an error encountered while the script was being executed; this is caused by errors that WSH doesn't know are errors until it actually tries them, such as trying to read from a file that doesn't exist or trying to calculate the square root of a negative number.

Lastly, the **Error** field shows a brief explanation of the error encountered, and the **Code** field shows the corresponding numeric error code (useful for searching Google or the Microsoft Knowledge Base if you can't figure out the problem yourself). Sometimes the error description is helpful, but most of the time it's either too vague or too cryptic to be of much help. This is where programming experience comes in handy for interpreting these messages and figuring out what caused them. The following are a few of the more common **Error** descriptions and what they mean:

Expected ')'
: Compilation error: you left out a closing parenthesis, such as at the end of an `InputBox` statement (see earlier). Note that sometimes you can have nested parentheses (e.g., `x=1+(6+7*(3-4))`), and you need to make sure you have an equal number of open and close parentheses.

Expected 'End'
: Compilation error: you left out a closing statement for a structure, such as `If`, `Sub`, or `For`. Make sure you include `End If`, `End Sub`, and `Next`, respectively. Note that WSH might report that the error occurred on line 37 of a 35-line file; this happens because in looking for a closing statement, WSH continues to search all the way to the end of the script, at which time, if the statement was not found, it will report the error. You'll have to look through the entire script for the unpaired beginning

statement. See the topics on flow control earlier in this chapter ("Creating Interactive Scripts with Conditional Statements," "Using Loops, Using Loops, Using Loops," and "Making Building Blocks with Subroutines and Functions") for more information on these commands.

Unterminated string constant
: Compilation error: you left out a closing quotation mark, usually required at the end of a "string of text."

Invalid procedure call or argument
: Runtime error: this usually means that a subroutine or function has been called with one or more improper parameters. This can occur, for example, if you try to do something WSH isn't capable of, such as calculating the square root of a negative number.

Type mismatch: '[undefined]'
: Runtime error: this means you've tried to use a command or function that VBScript doesn't recognize. You'll get this error whenever you try to use a VB command that doesn't exist in VBScript.

Object doesn't support this property or method
: Runtime error: because it can be difficult to find documentation on the various objects used in VBScript, you're likely to encounter this error frequently. It means that you've tried to refer to a property or method of an object (such as `WScript`) that doesn't exist (such as `WScript.Dingus`).

The system cannot find the file specified
: Runtime error: This error, obviously reporting that you've tried to access a file on your hard disk that doesn't exist, also appears when you try to delete a Registry key that doesn't exist. See "Accessing the Registry from Scripts" earlier in this chapter for a Registry function that solves this problem.

ActiveX component can't create object
: Runtime error: you'll get this when you try to use the `Set` statement (as described throughout this chapter) and, for whatever reason, WSH isn't familiar with the object you're trying to initialize. Typically, objects are extensions to WSH: some of which come with Windows XP, some of which are installed through Add or Remove Programs, and some of which come with third-party programs. The resolution usually involves installing the missing component (which usually can be found on the Web) but depends entirely upon the specific object reported by the error.

If you plan on distributing your scripts, you'll want to take steps to eliminate any error messages that may pop up. See the "Manipulating Files from

Scripts" script earlier in this chapter for more information on error trapping and the `On Error Resume Next` statement.

Finding a Better Editor

Notepad is a very rudimentary text editor. Although it serves our purpose, allowing us to write and save VBScript files, it doesn't go any further than it absolutely needs to. It has no toolbar, no syntax highlighting, no visible line numbers, and no macro feature. If you find yourself writing VBScript files often, you'll want to use a better editor. Now, Windows also comes with WordPad, although it doesn't do much more than Notepad in helping to write scripts, and it has that creepy Microsoft Word–like interface.

One direction to go is simply to use a better plain-text editor, such as UltraEdit-32 (*http://www.ultraedit.com*). It has many features prized by programmers, such as column selections, visible line numbers, a terrific multi-file search-and-replace, and many other goodies. However, it's still just a text editor and therefore doesn't provide any VBScript-specific assistance.

Most full-featured programming languages come with a rich programming environment that provides real-time syntax checking (similar to a spellchecker in your word processor; some even tell you right away if you missed a parenthesis), as well as context-sensitive help (you can get technical assistance as you're typing code). The problem is that Windows doesn't come with such an editor, nor am I aware of any decent VBScript editor at the time of this writing.

Some may suggest that you can use either the Visual Basic editor or the VBA editor that comes with Microsoft Office 97 or Office 2000 to write your scripts, but this should be taken with a grain of salt. Although VB and VBA do have a similar syntax to VBScript and even share many commands, the environments are different enough that it's more trouble than it's worth.

Further Study

Given that writing scripts for the Windows Script Host is a language-dependent endeavor, the most helpful reference material will be specific to the particular language you're using. Microsoft's support web site for all their scripting technologies, including WSH, can be found at *http://msdn.microsoft.com/scripting/*. In addition to documentation on VBScript and JScript, you can download updates to the WSH engine. Note that if you distribute scripts to other machines, you'll need to be careful about supporting features found only in newer releases of WSH.

Before committing to VBScript for a project, you may want to do some research on other supported languages listed here. Due to VBScript's heritage in web pages, security concerns have resulted in some limitations in the VBScript language, such as its inability to access the clipboard or link to external *.dll* files.

Given that JavaScript (which actually has nothing whatsoever to do with Sun Microsystems' Java programming language) was created by Netscape, you can find a lot of developer information at: *http://developer.netscape.com/tech/javascript/*. Keep in mind, however, that JScript is Microsoft's bastardized version of JavaScript and therefore not exactly the same language.

The Practical Extract and Report Language (Perl) is probably the most powerful and flexible scripting language available for the Windows Script Host at the time of this writing. It's traditionally very popular among the Unix crowd and has gained tremendous popularity for its use in writing CGI programs for web servers.

Unfortunately, Windows XP doesn't come with the Perl engine; you'll have to obtain a separate Perl add-on module from *http://www.activestate.com*. More information is available at *http://www.perl.com*.

Making a Startup Script

The process of making a startup script—a script that is executed automatically when Windows starts—is quite simple. Essentially, you create a script as you normally would, and then take steps to have it executed when Windows starts. There are a few different ways to do this:

Use the Startup folder
: Put a shortcut to the script in your Startup folder (usually *C:\Documents and Settings\{username}\Start Menu\Programs\Startup*). This is by far the easiest to implement but also the most fragile, because it's equally easy to disable (important if you're setting up a computer for someone else).

> If there is more than one user account on a computer, and you want the script to be executed regardless of the currently logged-in user, you can use the "All Users" Startup folder (usually *C:\Documents and Settings\All Users\Start Menu\Programs\Startup*) instead.

Use the Registry
: Open the Registry Editor (see Chapter 3), and expand the branches to `HKEY_CURRENT_USER\Software\Microsoft\Windows\CurrentVersion\Run`.

Select **New** and then **String Value** from the **Edit** menu, and type `startup script`. Double-click the new `Startup Script` value, type the name of your script (e.g., `c:\scripts\myscript.vbs`), and click **OK**. Although a little more difficult to implement, this setup is a little more robust and transparent than using the *Startup* folder.

Many viruses and spyware install themselves in this Registry key precisely because it's so transparent. See Chapter 6 for tips on how to remove malware from this key.

Likewise, you can implement this solution for all users rather than just the current user by adding the Registry value to `HKEY_LOCAL_MACHINE\Software\Microsoft\Windows\CurrentVersion\Run` instead.

Use the Group Policy Editor

This is probably the coolest solution, as it gives you the most control over precisely when the script is run, and it's the only way to facilitate a shutdown or logoff script as well. Open the Group Policy Editor (*gpedit.msc*), and expand the branches to `Computer Configuration\Windows Settings\Scripts (Startup/Shutdown)`. Double-click the **Startup** entry on the right side, and then click **Add**. Click **Browse** to locate a script file, and click **OK** when you're done. The script will be run every time you start your computer, but before the logon or Welcome screen appears (and before scripts specified in the Registry or Start Menu are ever run).

Likewise, double-click the **Shutdown** entry to specify a script to be run every time your computer shuts down.

Now, there's a similar folder called `Scripts (Logon/Logoff)`, located in the `User Configuration` branch. Like everything in the `User Configuration` branch, these settings apply only to the currently logged-on user (as opposed to all users). If you specify your startup script here (under `Logon`), instead of under Computer Configuration, the script will run after you log in. And, of course, a script specified under Logoff will be run when you log off, whether or not you actually shut down the computer.

A startup script can contain a list of programs that you want run in a specific order when Windows starts, such as connecting to the Internet and then checking your email. (Neither Explorer's Startup folder nor the Registry allow you to choose the order in which programs are run.) But there are other, less apparent uses for a startup script, such as for security or remote administration.

For example, say you've discovered a virus that has infected some or all the computers on a network. By writing a script that eliminates the virus by deleting key files or running an antivirus utility automatically with a startup script, you can effectively eliminate the virus from each computer.

But with scripts, you can take it even further: utilize a single script stored on a single computer that is run over the network on all computers. This way, you can make changes to the script once and have those changes propagated to all computers effortlessly. So, if you place the script *Startup.vbs* on a machine called *Server* in a folder called *c:\scripts* (drive *c*: would be shared as "c"), then each client machine should be configured to automatically execute *\\server\c\scripts\startup.vbs* (using one of the previous methods). The beauty of this is that when you don't want the script to do anything, you can simply leave it intact yet empty. If you find that you need to, say, make a Registry change or copy a group of files onto each computer, just type the appropriate commands into the script and turn on (or reboot) all the client computers. This can turn some administration tasks into very short work.

Automating Scripts with Scheduled Tasks

The Scheduled Tasks feature is fairly simple, allowing you to schedule any program or—more importantly in the context of this chapter—any script.

What's nice about the Scheduled Tasks feature is that it's actually a technology that is somewhat well integrated into the operating system. Any application can create a schedule for itself, and you can plainly see those that are in effect simply by opening the Scheduled Tasks folder. For the more forgetful among us, you can use it to schedule Disk Defragmenter to run once a month, Backup to run once a week, or Windows Update to check for new updates every morning.

The Scheduled Tasks feature also has its pitfalls. The Add Scheduled Task tool is cumbersome and very limited. It's also a rather passive service, and while that's an aspect I like, at least idealistically, it means that tasks can very easily be missed. Any scheduled tasks will not be performed if you've selected the **Stop Using Task Scheduler** option (in the **Advanced** menu), if your computer is turned off, if Windows isn't running, or if your portable computer is running off its battery. These situations may be obvious, but they can be easy to forget, and Windows will only tell you if you missed any tasks if you manually enable the **Notify Me of Missed Tasks** option.

There are several ways to create a new scheduled task, the most obvious of which is to double-click the **Add Scheduled Task** icon in the Scheduled Tasks folder. The overly verbose wizard should then walk you through the process of creating a new task. When the wizard prompts you to select a program (it just displays a list of all the applications listed in your Start Menu), click **Browse**, select an existing script or other application on your hard disk, and click **OK** when you're done. At this point, I recommend just clicking **Next** repeatedly here until the wizard is finished. Then right-click on the new task, and select **Properties** to configure the task with a more suitable and convenient tabbed interface.

Fortunately, there is a shortcut you can use to bypass the wizard entirely: just go to **File → New → Scheduled Task**, or right-click an empty area of the Scheduled Tasks folder, and select **New** and then **Scheduled Task**. Then, right-click the new task, and select **Properties**.

Finally, you can create a new task on the fly from the command prompt (or the Address Bar). Use the `at` command, like this:

```
at 11:15 /interactive c:\scripts\myscript.vbs
```

Naturally, you'll want to replace *`11:15`* with the time you actually want the task to run, and replace *`c:\scripts\myscript.vbs`* with the full path and filename of the application or script you wish to schedule. You can also use the `/every` option to specify a repeating day or date, or the /next option to specify only a single day:

```
at 15:45 /interactive /every:tuesday,thursday c:\scripts\myscript.vbs
at 15:45 /interactive /next:saturday c:\scripts\myscript.vbs
```

Type `at /?` at the command prompt for more options, or see *Windows XP in a Nutshell* (O'Reilly) for full documentation.

One thing to note is the two **Power Management** settings in the **Settings** tab of the Task's **Properties** dialog box. By default, tasks won't be run if your computer is running on batteries—a setting you may want to change if you need the task performed regardless of your computer's power source.

The use of a scheduler opens up some interesting possibilities. Scheduling helps with repetitive chores, such as running Disk Defragmenter or synchronizing network files; it also helps by taking care of things you may not remember to do yourself, such as backing up or sending an email to your grandmother on her birthday. See the following topics for more ideas.

Wacky Script Ideas

The point of scripting is that instead of using a canned application to perform a certain task, you can easily and quickly throw together a script that does exactly what you need. That said, you may need some inspiration to get you cooking.

The following examples use many of the custom subroutines and functions outlined earlier in this book, but for brevity and sanity, they won't be repeated in the forthcoming snippets of code.

Quick Floppy Backup Tool

The script in Example 9-2 starts by prompting you for the name of a folder to back up and checks to see if it exists. If not, it gives you an opportunity either to type another folder name or exit. Once a valid folder name has been entered, the script creates a backup of the entire folder on your floppy drive.

Example 9-2. Quick floppy backup tool

```
On Error Resume Next
Accepted = False
Do Until Accepted
  MyFolder = InputBox("Please enter the name of the folder _
       you want to back up.")
  If Not FolderExists(MyFolder) Then
    Answer = MsgBox("The folder you typed doesn't exist. _
       Try again?", 36, "")
    If Answer = 7 Then WScript.Quit
  Else
    Accepted = True
  End If
Loop

Answer = MsgBox("Please put a diskette in your floppy drive.", 33, "")
If FolderSize(MyFolder) > DriveFreeSpace("a") Then
  MsgBox "The folder you specified won't fit on the floppy.", 16
  WScript.Quit
End If

If FolderCreate("a:\Backup\") = False Then
  MsgBox "There was a problem writing to the diskette.", 16
  WScript.Quit
End If

Call FolderCopy(MyFolder, "a:\Backup\")

If Right(MyFolder, 1) <> "\" Then MyFolder = MyFolder & "\"
Call WriteToFile(MyFolder & "backuplog.txt", _
       "Last backed up: " & Now)
```

This script uses several MsgBox prompts and, if used unaltered, will probably irritate most users. (Hint: think about who will be using the scripts you write when you decide how much error checking and prompting is appropriate.) However, it also shows part of the power of interactive scripting. A little intelligent planning and error trapping can keep your scripts running smoothly, interrupting you only when necessary. Note the use of the `FolderExists` function at the beginning of the script; rather than risking encountering an error, the script checks for a potential problem (a missing file) and then takes the necessary steps to resolve it. Note also that if the folder doesn't exist and the user doesn't want to try again, the user can exit; always give your users a choice to get out if they want.

Because we have implemented some degree of error checking in this script, we include the line `On Error Resume Next` at the beginning of the script. This statement instructs WSH to simply ignore any errors it finds. This doesn't automatically resolve any errors; it just eliminates the error message that would otherwise appear in the event of an error, allowing the script to continue uninterrupted. This way, we're only bothered with the errors that concern us.

This example also uses the `Do...Loop` loop structure (which is similar to the `For...Next` loop, documented earlier in this chapter) at the beginning of the script. The code inside such a loop is repeated until a specific condition is met; in this case, the loop will repeat until the *Accepted* variable has a value of *True* (notice that it's set to *False* at the beginning of the script). The `If...Then` structures insure that the *Accepted* variable is only set to *True* if the folder actually exists.

The second part of the script compares the total size of the folder and all its contents with the amount of free space on the diskette currently inserted in the floppy drive. You could expand the script, so that if the diskette is not sufficient to store the folder, the user is given the opportunity to insert another diskette and try again. You'd need to use a similar `Do...Loop`, as described earlier.

Once the script has gone through all of the tests (eliminating the possibility of many errors), the `FolderCopy` subroutine is used to copy the folder to the floppy. Finally, the `WriteToFile` subroutine is used to record in a logfile that the folder was backed up. Note also the preceding line that adds a backslash (\) to the end of the `MyFolder` variable; this way, we can pass a valid filename (the folder name followed by a backslash and then the filename) to the `WriteToFile` subroutine.

This script requires the following subroutines, which are found earlier in this book: `DriveFreeSpace`, `FolderCopy`, `FolderCreate`, `FolderExists`, `FolderSize`, and `WriteToFile`.

Internet Fish Tank

Nothing exemplifies the power of the Internet more than an Internet-enabled fish tank. This, essentially, is a web page with a dynamic picture of the contents of a fish tank. There are several ways to do this, but the following instructions show that it can be done with nothing more than a script, a camera,* and a common FTP account.

These listings assume that all files are stored in the folder *c:\camera*. Start with the script shown in Example 9-3.

Example 9-3. Internet fish tank script

```
On Error Resume Next

ImageFile = "c:\camera\fish.jpg"
Call FileDelete(ImageFile)
Call RunProgram("c:\camera\camera.exe " & ImageFile, True)
If Not FileExists(ImageFile) Then WScript.Quit

Call RunProgram ("ftp -n -s:c:\camera\ftpscript.txt myhost.com", False)
```

The script starts by suppressing all error messages, as described in the previous example. The subsequent lines use the snapshot utility that comes with nearly all cheap video-conferencing digital cameras to take a photo and save it into a *.jpg* image file.† Note also the line that deletes the old file before the photo is taken, and the line thereafter that checks for the existence of the file before proceeding (in case something went wrong); this way, we never send the same photo twice. The inclusion of `True` in the `RunProgram` line instructs the script to wait for the *camera.exe* program to complete before the script continues, necessary for a script like this to work. You could alternatively incorporate a `Do...Loop` loop instead of the simple `If` statement to repeatedly check for the file over the course of several seconds.

The last line then runs the FTP utility that comes with Windows XP to transfer the JPG file to a web server (available for free from nearly all Internet service providers). Normally, FTP is an interactive program, requiring that the user type commands into the console, but the `-n` and `-s` options shown here eliminate the need for user interaction. Replace *`myhost.com`* with

* See "Add Wireless Support to Any Device" in Chapter 7 for information on wireless webcams.

† Refer to the instructions that come with your camera for the specific command-line syntax you should use. Alternatively, you could use the Timershot program, one of Microsoft's PowerToys for Windows XP, freely available at *http://www.microsoft.com/windowsxp/pro/downloads/powertoys.asp*, to automatically photograph your fish tank at regular intervals. You could then use a similar script to upload the file.

the name of the server containing your web account. Example 9-4 shows the FTP script used by the WSH script in Example 9-3; type it into a plain-text file, and save it as *ftpscript.txt*.

Example 9-4. FTP script for use with Internet-fish-tank script

```
user mylogin
pass mypassword
bin
cd public_html
put c:\camera\fish.jpg
bye
```

The FTP script, like a batch file (see Chapter 10), is simply a text file containing the commands (in order) that otherwise would be typed manually into the FTP console window. Naturally, you'll want to replace the specifics, like *mylogin* and *mypassword*, with your own login and password, respectively, and *public_html* with the directory containing your public HTML files. Note that all commands must be typed in lowercase. Type `FTP -?` at the command prompt for more command-line parameters, or see *Windows XP in a Nutshell* (O'Reilly) for more information on FTP.

Next, you'll want to set up a scheduled task to repeatedly run the script; the interval (5 seconds, 5 minutes, etc.) depends on your needs and the capabilities of your system. Lastly, if you haven't already done it, create a web page that references the *fish.jpg* photo; just visit the page to view a current picture of your fish tank, from anywhere in the world. You can even include JavaScript code in the page to automatically reload itself and update the picture after a certain delay.

This script requires the following subroutines, found earlier in this book: `FileDelete`, `FileExists`, and `RunProgram`.

Smart Phone Dialing

One of the things that scripting can add to a normal task is to make it conditional—that is, perform certain tasks based on predetermined conditions, eliminating user interaction. A simple example is that of a phone dialer that chooses a different phone number depending on the time of day. That phone number can be the prefix for a long-distance carrier or the number of an Internet service provider. Example 9-5 shows such a script.

Example 9-5. Smart dialer script

```
On Error Resume Next

If Hour(Now( )) >= 8 and Hour(Now( )) <= 17 then
```

Example 9-5. Smart dialer script (continued)

```
  Rem -- During the Day --
  Call RunProgram ("c:\links\daytime.lnk", False)
Else
  Rem -- At Night --
  Call RunProgram ("c:\links\nighttime.lnk", False)
End If
```

The script starts by suppressing all error messages, as described in the first script example. The rest of the script is one big `If...Then` structure, which executes a particular part of the script based on the time of day.

The test is performed with the `Hour( )` function, which is built into VBScript.* Similar to the `Minute( )`, `Second( )`, `Day( )`, `Week( )`, `Month( )`, and `Year( )` functions, the expected parameter is a valid time/date string. Here, I've used another built-in function, `Now( )`, which, not surprisingly, returns the current date and time in the proper format. Hence, `Hour(Now( ))` returns the current hour in 24-hour time; for 7:00 p.m., it would return 19.

If it is determined to be daytime (between 8:00 a.m. and 5:00 p.m.), the first code block is used; otherwise, the second code block is used. Naturally, you could put anything you want inside this structure, but for the sake of simplicity, this script just launches one of two shortcuts. The shortcuts could point to dial-up network connections or a phone-dialer utility.

This script requires the `RunProgram` subroutine, found earlier in this book.

Quick SendTo Shortcut Creator

Explorer's **SendTo** menu contains a list of programs and shortcuts to which any selected file can be sent. The idea is to list programs that could be used with any type of file, such as an email program or file viewer, without having to specifically set up file associations for each supported file type. The following script (Example 9-6) allows you to right-click on any application executable (*.exe* file), folder, or drive and create a shortcut in the *SendTo* folder on the spot.

Example 9-6. SendTo shortcut creator

```
SendToFolder = GetSpecialFolder("SendTo")
Call Shortcut("SendToFolder\Notepad.lnk", CommandLine(1))
```

Whenever we can, we want to make our scripts "smart." If we wanted to be lazy, all we would really need is the second line of this script, which creates

* A Visual Basic or VBScript reference will document more cool built-in functions like these.

a shortcut based on the command-line parameter (see "Using Command-Line Parameters in Scripts" earlier in this chapter for details). However, the first line uses the `GetSpecialFolder` function to obtain the location of the *SendTo* folder from the Registry, which is handy if there's more than one user account (each with its own *SendTo* folder), if you intend to use this script on more than one computer, or if you don't want to have to modify the script when Microsoft changes the location of the *SendTo* folder in the next version of Windows.

Once the script has been written, you'll need to associate it with all file types. The "*" file type (located in `HKEY_CLASSES_ROOT\*`) is a wildcard key, used to install context-menu items that affect all registered file types (discussed in "File Types: The Link Between Documents and Applications" in Chapter 4).

This script requires the following subroutines, found earlier in this book: `CommandLine`, `GetSpecialFolder`, and `Shortcut`.

Rename Files with Search and Replace

Although Explorer lets you rename more than one file at a time (as described in Chapter 2), it's not terribly flexible or intuitive. The Command Prompt provides a better multiple file-renaming tool (see the `Ren` command in Chapter 10), but it's not always convenient. Example 9-7 shows a script that will rename all the files in a given folder based on rules you choose.

Example 9-7. File renaming script

```
On Error Resume Next
FolderName = InputBox("Enter the name of the folder:")
If Not FolderExists(FolderName) Then WScript.Quit
SearchText = InputBox("Type the text to look for:")
ReplaceText = InputBox("Type the text with which to replace" _
                                            & SearchText & ":")
If SearchText = "" or ReplaceText = "" Then WScript.Quit

Set FileObject = CreateObject("Scripting.FileSystemObject")
Set FolderObject = FileObject.GetFolder(FolderName)
Set FilesObject = FolderObject.Files

FileCount = 0
For Each Filename in FilesObject
  If InStr(Filename.Name,SearchText) Then
    Filename.Name = Replace(Filename.Name,SearchText,ReplaceText)
    FileCount = FileCount + 1
  End If
Next
```

Example 9-7. File renaming script (continued)

```
If FileCount > 0 Then
  MsgBox FileCount & " files were renamed."
Else
  MsgBox "No filenames containing " & SearchText & " were found."
End If
```

The first section of code is responsible for asking the user for input, including the folder name, the text to look for, and the text with which to replace it. The next three lines set the appropriate objects (for further documentation on these objects, see *http://msdn.microsoft.com/scripting/*).

The `For...Next` structure that follows does the real work: this particular example uses a special form of the loop intended to cycle through all the elements of an object array. In this case, the array contains the filenames of all the files in the active folder. The `Replace` function (built into VBScript) then does the search and replace for each individual filename. Lastly, the `FileCount` variable keeps track of the number of files renamed, the result of which is tallied in the final code section.

Now, it may take some experience to understand the extensive use of objects in this example, but for the time being, just typing it in will serve as a good example that can be used in other circumstances.

This script requires the `FolderExists` subroutine, found earlier in this book.

Note that a far more powerful file-renaming utility, Power Rename (part of Creative Element Power Tools), is available for Windows XP (download it from *http://www.creativelement.com/powertools/*).

Mirror a Folder with Folder Shortcuts

This script is an automated way to perform the solution described in "Mirror a Folder with Folder Shortcuts" in Chapter 4. If you haven't read that section, it's very important that you do so before using this script (see Example 9-8).

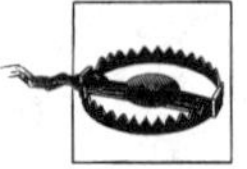

If you create a Folder Shortcut and then try to delete it, you will be deleting the target folder and all of its contents. Folder Shortcuts must be dismantled before they can be removed.

The solution in Chapter 4 essentially involves creating a folder, creating a shortcut, and creating a text file—all possible with a script.

Example 9-8. Folder Shortcut script

```
TargetName = CommandLine(1)
If TargetName = "" Then
  TargetName = InputBox("Type the name of the folder to link:")
End If
If FolderExists(TargetName) = False Then
  MsgBox "TargetName does not appear to be a valid folder."
  WScript.Quit
End If
If Right(TargetName,1) = "\" Then TargetName = Left(TargetName, Len(TargetName) - 1)

DesktopFolder = GetSpecialFolder("Desktop")
If Right(DesktopFolder,1) <> "\" Then DesktopFolder = DesktopFolder + "\"

X = 0
Do
  Y = X
  X = InStr(X + 1, TargetName, "\")
Loop until X = 0
NewTargetName = DesktopFolder + "Shortcut to " + Mid(TargetName, Y + 1)

If FolderExists(NewTargetName) = False Then
  MsgBox "NewTargetName already exists."
  WScript.Quit
End If

FolderCreate(NewTargetName)
Call Shortcut(NewTargetName + "\target.lnk", TargetName)

Text = "[.ShellClassInfo]" + chr(13) + chr(10) + _
"CLSID2={0AFACED1-E828-11D1-9187-B532F1E9575D}" + chr(13) + chr(10) + _
     "Flags=2" + chr(13) + chr(10) + _
"ConfirmFileOp=0" + chr(13) + chr(10)

Call WriteToFile(NewTargetName + "\desktop.ini", Text)
Call SetAttributes(NewTargetName + "\desktop.ini", 6)
```

This script is complex, but when broken down, it should be fairly easy to understand. First, the script asks for the name of an existing folder and checks to see if that folder exists. If a trailing slash is found, it is removed. The script then uses the `GetSpecialFolder` function to read the Registry and obtain the location of the current user's Desktop folder (where the new Folder Shortcut will be placed). The next block of code extracts the name of the folder from the path: if `c:\windows\temp` is typed, this code extracts the text `temp`. The script then forms a new path, checks to see if it already exists, and then creates the new folder.

Then, according to the steps described in "Mirror a Folder with Folder Shortcuts" in Chapter 4, a shortcut is created and several lines are written to the file *desktop.ini*. Lastly, the Hidden and System attributes for *desktop.ini* are turned on.

The beauty of this script is that it is almost entirely automated. It doesn't ask for any information it's able to safely retrieve itself. The very first line also checks to see if there's a command-line parameter specified. This enables you to use this script in a folder's context menu, so that you could right-click on any folder and select **Make Folder Shortcut**, and the script would do the rest. See "Using Command-Line Parameters in Scripts" earlier in this chapter and "Customize Context Menus" in Chapter 4 for details. For another similar example, see "Print Out a Folder Listing" in Chapter 4.

This script requires the following subroutines, which are found earlier in this book: `CommandLine`, `FolderCreate`, `FolderExists`, `GetSpecialFolder`, `RegistryRead`, `SetAttributes`, and `WriteToFile`.

This sample script does not accommodate Folder Shortcuts for FTP sites, although it can be modified to work with Internet Shortcut files instead of Folders.

Regardless, I leave it to you to put the final pieces together!

CHAPTER 10

The Command Prompt

If you don't quite have a grasp on the concept of DOS or the Command Prompt, here's a quick primer on this useful but oft-forgotten interface.

The Command Prompt in Windows XP is based on MS-DOS (Microsoft Disk Operating System), the operating system used by the first PCs and the basis for many versions of Windows, including 9x/Me. As explained in Chapter 1, however, the Windows XP/2000/NT platform has been designed from the ground up to be completely independent of DOS.

Fortunately, the DOS-like Command Prompt is still available from within Windows. If you don't have a **Command Prompt** item in your Start Menu, go to **Start → Run**, type `cmd`, and press **Enter**.

Windows XP also comes with the Command Prompt application found in Windows 9x/Me (*command.com*), but this should only be used if some DOS program won't work in the superior XP version (*cmd.exe*). Among other things, the XP Command Prompt has better support for long filenames and supports command-prompt extensions, used by some of the commands listed here.

When you open a Command Prompt window, you'll see a window that looks like the one shown in Figure 10-1. The cursor indicates the command line (where commands are typed), and the prompt usually shows the current working directory (here, *C:\Documents and Settings\Administrator\Desktop*), followed by a caret/angle bracket (>).

To run a program or execute a command, just type the name of the program or command at the command line (also called the *C prompt* because it usually looks like **C:\>**), and press **Enter**.

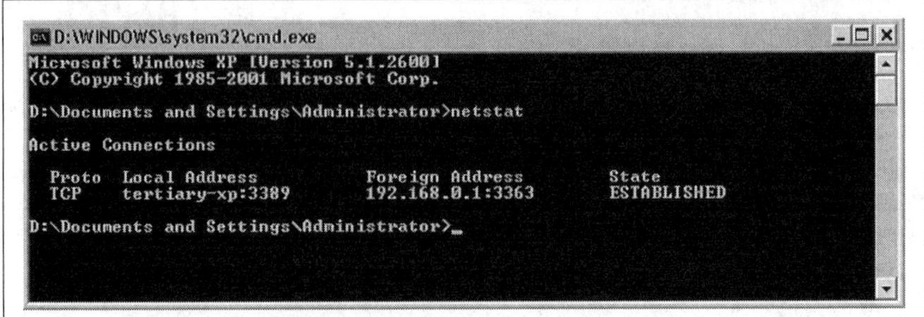
D:\WINDOWS\system32\cmd.exe
Microsoft Windows XP [Version 5.1.2600]
(C) Copyright 1985-2001 Microsoft Corp.
D:\Documents and Settings\Administrator>netstat
Active Connections
Proto Local Address Foreign Address State
TCP tertiary-xp:3389 192.168.0.1:3363 ESTABLISHED
D:\Documents and Settings\Administrator>_

Figure 10-1. The Command Prompt is used to implement some solutions in this book

Some command-prompt applications simply display information and then exit immediately. For example, Figure 10-1 shows some output from the Active Connections utility (*netstat.exe*) discussed in "Scan Your System for Open Ports" in Chapter 7.

DOS Commands

You should know the following basic DOS commands to be able to complete some of the solutions in this book and get by in the world of Windows.

This, however, should not be considered a comprehensive list of all DOS commands and their options. See *Windows XP in a Nutshell* (O'Reilly) for a more thorough reference, not only on the Command Prompt, but on all of the various utilities included with Windows XP that use the Command Prompt.

The commands shown here are in `constant width`, and any parameters (the information you supply to the command) are in *`constant width italic`*. It doesn't matter which case you use when you type them in the command prompt (DOS, like Windows, is not case-sensitive). If there is more than one parameter, each is separated by a space:

`attrib` *`attributes filename`*

Changes the attributes of a file or folder. The four attributes are `R` for *read only*, `S` for *system*, `A` for *archive*, and `H` for *hidden*.

In Explorer, you can right-click a file or group of files and select **Properties** to change the attributes; `attrib` is the DOS counterpart to this functionality. In addition, `attrib` lets you change the `S` (system) attribute, something Explorer doesn't let you do. Here are some examples:

`attrib +h` *`myfile.txt`*

- This turns *on* the `H` parameter for the file *`myfile.txt`*, making the file hidden.

`attrib -r "`*`another file.doc`*`"`

- This turns *off* the `R` (read-only) parameter for the file *another file.doc* (note that quotation marks are used because of the space in the filename).

Type `attrib /?` for additional options.

Command Prompt

`cd` *`foldername`*

Changes the working directory to `foldername`. If the prompt indicates you are in *C:\Windows* and you want to enter the *c:\Windows\System32* folder, type `cd system32`. You can also switch to any folder on your hard disk by including the full path of the folder. Type `cd ..` to go to the parent folder. Type `cd` by itself to display the current directory.

To switch to another drive, just type the drive letter, followed by a colon (:). For example, type `a:` to switch to the floppy drive.

`cls`

Clear the display and empty the buffer (the history of output accessible with the scrollbar.)

`copy` *`filename destination`*

Copies a file to another directory or drive, specified by `destination`. This is the same as dragging and dropping files in Explorer, except that the keyboard is used instead of the mouse. For example, to copy the file *myfile.txt* (located in the current working directory) to your floppy drive, type `copy myfile.txt a:\`. Type `copy /?` for additional options.

`del` *`filename`*

Deletes a file. For example, in order to delete the file *myfile.txt*, type `del myfile.txt`. This is not exactly the same as deleting a file in Windows, because the file will *not* be stored in the Recycle Bin. The advantage of the DOS variant is that you can more easily and quickly delete a group of files, such as all the files with the *.tmp* extension: `del *.tmp`. Type `del /?` for additional options.

`dir` *`name`*

Displays a listing of all the files and directories in the current working directory. Use `cd` to change to a different directory, or type `dir c:\files` to display the contents of *C:\Files* without having to first use the `cd` command. Type `dir /p` to pause the display after each page, useful for very long listings. You can also specify wildcards to filter the results; type `dir *.tmp` to display only files with the *.tmp* filename extension. Type `dir /?` for additional options.

`echo` *`text`*

Displays the specified text, *`text`*, on the screen, See "Variables and the Environment," later in this chapter.

`exit`
: Closes the Command Prompt window. In most situations, you can just click the close button [x] on the upper-right corner of the Window, but the `exit` command works just as well.

`md` *`foldername`*
: Stands for make directory. This command creates a new directory with the name *`foldername`*. The command will have no effect if there's already a directory or file with the same name.

`move` *`filename destination`*
: Is the same as `copy`, except that the file is moved instead of copied. Type `move /?` for additional options.

`rd` *`foldername`*
: Stands for remove directory. This command removes an existing directory with the name *`foldername`*. The command will have no effect if the directory is not empty. To remove a directory and all of its contents, use `deltree`.

`ren` *`oldfilename newfilename`*
: Renames a file to *`newfilename`*. This is especially useful, because you can use the `ren` command to rename more than one file at once—something Explorer doesn't let you do. For example, to rename *hisfile.txt* to *herfile.txt*, type `ren hisfile.txt herfile.txt`. To change the extensions of all the files in the current working directory from *.txt* to *.doc*, type `ren *.txt *.doc`. Type `ren /?` for additional options.

`set [`*`variable`*`=[`*`string`*`]]`
: When used without any arguments, displays a list of active environment variables (described in "Variables and the Environment," later in this appendix). The `set` command is also used to assign data to environment variables.

`TYPE` *`filename`*
: Displays the contents of a text file. Type `type filename | more` to display the file and pause between each page of information rather than display the whole file at once.

Batch Files: The Other Way to Do It

When it comes to quick-and-dirty scripting, it's hard to beat DOS batch files. Batch files, similar to WSH scripts (discussed in Chapter 9), are plain-text files with the *.bat* filename extension. However, rather than relying on a complex, unfamiliar scripting language, batch files simply consist of one or more DOS commands, typed one after another.

Using Long Filenames in the Command Prompt

Unlike the DOS window in Windows 9x/Me, the Windows XP Command Prompt fully supports long filenames. However, given the nature of the command line, there are times when specifying long filenames will cause a problem. Specifically, if the file or folder name you're typing contains a space, you may need to enclose the filename in quotes.

Say you wish to rename a file named *my stuff.txt* to *her stuff.doc*. Instinctively, you might type:

```
ren my stuff.txt her stuff.doc
```

However, this won't work, since the ren command believes that you've typed *four* parameters. Instead, you'll need to use quotation marks, like this:

```
ren "my stuff.txt" "her stuff.doc"
```

Now, this isn't always the case. For example, if you want to use the cd command to change the current working directory to *Program Files*, like this:

```
cd Program Files
```

the Command Prompt is smart enough to interpret this correctly, and no quotation marks are needed.

One of the problems with Windows-based scripting (see Chapter 9) is that it tries to control a graphical environment with a command-based language. Because DOS is a command-based interface, DOS-based scripting (batch files) is a natural extension of the environment.

Consider the following four DOS commands:

```
c:
cd \windows\temp
attrib -r *.tmp
del *.tmp
```

If you type these commands into a plain-text editor, such as Notepad, save it into a *.bat* file, and then execute the batch file by double-clicking or typing its name at the Command Prompt, it will have the same effect as if the commands were manually typed consecutively at the prompt. Obviously, this can be a tremendous time saver if you find yourself entering the same DOS commands repeatedly.

When you run a batch file, each command in the file will be displayed (echoed) on the screen before it's executed, which can be unsightly for the more compulsive among us. To turn off the echoing of any given command, precede it with the @ character. To turn off the printing of all commands in a batch file, place the command @echo off at the beginning of the batch file.

Batch files can be executed by double-clicking them in Explorer or by typing their names at a DOS prompt. You'll want to put more frequently used, general-purpose batch files in a folder specified in the system path (see "The Path Less Traveled," later in this chapter), so that they can be executed from the command prompt, regardless of the current working directory.

Although batch files can run Windows programs (just type `notepad` to launch Notepad), it's preferable to run Windows programs with Windows Script Host scripts, because they'll be able to run without having to first load a Command Prompt window.

In addition to the standard DOS commands, most of which are documented earlier in this chapter, batch files use a couple of extra statements to fill the holes. Variables, conditional statements, and `For...Next` loops are all implemented with statements that are ordinarily not much use outside of batch files.

The following topics cover the concepts used to turn a task or a string of DOS commands into a capable batch file.

Variables and the Environment

The use of variables in batch files can be somewhat confusing. All variables used in a batch file (with the exception of command-line parameters) are stored in the *environment*—an area of memory that is created when you first boot and is kept around until the computer is turned off. The environment variable space is discussed in more detail in "The Path Less Traveled," later in this chapter.

To view the contents of the environment, type `set` without any arguments. To set a variable to a particular value, type this command:

```
set VariableName=Some Data
```

Unlike VBScript (see Chapter 9), the `set` command is required and no quotation marks are used when setting the value of a variable. To remove the variable from memory, you set its value to nothing, like this:

```
set VariableName=
```

To then display the contents of the variable, use the `echo` command, as follows:

```
echo %VariableName%
```

Here, the percent signs (%) on both ends of the variable name are mandatory; otherwise, the `echo` command would take its arguments literally and display the name of the variable rather than the data it contains.

What's confusing is that in some cases, variables need no percent signs; sometimes they need one, sometimes two at the beginning, or sometimes one on each end. See the following topics for details.

Flow Control

Batch files have a very rudimentary, but easy-to-understand flow-control structure. The following example exhibits the use of the goto command:

```
@echo off
echo  Griff
echo  Asa
goto LaterOn
echo  Ox
:LaterOn
echo  Etch
```

The :LaterOn line (note the mandatory colon prefix) is called a label, which is used as a target for the goto command. If you follow the flow of the script, you should expect the following output:

```
Griff
Asa
Etch
```

because the goto command has caused the Ox line to be skipped. The label can appear before or after the goto line in a batch file, and you can have multiple goto commands and multiple labels.

Command-Line Parameters

Suppose you executed a batch file called *Demo.bat* by typing the following at the DOS prompt:

```
Demo file1.txt file2.txt
```

Both file1.txt and file2.txt are command-line parameters and are automatically stored in two variables, *%1* and *%2*, respectively, when the batch file is run.

The implication is that you could run a batch file that would then act with the parameters that have been passed to it. A common use of this feature is, as shown in the previous example, to specify one or more filenames, which are then manipulated or used in some way by the batch file. "Turn the Address Bar into a Command Prompt," later in this chapter, shows a batch file that utilizes command-line parameters.

The following two-line example uses command-line parameters and the FC utility to compare two text files. A similar example using the Windows Script

Host, shown in "Making Building Blocks with Subroutines and Functions" in Chapter 9, takes 22 lines to accomplish approximately the same task:

```
fc %1 %2 >c:\windows\temp\output.txt
notepad c:\windows\temp\output.txt
```

Save this batch file as *compare.bat*, and execute it like this:

```
compare c:\windows\tips.txt c:\windows\faq.txt
```

which will compare the two files, *tips.txt* and *faq.txt* (both located in your Windows folder), save the output to a temporary file, and then display the output by opening the file in Notepad. Note that the > character on the first line redirects the output of the FC program to the *output.txt* file, which would otherwise be displayed on the screen. The second line then opens the *output.txt* file in Notepad for easy viewing.

There are ways, other than typing, to take advantage of command-line parameters. If you place a shortcut to a batch file (say, *Demo.bat*) in your *SendTo* folder, then right-click on a file in Explorer, select **Send To** and then **Demo**, the *Demo.bat* batch file will be executed with the file you've selected as the first command-line parameter. Likewise, if you drag-drop any file onto the batch-file icon in Explorer, the dropped file will be used as the command-line parameter.*

Batch files have a limit of 9 command-line parameters (`%1` through `%9`), although there's a way to have more if you need them. Say you need to accept 12 parameters at the command line; your batch file should start by acting on the first parameter. Then, you would issue the `shift` command, which eliminates the first parameter, putting the second in its place. `%2` becomes `%1`, `%3` becomes `%2`, and so on. Just repeat the process until there are no parameters left. Here's an example of this process:

```
:StartOfLoop
if "%1"=="" exit
del %1
shift
goto StartOfLoop
```

Save these commands into *MultiDel.bat*. Now, this simple batch file deletes one or more filenames with a single command; it's used like this:

```
MultiDel file1.txt another.doc third.log
```

by cycling through the command-line parameters one by one using `shift`. It repeats the same two lines (`del %1` and `shift`) until the `%1` variable is empty

* If you drop more than one file on a batch-file icon, their order as arguments will be seemingly random, theoretically mirroring their ordering in your hard disk's file table.

(see "Conditional Statements," next, for the use of the if statement), at which point the batch file ends (using the exit command).

Conditional Statements

There are three versions of the if statement, which allow you to compare values and check the existence of files. The first version, which is usually used to test the value of a variable, is used as follows:

```
if "%1"=="help" goto SkipIt
```

Note the use of quotation marks around the variable name and the help text, as well as the double equals signs, all of which are necessary. Notice also there's no then keyword, which those of you who are familiar with VBScript (see Chapter 9) might expect. If the batch file finds that the two sides are equal, it executes everything on the right side of the statement; in this case, it issues the goto command.

The second use of the if command is to test for the existence of a file:

```
if exist c:\windows\tips.txt goto SkipIt
```

If the file *c:\windows\tips.txt* exists, the goto command will be executed. Similarly, you can you can test for the absence of a file, as follows:

```
if not exist c:\autoexec.bat goto SkipIt
```

The third use of the if command is to check the outcome of the previous command, as follows:

```
if errorlevel 0 goto SkipIt
```

If there was any problem with the statement immediately before this line, the errorlevel (which is similar to a system-defined variable) will be set to some nonzero number. The if statement shown here tests for any errorlevel that is greater than zero; if there is no error, execution will simply continue to the next command.

Here's a revised version of the file-compare example first shown in the "Command-Line Parameters" section earlier in this chapter:

```
if "%1"=="" goto problem
if "%2"=="" goto problem
if not exist %1 goto problem
if not exist %2 goto problem
fc %1 %2 >c:\windows\temp\output.txt
if errorlevel 0 goto problem
if not exist c:\windows\temp\output.txt goto problem
notepad c:\windows\temp\output.txt
exit
:problem
echo "A problem has been encountered."
```

This batch file is essentially the same as the original two-line example shown earlier, except that some error-checking statements that utilize the `if` statement have been added to make the batch file a little more robust. If you neglect to enter one or both command-line parameters, or if the files you specify as command-line parameters don't exist, the batch file will display the error message. An even more useful version might have multiple error messages that more accurately describe the specific problem that was encountered.

Loops

Batch files have a very simple looping mechanism, based loosely on the `For...Next` loop used in other programming languages. The main difference is that the batch file `for` loop doesn't increment a variable regularly, but rather cycles it through a list of values. Its syntax is as follows:

```
for %%i in ("Abe","Monty","Jasper") do echo %%i
```

Here, the variable syntax gets even more confusing; the reference to the `i` variable when used in conjunction with the `for...in...do` statement gets two percent signs in front of the variable name and none after. Note also that only single-letter variables can be used here.

If you execute this batch file, you'll get the following output:

```
Abe
Monty
Jasper
```

Note also the use of the quotation marks; although they aren't strictly necessary, they're helpful if one or more of the values in the list has a comma in it.

To simulate a more traditional `For...Next` statement in a batch file, type the following:

```
for %%i in (1,2,3,4,5) do echo %%i
```

Simulating Subroutines

Batch files have no support for named subroutines (as described in "Making Building Blocks with Subroutines and Functions" in Chapter 9). However, you can simulate subroutines by creating several batch files: one *main* file and one or more *subordinate* files (each of which can accept command-line parameters). You probably won't want to do this if performance is an issue.

This is useful in cases like the `for...in...do` statement (described in the preceding section), which can only loop a single command.

In one batch file, called *WriteIt.bat*, type:

```
if "%1"=="" exit
if exist %1.txt del %1.txt
echo This is a text > %1.txt
```

Then, in another batch file, called *Main.bat*, type the following:

```
for %%i in ("Kang","Kodos","Serak") do call WriteIt.bat %%i
```

Command Prompt

The single-line *Main.bat* batch file uses the `call` command to run the other batch file, *WriteIt.bat*, three times. The `call` command allows one batch file to run another batch file; if it's omitted, one batch file can still run another, but the first batch file will abruptly end upon running the second batch file.

When this pair of batch files is run, you should end up with three files, *Kang.txt*, *Kodos.txt*, and *Serak.txt*, all containing the text, "This is a text." The `if` statement, as well as the `for...in...do` loop, are explained in earlier sections.

Command Prompt Integration

Now that you know how to use the Command Prompt, you'll need to find ways to get to it quickly, so that it can be as useful as possible.

Turn the Address Bar into a Command Prompt

If you select **Run** from the Start Menu, the box that appears is essentially a limited command prompt; you can execute any program, open any folder, or launch any Internet URL simply by typing it here. Explorer and your taskbar also have the Address Bar, which essentially accomplishes the same thing as **Run**.

The problem with both the **Run** command and the **Address Bar** is that they can only be used to launch programs; they don't understand intrinsic DOS commands, like `dir` and `copy` (discussed earlier in this chapter). However, there is a way to have the Address Bar mimic all the functions of the Command Prompt and therefore have a true command prompt always within reach:

1. Start by making the Address Bar visible, if it's not already. Right-click on an empty area of your taskbar; select **Toolbars** and then **Address Bar**.*

* This solution focuses on the Address Bar on the taskbar, although it also works for the Address Bar in Explorer.

Your taskbar will then contain the Address Bar, which is dockable, resizable, and removable: you can move it around the taskbar or even tear it off by dragging it. Your taskbar will look something like Figure 10-2.

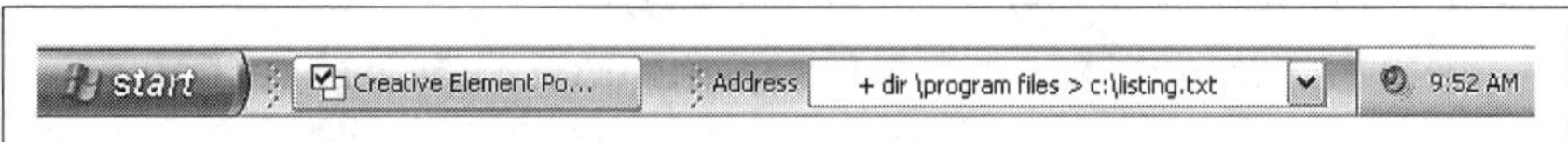

Figure 10-2. The Address Bar can be put to good use as a handy command prompt

2. You'll immediately be able to run programs, open folders, and launch URLs simply by typing them and pressing **Enter**.
3. To add DOS command functionality, you'll need the assistance of a batch file (discussed earlier in this appendix). Open a text editor, such as Notepad, and type the following:

```
@echo off
if "%1"=="" exit
if exist c:\windows\temp\temp.bat del c:\windows\temp\temp.bat
echo %1 %2 %3 %4 %5 %6 %7 %8 %9 > c:\windows\temp\temp.bat
call c:\windows\temp\temp.bat
if exist c:\windows\temp\temp.bat del c:\windows\temp\temp.bat
```

   You may have to change the references to *c:\windows\temp* to match the location of your *Temp* folder.
4. Save it as *+.bat* (just the plus sign followed by the *.bat* filename extension) in a convenient location, such as your *\Windows* folder.
5. Now, to run a DOS command from the Address Bar, simply precede it with a plus sign (+) and a single space, like this:

```
+ copy c:\bootlog.txt a:\
```

   You can even have the output of a DOS command redirected to a file, as follows:

```
+ dir c:\windows > c:\windir.txt
```

Here's how it works: the batch file reads what you've typed after the + and writes it to a new, but temporary, batch file. The new batch file is then executed, and the command you've typed is carried out. When it's finished, the temporary batch file is deleted.

The plus key was chosen for the name of the batch file because it's convenient and not likely to conflict with any other software or commands; the one on your keyboard's numeric keypad is usually more convenient than the one near your backspace key (**Shift-=**). However, you can certainly replace + with any other character, such as ` or -, as long as you rename the batch file accordingly.

There are some limitations to this design. Although it does mimic the Command Prompt, it only allows a single command at a time, after which the context is forgotten. What this means is that such commands as cd won't have much meaning—you can certainly type `+ cd directoryname`, but the "current directory" will be forgotten once the command has been executed. To get around this, include the full path with your commands. Instead of the following series of statements:

```
d:
cd \myfolder
del *.tmp
```

just type this:

```
+ del d:\myfolder\*.tmp
```

Of course, if you find that you need to type several consecutive commands, you can always just type cmd in the Address Bar to launch a full-fledged Command Prompt window.

Open a Command Prompt window in any folder

If you find yourself using the Command Prompt frequently, you'll probably benefit from the following solution. Instead of having to use the cd command to change to a given folder, you can simply open a Command Prompt window on the fly in Explorer, already rooted in the selected folder:

1. Open the Registry Editor (discussed in Chapter 3).
2. Expand the branches to: HKEY_CLASSES_ROOT\Directory\shell. See the discussion of file types in Chapter 4 for more information on the structure of this branch of the Registry.
3. Create a new key by going to **Edit → New → Key**, and type cmd for the name of this new key.
4. Double-click the (default) value in the new cmd key, and type the following for its contents:

   ```
   Open Command &Prompt Here
   ```

5. Next, create a new key here by going to **Edit → New → Key**, and type command for the name of the new key.
6. Double-click the (default) value in the new command key, and type the following for its contents:

   ```
   cmd.exe /k "cd %L && ver"
   ```

   This line launches the *cmd.exe* application, and then, using the /k parameter, instructs it to carry out the following two commands:

   ```
   cd %1
   ver
   ```

The first command changes the working directory to the folder that has been right-clicked, and the second displays the Windows version.

7. Close the Registry Editor when you're done; the change will take effect immediately. Just right-click any folder and select **Open Command Prompt Here** to open a Command Prompt at the selected folder.

The Path Less Traveled

Although it isn't really emphasized as much as it was in the heyday of DOS and Windows 3.x, the system path is still an important setting in Windows XP. It can be helpful as well as detrimental, depending on how it's used.

The system path is simply a listing of folder names kept in memory during an entire Windows session. If a folder name is listed in your system path, you'll be able to run a program contained in that folder *without* having to specify its location. This is most apparent when you use the Start Menu's **Run** command, Explorer's Address Bar, or a Command Prompt window, and type a program filename, such as `Notepad`. If all is well, Notepad will start, even though you didn't specify the full path (e.g. *c:\Windows*) of the folder containing the *notepad.exe* file. This is because *Notepad.exe* is located in a folder that, by default, is listed in the system path.

The path is one of several *environment variables* that are kept in memory from Windows startup until you shut down. In previous versions of Windows, the path was set with a line in the *Autoexec.bat* file (now obsolete); in Windows XP, all environment variables are set by going to **Control Panel → System → Advanced** tab **→ Environment Variables**.

By default, the system variable, *`Path`*, contains the following folders:

```
%SystemRoot%
%SystemRoot%\system32
%SystemRoot%\system32\WBEM
```

This means that an executable (*.exe* file) placed in any of these folders is instantly accessible from any folder on the system. The `%SystemRoot%` element represents the Windows folder, usually *c:\Windows*, and is so specified to account for systems where the Windows folder has been placed on a different drive or in a different folder.

One of the consequences of this design is that if two different versions of the same file are placed in two different folders in the path, only one of the available versions of the file—and not necessarily the most recent one—may be in use at any given time. Now, the same rules that apply to program executables also apply to shared files, such as *.dll*, *.vbx*, and *.vxd* files, so the issue of version control is an important one that can affect any application on your system.

How do you escape this trap? First, remove any unnecessary directories from your path variable. Next, if you suspect a conflict with a specific file, try searching your hard disk for the filename (select **Search** and then **For Files or Folders** from the Start Menu, and select **Local Hard Drives** from the **Look in** list). If you see more than one copy of the file in the search results window, it could potentially cause a conflict. Widen the **In Folder** column in the Search Results window so you can see where each file is located. If one of them is in *\Windows\System* (or any other Windows subdirectories, for that matter), then it most likely belongs there. Compare the versions of the files by right-clicking, selecting **Properties**, and clicking on the **Version** tabs. Now, you want to end up with only the newest file on your system, so what you can do at this point is simply delete (or temporarily rename, to be on the safe side) all versions but the most recent. Then move the newest file to your *\Windows\System32* folder if it's not already there.

Note that this solution by no means applies to all *.dll* files, which is why it's smart to back up any files before continuing. Some files have identical names only by coincidence, although this is rare. Of course, deleting a file just because there's another around by the same name is not a good idea unless you know that the files serve the same purpose. One way to make sure is to look through *all* the information in the **Version** tab; if the **Company Name** and **Product Name** are the same, you can be pretty sure that the files are duplicates. On the other hand, if the files have vastly different sizes, odds are that one is not a suitable replacement for the other.

APPENDIX A

Setting Locator

It shouldn't take you too long to find that the various options, switches, and adjustments that allow you to customize Windows are scattered throughout dozens of dialog boxes, property sheets, and add-on utilities. Understandably, this can turn a simple task into a monumental wild-goose chase. The following list contains more than 700 individual Windows XP settings and where to find them.

The settings are listed alphabetically and named in such a way that they should be easy to locate by context. For example, to find out how to turn off the Power Management icon in the Taskbar Notification Area, look under "Taskbar Notification Area, Power Icon." Note that a few settings have been duplicated with different labels to make them easier to find.

Settings made in the Registry (see Chapter 3) are not included here because of their complexity. Most Registry settings can be found by using the Registry Editor's Find tool or by looking through this book.

Of special note here is TweakUI, a special utility that Microsoft has made available to allow you to change some settings otherwise inaccessible in the Windows interface. TweakUI can be downloaded from the Microsoft web site or from *http://www.annoyances.org*.

Alphabetical Listing of All Windows XP Settings

Accessibility, additional settings for web pages
Control Panel → Internet Options → General tab → Accessibility

Accessibility, enable / disable warnings & notifications
Control Panel → Accessibility Options → General tab

Accessibility, move Magnifier with focus change in web pages
Control Panel → Internet Options → Advanced tag → Accessibility → Move system caret with focus/selection changes

Address Bar, Go button
See "Go button"

Address Bar, history settings
Control Panel → Internet Options → General tab → History section

Address Bar, search settings
Control Panel → Internet Options → Advanced tag → Search from the Address bar

Address Bar, show in Explorer
Explorer → View → Toolbars → Address Bar

Address Bar, show on taskbar
Right-click on empty area of taskbar → Toolbars → Address

Address Bar, show the full path of current folder
Control Panel → Folder Options → View tab → Display the full path in the address bar

Address Book, make the default contact list
Control Panel → Internet Options → Programs tab → Contact list

Address Book, profile assistant (enable/disable)
Control Panel → Internet Options → Advanced tag → Security → Enable Profile Assistant

Address Book, set default profile for AutoComplete
Control Panel → Internet Options → Content tab → My Profile

Administrative Tools, show in Start Menu (Classic Start Menu only)
Control Panel → Taskbar and Start Menu → Start Menu tab → Customize → "Advanced Start menu options" section → Display Administrative Tools

Administrative Tools, show in Start Menu (XP Start Menu only)
Control Panel → Taskbar and Start Menu → Start Menu tab → Customize → Advanced tab → "Start menu items" section → System Administrative Tools

Advanced Power Management, additional settings
Your computer's BIOS setup; see Appendix B

Advanced Power Management, effect on Offline files
Explorer → Tools → Synchronize → Setup → On Idle tab → Advanced → Prevent synchronization when my computer is running on battery power

Advanced Power Management, effect on Scheduled Tasks
Control Panel → Scheduled Tasks → right-click task → Properties → Settings tab → Power Management section

Advanced Power Management, enable / disable
Control Panel → Power Options → APM tab → Enable Advanced Power Management support

Alt Key, make it "sticky"
Control Panel → Accessibility Options → Keyboard tab → Use StickyKeys

Animation, enable / disable selectively
Control Panel → System → Advanced tab → Performance section → Settings → Visual Effects tab → Custom

TweakUI → General

Animation, fading between web pages
Control Panel → Internet Options → Advanced tag → Browsing → Enable page transitions

Animation, show animated GIFs in web pages
Control Panel → Internet Options → Advanced tag → Multimedia → Play animations in web pages

Animation, smooth scrolling of lists
TweakUI → Explorer → Enable smooth scrolling

Animation, smooth scrolling of web pages
Control Panel → Internet Options → Advanced tag → Browsing → Use smooth scrolling

Applications, ending
Task Manager (*taskmgr.exe*) → Applications tab

Applications, ending background processes
Task Manager (*taskmgr.exe*) → Processes tab

Applications, prevent from loading
Control Panel → Advanced tab → Performance → Settings → Data Execution Prevention tab

Applications, list loaded DLLs
System Information (*winmsd.exe*) → Software Environment → Loaded Modules

AutoComplete, edit data
Control Panel → Internet Options → Content tab → My Profile

AutoComplete, enable / disable
Control Panel → Internet Options → Advanced tag → Browsing → Use inline AutoComplete

AutoComplete, Profile Assistant (enable/disable)
Control Panel → Internet Options → Advanced tag → Security → Enable Profile Assistant

AutoComplete, settings
Control Panel → Internet Options → Content tab → AutoComplete

Autodial
See "Dialing"

Autoexec.bat, parse at logon
TweakUI → Logon

Automatic Windows Update settings
Control Panel → System → Automatic Updates tab

Autoplay
Explorer → right-click CD drive icon → Properties → AutoPlay tab

TweakUI → My Computer → AutoPlay

Background, create and modify
Paint (*mspaint.exe*) → save as *.bmp* in Windows folder

Background, select and configure
Control Panel → Display → Desktop tab

Balloon tips
(big tooltips that pop up from taskbar notification area)
TweakUI → Taskbar → Enable balloon tips

Browser, set default
Control Panel → Internet Options → Programs tab → Internet Explorer should check to see whether it is the default browser

Button color
Control Panel → Display → Appearance tab → Advanced → Item list → choose "3d Objects"

Calendar, default application
Control Panel → Internet Options → Programs tab → Calendar

Calling
See "Dialing"

Cascading Style Sheets
See "Style Sheets"

CD, autoplay
See "Autoplay"

CD Burning, folder location
TweakUI → My Computer → Special Folders

Certificates, check for revocation in Internet Explorer
Control Panel → Internet Options → Advanced tag → Security

Certificates, Internet Explorer settings for secure sites
Control Panel → Internet Options → Content tab → Certificates section

Certificates, warn about invalid certificates in Internet Explorer
Control Panel → Internet Options → Advanced tag → Security → Warn about invalid site certificates

Clock, show on the taskbar
Control Panel → Taskbar and Start Menu → Taskbar tab → Show the clock

Code page conversion table
Control Panel → Regional and Language Options → Advanced tab → Code page conversion tables

Color profiles, associate with device
Right-click on .icm file → Properties → Associate Device tab

Color profiles, management
Control Panel → Display → Settings tab → Advanced → Color Management tab

Colors, change for all display elements
Control Panel → Display → Appearance tab → Advanced

Colors, encrypted and compressed files
TweakUI → Explorer → Colors

Colors, in web pages
Control Panel → Internet Options → General tab → Colors

Colors, increase or decrease number of supported colors (color depth)
Control Panel → Display → Settings tab → Color Quality

Colors, show high contrast screen colors
Control Panel → Accessibility Options → Display tab → Use High Contrast

Combo boxes, enable / disable animation
Control Panel → System → Advanced tab → Performance section → Settings → Visual Effects tab → Custom

Command keys, customize
TweakUI → Explorer → Command Keys

Command Prompt, filename completion
TweakUI → Command Prompt

Command Prompt, settings
Command Prompt window → Control Menu

Compressed NTFS files, choose color
TweakUI → Explorer → Colors

Compressed NTFS files, differentiate with a different color
Control Panel → Folder Options → View tab → Show encrypted or compressed NTFS files in color

Contact list, default
Control Panel → Internet Options → Programs tab → Contact list

Control Panel, security policies
Group Policy (*gpedit.msc*) → User Configuration → Administrative Templates → Control Panel

Control Panel, categories (show/hide)
Control Panel → Tools → Options → General tab → Show common tasks in folders → Ok → Switch to Classic View or Switch to Category View

Control Panel, icons (show/hide)
TweakUI → Control Panel

Control Panel, show as menu in Start Menu (Classic Start Menu only)
Control Panel → Taskbar and Start Menu → Start Menu tab → Customize → "Advanced Start menu options" section → Expand Control Panel

Control Panel, show as menu in Start Menu (XP Start Menu only)
Control Panel → Taskbar and Start Menu → Start Menu tab → Customize → Advanced tab → "Start menu items" section → Control Panel

Control Panel, show in My Computer
Control Panel → Folder Options → View tab → Show Control Panel in My Computer

TweakUI → My Computer

Cookies, change settings (block, allow, prompt)
Control Panel → Internet Options → Privacy tab → Advanced → Override automatic cookie handling

Cookies, change settings for specific web sites (block, allow, prompt)
Control Panel → Internet Options → Privacy tab → Edit

Cookies, delete all
Control Panel → Internet Options → General tab → Temporary Internet Files section → Delete Cookies

Country, choose for dialing preferences
Control Panel → Phone and Modem Options → Dialing Rules tab → select location → Edit → Country/region

Country, choose for localized information
Control Panel → Regional and Language Options → Regional Options tab → Location section

Crashes, send reports to Microsoft
Control Panel → System → Advanced tab → Error Reporting

Critical Update Notification
Control Panel → System → Automatic Updates tab

Ctrl Key, make it "sticky"
Control Panel → Accessibility Options → Keyboard tab → Use StickyKeys

Ctrl-Alt-Del window, settings
Group Policy (*gpedit.msc*) → User Configuration → Administrative Templates → System → Ctrl+Alt+Del Options

Currency, customize display
Control Panel → Regional and Language Options → Regional Options tab → Customize → Currency tab

Cursor, mouse cursor
See "Mouse Cursor"

Cursor, text cursor
See "Text Cursor"

Data Execution Prevention (DEP) (enable/disable)
Control Panel → Advanced tab → Performance → Settings → Data Execution Prevention tab

Date, customize display
Control Panel → Regional and Language Options → Regional Options tab → Customize → Date tab

Date, set
Control Panel → Date and Time → Date & Time tab

Daylight Savings, enable / disable
Control Panel → Date and Time → Time Zone tab

Desktop, Cleanup Wizard runs every 60 days
Control Panel → Display → Desktop tab → Customize Desktop → General tab → Run Desktop Cleanup every 60 days

Desktop, color
Control Panel → Display → Desktop tab → Color

Control Panel → Display → Appearance tab → Advanced → Item list → choose "Desktop"

Desktop, folder, change location
TweakUI → My Computer → Special Folders

Desktop, icons
See "Icons"

Desktop, refresh
click on an empty portion of the desktop → press F5

Desktop, restrict installation of items
Control Panel → Internet Options → Security tab → Custom Level

Desktop, security policies
Group Policy (*gpedit.msc*) → User Configuration → Administrative Templates → Desktop

Desktop, show contents without minimizing applications
Right-click on taskbar → Toolbars → Show Desktop

Right-click on taskbar → Toolbars → Show Open Windows (to restore)

Explorer → open *Desktop* folder

Desktop, version (show/hide)
TweakUI → General → Show Windows version on desktop

Desktop, web content (enable/disable)
TweakUI → Explorer → Allow Web content to be added to the desktop

Desktop, web content, lock
TweakUI → Explorer → Lock Web content

Desktop, web pages, add / remove / hide
Control Panel → Display → Desktop tab → Customize Desktop → Web tab

Desktop, web pages, allow moving and resizing
Control Panel → Display → Desktop tab → Customize Desktop → Web tab → Lock desktop items

Desktop, web pages, automatic download of linked pages
Control Panel → Display → Desktop tab → Customize Desktop → Web tab → select item → Properties → Download tab

Desktop, web pages, automatic updates
Control Panel → Display → Desktop tab → Customize Desktop → Web tab → select item → Properties → Schedule tab

Desktop, web pages, automatic updates (enable/disable)
Control Panel → Internet Options → Advanced tag → Browsing → Enable offline items to be synchronized on a schedule

Devices
See "Hardware"

Dialing, area code settings
Control Panel → Phone and Modem Options → Dialing Rules tab → select location → Edit

Dialing, call waiting
Control Panel → Phone and Modem Options → Dialing Rules tab → select location → Edit → General tab → To disable call waiting...

Dialing, calling card
Control Panel → Phone and Modem Options → Dialing Rules tab → select location → Edit → Calling Card tab

Dialing, connect to the Internet when needed
Control Panel → Internet Options → Connection tab → Dial whenever / Always dial

Dialing, connect to the Internet when needed, depending on location
Control Panel → Network Connections → Advanced → Dial-Up Preferences

Dialing, default Internet connection
Control Panel → Internet Options → Connection tab → select connection → Set Default

Dialing, disconnect Internet connection when no longer needed
Control Panel → Internet Options → Connection tab → select connection → Settings

Dialing, operator-assisted dialing
Control Panel → Network Connections → Advanced → Operator-Assisted Dialing

Digital Camera, add as drive in Explorer (still camera only)
Control Panel → Scanners and Cameras → Add Device

Disconnect from Internet automatically
Control Panel → Internet Options → Connection tab → select connection → Settings

Display, force restart after changing resolution or color depth
Control Panel → Display → Settings tab → Advanced → General tab → Compatibility section

Display, list all possible combinations of resolution and color depth
Control Panel → Display → Settings tab → Advanced → Adapter tab → List All Modes

Display, refresh rate
Control Panel → Display → Settings tab → Advanced → Monitor tab → Screen refresh rate

Display, resolution
Control Panel → Display → Settings tab → Screen resolution

Display, show amount of memory installed on display adapter
Control Panel → Display → Settings tab → Advanced → Adapter tab → Adapter Information section

Display, size
Control Panel → Display → Settings tab → Screen resolution

Display, style
Control Panel → Display → Appearance tab → Windows and buttons list

Display, style, apply to controls in web pages
Control Panel → Internet Options → Advanced tag → Browsing → Enable visual styles on buttons and controls in web pages

Display, troubleshooting
Control Panel → Display → Settings tab → Advanced → Troubleshoot tab

Display, turn off to save power
Control Panel → Power Options → Power Schemes tab → Turn off hard disks

Document templates, manage
TweakUI → Templates

Document templates, relocate folder
TweakUI → My Computer → Special Folders

Documents, history, clear on exit
TweakUI → Explorer → Clear document history on exit

Documents, history, maintain
TweakUI → Explorer → Maintain document history

Documents, show on Start Menu (Classic Start Menu only)
TweakUI → Explorer → Show My Documents on classic Start Menu

Documents, show on Start Menu (XP Start Menu only)
TweakUI → Explorer → Allow Recent Documents on Start Menu

Double-click required to open icons
Control Panel → Folder Options → General tab → Double-click to open an item

Download Complete message, enable / disable
Control Panel → Internet Options → Advanced tag → Browsing → Notify when downloads complete

Drivers
See "Hardware"

Drives, show/hide in My Computer
TweakUI → My Computer → Drives

Drives, warn when low on free space
TweakUI → Taskbar → Warn when low on disk space

DVD drive, autoplay enable / disable
Explorer → right-click DVD drive icon → Properties → AutoPlay tab

Effects, display settings
Control Panel → Display → Appearance tab → Effects

Email icon, show in Start Menu (XP Start Menu only)
Control Panel → Taskbar and Start Menu → Start Menu tab → Customize → General tab → E-mail

Email program, default
Control Panel → Internet Options → Programs tab → E-mail

Encrypted NTFS files, customize color
TweakUI → Explorer → Colors

Encrypted NTFS files, differentiate with a different color
Control Panel → Folder Options → View tab → Show encrypted or compressed NTFS files in color

Encrypted NTFS files, use with Offline files
Control Panel → Folder Options → Offline Files tab → Encrypt offline files to secure data

Environment variables
Control Panel → System → Advanced tab → Environment variables

Error messages, font
Control Panel → Display → Appearance tab → Advanced → Item list → choose "Message Box"

Error messages, sound
Control Panel → Sounds and Audio Devices → Sounds tab

Error messages, text color
Control Panel → Display → Appearance tab → Advanced → Item list → choose "Window"

Error Reporting, advanced settings
Group Policy (*gpedit.msc*) → Computer Configuration → Administrative Templates → System → Error Reporting

Error Reporting, enable / disable
Control Panel → System → Advanced tab → Error Reporting

Explorer
See "Windows Explorer"

Extensions, show/hide filename extensions
Control Panel → Folder Options → View tab → Hide extensions for known file types

Favorites, hide infrequently used items
Control Panel → Internet Options → Advanced tag → Browsing → Enable Personalized Favorites Menu

Favorites, links (show/hide)
TweakUI → Explorer → Show Links on Favorites menu

Favorites, navigation key
TweakUI → Explorer → Command Keys

Favorites, relocate folder
TweakUI → My Computer → Special Folders

Favorites, show in Start Menu (Classic Start Menu only)
Control Panel → Taskbar and Start Menu → Start Menu tab → Customize → "Advanced Start menu options" section → Display Favorites

Favorites, show in Start Menu (XP Start Menu only)
Control Panel → Taskbar and Start Menu → Start Menu tab → Customize → Advanced tab → "Start menu items" section → Favorites menu

Fax service, install support
Control Panel → Printers and Faxes → File → Set Up Faxing

File dialogs, options
TweakUI → Common Dialogs

Files, differentiate encrypted or compressed NTFS files with a different color
Control Panel → Folder Options → View tab → Show encrypted or compressed NTFS files in color

Files, display size in folder tips
Control Panel → Folder Options → View tab → Display file size information in folder tips

Files, double-click sensitivity
TweakUI → Mouse

Files, downloads (enable/disable)
Control Panel → Internet Options → Security tab → Custom Level

Files, drag-drop (enable/disable)
Control Panel → Internet Options → Security tab → Custom Level

Files, drag-drop sensitivity
TweakUI → Mouse

Files, extensions (show/hide)
Control Panel → Folder Options → View tab → Hide extensions for known file types

Files, filename completion in Command Prompt
TweakUI → Command Prompt

Files, hidden files (show/hide)
Control Panel → Folder Options → View tab → Hidden files and folders

Files, Indexing Service
See "Indexing Service"

Files, system files (show/hide)
Control Panel → Folder Options → View tab → Hide protected operating system files

Firewall
See "Windows Firewall"

Focus, prevent applications from stealing
TweakUI → General → Focus

Folders, cache settings for offline access
Explorer → right-click folder icon → Sharing → Caching

Folders, close automatically when Favorites or History folder is shown
Control Panel → Internet Options → Advanced tag → Browsing → Close unused folders in History and Favorites

Folders, columns in details view
Folder window → View → Details → View → Choose Details

Folders, display file size in folder tips
Control Panel → Folder Options → View tab → Display file size information in folder tips

Folders, group similar items
Folder window → View Arrange Icons by → Show in Groups

Folders, history settings
Control Panel → Internet Options → General tab → History section

Folders, Indexing Service
See "Indexing Service"

Folders, open each folder in its own window
Control Panel → Folder Options → General tab → Open each folder in its own window

Folders, open in separate process
Control Panel → Folder Options → View tab → Launch folder windows in separate process

Folders, refresh view
Folder window → View → Refresh or press F5

Folders, remember individual settings
Control Panel → Folder Options → View tab → Remember each folder's view settings

Folders, reopen all folder windows that were left open when system was last shut down
Control Panel → Folder Options → View tab → Restore previous folder windows at logon

Folders, reset default appearance to Windows default
Control Panel → Folder Options → View tab → Reset All Folders

Folders, reuse folder windows
Control Panel → Folder Options → General tab → Open each folder in the same window

Folders, reuse folder windows when launching Internet shortcuts
Control Panel → Internet Options → Advanced tag → Browsing → Reuse windows for launching shortcuts

Folders, set default appearance
Open any folder and configure it as you wish → Tools → Folder Options → View tab → Apply to All Folders

Folders, share on network
Explorer → right-click folder icon → Sharing → Share this folder

Folders, show/hide hidden folders
Control Panel → Folder Options → View tab → Hidden files and folders

Folders, show background images
Control Panel → System → Advanced tab → Performance section → Settings → Visual Effects tab → Custom

Folders, show common tasks
Control Panel → System → Advanced tab → Performance section → Settings → Visual Effects tab → Custom

Folders, show contents of system folders
Control Panel → Folder Options → View tab → Display the contents of system folders

Folders, show Digital Camera memory as a folder (still camera only)
Control Panel → Scanners and Cameras → Add Device

Folders, show FTP site as folder in Internet Explorer
Control Panel → Internet Options → Advanced tag → Browsing → Enable folder view for FTP sites

Folders, show lines in Explorer tree view
Control Panel → Folder Options → View tab → Display simple folder view in Explorer's Folders list

Folders, show the full path in the address bar
Control Panel → Folder Options → View tab → Display the full path in the address bar

Folders, show the full path in the titlebar
Control Panel → Folder Options → View tab → Display the full path in the title bar

Fonts, change DPI of all screen fonts
Control Panel → Display → Settings tab → Advanced → General tab → DPI setting list → select "Custom setting"

Fonts, determine link between font filename and font screen name
Control Panel → Fonts → View → Details

Fonts, downloads (enable/disable)
Control Panel → Internet Options → Security tab → Custom Level

Fonts, eliminate duplicates
Control Panel → Fonts → View → List Fonts by Similarity

Fonts, in web pages
Control Panel → Internet Options → General tab → Fonts

Fonts, in windows, menus, and icons
Control Panel → Display → Appearance tab → Advanced

Fonts, install
Control Panel → Fonts → File → Install New Font

Fonts, repair folder
TweakUI → Repair

Fonts, size in applications
Control Panel → Display → Appearance tab → Font size

Fonts, smooth edges (enable/disable)
Control Panel → System → Advanced tab → Performance section → Settings → Visual Effects tab → Custom

Fonts, smooth edges (settings)
Control Panel → Display → Appearance tab → Effects → Use the following method to smooth edges of screen fonts

Fonts, uninstall
Control Panel → Fonts → delete a font file to uninstall it

Fonts, view & compare
Control Panel → Fonts → double-click any font

FTP, server restrictions
Control Panel → Network Connections → right-click connection → Properties → Advanced tab → Settings → Services tab

FTP, show as folder in Internet Explorer
Control Panel → Internet Options → Advanced tag → Browsing → Enable folder view for FTP sites

FTP, use passive mode
Control Panel → Internet Options → Advanced tag → Browsing → Use Passive FTP

Go button, show in Address Bar
Control Panel → Internet Options → Advanced tag → Browsing → Show Go button in Address Bar

Right-click on empty portion of address bar → Go Button

Hang up Internet Connection automatically
Control Panel → Internet Options → Connection tab → select connection → Settings

Hard Disk, cache settings for offline access
Explorer → right-click drive icon → Sharing → Caching

Hard Disk, check for errors
Explorer → right-click drive icon → Properties → Tools tab → Check Now

Hard Disk, clean up
Explorer → right-click drive icon → Properties → General tab → Disk Cleanup

Hard Disk, compress drive
Explorer → right-click drive icon → Properties → Compress drive to save disk space

Hard Disk, convert to dynamic disk
Disk Management (*diskmgmt.msc*) → View → Top → Disk List → right-click on drive in top pane → Convert to Dynamic Disk

Hard Disk, defragment
Explorer → right-click drive icon → Properties → Tools tab → Defragment Now

Hard Disk, enable / disable write caching
Device Manager → right-click drive → Properties → Policies tab → Enable write caching on the disk

Hard Disk, Indexing Service
See "Indexing Service"

Hard Disk, list volumes
Device Manager → right-click drive → Properties → Volumes tab → Populate

Hard Disk, quota management
Explorer → right-click folder icon → Properties → Quota tab

Hard Disk, quota security policies
Group Policy (*gpedit.msc*) → Computer Configuration → Administrative Templates → System → Disk Quotas

Hard Disk, share on network
Explorer → right-click drive icon → Sharing → Share this folder

Hard Disk, turn off to save power
Control Panel → Power Options → Power Schemes tab → Turn off monitor

Hardware, change the driver for a device
Device Manager → right-click on device → Properties → Driver tab → Update Driver

Hardware, driver information for a device
Device Manager → right-click on device → Properties → Driver tab → Driver Details

Hardware, driver signing options
Control Panel → System → Hardware tab → Driver Signing

Hardware, enable / disable
Device Manager → right-click on device → Properties → General tab → Device usage

Hardware, install
Control Panel → Add Hardware

Hardware, IRQ Steering settings
Device Manager → Computer → right-click sole entry → Properties → IRQ Steering tab

Hardware, list devices
System Information (*winmsd.exe*) → Components

Hardware, list drivers
System Information (*winmsd.exe*) → Software Environment

Hardware, list resources used
System Information (*winmsd.exe*) → Hardware Resources

Hardware, places to look for drivers
Group Policy (*gpedit.msc*) → User Configuration → Administrative Templates → System

Hardware, profile settings
Control Panel → System → Hardware tab → Hardware Profiles

Hardware, resources in use by a device
Device Manager → right-click on device → Properties → Resources tab

Hardware, security policies
Group Policy (*gpedit.msc*) → Computer Configuration → Windows Settings → Security Settings → Local Policies → Security Options

Hardware, show all installed devices
Device Manager

Hardware, uninstall
Device Manager → right-click on device → Uninstall

Hardware, Universal Plug and Play support
Control Panel → Network Connections → Advanced → Optional Networking Components → Networking Services

Help, pop-up help windows
See "Tooltips"

Help, show in Start Menu (XP Start Menu only)
Control Panel → Taskbar and Start Menu → Start Menu tab → Customize → Advanced tab → "Start menu items" section → Help and Support

TweakUI → Explorer → Allow Help on Start Menu

Hibernation, enable / disable
Control Panel → Power Options → Hibernate tab → Enable hibernation

Hidden files and folders, show/hide
Control Panel → Folder Options → View tab → Hidden files and folders

Hourglass, change icon
Control Panel → Mouse → Pointers tab

HTML editor, default
Control Panel → Internet Options → Programs tab → HTML Editor

Icons, desktop icons (show/hide)
Control Panel → Display → Desktop tab → Customize Desktop

TweakUI → Desktop

Icons, highlight color & font
Control Panel → Display → Appearance tab → Advanced → Item list → choose "Selected Items"

Icons, repair
TweakUI → Repair

Icons, show shadows under icon captions
Control Panel → System → Advanced tab → Performance section → Settings → Visual Effects tab → Custom

Icons, show translucent selection rectangle when highlighting multiple icons
Control Panel → System → Advanced tab → Performance section → Settings → Visual Effects tab → Custom

Icons, single-click or double-click
Control Panel → Folder Options → General tab → Click items as follows

Icons, size on desktop and in folders
Control Panel → Display → Appearance tab → Effects → Use large icons

Control Panel → Display → Appearance tab → Advanced → Item list → choose "Icon"

Icons, spacing on desktop and in folders
Control Panel → Display → Appearance tab → Advanced → Item list → choose "Icon Spacing (Horizontal)" or "Icon Spacing (Vertical)"

Icons, underline captions
Control Panel → Folder Options → General tab → Click items as follows

Images, show as thumbnails in Explorer
Explorer → View → Thumbnails

Images, show in web pages
Control Panel → Internet Options → Advanced tag → Multimedia → Show pictures

Images, show placeholders in web pages (if pictures are disabled in web pages)
Control Panel → Internet Options → Advanced tag → Multimedia → Show image download placeholders

Indexing Service, enable / disable for individual drives
Explorer → right-click drive icon → Properties → General tab → Allow Indexing Service to index this disk for fast file searching

Insertion Point, change
Control Panel → Mouse → Pointers tab → choose "Text Select" from "Customize" list

Install On Demand, enable / disable
Control Panel → Internet Options → Advanced tag → Browsing → Enable Install On Demand

Internet Call, default application
Control Panel → Internet Options → Programs tab → Internet Call

Internet Connection, set up
Control Panel → Internet Options → Connection tab → Setup

Internet Control Message Protocol (ICMP)
Control Panel → Windows Firewall → Advanced tab → Network Connection Settings → select connection → Settings → ICMP tab

Control Panel → Windows Firewall → Advanced tab → ICMP → Settings

Internet Explorer, abbreviate link addresses in status bar
Control Panel → Internet Options → Advanced tag → Browsing → Show friendly URLs

Internet Explorer, ActiveX settings
Control Panel → Internet Options → Security tab → Custom Level

Internet Explorer, additional security policies
Group Policy (*gpedit.msc*) → Computer Configuration → Administrative Templates → Windows Components → Internet Explorer

Group Policy (*gpedit.msc*) → User Configuration → Administrative Templates → Windows Components → Internet Explorer

Internet Explorer, animated GIFs (enable/disable)
Control Panel → Internet Options → Advanced tag → Multimedia → Play animations in web pages

Internet Explorer, AutoComplete settings
See "AutoComplete"

Internet Explorer, automatically check for updates
Control Panel → Internet Options → Advanced tag → Browsing → Automatically check for Internet Explorer updates

Internet Explorer, automatically download linked pages for desktop web pages
Control Panel → Display → Desktop tab → Customize Desktop → Web tab → select item → Properties → Download tab

Internet Explorer, automatically update desktop web pages
Control Panel → Display → Desktop tab → Customize Desktop → Web tab → select item → Properties → Schedule tab

Internet Explorer, buttons & controls, use display settings
Control Panel → Internet Options → Advanced tag → Browsing → Enable visual styles on buttons and controls in web pages

Internet Explorer, cache settings
Control Panel → Internet Options → General tab → Temporary Internet Files section → Settings

Internet Explorer, cache settings for encrypted pages
Control Panel → Internet Options → Advanced tag → Security → Do not save encrypted pages to disk

Internet Explorer, cache, clear automatically when browser is closed
Control Panel → Internet Options → Advanced tag → Security → Empty Temporary Internet Files folder when browser is closed

Internet Explorer, certificates for secure sites
See "Certificates"

Internet Explorer, check to see if it is the default browser
Control Panel → Internet Options → Programs tab → Internet Explorer should check to see whether it is the default browser

Internet Explorer, colors & fonts
Control Panel → Internet Options → General tab

Internet Explorer, cookies
See "Cookies"

Internet Explorer, default home page
Control Panel → Internet Options → General tab → Home page

Internet Explorer, desktop icon
Control Panel → Display → Desktop tab → Customize Desktop

Internet Explorer, disable compositing effects when using Terminal Server
Control Panel → Internet Options → Advanced tag → Browsing → Force offscreen compositing even under Terminal Server

Internet Explorer, download-complete notification
Control Panel → Internet Options → Advanced tag → Browsing → Notify when downloads complete

Internet Explorer, enable / disable HTTP 1.1
Control Panel → Internet Options → Advanced tag → HTTP 1.1 settings

Internet Explorer, enable / disable moving or resizing web page items on desktop
Control Panel → Display → Desktop tab → Customize Desktop → Web tab → Lock desktop items

Internet Explorer, enlarge picture boxes to accommodate "ALT" captions (if pictures are disabled in web pages)
Control Panel → Internet Options → Advanced tag → Accessibility → Always expand ALT text for images

Internet Explorer, explain server error messages
Control Panel → Internet Options → Advanced tag → Browsing → Show friendly HTTP error messages

Internet Explorer, fading animation when moving from one web page to another
Control Panel → Internet Options → Advanced tag → Browsing → Enable page transitions

Internet Explorer, Go button
See "Go button"

Internet Explorer, hand icon (change)
Control Panel → Mouse → Pointers tab → choose "Link Select" from "Customize" list

Internet Explorer, hide infrequently used Favorites
Control Panel → Internet Options → Advanced tag → Browsing → Enable Personalized Favorites Menu

Internet Explorer, History settings
Control Panel → Internet Options → General tab → History section

Internet Explorer, icon, change
Control Panel → Display → Desktop tab → Customize Desktop → General tab → select icon → Change Icon

Internet Explorer, icon, show on desktop
Control Panel → Display → Desktop tab → Customize Desktop → General tab → Internet Explorer

Internet Explorer, image placeholders (if pictures are disabled in web pages)
Control Panel → Internet Options → Advanced tag → Multimedia → Show image download placeholders

Internet Explorer, Image Toolbar (enable/disable)
Control Panel → Internet Options → Advanced tag → Multimedia → Enable Image Toolbar

Internet Explorer, Java
See "Java"

Internet Explorer, Link underline
Control Panel → Internet Options → Advanced tag → Browsing → Underline links

Internet Explorer, list additional settings
System Information (*winmsd.exe*) → Internet Settings → Internet Explorer

Internet Explorer, Media Bar content
Control Panel → Internet Options → Advanced tag → Multimedia → Don't display online media content in the media bar

Internet Explorer, navigation keys
TweakUI → Explorer → Command Keys

Internet Explorer, plug-ins (enable/disable)
Control Panel → Internet Options → Advanced tag → Browsing → Enable third-party browser extensions

Internet Explorer, print background colors and images when printing web pages
Control Panel → Internet Options → Advanced tag → Printings → Print background colors and images

Internet Explorer, profile assistant (enable/disable)
Control Panel → Internet Options → Advanced tag → Security → Enable Profile Assistant

Internet Explorer, restrict certain sites
Control Panel → Internet Options → Content tab → Content Advisor section

Internet Explorer, reuse folder windows when launching shortcuts
Control Panel → Internet Options → Advanced tag → Browsing → Reuse windows for launching shortcuts

Internet Explorer, save form data
Control Panel → Internet Options → Content tab → AutoComplete

Internet Explorer, saved web pages, link to image folder
TweakUI → Explorer → Manipulate connected files as a unit

Internet Explorer, saved web pages, link to image folder
Control Panel → Folder Options → View tab → Managing pairs of Web pages and folders

Internet Explorer, script debugging
Control Panel → Internet Options → Advanced tag → Browsing → Disable script debugging

Internet Explorer, script error notification
Control Panel → Internet Options → Advanced tag → Browsing → Display a notification about every script error

Internet Explorer, search, choose prefixes
TweakUI → Internet Explorer → Search

Internet Explorer, search, from the Address Bar
Control Panel → Internet Options → Advanced tag → Search from the Address bar

Internet Explorer, search, use classic
TweakUI → Explorer → Use Classic Search in Internet Explorer

Internet Explorer, show web page on desktop
Control Panel → Display → Desktop tab → Customize Desktop → Web tab

Internet Explorer, shrink large images to fit browser window
Control Panel → Internet Options → Advanced tag → Multimedia → Enable Automatic Image Resizing

Internet Explorer, smooth scrolling
Control Panel → Internet Options → Advanced tag → Browsing → Use smooth scrolling

Internet Explorer, sounds (enable/disable)
Control Panel → Internet Options → Advanced tag → Multimedia → Play sounds in web pages

Internet Explorer, SSL settings
Control Panel → Internet Options → Advanced tag → Security

Internet Explorer, status bar shows abbreviated link addresses
Control Panel → Internet Options → Advanced tag → Browsing → Show friendly URLs

Internet Explorer, toolbar background
TweakUI → Internet Explorer

Internet Explorer, underline links
Control Panel → Internet Options → Advanced tag → Browsing → Underline links

Internet Explorer, use passive mode in FTP
Control Panel → Internet Options → Advanced tag → Browsing → Use Passive FTP

Internet Explorer, video clips (enable/disable)
Control Panel → Internet Options → Advanced tag → Multimedia → Play videos in web pages

Internet Explorer, view source, choose program
TweakUI → Internet Explorer → View Source

Internet Explorer, warning for redirected form submission
Control Panel → Internet Options → Advanced tag → Security → Warn if forms submittal is being redirected

Internet Explorer, warnings, enable / disable
Control Panel → Internet Options → Security tab → Custom Level

Internet icon, show in Start Menu (XP Start Menu only)
Control Panel → Taskbar and Start Menu → Start Menu tab → Customize → General tab → Internet

Internet Shortcuts, use same folder window or Explorer window to open web page
Control Panel → Internet Options → Advanced tag → Browsing → Reuse windows for launching shortcuts

Java, compile applets before running using the JIT (Just In Time) compiler
Control Panel → Internet Options → Advanced tag → Microsoft VM → JIT compiler for virtual machine enabled

Java, console
Control Panel → Internet Options → Advanced tag → Microsoft VM → Java console enabled

Java, logging
Control Panel → Internet Options → Advanced tag → Microsoft VM → Java logging enabled

Java, security settings
Control Panel → Internet Options → Security tab → Custom Level

Joystick settings
Control Panel → Game Controllers

Keyboard shortcuts, hide until Alt key is pressed
Control Panel → Display → Appearance tab → Effects → Hide underlined letters for keyboard navigation until I press the Alt key

Keyboard shortcuts, show in menus and windows
Control Panel → Accessibility Options → Keyboard tab → Show extra keyboard help in programs

Keyboard, choose international layout

Control Panel → Regional and Language Options → Language tab → Details

Keyboard, enable alternative device

Control Panel → Accessibility Options → General tab → Use Serial Keys

Keyboard, ignore brief or repeated keystrokes

Control Panel → Accessibility Options → Keyboard tab → Use FilterKeys

Keyboard, specify type

Control Panel → Keyboard → Hardware tab → Properties → Driver tab → Update Driver → Install from a list of specific location → Next → Don't search → Next

Keyboard, speed (repeat rate and delay)

Control Panel → Keyboard → Speed tab → Character repeat section

Keyboard, Windows logo key combinations (enable/disable)

TweakUI → Explorer → Enable Windows+X hotkeys

Language settings in web pages

Control Panel → Internet Options → General tab → Languages

Language, settings for non-Unicode applications

Control Panel → Regional and Language Options → Advanced tab → Language for non-Unicode programs

Language, settings for text entry

Control Panel → Regional and Language Options → Language tab → Details

Language, use more than one

Control Panel → Regional and Language Options → Language tab → Details → Settings tab → Add

Listboxes, enable / disable animation

Control Panel → System → Advanced tab → Performance section → Settings → Visual Effects tab → Custom

Log off, show in Ctrl-Alt-Del window

Group Policy (*gpedit.msc*) → User Configuration → Administrative Templates → System → Ctrl+Alt+Del Options

Log off, show in Start Menu (Classic Start Menu only)

Control Panel → Taskbar and Start Menu → Start Menu tab → Customize → "Advanced Start menu options" section → Display Log Off

TweakUI → Explorer → Allow Logoff on Start Menu

Log on, automatic log on

TweakUI → Logon

Log on, parse Autoexec.bat

TweakUI → Logon

Log on, scripts policies

Group Policy (*gpedit.msc*) → Computer Configuration → Administrative Templates → System → Scripts

Group Policy (*gpedit.msc*) → User Configuration → Administrative Templates → System → Scripts

Log on, security policies

Group Policy (*gpedit.msc*) → Computer Configuration → Windows Settings → Security Settings → Local Policies → Security Options

Group Policy (*gpedit.msc*) → Computer Configuration → Administrative Templates → System → Logon

Group Policy (*gpedit.msc*) → User Configuration → Administrative Templates → System → Logon

Log on, use Welcome screen

Control Panel → User Accounts → Change the way users log on or off → Use the Welcome screen

Magnifier, move with focus change in web pages

Control Panel → Internet Options → Advanced tag → Accessibility → Move system caret with focus/selection changes

Mail Server, restrictions
Control Panel → Network Connections → right-click connection → Properties → Advanced tab → Settings → Services tab

Memory, priorities
Control Panel → System → Advanced tab → Performance section → Settings → Advanced tab → Memory usage section

Memory, show amount of memory installed on display adapter
Control Panel → Display → Settings tab → Advanced → Adapter tab → Adapter Information section

Memory, show amount of system memory installed
Control Panel → System → General tab

Memory, virtual memory
See "Virtual Memory"

Menus, animation (enable/disable)
Control Panel → Display → Appearance tab → Effects → Use the following transition effect for menus and tooltips

Control Panel → System → Advanced tab → Performance section → Settings → Visual Effects tab → Custom

TweakUI → General → Enable menu animation

Menus, fading (enable/disable)
TweakUI → General → Enable menu fading

Menus, fonts & colors
Control Panel → Display → Appearance tab → Advanced → Item list → choose "Menu"

Menus, highlight color & font
Control Panel → Display → Appearance tab → Advanced → Item list → choose "Selected Items"

Menus, shadows (enable/disable)
Control Panel → Display → Appearance tab → Effects → Show shadows under menus

Menus, size
Control Panel → Display → Appearance tab → Advanced → Item list → choose "Menu"

Menus, speed
TweakUI → Mouse

Menus, underlined keyboard shortcuts (show/hide)
Control Panel → Display → Appearance tab → Effects → Hide underlined letters for keyboard navigation until I press the Alt key

Message boxes, font
Control Panel → Display → Appearance tab → Advanced → Item list → choose "Message Box"

Message boxes, sound
Control Panel → Sounds and Audio Devices → Sounds tab

Message boxes, text color
Control Panel → Display → Appearance tab → Advanced → Item list → choose "Window"

Modems, settings
Control Panel → Phone and Modem Options → Modems tab

Mouse, auto-raise windows
TweakUI → Mouse → X-Mouse

Mouse, control with keyboard
Control Panel → Accessibility Options → Mouse tab

Mouse, detect accidental double-clicks
TweakUI → Explorer → Detect accidental double-clicks

Mouse, double-click speed
Control Panel → Mouse → Buttons tab → Double-click speed section

Mouse, double-click sensitivity
TweakUI → Mouse

Mouse, drag-drop sensitivity
TweakUI → Mouse

Mouse, drag without holding down buttons
Control Panel → Mouse → Buttons tab → ClickLock section

Mouse, enable alternative device
Control Panel → Accessibility Options → General tab → Use Serial Keys

Mouse, hide when typing
Control Panel → Mouse → Pointer Options tab → Hide pointer while typing

Mouse, hot-tracking effects
TweakUI → General → Enable mouse hot tracking effects

Mouse, hot-tracking effects color
TweakUI → Explorer → Colors

Mouse, hover sensitivity
TweakUI → Mouse → Hover

Mouse, left-handed use
Control Panel → Mouse → Buttons tab → Switch primary and secondary buttons

Mouse, move to default button when window is opened
Control Panel → Mouse → Pointer Options tab → Automatically move pointer to the default button in a dialog box

Mouse, pointer
Control Panel → Mouse → Pointers tab

Mouse, precise control enhancement
Control Panel → Mouse → Pointer Options tab → Enhance pointer precision

Mouse, sensitivity
TweakUI → Mouse

Mouse, shadow
Control Panel → Mouse → Pointers tab → Enable pointer shadow
TweakUI → General → Enable cursor shadow

Mouse, show location with animated circles when Ctrl is pressed
Control Panel → Mouse → Pointer Options tab → Show location of pointer when I press the Ctrl key

Mouse, specify type
Control Panel → Mouse → Hardware tab → Properties → Driver tab → Update Driver → Install from a list of specific location → Next → Don't search → Next

Mouse, speed
Control Panel → Mouse → Pointer Options tab → Motion section

Mouse, switch left and right buttons
Control Panel → Mouse → Buttons tab → Switch primary and secondary buttons

Mouse, trails
Control Panel → Mouse → Pointer Options tab → Display pointer trails

Mouse, wheel, use for scrolling
TweakUI → Mouse → Wheel

My Computer, change icon
Control Panel → Display → Desktop tab → Customize Desktop → General tab → select icon → Change Icon

My Computer, show Control Panel
Control Panel → Folder Options → View tab → Show Control Panel in My Computer

My Computer, show first on desktop
TweakUI → Desktop → First Icon

My Computer, show icon on desktop
Control Panel → Display → Desktop tab → Customize Desktop → General tab → My Computer

My Computer, show in Start Menu (XP Start Menu only)
Control Panel → Taskbar and Start Menu → Start Menu tab → Customize → Advanced tab → "Start menu items" section → My Computer

My Documents, change icon
: Control Panel → Display → Desktop tab → Customize Desktop → General tab → select icon → Change Icon

My Documents, clear recently opened documents from Start Menu (Classic Start Menu only)
: Control Panel → Taskbar and Start Menu → Start Menu tab → Customize → Clear

My Documents, clear recently opened documents from Start Menu (XP Start Menu only)
: Control Panel → Taskbar and Start Menu → Start Menu tab → Customize → Advanced tab → Clear List

My Documents, folder location
: TweakUI → My Computer → Special Folders

My Documents, show as menu in Start Menu (XP Start Menu only)
: Control Panel → Taskbar and Start Menu → Start Menu tab → Customize → Advanced tab → "Start menu items" section → Expand My Documents

My Documents, show first on desktop
: TweakUI → Desktop → First Icon

My Documents, show icon on desktop
: Control Panel → Display → Desktop tab → Customize Desktop → General tab → My Documents

My Documents, show in Start Menu (Classic Start Menu only)
: Control Panel → Taskbar and Start Menu → Start Menu tab → Customize → "Advanced Start menu options" section → My Documents

My Documents, show recently opened on Start Menu (XP Start Menu only)
: Control Panel → Taskbar and Start Menu → Start Menu tab → Customize → Advanced tab → "Recent documents" section

My Music, repair folder
: TweakUI → Repair

My Music, show as menu Start Menu (XP Start Menu only)
: Control Panel → Taskbar and Start Menu → Start Menu tab → Customize → Advanced tab → "Start menu items" section → My Music

My Network Places, history (enable/disable)
: TweakUI → Explorer → Maintain network history

My Network Places, icon, change
: Control Panel → Display → Desktop tab → Customize Desktop → General tab → select icon → Change Icon

My Network Places, icon, show on desktop
: Control Panel → Display → Desktop tab → Customize Desktop → General tab → My Network Places

My Network Places, show in Start Menu (XP Start Menu only)
: Control Panel → Taskbar and Start Menu → Start Menu tab → Customize → Advanced tab → "Start menu items" section → My Network Places

My Network Places, View workgroup computers in common task pane (show/hide)
: TweakUI → Explorer → Show "View workgroup computers" in Net Places

My Pictures, folder location
: TweakUI → My Computer → Special Folders

My Pictures, repair folder
: TweakUI → Repair

My Pictures, show as menu in Start Menu (Classic Start Menu only)
: Control Panel → Taskbar and Start Menu → Start Menu tab → Customize → "Advanced Start menu options" section → Expand My Pictures

My Pictures, show in Start Menu (Classic Start Menu only)
: TweakUI → Explorer → Show My Pictures on classic Start Menu

My Pictures, show in Start Menu (XP Start Menu only)
Control Panel → Taskbar and Start Menu → Start Menu tab → Customize → Advanced tab → "Start menu items" section → My Pictures

My Videos, repair folder
TweakUI → Repair

Navigation keys on special keyboards, customize
TweakUI → Explorer → Command Keys

NetMeeting, make the default for Internet Calls
Control Panel → Internet Options → Programs tab → Internet Call

Network, add new connection
Control Panel → Network Connections → New Connection Wizard

Network, advanced adapter settings
Device Manager → right-click adapter → Properties → Advanced tab

Network, Authentication
Control Panel → Network Connections → right-click connection → Properties → Authentication tab

Network, bindings
Control Panel → Network Connections → Advanced → Advanced Settings → Adapters and Bindings tab

Control Panel → Network Connections → right-click connection → Properties → General tab → turn on or off listed protocols and services

Network, bridge two connections
Control Panel → Network Connections → select two connections → Advanced → Network Bridge

Network, computer description
Control Panel → System → Computer Name tab

Network, computer name
Control Panel → System → Computer Name tab → Change

Network, connect to shared printer
Control Panel → Printers and Faxes → Add Printer → Next → A network printer, or a printer attached to another computer

Network, connection status
Control Panel → Network Connections → double-click connection → General tab

Network, disconnect mapped network drive
Explorer → Tools → Disconnect Network Drive

Network, DNS settings
Control Panel → Network Connections → right-click connection → Properties → General tab → Internet Protocol (TCP/IP) → Properties → Advanced → DNS tab

Network, enable / disable
Control Panel → Network Connections → right-click connection → Enable or Disable

Network, Firewall
See "Internet Connection Firewall"

Network, include in Files or Folders search
Control Panel → Folder Options → View tab → Automatically search for network folders and printers

Network, install a network protocol or service
Control Panel → Network Connections → right-click connection → Properties → General tab → Install

Network, IP address and other connection information
Control Panel → Network Connections → double-click connection → Support tab

Network, join a Windows NT domain
Control Panel → System → Computer Name tab → Change

Network, map network drive
Explorer → Tools → Map Network Drive

Network, preliminary setup
Control Panel → Network Connections → Network Setup Wizard

Network, priorities
Control Panel → Network Connections → Advanced → Advanced Settings → Provider Order tab

Network, protocol, enable or disable for a connection
Control Panel → Network Connections → right-click connection → Properties → General tab → check or uncheck entries in list

Network, security policies
Group Policy (*gpedit.msc*) → Computer Configuration → Windows Settings → Security Settings → Local Policies → Security Options

Group Policy (*gpedit.msc*) → Computer Configuration → Administrative Templates → Network

Group Policy (*gpedit.msc*) → User Configuration → Administrative Templates → Network

Network, set IP address
Control Panel → Network Connections → right-click connection → Properties → General tab → Internet Protocol (TCP/IP) → Properties → Use the following IP address

Network, set multiple IP addresses
Control Panel → Network Connections → right-click connection → Properties → General tab → Internet Protocol (TCP/IP) → Properties → Advanced → IP Settings tab

Network, share printer
Control Panel → Printers and Faxes → right-click printer → Sharing → Shared as

Network, show icon in taskbar notification area when connected
Control Panel → Network Connections → right-click connection → Properties → General tab → Show icon in notification area when connected

Network, SNMP components (install / uninstall)
Control Panel → Network Connections → Advanced → Optional Networking Components → Management and Monitoring Tools

Network, TCP/IP filtering
Control Panel → Network Connections → right-click connection → Properties → General tab → Internet Protocol (TCP/IP) → Properties → Advanced → Options tab → TCP/IP filtering → Properties

Network, TCP/IP settings
Control Panel → Network Connections → right-click connection → Properties → General tab → Internet Protocol (TCP/IP) → Properties

Network, uninstall a protocol or service
Control Panel → Network Connections → right-click connection → Properties → General tab → Uninstall

Network, WINS settings
Control Panel → Network Connections → right-click connection → Properties → General tab → Internet Protocol (TCP/IP) → Properties → Advanced → WINS tab

Network Connections, automatically dial
Control Panel → Internet Options → Connection tab

Network Connections, security policies
Group Policy (*gpedit.msc*) → User Configuration → Administrative Templates → Network → Network Connections

Network Connections, show as menu in Start Menu (Classic Start Menu only)
Control Panel → Taskbar and Start Menu → Start Menu tab → Customize → "Advanced Start menu options" section → Expand Network Connections

Network Connections, show in Start Menu (Classic Start Menu only)
TweakUI → Explorer → Show Network Connections on classic Start Menu

Network Connections, show in Start Menu (XP Start Menu only)
Control Panel → Taskbar and Start Menu → Start Menu tab → Customize → Advanced tab → "Start menu items" section → Network Connections

Newsgroup reader, default
Control Panel → Internet Options → Programs tab → Newsgroups

Notification Area
See "Taskbar Notification Area"

Numbers, customize display
Control Panel → Regional and Language Options → Regional Options tab → Customize → Numbers tab

ODBC data sources, restrict access
Control Panel → Internet Options → Security tab → Custom Level

Offline Files, action to take when network connection is lost
Control Panel → Folder Options → Offline Files tab → Advanced

Offline Files, automatic synchronization
Explorer → Tools → Synchronize → Setup → Logon/Lofoff tab → Automatically synchronize the selected items...

Offline Files, automatic synchronization on idle
Explorer → Tools → Synchronize → Setup → On Idle tab → Advanced

Offline Files, compatibility with computers running on batteries
Explorer → Tools → Synchronize → Setup → On Idle tab → Advanced → Prevent synchronization when my computer is running on battery power

Offline Files, enable scheduling of desktop web page updates
Control Panel → Internet Options → Advanced tag → Browsing → Enable offline items to be synchronized on a schedule

Offline Files, security policies
Group Policy (*gpedit.msc*) → User Configuration → Administrative Templates → Network → Offline Files

Offline Files, settings
Control Panel → Folder Options → Offline Files tab

Explorer → Tools → Synchronize → Setup

Offline Files, synchronize
Explorer → Tools → Synchronize

Outlook Express, make the default
Control Panel → Internet Options → Programs tab → E-mail or Newsgroups

Outlook Express, repair unread mail count
TweakUI → Repair

Parental Control of web sites
Control Panel → Internet Options → Content tab → Content Advisor section

Passwords, automatic logon
Control Panel → Internet Options → Security tab → Custom Level → User Authentication

Passwords, change
Control Panel → User Accounts → select an account → Change my password

Passwords, expiration
Group Policy (*gpedit.msc*) → Computer Configuration → Windows Settings → Security Settings → Account Policies → Password Policy

Setting Locator

Passwords, prevent forgotten passwords
Control Panel → User Accounts → select an account → Related Tasks section → Prevent a forgotten password

Passwords, require for exiting screensaver
Control Panel → Display → Screen Saver tab → On resume, password protect

Passwords, require for resuming from standby mode
Control Panel → Power Options → Advanced tab → Prompt for password when computer resumes from standby

Passwords, saving in web pages
Control Panel → Internet Options → Content tab → AutoComplete

Passwords, security policies
Group Policy (*gpedit.msc*) → Computer Configuration → Windows Settings → Security Settings → Account Policies → Password Policy

Passwords, show "Change Password" in Ctrl-Alt-Del window
Group Policy (*gpedit.msc*) → User Configuration → Administrative Templates → System → Ctrl+Alt+Del Options

Path, show full path in folder windows
Control Panel → Folder Options → View tab → Display the full path in the title bar / Display the full path in the address bar

Personalized menus, Favorites
Control Panel → Internet Options → Advanced tag → Browsing → Enable Personalized Favorites Menu

Pictures
See "Images"

Places bar, customize
TweakUI → Common Dialogs

Pointer
See "Mouse"

Pop-up help windows
See "Tooltips"

Power Management
See "Advanced Power Management"

Print Server settings
Control Panel → Printers and Faxes → File → Server Properties

Printers, advanced settings
Group Policy (*gpedit.msc*) → Computer Configuration → Administrative Templates → Printers

Group Policy (*gpedit.msc*) → User Configuration → Administrative Templates → Printers

Printers, cancel printing of all documents
Control Panel → Printers and Faxes → right-click printer → Cancel All Documents

Printers, cancel printing of one document
Control Panel → Printers and Faxes → double-click printer → right-click document → Cancel

Printers, change settings for a single application
Open application → File → Print or Printer Setup

Printers, change settings for all applications
Control Panel → Printers and Faxes → right-click printer → Properties

Printers, connect to a printer on your network
Control Panel → Printers and Faxes → Add Printer → Next → A network printer, or a printer attached to another computer

Printers, install
Control Panel → Printers and Faxes → Add Printer

Printers, pause printing
Control Panel → Printers and Faxes → right-click printer → Pause Printing

Printers, print background colors and images when printing web pages
Control Panel → Internet Options → Advanced tag → Printings → Print background colors and images

Printers, set default printer
Control Panel → Printers and Faxes → right-click printer → Set as Default Printer

Printers, share with other computers on network
Control Panel → Printers and Faxes → right-click printer → Sharing → Shared as

Printers, show as menu in Start Menu (Classic Start Menu only)
Control Panel → Taskbar and Start Menu → Start Menu tab → Customize → "Advanced Start menu options" section → Expand Printers

Printers, show in Start Menu (XP Start Menu only)
Control Panel → Taskbar and Start Menu → Start Menu tab → Customize → Advanced tab → "Start menu items" section → Printers and Faxes

Printers, uninstall
Control Panel → Printers and Faxes → right-click printer → Delete

Printers, view status
Control Panel → Printers and Faxes → double-click printer

Processor, priorities
Control Panel → System → Advanced tab → Performance section → Settings → Advanced tab → Processor scheduling section

Processor, show details
Control Panel → System → General tab

Profile Assistant, enable / disable
Control Panel → Internet Options → Advanced tag → Security → Enable Profile Assistant

Proxy settings
Control Panel → Internet Options → Connection tab → LAN Settings

Quick Launch toolbar, show on Taskbar
Control Panel → Taskbar and Start Menu → Taskbar tab → Show Quick Launch

Right-click on taskbar → Toolbars → Quick Launch

Recent Documents
See "Documents"

Recycle Bin, desktop icon
Control Panel → Display → Desktop tab → Customize Desktop

Registered User, view
Control Panel → System → General tab

Registry Editor, repair
TweakUI → Repair

Remote Assistance, allow invitations to be sent
Control Panel → System → Remote tab → Remote Assistance tab

Remote Desktop, enable incoming connections
Control Panel → System → Remote tab → Remote Desktop tab

Report crashes to Microsoft
Control Panel → System → Advanced tab → Error Reporting

Run, show in Start Menu (Classic Start Menu only)
Control Panel → Taskbar and Start Menu → Start Menu tab → Customize → "Advanced Start menu options" section → Display Run

Run, show in Start Menu (XP Start Menu only)
Control Panel → Taskbar and Start Menu → Start Menu tab → Customize → Advanced tab → "Start menu items" section → Run Command

Scheduled Tasks, add a task
Control Panel → Scheduled Tasks → Add Scheduled Task

Scheduled Tasks, choose user for a single task
Control Panel → Scheduled Tasks → right-click task → Properties → Task tab → Run as

Scheduled Tasks, choose user for AT service
Control Panel → Scheduled Tasks → Advanced → AT Service Account

Scheduled Tasks, compatibility with computers running on batteries
Control Panel → Scheduled Tasks → right-click task → Properties → Settings tab → Power Management section

Scheduled Tasks, delete a task
Control Panel → Scheduled Tasks → right-click task → Delete

Scheduled Tasks, delete completed tasks automatically
Control Panel → Scheduled Tasks → right-click task → Properties → Settings tab → Delete the task if it is not scheduled to run again

Scheduled Tasks, enable / disable
Control Panel → Scheduled Tasks → Advanced → Stop Using Task Scheduler or Start Using Task Scheduler

Scheduled Tasks, enable / disable a single task
Control Panel → Scheduled Tasks → right-click task → Properties → Task tab → Enabled

Scheduled Tasks, log
Control Panel → Scheduled Tasks → Advanced → View Log

Scheduled Tasks, missed task notification
Control Panel → Scheduled Tasks → Advanced → Notify Me of Missed Tasks

Scheduled Tasks, pause
Control Panel → Scheduled Tasks → Advanced → Pause Task Scheduler

Scheduled Tasks, perform only if computer is idle
Control Panel → Scheduled Tasks → right-click task → Properties → Settings tab → Idle Time section

Scheduled Tasks, repeat settings for a single task
Control Panel → Scheduled Tasks → right-click task → Properties → Schedule tab → Advanced

Scheduled Tasks, schedule settings for a single task
Control Panel → Scheduled Tasks → right-click task → Properties → Schedule tab

Scheduled Tasks, security policies
Group Policy (*gpedit.msc*) → Computer Configuration → Administrative Templates → Windows Components → Task Scheduler

Group Policy (*gpedit.msc*) → User Configuration → Administrative Templates → Windows Components → Task Scheduler

Scheduled Tasks, stop hung tasks
Control Panel → Scheduled Tasks → right-click task → Properties → Settings tab → Stop the task if it runs for...

Screen
See "Display"

Screensaver settings
Control Panel → Display → Screen Saver tab

Scrollbars, color
Control Panel → Display → Appearance tab → Advanced → Item list → choose "3d Objects"

Scrollbars, size
Control Panel → Display → Appearance tab → Advanced → Item list → choose "Scrollbar"

Search, Address Bar
Control Panel → Internet Options → Advanced tag → Search from the Address bar

Search, classic search in Explorer
TweakUI → Explorer → Use Classic Search in Explorer

Search, customize navigation key
TweakUI → Explorer → Command Keys

Search, include network folders and printers
Control Panel → Folder Options → View tab → Automatically search for network folders and printers

Send To, folder location
TweakUI → My Computer → Special Folders

Services, allow only essential services
Control Panel → Advanced tab → Performance → Settings → Data Execution Prevention tab

Setup, location of setup files
TweakUI → My Computer → Special Folders → Installation Path

Shared folders, include in searches
Control Panel → Folder Options → View tab → Automatically search for network folders and printers

Shared folders, make accessible to all users
Control Panel → Folder Options → View tab → Use simple file sharing

(Turn this off to further restrict access to shared resources.)

Shift Key, make it "sticky"
Control Panel → Accessibility Options → Keyboard tab → Use StickyKeys

Shortcuts, overlay icon
TweakUI → Explorer → Shortcut

Shortcuts, show "Shortcut to" prefix
TweakUI → Explorer → Prefix "Shortcut to" on new shortcuts

Single-click required to open icons
Control Panel → Folder Options → General tab → Single-click to open an item

Software, install or uninstall
Control Panel → Add or Remove Programs

Software, install or uninstall (network components)
Control Panel → Network Connections → Advanced → Optional Networking Components

Software, installation security policies
Group Policy (*gpedit.msc*) → Computer Configuration → Administrative Templates → Windows Components → Windows Installer

Group Policy (*gpedit.msc*) → User Configuration → Administrative Templates → Windows Components → Windows Installer

Sounds, beep on errors
TweakUI → General → Beep on errors

Sounds, default audio devices for playback, recording, and MIDI
Control Panel → Sounds and Audio Devices → Audio tab

Sounds, disable unwanted audio devices
Control Panel → Sounds and Audio Devices → Audio tab → Use only default devices

Sounds, events that trigger sounds
Control Panel → Sounds and Audio Devices → Sounds tab

Sounds, list devices
Control Panel → Sounds and Audio Devices → Hardware tab

Sounds, mute all
Control Panel → Sounds and Audio Devices → Volume tab → Mute

Sounds, navigation keys on special keyboards
TweakUI → Explorer → Command Keys

Sounds, play in web pages
Control Panel → Internet Options → Advanced tag → Multimedia → Play sounds in web pages

Sounds, play sounds when Caps Lock, Num Lock, or Scroll Lock is pressed
Control Panel → Accessibility Options → Keyboard tab → Use ToggleKeys

Sounds, show visual notification
Control Panel → Accessibility Options → Sound tab

Sounds, speaker, enable/disable PC speaker
TweakUI → General → Beep on errors

Sounds, speaker orientation
Control Panel → Sounds and Audio Devices → Volume tab → Speaker settings section → Advanced → Speakers tab

Sounds, speaker troubleshooting
Control Panel → Sounds and Audio Devices → Volume tab → Speaker settings section → Advanced → Performance tab

Sounds, speaker volume
Control Panel → Sounds and Audio Devices → Volume tab → Speaker settings section → Speaker Volume

Sounds, surround-sound setup
Control Panel → Sounds and Audio Devices → Volume tab → Speaker settings section → Advanced → Speakers tab

Sounds, volume
Control Panel → Sounds and Audio Devices → Volume tab

Sounds, volume from keyboard
TweakUI → Explorer → Command Keys

Speech, recording voice
See "Voice"

Speech, select preferred audio device
Control Panel → Speech → Text to Speech tab → Audio Output

Speech, speed
Control Panel → Speech → Text to Speech tab → Voice speed section

Speech, voice selection
Control Panel → Speech → Text to Speech tab → Voice selection section

Speech, volume
Volume Control (*sndvol32.exe*) → adjust master or "Wave" controls

Start Menu, button look and feel
Control Panel → Display → Appearance tab → Windows and buttons list

Start Menu, clear list of recently opened applications
Control Panel → Taskbar and Start Menu → Start Menu tab → Customize → General tab → Clear List

Start Menu, enable dragging and dropping (Classic Start Menu only)
Control Panel → Taskbar and Start Menu → Start Menu tab → Customize → "Advanced Start menu options" section → Enable Dragging and Dropping

Start Menu, enable dragging and dropping (XP Start Menu only)
Control Panel → Taskbar and Start Menu → Start Menu tab → Customize → Advanced tab → "Start menu items" section → Enable Dragging and Dropping

Start Menu, folder location
TweakUI → My Computer → Special Folders

Start Menu, Frequently Used Programs, ban items from list
TweakUI → Taskbar → XP Start Menu

Start Menu, hide infrequently accessed applications (Classic Start Menu only)
Control Panel → Taskbar and Start Menu → Start Menu tab → Customize → "Advanced Start menu options" section → Use Personalized Menus

Start Menu, highlight newly installed programs (XP Start Menu only)
Control Panel → Taskbar and Start Menu → Start Menu tab → Customize → Advanced tab → Highlight newly installed programs

Start Menu, look and feel
Control Panel → Taskbar and Start Menu → Start Menu tab → "Start menu" or "Classic Start menu"

Start Menu, number of recently opened applications to show (XP Start Menu only)
Control Panel → Taskbar and Start Menu → Start Menu tab → Customize → General tab → "Programs" section

Start Menu, open menus when hovering with mouse (XP Start Menu only)
Control Panel → Taskbar and Start Menu → Start Menu tab → Customize → Advanced tab → Open submenus when I pause on them with my mouse

Start Menu, size of icons (Classic Start Menu only)
Control Panel → Taskbar and Start Menu → Start Menu tab → Customize → Advanced tab → "Start menu items" section → Show Small Icons in Start Menu

Start Menu, size of icons (XP Start Menu only)
Control Panel → Taskbar and Start Menu → Start Menu tab → Customize → General tab → "Select an icon size for programs" section

Startup, folder location
TweakUI → My Computer → Special Folders

Startup, log
Control Panel → System → Advanced tab → Startup and Recovery section → Settings → System failure section

Startup, multiboot menu settings
Control Panel → System → Advanced tab → Startup and Recovery section → Settings → System startup section

Startup, sound
See "Sounds"

Status Bar, show in Explorer
Explorer → View → Status Bar

Style sheets, impose a single style sheet for all web pages
Control Panel → Internet Options → General tab → Accessibility → Format documents using my style sheet

Style, apply to controls in web pages
Control Panel → Internet Options → Advanced tag → Browsing → Enable visual styles on buttons and controls in web pages

Style, enable / disable all styles
Control Panel → System → Advanced tab → Performance section → Settings → Visual Effects tab → Custom

Style, visual style of windows and buttons
Control Panel → Display → Appearance tab → Windows and buttons list

Swapfile, size and location
See "Virtual Memory"

Synchronize
See "Offline Files"

System Restore, disk space usage
Control Panel → System → System Restore tab → Disk space usage section

System Restore, enable / disable
Control Panel → System → System Restore tab → Turn off System Restore

System Restore, policies
Group Policy (*gpedit.msc*) → Computer Configuration → Administrative Templates → System → System Restore

System Restore, status
Control Panel → System → System Restore tab → Status section

Task, show extra task pane in folder windows
Control Panel → Folder Options → General tab → Tasks section

Task Manager, show in Ctrl-Alt-Del window
Group Policy (*gpedit.msc*) → User Configuration → Administrative Templates → System → Ctrl+Alt+Del Options

Task Scheduler
See "Scheduled Tasks"

Taskbar, flash buttons
TweakUI → General → Focus

Taskbar, group buttons by application
Control Panel → Taskbar and Start Menu → Taskbar tab → Group similar taskbar buttons

Taskbar, group buttons by application (customize)
TweakUI → Taskbar → Grouping

Taskbar, hide when not in use
Control Panel → Taskbar and Start Menu → Taskbar tab → Auto-hide the taskbar

Taskbar, keep on top of other windows
Control Panel → Taskbar and Start Menu → Taskbar tab → Keep the taskbar on top of other windows

Taskbar, move to a different screen location
Click on an empty portion of the taskbar and drag

Taskbar, prevent moving and resizing
Control Panel → Taskbar and Start Menu → Taskbar tab → Lock the taskbar

Right-click on taskbar → Toolbars → Lock the taskbar

Taskbar, resize
Drag the border of the taskbar to make it larger or smaller

Taskbar, sliding button animation (enable/disable)
Control Panel → System → Advanced tab → Performance section → Settings → Visual Effects tab → Custom

Taskbar, style
Control Panel → Display → Appearance tab → Windows and buttons list

Taskbar Notification Area, hide infrequently accessed applications
Control Panel → Taskbar and Start Menu → Taskbar tab → Hide inactive icons

Taskbar Notification Area, network icon
Control Panel → Network Connections → right-click connection → Properties → General tab → Show icon in notification area when connected

Taskbar Notification Area, power icon
Control Panel → Power Options → Advanced tab → Always show icon on the taskbar

Taskbar Notification Area, volume control (yellow speaker)
Control Panel → Sounds and Audio Devices → Volume tab → Place volume icon in the taskbar

Telephony settings
Control Panel → Phone and Modem Options → Advanced tab

Telnet Server, restrictions
Control Panel → Network Connections → right-click connection → Properties → Advanced tab → Settings → Services tab

Temporary Internet Files, clear automatically when browser is closed
Control Panel → Internet Options → Advanced tag → Security → Empty Temporary Internet Files folder when browser is closed

Temporary Internet Files, policy regarding encrypted pages
Control Panel → Internet Options → Advanced tag → Security → Do not save encrypted pages to disk

Temporary Internet Files, settings
Control Panel → Internet Options → General tab → Temporary Internet Files section → Settings

Terminal Server, disable compositing effects in Internet Explorer
Control Panel → Internet Options → Advanced tag → Browsing → Force offscreen compositing even under Terminal Server

Terminal Server, security policies
Group Policy (*gpedit.msc*) → Computer Configuration → Administrative Templates → Windows Components → Terminal Services

Group Policy (*gpedit.msc*) → User Configuration → Administrative Templates → Windows Components → Terminal Services

Text Cursor, blink rate
Control Panel → Keyboard → Speed tab → Cursor blink rate

Text Cursor, blink rate & size
Control Panel → Accessibility Options → Display tab → Cursor Options section

Text Cursor, change mouse "I-beam" cursor
Control Panel → Mouse → Pointers tab → choose "Text Select" from "Customize" list

Themes
Control Panel → Display → Themes tab

Thumbnails, cache (enable/disable)
Control Panel → Folder Options → View tab → Do not cache thumbnails

Thumbnails, image quality
TweakUI → Explorer → Thumbnails

Thumbnails, show in Explorer
Explorer → View → Thumbnails

Thumbnails, size
TweakUI → Explorer → Thumbnails

Time, customize display
Control Panel → Regional and Language Options → Regional Options tab → Customize → Time tab

Time, set
Control Panel → Date and Time → Date & Time tab

Time, synchronize with Internet time server automatically
Control Panel → Date and Time → Internet Time tab

Time, time service policies
Group Policy (*gpedit.msc*) → Computer Configuration → Administrative Templates → System → Windows Time Service

Time, time zone
Control Panel → Date and Time → Time Zone tab

Titlebar, font, color, and size
Control Panel → Display → Appearance tab → Advanced → Item list → choose "Active Title Bar" or "Inactive Title Bar"

Titlebar, size only
Control Panel → Display → Appearance tab → Advanced → Item list → choose "Caption Buttons"

Toolbar, size and font for floating toolbar captions
Control Panel → Display → Appearance tab → Advanced → Item list → choose "Palette Title"

Tooltips, animation
Control Panel → Display → Appearance tab → Effects → Use the following transition effect for menus and tooltips

TweakUI → General → Enable tooltip animation

Tooltips, animation (enable/disable)
Control Panel → System → Advanced tab → Performance section → Settings → Visual Effects tab → Custom

Tooltips, enable / disable (desktop, taskbar, and Explorer only)
Control Panel → Folder Options → View tab → Show pop-up description for folder and desktop items

Tooltips, fade (enable/disable)
TweakUI → General → Enable tooltip fade

Tooltips, font & color
Control Panel → Display → Appearance tab → Advanced → Item list → choose "ToolTip"

Tooltips, big "balloon" tooltips that pop up from taskbar notification area
See "Balloon tips"

Transition effects, enable / disable
Control Panel → Display → Appearance tab → Effects → Use the following transition effect for menus and tooltips

Tray
See "Taskbar Notification Area"

Uninstall Hardware
Control Panel → Add Hardware

Uninstall Software
Control Panel → Add or Remove Programs

Uninterruptible Power Supply (UPS) settings
Control Panel → Power Options → UPS tab

User names in web pages, saving
Control Panel → Internet Options → Content tab → AutoComplete

Users, add new user account
Control Panel → User Accounts → Create a new account

Users, allow fast switching between users
Control Panel → User Accounts → Change the way users log on or off → Use Fast User Switching

Users, multiple profiles for each user account
Control Panel → System → Advanced tab → User Profiles section → Settings

Users, passwords
See "Passwords"

Users, registered user
See "Registered User"

Users, security policies
Group Policy (*gpedit.msc*) → Computer Configuration → Windows Settings → Security Settings → Local Policies → User Rights Assignment

Group Policy (*gpedit.msc*) → Computer Configuration → Administrative Templates → System → User Profiles

Group Policy (*gpedit.msc*) → User Configuration → Administrative Templates → System → User Profiles

Users, security policies for groups
Group Policy (*gpedit.msc*) → Computer Configuration → Administrative Templates → System → Group Policy

Group Policy (*gpedit.msc*) → User Configuration → Administrative Templates → System → Group Policy

Video, play in web pages
Control Panel → Internet Options → Advanced tag → Multimedia → Play videos in web pages

Virtual memory, settings
Control Panel → System → Advanced tab → Performance section → Settings → Advanced tab → Change

Voice, calibrate volume settings
Control Panel → Sounds and Audio Devices → Voice tab → Test hardware

Voice, playback and recording volume
Control Panel → Sounds and Audio Devices → Voice tab

Voice, speech synthesis
See "Speech"

Volume
See "Sounds"

Wallpaper
See "Background"

Warnings in web pages, enable / disable
Control Panel → Internet Options → Security tab → Custom Level

Web pages
See "Internet Explorer"

Web pages, set default browser
Control Panel → Internet Options → Programs tab → Internet Explorer should check to see whether it is the default browser

Web pages, set default editor
Control Panel → Internet Options → Programs tab → HTML Editor

Web Server, restrictions
Control Panel → Network Connections → right-click connection → Properties → Advanced tab → Settings → Services tab

Welcome screen, enable / disable
Control Panel → User Accounts → Change the way users log on or off → Use the Welcome screen

Windows, background of MDI (multiple document interface) windows
Control Panel → Display → Appearance tab → Advanced → Item list → choose "Application Background"

Windows, background of non-MDI windows
Control Panel → Display → Appearance tab → Advanced → Item list → choose "Window"

Windows, cascade all open application windows
Right-click on taskbar → Cascade Windows

Windows, closing crashed applications
Task Manager (*taskmgr.exe*) → Applications tab

Windows, closing hidden applications
Task Manager (*taskmgr.exe*) → Processes tab

Windows, color of borders
Control Panel → Display → Appearance tab → Advanced → Item list → choose "3d Objects"

Windows, minimize all open application windows
Windows Logo Key + D

Windows, minimize/maximize animation
TweakUI → General → Enable window animation

Windows, show outline or full window when dragging
Control Panel → Display → Appearance tab → Effects → Show window contents while dragging

Windows, tile all open application windows
Right-click on taskbar → Tile Windows Horizontally or Tile Windows Vertically

Windows, titlebar font, color, and size
Control Panel → Display → Appearance tab → Advanced → Item list → choose "Active Title Bar" or "Inactive Title Bar"

Windows Explorer, access digital-camera memory as a drive (still camera only)
Control Panel → Scanners and Cameras → Add Device

Windows Explorer, additional security policies
Group Policy (*gpedit.msc*) → User Configuration → Administrative Templates → Windows Components → Windows Explorer

Windows Explorer, columns in details view
Explorer → View → Details → View → Choose Details

Windows Explorer, group similar items
Explorer → View Arrange Icons by → Show in Groups

Windows Explorer, refresh view
Explorer → View → Refresh or press F5

Windows Explorer, reuse window when launching Internet shortcuts
Control Panel → Internet Options → Advanced tag → Browsing → Reuse windows for launching shortcuts

Windows Explorer, search
See "Search"

Windows Explorer, show lines in tree view (Folders Explorer bar)
Control Panel → Folder Options → View tab → Display simple folder view in Explorer's Folders list

Windows Explorer, show Status Bar
Explorer → View → Status Bar

Windows Explorer, toolbar, background
TweakUI → Internet Explorer

Windows Explorer, toolbar, customize
Explorer → View → Toolbars → Customize

Windows Explorer, toolbar, icon size
Explorer → View → Toolbars → Customize → Icon options

Windows Explorer, toolbar, prevent being moved
Explorer → View → Toolbars → Lock the Toolbars

Windows Explorer, toolbar, text captions
Explorer → View → Toolbars → Customize → Text options

Windows File Protection, advanced settings
Group Policy (*gpedit.msc*) → Computer Configuration → Administrative Templates → System → Windows File Protection

Windows Firewall, allow Internet server services
Control Panel → Windows Firewall → Advanced tab → Network Connection Settings → select connection → Settings

Windows Firewall, allow programs to run
Control Panel → Windows Firewall → Exceptions tab

Windows Firewall, enable / disable
Control Panel → Windows Firewall

Control Panel → Network Connections → right-click connection → Properties → Advanced tab → Settings

Windows Firewall, Internet Control Message Protocol (ICMP)
See "Internet Control Message Protocol (ICMP)"

Windows Firewall, logging
Control Panel → Windows Firewall → Advanced tab → Security Logging → Settings

Windows Media Player, change as default for CDs
TweakUI → My Computer → AutoPlay

Windows Registered User information
Control Panel → System → General tab

Windows Update
Internet Explorer → Tools → Windows Update

Windows Update, automatic updating
Control Panel → System → Automatic Updates tab

Windows version
Control Panel → System → General tab

Windows XP Style for screen elements
Control Panel → Display → Appearance tab → Windows and buttons listbox

APPENDIX B
BIOS Settings

The BIOS, or Basic Input-Output System, is the program (stored in a chip on your motherboard) responsible for booting your computer and starting your operating system. It also handles the flow of data between the operating system and your peripherals (keyboard, mouse, hard disk controller, video adapter, etc.). Your BIOS has a special "setup" screen that allows you to customize its settings to enable or disable motherboard features, improve performance, and, sometimes, fix problems.

The BIOS setup is usually accessed by pressing a key—such as **Del**, **F2**, or **Esc**—immediately after powering on your system and before the initial beep. The screen that appears before the Windows logo typically identifies the key you need to press to enter setup; consult your computer's manual if you need further help.

The settings available in a computer's BIOS setup screen will vary significantly from one system to another, but there are some settings that are common among them all. The problem is that motherboard and computer manufacturers are notorious for poorly documenting BIOS settings, so it can be difficult to determine what the settings mean, let alone how they should be set.

Here are some tips for working with BIOS settings and the descriptions in this appendix:

- If you're trying to fix a problem, don't change more than one BIOS setting at a time. Although it may take longer, it means you can determine which setting is responsible for fixing the problem (or causing a new one).
- The BIOS is typically stored on a "flash" chip, which means it can be updated with newer versions. Check with your motherboard

manufacturer to see if a newer BIOS is available for your system. In most cases, BIOS updates only fix bugs, but they occasionally can improve performance or add support for new hardware. If you're unable to install Windows XP (or its successor) on your system, an outdated BIOS may be to blame.

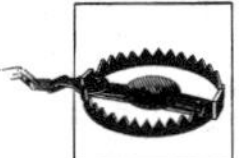

Flashing (updating) a BIOS is a risky procedure. If something goes wrong (i.e., if the power goes out, or the BIOS turns out to be corrupted or the wrong version), your computer will probably not boot. Most motherboard manufacturers provide a BIOS recovery method, typically involving a floppy diskette and a special keystroke combination, but if the computer won't boot, you won't be able to look up the solution on the Web after the fact. For this reason, you'll want to make sure you've familiarized yourself with the procedure *before* you attempt to update your BIOS.

- Keep in mind that the names of BIOS settings listed here may vary, and one appendix can't possibly accommodate them all. For example, a setting named **Event Log** on one system might be called **System Event Log** on another. If you can't find a particular setting, try looking through the list for variations.
- One of the problems with the BIOS setup screen is that you can't access it from within Windows, which means you can't look up settings on the Web, you can't take screenshots, and you can't take notes without using a pen and paper. However, a digital camera can be very handy in this situation; just take one or more photos of your screen (with the flash turned off, of course) to quickly record all your BIOS settings.

Table B-1 lists many common BIOS settings, along with brief explanations and some tips. For more extensive BIOS setting information and advice, check out the "The Definitive BIOS Optimization Guide" at *http://www.rojakpot.com/bog.aspx*.

Table B-1. Common BIOS settings and what they do

Setting	Description
AC Power Recovery	Determines whether or not the computer turns on automatically when power is applied (such as recovering from a power loss or using an external power switch).
ACPI Aware O/S	See "Power Management."
AddOn ROM Display Mode	Choose whether the startup screen is handled by the primary BIOS or a secondary "add-on" BIOS. In most cases, you'll want to disable this option.

Setting	Description
Address Range Shadowing	Various hardware address ranges can be "shadowed," which means that pieces of faster system RAM are substituted for them. In most cases, this is not a good idea, so it is recommended that shadowing be disabled for all address ranges.
AGP 2X/4X Mode	The AGP 2X and 4X modes double and quadruple the bandwidth to your AGP video card, respectively, but can only be used if your video card supports 2X or 4X.
AGP Aperture/Device Address Space Size	This sets the amount of system memory used to store textures for 3D graphics. The more video memory you have, the lower this setting should be. Many video problems are caused by this value being set too high. Try a value of 32MB.
Anti-Virus Protection	Actively scans your hard disk for boot sector viruses. Despite the apparent usefulness of a feature like this, you should always disable it, as it typically interferes with Windows and causes all sorts of problems.
APM Enable	See "Power Management."
Assign IRQ For USB	See "Legacy USB Support."
Assign IRQ For VGA	This should be enabled only if your video card does not need its own IRQ *and* you need an extra IRQ for another device.
Auto Power On	See "AC Power Recovery."
Boot Device Priority/ Boot Sequence	Specifies the order in which your computer looks through the various drives in your system for a drive with a bootable operating system. For example, if your CD drive has a higher boot priority than your hard drive, then your computer will look for a bootable CD in your CD drive before it attempts to boot off the hard disk. If the CD drive has a *lower* boot priority, and Windows is installed on your hard disk, your computer will ignore bootable CDs.
Boot Other Device	If an operating system isn't found on the first boot drive (see "Boot Device Priority/ Boot Sequence") and this setting is enabled, your computer will attempt to boot off of other drives.
Boot Sector Virus Protection	See "Anti-Virus Protection."
Boot to OS/2	Changes how memory above 64 MB is handled for compatibility with IBM's defunct OS/2 operating system. For obvious reasons, this option should be disabled.
Bootup CPU Speed	This is a remnant of the "turbo" button found on old 486 computers, allowing you to slow down the machine for old games. There's little reason you'd want any setting other than `Fast` here.
Bootup Numlock Status	See "Numlock State."
C000/C400/C800/CC00 16k Shadow	See "Address Range Shadowing."
Chassis Fan	This shows the RPM of the fan connected to the "Chassis Fan" connector on your motherboard. This is typically a read-only setting.
CPU Current Temperature	This shows the measured temperature of your processor. For dual-processor systems, you'll see two such settings. This is typically a read-only setting.
CPU Fan	This shows the RPM of the fan connected to the "CPU Fan" connector on your motherboard. For dual-processor systems, you'll see two such settings. This is typically a read-only setting.

Table B-1. Common BIOS settings and what they do (continued)

Setting	Description
CPU Level 1 Cache/ Level 2 Cache	These settings allow you to disable your processor's primary (level 1) and secondary (level 2) cache, respectively. These settings should always be enabled.
CPU to PCI Write Buffer	Enables or disables the buffer used for data sent to the PCI bus by the processor. This should be enabled.
D000/D400/D800/DC00 16k Shadow	See "Address Range Shadowing."
Delayed Transaction	See "PCI 2.1 Compliance."
Diskette	See all "Floppy" entries.
DRAM Data Integrity Mode	If you're using ECC (Error Checking and Correction) memory, set this to `ECC`. Otherwise, choose `Non-ECC`.
EMM386 Support	Enable this only if you're booting to DOS and need to support the now-defunct *EMM386.SYS* driver.
Event Log	Your motherboard can log errors (such as BIOS problems and hard disk boot problems) it encounters during startup. Settings in this section allow you to enable or disable logging, view the log, erase the log, etc.
Fast Boot	See "Quick Boot."
First Boot Device	See "Boot Device Priority/Boot Sequence."
Flash BIOS Protection	This prevents the BIOS from being overwritten or updated. You'll need to disable this to update your BIOS, as explained at the beginning of this appendix. Otherwise, leave this enabled to protect against viruses that attack BIOSes.
Floppy Drive A/B	Use these settings to define the floppy diskette drives you have connected to your computer.
Floppy Drive Seek	When enabled, this option will send a signal to your floppy drive(s) to help detect certain drive characteristics. Leave this off for a quicker boot.
Floppy Write Protect	This prevents anyone from writing data to a diskette in your floppy drive, useful if the computer is in a public place and you don't want people copying data to floppies.
GART W2K Miniport Driver	The GART (Graphics Address Remapping Table) is part of the AGP subsystem. In most cases, you want to disable this option.
Green PC Monitor Power State	If you're using an APM (advanced power management)-compliant "Green PC" monitor, this setting allows you to automatically shut it off after a certain perioud of inactivity, in lieu of a screensaver. With these types of settings, it's best to let Windows XP control how and when devices are shut off.
Hard Disk Power Down Mode	Windows can shut down your hard disk to save power after a certain period of inactivity. With these types of settings, it's best to let Windows XP control how and when devices are shut off.
Hard Disk Write Protect	This option write-protects your hard disk so data can't be written to it. You won't want to use this on a Windows XP machine.
Hard-Disk Drive Sequence	If you have more than one hard disk drive on your IDE controller, this option allows you to choose the order in which your computer looks for bootable drives. Used in conjunction with "Boot Device Priority/Boot Sequence."

Table B-1. Common BIOS settings and what they do (continued)

Setting	Description
Hardware Reset Protect	Prevent the computer from being restarted with the Reset button on the front of your computer's case. Helpful if you have a dog who likes to wag his/her tail while standing next to your computer.
HDD S.M.A.R.T. Capability	Enables the S.M.A.R.T. (Self Monitoring Analysis And Reporting Technology) feature, supported by most modern hard disks, that helps predict potential problems before they happen. Most users don't need it and are probably better off disabling this feature.
Hit DEL Message Display	Turns on or off the message on the POST (Power On Self Test) screen that says "Press DEL to enter Setup."
IDE BusMaster	See "PCI IDE BusMaster."
IDE Controller	Enable or disable either or both of the IDE controllers on the motherboard. Each controller supports up to two devices (a "master" and a "slave"), but if you only have two devices, you can hook them both up to your primary IDE controller and disable the secondary controller. Disabling the controllers you don't need frees IRQs for other devices in your system, but distributing your devices across your controllers can improve performance.
IDE HDD Block Mode	Although enabling this option should improve performance on some systems, it should not be used with Windows XP.
Internal Cache	See "CPU Level 1 Cache/Level 2 Cache."
IRQ3, IRQ4, IRQ5, etc.	There are two different settings named for IRQs. One, used with power management, determines whether or not your computer monitors a given IRQ for activity (used to "wake up" the system). The other, typically found in the **PCI** section, allows to you "reserve" an IRQ and prevent the Plug and Play system from automatically assigning it to a device.
Legacy USB Support	Enable this option if you're using a USB keyboard or USB mouse and you want to use them in the BIOS setup screen, DOS, or some other environment outside of Windows.
Master/Slave Drive UltraDMA	This should be enabled for drives that support UltraDMA, and disabled otherwise. In most cases, it should be set to `Auto`.
Memory Hole at 15M-16M	Enable this option to reserve this segment of your computer's memory for use by some older ISA cards. Unless you specifically need it, this option should be disabled.
Memory Write Posting	This option may improve performance on older systems, but will likely degrade performance—and even cause video corruption—on newer systems. Disable this option unless you're willing to experiment with it.
MPS Version Control	This allows you to choose the multiprocessor specification version supported by your operating system. Windows XP supports version 1.4, although some other operating systems do not.
Numlock State	Turn this on if you want the **Num Lock** keyboard light turned on when the system starts. Turn this off if you typically use the numeric keypad to move your cursor, instead of the "inverted T" cursor keys.
Onboard FDD Controller	This enables or disables the floppy diskette drive controller on your motherboard.
Onboard IR Function	This enables or disables the infrared port on your motherboard.

Table B-1. Common BIOS settings and what they do (continued)

Setting	Description
Onboard SCSI	This enables or disables the SCSI controller on your motherboard. Note that SCSI settings will typically be set with a separate SCSI BIOS utility. For instance, most Adaptec controllers are configured by pressing **Ctrl-A** at the screen that lists SCSI devices during bootup.
Overheat Warning Temperature	This sets the temperature above which the overheat warning is triggered. See "System Overheat Warning," later in this appendix, for more information.
Parallel Port	This enables or disables the parallel (printer) port on your motherboard.
Parallel Port Mode	Use this to choose between the various parallel (printer) port modes: `ECP`, `EPP`, `ECP+EPP`, `Normal (SPP)`. In most cases, you'll want `ECP`; only choose one of the lesser options if you run into a compatibility problem. Note that such problems are more commonly caused by incorrect or faulty printer cables.
PCI 2.1 Compliance	This should be enabled, unless you have one or more PCI cards that are not compatible with the PCI 2.1 specification.
PCI IDE BusMaster	Enables or disables bus mastering for the IDE controller, which helps reduce load on the processor when data is transferred to and from IDE devices. Disable if you're using older drives that don't support bus mastering.
PCI IRQ Assignment	This setting (usually a group of settings) allows you to assign IRQs to specific PCI slots.
PCI Latency Timer	This sets the number of cycles during which a single PCI device can monopolize the PCI bus. Increase this value for better performance, or decrease it if you run into problems. The default is typically 32 cycles, but you may have success with 64 or 128 cycles.
PCI Pipelining	Enable this to improve performance with your video adapter.
PME Resume	See "Remote Wake Up."
PnP OS Installed	This allows your operating system's Plug and Play feature to control the resources used by the various devices in your system. Enable this option for Windows XP, or disable it if you're using an OS that doesn't support PnP.
Power Button Mode	This allows you to choose whether your computer's power button shuts off the computer (after holding it for four seconds) or forces your computer to enter a "hibernate" state.
Power Lost Control	Determines what happens when power is lost and then reapplied to the system. Choose `Always On` if you want the system to power up automatically(useful for servers), or `Always Off` to leave it off until the power button is pressed. Note that some systems will power themselves on after a power outage, even if they were powered down beforehand.
Power Management	This allows your operating system's APM (Advanced Power Management) feature to turn off the various devices in your system to save power. Enable this option for Windows XP, or disable it if you're using an OS that doesn't support APM.
Power On Function	Use this option to enable other ways to turn on your computer, such as the "power on" button on your keyboard (if applicable).
Primary Display	Allows you to choose whether your PCI or AGP adapter is used as your primary display when using multiple video cards.
Primary IDE Master	Specify the type of drive connected to your primary IDE controller, and set as the "master" (typically with a jumper).

Table B-1. Common BIOS settings and what they do (continued)

Setting	Description
Primary IDE Slave	Specify the type of drive connected to your primary IDE controller, and set as the "slave" (typically with a jumper).
Processor Serial Number	Enable this only if you want your operating system to be able to read the serial number of your processor. Since this can cause substantial security and privacy problems, this option should be disabled unless you specifically need it.
Processor Speed	This is typically a read-only setting that shows the speed of your processor (in Mhz or Ghz). Some motherboards allow you to "overclock" your processor, forcing it to run faster than its rated speed.
Processor Type	This read-only setting tells you what type of processor is currently installed.
PS/2 Mouse Support	Use this to enable or disable your PS/2 mouse port. Disable this if you're using a USB or serial-port mouse, and wish to free up IRQ 12 for another device.
PXE Resume	See "Remote Wake Up."
Quick Boot	Turn this on to skip the thorough, slow memory test performed when the computer is first turned on, allowing a faster boot. It's a good idea to disable this option and sit through the test when first installing new RAM, but once the memory has been tested, it's fine to skip it.
Quiet Boot	A "quiet" boot is one in which your motherboard manufacturer's logo is displayed on the screen instead of the details, such as the amount of memory, detected disks, and BIOS revision date. Disable this option (or press ESC while looking at the logo) to show this information.
Read-Around-Write	When this setting is enabled, your processor can read directly from the cache, without waiting for it to be written to memory first. Enable this feature for better performance.
Remote Wake Up	This feature allows your computer to be turned on by a signal from another computer on your network. Disable this feature unless you specifically need this functionality. See *http://www.annoyances.org/exec/show/article04-101* for details.
Report no FDD for Win95	If this setting is disabled, your BIOS will not identify a missing floppy diskette drive in a Windows 9x/Me system. Enable this option for Windows XP.
Reset Config Data	If enabled, the PnP (Plug and Play) subsystem will reset and reconfigure all of your PnP devices every time your system starts. Use this only if one or more devices needs to be reset to function.
SDRAM CAS Latency	In theory, set this to `CAS2` if your memory is rated at CAS Latency 2; otherwise, use `CAS3`. Interestingly, you should be able to use the faster `CAS2` setting regardless of the type of installed memory; use `CAS3` only if instability results.
Second Boot Device	See "Boot Device Priority/Boot Sequence."
Secondary IDE Master	Specify the type of drive connected to your secondary IDE controller, and set as the "master" (typically with a jumper).
Secondary IDE Slave	Specify the type of drive connected to your secondary IDE controller, and set as the "slave" (typically with a jumper).

Table B-1. Common BIOS settings and what they do (continued)

Setting	Description
Serial Port 1/2 Serial Port A/B	The numbers (or letters) have no correlation to the well-known COM1/COM2 designations, but rather to each of the two physical ports on your motherboard. Set the ports as follows: `3F8/IRQ4` to assign the port to COM1, `2F8/IRQ3` for COM2, `3E8/IRQ4` for COM3, or `2E8/IRQ3` to make it COM4. Disable any port you're not using so it won't consume any resources you can use for other devices. Make sure the two ports don't conflict with each other, or any other devices in your system (such as your modem).
Supervisor Password	This setting allows you to password-protect your BIOS setup. Note that if you forget the password (or simply wish to bypass such a restriction), just reset the BIOS configuration; this is typically done with a jumper, but can also be accomplished by disconnecting the motherboard battery for about twenty minutes.
Suspend Mode	Choose whether the computer is placed in `suspend` or `hibernate` power-saving modes.
Suspend Timeout	Specifies the number of minutes of inactivity before the system is placed in `suspend` power-saving mode.
System BIOS Cacheable	This is similar to "Address Range Shadowing," except that it works with your motherboard's BIOS. Disable this option for best performance.
System Date/Time	Sets your computer's internal clock. This can also be changed by going to **Control Panel → Date and Time.**
System Keyboard	Disable this option if there's no keyboard attached.
System Memory	In most computers, this will be a read-only setting that displays the amount of installed RAM. However, as a holdover from older computers, you may have to enter the BIOS setup screen and then exit for the computer to recognize newly installed memory, even though you won't be able to directly modify this setting.
System Overheat Warning	Enable this to sound an alarm or flash a light if your computer's internal temperature exceeds the value set with the "Overheat Warning Temperature"
Third Boot Device	See "Boot Device Priority/Boot Sequence."
Typematic Rate/Delay	Faster settings will make your keyboard more responsive outside of Windows, but within Windows, these settings are overridden by those found in Control Panel → Keyboard.
USB Function	See "Legacy USB Support"
VGA Palette Snoop	Enable this only if you're using an add-on card that connects to the "Feature Connector" found on older video cards, and then only if the device specifically requires this setting.
Video BIOS Shadow/ Video BIOS Cacheable	This is similar to "Address Range Shadowing," except that it works with the BIOS of your video adapter. This is a holdover from early video cards, and should be disabled in any modern system.
Video Power Down	If enabled, your computer will be able to shut down your video card and monitor to save power. Typically, it's best to have Windows control power-saving features by going to **Control Panel → Power Options**.
Video RAM Cacheable	This is similar to "Address Range Shadowing," except that it works with the memory installed on your video card. This option should always be disabled.
Virus Warning	See "Anti-Virus Protection."

Table B-1. Common BIOS settings and what they do (continued)

Setting	Description
Wait for F1 if Error	If this option is disabled, your computer will continue to boot, even if an error is found; otherwise, you'll have to press **F1** before the system will boot. Such errors include a missing keyboard, a missing video adapter, and an unexpected quantity of installed memory.
Write combining	Enable this option for better video performance, but disable it if you encounter video corruption or system crashes. A related setting can be found in **Control Panel → Display → Settings** tab **→ Advanced → Troubleshoot** tab.

APPENDIX C

TCP/IP Ports

When your web browser or email program connects to another computer on the Internet, it does so through a TCP/IP port. If you have a web server or FTP server running on your computer, it opens a port to which other computers can connect. Port numbers are used to distinguish one network service from another.

Mostly, this is done invisibly behind the scenes. However, knowing which programs use a specific port number becomes important when you start considering security. A firewall uses ports to form its rules about which types of network traffic to allow and which to prohibit. And the Active Connections utility (*netstat.exe*), used to determine which ports are currently in use, allows you to uncover vulnerabilities in your system using ports. Ports, firewalls, and the Active Connections utility are all discussed in Chapter 7.

Some firewalls make a distinction between TCP (Transmission Control Protocol) and UDP (User Datagram Protocol) ports, which is usually unnecessary. In most cases, programs that use the more common TCP protocol will use the same port numbers as their counterparts that use the less-reliable UDP protocol.

Ports are divided into three ranges:

Well-known ports: 0–1023
Registered ports: 1024–49151
Dynamic and/or private ports: 49152–65535

Since a complete port listing would consume about a hundred pages of this book, only the most commonly used ports are listed here. For a more complete listing, see any of these resources:

http://www.portsdb.org/
http://www.iana.org/assignments/port-numbers
http://www.faqs.org/rfcs/rfc1700.html

Table C-1 lists the more commonly used TCP/IP ports.

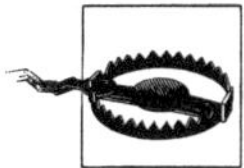

Those ports marked with an ✗ in Table C-1 are commonly exploited by worms and other types of remote attacks. Unless you specifically need them, you should block them in your firewall or router.

Table C-1. Commonly used TCP/IP Ports and how they're used

Port number	Description
21	FTP (File Transfer Protocol)
22	SSH (Secure Shell)
23	Telnet
25	SMTP (Simple Mail Transfer Protocol), used for sending email
43	WhoIs
50–51	IPSec (PPTP Passthrough for VPN, Virtual Private Networking)
53	DNS (Domain Name Server), used for looking up domain names
69 ✗	TFTP
70	Gopher
79	Finger
80	HTTP (Hypertext Transfer Protocol), used by web browsers to download standard web pages
81	Kerberos
110	POP3 (Post Office Protocol, version 3), used for retrieving email
119	NNTP (Network News Transfer Protocol), used for newsgroups
123	NTP (Network Time Protocol), used for XP's Internet Time feature
135 ✗	RPC (Microsoft Windows Remote Procedure Call)
139 ✗	NETBIOS Session Service
143	IMAP4 (Internet Mail Access Protocol version 4)
161, 162	SNMP (Simple Network Management Protocol)
220	IMAP3 (Internet Mail Access Protocol version 3)
443	HTTPS (HTTP over TLS/SSL), used by web browsers to download secure web pages
445 ✗	File sharing for Microsoft Windows networks
500	IPSec (PPTP Passthrough for VPN, Virtual Private Networking)
563	NNTPS (Network News Transfer Protocol over SSL), used for secure newsgroups
593 ✗	RPC (Microsoft Windows Remote Procedure Call) over HTTP
1026 ✗	Windows Messenger - pop-ups (spam)
1352	Lotus Notes mail routing
1503	Windows Messenger - application sharing and whiteboard
1701	VPN (Virtual Private Networking) over L2TP

TCP/IP Ports

Table C-1. Commonly used TCP/IP Ports and how they're used (continued)

Port number	Description
1723	VPN (Virtual Private Networking) over PPTP
1863	Windows Messenger - instant messenging
3389	Remote Desktop Sharing (Microsoft Terminal Services), used for remote control
4444 ✗	W32.BLASTER.WORM virus
5004 and up	Windows Messenger - audio and video conferencing (port is chosen dynamically)
5010	Yahoo! Messenger
5190	AOL Instant Messenger
5631, 5632	pcAnywhere, used for remote control
5800, 5801 5900, 5901	VNC (Virtual Network Computing), used for remote control
6699	Peer-to-peer file sharing, used by Napster-like programs
6891–6900	Windows Messenger - file transfer
7648, 7649	CU-SeeMe video conferencing

APPENDIX D

Class IDs (CLSIDs) of System Objects

Windows keeps track of its various components with Class IDs, 33-digit codes consisting of both letters and numbers, enclosed in curly braces { }. Table D-1 shows a list of commonly used system objects.

Table D-1. Commonly used system objects and their corresponding Class IDs

Object	CLSID
ActiveX Cache Folder	{88C6C381-2E85-11d0-94DE-444553540000}
Briefcase	{85BBD920-42A0-1069-A2E4-08002B30309D}
Compressed Folder	{E88DCCE0-B7B3-11d1-A9F0-00AA0060FA31}
Control Panel	{21EC2020-3AEA-1069-A2DD-08002B30309D}
Desktop	{00021400-0000-0000-C000-000000000046}
Dial-Up Networking	{992CFFA0-F557-101A-88EC-00DD010CCC48}
Favorites	{1A9BA3A0-143A-11CF-8350-444553540000}
Fonts	{BD84B380-8CA2-1069-AB1D-08000948F534}
Internet Explorer	{FBF23B42-E3F0-101B-8488-00AA003E56F8}
Internet Explorer Cache	{7BD29E00-76C1-11CF-9DD0-00A0C9034933}
My Computer	{20D04FE0-3AEA-1069-A2D8-08002B30309D}
My Documents	{450D8FBA-AD25-11D0-98A8-0800361B1103}
My Network Places	{208D2C60-3AEA-1069-A2D7-08002B30309D}
Printers	{2227A280-3AEA-1069-A2DE-08002B30309D}
Recycle Bin	{645FF040-5081-101B-9F08-00AA002F954E}
Scheduled Tasks	{D6277990-4C6A-11CF-8D87-00AA0060F5BF}
Subscriptions	{F5175861-2688-11d0-9C5E-00AA00A45957}
The Internet	{3DC7A020-0ACD-11CF-A9BB-00AA004AE837}
The Microsoft Network	{00028B00-0000-0000-C000-000000000046}
URL History Folder	{FF393560-C2A7-11CF-BFF4-444553540000}

Here are some tips for working with Class IDs:

- Class IDs are stored in the Registry under `HKEY_CLASSES_ROOT\CLSID`. Locate the key named for a Class ID under this branch to change any settings or behavior of the corresponding object. Use the Registry Editor's search feature to find the Class ID for an object not listed here by searching for the name of the object.
- A good way to avoid having to type these codes is to do a search in the Registry. For example, if you're looking for the Recycle Bin Class ID, do a search in the Registry Editor for `Recycle Bin`. When it's found, make sure the code matches the one listed here (because there may be more than one). Right-click on the key named for the code, then select **Rename**. Next, right-click on the highlighted text in the rename field, and select **Copy**. The Class ID will then be placed on the clipboard, waiting to be copied anywhere you please.
- To create a copy of a virtual folder or system object, such as Dial-Up Networking, create a new folder anywhere (such as on your Desktop or anywhere on your hard disk), and call it `Dial-Up Networking.{992CFFA0-F557-101A-88EC-00DD010CCC48}`. Make sure to include the dot between the name and the Class ID. Replace the name and ID with any others from the table. Note that all objects listed here should be able to exist as movable folders, except for **Network Neighborhood**. See "Make the Control Panel More Accessible" in Chapter 2 for more information.
- By placing references to Class IDs in other parts of the Registry, you can make Windows do cool tricks. See "Customizing My Computer and Other System Folders" in Chapter 4 for more information.

Index

Numbers

Symbols

A

We'd like to hear your suggestions for improving our indexes. Send email to *index@oreilly.com*.

B

C

D

F

G

H

J

K

L

M

O

Q

R

S

T

U

V

W

Y

Z

About the Author

David A. Karp, educated in Mechanical Engineering at U.C. Berkeley, consults on Internet technology, user-interface design, and software engineering. He is the author of eight power-user books, currently available in ten different languages, including several installments of the best-selling *Windows Annoyances* series. And from the "out of left field" department, he also wrote *eBay Hacks* and served as the editor for *PayPal Hacks* (both from O'Reilly).

His web site, Annoyances.org, is one of the most respected and popular computer help sites on the Internet. He has also written for a number of magazines, including *PC Magazine*, *Windows Sources Magazine*, *Windows Pro Magazine*, and *New Media Magazine*, and is a contributing editor for *ZTrack Magazine*. Notable recognition has come from *PC Computing*, *Windows Magazine*, the *San Francisco Examiner*, and the *New York Times*.

David often inserts arcane pop culture references into his writing to keep himself awake late at night (e.g. "Let's get sushi and not pay"). He spends much of his spare time outside on a bicycle or holding a camera—that is, when he can tear himself away from a good movie. David also likes hiking and skiing, almost as much as he enjoys talking about them. He often takes weeks to unpack from long trips. He scored 30.96647% on the Geek Test (*http://www.innergeek.us/*), earning a rating of "Total Geek." And once, using only three wooden stakes and a glass of water, he single-handedly defended a small village from an attack of ferocious ants. Animals and children trust him. He can make 15-minute brownies in less than 10 minutes, and never gets tired of The Simpsons.

Colophon

Our look is the result of reader comments, our own experimentation, and feedback from distribution channels. Distinctive covers complement our distinctive approach to technical topics, breathing personality and life into potentially dry subjects.

The animal on the cover of *Windows XP Annoyances for Geeks*, Second Edition is a Surinam toad (also known as *Pipa Pipa*). Surinam toads are entirely aquatic, never venturing onto land from the dark, muddy South American rivers where they dwell. Adapted to life in a constantly murky environment, the eyes of the Surinam toad are little more than small dark spots on its evenly brown body. Adult toads are about six inches long with a broad, flat, almost rectangular appearance. They have large, heavily webbed hind feet and small sensory feelers on their front feet and around their mouths. They use these feelers to aid in the search for food along the muddy river bottom. Once a morsel is located, the toad uses its front feet to stir up the water and swish the food into its gaping, tongueless mouth. It will consume anything it can swallow, dead or alive.

Surinam toads are remarkable even among the several other similar species of aquatic frogs. Rather than depositing her eggs in a secluded location and leaving their fate to chance, the female toad relies on the male to direct the fertilized eggs onto the softened skin of her back. Over the course of several hours the skin swells and completely envelops the eggs. Here the young remain for several months until metamorphosis is complete, emerging as tiny, fully developed toads.

Sanders Kleinfeld was the production editor and proofreader for *Windows XP Annoyances for Geeks*, Second Edition. Genevieve d'Entremont and Colleen Gorman provided quality control. Julie Hawks wrote the index.

Ellie Volckhausen designed the cover of this book, based on a series design by Edie Freedman. The cover image is a 19th-century engraving from the Dover Pictorial Archive. Emma Colby produced the cover layout with QuarkXPress 4.1 using Adobe's ITC Garamond font.

David Futato designed the interior layout. This book was converted to FrameMaker 5.5.6 with a format conversion tool created by Erik Ray, Jason McIntosh, Neil Walls, and Mike Sierra that uses Perl and XML technologies. The text font is Linotype Birka; the heading font is Adobe Myriad Condensed; and the code font is LucasFont's TheSans Mono Condensed. The illustrations that appear in the book were produced by Robert Romano and Jessamyn Read using Macromedia FreeHand MX and Adobe Photoshop CS. The tip and warning icons were drawn by Christopher Bing. This colophon was written by Sarah Sherman.

Related Titles Available from O'Reilly

Windows Users

Access Cookbook, *2nd Edition*
Access Database Design & Programming, *3rd Edition*
Excel Hacks
Excel Pocket Guide
Outlook 2000 in a Nutshell
Outlook Pocket Guide
PC Annoyances
Windows XP Annoyances
Windows XP Hacks
Windows XP Home Edition: The Missing Manual
Windows XP in a Nutshell
Windows XP Pocket Guide
Windows XP Power User
Windows XP Pro: The Missing Manual
Windows XP Unwired
Word Hacks
Word Pocket Guide, *2nd Edition*

Keep in touch with O'Reilly

1. Download examples from our books

To find example files for a book, go to:

www.oreilly.com/catalog

select the book, and follow the "Examples" link.

2. Register your O'Reilly books

Register your book at *register.oreilly.com*

Why register your books? Once you've registered your O'Reilly books you can:

- Win O'Reilly books, T-shirts or discount coupons in our monthly drawing.
- Get special offers available only to registered O'Reilly customers.
- Get catalogs announcing new books (US and UK only).
- Get email notification of new editions of the O'Reilly books you own.

3. Join our email lists

Sign up to get topic-specific email announcements of new books and conferences, special offers, and O'Reilly Network technology newsletters at:

elists.oreilly.com

It's easy to customize your free elists subscription so you'll get exactly the O'Reilly news you want.

4. Get the latest news, tips, and tools

http://www.oreilly.com

- "Top 100 Sites on the Web"—PC Magazine
- CIO Magazine's Web Business 50 Awards

Our web site contains a library of comprehensive product information (including book excerpts and tables of contents), downloadable software, background articles, interviews with technology leaders, links to relevant sites, book cover art, and more.

5. Work for O'Reilly

Check out our web site for current employment opportunities:

jobs.oreilly.com

6. Contact us

O'Reilly & Associates
1005 Gravenstein Hwy North
Sebastopol, CA 95472 USA

TEL: 707-827-7000 or 800-998-9938
(6am to 5pm PST)

FAX: 707-829-0104

order@oreilly.com
For answers to problems regarding your order or our products.
To place a book order online, visit:

www.oreilly.com/order_new

catalog@oreilly.com
To request a copy of our latest catalog.

booktech@oreilly.com
For book content technical questions or corrections.

corporate@oreilly.com
For educational, library, government, and corporate sales.

proposals@oreilly.com
To submit new book proposals to our editors and product managers.

international@oreilly.com
For information about our international distributors or translation queries. For a list of our distributors outside of North America check out:

international.oreilly.com/distributors.html

adoption@oreilly.com
For information about academic use of O'Reilly books, visit:

academic.oreilly.com

O'REILLY®

Our books are available at most retail and online bookstores.
To order direct: 1-800-998-9938 • *order@oreilly.com* • *www.oreilly.com*
Online editions of most O'Reilly titles are available by subscription at *safari.oreilly.com*